THE EMERALD HANDBOOK OF NARRATIVE CRIMINOLOGY

THE EMERALD HANDBOOK OF NARRATIVE CRIMINOLOGY

Edited By

JENNIFER FLEETWOOD
Goldsmiths, University of London, UK

LOIS PRESSER
University of Tennessee, USA

SVEINUNG SANDBERG
University of Oslo, Norway

THOMAS UGELVIK
University of Oslo, Norway

emerald PUBLISHING

United Kingdom – North America – Japan – India – Malaysia – China

Emerald Publishing Limited
Howard House, Wagon Lane, Bingley BD16 1WA, UK

First edition 2019

Selection and editorial matter © 2019 Jennifer Fleetwood, Lois Presser, Sveinung Sandberg, Thomas Ugelvik. Individual chapters © respective authors.

Published under exclusive licence by Emerald Publishing Limited.

Reprints and permissions service
Contact: permissions@emeraldinsight.com

No part of this book may be reproduced, stored in a retrieval system, transmitted in any form or by any means electronic, mechanical, photocopying, recording or otherwise without either the prior written permission of the publisher or a licence permitting restricted copying issued in the UK by The Copyright Licensing Agency and in the USA by The Copyright Clearance Center. Any opinions expressed in the chapters are those of the authors. Whilst Emerald makes every effort to ensure the quality and accuracy of its content, Emerald makes no representation implied or otherwise, as to the chapters' suitability and application and disclaims any warranties, express or implied, to their use.

British Library Cataloguing in Publication Data
A catalogue record for this book is available from the British Library

ISBN: 978-1-78769-006-6 (Print)
ISBN: 978-1-78769-005-9 (Online)
ISBN: 978-1-78769-007-3 (Epub)

Printed and bound by CPI Group (UK) Ltd, Croydon, CR0 4YY

ISOQAR certified Management System, awarded to Emerald for adherence to Environmental standard ISO 14001:2004.

Certificate Number 1985 ISO 14001

INVESTOR IN PEOPLE

Table of Contents

List of Figures, Illustrations and Tables   ix

List of Contributors   xi

Chapter 1   Introduction   *1*
Jennifer Fleetwood, Lois Presser, Sveinung Sandberg and Thomas Ugelvik

PART I: COLLECTING STORIES

OBSERVATIONS AND FIELDWORK

Chapter 2   Narrative Ethnography under Pressure: Researching Storytelling on the Street   *27*
Sébastien Tutenges

Chapter 3   Storied Justice: The Narrative Strategies of US Federal Prosecutors   *45*
Anna Offit

Chapter 4   Narrative Convictions, Conviction Narratives: The Prospects of Convict Criminology   *63*
Rod Earle

INTERVIEWS

Chapter 5   Reflections after 'Socrates Light': Eliciting and Countering Narratives of Youth Justice Officials   *87*
Olga Petintseva

vi Table of Contents

Chapter 6 Stories that Are Skyscraper Tall: The Place of 'Tall Tales' in Narrative Criminology *109*
Carmen Wickramagamage and Jody Miller

TEXTS

Chapter 7 By Terrorists' Own Telling: Using Autobiography for Narrative Criminological Research *131*
Simon Copeland

Chapter 8 Stories of Environmental Crime, Harm and Protection: Narrative Criminology and Green Cultural Criminology *153*
Avi Brisman

BEYOND 'TEXTS': IMAGES AND OBJECTS

Chapter 9 The Stories in Images: The Value of the Visual for Narrative Criminology *175*
Heith Copes, Andy Hochstetler and Jared Ragland

Chapter 10 Reading Pictures: Piranesi and Carceral Landscapes *197*
Eamonn Carrabine

Chapter 11 The Tales Things Tell: Narrative Analysis, Materiality and my Wife's Old Nazi Rifle *217*
Thomas Ugelvik

PART II: ANALYSING STORIES

STUDYING THE VICTIM

Chapter 12 Excavating Victim Stories: Making Sense of Agency, Suffering and Redemption *239*
Elizabeth A. Cook and Sandra Walklate

Chapter 13 Narrative Victimology: Speaker, Audience, Timing *259*
Kristen Lee Hourigan

Chapter 14 Finding Victims in the Narratives of Men Imprisoned for Sex Offences	*279*
Alice Ievins	

CATEGORISATIONS, PLOTS AND ROLES

Chapter 15 Narratives of Conviction and the Re-storying of 'Offenders'	*303*
Bernd Dollinger and Selina Heppchen	
Chapter 16 Police Narratives as Allegories that Shape Police Culture and Behaviour	*321*
Don L. Kurtz and Alayna Colburn	
Chapter 17 Revealing Criminal Narratives: The Narrative Roles Questionnaire and the Life as a Film Procedure	*343*
David Canter, Donna Youngs and David Rowlands	

NARRATIVE DIALOGUE, THE UNCONSCIOUS AND ABSENCES

Chapter 18 Doing Dialogical Narrative Analysis: Implications for Narrative Criminology	*367*
Dan Jerome S. Barrera	
Chapter 19 'Protecting and Defending Mummy': Narrative Criminology and Psychosocial Criminology	*389*
Alfredo Verde and Nicolò Knechtlin	
Chapter 20 The Story of Antisociality: Determining What Goes Unsaid in Dominant Narratives	*409*
Lois Presser	

CONNECTING STORIES, POWER AND SOCIAL INEQUALITIES

Chapter 21 The Archived Criminal: Mandatory Prisoner Autobiography in China	*427*
Xiaoye Zhang and Xianliang Dong	

**Chapter 22 Opposing Violent Extremism through
Counternarratives: Four Forms of Narrative Resistance**   *445*
Sveinung Sandberg and Jan C. Andersen

**Chapter 23 Researching Sex Work: Doing Decolonial,
Intersectional Narrative Analysis*   *467*
Floretta Boonzaier

Index   *493*

List of Figures, Illustrations and Tables

Chapter 5

Table 5.1   Doxastic Interviews Compared to Epistemic Interviews 94

Chapter 9

Image 9.1   Chico Stands in the Doorway of His Trailer, Sand Mountain, Marshall County, Ala 182

Image 9.2   Chico in His Yard, Sand Mountain, Marshall County, Ala 182

Image 9.3   Chico Stands in His Yard, Sand Mountain, Marshall County, Ala. Nearby a Hand-painted Sign Reads, 'DON'T GET CAUGHT BEING STUPID' 183

Image 9.4   Chico's Trailer, Sand Mountain, Marshall County, Ala 185

Image 9.5   A 'DRUG FREE ZONE' Sign Is Posted to a Tree in Chico's Front Yard, Sand Mountain, Marshall County, Ala 186

Image 9.6   An Effigy Is Attached to a Noose in Chico's Front Yard, Sand Mountain, Marshall County, Ala . . . 187

Image 9.7   Chico Holds a Propane Torch between Taking Hits of Meth and Smoking Marijuana Inside His Home on Sand Mountain, Marshall County, Ala 188

Image 9.8   Chico Wearing a Dia de los Muertos Masks, Sits in His Living Room Underneath a Swastika, Copy of the US Constitution and a Confederate Battle Flag   188

Image 9.9   Chico and Alice Sit in the Front Yard of Chico's Trailer on Sand Mountain, Marshall County, Ala   190

Chapter 10

Figure 10.1   Giovanni Battista Piranesi, *Carceri*, pl X, First State, c.1745 205

x List of Figures, Illustrations and Tables

Figure 10.2	Ferdinando Galli de Bibiena, Illustration of a Scene Design from *Direzioni della Prospettiva Teorica*, c.1711	206
Figure 10.3	Canaletto *The Mouth of the Grand Canal Looking West towards the Carità*, c.1729–1730	208
Figure 10.4	Giovanni Paolo Panini, *Roman Capriccio: The Pantheon and Other Monuments*, 1735	209
Figure 10.5	Giovanni Battista Piranesi, *Vedute di Roma: the Fontana dell' Acqua Giulia*, c.1753	210
Figure 10.6	Giovanni Battista Piranesi, *Carceri*, pl XIII, Second State, c. 1761	212

Chapter 11

Image 11.1	Ugelvik Family Mauser Rifle	221
Image 11.2	Ugelvik Family Maser Rifle; Detail with Wehrmacht Symbols	221
Image 11.3	Ugelvik Family Mauser; Detail with Wehrmacht symbols	222

Chapter 17

Figure 17.1	SSA-I Results for 71 Offenders' Responses on Roles Questionnaire	349
Table 17.1	Indicative Statements that Define Themes of Narrative Roles Taken from Narrative Roles Questionnaire	350
Table 17.2	Narrative Integration of Affective, Cognitive and Offence-specific Identity Components of Offending	351

Chapter 18

Table 18.1	Profile of the Data Analysed	375
Table 18.2	The Stories that Occupy the Civil Sphere in the Philippines from 2015 to 2017	376
Figure 18.1	Types of Drug War Stories that Proliferated in the Philippine Civil Sphere, 2015–2017	384

Chapter 23

Table 23.1	Phase One: Useful Analytic Questions	474
Table 23.2	Phase Two: Useful Analytic Questions	480
Table 23.3	Phase Three: Useful Analytic Questions	484

List of Contributors

Jan C. Andersen, *University of Oslo, Norway.*
Jan is a Scientific Assistant at the University of Oslo, Norway. He has a Masters in Criminology from the University of Oslo. His research focusses on IS propaganda on the Internet and the everyday religion of young Muslims.

Dan Jerome S. Barrera, *Negros Oriental State University, Philippines.*
Dan Jerome is affiliated with the College of Criminal Justice Education of Negros Oriental State University – Main, Bayawan-Sta. Catalina, and Siaton Campuses in Negros Oriental, Philippines. He is interested in the power of narratives to influence actions among criminal justice clients and agents.

Floretta Boonzaier, *University of Cape Town, South Africa.*
Floretta is Professor in Psychology at the University of Cape Town, South Africa. She is Codirector of the Hub for Decolonial Feminist Psychologies in Africa and she works and teaches in feminist, critical, social and decolonial psychologies.

Avi Brisman (MFA, JD, PhD) is an Associate Professor in the School of Justice Studies at Eastern Kentucky University, USA, an Adjunct Associate Professor in the School of Justice at Queensland University of Technology, Australia, and a Conjoint Associate Professor in the Newcastle Law School at the University of Newcastle, Australia.

David Canter, Emeritus Professor at the University of Liverpool, UK, has published widely in many aspects of applied social psychology over the past half century. He is best known for developing Environmental Psychology in the 1970s and Investigative Psychology a quarter of a century ago.

Eamonn Carrabine is a Professor of Sociology at the University of Essex, UK. His books include *Crime in Modern Britain* (co-authored, 2002), *Power, Discourse and Resistance: A Genealogy of the Strangeways Prison Riot* (2004), *Crime, Culture and the Media* (2008) and *Crime and Social Theory* (2017).

Alayna Colburn is a Doctoral Candidate in the Department of Sociology, Anthropology and Social Work at Kansas State University, USA. She also serves as a Junior Research Scientist for New York University. Her research focusses on domestic violence, policing and the military. Her dissertation examines domestic violence perpetrated by soldiers post deployment.

Elizabeth A. Cook is an ESRC Postdoctoral Research Fellow at the University of Oxford, UK. Before that she worked at the University of Manchester and University of Sheffield. Her research interests include cultural victimology, victim stories and the experiences of bereaved families in the aftermath of violence.

Simon Copeland is a Doctoral Researcher at Lancaster University, UK. Part of the Centre for Research and Evidence on Security Threats, his research explores kin and peer networks and militancy. His article applying narrative approaches to militants' self-accounts won the 2018 Society for Terrorism Research best student paper award.

Heith Copes is Professor in the Department of Criminal Justice at the University of Alabama at Birmingham, USA. His primary interest is in understanding the decision-making process and identity construction of people who engage in crime and drug use.

Bernd Dollinger is a Professor of Pedagogy and Social Work at the University of Siegen (Germany). He completed his academic career at the Universities of Bamberg and Freiburg (Germany). His approach to criminological research revolves around professional, political and subjective accounts which, in their interplay, constitute crime as a cultural phenomenon.

Xianliang Dong is a PhD Candidate in Chinese and History of the City University of Hong Kong, China. His research specialises in the medical history of China and Hong Kong, with broader interests in performance studies and dramaturgy. His articles have appeared in *Taiwan: A Radical Quarterly in Social Studies* and *Router: A Journal of Cultural Studies*.

Rod Earle is Senior Lecturer at The Open University, UK. Rod has worked as a printer, in youth justice and currently enjoys life as an academic. He is a member of the British Society of Criminology and in 2019 helped to establish the BSC Race Matters Network.

Jennifer Fleetwood is Senior Lecturer in Criminology at Goldsmiths College, University of London, UK. Before that she worked at the University of Leicester and the University of Kent. Her book, *Drug Mules: Women in the International Cocaine Trade*, won the 2015 British Society of Criminology Book Prize.

Selina Heppchen is an Academic Assistant at the University of Siegen (Germany). Her research interest involves subjective perceptions of crime, their interactive production and the communication of social categories. In her recent publications, she analyses youth crime as a social phenomenon based on interpersonal ascriptions.

Andy Hochstetler is Professor of Sociology at Iowa State University, USA. He mainly writes on self-conception and the choice to offend. Currently, he is working on two grant projects with the US Department of Agriculture and National Institute of Justice funding.

List of Contributors xiii

Kristen Lee Hourigan is Assistant Professor in the Sociology Department at California State University, Los Angeles. Her work bridges the subfields of victimology and social psychology, focussing upon the transformation of emotion and identity following traumatic loss.

Alice Ievins is a Research Associate at the Institute of Criminology, University of Cambridge, UK. Her research to date concerns the relationship between punishment and moral communication, with a particular focus on men convicted of sex offences.

Nicolò Knechtlin, licensed psychologist and criminologist, has worked in therapeutic communities hosting mentally ill offenders, and is currently working as psychologist in the field of human resources. He is also currently conducting a research project on Italian soccer 'ultras'.

Don L. Kurtz is Professor of Social Work and the Social Work Program Coordinator at Kansas State University, USA. His research interests include police stress, youth violence, police storytelling and narrative development, and his work is published in many highly regarded criminology and criminal justice journals.

Jody Miller is Distinguished Professor in the School of Criminal Justice at Rutgers University, USA, and Fellow of the American Society of Criminology. She is author of *One of the Guys: Girls, Gangs and Gender* and *Getting Played: African American Girls, Urban Inequality, and Gendered Violence*.

Anna Offit is an Assistant Professor of Law at SMU Dedman School of Law. She previously worked as a Research Fellow at New York University School of Law. She holds a PhD and MA in Anthropology from Princeton University, an MPhil in Social Anthropological Analysis from the University of Cambridge and a JD from the Georgetown University Law Center.

Olga Petintseva is a Postdoctoral Fellow of the Research Foundation – Flanders, affiliated with Ghent University and Free University Brussels, Belgium. Olga's expertise is located at the intersection of criminology, migration studies and sociolinguistics. Her most recent book *Youth, Justice and Migration: Discursive Harms* was published in 2018 by Palgrave Macmillan.

Lois Presser is Professor of Sociology at the University of Tennessee, USA. Her research concerns narrative, harm, identity and restorative justice. She is the author of *Been a Heavy Life: Stories of Violent Men*, *Why We Harm*, *Narrative Criminology* (coedited with Sveinung Sandberg) and *Inside Story: How Narratives Drive Mass Harm*.

Jared Ragland is the Visual Media and Outreach Coordinator for the Department of Art & Art History at the University of Alabama at Birmingham, USA. He served as a White House Photo Editor under the Bush and Obama Administrations. He has published with National Geographic books and has exhibited his fine art work internationally.

David Rowlands is a Doctoral Student at the University of Huddersfield, UK. He has worked for many years in drug rehabilitation.

Sveinung Sandberg is Professor in Criminology at the University of Oslo, Norway. His research focusses on processes of marginalisation, violence, masculinity, illegal drugs, radicalisation and social movements often using a narrative or discourse analytical approach.

Sébastien Tutenges is Assistant Professor at the Department of Sociology at Lund University, Sweden. He completed this chapter whilst a postdoctoral fellow at the Department of Criminology and Sociology of Law at the University of Oslo, Norway. His research is broadly concerned with intoxication, drug dealing, fights and terrorism.

Thomas Ugelvik is Professor in Criminology at the University of Oslo, Norway. He is the author of *Power and Resistance in Prison* (Palgrave, 2014), and the founding coeditor of *Incarceration: An International Journal of Imprisonment, Detention and Coercive Confinement* (Sage, first volume 2020).

Alfredo Verde, a psychologist and psychoanalyst, applies a narrative approach to criminology, from offender narratives, to social control narratives (including criminological ones). He is currently Professor of Criminology at the University of Genoa, Italy. He has translated into Italian Gadd & Jefferson's *An Introduction to Psychosocial Criminology* (Milan: Franco Angeli, 2016) and is author of several contributions in the field, including a criminological manual in Italian.

Sandra Walklate is the Eleanor Rathbone Chair of Sociology at the University of Liverpool, UK, and conjoint Chair of Criminology at Monash University, Australia. She is internationally recognised for her work on criminal victimisation generally and more recently on victimisation and war. Her forthcoming work includes, *A Criminology of War?* with Ross McGarry.

Carmen Wickramagamage has been teaching English at the Department of English, University of Peradeniya, Sri Lanka, since 1986. She has taught briefly as Visiting Assistant Professor and Visiting Professor at Colleges in the US, including Carleton College, Holy Cross College, Whitman College and Bowdoin College.

Donna Youngs is Reader in Investigative Psychology at the University of Huddersfield, UK. Her early work examining the psychological processes differentiation styles of criminal action led her to develop a framework for eliciting and distinguishing the psychological narrative forms that underpin a person's life story and identity.

Xiaoye Zhang is a recent PhD graduate of Criminology from City University of Hong Kong, China. Zhang obtained her MA degree of Applied Theatre from Goldsmith College, University of London, where she began working with incarcerated persons and prison officers. Prison sociology with a focus on arts in prison is Zhang's current research area. Zhang is currently based at the Criminal Justice Department of East China University of Political Science and Law.

Chapter 1

Introduction

Jennifer Fleetwood, Lois Presser, Sveinung Sandberg and Thomas Ugelvik

Rosario Castellanos' (1962) *The Book of Lamentations* and Mario Vargas Llosas' (1981) *The War of the End of the World* tell epic stories of poor indigenous people fighting for their physical and spiritual lives. Both describe fictional characters, inhabiting the impoverished states of Chiapas in Mexico (Castellanos) and Bahia in Brazil (Llosas), who were inspired by real people and events to revolt. As in these books so in 'life': intertwined Catholic and local beliefs have been narrative resources in actual indigenous revolts against ethnic, class and colonial hierarchies. Narratives can also legitimise conquest, and not just rebellion, as Keeton (2015) shows in his analysis of the link between Old Testament narratives and the colonisation of the US. Biblical stories *move*: they are carried and passed on by people, traversing continents and oceans. Narratives also travel in time, enduring thousands of years, continuously changing and intermingling with other stories.

Narratives undergird power as well as resistance. They have created some of the darkest moments in human history. The Third Reich built its legitimacy on epic stories of valour and glory adapted from a mythical northern European past. Narratives can also challenge harms; tales of native people's resistance were crucial for the renowned Zapatista uprising of 1994. These events, motivated by stories, are rewritten in the present, acquiring new emphases and significance. Stories move in and out of 'reality'. Some have an historical point of reference, others do not; it is their 'storiness' (Hogan, 2003, p. 203) that gives them their unique power. Power to defend the established order and do harm, but also power to change society and better the conditions under which people live. The capacity of stories to explain, guide, and arouse is at the heart of narrative criminology. Put simply, stories shape our social world; they inspire us to do or resist harms. With careful and close attention, they can tell us a great deal.

Hence this volume. For ease, we have organised it by moment in the process of research – collecting versus analysing stories. Around this somewhat arbitrary binary is a profusion of discoveries as to what narrative criminology – indeed, criminology – can do and be. This chapter introduces the volume and addresses three key questions. First: where have we been? What research has been done to date in narrative criminology? What have we learnt? Second: what are this Handbook's specific contributions to the field? Third: what are some important future directions in narrative criminology? What has narrative criminology yet to grasp, hone or pay attention to? What good could it do in the world?

Looking Back

Stories connect the present with the past and future, and so too are the present and future of narrative criminology closely connected to its past in any recognisable account. Where did narrative criminology come from? Several origin stories have been told (Maruna, 2015; Presser & Sandberg, 2015a, Sandberg & Ugelvik, 2016a). Linkages to mid-century American sociology are often highlighted. Sykes and Matza's (1957) description of how delinquents use 'techniques of neutralisation' to make their offending behaviour morally justifiable is said to be an important inspiration, as is Mills' (1940) elucidation of 'vocabularies of motive'. Similarly, Scott and Lyman's (1968) study of how people's accounts of their own actions bridge the gap between action and expectation is said to be another core text. These works related socially structured discourse to individual action. Labelling theories, as well as theories of gendered action, would emphasise identity mechanisms driving that relationship. For example, narrative criminology owes a profound debt to Becker's demonstration in *Outsiders* (1963) that deviance is not an attribute of any act but rather the meanings attached to it. Building on insights from symbolic interactionism and especially Goffman, Katz (1988) showed that crimes are an acting out of certain narrative scripts and thus actions in general are shaped by their storytelling potential.

Maruna's (2001) *Making Good*, which set out the close connections between desistance from crime and narrative reconfigurations of self-image, was a rigorous take on the idea that behaviour reversals are founded on stories. Outside criminology, myriad studies have theorised specific mass harms (e.g. violent attacks on abortion clinics, criminal executions, war, terrorism) in narrative terms. In psychology, anthropology, political science, medicine, geography and still other nonliterary disciplines, the narrative turn had already taken place. Hence an alternative origin story might be that, bolstered by the development of cultural, constitutive and psychosocial criminologies, the moment had finally come for narrative criminology.

When Presser coined the term 'narrative criminology' in her 2009 article in *Theoretical Criminology*, there existed a reservoir of evidence and theory to draw from. Her paper was a timely and productive intervention that drew together and summarised several coinciding developments in the social sciences. Looking back, one is tempted to say that it was like a spark in a fireworks factory. Narrative criminology was quickly adopted by a number of scholars internationally. Sandberg further developed the framework (Sandberg, 2010, 2013, 2016) when with colleagues he analysed the importance of stories for phenomena such as terrorism, illegal drugs, drinking, violence and humour. Connections were made with visual criminology (Sandberg & Ugelvik, 2016b) and Bourdieusian criminology (Sandberg & Fleetwood, 2017, see also Fleetwood, 2014, 2016). Presser, for her part, developed narrative criminology further. Her book *Why We Harm* (2013) pivots from 'crime' in the narrow sense to encompass legal and routine harms. In *Inside Story* (2018) she explores why and how stories captivate audiences and drive mass harm.

As a criminological subdiscipline, narrative criminology reached maturity with the publication of the edited collection *Narrative Criminology: Understanding Stories of Crime* (Presser & Sandberg, 2015a). This volume includes a range of different studies with a variety of topics – prisoners' work on the self, drug users' use of narratives and the connection between bad trip stories and folk tales about magical creatures and dark forces. It also covers stories justifying mass atrocities and sex offences, and the relationship between cultural and narrative criminology. The anthology was followed by a special issue of the journal *Crime, Media, Culture* (Sandberg & Ugelvik, 2016a). This special issue covered issues such as forms of narrative, narrative habitus, boundary work, media narratives and the relationship between narrative and image.

Recent Developments

Narrative criminology is, formally speaking, only 10 years old, but it is already moving in new directions, especially around a deepening understanding of human experience and meaning making. The field is still expanding, with novel research topics, analytical perspectives and methodological options. Indeed, the last year or two has seen a rapid proliferation of narrative perspectives across various criminological areas.

Continuing narrative criminology's core interest in understanding violence, Henriksen and Bengtsson (2018) find that marginalised Danish youths describe violence as 'nothing special'; as an acceptable and even trivial part of their lives. Colvin and Pisoiu (2018) examine the narratives of members of present-day right-wing groups in Germany, finding that violence is neutralised through tropes such as pragmatic realpolitik (a way of 'getting results') and the mythical race of *Herrenmensch*. Looking at a very different group – serial killers – James and Gossett (2018) show how even people who have committed the most heinous of crimes are able to narratively reconstruct themselves as people with high moral standards. Raitanen, Sandberg, and Oksanen (2019) explore connections between the master narrative of school shootings and personal stories of being bullied. The same kind of micro–macro link is drawn in Banks and Albertson's (2018) study of violence committed by ex-service personnel. These authors locate such violence in both personal biographies and individual psyches, and the structural conditions of advanced capitalism. Lastly, Sandberg, Copes, and Pedersen (2019) expand the traditional focus on violent populations, to 'peaceful people', arguing that narrative analysis far exceeds approaches such as subcultural and neutralisation theory in understanding engagement in violence.

An emerging literature concerns the narrative dimensions of representations of *armed conflict and war*. Following Houge's (2016) study of perpetrators of mass violence in postconflict international tribunal proceedings, Rauschenbach (2018) studies the tension between 'judicial truth' and other kinds of truths in interviews with individuals accused by the International Criminal Tribunal for the Former Yugoslavia. Walklate (2019) shows how images of violence and atrocity play an important part in the political aftermath of such incidents, a point that is also made by Houge (2018) in her study of international criminal tribunals as sites that impact on societal understandings of mass violence, promoting a particular kind of story.

Another core interest in narrative criminology is *drug crime*. In research by Webb, Copes, and Hendricks (2019), people engaged in so-called microdosing of psychedelics talk about their drug use as rational and normal, narratively emphasising connections to conventional citizens who hold middle-class values. Rather similarly, Arnull and Ryder (2019) describe how young women normalise their alcohol and marihuana use by telling stories in which they are in control of their substance use and it is all just 'good fun'. Hammersvik's (2018) study of cannabis growers and dealers highlights camaraderie. His participants reconstruct their growing and selling of illegal drugs as a way of helping their friends. Narratives have also become important for scholars who wish to understand the absence of crimes and harm. One novel contribution here is Rowlands, Youngs, and Canter's (2019) exploration of the role of narrative identity change in substance misuse recovery.

Several recent papers offer *meta arguments* unpacking what narrative criminology is, what it can and should be, and how different analytical and methodological perspectives can be brought into and add to the original conceptualisation of narrative criminology. Wesely (2018) contends that, given that much narrative criminology research has been interview-based, narrative criminologists should look more closely at how interview dynamics and the narrative techniques both participants and interviewers deploy during interviews impact our analyses. Brisman (2019) shows how values that contribute to pollution and thus climate change are reproduced in stories for children. He contends that narrative criminology can very beneficially analyse fictional narratives and situates his ecology-focused work under the rubric of green cultural criminology. Presser and Sandberg (2019) have connected narrative criminology to critical criminology, arguing among other things that narrative criminology is rooted in a concern with harm, legal or illegal.

Walklate has, with her colleagues, developed narrative criminology in the direction of a narrative *victimology* (Walklate, Maher, McCulloch, Fitz-Gibbon, & Beavis, 2018), as have Pemberton, Mulder, and Aarten (2018), who claim great potential for the study of the multiple ways victimisation experience is embedded in life stories. Pemberton, Aarten, and Mulder (2018) highlight the need for victims to own their stories to avoid secondary victimisation. Together, these authors point to the potential for narrative approaches for understanding how victimisation is made sense of and told about, as well as how these narratives may (or may not) catalyse responses by the criminal justice system or policy makers.

Narratives of victimisation are both personally and existentially significant *and* motivators for political and social change. Analysis of both depends on a keen attentiveness to questions of power that infuse who can tell a victim narrative.

Narrative criminology was originally explicitly centred on the narratives of offenders. There is now a sizeable literature on the *narrative lives of professionals* working in the social control professions. Kurtz and Upton (2018) continue this recent development and reveal that a certain kind of masculine police culture is reproduced through the sharing of stories. Similarly, Petintseva examines the narratives of youth justice workers (2018) and Baker (2018) looks at how believable truths are constructed narratively in coroners' reports. Whilst criminology has long attended to the discursive qualities of law and criminal justice institutions, studying personal narratives opens up daily practice for analysis, and the ways that individuals draw on, reproduce and adapt narratives about crime and justice. Whilst studying the 'texts' of law is important, narrative criminology emphasises the importance of storytelling as a form of social action – the daily performance of stories in working lives.

Narrative criminologists have mainly, although not exclusively, used qualitative methods. Canter and Youngs (e.g. Canter & Youngs, 2012; Youngs & Canter, 2012a, 2012b) have done *quantitative research* on the narratives of offenders for some time. Their methodological example has provided notable inspiration, especially their commitment to standardised methodological approaches reflecting their psychological approach to studying offenders. Recently, using quantitative analysis, Goodlad, Ioannou, and Hunter (2018) have explored how offenders with personality disorders and psychopathy experience committing a crime. Ciesla, Ioannou, and Hammond (2019) surveyed female prisoners to examine their narrative and emotional experiences. Kruttschnitt and Kang (2019) studied persistent offenders' understanding of their past crimes using Canter and Young's narrative 'life as a film' method (see also Ioannou, Synnott, Lowe, & Tzani-Pepelasi, 2018). Through analysis of stock narratives, they draw out the significance of structural disadvantages in their analysis, for both experience and storytelling, attending to the intersections of race and gender in particular.

A literature has also flourished concerning how prisoners narratively come to terms with their sentence. Rather than examine how narratives contribute to crime and other harmful actions, these researchers address traditional questions from the field of *penology*, but from a narrative theory perspective, such as how prisoners use discursive resistance strategies to deal with confinement and related humiliations. Following Ugelvik's (2012, 2015) narrative studies of prison environments, Vannier (2018) highlights the importance of letter-writing for prisoners who have to endure the most extreme kinds of imprisonment, and also the analytical potential these letters have for researchers. Warr (2019) studies how prisoners sentenced to long periods of custody must undertake 'narrative labour' to manage the carceral identity imposed upon them, including their daily struggle to construct an acceptable narrative identity. Finally, Easterling, Feldmeyer, and Presser (2018) describe the narrative strategies of incarcerated mothers managing the identity threats that incarceration presents for them as mothers. These are, in effect, studies of narrative responses to what Sykes (1958) called 'the pains of imprisonment'. Narrative criminologists are poised to revisit classic ideas from criminology, connecting them with the idea of stories' productive potential.

The above overview of publications in narrative criminology from the last 2 years gives a flavour of recent research in narrative criminology, updating previous reviews (Presser & Sandberg, 2015a, 2019; Sandberg & Ugelvik, 2016a). The study of narrative is inherently interdisciplinary, and it is hard to do justice to the array of interesting and creative ways narrative approaches have been deployed across varied disciplines and subfields. As well as expanding the methodological toolkit, the following chapters continue to broaden our understanding of the ways in which stories matter for understanding contemporary issues of harm, crime and justice.

Chapters of this Handbook

The book is structured along two broad methodological dimensions. The first part explores different ways of *collecting* stories, including ethnography, interviews, texts and images and objects. While authors address the particularities of each of these methods of collecting data to varying degrees, we want readers to get an idea of the many ways stories can be 'found'. For good reasons, narrative criminology has tended towards using interviews to generate narratives, and hopefully these chapters presenting alternative methodological approaches will inspire researchers to expand the pool of stories studied. Chapters also suggest innovative ways to work with interview data, suggesting ways to be more reflexive and systematic when using interview data. The second part of the book concerns ways of *analysing* stories. Previous work in narrative criminology has used a multitude of analytical approaches, but in this volume the tool box is expanded further to include membership categorisation analysis, psychoanalysis, dialogical analysis, 'life as a film' and counter narrative analysis.

Part I: Collecting Stories

Thus far narrative criminologists have been mostly concerned to draw linkages between harm and story, paying less attention to the 'places' where stories can be found. In this first part of the Handbook we highlight different ways of accessing stories, through ethnography, interviews, texts, images and objects.

Observations and Fieldwork

Ethnography is 'the study of people in naturally occurring settings or "fields" by methods of data collection which capture their social meanings and ordinary activities. It involves the researcher participating directly in the setting, if not also the activities, in order to collect data in a systematic matter' (Brewer, 2000, p. 172). Traditionally, ethnography involves one or a few researchers engaging with a small group for a relatively long period, with a high level of engagement and commitment, and with the aim of understanding the culture, perspective and organisation of that group. Lately, ethnography has expanded to include forms such as autoethnography, netnography, multi-sited ethnography and narrative ethnography. This last is conceptualised as 'aimed at close scrutiny of social situations, their actors, and actions in relation to narratives' (Gubrium & Holstein, 2008, p. 250). The narrative ethnographer documents the vagaries of story construction within concrete social interactions.

Sébastien Tutenges, in Chapter 2, describes how to access, collect and process the stories of street-level offenders using ethnographic fieldwork. In what he describes as 'narrative ethnography under pressure' at a street drug scene, he details the advantages of being deeply embedded in the cultural context where narratives emerge, to get a better understanding of narrative performances and the impact they have. His rendering of narrative ethnography enables researchers to use all senses when studying storytelling and see how they evolve and change across time and space. Chapter 3 is similarly based on a traditional approach to ethnographic fieldwork. Here Anna Offit continues the argument for narrative ethnography in a study of American federal prosecutors. Participating in their daily work and ongoing discussions of trial opening and closing statements, she gains unique insight into how justice is continually negotiated in narratives. She demonstrates that generally stories are made and remade by narrators in collective story-making processes.

In Chapter 4 Rod Earle works from interviews with fellow convict criminologists but also explores the potential of narrative autoethnography. He argues that first-hand experience of imprisonment may be helpful to understand not only prison conditions but recent carceral expansions as well. He puts narrative criminology into dialogue with convict criminology, whose stories are potentially a form of activism – a means to take down the carceral regime. The chapter speaks to problems of making collective narratives – or counternarratives – out of personal narratives and demonstrates the advantages of combining different data when studying narrative. Narratives are not confined to one particular setting; they move back and forth from mainstream media, popular culture and social media, to individual, groups and communities – and they are increasingly transnational and global in scope.

Interviews

A classic definition of interviewing is 'a face-to-face verbal exchange, in which one person, the interviewer, attempts to elicit information of expression of opinion or belief from another person or persons' (Maccoby & Maccoby, 1954, p. 449). Against this commonly accepted formal definition, it has been said that we inhabit an 'interview society' (Atkinson & Silverman, 1997), in which interviewing is part of everyday life and a common way to seek and obtain information (data) or just a feel for what goes on in a particular locale. As chapters in this Handbook illustrate, interviewing has become so assimilated into ways of knowing, including but not limited to research, that it is seldom reflected upon. The chapters in this section address the interview situation pointedly.

Practitioners of 'justice work' tell stories about their charges and those stories have implications for practice. In Chapter 5, recognising that professional stories reproduce racist treatment and subordination, Olga Pentintseva describes experimenting with discursive intervention during interviews with youth justice professionals in Belgium. The method, which she calls a 'light' form of Socratic dialogue, reminds us that we cannot treat narratives as simply 'there'. Pentintseva shaped the narratives overtly and with a transformative agenda, but she nonetheless reminds us that even passive 'collectors' of narrative data – minimally probing interviewers and archivists, for instance – can powerfully shape their data. Chapter 6 similarly explores and reflects upon the interview situation by asking what to do about 'tall tales' in interviews, when participants are obviously making up stories. Here Carmen Wickramagamage and Jody Miller offer a vantage on the sometimes messy world of interview research. They also reflect on the complex relations between 'truth,' 'fiction' and 'lies', showing that even tall tales can teach us a great deal about research participants and perhaps also researchers.

Many other chapters in this Handbook use interview data as well, illustrating the prominence of this approach in narrative criminology as in qualitative research generally. Close attention to narrative, however, invites new ways to scrutinise interviews, getting more out of them than reports about 'facts'. Chapters in the second part based on interviews include Canter, Youngs and Rowland's quantitative approach to interviewing, and Sandberg and Andersen's description of how interviews can benefit from being done collectively by research groups. Cook and Walklate, Ievins, Dollinger and Heppchen, Kurtz and Colburn, Verde and Knechtlin, and Boonzaier also all use narrative interviews in their contributions.

Texts

Document or textual analysis is often seen as a separate category in methodological literature, sometimes associated with discourse analysis. Yet, for the sake of narrative analysis there is little difference whether we have documents or other texts, interviews or ethnographic data. We are still searching for elements of narrative, characters, metaphors etc. There are many advantages to working with already finished texts, however. They can be easy to access; and in a society where many of us engage more with texts (e.g. on social media) than with 'real' people, and where most public policies are firmly anchored in texts, they are important sociological data. This section offers examples of rather different texts that can be relevant for narrative criminologists.

In Chapter 7 Simon Copeland uses the case of an American jihadist to argue that autobiographies are rare resources for doing narrative criminology. His is a detailed account of how and why to study autoethnographies. Drawing on literary criticism, Copeland shows how autobiographies, like narratives, are shaped both individually and collectively by genre. Chapter 8 by Avi Brisman starts from fiction, showcasing the value of narrative criminology for green criminology – or the study of environmental harm – and the sustenance given to harm-genic stories from works of fiction. Brisman also reports from web- and interview-based studies to illustrate the importance of stories for environmental harm. Texts in all forms, including news coverage (e.g. Barrera's chapter later in this volume), official documents (e.g. Xiaoye and Xianliang's chapter), criminological texts (e.g. Presser's chapter), text messages, social media and webpages etc., are clearly of great value for anyone interested in stories. We have only seen the start of how such resources can be used.

Beyond the Text: Images and Objects

Ethnographies, interviews and texts are much-used troves of narrative data. In this final section on collecting stories we turn to novel sources. Narrative criminology takes as its point of departure that stories can be found everywhere, following Barthes' (1977, p. 79) famous observation which begins: 'The narratives of the world are numberless. Narrative is first and foremost a prodigious variety of genres, themselves distributed amongst different substances – as though any material were fit to receive man's stories.' The authors of this section's chapters likewise argue that we can find narratives in a variety of nontextual representations: photographs, art and objects, drawing on exciting synergies between narrative and art history, photography and material culture.

In Chapter 9 Heith Copes, Andy Hochstetler and Jared Ragland tell the story of Chico, a meth user, through visual and 'textual' means. As much as traditional (written and spoken) narratives, visual symbols on Chico's body, property and in his home reveal him to be both rebellious and caring. The authors argue that images also can be used to elicit oral storytelling and describe the process whereby they engage a dialogue with Chico around the photographs they have taken. These prompt him to reflect on his life and further expand on his self-story. Eamonn Carrabine (Chapter 10) likewise emphasises the visual by scrutinising Giovanni Battista Piranesi's images of fantasy prisons, and laying out in more theoretical detail the relationship between narrative and image. His chapter delves into the relationships between narrative criminology and visual methods through parallels to scholarship in art history, such as where 'word' and 'image' are related and juxtaposed.

Finally, in Chapter 11, Thomas Ugelvik pushes the boundaries of narrative criminology still further by finding stories in an object – in this case his wife's hunting rifle. Ugelvik lays out the possibilities and problematics. If objects narrate – if stories are already out there in the physical and not only cultural world – what autonomy is left for humans? The question gets to the core of studies in narrative criminology and social sciences in general. Combined, the three chapters compel the view that narrative criminologists ought not limit themselves to 'texts' – whether obtained from fieldwork, interviews or already existing writings – when exploring for the impact and importance of narrative. Note too that Ugelvik's chapter, like Earle's, draws upon personal biography in the analysis, thus expanding the pool of stories that researchers can study to include their own.

Part II: Analysing Stories

The second part of the book turns from how stories can be collected to how they can be analysed. Here new analytical approaches are introduced and the emphasis is mainly on what to do with data already collected. We start with approaches to victimhood and the role of the victim before we turn to approaches scrutinising categorisations, roles and plots, the dialogical nature of narrative and narrative absences. Finally, while many if not most of the contributions in this volume consider asymmetric relations of power, we end with those chapters that most explicitly address such issues.

Studying the Victim

Like criminology in general, narrative criminology has tended to foreground harm-doers. Their stories are not the only ones relevant for understanding harm as storied. Alongside the burgeoning of victimology as an academic discipline, victim voices and characters are increasingly being studied within narrative criminology. In the first part of the analytical section, then, we position work that either directly or indirectly studies victim narratives.

In Chapter 12, Elizabeth A. Cook and Sandra Walklate ask what narrative victimology and narrative criminology can learn from one another. By exploring in great depth the narrative of a mother who lost her son to violent crime, they show that storytelling, long held to be essential for recovering from trauma (see Herman, 1997), is also parcel to political struggle and community engagement. Their chapter reveals the importance of religious storylines for 'narrative recovery' and explores the complexity of victim voices in policy. Kristen Lee Hourigan, in Chapter 13, extends narrative victimology with insights from narrative ethnography (see also chapters by Tutenges and Offit) with those who have lost loved ones to murder. Emphasising different elements of the storytelling process – speaker, audience, timing – Hourigan shows how important it is to appreciate narratives across different settings; victim narratives are contingent, deeply personal and sometimes public and political. Both of these chapters are firmly situated within the burgeoning perspective of narrative victimology, and those interested in this perspective should also read Boonzaier's chapter, the last one in the Handbook.

Alice Ievins (Chapter 14) moves the victim focus from voices of victims to representations of victims in offenders' stories, thereby blurring the lines between traditional 'victim' and 'offender' approaches. Noting that narrative can be a strategy for shame management, she demonstrates that crime victims haunt sex offenders' stories. In narrative terms, they are characters, perhaps the most important characters in their stories. The UK prisoners she interviewed often tried to challenge simple categorisations of 'victims' and 'prisoners' in their attempts to display penitence and reform. Some expressed remorse, some marginalised having hurt a victim and some denied offender status altogether. Finally, Ievins directs attention upward, asking what sorts of stories the state facilitates concerning victims and victimisation, thereby connecting to Xiaoye and Xianliang's chapter concerning Chinese prisoners that appears later in this book. Combined, they raise complex questions about who really creates the stories that are being told in institutional environments.

Categorisations, Plots and Roles

The next section of the book goes into greater depth on narrative analytical techniques and concepts. An almost endless supply stocks the narrative criminologist's repertoire, and only imagination as well as each individual scholar's capability to orient herself within the narrative literature set the limits. As opposed to attempting an overview of possible narrative strategies, this section therefore provides examples of some fruitful ways to approach stories within the framework of narrative criminology.

In Chapter 15, Bernd Dollinger and Selina Heppchen demonstrate the value for narrative criminology of classic ethnomethodology and membership categorisation analysis. In-depth analysis of interviews with Dave, a youth charged with sex offences in Germany, allows them to show how he balances between the categories (or stories) of psychiatry or social work and law, with potential consequences for the verdict in his case. The work of categorising both Dave and the offences he allegedly has committed is partly done by the youth himself, but institutional interests and voices are also involved. Dollinger and Heppchen show how competing narratives constitute the reality of crime, which is an important insight for narrative criminology. In Chapter 16, Don L. Kurtz and Alayna Colburn continue the emphasis on institutions, exploring police narratives in the US and showing how important they are for police action. Here, narrative criminology takes on the harm of police activity as opposed to the harm of 'offenders'. A corrective to notions of police subculture, these authors show us that police narratives reflect broad, conventional themes – and they discuss the many links between police narratives and popular culture. The plots and metaphors they identify in police officers' stories are crucial to understand the culture behind police authority and engagements.

Chapter 17 is the only contribution in the Handbook that takes a quantitative approach. David Canter, Donna Youngs and David Rowland give an instructive overview of some of the methodological and analytical tools they have used over the years, focussing on the Narrative Role Questionnaire (NRQ) and Life As A Film (LAAF). Distinguishing between the professional, the revenger, the victim and the hero, this chapter outlines fruitful ways of analysing narrative roles and themes in stories. Using a systematic approach to interviewing and data collection, their work counters the usual criticism of narrative analysis as anecdotal and subjective. Great potential exists in further developing these quantitative approaches to data analysis in narrative criminology.

All three chapters in this section present new and important ways to expand narrative criminology, developing new theoretical perspectives and analytical models, taking up and reinvestigating classic ones – and not least, including new forms of data such as stories from the criminal justice 'system' and surveys. The emphasis on combining narrative criminology with other established traditions continues in the next section.

Narrative Dialogue, the Unconscious and Absences

Narratives are complex and ambiguous discursive formations. They contain multiple voices as well as impactful silences. And they are 'heard' in as many ways as there are interlocutors/audience members and readings. Researchers may discern a narrative 'on paper', equipped with a formal definition, but narratives also exist as cognitive schemes in the minds of audiences. Thus, it may be necessary for narrative analysts to cross over to boldly interpretative perspectives, from identifying to reconstructing narratives. Chapters in this section move narrative criminology in this direction, emphasising narrative dialogue, the unconscious and narrative absences.

Chapter 18 starts out with a detailed description of socionarratology and dialogical narrative analysis (DNA), showing how it can be applied in a particular case study. Dan J. S. Barrera argues that media narratives have a close relationship with the ongoing drug war in the Philippines. He links apocalyptic narratives from leading politicians in media to an 'apocalyptic style of war on drugs'. It is not always an easy and direct relationship however and the dialogical and often ambiguous nature of stories makes narrative analysis difficult. Indeed, narrative analysis is an ongoing project, never finalised and full of contradictions. Alfredo Verde and Nicolò Knechtlin take this idea further in Chapter 19 by pointing out the many similarities between psychoanalysis and narrative criminology. The relevance of psychoanalysis for narrative criminology is demonstrated in an interview with an Italian football 'hooligan'. The justifications often studied by narrative criminologists, for example, are, like defence mechanisms, not entirely known to the subject. Offenders are multifaceted, stories are co-constructed to deal with inner and outer tensions and samples are often small. Illustratively, several of the chapters in this volume are based on a single case, as is theirs.

Stories speak – they put things 'out there' – but they also contain absences. Lois Presser contends in Chapter 20 that the narrative sustaining penal harm in the US and elsewhere leaves much consequential 'stuff' unsaid concerning proper living. She demonstrates *how* we might rigorously locate the 'not said' in stories, including but not limited to the impactful stories that criminologists tell. Her methods include coding for figurative devices and ambiguation. Her vantage is critical, connecting to notions of ideological control and the silencing of the subaltern. Combined, the chapters in this section call for further engagement with narrative traditions in the social sciences and elsewhere. They demonstrate the potential depth of narrative analysis in criminology.

Connecting Stories, Power and Social Inequalities

The final section of the book contains chapters that explicitly take on one of the greatest challenges of narrative criminology: taking power and social inequalities into account. Narratives do not exist in a vacuum. Many contributors to this volume raise similar concerns (e.g. Earle, Pentintseva, Brisman, Presser, Kurtz and Colburn, Dollinger and Heppchen), but the authors of these final chapters confront social hierarchy as a central issue. In rather different ways, they show a way forward for narrative criminology that includes challenging established truths and knowledge regimes – while also pointing to alternatives.

In Chapter 21 Zhang Xiaoye and Dong Xianliang study Chinese penal policy where by prisoners write autobiographical essay, as part of the admissions process. These accounts are a great resource for narrative scholars and shed light on Chinese prison reforms and society. They raise the question: Who tells the story when the story is ordered by officials? The inmate's official story is moulded by the prison into a testament to reform. In this way, Xiaoye and Xianliang question previous research that assumes prisoners' stories function as counternarratives – and claim that inmates are engaged in a narrative combat they can never win. Their chapter shows that certain contemporary practices of autobiographical writing in China must be viewed in light of the Chinese literary tradition and the 'confession movement' initiated by the Communist party. Power relations surrounding literary genres and political environments shape texts.

Sandberg and Andersen conceive of opposition to harm-doing as a narrative accomplishment in Chapter 22. Their primary aim is not only to identify but also to challenge narrative consensus, in this case the established belief that Islam is a religion of war. Their study centres on narrative resistance to jihadist terrorism among young Norwegian Muslims. The chapter discloses the nature of such resistance – distinguished as factual, emotional and humorous counternarratives – and silencing as a narrative strategy for those that are narratively and otherwise largely excluded from the mainstream. Our final chapter by Floretta Boonzaier (Chapter 23) makes the case for a decolonial, intersectional approach to narrative criminology, drawing on interviews with women sex workers about their experiences of gendered violence in South Africa. Boonzaier illuminates the multiple and intersectional nature of the women's subjugation, focussing her analysis on convergences of power abuse at material, representational and structural levels. In their stories the women blur boundaries between 'types of crime' rather in contrast to criminology including narrative criminology has largely attended to factors/stories behind one crime. This blurring reflects the lived experience of intersecting forms of oppression.

Narrative criminology is intrinsically critical; it questions established truths and reveals power structures and hegemonies of consensus. Social justice lurks as an inspiration of most of the chapters in this Handbook. Closing with these three chapters highlights the critical and emancipatory potential of narrative criminology.

Future Directions

Stories connect the present, with the past and future. Reflecting upon the future directions of narrative criminology in the present also means telling a story with potential self-fulfilling implications. So what might the future hold for narrative criminology? Perhaps we can begin to think this through by telling another story.

In the spring of 2019, just as we were finishing work on this book, news circulated about a man who shot and killed 51 people and injured dozens more, as they prayed at a mosque in Christchurch, New Zealand. Chillingly, he live-streamed the attack on several social media platforms, carrying a gun inscribed with the names of previous mass shooters who had come before. His manifesto has been subsequently banned; likewise, news media have agreed not to circulate his footage. Following Prime Minister Jacinda Arden's vow to never mention the shooter by name, most news media have followed suit. This event all too clearly exemplifies the narrative motivations of mass violence. Stills from the footage, recorded on body worn video, are uncannily like a first-person shooter video game. Inscribing the names of other mass shooters makes evident his intention to enact a similar plotline. At the same time, this incident also tells of the contemporary politics of silencing; a refusal to retell the killer's story or even to acknowledge him by name. It also points to the global circulation of narratives, and their importance, in a contemporary age.

Shortly after the attack, another video circulated online. The Black Power Gang, a biker gang, which takes inspiration from the Black Panthers, performed a Haka outside the mosque. A group of men, instantly recognisable as gang members, in matching leather jackets and bandanas, moved together to the sound of their shouts in Maori, telling a powerful story about nationhood, mourning and belonging. That story conveys grief and anger as well as solidarity and common feeling. Soon after, further videos circulated of Hakas by school children and even other gangs. Despite lasting only a couple of minutes each, these complex performances challenge contemporary and historic marginalisation. The performance calls to mind New Zealand's own violent, colonial history. Performed by a group of outlaws, it challenges who can deliver justice, or even what justice might be.

These events raise many potential questions for narrative criminology. The performance is surely embedded in stories and relies on stories to be understood. But can a dance or performance *be* a story? How can we analyse it narratively? Furthermore, what happens to 'the story of the dance' when it is performed by subsequent groups? Or when it continues its travel as a film clip to global mainstream media? Can it be part of a counternarrative opposing xenophobia, racism and religious extremism worldwide? And what happens when the story 'comes back'? Will it be at all recognisable for those that initially performed the dance? We do not have the answers, but we believe these are all crucial questions for narrative criminologists in an increasingly global world.

Travelling Stories

Narrative criminology is well placed to explore how stories of 'crime' travel across time and space, nationally and internationally. Crucially, the movement of stories ought not be considered organic agency is implicated. Thus, we see two key future directions in narrative criminology research as interconnected – global traffic in stories and the deployment of stories to advance, uphold or contest power relations and inequalities. Along with stories of divine will and folk heroism, stories of 'criminals', 'crime' and 'authorities' migrate with dramatic ramifications. Iconic tales of Wild West Sheriffs influence contemporary policing, and can be traced to earlier stories of the valiant soldiers of the King's Army. Stories of The Knights Templar defending Christian holy sites in the twelfth century reappeared in the manifesto of a Norwegian mass murderer in 2011. In the same way, 'gangster narratives' have travelled a long way to today's popular culture through the idealisation of outlaws in the medieval period. The Robin Hood story still colours contemporary characterisations of tough men of honour fighting 'the system' – seen in contemporary Mexican *narcocorrido* or North American gangsta rap. More commonly, however, 'criminals' are portrayed as imposters and villains across contemporary societies.

Thus, rather than focussing on a single field or group of storytellers, we might examine the way narratives and their meanings circulate and may change their meaning in different contexts. For example, Fraser and Atkinson's (2014) parallel ethnography looks at how young people in Glasgow sought to narrate themselves as gang members on their social media pages, for example by 'friending' well-known criminals, posing with gang graffiti and so on. In the context of the street, gang membership was fluid. These pages, once read and documented by civilian intelligence analysts, could constitute evidence of being at risk of gang membership – a classification with potentially far-reaching consequences. Similarly, Lindegaard (2018) explores how young men navigate different contexts, schools, jobs and 'the street,' and different neighbourhoods in Cape Town, South Africa. Her emphasis is not on stories but could have been. The 'ghetto chameleons' drew upon – and were constrained by – embodied stories developed in one context and transplanted in another. These stories were the product not only of individual lives, neighbourhoods and particular institutions, but also political context, mainstream discourses and popular culture.

Crime discourses emanating from the US have been spectacularly mobile. Whereas 'three strikes' derives from baseball, America's alleged national pastime, it reappears as a trope for commonsense punishment in the US, the UK (Jones & Newburn, 2006) and farther afield. We might consider what specific ideas about crime and justice lend themselves to adaptation elsewhere. We should also wonder about the role of geopolitics in the unequal transnational transfer of ideas about crime and punishment (de Sousa Santos, 2006). Furthermore we might examine how different narrators story the same event. And, beyond that – how such narratives might anticipate, respond to or contest that of the other group. Storytelling always anticipates and responds to present or distant, real or imagined audiences.

To study stories' reworkings and routes demands multi-sited data collection. It also demands a sensitivity to varied forms for the same basic prototype: these are the forms covered in this Handbook – diverse texts, images and objects, grasped through ethnographic observation, interviews, archives and so forth. Studying how stories travel would move our narrative perspective even further away from a traditional focus on individuals (and their storytelling) to an emphasis on stories as points of interest and research units.

Harm, Power and Inequality

Narrative criminology is fundamentally committed to understanding issues of harm, power and inequality (Presser & Sandberg, 2019). Whatever topics, concepts and methodologies steer their work, narrative criminologists should remain attentive to power. This will continue to mean studying harms done by the state as well as criminalised individuals and groups. It means more enquiries into those narratives that challenge harms.

We can very usefully attend to questions of power and inequality in the research process. We must attend to the 'narrative environment' (Gubrium & Holstein, 2008, p. 252) – and to which speakers are empowered to speak. Institutions (e.g. prisons, courts, schools) empower some narrators and not others. When we conduct research in these places, we inevitably become part of the power dynamics (Presser, 2005). These environments also shape the things that people feel free to say. We must attend to the ways that narrative conventions and patterns make available some kinds of realities whilst ruling out others. These issues surface in many of the Handbook chapters.

In addition to attending to power and inequality in the research process, we might also consider which individuals or groups our research stories make visible, or invisible. In order to extend criminology beyond the Global North, we should also be cognisant of criminology's geopolitical divisions (Aas, 2012). Indeed, there is a neat synergy between narrative criminology and 'southern' criminology since both question where a particular story (or theory) comes from, and whose purposes such a story might serve. Whilst criminologists question whether theories developed in the Anglophone north might effectively travel (Carrington, Hogg, & Sozzo, 2016; see also; Cain, 2000). Nonetheless, we still contend that narrative criminology may be more transposable than most criminological theories (Fleetwood, 2014).

Furthermore, narrative criminology is poised to take all kinds of 'stories' seriously, and has the potential to attend to historic 'silences'. We might direct our attentions to indigenous arts or crafts that tell stories about colonialism, violence and ongoing injustices (Cunneen, 2011). For narrative criminological theory to move beyond the Global North, we need to be better able to think about race, colonialism and postcoloniality, such as understanding that when stories move from the Global South to the Global North and vice versa their travels are deeply embedded in power structures and global inequalities.

Lastly, as narrative criminologists, we might consider if or when it is our duty not just to analyse narratives, but to try to change them. How might our work amplify the potential power of counternarratives that seek to confront or challenge harmful narratives? Not all of us undertake the kind of work that melds well with activism, but we might all ask – what role can we play in exposing or supporting particular narratives beyond the academy.

Conclusion

In compiling this edited volume, we have tried to reflect the 'state of the art' in narrative criminology. Whilst we draw on the work of some familiar names, we have especially tried to include early career scholars, and to aim for an international representation. The result is an extensive and varied selection of scholarship. The 23 chapters of this Handbook are empirically, geographically, topically and thematically diverse. They share an interest in – and more thorough engagement with – methods than previous work within narrative criminology (but see Presser & Sandberg, 2015b). The chapters demonstrate that narrative criminology is not wedded to any one data source or form of analysis. There is a methodological openness towards any approach that can assist in explorations of how stories motivate, sustain or prevent harmful action. As one of the last disciplines to have its own 'narrative turn', criminology is able to draw on an already-established set of research tools. Whilst we cannot predict what future developments in methodology await, we can point to the fruitfulness of continuing to draw on this interdisciplinary scholarship on narrative.

The chapters in this Handbook expand the horizon of narrative criminology in many other ways too; most importantly, extending what we approach as 'story', and what or whom we think of as storytellers. In this volume, people, but also texts, objects and pictures, tell stories – and these stories are analysed in new ways, emphasising absences, dialogue, allegories, humour and elements of tall tales. The political dimension is more present than ever. Chapters explore intersectionality, narrative agency and narrative resistance in meetings with injustice and powerful hegemonic consensuses. All chapters work from the fundamental premise that 'crime' is constituted in and through stories. This is a simple idea, but as these chapters show, one that inspires creative, innovative and critical scholarship.

Like stories, academic perspectives travel, and live their own lives beyond the control of those that initially framed them. We thus encourage readers to do as the contributors in this book have done, and make narrative criminology 'their own'. This can help us move forward in directions we had not anticipated. Our hope is that narrative criminology can be a tool for critique and thus inspire counternarratives at the same time as it remains guided by the empirical data (stories), and committed to intellectual openness and integrity. Most of all, we hope that narrative criminology can inspire researchers to *do good work* – in academia and beyond. At the core of this is the difficult task of connecting intimate, narrative imaginaries to the vast horizons of a world out there.

References

Aas, K. F. (2012). 'The Earth is one but the world is not': Criminological theory and its geopolitical divisions. *Theoretical Criminology*, *16*(1), 5–20.

Arnull, E., & Ryder, J. (2019). 'Because it's fun': English and American girls' counter-hegemonic stories of alcohol and marijuana use. *Journal of Youth Studies*, pp. 1–17.

Atkinson, P., & Silverman, D. (1997). Kundera's Immortality: The interview society and the invention of the self. *Qualitative Inquiry*, *3*(3), 304–325.

Baker, D. (2018). Using narrative to construct accountability in cases of death after police contact. *Australian and New Zealand Journal of Criminology*, *52*(1), 60–75.

Banks, J., & Albertson, K. (2018). Veterans and violence: An exploration of pre-enlistment, military and post-service life. *European Journal of Criminology*, *15*(6), 730–747.

Barthes, R. (1977). Introduction to the structural analysis of narratives. In S. Heath (Trans.), *Image, music, text* (pp. 79–124). New York, NY: Hill & Wang.
Becker, H. S. (1963). *Outsiders*. New York, NY: Free Press of Glencoe.
Brewer, J. D. (2000). *Ethnography*. Buckingham: Open University Press.
Brisman, A. (2019). The fable of The Three Little Pigs: Climate change and green cultural criminology. *International Journal for Crime, Justice and Social Democracy*, *8*(1), 46–69.
Cain, M. (2000). Orientalism, occidentalism and the sociology of crime. *British Journal of Criminology*, *40*(2), 239–260.
Canter, D., & Youngs, D. (2012). Narratives of criminal action and forensic psychology. *Legal and Criminological Psychology*, *17*(2), 262–275.
Carrington, K., Hogg, R., & Sozzo, M. (2016). Southern criminology. *British Journal of Criminology*, *56*(1), 1–20.
Castellano, R. (1962). *The book of Lamentations*. London: Penguin Books.
Ciesla, K., Ioannou, M., & Hammond, L. (2019). Women offenders' criminal narrative experience. *Journal of Criminal Psychology*, *9*(1), 23–43.
Colvin, S., & Pisoiu, D. (2018). When being bad is good? Bringing neutralization theory to subcultural narratives of right-wing violence. *Studies in Conflict & Terrorism*, 1–16. doi:10.1080/1057610X.2018.1452754
Cunneen, C. (2011). Postcolonial perspectives for criminology. In M. Bosworth & C. Hoyle (Eds.), *What is criminology?* Oxford: Oxford University Press.
Easterling, B. A., Feldmeyer, B., & Presser, L. (2018). Narrating mother identities from prison. *Feminist Criminology*. doi:10.1177/1557085118773457
Fleetwood, J. (2014). *Drug mules: Women in the international cocaine trade*. Basingstoke: Palgrave Macmillan.
Fleetwood, J. (2016). Narrative habitus: Thinking through structure/agency in the narratives of offenders. *Crime, Media, Culture*, *12*(2), 173–192.
Fraser, A., & Atkinson, C. (2014). Making up gangs: Looping, labelling and the new politics of intelligence-led policing. *Youth Justice*, *14*(2), 154–170.
Goodlad, K., Ioannou, M., & Hunter, M. (2018). The criminal narrative experience of psychopathic and personality disordered offenders. *International Journal of Offender Therapy and Comparative Criminology*, *63*(4), 523–542.
Gubrium, J. F., & Holstein, J. A. (2008). Narrative ethnography. In S. N. Hesse-Biber & P. Leavy (Eds.), *Handbook of emergent methods*. New York, NY: Guilford Press.
Hammersvik, E. (2018). Making sense of 'helping friends': 'Flexing' motivational accounts of cannabis growing. *Journal of Contemporary Ethnography*, *47*, 88–112.
Henriksen, A.-K., & Bengtsson, T. T. (2018). Trivializing violence: Marginalized youth narrating everyday violence. *Theoretical Criminology*, *22*(1), 99–115.
Herman, J. L. (1997). *Trauma and recovery: The aftermath of violence – from domestic abuse to political terror* (2nd ed.). New York, NY: Basic Books.
Hogan, P. C. (2003). *The mind and its stories: Narrative universals and human emotions*. Cambridge: Cambridge University Press.
Houge, A. B. (2016). Re-presentations of defendant perpetrators in sexual war violence cases before international and military criminal courts. *British Journal of Criminology*, *56*(3), 419–437.

Houge, A. B. (2018). Narrative expressivism: A criminological approach to the expressive function of international criminal justice. *Criminology and Criminal Justice*, *19*(3), 277–293.

Ioannou, M., Synnott, J., Lowe, E., & Tzani-Pepelasi, C. (2018). Applying the criminal narrative experience framework to young offenders. *International Journal of Offender Therapy and Comparative Criminology*, *62*(13), 4091–4107.

James, V., & Gossett, J. (2018). Of monsters and men: Exploring serial murderers' discourses of neutralization. *Deviant Behavior*, *39*(9), 1120–1139.

Jones, T., & Newburn, T. (2006). Three strikes and you're out: Exploring symbol and substance in American and British crime control politics. *British Journal of Criminology*, *46*(5), 781–802.

Katz, J. (1988). *Seductions of crime: Moral and sensual attractions in doing evil*. New York, NY: Basic Books.

Keeton, R. M. (2015). 'The race of pale men should increase and multiply': Religious narratives and indian removal. In L. Presser & S. Sandberg (Eds.), *Narrative criminology: Understanding stories of crime*. New York, NY: New York University Press.

Kruttschnitt, C., & Kang, T. (2019). Do intersectional variations shape prisoners' understanding of their past lives? An examination of the stock narratives of persistent offenders. *Justice Quarterly*, 1–28. doi:10.1080/07418825.2019.1575456

Kurtz, D. L., & Upton, L. L. (2018). The gender in stories: How war stories and police narratives shape masculine police culture. *Women & Criminal Justice*, *28*(4), 282–300.

Lindegaard, M. R. (2018). *Surviving gangs, violence and racism in Cape Town: Ghetto chameleons*. London: Routledge.

Llosa, M. V. (1981). *The war of the end of the world*. London: Picador.

Maccoby, E. E., & Maccoby, N. (1954). The interview: A tool of social science. In G. Lindzey (Ed.), *Handbook of social psychology*. Theory and method (Vol. 1, pp. 449–487). Reading, MA: Addison-Wesley.

Maruna, S. (2001). *Making good: How ex-convicts reform and rebuild their lives* (1st ed.). Washington, DC: American Psychological Association.

Maruna, S. (2015). Foreword: Narrative criminology as the new mainstream. In L. Presser & S. Sandberg (Eds.), *Narrative criminology: Understanding stories of crime*. New York, NY & London: New York University Press.

Mills, C. W. (1940). Situated actions and vocabularies of motive. *American Sociological Review*, *5*(6), 904–913.

Pemberton, A., & Aarten, P. G. (2018). Narrative in the study of victimological processes in terrorism and political violence: An initial exploration. *Studies in Conflict & Terrorism*, *41*(7), 541–556.

Pemberton, A., Mulder, E., & Aarten, P. G. M. (2018). Stories of injustice: Towards a narrative victimology. *European Journal of Criminology*. *16*(4), 391–412. doi:10.1177/1477370818770843

Petintseva, O. (2018). *Discursive harms: Youth justice and migration*. Basingstoke: Palgrave Macmillan.

Presser, L. (2005). Negotiating power and narrative in research: Implications for feminist methodology. *Signs: Journal of Women in Culture and Society*, *30*(4), 2067–2090.

Presser, L. (2009). The narratives of offenders. *Theoretical Criminology*, *13*(2), 177–200.

Presser, L. (2013). *Why we harm*. New Brunswick, NJ & London: Rutgers University Press.

Presser, L. (2018). *Inside story. How narratives drive mass harm*. Oakland, CA: University of California Press.

Presser, L., & Sandberg, S. (2015a). *Narrative criminology: Understanding stories of crime*. New York, NY & London: New York University Press.

Presser, L., & Sandberg, S. (2015b). Research strategies for narrative criminology. In J. Miller & W. Palacios (Eds.), *Qualitative research in criminology. Advances in criminological theory* (Vol. 20, pp. 85–100). New Brunswick, NJ: Transaction Publishers.

Presser, L., & Sandberg, S. (2019). Narrative criminology as critical criminology. *Critical Criminology*, *27*(1), 131–143.

Raitanen, J., Sandberg, S., & Oksanen, A. (2019). The bullying-school shooting nexus: Bridging master narratives of mass violence with personal narratives of social exclusion. *Deviant Behavior*, *40*(1), 96–109.

Rauschenbach, M. (2018). Individuals accused of international crimes as delegitimized agents of truth. *International Criminal Justice Review*, *28*(4), 291–316.

Rowlands, D., Youngs, D., & Canter, D. (2019). Exploring an agency-communion model of identity transformation in recovery from substance misuse. *Journal of Substance Use*, *24*(3), 265–272.

Sandberg, S. (2010). What can "lies" tell us about life? Notes towards a framework of narrative criminology. *Journal of Criminal Justice Education*, *21*(4), 447–465.

Sandberg, S. (2013). Are self-narratives unified or fragmented, strategic or determined? Reading Breivik's manifesto in light of narrative criminology. *Acta Sociologica*, *56*(1), 65–79.

Sandberg, S. (2016). The importance of stories untold: Life-story, event-story and trope. *Crime, Media, Culture*, *12*(2), 153–171.

Sandberg, S., Copes, H., & Pedersen, W. (2019). When Peaceful People Fight: Beyond neutralization and subcultural theory. *British Journal of Criminology*. doi:10.1093/bjc/azz032

Sandberg, S., & Fleetwood, J. (2017). Street talk and Bourdieusian criminology: Bringing narrative to field theory. *Criminology and Criminal Justice*, *17*(4), 365–381.

Sandberg, S., & Ugelvik, T. (Eds.). (2016a). *Crime, Media, Culture: International Journal*, *12*(2).

Sandberg, S., & Ugelvik, T. (2016b). "Why do offenders tape their crimes? Crime and punishment in the age of the selfie. *British Journal of Criminology*, *57*, 1023–1040.

Scott, M. B., & Lyman, S. M. (1968). Accounts. *American Sociological Review*, *33*(1), 46–62.

de Sousa Santos, B. (2006). Globalizations. *Theory, Culture & Society*, *23*(2–3), 393–399.

Sykes, G. M. (1958). *The society of captives: A study of a maximum security prison*. Princeton, NJ: Princeton University Press.

Sykes, G. M., & Matza, D. (1957). Techniques of neutralization: A theory of delinquency. *American Sociological Review*, *22*(6), 664–670.

Ugelvik, T. (2012). Prisoners and their victims: Techniques of neutralization, techniques of the self. *Ethnography, 13*(3), 259–277.

Ugelvik, T. (2015). The rapist and the proper criminal: The exclusion of immoral others as narrative work on the self. In L. Presser & S. Sandberg (Eds.), *Narrative criminology: Understanding stories of crime*. New York, NY & London: New York University Press.

Vannier, M. (2018). The power of the pen: Prisoners' letters to explore extreme imprisonment. *Criminology and Criminal Justice*. doi:10.1177/1748895818818872

Walklate, S. (2019). Images of atrocity: From victimhood to redemption and the implications for a (narrative) victimology. In R. Lippens & E. Murray (Eds.), *Representing the experience of war and atrocity: Interdisciplinary explorations in visual criminology* (pp. 73–92). Cham: Springer International Publishing.

Walklate, S., Maher, J., McCulloch, J., Fitz-Gibbon, K., & Beavis, K. (2018). Victim stories and victim policy: Is there a case for a narrative victimology? *Crime, Media, Culture*. doi:10.1177/1741659018760105

Warr, J. (2019). 'Always gotta be two mans': Lifers, risk, rehabilitation, and narrative labour. *Punishment & Society*. doi:10.1177/1462474518822487

Webb, M., Copes, H., & Hendricks, P. S. (2019). Narrative identity, rationality, and microdosing classic psychedelics. *International Journal of Drug Policy, 70*, 33–39.

Wesely, J. K. (2018). Co-constituting narrative: The role of researcher identity bids in qualitative interviews with women ex-offenders. *Criminal Justice Studies, 31*(3), 213–229.

Youngs, D., & Canter, D. V. (2012a). Narrative roles in criminal action: An integrative framework for differentiating offenders. *Legal and Criminological Psychology, 17*(2), 233–249.

Youngs, D., & Canter, D. V. (2012b). Offenders' crime narratives as revealed by the Narrative Roles Questionnaire. *International Journal of Offender Therapy and Comparative Criminology, 57*(3), 289–311.

PART I: COLLECTING STORIES

OBSERVATIONS AND FIELDWORK

Chapter 2

Narrative Ethnography under Pressure: Researching Storytelling on the Street

Sébastien Tutenges

Introduction

Narrative researchers have traditionally prioritized the study of written texts, such as the stories found in letters, diaries, newspapers, official documents and books by classical authors such as Shakespeare and Poe. Comparatively little attention has been placed on oral stories and their performance. Written stories – especially the classics – are perpetually and ritualistically scrutinized, whereas oral narrative performances tend to be neglected or even devalued in the research literature (Bauman, 1982; Finnegan, 1992, p. 155). In the words of Richard Bauman (1986), oral stories are widely treated as, 'simple, formless, lacking in artistic quality and complexity, the collective expression of unsophisticated peasants and primitives' (p. 7). Bauman calls for an ethnographic shift in narrative research in order to explore the performance of oral stories in their everyday context.

In this chapter, I will share both experiences and advice on conducting ethnographic research on storytelling, drawing on recent fieldwork among Muslim drug dealers in an open drug market in Oslo called 'Godka'. The purpose of the fieldwork was to understand the relationship between street youths and jihadist groups such as ISIS and al-Shabaab. The basic question was what characterizes the narratives and counternarratives about jihadism that circulate among Muslim street youths? The aim of this chapter is not to answer this question, but rather to describe where and how I went about investigating it. In short, I argue that an ethnographic approach to storytelling allows for consideration of the storying process as it evolves and changes across time and space. Moreover, I suggest that narrative researchers may benefit from studying storytelling with all of their senses – not just hearing or reading words, but actively sensing narrative performances with their entire bodies.

The chapter is organized as follows. First, I present the main research traditions that inspire my study, namely narrative ethnography and narrative criminology. Second, I describe the first day of my fieldwork in Godka, focussing on how I gained access to the dealers and the narrative conventions that govern their interactions. Third, I describe my encounter with two young men and how I proceeded to open them, as well as myself, to the mutuality of storytelling. Finally, I offer some methodological conclusions and a summary of the basic characteristics that define Godka as a narrative environment.

Narrative Ethnography and Criminology

A key inspiration in my narrative research comes from anthropological, folkloristic and sociological studies that consider stories and storytelling as valuable mediums through which local cultures are expressed and experienced. To borrow the words of Ray Cashman (2012), I strive to 'appreciate vernacular expressive culture – particularly narrative – as a window into aesthetics, values, beliefs, preoccupations, and habits of mind that may be shared (or contested) among a given group' (p. 182). Stories and storytelling are culturally contingent phenomena. The way people speak, gesticulate and listen varies cross-culturally, and the meaning of a story, or even of a single word, can be drastically different in different contexts (Polletta, 2006, p. 167). Indeed, a joke may provoke laughter, tears, yawns or criminal prosecution depending on the time, place and manner of its telling (Brown, Esbensen, & Geis, 2010, p. 49). Hence, narrative performances must be researched in their cultural context.

The approach taken in my Oslo fieldwork may be termed narrative ethnography because it uses ethnographic methods to study the cultural context, occasions and processes of narrative activity (Gubrium & Holstein, 2008). Gubrium and Holstein (2009, p. vii) explain that whereas traditional narrative research considers stories mainly for their internal organization and meaning, narrative ethnography widens the focus to examine stories as they are being performed on specific social occasions. This widened focus requires ethnographic attention to an array of situational factors, most notably the cultural context from which narratives emerge; the locations in which narratives are performed or not performed; the expressive means used during narrative performances; the sequence of actions that make up the scenario of performances; and the impact performances have on the narrators and their audiences (Bauman, 1986, p. 4).

There is a close connection between the traditions of narrative ethnography and narrative criminology. Both are based on the view of stories as dynamic interactional accomplishments with meanings that vary depending on where they are told, when, how, among whom and for what purposes. One of the founders of narrative criminology, Lois Presser (2010), thus emphasizes that researchers who use narrative data 'must take the contexts of story telling into account. If they do not – and usually they do not – they risk making mistakes about what the story and its delivery mean' (p. 441). One of Presser's major studies is based on interviews conducted in prisons, which turned out to be a context that significantly shaped the storytelling of her male interviewees. 'The circumstance of incarceration,' she writes (2010), 'clarifies the efforts by many of the men to be in control in the interview' (p. 442). She describes (2005), moreover, how the men she interviewed structured their stories to obtain certain effects, such as eliciting empathy and understanding from her. In other words, the men's stories were shaped not only by the events that they recounted but also by the circumstances in which they were told (see also Bauman, 1986, p. 2). Presser (2005) therefore argues that '[t]he researcher's goal is not to emancipate the authentic story of the narrator – none exists – but rather to expose as much as she can of the relations that influence the construction of the story that is told' (p. 2087).

Another narrative criminologist, Jennifer Fleetwood (2014), explicitly uses the expression 'narrative ethnography' to describe her work (p. 11). Drawing on ethnographic observation and interviews, she collected data over a 16-month period inside Ecuadorian prisons. Sustained copresence with prisoners allowed her to immerse herself in their situation and understand some of the narrative conventions governing their day-to-day interactions. Fleetwood (2016) emphasizes the importance of being present and patiently building trustful relationships, arguing that with interview data alone she might have 'ignored the particular narrative forms common in prisons' (p. 27). Sustained ethnographic fieldwork among criminal offenders – be that inside or outside of prison – may at times be 'exhausting' (Fleetwood, 2014, p. 11), even dangerous (Bucerius, 2014, p. 82), but can also provide moments of laughter (Sandberg & Tutenges, 2018), friendship (Copes, 2018) and appreciation of the common humanity behind stereotypes.

One of the advantages of doing extensive ethnographic fieldwork – in contrast to, say, document studies or hit-and-run interviews – is that it facilities embodied engagement and understandings of other people's situation (Tutenges, forthcoming). The thorough ethnographer (and the thorough interviewer, for that matter) does not attend to words only, but also to various nonverbal signals such as dress, gesticulation, facial expressions, intonation and pace of speech. This is important, also for the narrative researcher, given the embodied nature of storytelling. As Bret Smith (2007) puts it, 'we tell stories about, in, out of, and through our bodies', and our bodies, in turn, are significantly shaped by the stories we are exposed to (p. 395). Consider the way children sometimes mimic, in movement and speech, their favourite character from children's movies. We humans are mimetic creatures who move and narrate in ways that significant others have done before us. All of this calls for 'an embodied rather than a disembodied narrative inquiry' (Smith, 2007, p. 395), such as that of narrative ethnography. By applying all of the senses during fieldwork and attending to both verbal and nonverbal stimuli, the narrative ethnographer may develop a feel or knack for the stories people are telling.

Ditte Andersen's (2015b) research on drug treatment is a good example of how the narrative ethnographer may develop embodied sensibilities of storytelling in the field. Her fieldwork was conducted over a 5-month period in two different treatment facilities. As her work progressed, she became aware of the widespread uses and effects of humour in various treatment situations. Whereas the professionals generally considered their humour as good-natured attempts to lift the mood, Andersen sensed that the humour also had a dark side, both for her and for the youth in treatment. She (2015b) writes of how witnessing the professionals' funny stories (for example, on how to 'improve' suicide attempts) felt 'strenuous, almost tormenting,' giving her 'aching cheeks caused by continuously forcing artificial smiles' (p. 270). Her reactions were important sources of data on the elusive dynamics of humour in day-to-day interactions.

She also tried to use interviews to collect data about humour, but with poor results. The young interviewees 'did not provide details about how they experienced professionals' use of humour,' perhaps because this topic was too abstract or embarrassing for them to talk about in a formal interview situation (p. 270). Andersen's work illustrates the importance of narrative ethnographers using their own bodies and senses during fieldwork in order to make explicit the implicit conventions of speech and storytelling (see also Andersen, 2015a). This can be time-consuming and wearing, especially for those of us studying crime and deviance.

The primary concern in narrative criminology is to examine how stories inspire, sustain or prevent harmful action (Presser & Sandberg, 2015, p. 11). Ethnographers are well placed to make such examinations within and, importantly, beyond the interview situation. Sociologist Curtis Jackson-Jacobs' (2009) research on the social organization of fights highlights some of the strengths and challenges of deep immersion ethnography. He conducted participant observation and interviews among brawlers over the course of more than 4 years. He hung out with them in their homes and at bars. He saw them fighting and listened to them talk about fights. And he also participated in fights himself, breaking an arm in the process. These prolonged, embodied engagements earned him unique insights into the human tendency to undertake certain actions in order to create desired stories. Jackson-Jacobs (2009) observes that, '[w]hen people fight, they often do things to make good storytelling details. They perform for future storytellers, for present audiences, and also for themselves, appreciating their own conduct much as audiences do' (p. 177). Indeed, we sometimes do things to get good stories out of it, and good stories sometimes influence the way we do things (Tutenges & Sandberg, 2013). We make and are made by stories.

I observed these dynamics during fieldwork at nightlife resorts in Southern Europe (Tutenges, 2012). In these settings, there is a tendency among young tourists and tour guides to perform drunken, histrionic transgressions, such as doing stripteases, having public sex, wrecking hotel rooms, climbing on rooftops, playing 'I dare you' games and jumping from balconies into swimming pools. Such performances are typically, though not always, undertaken in groups or in front of an audience, and they are almost always followed by engrossing storytelling sessions about what happened, who did what, with whom and so forth. Of course, drunken transgressions may be rewarding in and of themselves, giving those involved a sense of excitement and freedom from restraint. But the reward is often also narrative. People sometimes risk their necks, quite literally, in the pursuit of a story that they can use, for instance, to entertain their friends and gain local fame (Tutenges & Sandberg, 2013). My fieldwork allowed me to observe a number of drunken antics as they unfolded across time and social situations: from their anticipation, to their enactment and finally to their narration on one or more occasions (see also Tutenges, 2015, p. 289).

This is not to argue that fully-fledged ethnography is the only or best way to study stories and storytelling. There are circumstances that can make it unwise, unnecessary or outright impossible to conduct prolonged observation and engagement with research participants. Our choice of methods should be guided not by rigid principles or personal preferences, but by the empirical realities that we wish to explore. And as cofounder of narrative criminology, Sveinung Sandberg (2010b), points out, having been there in the field over long stretches of time is no guarantee of insightful or reliable findings. My argument is that ethnographic fieldwork can provide certain advantages for the narrative researcher, most notably that of allowing close consideration of the storying process as it occurs over time and in different situations. This may enable embodied understandings of narrative activities in their cultural context. The following section tells the story of the first day of my fieldwork in a drug market in Oslo. Focus is on how I gained access to this particular narrative environment and how I understand its defining characteristics.

Inside Godka

It took me some weeks of searching and asking around before I decided to settle on one primary site for my fieldwork: a large open drug market in downtown Oslo. The main part of the market was, and still is, spread across a public square with a broad bridge running over it. Many people are often rushing to and fro for various purposes, such as catching the metro, buying groceries, getting a kebab and praying in the nearby mosque. The place is in motion, except for the people looking for drugs who tend to stand still until approached by a dealer. By calling the market 'open' I mean to say that it is publicly visible, easily accessible and attracts a broad clientele who can choose freely between dealers while retaining their anonymity as they purchase drugs (Pitts, 2008, pp. 76–77). On an average evening during the period when I was conducting fieldwork (2017–2018), there were between 5 and 10 dealers operating the market. Most of the dealers are in their teens or early twenties and with immigrant backgrounds. Some have Norwegian citizenship but others are in the country illegally. The dealers who operate the market are constantly changing, as are the hierarchical relations between them. There are no formalized rules or rulers, and police officers often interfere to make arrests. The area goes by many names, including 'The River' and 'Godka,' which means 'Hole' in Somali. Pretty much anyone with the right attitude, body language and connections can meet up and earn fast money from selling cannabis and other drugs. But one easily gets stuck, the dealers say. You get used to the money, the action and the authority that comes from being an experienced drug dealer.

It was winter and freezing cold when I first visited Godka. I was in the company of two outreach workers from 'Uteseksjonen' ['Outreach Section'] in Oslo, a public organization that specializes in helping at-risk populations on the streets. They had kindly agreed to show me around and introduce me to some of the youths in the area, and it did not take long before they presented me to a young Somali dealer called Ibrahim.[1] He had a long, fresh scar on his neck and was reeling drunk. He looked me over and laughed skeptically, but one of the

---

[1]The names of all research participants and a few unimportant details have been altered to protect anonymity.

outreach workers, Felicia, convinced him that I was not a cop and that I could be trusted. Her word bore a lot of weight because she had been around for a long time and had helped numerous street youths out of all sorts of trouble. So Ibrahim and I walked off towards a tunnel that would take us underground to a fast-food restaurant where we could talk. But, our passage was barred by a group of dealers. One of them pulled Ibrahim aside and another one aggressively asked me who I was and what I wanted. I explained my project while he stared me down and frisked me. 'I'm a researcher from the University of Oslo. I study street culture, religion, and crime,' I said, consciously avoiding controversial words such as 'jihadism' and 'Islamism.' What if he found the two audio recorders in my pocket? Would that put me in the category of 'a problem'? The moment felt unreal, as if I was in some gangster movie. Ibrahim kept joking and laughing and said, 'it's OK,' and other things I could not understand. The guy in front of me puffed himself up even more, his eyes now bulging out with rage. Then he turned around and gave a loud laugh. We could go.

Speaking with ethnographers can come at a cost, especially when you are part of a secretive subculture that views public agents with suspicion (Anderson, 1999). Indeed, to leak insider stories to outsiders can be outright dangerous in criminal milieus like Godka. Doing so may lead to the unshakable stigma of being a 'snitch,' a 'rat' or an 'informer' (Rosenfeld, Jacobs, & Wright, 2003). This is why criminally active individuals are sometimes referred to as, 'hard to reach,' 'hard to access' and 'high risk' (for a critical discussion of these terms, see Glynn, 2013, pp. 50, 67–68). They may be rather easy to find, but they do not share their stories with just anyone. Like so many other urban ethnographers before me, I was under suspicion of being a cop (e.g. Liebow, 2003, p. 155). The drunken Ibrahim, meanwhile, was under suspicion of violating the all-important code of the street: no snitching.

I checked my breathing and heartbeat as we walked down the tunnel. I was excited, not panicky.[2] We had left Felicia and her colleague, but knowing that they were in the vicinity reassured me. Felicia had vouched for me to Ibrahim – perhaps to other dealers as well – and I had been seen in her company. To mess with me would indirectly be to mess with her. She acted, in other words, like my 'sponsor' or 'gatekeeper,' somewhat like 'Doc' did in the classical fieldwork of William Foote Whyte (1993), or 'Tally' in the work of Elliot Liebow (2003) or 'Herman' in the work of Elijah Anderson (2003). The ethnographic literature on sponsors and gatekeepers often emphasizes the *practical importance* these people have for providing information on local customs, clarifying 'dos and don'ts,' ensuring physical safety and opening doors to otherwise closed social circles (see, for example, Hammersley & Atkinson, 1995, pp. 55–67). However, sponsors and gatekeepers can also be of *emotional importance*. They can, for instance, make the fieldworker feel less scared, awkward and alone in the field. I for one felt more at ease, especially during the first weeks of my fieldwork, when I was in the company

---

[2] Much to my own surprise, I rarely felt scared or sad whilst in the field. However, strong negative emotions generally hit me when I came home, especially during the first days immediately following intensive bouts of fieldwork.

Narrative Ethnography under Pressure   33

of Felicia and my other main contact from Uteseksjonen. I could not share any confidential data with them, but I could ask them for advice and consult them for informal debriefing.

Ibrahim and I reached the fast-food restaurant and sat down. This was certainly not the ideal place for holding an interview. The place was crowded and noisy, making it difficult to understand what Ibrahim was saying. Besides, he was too drunk to comprehend fully the implications of being interviewed. There was no way I could get his 'informed consent.' So I just showed him my interview guide and chitchatted to make him feel comfortable; but he looked anything but comfortable. In came the guy who had frisked me, Hetav, in the company of four other guys. They wanted to know what we were doing. Hetav was still the most confrontational, and I decided to direct all my attention on him. I asked if he was religious, what he believed in and other such dry questions that an undercover policeman would probably not have asked. Hetav stopped asking me questions and instead began answering mine. He was talking at high speed and often interrupted himself to look around, eat some fried chicken and say something to somebody from his group. They all seemed stressed out. There were so many people coming in and out of the restaurant, and there was so much noise, along with countless interruptions. In my field notes I described Hetav as, 'restless, edgy, almost in a state of alarm,' and I described the overall mood as 'action packed.' My notes continue: 'This is where it happens. They are busy. So much happening. They obviously like it, to be here in this environment. It's fun, intense, draining.'

Then Hetav shifted into storytelling mode. I am not sure exactly how, but right there in the middle of all the commotion he managed to establish a sort of narrative bubble within which he could tell his story without interruption for an entire 2 or 3 minutes. All ears around the table were on him. Nobody else said anything. The mood, as I experienced it, was concentrated, almost solemn. It was a desistance story that centred on a religious epiphany that he recently had in a mosque. The experience had been a turning point in his life. He no longer committed any crimes. I was deeply moved by the story and by the earnest way he told it. Such openness, and so suddenly. This was an unexpected breakthrough in my fieldwork. After he had finished his story, I said that I found it absolutely fascinating and asked if he could tell it again so I could record it. He consented and I put my audio recorder on the table. I quickly glanced around but saw no raised eyebrows or looks of discomfort. I guess I was no longer under suspicion of being a cop.

I said that he should not mention any names, not even his own, and that he should leave out all details that could put anyone in trouble. He laughed and sang out what sounded like lyrics from a rap tune, 'No face, no case.' I cued him in: 'So just to sum up, two weeks ago you were in the mosque, and you had this talk with the....' 'The Imam, yeah,' he said, picking up the thread. 'He started talking about, you know, a verse from the Quran, right. And I didn't listen that much, but what I realized was that, either you pray or you get prayed on, right. You choose. So that got me thinking differently about everything, you know. 'Cause the meaning is, if you do your sins and sins and sins, you understand what I...?' I said that I understood what he meant. If you do not pray, you sin, and then other people will pray for your sins. We were on the same page, more or less. I prompted him to tell me, again, about his religious experience. He explained that he had not been in the mosque for several years, but after the talk with the Imam he went there and prayed. 'I felt good. It was so nice to feel connected with God again, you understand. And since I prayed that day, all my goals, everything, I've achieved all that I want, you know. So I thought to myself, if this can happen, why not pray a little and then a little more and more and get a great life, you know. That's it.'

End of story. The moment I had turned on my audio recorder, Hetav began speaking in short sentences and with little engagement. All the magic of his first telling was gone. Perhaps it was the audio recorder that sabotaged his story, or perhaps it was the fact that he had to repeat himself. It is said that one should not tell the same joke twice, and I suppose that this is true also for other types of storytelling. You do not tell the same story twice within minutes to the same group of people. What also bothered me was that the first and second version of Hetav's story had a slightly different cast of protagonists and localities. Was it the Imam or a friend who had said, 'either you pray or get prayed on'? Did the conversation take place in the mosque or not? Hetav was getting more and more jittery. His phone was ringing and people outside the restaurant were calling on him. Nonetheless, I was very satisfied with the interview. The sheer fact that I had found street youths willing to talk was a scoop. And after all, his message was clear: His religion had made him law-abiding. He emphasized this point just before leaving: 'If you are in a situation and you have to strangle someone, for example, if you're gonna squeeze him, you start to think, poor guy. Empathy, you know. He breaths and bleeds just like me. People hit people for no reason, right. I would never do that, because of the Quran.' He then apologized himself and went off.

A few minutes later I was up on the square next to Hetav who was busy selling drugs. The discrepancy between what he had just told and what he was now doing seemed not to bother him in the least. No signs of qualms whatsoever. Earlier, during the interview, his words and body language had not indicated to me that he was making things up, and his friends also seemed to accept his story. Had he invented a story that he thought I would like to hear? Was his story true on some level? Had he used the interview as a pretext for fantasizing about how his life could have been? Had it all just been a game to test me? In any case, on that first day in Godka, I was able to demonstrate to quite a few people exactly what my work consisted of: I asked questions about crime and religion; I recorded stories with my audio recorder; and I hung out with people to observe them.

Over the course of my fieldwork, I heard many stories akin to Hetav's and have come to understand them as a form of *imaginative small talk*, which I consider a significant subtype of conventional 'small talk' (Coupland, 2000; see also Kalkan, 2018, pp. 393–399). Imaginative small talk is informal communication that centres on fictional speech acts.[3] This communication does not have to

---

[3] What I refer to as imaginative small talk is akin to what Malinowski calls 'phatic talk' (2003). I do not use Malinowski's expression because of its pejorative elements. I agree with his argument that 'phatic talk' is an important type of communication 'in which ties of union are created by a mere exchange of words' (2003, p. 10), but I am critical of his description of 'phatic talk' as aimless and uninteresting.

be accurate, plausible or carry any specific messages. That does not mean, however, that it is empty or simple lying. Imaginative small talk can serve multiple interactional purposes: to fill out silences; to capture people's attention; to exhibit storytelling virtuosity; to engage others in the same conversational activity; to create a shared mood; to establish, sustain, and improve relationships; to turn awareness away from potential conflicts; or to perform a certain identity. Moreover, although imaginative small talk can be rather poor in *factual truths*, it may be rich in *existential truths* in the sense of corresponding to the realities of a person's feelings, dreams and beliefs. For example, Hetav's desistance story might have reflected something existentially pertinent to him, like the feeling of leading a sinful life, the dream of a new beginning and the belief that religion holds the key to positive change.

It is impossible to know exactly why Hetav told his desistance story, but it had the palpable effect of turning an awkward encounter into engrossing conversation. What gave the story this effect was not only Hetav's skills as a storyteller but also his high status among the dealers in Godka. He had a commanding presence, a fun disposition, good connections and access to top quality drugs. When he talked, people usually listened. Moreover, his story was something of a classic in Godka, a sort of 'formula story' (Loseke, 2012) in the sense that it is widely circulating and features recognizable characters (e.g. 'the religious person' and 'the criminal'), predictable plot lines (e.g. from crime to religion) and standard moralities (e.g. crime is bad, religion is good). I think that Hetav's story was so readily and respectfully received by his friends because they recognized and appreciated the scenario of a criminal turning into a devout believer. Many Muslim drug dealers in Oslo (Sandberg, 2010a) and elsewhere (Bucerius, 2014) nurture hopes that one day their religion will save them from their crime-ridden lives.

I never got the chance to interview Hetav again, but I had several casual conversations with him, mostly about the cold weather, drug dealing, the police, the good life and my ongoing fieldwork. We gradually became used to each other's presence and developed new stories about one another. Importantly, the story about me being a cop was replaced by other, more realistic stories. One that soon gained popularity among the dealers framed me as a 'school boy' ['skolegutt'] from Denmark studying street culture. This did not just happen through random chitchat. Rather, it required continuous effort on my part to remove the cop stigma that the dealers invariably placed on me during our first encounters. This effort was also narrative because it involved me telling and retelling stories about myself that were fitting for my purposes. To quote Presser, what I did was to, 'perform a preferred self-story and thereby to construct a sought-after identity – a desired character' (Presser, 2018, p. 13). In my self-presentation, I often emphasized that I was working for the University of Oslo, that I lived in another country (Denmark), that I had no permanent place to stay during my visits to Oslo and that I thought the prices in Norway were outrageous. I thus presented myself as an ordinary, noncop guy with my own, ordinary, noncop problems.

This negotiation and renegotiation of self-stories is key to narrative ethnography. Especially as an ethnographer of crime and deviance, one must continuously monitor and modify the stories participants have about you. If they get the wrong story, the consequences can be dire. This also cuts the other way. Narrative ethnographers obviously also have to monitor and modify the stories they hold about their research participants. In my case, I struggled with unrealistic gangsta stories, which ran through my head during my early visits to Godka. When I first met Hetav, what I saw was an archetypal gangsta similar to the gangstas I had encountered in fictional books, music and movies. I suppose this is only natural given that, at the time, my knowledge about street culture was based mainly on fiction. Moreover, Hetav has to be credited for his convincing performance of the archetypal gangsta, notably when he frisked and stared me down with feigned fury. What was he doing, if not enacting some fictional, gangsta character: Scarface on cocaine, perhaps? Indeed, real life sometimes resembles stories, not only because stories mimic real life but also because people act in accordance with stories they are familiar with and that prevail in their social environment (Sandberg, 2016, p. 159).

Opening up to Storytelling

Establishing trust is essential to narrative ethnography. Without it, people are unlikely to open up their lives and tell their stories. One may seek to establish trust through assurances of confidentiality and by trying to conform to at least some of the local conventions of the people being studied. Conforming to local conventions, such as those of appropriate conversation, is a way to affirm that one respects what people stand for and who they are. This may in turn create a rapport. To be honest and nonjudgmental is also essential, especially when studying individuals who have been deceived and rejected much too often in their lives. Trust-building can take time, but as 'people learn that the ethnographer will respect and protect their conversation, they open up a little more each day in the belief that the researcher will not betray their trust' (Fetterman, 2010, p. 145). Three supplementary strategies that I often found myself using are humouring people; offering small tokens of my good intentions and loyalty; and exposing some of my personal problems and vulnerabilities. One of the times that I used a combination of these strategies was when I first encountered Abdel. This happened in the fall of 2018, 7 months into my fieldwork.

It was around noon and I was standing on my usual spot by the tunnel leading down to the metro. There were only a few dealers around, but not far from me was Abdel. He occasionally sent me a worried glance, probably considering whether I was a cop. I pulled myself together and went over to introduce myself and my project – something I always found difficult, especially in Godka. It made me feel phony, like some salesman offering useless products to people who were busy selling their own products.

'So you study street culture?' he said, looking somewhat relieved. He began explaining the art of drug dealing: 'Rule number one is to avoid the cameras. Always avoid the cameras. You have to protect yourself.' He tapped himself on the chest with a heavy hand. 'I get it,' I replied, gesturing with my thumb in the direction of the camera on the wall just behind us: 'Always avoid the cameras.' He turned and yelled with surprise: 'What the fuck!! I didn't notice that one. Fuck!!

I've been standing right here selling.' We laughed, him with what seemed to be a mix of disbelief and embarrassment.

Humour is a form of communication that can serve to ease tension and create a rapport, but it is generally also highly ambivalent and therefore easily misunderstood (Sandberg & Tutenges, 2018). I had called Abdel's bluff of being an experienced drug dealer, but the fact that he joined my laughter suggested to me that he took my remark well and for what it was: a friendly joke, not an insult. Also, perhaps he appreciated that I had shown him the hidden camera. I told him not to worry too much about the cameras: 'I don't think the police care about the sales. They come storming in when people fight, but I don't think that they pay attention to the dealing.'

We continued with this kind of chitchat about drug dealing. I gave him my assessment of a 'crazy' customer who was roaming around not far from us, and I shared my concern about an ongoing conflict in the Godka area where guns and machetes were being used. The conflict was mainly between groups of Somali youths, but the situation was so heated that random people had been assaulted because they happened to be in 'the wrong place at the wrong time.' By sharing these worries and pieces of advice with him, I demonstrated that I meant him well and was on his side. He responded positively by offering me cannabis for free and, more importantly, his good company and conversation. The ground had been set for storytelling between Abdel and me.

Other dealers never wanted anything to do with me for reasons I never found out. They stayed away from me and indicated that I should stay from them, which I did as best as I could. However, most of the dealers eventually opened up and provided me with, if not stories, at least a bit of company and small talk. Their openness was quite striking and was a result not only of my sustained efforts to build trust but also of the nature of my project. I was studying street culture and jihadism, topics that the dealers generally had very strong opinions about and were willing to discuss with me, as long as our talks were kept anonymous and away from Godka. Moreover, almost all of the drug dealers I got to know were clearly and fervently opposed to jihadism, and they saw me as an ally – someone they wanted to help and who could give them a public voice.

Ismael, who originated from Somalia, was among the most eager contributors to my project. I first met him at a youth centre where I and some of the dealers sometimes went to get a bit of respite from the stress and cold outside. After having heard who I was and what I was doing, he pulled me aside so nobody would hear us. 'Some of these brothers,' he said, nodding angrily in the direction of a group of youths. He paused and continued in a whisper, 'The other day this guy comes up to me. Never seen him before. And he tells me about ISIS and how great they are, you know. I have never seen him before!' We were soon interrupted, but he handed me his phone number. He said that my project was important and that I could call anytime.

Three months later, I met Ismael again close to the youth centre. We found an empty room at the centre and sat down for an interview with the door firmly closed. He still very much wanted to help with my project, but it clearly was not easy for him to talk about jihadism. He felt that the jihadists posed a direct threat to his religion, his identity and his way of life. The mere mention of the word 'jihad' put him on edge. He had met Muslim extremists on the streets of Oslo on two occasions, he said. Although he knew all about 'the gang life' and had committed innumerable dangerous crimes, something about religious extremists scared him. Perhaps they might succeed in convincing street youths about their extremist ideas, or perhaps they might come after him if they found out how much he hated them. He had previously been in violent confrontations with neo-Nazis, and he could envision this happening with jihadists too. In Godka, he explained, 'people want to be gangsters and not talk about religion. The fact is, when somebody leaves the gang they have the sick, dirty mentality of causing mayhem and terror, so what they do is to listen to the imam that speaks terror at the mosques. What happens is that they use the sick mentality in the name of Islam.'

When Ismael spoke about the jihadists, his face turned dark with negative emotions and his voice became hard. He said that the extremists produced top-class propaganda videos: 'Some people might actually like these videos and end up following them. Which is happening! Which is actually happening! People flying out from Europe, England, America, all the way to Iraq! And getting raped and murdered!' He slammed together his hands, perhaps so as to emphasize this horrible fact. He had watched a propaganda video himself, he said, not knowing what it was to begin with: 'When I started watching that video I actually felt this attraction, like "yeah, from my religion," this that, "it's all about my religion, yeah." Then when I saw the execution. You really cry like a baby. I cried like a baby because I was thinking about how many people are going to love this, are going to fall for it and end up following it, and end up going towards it? It scared me. Do you know when you feel like someone just took something through, just like from inside of you, ripping your chest, when you feel like you've been backstabbed? It felt like that.'

He continued with an exasperated laugh. 'Oh, I broke my phone. I actually broke my phone that day. My sisters and mom were really crazy at me, yeah, they were like "what the hell are you doing?" It was my brand new phone. I had it for a few months and I smashed it in pieces.' He sniffled. 'Yeah man, I can never forget that. I smashed that and I, the reason I smashed it was because I was upset. Imagine if you hear a lullaby since you were little, and your mom's like, telling you this lullaby since you were little and you've been raised by it, and you love this thing, it's like a very nice green image in your head of peace. I always heard it back in Somalia, as I grew up. And then another guy comes along and uses the same lullaby to beat someone up. Wouldn't you feel destroyed inside? Like I heard this all my life and it's always warmed me inside. And all of a sudden, you're using it for something evil. It's like, do you understand what I mean now? That's what I mean, that's how I felt. And I felt like destroying everything, like around me, I felt like I was completely lost. I was like, "what is this man?" Like, my mom, I'd been raised with like, hearing the blessings of the Quran and stuff, and all of a sudden these people are coming up on the internet and using this nice accent and this like way of reading it and stuff sounds really nice.'

Not only did Ismael hate the jihadists, he hated them with a passion and actively tried to undermine their cause. On the street, I saw him preaching to fellow

Muslims that Islam was all about love, not violence. He told me that he had confronted jihadists on a couple of occasions to question their interpretation of Islam. He also claimed that he had contacted the authorities to warn them against a person with extremist ideas whom he knew to be in direct contact with a terrorist organization. In other words, he had 'snitched' and was proud of it, perhaps because the jihadists did not play by the rules of the street: they used violence against innocent people; they killed women and children; and they had placed a bomb in the Godka area for no apparent reason (the bomb was discovered and brought to controlled explosion by the police). Ismael's position was echoed by many others in Godka. Snitching on ordinary criminals was considered morally wrong, whereas snitching on jihadists was considered morally right.

Ismael probably embellished his accounts, and he may even have made up certain things. However, I found his claims of being against jihadism most convincing. This anti-jihadism was both intellectually and emotionally founded. He disagreed with the jihadists' interpretation of Islam and had theological arguments to prove them wrong. At the same time he felt very strongly against them and what they stand for. Ismael conveyed these feelings in his choice of words and frequent use of metaphors, such as when he described himself as 'crying like a baby' and feeling 'backstabbed.' Such metaphors are powerful devices for representing and inducing emotional intensity, much more so than literal language (Presser, 2018, p. 73). Importantly, he also expressed himself nonverbally with hand gestures, facial expressions, body postures, vocal tones and speech rhythms. He thus bodied forth his stories, using his physique to deliver his messages. Indeed, storytelling is an embodied activity (Smith, 2007). This is why narrative ethnographers should pay attention to both verbal and nonverbal aspects of the storying process – and by paying attention, I mean applying all of the senses in order to understand the multisensory dynamics of storytelling. Listening with the ears is not enough. Concentrating on words alone will only give us half the story.

Conclusion

Open drug markets are often located in marginal urban areas with grim reputations; Godka conforms to this stereotype. The Norwegian media tend to portray it in purely negative terms, as a place of criminality and danger. The police have warned people from going there alone in the night-time, and social workers have long considered it a notoriously difficult place to carry out their duties. However, like any other place where people meet and interact, Godka has culture (Gubrium & Holstein, 2009, p. 139). It constitutes a narrative environment with distinct rules that influence how people talk – as well as when, with whom, about what, to what extent and for what purposes. In this chapter, I have described my ethnographic efforts to access this narrative environment and understand the way it operates, with a special focus on how Muslim drug dealers talk about jihadism.

I have labelled my approach a blend of 'narrative ethnography' and 'narrative criminology' because it consists of using ethnographic methods to study the occasions, settings and processes of narrative activity among individuals engaged in crime. Accordingly, my interest is less in deciphering the internal organization of stories about jihadism than in understanding how these stories are performed in face-to-face interaction. I consider storytelling as an embodied, intersubjective act that consists of much more than the exchange of words. I am skeptical, therefore, of the traditional procedure in the social sciences to focus narrowly on recording, transcribing and analyzing stories to understand how they organize and construct what they are about (Gubrium & Holstein, 2009, p. xv). This approach tends to reduce people's stories to mere texts, far removed from the embodied, emotional and sensory dynamics of the storytelling process.

This is not an argument against the interview as a method of narrative inquiry. Interviews can potentially generate excellent, multisensory data if the interviewer makes sure to register more than just verbal utterances (Pink, 2015, p. 74). This can be done with the old-school, low-tech method of taking notes during or immediately after interviews. In my experience, taking notes does not require much attention and rarely intimidates interviewees. The information that I write down in my notes are typically about the interview setting (e.g. the décor in a bar), significant sounds (e.g. laughter), smells (e.g. of cannabis), bodily movements (e.g. the slamming together of hands) and the situational mood (e.g. gloomy). I may also write about my own physical reactions during interviews (e.g. pounding heart) or how I feel (e.g. sadness). Such details can be important sources of insight into one's own prejudices and vulnerabilities (Thurnell-Read, 2011), and they may also shed light on ambiguous communication such as humour (Andersen, 2015b).

By way of conclusion, I would like to describe Godka as a narrative environment with three defining characteristics, all of which proved decisive for my efforts to research storytelling about jihadism. First, Godka is characterized by lots of small talk, including imaginative small talk. People share rumours, invent gossip, joke around, call each other funny names, exchange formulaic phrases about business, brag about how tough they are and comfort themselves with narrative fantasies about how life will be once they get a few things sorted out. This type of talk imbues the harsh realities of street life with dreamlike qualities and distraction. It may not be particularly true, accurate or sensible, but this does not matter so much, as long it raises the mood and entertains (Collins, 2004, p. 85). Small talk, whether imaginative or not, can be valuable for making everyday conversations flow – and for the narrative researcher, it can provide important insights into the discursive forms that animate people's perceptions, values and behaviours (Fleetwood & Sandberg, forthcoming). In my case, observing and engaging in small talk taught me a great deal about street culture and how it differs from jihadi culture.

Second, Godka is an environment with high levels of interactional stress. Some of the factors that create this stress among the dealers include sleep deprivation; poor nutrition; excessive substance use; the need to earn money and pay off debts; the risk of being spotted and socially sanctioned by disapproving family members; the threat of being caught and legally punished by the police; and the danger of being assaulted by unstable customers or rival drug dealers. The stress of it all is tangible and is reflected in the dealers' tendencies for brisk body language, gaze aversion, fast speech and irritability. Conflicts are never far away. One wrong word can be enough to transform a pleasant conversation into a quarrel. Therefore, as an ethnographer it is important not to blurt out questions, opinions or sentiments to just anyone at any time or place.

Third, Godka is a place where conversational taboos loom large. These taboos are most pronounced in interactions with social out-groups, above all the police: 'Don't talk to cops!' and 'don't snitch!' are phrases often heard among the dealers. However, even among close associates, there are certain topics that tend to be avoided while in Godka. People rarely say anything about their personal problems and weaknesses, for instance, allegedly because such information may be abused by others who want to gain power or 'make fun.' The topic of Islam is also rarely brought up because it is considered inappropriate to even mention it in an impure place like Godka. As for jihadism, this is a topic that is generally avoided on the grounds that it may trigger negative emotions and cause conflicts between individuals belonging to different clans and schools of Islam. Godka was a good place for me to meet people and establish trust, but I generally had to go elsewhere before they would share stories about personal issues, religion and jihadism.

Acknowledgement

The study was funded by the Norwegian Research Council (project number 259541).

References

Andersen, D. (2015a). Stories of change in drug treatment: A narrative analysis of 'whats' and 'hows' in institutional storytelling. *Sociology of Health & Illness, 37*(5), 668–682. doi:10.1111/1467-9566.12228

Andersen, D. (2015b). What's so funny? Towards a client perspective on professionals' use of humour in drug treatment. *Drugs: Education, Prevention & Policy, 22*(3), 263–271. doi:10.3109/09687637.2015.1016399

Anderson, E. (1999). *Code of the street: Decency, violence, and the moral life of the inner city*. New York, NY: W. W. Norton & Company.

Anderson, E. (2003). *A place on the corner*. Chicago, IL: University of Chicago Press.

Bauman, R. (1982). Conceptions of folklore in the development of literary semiotics. *Semiotica, 39*(1–2), 1–20. doi:10.1515/Semi.1982.39.1-2.1

Bauman, R. (1986). *Story, performance, and event: Contextual studies of oral narrative*. Cambridge: Cambridge University Press.

Brown, S. E., Esbensen, F.-A., & Geis, G. (2010). *Criminology: Explaining crime and its context*. 7th ed., New Providence, NJ: LexisNexis/Anderson Publishing.

Bucerius, S. M. (2014). *Unwanted: Muslim immigrants, dignity, and drug dealing*. Oxford: Oxford University Press.

Cashman, R. (2012). Situational context and interaction in a folklorist's ethnographic approach to storytelling. In J. A. Holstein & J. F. Gubrium (Eds.), *Varieties of narrative analysis* (pp. 181–204). Los Angeles, CA: SAGE Publications.

Collins, R. (2004). *Interaction ritual chains*. Princeton, NJ: Princeton University Press.

Copes, H. (2018). "Did I just get caught being stupid?" Experiencing and managing the emotional labor of fieldwork. In S. K. Rice & M. D. Maltz (Eds.), *Doing ethnography in criminology: Discovery through fieldwork* (pp. 75–81). Cham: Springer International Publishing.

Coupland, J. (2000). *Small talk*. New York, NY: Longman.

Fetterman, D. M. (2010). Walking softly through the wilderness: Ethics. In D. M. Fetterman (Ed.), *Ethnography: Step-by-step*. Los Angeles, CA: SAGE Publications.

Finnegan, R. H. (1992). *Oral poetry: Its nature, significance, and social context*. Bloomington, IN: Indiana University Press.

Fleetwood, J. (2014). *Drug mules: Women in the international cocaine trade*. Basingstoke: Palgrave Macmillan.

Fleetwood, J., & Sandberg, S. (forthcoming). Narrative ethnography and narrative criminology. In K. Haggerty, S. Bucerius, & L. Berardi (Eds.), *The Oxford handbook of ethnograpies of crime and criminal justice*. Oxford: Oxford University Press.

Fleetwood, J. S. (2016). Entering the global field: Talk, travel and narrative practice in Ecuadorian prisons. *British Journal of Community Justice, 14*(2), 13–32.

Glynn, M. (2013). *Black men, invisibility and desistance from crime: Towards a critical race theory of desistance*. Abingdon: Routledge.

Gubrium, J. F., & Holstein, J. A. (2008). Narrative ethnography. In S. N. Hesse-Biber & P. Leavy (Eds.), *Handbook of emergent methods* (pp. 241–264). New York, NY: Guilford Press.

Gubrium, J. F., & Holstein, J. A. (2009). *Analyzing narrative reality*. London: SAGE Publications.

Hammersley, M., & Atkinson, P. (1995). *Ethnography: Principles in practice*. London: Routledge.

Jackson-Jacobs, C. (2009). *Tough crowd: An ethnographic study of the social organization of fighting*. Unpublished thesis, University of California, Los Angeles, CA.

Kalkan, H. (2018). *Shababs: Gadekultur, gadens økonomi og respekt - på Nørrebro*. Unpublished thesis, Copenhagen: Copenhagen University.

Liebow, E. (2003). *Tally's corner: A study of Negro streetcorner men*. Lanham, MD: Rowman & Littlefield.

Loseke, D. R. (2012). The empirical analysis of formula stories. In J. A. Holstein & J. F. Gubrium (Eds.), *Varieties of narrative analysis* (pp. 251–271). London: SAGE Publications.

Malinowski, B. (2003). The problem of meaning in primitive languages. In J. Maybin (Ed.), *Language and literacy in social practice* (pp. 1–10). Clevedon: The Open University.

Pink, S. (2015). *Doing sensory ethnography*. London: SAGE Publications.

Pitts, J. (2008). *Reluctant gangsters: The changing face of youth crime*. Portland, OR: Willan Publishing.

Polletta, F. (2006). *It was like a fever: Storytelling in protest and politics*. Chicago, IL: University of Chicago Press.

Presser, L. (2005). Negotiating power and narrative in research: Implications for feminist methodology. *Signs: Journal of Women in Culture and Society, 30*(4), 2067–2090.

Presser, L. (2010). Collecting and analyzing the stories of offenders. *Journal of Criminal Justice Education, 21*(4), 431–446.

Presser, L. (2018). *Inside story: How narratives drive mass harm*. Berkeley, CA: University of California Press.
Presser, L., & Sandberg, S. (2015). *Narrative criminology: Understanding stories of crime*. New York, NY: New York University Press.
Rosenfeld, R., Jacobs, B. A., & Wright, R. (2003). Snitching and the code of the street. *British Journal of Criminology*, *43*(2), 291–309.
Sandberg, S. (2010a). 'The sweet taste of sin'—A Muslim drug dealer in a Nordic welfare state. *Journal of Scandinavian Studies in Criminology and Crime Prevention*, *11*(2), 103–118. doi:10.1080/14043858.2010.522819
Sandberg, S. (2010b). What can "lies" tell us about life? Notes towards a framework of narrative criminology. *Journal of Criminal Justice Education*, *21*(4), 447–465. doi: 10.1080/10511253.2010.516564
Sandberg, S. (2016). The importance of stories untold: Life-story, event-story and trope. *Crime, Media, Culture*, *12*(2), 153–171. doi:10.1177/1741659016639355
Sandberg, S., & Tutenges, S. (2018). Laughter in stories of crime and tragedy: The importance of humor for marginalized populations. *Social Problems*, 1–16. doi: 10.1093/socpro/spy019
Smith, B. (2007). The state of the art in narrative inquiry – Some reflections. *Narrative Inquiry*, *17*(2), 391–398. doi:10.1075/ni.17.2.13smi
Thurnell-Read, T. (2011). 'Common-sense' research: Senses, emotions and embodiment in researching stag tourism in Eastern Europe. *Methodological Innovations Online*, *6*(3), 39–49.
Tutenges, S. (2012). Nightlife tourism: A mixed methods study of young tourists at an international nightlife resort. *Tourist Studies*, *12*(2), 131–150. doi:10.1177/1468797612454250
Tutenges, S. (2015). Pub crawls at a Bulgarian nightlife resort: A case study using crowd theory. *Tourist Studies*, *15*(3), 283–299. doi:10.1177/1468797615597856
Tutenges, S. (forthcoming). Nightlife ethnography: A phenomenological approach. In K. Haggerty, S. Bucerius, & L. Berardi (Eds.), *The Oxford handbook of ethnograpies of crime and criminal justice*. Oxford: Oxford University Press.
Tutenges, S., & Sandberg, S. (2013). Intoxicating stories: The characteristics, contexts and implications of drinking stories among Danish youth. *International Journal of Drug Policy*, *24*(6), 538–544. doi:10.1016/j.drugpo.2013.03.011
Whyte, W. F. (1993). *Street corner society: The social structure of an Italian slum*. Chicago, IL: University of Chicago Press.

Chapter 3

Storied Justice: The Narrative Strategies of US Federal Prosecutors

Anna Offit

Introduction

Narrative criminologists have demonstrated the vital role that stories play in legal actors' efforts to make sense of their experience and behaviour – whether in jail or on city streets (Presser & Sandberg, 2015). This is particularly true in adversarial legal systems, where so-called 'factual' accounts of wrongdoing emerge from the rival construction and performance of courtroom narratives. Building on ethnographic work alongside those engaged in criminal activity (Hammersvik, 2018; Tutenges, 2019) and those serving prison sentences (Fleetwood, 2015; Ugelvik, 2015), this chapter turns to the narrative practices of state actors with discretion to define criminality to begin with: American federal prosecutors.

Focussing on prosecutors' opening and closing statements, which book-end criminal trials, this chapter examines the extent to which narratives of crime offer a resource with which lawyers make sense of their obligation to seek justice. The first part of the chapter outlines a theoretical rationale for using ethnographic methods to scrutinise the ethical work behind seemingly polished legal narratives. The second part draws on illustrative examples from fieldwork to highlight aspects of real-time story creation that aid lawyers' professional self-definition. My central argument is that ethnographic research, and participant observation in particular, is an essential methodological tool for studying attorneys' creation of trial narratives.

Ethnography and the Study of Real-time Narrative Creation

Since criminology's 'narrative turn' was documented and systematised (Presser, 2016), narrative criminologists have made broad use of ethnographic methods including formal and open-ended interviews and participant observation. Of particular relevance to this study, Thomas Ugelvik's fieldwork in Oslo Prison revealed how inmates narratively identified themselves as ethical individuals. In the course of numerous informal interactions, conversations and games of pool with inmates convicted of violent and drug-related crime, Ugelvik learnt that his informants routinely defined themselves in opposition to those convicted of sexual crimes whom they shunned and avoided. To the extent that these narratives affirmed the moral worth of their tellers, they were constitutive of a collective process of moral 'sense making' (Ugelvik, 2015, p. 27). Here, participant observation not only made it possible to analyse inmates' *talk* of exclusion but enabled Ugelvik to see firsthand how convicted rapists were routinely excluded from social spaces, activities and leadership roles.

Jennifer Fleetwood's research in a women's prison in Ecuador shed similar light on the generative capacity of storytelling for inmates' formulations of their identities as mothers, partners and (sometimes unwitting) drug mules. In this context, women claimed interpretive authority over their experience through private narrations of the circumstances of their incarceration with Fleetwood. Unlike the static accounts that can emerge from one-off interviews, Fleetwood demonstrated how ethnography:

> reveals the multilayered aspects of agency, and in the process exposes the agency involved in constructing an account, including the strategic adoption of passive subject positions (Fleetwood, 2015, p. 62).

Her emphasis on the multiple, flexible and strategic accounts of informants resonates with a subsequent ethnographic study of indoor cannabis growers. Through informal interactions with growers as they socialised at parties, concerts and in bars (among other locales), researcher Eirik Hammersvik observed the way his interlocutors tailored their accounts to fit different 'interactional conditions' (Hammersvik, 2018, p. 97). Here, again, participant observation was key. As a preliminary matter, it took months of observation – and being physically present at his fieldsite – for Hammersvik to build a trusting and unselfconscious relationship with his primary informant, Bill. It was only with the benefit of daily interactions with Bill in the months that followed that Hammersvik was able to observe shifts in Bill's rationales for running a large-scale drug production operation.

Jaber Gubrium and James Holstein's (2008) exposition of 'narrative ethnography' has been an instructive and influential point of departure for these and other narrative criminologists. Notably, Gubrium and Holstein emphasise the complex interplay between the contextual circumstances and content of a story, underscoring the need for researchers engaged in the 'close scrutiny of social situations, their actors, and actions in relation to narratives' (Gubrium & Holstein, 2008, p. 250). In describing the temporal and social contingency of storytelling, they write: 'the environments of storytelling shape the content and internal organisation of accounts, just as internal matters can have an impact on one's role as a storyteller' (p. 247). Sébastien Tutenges's chapter in this volume draws out the implications of this insight powerfully; depending on the time of day, listeners and presence of an audio recorder, 'imaginative small talk' assumed different forms or could feature altogether different characters (Tutenges, 2019).

Narrative ethnography has the benefit of mitigating a widely acknowledged challenge of narrative analysis in legal contexts: its retrospective orientation. Or, in other words, the tendency of interdisciplinary legal scholars to focus on outcomes (e.g. verdicts, judicial opinions) and adopt backward-looking reasoning from already settled ends (Barthes, 1966). American anthropologist Clifford Geertz has described this analytic tendency as a '"how-to" bias' that treats the effects of legal practice as constitutive of law more generally (Geertz, 2000).

My study alongside federal prosecutors, in contrast, reveals that legal practice, like narrative practice, is dialogic, interactive and collaborative. Barriers to accessing prosecutors in the context of their work, however, have meant that they have not been subjects of sustained ethnographic engagement apart from the narratives they coproduce in courtrooms (Matoesian, 2001). This study thus reflects a novel application of narrative criminology – enriched by an ethnographic approach – to an otherwise opaque site of elite and highly discretionary law enforcement work in America.

Studying Prosecutorial Narratives: A Case Study

The present study of federal prosecutors included participation in meetings that featured the rehearsal, critique and discussion of criminal case narratives for jurors. In the course of this undertaking, prosecutors' efforts to negotiate and forge unified professional self-narratives came into relief. My ability to take verbatim notes during prosecutors' discussions of opening and closing statements aided my ability to analyse the way their accounts – and colleagues' critiques – changed over time. Analysis of these notes consisted of identifying patterns in prosecutors' suggestions and rationales for the revision of colleagues' narratives. As a preliminary matter, this entailed reading and annotating full-length drafts before listening to rehearsals of trial narratives in group settings. Prosecutors then shared and elaborated their written lists of recommended modifications of these narratives–including to their length, word choice, inclusion of detail, reference to particular pieces of evidence, and inclusion of legal instructions. This structured round of feedback often gave way to more pointed discussion of sources of disagreement.

To accommodate busy schedules, such meetings were often scheduled late in the day and attended by supervisors and colleagues who were willing to offer feedback. I was often implicitly (or explicitly) treated like a proxy juror to the extent that my opinion was elicited alongside those of Assistant US Attorneys in the office. On one occasion my status as a 'nonprosecutor' was invoked to assert the value of my opinion as someone who could comment on the narrative framing of a case from a position of detachment.

Over the course of these meetings, I captured comments in real time to the extent possible, recognising that my synthesis of rapidly unfolding events would benefit from examining the notes as a whole, allowing theoretical insights to take shape from the ground up (*see* Geertz, 2000). A practical advantage of this approach was the opportunity it afforded to identify recurring themes in lawyers' narratives and critiques that were not immediately apparent. It also highlighted the extent to which lawyers' face-to-face communication was constitutive of their social and professional identities (Philips, 2013, p. 94).

It is of course possible that efforts to analyse representative discussions in real time reflected a conscious attempt to emulate the work of my interlocutors who eagerly generated and consulted detailed handwritten notes themselves as meetings – or arguments in court – were underway. I distinguished these contemporaneous notes from the later coding and synthesis of my ethnographic data. H.R. Bernard's discussion of 'analytic notes' helpfully differentiates these distinct temporalities. That is, where verbatim notes were taken in real time, analytic notes were products of later analysis that came about through 'organizing and working with descriptive and methodological notes over a period of time' (Bernard, 2011, p. 300).

The value of this approach to the present study was the opportunity it created to revisit and analyse interactions that might have been overlooked as they unfolded. In writing on ethnographic research, Marilyn Strathern has helpfully emphasised the value of generating contemporaneous fieldnotes. Unlike post hoc reflections, ethnographic notes in real time can be attuned to rapid shifts in social interaction as the researcher gathers 'more data than the investigator is aware of at the time of collection... a participatory exercise which yields materials for which analytical protocols are often devised after the fact' (Strathern, 2004, pp. 5–7 cited by Marcus, 2009). She goes on to explain that ethnography allows:

> one to recover the antecedents of future crises from material not collected for the purpose... to anticipate a future need to know something that cannot be defined in the present. *Id.* at 507.

Efforts to observe processes of narrative construction and revision as they unfold can thus set the stage for unexpected future lines of inquiry (Marcus, 2009, pp. 28–29). In so doing, this approach treats fieldnotes as part of a 'reinterpretable and contradictory patchwork of perspectives' rather than a stable repertoire of data (Lederman in Sanjek, 1990, p. 90) and facilitates discovery (Jacobsson, 2008; Sanjek, 1990, p. 90). In this vein, it was only after years of participant observation in a US Attorney's office that prosecutors' emphasis on character traits like equanimity came into relief with the benefit of analysing their exchanges in the aggregate.

Much of the trial narrative generation that I focus on here emerged as the product of lawyers' formal and informal discussions with one another. Though initial draft writing was a typically solitary endeavour that entailed the review of personal (or colleagues') notes and past work product, informal conversation among peers and supervisors was continual. Draft trial narratives also often included input from or acknowledgement of the reactions of case agents.

To assimilate the varying and often informal reflections on office life that unfolded in the course of a day, an ethnographic research approach was essential. As both an observer and a participant in everyday case conversations, I could analyse lawyers' narrative work in real time. Participant observation was particularly well suited for the study of criminal trial narratives. This is because prosecutors' decision-making in advance of – and during – trial was rarely a subject of spontaneous, reflexive commentary in the absence of group interaction. To the extent that I participated in opening and closing statement moot sessions, my own strategic suggestions prompted reactions and counterarguments that could generate new opportunities for elaboration. Openings for reflexive professional critique also arose as prosecutors challenged colleagues' supervisors', and case agents' approaches to narratively framing witness testimony and other evidence. Sources of disagreement in these contexts, however fleeting or far afield, offered a valuable window into how prosecutors understood and formulated their chosen approaches to narrating their cases-in-progress.

To the extent that lay participation in the US legal system has been studied by social scientists, the staging of mock trials, simulated jury deliberations, post hoc interviews, surveys and analyses of trial transcripts have been common methods. What these studies are not positioned to capture, however, is an understanding of the jury system's practical and symbolic role in the everyday work of professional legal actors (Broeder, 1964). Much is lost when case presentations are analyzed without attending to the circumstances of their telling 'at a particular moment, with a particular audience and purpose in mind' (Fleetwood & Sandberg, forthcoming). By situating the researcher in spaces of spontaneous, informal and unselfconscious practice, ethnography offers narrative criminologists access to off-the-record and behind-the-scenes legal contexts. A researcher's capacity to communicate and participate in the professional activities she studies is also integral to illuminating and analysing tacit and taken-for-granted practices.

Jurors at the Centre of Opening and Closing Statements

Jurors' potential interpretations of evidence were at the heart of prosecutors' discussions of case narratives. Although accessing jurors' impressions was an inherently speculative endeavour, prosecutors nonetheless developed robust beliefs about their future lay decision-makers (Zalman & Tsoudis, 2005). In some cases, prosecutors explicitly identified 'average' jurors as individuals who were middle-class, employed and lived in the suburbs, like themselves (Offit, 2016, p. 180). In other cases, prosecutors' understandings of jurors stemmed from knowledge about their own family members or friends who shared characteristics in common with them (e.g. occupations, counties of residence) and were thus regarded as proxy jurors.

When it came time to prepare opening and closing statements, the distinction between prosecutors' interpretive capacities and those of the jurors they imagined was ambiguous at best. Lawyers, in other words, became surrogate jurors for each other. For some, the aim of preparation meetings was to discuss and refine language that might resonate with laypeople. For others, presentation style was a narrative priority, as prosecutors likened themselves to teachers. In both cases, jurors' perspectives were invoked and imaginatively enacted by prosecutors as part of a practice of distancing themselves from cases to offer critiques from a position of detachment.

Crafting Language with Jurors in Mind

In examining authors' writing practices, narrative theorists have considered the integral role of readers and listeners to the imaginative process of creating stories. Umberto Eco, for example, suggests that texts not only presuppose particular 'model readers' but explicitly aim to constitute them along specific lines by contributing to their competence (Eco, 1984, pp. 7–8). Likewise, prosecutors sought to craft stories that would be uniquely positioned to shape jurors' conceptions of justice and perspectives on their evidence. To this end a number of prosecutors emphasised the importance of integrating analogies into their narratives that would resonate with jurors. This included attorneys who kept lists of details about jurors to invoke during opening statements that included reference to their occupations among other details. If a prosecutor had a math tutor on her jury, for instance, references to statistics and exams might enter an otherwise legalese description of the facts of a case. One prosecutor thought she could tell when jurors were particularly receptive to metaphors based on seeing their eyes widen – which suggested to her that they were paying close attention. When another prosecutor learnt that members of her jury were parents of small children, she incorporated references to schoolyard recess and specific childhood games into her characterisations of evidence.

In the similar spirit of keying language used in opening and closing statements to model jurors' likely experiences outside the courtroom, another prosecutor chose presentation styles that future listeners might be receptive to. Consideration of jurors' divergent backgrounds thus prompted creative discussion of how cases might appear to unfamiliar observers. Recognising that people rely on analogies to reconcile informational gaps in everyday life (Douglas, 1986, p. 65; Lakoff & Johnson, 1980, p. 119; Rosen, 2006, p. 9), prosecutors eagerly reframed evidence to align with knowledge systems that might bring clarity to sources of confusion in court. In an effort to use language that might resonate with jurors, prosecutors recognised the importance of drawing on local knowledge when formulating their arguments. Some accessed this knowledge by drawing on vocabulary from divergent professional registers (e.g. analogies tailored to carpenters, nurses or athletes) or from opinions elicited during voir dire (e.g. related to DNA evidence and abuse). Consideration of jurors' perspectives thus blurred lay and professional expertise – both of which permeated prosecutors' narrative labour.

Making Evidence Intelligible to Lay Decision-makers

Prosecutors' opening statement narratives, which could range from 10 minutes to several hours, were selective by necessity; they sounded more like previews than fulsome stories. For the prosecutors who practiced, critiqued and ultimately delivered them, this was by design. These statements were intended to offer jurors a broad brush understanding of the charges and evidence in cases and to pare down complex or unpredictable testimony into simple narratives. A benefit of this approach, as prosecutors saw it, was the possibility that concise narratives would be more compelling and memorable than detailed or long-winded ones. To refine their stories, prosecutors critiqued each other's presentations from the vantage point of hypothetical lay decision-makers. This meant that suggestions for revision could be articulated in impersonal terms as prosecutors scrutinised evidence with fresh eyes. It also assumed that prosecutors' concerns could be substituted in conversation for those of future jurors.

Nevertheless, aided by colleagues, many prosecutors viewed their task in crafting opening statements as one of making the facts of a case and elements of a crime intelligible to an imagined lay audience. As part of this effort, which some viewed as central to their job, prosecutors encouraged each other to transform evidence into units of information that model listeners could easily understand and assimilate. Another prosecutor referred to his professional obligation to translate legal language for laypeople as a burden of 'coherence' (in addition to proof). He considered gaps in the narrative he was formulating for jurors detrimental to his case. Others similarly analogised their roles *vis-à-vis* jurors to those of teachers – viewing it as their duty to clearly delineate why particular pieces of evidence were significant. Exemplifying this approach, a supervisor suggested that paragraphs of an opening statement be revised to sound like a primer for jurors. The imagined perspectives of individuals who lacked professional training thus helped prosecutors deconstruct and evaluate evidence in their cases from a new perspective.

To aid jurors' comprehension of cases, colloquial language was preferable to legalese, as prosecutors sought to craft stories in terms used and heard outside of court. During preparation meetings for a white-collar case, for example, prosecutors' critiques of opening statements distinguished between the level of precision and detail one might expect from a written brief and oral story. In a brief, a prosecutor explained, it might be appropriate to list the monetary values of fake checks or note the number of days between transactions. In the context of an oral opening statement, however, quantitative description would likely contribute little to jurors' understanding. In this prosecutor's view, an opening statement narrative would suffer for sounding excessively long and complicated.

In a number of different types of cases, references to jurors' fictive perspectives informed prosecutors' critiques of colleagues' language use. In the process, prosecutors sometimes clarified aspects of cases for themselves. An opening statement for a child pornography case, for example, prompted discussion of substantive legal questions. In this context a colleague asked the narrative's presenter about the relationship between 'child abuse' and 'child pornography' as different types of crime. In the discussion that followed prosecutors tacked back and forth between their need to refine and 'translate' legal characterisations of sexually explicit images for lay listeners and for each other. Requests for a clear road map, topic sentences and colloquial definitions highlighted the meeting's role as an editorial resource and context in which legal knowledge was tested and exchanged.

In sum, talk of jurors permeated prosecutors' discussions of their case narratives. Notwithstanding the infrequency of jury trials and prosecutors' lack of contact with jurors (Offit, 2019), this focus underscored the centrality of lay intuitions and stories about justice to prosecutors' conceptions of their role.

Perhaps the greatest reflection of the value conferred on the narrative art of opening and closing statement construction was the inordinate amount of time prosecutors devoted to the process. Prosecutors in the office spent solitary hours hunched over their keyboards. Along with prosecutors' family members and friends, I was enlisted to listen and share reactions to drafts at all hours. Implicit in this exercise was recognition that prosecutors' critics were unpredictable and would hold subjective views – an understandably frustrating feature of professional and social life for many of us.

Professional Identity Formation through Narrative

As prosecutors critiqued colleagues' case narratives they distinguished accounts that embodied the personal and professional character traits they viewed as central to their work. As we see in the sections that follow, prosecutors' self-consciousness about their perceived reliability and fairness loomed large in these discussions. Narrative criminologists (Presser & Sandberg, 2015) and other interdisciplinary scholars (Frank, 2010, p. 51) have underscored the extent to which stories interpolate – or impose identities on – characters within them. As authors, narrators and preliminary listeners to such stories, prosecutors' opening and closing statements offered valuable data about themselves. The component parts of their stories, as we will see, illuminated their preferences, values and self-imagination as reliable, scrupulous and neutral officers of the court.

Honesty

As prosecutors co-constructed trial stories, they were eager to present themselves as trustworthy. In practice, however, they took divergent approaches to curating presentations of their honesty. For many, this involved prioritising the alignment of opening statement narratives with evidence they expected (or hoped) jurors would see and hear during trial. For others it also involved exemplifying a professional who was prepared, framed herself as a teacher and substituted personal argument with corroborating evidence whenever possible.

In the course of my fieldwork, prosecutors devoted an inordinate amount of narrative attention to the possibility that they would *mischaracterise* evidence during their opening statements. Underlying this concern was a pervasive assumption that a juror whose expectations were betrayed by later inconsistencies would call a prosecutor's character into question and thus imperil the entire case. The stories prosecutors fashioned for jurors were critiqued as though they were promises. Violations of this trust, in turn, were referred to as instances of narratively 'overselling' one's case.

Where prosecutors positively reinforced opening statement narratives that used precise language, vagueness was a source of disagreement. This is because the extent of a particular word or phrase's ambiguity was negotiable. In one discussion, for example, a prosecutor's appeal to 'common sense' was perceived as signalling that the trial team's evidence was insufficient, requiring that jurors make an excessive inferential leap to convict a defendant. Common sense, in this prosecutor's view, was too indeterminate and subjective a metric for lay decision-makers. In another instance, a prosecutor criticised a colleague's suggestion that jurors might 'learn things' during the trial that departed from the rehearsed opening statement. Though the trial team wanted to anticipate contrary arguments from defence counsel, a colleague warned that such ambiguity might lead jurors to believe they would hear exculpatory evidence – or something that would detract from the Government's case. Here, the author of the opening statement showed an interest in foreshadowing potentially adverse information – akin to film theorists' discussions of the 'payoff' experienced by viewers who have followed cues, drawn inferences and made assumptions about the direction of an unfolding plot (Bordwell, 1985, p. 39). In his colleague's view, however, the ultimate payoff for jurors ought to bolster rather than undermine their confidence in the case at hand.

At the same time that prosecutors considered the risk of later contradiction (or benefit of later corroboration), they also did not want their narratives to create the impression they had chosen to *withhold* relevant evidence. To the extent that pieces of evidence had unfavourable interpretations, prosecutors referred to their presentation as 'fronting' pieces of information. An aim of this technique was to perform their candour, as though to emphasise there was nothing to hide. In a case involving the alleged forgery of bank documents, for example, a prosecutor was not certain how defence counsel would use evidence that a defendant had only made counterfeit copies of a portion of the forms in question. A supervisor encouraged him to bring the limitation of this evidence out into the open lest jurors think to themselves, upon making the discovery, 'they never told us *that*!'

Prosecutors also sought to demonstrate their credibility by inviting *jurors* to construct narratives of their own. This entailed presenting themselves as neutral purveyors of independent and mutually reinforcing evidence of wrongdoing. As a practical matter, this also meant emphasising that distinct pieces of evidence could lead one to the same conclusion about a defendant's guilt. Jurors could interpret complementary, overlapping, or 'lined up' accounts of a defendant's actions, in other words, as evidence of their facticity as though each existed in a vacuum. The skillful closing statement or rebuttal, in contrast, directed jurors' attention to 'all those things taken together.'

The narrative significance of corroborating evidence emerged with particular force during a case of alleged medical neglect of children. In this context, the lead prosecutor planned to show the jury medical records that documented doctors' referrals to seek immediate follow-up treatment and the defendants' subsequent failure to follow through. She then planned to show the jury records generated by administrators listing numerous appointments the defendants had cancelled or missed. Like many of her colleagues, this prosecutor's narrative intuitions revealed the value she conferred on offering several accounts of the same conduct to reinforce her *own* credibility in the event that jurors chose not to believe a particular witness. With this strategy in mind, other prosecutors' closing statements and rebuttals stressed their cases' reliance on distinct but complementary pieces of evidence to anticipate or address defence counsel's arguments. This was a move that explicitly left interpretive and inferential work to jurors. If lay decision-makers connected the dots themselves, the prosecutor might emerge as a neutral and therefore more reliable curator of the evidence.

Prosecutors also considered the potential for jurors to view witnesses' later narratives as corroborating their own opening statements. Recognising the additive value of these contextualising accounts, one prosecutor described them as a 'a stamp on all the arguments and evidence you've presented' and a means of 'buttressing' particular witnesses' credibility. Illustrating the position further, another prosecutor noted, in reference to a cooperating witness's testimony, that it bolstered her *own* credibility if a juror recalled hearing about aspects of the case for a second time despite the fact that opening statements did not constitute evidence in the case. This view acknowledged the possibility that jurors would notice inconsistencies between opening and closing statements, leading colleagues to urge trial partners to reconcile their own conflicting narratives before trial.

Underlying some prosecutors' careful attention to word choice was broader concern that jurors form favourable impressions of their character as professionals. Prosecutors' critical narrative interventions as opening statements came together thus embraced an obligation to layer factual accounts in such a manner as to create the impression that evidence of crime was ample and beyond reproach. The creation of a believable case story and credible prosecutor was thus part of the same project. Prosecutors applied themselves to this task by bringing their most biting questions and scepticism to aspects of colleagues' narratives that deviated from their own commonsense understandings of crime.

Performance

In addition to actively constituting model listeners, prosecutors were attentive to how the performance of their narratives might inform jurors' perceptions of their own professional character. The view that narratives generate professional identities resonates with the anthropological writing of Helen Schwartzman and others who are attentive to story-telling as a fundamentally social and participatory exercise (Bauman, 1986, pp. 112–115; Schwartzman, 1989, p. 259). In the organisational context of a US Attorney's Office, as in other work places, trial narratives play a significant role in generating, interpreting and transforming professional life (Bauman, 1986, pp. 112–115; Schwartzman, 1989, p. 259). In her study of a mental health organisation, Schwartzman focuses on the extent to which stories are shared through 'ordinary turn-by-turn-talk'. In this context of this analysis, the types of stories that research subjects introduced into their everyday talk related to the organisation in which they worked, individuals in the office, and meetings. Here, in contrast, the creation of stories was a formative feature and – indeed – a direct aim of formal meetings that were convened.

Concern about narrative performance more explicitly intervened as prosecutors critiqued the manner in which colleagues communicated their case stories – including tempo, tone and memorisation. Prosecutors' commitment to maintaining jurors' trust led some to make a concerted effort to communicate in an informal, relatable and conversational manner. In one such case, a prosecutor's effective connection with her listeners during a preparation meeting was lauded as the culmination of continued practice. The absence of such a connection was considered a shortcoming in other prosecutors' presentations. The stakes of establishing a rapport with jurors, in some prosecutors' view, were high. One prosecutor explained, for example, that if he seemed like someone a juror would want to socialise with, that person might be more likely to listen to and trust him. Others were attuned to whether they (or their trial partners) felt a personal connection with their lay listeners during jury selection.

In an effort to perform their preparedness, some prosecutors felt that memorising details in their cases signalled to jurors that they took their jobs and audience seriously. In a gun case, for example, a prosecutor emphasised the importance of confidently describing the weapon's name, model, size and place of origin. Echoing this sentiment, another prosecutor agreed that references to minute details demonstrated that prosecutors' were in command of their cases. Detailed references, the theory went, might enhance a trial team's perceived credibility, as they exhibited proficiency in the complex factual patterns of their cases. Correspondingly, in light of the value conferred on precision, prosecutors' misstatements of evidence – or displays of inconsistent facts on PowerPoint slides – were sharply criticised during meetings due to their anticipated undermining effect.

Prosecutors' efforts to appear trustworthy extended to their narrative presentations of defendants' conduct, and, in particular, their moves to highlight the criminality of this conduct. To this end, prosecutors pushed for characterisations of evidence that emphasised their illegitimate and illegal dimensions when faced with the possibility of multiple interpretations. Comments from a meeting in preparation for a criminal trial exemplified this approach. Here, a prosecutor pointed out that when references were made to defendants' 'employees' or the 'contracts' they had signed, jurors might interpret such behaviour as commonplace. Echoing this view a colleague advised the trial team to refer to 'co-conspirators' rather than business associates, partners or profits.

These comments amplified others in criminal cases in which colleagues recommended referring to defendants as defendants (rather than 'he' or 'she'), cooperators as co-conspirators, and using words that connoted illegal abuse rather than physical discipline. Prosecutors also recommended using active voice in characterisations of defendants' alleged actions to underscore their culpability relative to other parties. Rather than note in a white-collar case, for example, that files were hidden, colleagues agreed that a defendant should be described as hiding files herself.

A corruption case raised similar concerns for one prosecutor who observed that though a case involved the acceptance of illegal kickback payments, the trial team's characterisation of the defendant's behaviour did not make this clear. A colleague who participated in a meeting about this case suggested that the trial team's draft opening statement be revised to make the alleged conduct sound 'bribe-ier.' Despite the narrative's strong delivery, he suggested, it could be improved upon by emphasising the charges of fraud and extortion that lay at the heart of the prosecution. Listeners, in other words, took issue with the story's insufficiently compelling performance.

In other contexts, however, prosecutors criticised visual aids and language perceived to exaggerate the strength or moral outrage prompted by a case. Discomfort displaying photographs prompted one prosecutor to refer to their inclusion as turning an opening statement into a dog and pony show and another to question the need for their blockbuster effect. Some cautioned each other, for example, against 'overcommitting' to evidence that may not be presented to jurors as expected. This sense of the value of 'exact' language was shared by a prosecutor who cautioned the deliverer of another opening statement not to set jurors up to expect something earth-shattering that might not be perceived as such. To this end, another prosecutor advised a colleague not to conflate the inclusion of a 'grabber' opening line with an explosive opening to a story. Performances that preserved ambiguity and vagueness – when expeditious – were believed to help mitigate the unpredictability attendant to trial.

In another illustrative exchange, prosecutors debated whether opening statements should begin with a delineation of the laws being violated – or, instead, to begin with a hook – or 'grabber fact' meant to catch jurors' attention. In this context, one could quickly appreciate the group's attentiveness to the question of whether an opening statement should be engaging or focus on the laws that a defendant was charged with having broken. The stakes of this decision for some who discussed it, however, were higher. What if jurors saw nothing wrong with a defendant's conduct? Several prosecutors emphasised the possibility that for a layperson unfamiliar with laws restricting felons' right to possess guns, a narrative that failed to flag this fact might confuse jurors – or worse – make them question prosecutors' judgement. Ideas about narrative performance were thus tied to conceptions of prosecutors' professional obligation to seek justice. Accepting the risk of boring jurors, some prosecutors felt strongly that a trial team's obligation to assert the legitimacy of a case should trump concern about how to animate the events in their story.

Prosecutors' recurrent critiques of colleagues' performances of opening and closing statements highlight the importance of ethnography, and participant observation in particular, to the study of legal narratives in the environments of their making. This is because oral storytelling arises from 'performance events' rooted in particular institutional contexts and communicative norms (Bauman, 1986, pp. 3–4). Likewise, and as Bauman (1986) helpfully delineates, the conventions of prosecutors' opening statement critiques not only led to the refinement of claims about their legal duties, but enabled them to perform proficiency about such traits to the supervisors who convened and participated in such meetings and could selectively dismiss or incorporate colleagues' opinions in the framing of their own suggestions. Anthropologist Elizabeth Mertz describes an analogue to this process, as students learn to 'think like lawyers' through professors' subtle redirection of their attention to aspects of cases narrative in classroom settings (Mertz, 2007, p. 83). As in prosecutors' meetings, professional acculturation occurs through a process of public performance and, in turn, the public critique and reorientation of such performances. Without the benefit of attention to the social circumstances of legal narrative creation, the constitutive role of such stories – a central feature of narrative criminologists' inquiries – would be unavailable to a researcher.

Impartiality

To the extent that prosecutors' formulations of their professional identity assumed a unified and coherent form, the diplomatic and nonzealous prosecutor often surfaced as an ideal type in their talk. In critiquing opening statements, prosecutors thus focused on behaviour that a hypothetical juror might perceive as overzealous. Though not defined explicitly, prosecutors articulated generalised indices of this undesirable quality. This included appearing excessively argumentative, confrontational, disrespectful or dismissive when characterising witnesses or evidence. Jurors' presence, even in hypothetical form, thus invited prosecutors to share their own commonsense understandings of how to distinguish reasonable from excessive advocacy in criminal prosecutions.

In one illustrative reflection, a prosecutor challenged colleagues' decision to have a defendant's mother testify against him in court despite the fact that her name, address and forged signature appeared on documents that would be relied upon during a future potential trial. Despite the legality of calling a defendant's family member as a witness, another prosecutor explained to me – as he had to colleagues – that jurors would share his intuition that this tactic was distasteful and unfair, particularly given any decent person's willingness to lie in defence of a close family member. Though the case never proceeded to trial, like most in the office, colleagues who found these arguments compelling chose to pursue an alternative approach to narrating – and thus proving – the fraudulence of the paperwork in question. The group settled on using tax documents rather than a relative's firsthand account.

Prosecutors' sensitivity to jurors' perception of overzealousness also informed their approaches to characterising the strength of cooperating witness's testimony. As a general matter, cooperators' utility to prosecutions was undeniable. Yet most promised to tell the truth in the hope of receiving lighter sentences despite being involved in criminal activity themselves. Though prosecutors did not want to endorse behaviour that brought cooperating witnesses in contact with law enforcement agents, they navigated this fraught relationship with care. One prosecutor, for example, criticised a colleague's use of derogatory language to describe cooperating witnesses while acknowledging that her opinion might shift from one case to the next. Rather than call cooperating witnesses crooks, she invited her colleague to consider less argumentative language. To the extent that prosecutors relied on the credibility and persuasiveness of such witnesses, they presented a continuing dilemma as prosecutors attempted to narratively distinguish themselves from admitted criminals.

Opening statements that appeared to vouch for, praise or depict cooperating witnesses as victims were also subject to criticism. This is because one could not predict exactly what such witnesses would say or how truthful their testimony would seem to jurors. In one illustrative case, a prosecutor suggested that a colleague frame a case narrative by emphasising that the cooperator *said* he did not know a transaction had taken place, rather than assert this fact herself. This would prevent the deliverer of the opening statement from implicitly vouching for its truthfulness. Likewise, another prosecutor's remark that a cooperator wanted to testify truthfully in any effort to live life with a clean slate was cautioned to revise this narrative detail due to the inherent uncertainty of future jurors' interpretation of the cooperator's intentions. A theme in prosecutors' reflections was that behaviour that might tarnish a jury's opinion of cooperators might also undermine their confidence in prosecutors who appeared to take them at their word.

In an effort to narratively mitigate jurors' perceptions that prosecutors personally identified with the co-operators whose accounts supported their cases, they avoided colloquial phrases that might imply a personal affinity for or alliance with such witnesses. In discussion, prosecutors suggested to colleagues that impersonal constructions be used to characterise cooperating witnesses' testimony including, for instance, saying *the evidence is going to show* rather than suggest a *trial team* would provide evidence. In another illustrative case a prosecutor encouraged a colleague to explain that a *defendant* chose cooperating witnesses. If jurors disliked a particular cooperator, the theory went, they might transfer such distrust – or animus – to a party viewed as closely aligned with the witness.

Prosecutors also critiqued opening statements that appeared to empathise with witnesses. When an opening statement involved witnesses who were undocumented immigrants, for example, a supervisor objected to a section of a draft that described them as saving "hard-earned" money. In light of pervasive political anti-immigrant rhetoric, some worried that jurors might view undocumented witnesses as earning money at the expense of law-abiding citizens – thus complicating their presentation as sympathetic victims. In this context, prosecutors' assessments of case narratives were shaded by broader concern about jurors' alignment with exclusionary immigration discourse. Lawyers' narrative strategies for prosecuting worthy cases thus grappled with the possibility that stories would be received and interpreted by an *unjust* audience of jurors.

Others more explicitly translated the prosecutor's desired status as an equanimous, honest broker into a stated preference for precise language. During one discussion, for instance, a prosecutor emphasised the need to sound like a 'regular' person – in enunciating words and effectively assuming the role of a teacher – when describing evidence of illegal bank transactions. Along similar lines, another prosecutor was told that an excessively dramatic delivery of the beginning of an opening statement distanced the lawyer from her listeners. Instead, she was told, virtue lay in a calm and natural performance.

In preparation for cases with ambiguous evidence, prosecutors thus encouraged each other to err on the side of understatement, weighing emphatic claims against jurors' imagined scepticism and defence counsel's imagined counterarguments. In a fraud case, for example, a supervisor implored the deliverer of an opening statement not to characterise a defendant's confession as devastating evidence. Since the defendant had not conceded that he had lied to a victim – or committed any crime at all, for that matter – this prosecutor encouraged the trial team to proceed with caution. He explained that when he heard about confessions, the scene he imagined was a person being robbed at gunpoint. The confession in *this* case, in contrast, would strike a likeminded juror as less dramatic and therefore less befitting such hyperbolic description.

In sum, the creative and imaginative labour that prosecutors devoted to reformulating case stories revealed a relationship many articulated between tempered advocacy and professionalism. Though overzealousness – like an attorney's obligation to seek justice – lacked explicit definition, colloquial critiques of opening and closing statements highlighted the importance of performing neutrality. As an opening for disagreement and critical engagement, hypothetical jurors offered a vital resource for bringing divergent understandings of narrative priorities to colleagues' attention.

As a rhetorical device, imagined jurors thus served as proxies for the imaginary audiences conjured by writers, performers, teachers and others whose livelihoods depend on the receptiveness of strangers. Literary critic Wayne C. Booth helpfully distinguished analogous types of implied readers for authors of works of fiction (Booth, 1961). Among the 'flesh-and-blood people' writers imagine when creating a narrative, Booth wrote, were unpredictable listeners or readers 'immeasurably complex and diverse in their responses,' and those believed to largely share (or be influenced by) a writer's values (p. 428). In the context examined here, prosecutors prepared for both audiences. On the one hand, they hoped to perform and craft opening statements in such a way that law-abiding jurors might identify and respect a law-enforcing narrator. On the other hand, prosecutors' intensive work of narrative revision recognised the inherent mystery of their lay critics.

Conclusion

Prosecutors revised case stories to not only manage jurors' impressions of them, but to clarify their professional and ethical commitments to themselves. In the process of composing these narratives, they formulated and shared their own understandings of their inchoate obligation to 'seek justice.' Attention to this dimension of 'narrative practice' (Booth, 1961) contributes to narrative criminology by focussing on legal elites who exercise broad discretion in their work to enforce federal law. In so doing, it highlights the implications of lawyers' narrative preferences for their understandings – and thus enactments – of justice as they prepare cases.

Prosecutors' practices of narrative self-imagination affirmed a central insight of narrative criminology: stories structure experience (Maruna, 2007, p. 86). Justice, in other words, is animated by the stories we tell about it – as well as the attorney stories that later map onto prosecutions. In the context of studies of prosecutorial decision-making, a focus on how lawyers produce coherence in their accounts of evidence for jurors brings to light the social contingency at the heart of the laws they enforce. Narrative ethnography is key to this endeavour, since it can bring the researcher in contact with 'both the substantive and the dynamic agentic sides of story-in-use' (Gubrium & Holstein, 1998, p. 166). By scrutinising aspects of their cases and evidence through the eyes of imagined jurors, prosecutors keyed their professional roles to extralegal considerations, including the extent to which decisions aligned with commonsense understandings of fairness. Ordinary citizens, both real and imagined, were thus tied to the collaborative process of narrative composition and critique.

The professional identity traits that emerged as salient included, first, prosecutors' honesty – evinced by their use of precise, detailed and instructive language. They also emphasised the importance of refraining from overly argumentative or aggressive techniques of persuasion that could be viewed as overzealous. Measured, diplomatic and equanimous presentations of case narratives – in contrast – were perceived to signal confidence in evidence drawn from different but mutually reinforcing sources. Though prosecutors might have agreed on the value of these types of attributes in the abstract, their practical application to the framing of case narratives was an interpretively open question. One person's 'dog and pony show' might be another person's earnest attempt at persuasion. Participant observation, which gave me a seat at conference room tables and a voice in discussions, afforded key analytic access to the numerous contingencies that guided narrative decisions.

A benefit of narratively reinforcing professional characteristics with broad and unsettled meaning was the space this created for collaborative work. In the context of civil cases that required translating complex and often ambiguous evidence for laypeople, inviting disparate perspectives and critiques could be illuminating for a trial team long in the weeds of their work. And in criminal cases, too, it was not obvious how to present the testimony of 'scumbag' cooperating witnesses without implicitly vouching for it (Offit, 2019, p. 1093). Conscious of the broad discretion they exercised in selecting and assembling evidence, prosecutors relied on each other as sounding boards for narrative presentations that would have to pass muster with discerning and potentially sceptical lay interlocutors.

As this chapter suggests, prosecutors' conceptions of the just prosecutor – and just prosecutions – were subject to discussion and reformulation as trial narratives took shape. Through references to jurors' perspectives, prosecutors explained their professional commitments to each other and to themselves. In the process of 'storying' (Presser & Sandberg, 2015, pp. 4–5) their cases, prosecutors explicitly and implicitly gave expression to values they viewed as central to their jobs and identities. Reflecting on the role of lay decision-makers during case preparation, one prosecutor explained that reference to future jurors prompted her and her colleagues to reflect on whether they 'should' do something in a particular case. As we have seen, the 'should' of justice is ever-evolving, subject to shift as prosecutors revise the stories that organise and guide their work. It is only with the benefit of narrative ethnography, however, that the variability and stakes of their revisions come to light.

References

Barthes, R. (1966). Introduction to the Structural Analysis of Narrative. In S. Sontag (Ed.), *The Barthes Reader* (p. 266). New York: Hill and Wang, 1982.

Bauman, R. (1986). *Story, performance, and event: Contextual studies of oral narrative.* Cambridge; New York, NY: Cambridge University Press.

Bernard, R. H. (2011). *Research Methods in Anthropology: Qualitative and Quantitative Approaches* (5th ed.). United Kingdom: AltaMira Press.

Booth, W. C. (1961). *The rhetoric of fiction.* Chicago, IL: University of Chicago Press.

Bordwell, D. (1985). *Narration in the fiction film.* Madison, WI: University of Wisconsin Press.

Broeder, D. W. (1964). Voir dire examinations: An empirical study. *Southern California Law Review, 38*, 503. https://heinonline-org.proxy.library.nyu.edu/HOL/Page?handle=hein.journals/scal38&div=53&g_sent=1&casa_token=&collection=journals. Accessed on July 21, 2019.

Douglas, M. (1986). *How institutions think.* Syracuse, NY: Syracuse University Press.

Eco, U. (1984). *The role of the reader: Explorations in the semiotics of texts.* Bloomington, IN: Indiana University Press.

Fleetwood, J., & Sandberg, S. (forthcoming). Narrative Ethnography. In S. Bucerius, K. Haggerty & L. Berardi (Eds.), *Oxford Handbook on Ethnographies of Crime and Criminal Justice.* Oxford: Oxford University Press.

Frank, A. W. (2010). *Letting stories breathe: A socio-narratology.* Chicago, IL: University of Chicago Press.

Geertz, C. (2000). *Local knowledge: Further essays in interpretive anthropology* (3rd ed.). New York, NY: Basic Books.

George, M. E. (2009). Introduction: Notes toward an ethnographic memoir of supervising graduate research through anthropology's decades of transformation. In J. D. Faubion & G. E. Marcus (Eds.), *Fieldwork Is Not What It Used To Be*, (pp. 1–34). Ithaca, NY: Cornell University Press.

Gubrium, J. F., & Holstein, J. A. (1998). Narrative practice and the coherence of personal stories. *The Sociological Quarterly, 39*(1), 163–187.

Hammersvik, E. (2018). Making sense of 'helping friends': 'Flexing' motivational accounts of cannabis growing. *Journal of Contemporary Ethnography, 47*(1), 88–112. doi:10.1177/0891241616662506

Jaber, G., & James, H. (2008). *Handbook of Emergent Methods, edited by Sharlene Nagy Hesse-Biber and Patricia Leavy.* The Guilford Press. Retrieved from https://www.guilford.com/books/Handbook-of-Emergent-Methods/Hesse-Biber-Leavy/9781609181468; https://sociology.missouri.edu/sites/default/files/people/narr._ethnographyhessebiber-ch12_0.pdf

Jacobsson, K. (2008). 'We can't just do it any which way' – Objectivity work among Swedish prosecutors. *Qualitative Sociology Review, 4*(1), 46–67.

Lakoff, G., & Johnson, M. (1980). *Metaphors we live by.* Chicago, IL: University of Chicago Press.

Maruna, S. (2007). *Making good: How ex-convicts reform and rebuild their lives.* Washington, DC: American Psychological Association.

Matoesian, G. M. (2001). *Law and the language of identity: Discourse in the William Kennedy Smith rape trial.* Oxford; New York, NY: Oxford University Press.

Mertz, E. (2007). *The language of law school: Learning to "think like a lawyer"*. Oxford; New York, NY: Oxford University Press.

Offit, A. (2016). Peer review: Navigating uncertainty in the United States jury system. *UC Irvine Law Review, 6*, 169.

Offit, A. (2019). Prosecuting in the shadow of the jury. *Northwestern University Law Review, 113*, 1093.

Philips, S. (2013). Method in anthropological discourse analysis: The comparison of units of interaction. *Journal of Linguistic Anthropology, 23*(1), 82–95. doi:10.1111/jola.12011

Presser, L. (2016). Criminology and the narrative turn. *Crime, Media, Culture, 12*(2), 137–151. doi:10.1177/1741659015626203

Presser, L., & Sandberg, S. (Eds.). (2015). *Narrative criminology: Understanding stories of crime*. New York, NY; London: New York University Press.

Rosen, L. (2006). *Law as culture: An invitation*. Princeton, NJ; Oxford: Princeton University Press.

Sanjek, R. (1990). *Fieldnotes: The makings of anthropology*. Ithaca, NY; London: Cornell University Press.

Schwartzman, H. B. (1989). *The Meeting: Gatherings in Organizations and Communities* (p. 259). New York, NY: Plenum Press.

Strathern, M. (2004). *Commons and Borderlands: Working Papers on Interdisciplinarity, Accountability, and the Flow of Knowledge*. Oxford: Sean Kingston Publishing.

Tutenges, S. (2019). Narrative ethnography under pressure: Researching storytelling on the street. In J. Fleetwood, L. Presser, S. Sandberg & T. Ugelvik (Eds.), *The Handbook of Narrative Criminology*, (pp. 27–43). Bingley: Emerald Publishing Limited.

Zalman, M., & Tsoudis, O. (2005). Plucking weeds from the garden: Lawyers speak about voir dire. *Wayne Law Review, 51*(163), 195–198.

Chapter 4

Narrative Convictions, Conviction Narratives: The Prospects of Convict Criminology

Rod Earle

Introduction: Slants on Truth[1]

In the 1950s C. Wright Mills (1951, p. xx) urged sociologists to locate themselves and their own experiences in the 'trends of their epoch'. In this chapter I examine how narrating personal experience of imprisonment can help criminologists provide more meaningful and insightful accounts of the trend towards the use of imprisonment in many Western democracies over the last 50 years. Using interviews with a small group of British criminologists who have such experience of imprisonment, I explore the connections between personal stories and collective narratives. Drawing reflexively from my own professional trajectory, experiences of prison research and imprisonment, I consider the difficulties and potential of crafting a collective criminological project from disparate and profoundly personal experiences of imprisonment. The chapter combines methodological reflections on the use of autoethnography and vignettes as a means to an end: establishing collective narratives from personal stories. I argue that the task of connecting these narratives to the 'trends of the epoch' that manifest in expanding prison populations is developing some momentum in convict criminology. By focussing on personal experience I do not mean to suggest that there are 'biographical solutions to structural problems' (Beck, 1992, p. 137) but seek to extend a critical reflexivity that is inclusive of the epistemological potentials of personal experience.

Criminologists rarely write about themselves for the simple reason that they do not generally think of themselves as the story. As such, criminologist tend to see themselves as being in the business of other people's stories – specifically other people's troubles with crimes, punishments and wider issues of social control, conformity, transgression, law and order. Criminologists are trained to write with

---

[1]Tell all the truth but tell it slant,
Success in circuit lies.
- Emily Dickson

The Emerald Handbook of Narrative Criminology, 63–83
Copyright © 2019 Rod Earle
All rights of reproduction in any form reserved
doi:10.1108/978-1-78769-005-920191009

analytical detachment, in part because the credibility of their accounts, and hence the discipline, depends on establishing this status. To do otherwise is to compromise scientific principles of inquiry, trespassing recklessly into the realm of fictions rather than facts (Law, 2000).

While the conventional criminologists might ask 'what does prison do to these people', or variants along that line of questioning, the convict criminologist is presented with another line of enquiry: 'what has prison done to me?' or 'how and what do I know of prison life from my own time in prison'. There is the possibility of a dialogue between criminology and their own lives. This kind of purposeful storytelling and experience connects narrative criminology's interest in how stories are told with convict criminology's emphasis on whose stories are told and who is doing the telling (Berger & Quinney, 2005; Presser & Sandberg, 2015). It is a connection that leads towards autobiographical writing and narrative techniques. It brings subjective language and 'unverifiable facts' (Gander, 2013) into closer correspondence with the sociological imagination that C. Wright Mills (1959) made such a strong case for. In the words of Lillian Smith (1963, p. 13) it involves a form of writing that 'has to true itself with facts but also with feelings and symbols, and memories that are never quite facts but sometimes closer to the truth than is any fact'. It is writing that, as she puts it, explores both the 'horizontal and vertical', writing that slants between the humanistic, the lyrical, the evocative and the empirical (Russell-Brown, 1992).

Inside and Outside Insights – Prisoner's Autobiographies versus Prison Ethnographies

Contemporary penal studies in the UK have a relatively strong track record of using the subjective accounts of prisoners as a tool to develop more thorough understandings of prison life, prison policy and penal dynamics (Crewe, 2009; Jewkes, 2002; Leibling, 2004; Phillips, 2012). They have done this by adopting qualitative research strategies that can include and appreciate prisoner's perspectives. Ethnographic studies of imprisonment, such as Gresham Sykes (1958) *The Society of Captives*, have become celebrated as 'classic', 'landmark' texts (Drake et al., 2014). Notwithstanding Wacquant's (2002) lament for the 'eclipse' of such studies in the US as its penal population exploded in the 1990s, prison ethnographers have worked hard to reveal and represent prisoner's lives. They have undoubtedly generated important insights about prison life (Drake et al., 2014).

However, due to the comparative richness of ethnographic accounts of imprisonment it is sometimes overlooked that prisoners themselves may have something important to say about imprisonment without third-party ethnographic conveyancing. Their stories can become overshadowed by the more conventionally academic literature. Nonetheless, prisoners and ex-prisoners have been writing important narratives about prison ever since there have been prisons. Almost as soon as Benjamin Rush had established in 1790 the Pennsylvania prison that modelled his ideas about the need for 'houses of repentance', released prisoners began to present a counternarrative about life inside them.

As Bamberg and Andrews (2004) explain, counternarratives are 'the stories which people tell and live which offer resistance, either implicitly or explicitly, to dominant cultural narratives'. For example, John Palmer's account of his 2 years in the Maine State Prison in the late 1820s reveals his firm belief that it was nothing more than a 'house of pretended reform' (1831, cited in Kann, 2005, p. 227). Henry Tufts' spell inside Massachusetts State Prison taught him that the impact of these new prisons on convicts 'served only to increase their vicious habits and to inspire them with a spirit of revenge' (1807, cited in Kann, 2005, p. 227). William A. Coffey's training as a lawyer provided him with the resources to publish perhaps the most systematic 'insider' critique of the newly emergent penitentiary system. He denounced the reformed prison system as an 'utter failure', identified the source of the failure in the systemic brutality of the guards and excoriated the hypocrisy that allowed 'the umbrage of law' to conceal such routine and repeated failure (1823, cited in Kann, 2005, p. 228). Women's accounts, such as those of Dorah Mahony (1835 cited in Kann, 2005, p. 229), Lucretia P. Cannon (1841 cited in Kann, 2005, p. 229) and Josephine Perkins (1839 cited in Kann, 2005, p. 229), present vivid testimony of the harsh gender regimes imposed on women in the new prisons, and their resistance to them.

The accounts of black prisoners, whose disproportionate presence in the new penitentiaries is partially exposed in some of these accounts by white prisoners, are less readily identifiable in the historical narrative. In his extensive penal commentaries Rush did not comment on the racial dimensions of disproportionality because black people in general did not feature within the grand schemes of penal rehabilitation being formulated in the penitentiaries. As slaves or former slaves, black people were commonly regarded as dispensable, subordinate, 'a lesser breed outside the law' (Gilroy, 1987). When they absconded from plantations and became fugitives from slavery, black people were subject to property laws that rendered them 'thieves of themselves' (Best & Hartman, 2005) because they deprived their 'owner' of a possession (a slave). Their peculiar crime was beyond the conventional reforming scope of the penitentiary that sought to reinsert prisoners into the social relations of liberalism. For black people, self-possession as a liberal political subject was never the same political option it was for white people. They were regarded as exempt from the rehabilitative vision of the prison by virtue of their imagined racial inferiority. Rush's emerging and influential penal philosophies regarded the 'problem' of free black slaves as being beyond the writ of prison and instead he 'contemplated putting all blacks into internal US colonies that could accommodate their huge numbers' (Alexander, 2012; Kann, 2005, p. 107). They simply belonged elsewhere. Race was thus carved deep into US penal thinking and white reforming sensibilities, helping to establish its white separatist dimensions and the differential 'wages of whiteness' identified by Du Bois (1903).

The counternarratives provided by ex-prisoners, including, in Europe, the accounts of the anarchist Peter Kropotkin (1887, see Earle, 2016), consistently portray the newly designed penitentiary regimes as disastrous failures engineering new forms of tyranny and brutality. They expose the penitentiary as producing criminality far more effectively than they contain or deter it. These early nineteenth-century ex-convict narratives correspond very closely with the critical, abolitionist, criminology that emerged in the second half of the twentieth century in the UK and US, but they are narratives that have 'had no discernible impact on penal reformers or public officials' (Kann, 2005, p. 233), a bit like critical criminology. As Kann suggests, public sentiment, penal policy and their misshapen or perverse outcomes tend towards the side of the punishers rather than the punished.

The lived experience of prisoners and ex-convicts has only rarely troubled the hegemony of benevolent, well-intentioned liberal penal reform. Critical criminology has drawn from prison ethnographies principally to demonstrate the recurring gruesome consequences of 'fine ideas' and 'good intentions', the gap between the sanitised rhetoric of penal policy and the 'distasteful ugliness' (Pratt, 2002, p. 97) of day-to-day prison life that is so much part of the lived experience of prisoners. Kann (2005, p. 227) identifies that 'the most consistent and salient themes' of these ex-convict narratives are 'that penitentiaries produced crime and prison officials practiced tyranny'. In short, imprisonment involved personal exposure to the profoundly affecting hypocrisy that thrives in the enormous gap between penal rhetoric and penal reality. It is an intimate, visceral encounter with a travesty of epic proportions that has simply magnified and multiplied since the 1800s, only to resurface in the accounts of contemporary convict criminology (Earle, 2016, 2018a, 2018b; Ross & Richards, 2003).

The Lights of Exposure, the Narrative of Art

Prisoners' counternarratives can help develop understandings of imprisonment because they implicitly and explicitly undo the isolating work of the prison that seeks to render prisoners voiceless and invisible. Counternarratives give agency and offer presence to the otherwise excluded. They act against 'received narratives' (Chatterjee, 2011) to offer powerful accounts of how prisoners have lived through the hardships, contradictions, ambiguities and entanglements that critical criminologists helpfully identify in their studies (Brown & Clare, 2005). Perhaps unsurprisingly, counternarratives have a tendency to reveal prisoners as neither the mutes nor the brutes of popular imagination but as people fashioning themselves to their circumstances with the usual distinguishing features of human agency; dignity, humour, intelligence and integrity. As the artist Antony Gormley noted in his curation of the 2017 Koestler exhibition[2] of prisoners' art and writing, their work presents the prisoner as a creative being rather than a contained one, and almost inevitably subverts their conventional representation as beasts best kept out of sight and in cages.

Gormley goes so far as to describe the finest prison artists as 'the psychonauts of the twenty-first century, telling us things we do not know about inside worlds,

---

[2] Arthur Koestler was a writer who campaigned throughout the 1950s in the UK for the abolition of capital punishment and then established a fund to foster ways of 'stimulating the mind and spirit of the prisoner'. https://www.koestlertrust.org.uk/exhibitions/developments.

the truths we lock up, and thus helping the outside world to know itself better.' (Gormley, 2017). Creating work from the 'induced paralysis' of prison, the prison artist is an 'expert witness', says Gormley, on what prison does and how it can be seen. They produce narratives from the 'front line of the human imagination', 'phenomenal testimony' about how to live in lifeless conditions. Gormley himself speaks from personal experience of imprisonment in the UK (for drugs), Iran and Afghanistan (for art).

Authentic as prisoner's literary arts may be, there are caveats to bear in mind. Such writing cannot necessarily be taken as representative of the general prison population (Brown & Clare, 2005). Prisoner autobiographies in particular have a tendency to be propelled, reasonably enough, by a variety of specific motives such as personal innocence, a particular miscarriage of justice, or straightforward journalistic ambition (Morgan, 1999). They are narratives often presented to advise future generations in a way that consolidates the author's new sense of self and their desistance from crime.

Autobiographical resources are ones that convict criminology is well placed to exploit. They can be written from within the discipline and theorised from personal experience of its most iconic institution – the prison. The developing and diverse narratives of UK convict criminology (Aresti, Darke, & Manlow, 2016; Davies, 2018; Earle, 2016, 2018a, 2018b; Honeywell, 2013, 2015) can shift the emphasis from the peripheral incidental benefit provided by autobiographical accounts generated outside the discipline (with all their compensatory subjective vitality) to a more central role in transforming the prison. They promise a shift in position from a passive witness to criminology, at worst its showroom dummy, at best, a useful bystander, to one that can extend its sensibilities and reach. These narratives decline a neutral, placeless objectivity in favour of a more embodied, situated 'optic of knowing' (Haraway, 1988). By combining an uncommon double exposure to prison, as a prisoner and as an academic, the convict criminologist can offer fresh phrasing and new kinds of narratives on the mechanics and ethics of imprisonment, criminal justice and punishment.

Narrative criminology applies to convict criminology because of the way it studies how narratives inspire and motivate human action, and how they are used to make sense of social phenomena. Narrative criminology provides a primacy to narrative in human action but is an approach that involves recognising narratives as complex constructions. Narrative approaches to criminology eschew a singular or exclusive methodology by drawing selectively from a variety of perspectives and methodologies (Presser & Sandberg, 2015). Narrative criminology also insists that narratives are more than stories, more than accounts of experience and reckonings with voices. Narratives produce experience and manufacture voices. Narrative is recognised as being constitutive as much as it is representational, and both dynamics are at work in the convict criminology developed here.

Writing from a convict criminology perspective often involves moving from the established conventions of ethnography towards autoethnography. The reflexive practice of self-referential narrative involved in autoethnography is sometimes considered an academic indulgence and of limited value, adding only literary or poetic embellishment to an unhelpfully singular form of analysis that can only be true to itself, and unreliably so at that (see Law's (2000, pp.7–8) discussion on 'vanity ethnography'). However, despite being dismissed by mainstream metric criminology, these 'literary truths' have a habit of fuelling the sociological imagination in ways that conventional social scientific writing is rarely capable of doing.

Telling Tales of Autoethnography: A Vignette of Green Slime

Autoethnography 'is an approach to research and writing that seeks to describe and systematically analyse (graphy) personal experience (auto) in order to understand cultural experience (ethno)' (Ellis, Adams, & Bouchner, 2011, p. 1). It is a kind of writing that uses personal, first-person accounts intended to be emotionally and intellectually evocative of various sociological or anthropological themes. It implies that a personal narrative is being developed and used for a purpose beyond the simple telling of a story to a particular audience. Autoethnography is a process of structured reflection and reviewing of lived experience which may seek to bring past experience into the present for a variety of analytic, heuristic or hermeneutic purposes. These are potentials that convict criminology needs to exploit but require commitment and courage (c.f. Wakeman, 2014).

In my case, the more I found myself writing about my prison research conducted in 2006–2008, the more I found myself stumbling over memories of my own brief period of incarceration in 1982. I could not find a place for these memories in the accounts I gave of that research (Earle, 2011, 2012; Earle & Phillips, 2013) but their absence was continually troubling, amounting to an exclusion that, like missing data in a quantitative dataset, I knew should be accounted for. In quantitative analysis, missing data refer to the absence of one or more values within a study variables dataset. They may be missing because, for example, survey respondents have chosen not to offer a response to a survey item. Quantitative analysts are careful to declare absences and assess their significance for the conclusions they might draw from their data. For qualitative researchers to do something similar should not be a methodological indulgence but a reflexive obligation, a more 'exact description of the apparatus used' as Malinowski (2010, p. 2) urged.

I eventually found a place for my first-hand experiences of criminal justice procedures and their culmination in a prison sentence in my book *Convict Criminology – Inside and Out* (Earle, 2016). The key was to open each chapter in the book with a short autobiographical vignette. In part, this was inspired by the writing of W. E. B Du Bois (1903) whose much neglected sociological craft pioneered affective, lyrical and autobiographical approaches (Back & Tate, 2014). I am wary, as someone who is white, of making any kind of analogy to the varieties of black experience, of finding any kind of affinity to the forms of identification, objectification or subjectification involved in racialisation, but Du Bois's 'double consciousness' in which the sense of always looking at one's self through the eyes of others, of being a construction of others making, has something of the enduring exclusions of criminal labelling about it. Du Bois remains a source of inspiration, and as I explore later, the reflexive and narrative methods of critical race theory can provide important lessons for convict criminology. They demonstrate how the twin constitutive and representational aspects of narrative criminology generate affinities across the nominal boundaries of an expanding discipline, linking it to convict criminology.

The eight vignettes I used to open each chapter provided both a vehicle to drive the book's narrative, and a thread through the tentative assemblage of a convict criminology narrative. The first begins with the prison experience etched most strongly into my memory, one that connected directly to my research fieldwork around prison exercise yards, and one that has simply refused to go away.

A Ring of Green Slime

I had only been in prison one day. It was time to go out into the exercise yard and I was anxious because it was clearly a kind of informal and vaguely social occasion. The exercise yard? It sounded like a prison cliché. As I emerged through the door into a high walled compound I could see the walking circle of prisoners forming, and couldn't quite believe it. It was just like in the movies, except they weren't wearing stripped uniforms, just shabby grey trousers and jumpers. Walking round and round in a circle, going nowhere, like the cliché. It seemed an unreal stereotype of meaninglessness. Prison life. Do I go with the flow or what? I didn't know what else to do, so I wandered slowly toward the circulating straggle of men, and fell into step.

It was 1982. I was 24. I have crowded fragments of indistinct memories about the occasion, but one that has always stayed with me is the awful ring of green slime that had formed on the inside of the circle from the men's accumulated gobbits of phlegm. A string of men walking slowly round and round in a circle, three times a day, and like some kind of human-formed seaweed on the tarmac, the accumulated expectorations of 200 men disfigured the exercise yard with passively malign intent. Prison. Men. All in it together. (Earle, 2016, p. 1).

A vignette is defined as 'a short piece of writing that expresses the typical characteristics of something or someone' (Cambridge Dictionaries Online, 2018). It is a piece of writing that attempts to capture a snapshot of a larger picture and also tries to evoke some dimensions of that larger picture. Vignettes allude to a wider reality without necessarily specifying it. Each of the eight vignettes I use in *Convict Criminology* are short snatches of a bigger picture of various personal experiences of crime, policing, arrests, trials and prison. They are the selective result of a conscious process of retrieval and construction. The assemblage of the first vignette led to another, then another. They do not follow a chronological pattern, but each is built around a powerful experience or lingering memories that had surfaced at various stages of my later working life as a criminologist. They frequently pivoted around the dual experience of being someone subject to criminal justice interventions, such as arrest and detention, and its potential significance as a criminological artefact. Assembling the vignettes involved a conscious selection of 'stories' that I felt would 'work', and was not intended as a comprehensive retelling of all my crimes and misdemeanours, or my life.

The 'ring of green slime' vignette was chosen because the circle of walking men is such an iconic penal image, an image captured in Van Gogh's famous picture of a prison exercise yard, and the picture that adorns the front cover of my copy of Foucault's *Discipline and Punish*. Placing myself in that circle, figuratively speaking, seemed consistent with the aim of convict criminology to combine personal experience of imprisonment with critical, reflexive analysis of criminology's role in theorising imprisonment. Being in that circle was an experience that communicated something powerful to me – the men's contempt for their environment and the opportunity for its expression by spitting on the ground; an innocent, approximately social, masculine habit indicative of nothing and everything about what it means to be a man and a man in prison. Passive, aggressive and neither; visceral, embodied and placed, it communicated men's reluctantly collective inhabitation of a ruined social life. The refusal of the prison guards to clean the mess we left and allow its accumulation into the ring of slime told me something powerful about prison life, the limits of its care and the mutual contempt that lurked not very far around its corners. The distance between carelessness and incarceration is narrow.

My subjective understandings of imprisonment will always be conditioned by this experience, this personal knowledge will qualify every book I ever read about prison and every prison I ever visit as a researcher or as a teacher, and it only seems ethical as a criminologist to declare this slant. Calling it convict criminology makes it sound more like an academic tool kit than a bias, though it inevitably adds some unwelcome weight of expectation. Without unduly labouring the point, the experience is loosely analogous to the distinction made by Edward Said (1993, p. 77) that you don't have to be from 'the colonies' to do postcolonial analysis but 'an Indian or an African scholar of English literature will read *Kim*, say, or *Heart of Darkness* with a critical urgency not felt in quite the same way by an American or a British one'.

There are longstanding disputes over the epistemological significance of experience and its relationship to truth and reality in social science, philosophy and literature. Feminist scholars in the 1980s cut a path that challenged and diverted the standard narratives of social science, asking how and why women's experience counted for so little (Harding, 1987; Stanley, 1990). In cultural studies Raymond Williams developed his concept of 'structures of feeling' to offer a theoretical account of the tensions between the vitality of experience as an aspect of personal agency and the morbid anonymity of structuralist theories of historical change. As a theoretical framework 'structures of feeling' address questions about the unintelligible qualities of lived experience that often operate below the level of narrative because they cannot be easily expressed, lack available vocabularies and exist only on the margins of semantic availability:

> ...the peculiar location of a structure of feeling is the endless comparison between the articulated and the lived. The lived is only another word, if you like, for that experience: but you have to find a word for that level. For all that is not fully articulated, all that comes through as disturbance, tension, blockage, emotional trouble seems to me precisely a source of major changes in the relation between the signifier and the signified. (Williams, 2015, p. 242).

Structures of feeling are lived even as they are negotiated, inhabited and performed. Making narratives of personal experience and finding words that do not, in Williams' (2015, p. 242) memorable phrasing, 'make a god out of unexamined subjectivity' is where ethnographic traditions and most specifically, autoethnography can be helpful (Geertz, 1988).

Autoethnography and the use of vignettes are an increasingly prevalent feature of service-user and expert-by-experience research (Robertson, Carpenter, & Donovasn-Hall, 2017). They have both developed especially strongly from mental health practice and therapies that continually ask service users to 'tell their stories' as an aspect of clinical interventions, so that a suitable diagnosis can be completed and an appropriate treatment formulated for them. In mental health services, alternative possibilities for overcoming trauma and recovering a life have adopted narrative as a technique that allows individuals to provide accounts of themselves and for themselves so that they acquire the power to tell their stories and frame their 'narrative of recovery' (Slade, 2009). They are referred to by Jason Warr (2019), in the context of prisoners serving life or indeterminate sentences, as a form of 'narrative labour'. This narrative approach is emerging through the collaborations and affinities being developed by narrative criminology. The voices of former or existing prisoners that have been relatively muted within criminology are starting to emerge (Warr, 2019). Narrative methods offer them a remedy for their degraded penal status, providing for their voice to be heard and opportunities to fashion the context and substance from which they are made (Couldry, 2010). In the next section I discuss how the establishment of British Convict Criminology (BCC) is encouraging these developments.

Criminology with Conviction

The BCC group was launched at the 2011 conference of the British Society of Criminology (BSC), with papers from the cofounders Dr Andreas Aresti and Dr Sacha Darke from the University of Westminster, and myself. Since then it has presented panels and academic papers at each subsequent BSC annual conference, and slowly established a small network of scholars and students who identify with its aims. In 2016 I invited six academics who meet the convict criminology criteria of having served a prison sentence and completed, or being in the process of completing, a criminology or related PhD, to participate in interviews about their views on convict criminology. All are working within British criminology in various capacities but not all are active in the BCC group or align themselves with convict criminology.

The criminological demographics of this interview group ($n = 6$) are relatively predictable, reflecting much of the conventional criminological wisdom and established 'criminological facts' of crime: it's mostly about wayward white men. However, there was one woman among the respondents. All but one (mixed ethnicity) are white, but diversely so, qualifying their white ethnicity with a variety of 'secondary whiteness' markers (Alexander, 2017). Between them the group have nearly 80 convictions, although again, this simple aggregation belies a complex distribution. For one person, seven convictions arise from a single trial resulting in a custodial sentence that marks the beginning and end of criminal sanctioning at a relatively late age (mid-30s). For another respondent, criminal sanctions began age 11 (formal police caution) and ended 6 years later, aged 17, with a long sentence. The prison sentences range from the very short, 3 months, to the notorious 'indeterminate', open-ended detention. Some served their sentence in a single prison, some in several. With more than 30 years of custodial experience, the group collectively inhabits nearly all the categories of penal detention, from pretrial remand, youth detention, military detention, high security prisons, punishment blocks and open conditions dating back to the 1980s.

The interviews were designed to foster a semi-structured dialogue to share and compare experiences. My own position and experience as someone with convictions and a career in criminology were fully disclosed. The interviews were complemented by a day-long symposium, funded by a Small Groups grant from the Independent Social Research Foundation (ISRF) which provided an opportunity for a larger round table discussion attended by undergraduate criminology students with criminal convictions and nonconvicted academics and voluntary sector supporters (see Larsen, 2017).

Criminologists with, and without, Convict Narratives

Although all those interviewed had criminal convictions resulting in imprisonment, not all of them were reconciled to the implied or 'received' narrative of convict criminology. A significant feature of the discussions and interviews was the extent to which the diversity of penal experience could be combined to generate a distinctive form of criminological knowledge, and, further, the relationship between the production of this knowledge and other forms of criminological practice, such as teaching. Each of the people interviewed had substantial first-hand experience of criminal justice, something in common with each other but unusual in the wider academic community of criminology. Notwithstanding this commonality, at least two of the interviewees expressed doubts that the experiences should define their academic identity in the ways implied by any formal alignment with convict criminology. For 'Mike[3]' 'it needs to come with me, as part of me, be complementary to who I am, but not define who I am'. For 'Marcus', the very idea of becoming a criminologist after spending so much time in prison seemed absurd, at first:

> *What I didn't want was to get out of prison and be a criminologist. Come out of prison, talk about prisons, write about prisons, be a prisons' researcher??!!. I didn't want that! Because I needed to rebuild my life, I wanted some distance.*

For Marcus, a series of pivotal interactions with well-established and supportive criminologists inspired him to believe in his academic potential, and his success as a criminologist is woven around a long academic apprenticeship in a range of disciplines. The opportunities for disciplinary rendezvous that criminology provides are its principal attraction, according to Marcus, rather than his biographical connection. Criminology can satisfy his wide-ranging appetite for psychology, law, sociology, history and literature. While he relishes the opportunity for his penal experience to act as an occasional 'reality checker' or 'bullshit detector' in teaching encounters with, for example, prison officers or probation officers, his fidelity is to methodological and epistemological rigour. This, he insists, is partly a defensive strategy built to deflect the anticipated critiques of his work as being partial, partisan or otherwise biased by his prison experience. For example, he recognises that his encounters with criminal justice professionals studying criminology are inevitable, and potentially problematic:

> *And the minute I allow* my *personal history to start shaping the way that I explain their* lived experiences [as prison officers]*, I'm not really doing science as I understand it; I'm doing journalism. And for me I have to make that distinction, because it's so overwhelming in my background. I have to make a very conscious decision not to do that.*

For Mike, the idea of being seen as a convict criminologist is restrictive and potentially limiting because of the way it would always signal to the people he wants to interact with as an academic, only a narrow range of his hinterland obscuring equally significant aspects of his biography: 'My experience of prison life is a strand of a number of experiences that I draw on, as well as coming from an estate, as well as being excluded from school'. Mike is also wary of being patronised by established, middle-class academics and dismissive of the kind of pretentious intellectual capital they sometimes trade in. Mike resents the way his well-proven, hard-earned academic capabilities can be so easily traduced by

---

[3]Pseudonyms have been used because although several respondents are openly aligned with convict criminology, others are not and the process of disclosure should always remain with the individual concerned.

middle-class preferences for the 'authenticity' of his worldly experience, of his imprisonment:

> *So it is known in my work that I do come from this [ex-convict] perspective. I think it's important, and I deal with it through my discussion of methodology, and how it's important to critically engage with what that experience is, and what the limitations are and what the advantages are. I think what I want to be careful of, and this is quite hard to say, is I don't want to be like 'oh here's a convict, this guy who's been away [in prison]. We can't really challenge him too much. His work's a bit shit and he doesn't really think things through properly, you know, but better not say so, because he's from prison'. I don't want to eat out on my [convict] identity. I don't want people to be clapping my ex-convict back, patting me on the head. But I want it recognised as well though.*

Like Marcus, Mike has had to struggle in his research with the fact that 'those guys knew I knew more than your average academic' and that his experiences of withdrawal from drugs, for example, equip him with service user and experiential insights he can reveal and share, or withhold, according to circumstance. Negotiating the boundary, he says with telling feeling 'is really hard sometimes'.

Mike is sanguine about the limitations that accompany the insider researcher position, citing not only Merton's (1972) early identification of the dilemma but also his research experiences. He has found disclosure of his ex-convict status can shut doors, as well as open them. Some of the young men he has interviewed in prison seemed keen to test his experience against theirs, and he sensed their accounts were modified according to their revised understanding of his. Some of this derived from his dual status as a former drug user and ex-prisoner, personally familiar with the routines of drug dependency as well as cell life:

> *Part of my reservations about disclosing during prison research is because of exactly those things that play out in convict criminology… And then that guy's narrative is going to be impacted by whether he feels your positioning or your prison experience is less or more than his.*

In sharp contrast, for three of the interview group, 'Steve', 'Ron' and 'Gavin', convict criminology offered a pathway into academic life, rather than a route to be avoided. For Gavin, learning of the existence of the US group and helping to establish the UK group provided a structure for solidarity and support, and a welcome intelligibility to his personal circumstances: 'trying to make sense of my own situation was what drew me to the criminology'. He concedes that despite all the considerable obstacles he has had to overcome because of his prison sentence, it is now working as a positive asset rather than a hindrance:

> *I'm doing a lot of things because of the very fact that I've been in prison. And I'm in a privileged position, and I sort of think well if I hadn't have been [in prison] I wouldn't be getting invited to do these talks here, there and around the country. There's obstacles, there's other things that I have to deal with, but generally at least in academic terms and career terms it's actually working in my favour. Convict criminology as a project has taken me places, as it has other members of the group. There is that sense of belonging for sure. You're not alone in this, and you've got these people there.*

The narrative arcs of Gavin, Ron and Marcus's convictions may differ but each share moving testimonies on the tribulations involved in the transition from prison cell to academic office, and the numerous job rejections they received in which their old criminal disqualification trumped their newest academic qualification. Both Ron and Marcus say they acquired a new moral compass in prison, developed by introspection, reflection and faith in their own moral integrity rather than contrition over the error of their ways, the arc of the conventional liberal narrative.

Other similarities and experiences in common are significant but relatively submerged in the interviews. For all six, substance misuse, drugs and violence have played a major or at least partial role in their route to incarceration, implicated in various contributory combinations to their convictions. For four of the six substance misuse, dependency and alcoholism have been part of the journey into prison. Trying to stay free of these has been part of the journey least talked about. As Mike reflects, these are often aspects of working-class life that leave many men vulnerable to criminal justice interventions when the harms he and his generation have endured, or imposed on others, could have been prevented by more comprehensive health services and more egalitarian educational opportunities responsive to their needs and circumstances. The convict route to criminology is more likely to be a working-class route than the usual college route of the well-supported, conventional middle-class student. Ron is not alone when he declares:

> *I was the first person in my family, going back forever, and wider family, ever to go to university, so for me seeing if I could get in, seeing if I could complete it, were the main thing, and then the excitement of where it might lead my life in future.*

When discussing the dilemma of 'whether to prostitute my past to get to my future', i.e. the issue of how his criminal career might contribute to his academic career, Ron was encouraged by his professorial mentor who insisted: 'look, you've got an important voice, you'll find a place somewhere'. The 'imposter syndrome' that bothers many early career academics doesn't worry him and he's happy to call himself, tongue in cheek, 'a tall fraud': 'I don't really class myself as an academic. I'm here just because I've been to prison and I've got a bit of a gob on me that's prepared to shout about it.' For Ron a passion for teaching, his long-standing work ethic and creative talent in forging novel partnerships between his university and the local prison sustain his interest in convict criminology. As far as he is concerned, he has nothing to hide, nothing to fear and nothing to be ashamed of. He has paid his dues: 'I paid a price to get this knowledge, and the price I paid I'll never get back'. For Ron, establishing himself with an explicit profile as a convict criminologist is simply fair game.

Similar sentiments have propelled 'Steve' from a series of substantial prison sentences, starting in his youth, to a successfully concluded PhD and a lectureship in criminology. He describes a moment in his final prison sentence:

> *while I was in there and studying it just came to me really, it was a bit like a light being switched on. I thought I can study my own people here, I can become a criminologist, I can become a lecturer, this is what I want to do, this is where I want to go, so I'd planned on doing what I'm doing now way back then, and I've stuck to that.*

Steve has wrestled with the same kind of dilemmas that concerned Marcus. Having spent much of his life in prison, why would he want to spend the rest of it studying the place rather than leaving it well alone? He is reconciled now to the prison being an area of expertise around which he can make a distinctive contribution, but his immersion in it can still be troubling in ways that C. Wright Mills (see below) may have failed to fully appreciate:

> *it isn't just a job is it, it's my life as well. My self is incorporated into my career. It's what I am as well. What I'm teaching is what I'm part of. I mean it's not a nine until five job. It's there with me 24/7. Sometimes I think 'is this dominating myself, am I sort of imprisoning myself here to be always this ex-convict talking about the same old thing over and over again?'*

For Ron, Steve and Gavin, a particular feature of convict criminology is the way it brings their prison past into the lecture theatre, and allows them to take their lectures and students into prison. In this teaching modality, convict criminology presents a more ontological face where the simple existence of the lecturer as an ex-convict, an expert by experience, is the essence of the practice. The epistemological claims of convict criminology to be a distinctive way of generating knowledge of the prison, and other criminological objects, are harder to pin down.

Hazel's experiences as an academic studying crime have been transformed by her first-hand experience of trial and conviction. She contrasts her reading of academic literature on trial procedures as 'dramatisation' consisting of scripts and carefully stage-managed rituals, with the actuality of being prosecuted. Her feelings of helplessness in the face of what she felt to be callous disinterest masquerading as politeness remain raw and unsettling. The image of the prosecuting barrister leafing through the case notes of his next trial as he awaited her life-changing verdict may appear mundane but were devastating to Hazel: 'I can't unsee that'. It confirmed her status as a mere procedural object, a life transacted. She compares her visceral rage in the trial and in the moment, with the accounts of trials she had drawn from her research respondents:

> *And it wasn't that I disbelieved them because I believed them, but I thought perception is a lot, isn't it, in those situations, in a stressful situation, so you have to always kind of slightly try to look at it from all sides. But then you go through that experience and you go they were right! They were right!*

The revelations of first-hand experience recur at various stages of her sentence, particularly around the extent of self-harm and the physically degrading features of women's imprisonment, but Hazel is also acutely aware of her exceptional circumstances as a woman in convict criminology. For Hazel the potentials of convict criminology lie in its capacity to bring new voices into the discipline, and make it more aware of its deficiencies. Her experiences in prison, inside the criminal justice system, have made her more critical of the way criminology inevitably reifies crime and obsesses over criminal identities. Having spent a number of years in prison she declares: 'I haven't met anybody that describes themselves as having a criminal identity. I haven't met any people that say that kind of thing. Can we stop calling it crime? It's not a real thing.'

The attractions of using her own experience and identifying with convict criminology are considerable for Hazel, but she remains ambivalent and circumspect. 'I think firstly it's about acknowledging the epistemological value of direct experience. You don't exclude that from any other form of academia, do you? It needs to be rigorous. I think you can contribute to the rigour of that by not just talking about yourself, and that it's not only about "this was my experience" so therefore.... It's not autobiographical in that way. It might be autoethnographical. But you're not in criminology to tell somebody your life story.'

In the final section I consider if the new horizons of narrative criminology might help qualify some of this scepticism and offer a way of fulfilling the positive potentials of convict criminology.

From Convictions to Sentences: Narrative and Voice in Convict Criminology

C Wright Mills' advice on the development of a sociological imagination is pretty straightforward:

> ...you must learn to use your life experience in your intellectual work: continually to examine and interpret it. In this sense craftsmanship is the centre of yourself and you are personally involved in every intellectual product upon which you work. (Mills, 1959, p. 196).

The implications for a convict criminologist are relatively obvious, literally self-evident, but the task of narrating oneself as a convict criminologist is far from simple. Steve's narrative combines the pain and anguish of the past with possibilities of the future in a familiar narrative arc that bends towards hope, but is never purged of a troubling ambivalence: will he ever escape the penal gaze? As Hazel's pithy observation indicates although you may not be in criminology just to tell your life story, if you are a criminologist and have a criminal story to tell, narrative criminology provides some helpful avenues through which to develop your intellectual contribution to the discipline.

Presser (2009, p. 178) notes how '[c]riminologists are concerned with that sequence of events culminating in crime' and as a convict criminologist you are intimate with the narrative implications of this sequence, even if only in the details of your own case. You also carry around a truncated narrative of the sequence of events given to you by a court of law: a criminal conviction and a sentence of imprisonment. In becoming a prisoner, the narrative culminates in you becoming the property of the state, an object of its criminal law. It is not a narrative of your own making (even if a guilty plea was entered) and it is a uniquely compressed and condensed narrative presented in headline form for public consumption and almost unending bureaucratic administration. Presser (2009) notes how, in response, the narratives she finds offenders generating of themselves are often profound social constructs, self-consciously manufactured by the person against the master narrative of 'offender', and textured by the qualities of the interview context (Presser, 2009).

In receiving a conviction, the 'offender', the convicted person, is made unusually self-conscious of themselves as a social construct, the product of another's narrative to which theirs, as and when they fashion it, is almost inevitably a counternarrative. Other abstract constructs of the liberal penal imagination, the received narrative, such as being a reformed political subject, a bearer of liberal freedoms, a party to a social contract, are all clustered around the prisoner in their involuntary, intimate and embodied proximity to the foundational touchstones of liberal society (Easton, 2018; Hesse, 2014). It's the reason the prison cell is such an evocative literary device and the source of so much criminological fascination but it places the (ex)prisoner in some degree of narrative jeopardy, forever required to maintain one narrative over another. This involves unusually explicit investment in narrative labour (Warr, 2019) with all its predicaments and dilemmas (Earle, 2018a).

Narrative, to paraphrase Bakhtin (1981, p. 259), is 'overpopulated with the intentions of others' and has become a popular portmanteau term in social science (Squire, 2014). For a convict criminologist the first lessons of narrative are taught to them in a courtroom rather than a classroom; their personal story is subordinate to law's grand narrative of liberal freedom and its removal. It is one of the sweeter ironies of convict criminology to take the courtroom narrative back into the classroom, not with the punitive intention of 'teaching someone a lesson' as they do in court, but with the pedagogic intention of helping students learn reflexively about the power of law in the raw and the fiascos of liberal penality (Drake, 2018) in the person of their teacher. These are narratives that come through strongly in my interviews with Steve, Ron and Gavin. In the words of

C. Wright Mills (1979, p. 370) they tell their students they are 'in touch with the realities of themselves and their world'.

For a convict criminologist academic life begins with a sentence just as any narrative must, but there will always be a double entendre at play, a double meaning intelligible only from a particular and usually private perspective. The official, legal, story starts in a court of law where the sentence is the source of a powerful narrative that becomes fixed to a person and defines their character to a particular social audience, and becomes their conviction. In this linguistic sense, 'criminals' are the syntax of criminology, its functional characters. As Hazel discovered in court, there is a narrative violence involved in this reduction to a single, legalistic story, a violence eloquently described in the context of race by the Nigerian novelist Chimamanda Adichie (2009):

> The single story creates stereotypes and the problem with stereotypes is not that they are untrue, but that they are incomplete. They make one story the only story. The consequence of the single story is this: it robs people of dignity. It makes our recognition of our equal humanity difficult. It emphasizes how we are different rather than how we are similar. Stories matter. Many stories matter. Stories have been used to dispossess and to malign, but stories can also be used to empower and to humanize. Stories can break the dignity of a people, but stories can also repair that broken dignity.

Autoethnography can bring personal narratives into the sociological imagination by linking personal troubles to public issues, as recommended with such force and vigour by C Wright Mills. Producing these narratives is an important kind of criminological activism and a significant form of sociological introspection (Ellis, 2009). Lived experience only becomes intelligible and tellable through narratives, but convict criminology narratives are fraught with tensions and difficulties. As my interviews indicate, there are several degrees of narrative jeopardy involved. Some of these can be attributed to familiar 'insider/outsider' dilemmas described by Mike, but they are complicated by further methodological conundrums on 'going native' and 'staying native' (Gillard et al. 2010; Earle, 2018a), as described by Marcus. Both Mike and Marcus are concerned that convict criminology narratives are prone to lapses of 'narrative bad faith' (Craib, 2004) in which the currency of the convictions is too readily coined to academic advantage. The narrative capital can be inflated by the toxic gas of middle-class condescension. Against this, Ron, Gavin and Steve find the tensions produced by their unsettling presence in criminology productive; stimulating and just returns for hard work and the pains of imprisonment they have endured, a creative anomaly.

Lived experience is full of lived contradictions. The emotional process of using lived experience and presenting one's subjectivity to wider scrutiny is full of risks, but convict criminology may grow stronger if it looks to other critical perspectives in service user movements, such as in mental health, and radical social movements where these methods are accepted and productive. Experiential narratives have been central to the development of critical race theory (Delgado & Stefanic, 2001) where the need to develop counternarratives to the dominant theme of the declining salience of race in US social life has been an urgent priority. Critical race theory foregrounds everyday experience in the form of stories and retelling conventional (white) narratives from unconventional (black) perspectives, frequently around issues of law and order, courtrooms and jails.

According to Roland Barthes (1975) narrative is one of the great cognitive categories that enables us to understand and organise the world. For Paul Ricoeur (1984) it is impossible to conceive of a culture without narrative, so basic is it to human interaction. Giving an account of ourselves is the signature of our humanity, according to Judith Butler (2005), allowing us to recognise ourselves and each other. To have a narratable life is to have a liveable life and both are becoming increasingly untenable in the prevailing rationalities of neoliberal racial capitalism. These are rationalities that depend on, and generate, the unintelligibility of everyday life, the irrelevance of the future and the disposability of the past. In this context experience, voice and narrative are the raw materials of struggle and resistance (Couldry, 2012).

Part of this struggle is to allow time for convict criminology narratives to emerge. Each convict criminologist is 'sailing at once in several seas' (Geertz, 1988, p. 77) and has their own tale to tell, their own corrections or amendments to construct against their conviction and their sentence, their received narrative. The recourse to personal narrative can seem facile but is necessary and difficult work because only by generating these individual narratives can something more substantial, more collective emerge through the vital 'entanglement of our stories with the stories of others' (Ricoeur, 1995, p. 15). In convict criminology making these narratives disrupts 'the silence of being relegated to oneself' (Kierkegaard, 1954, p. 167) and presents new slants on the vast truths of prison life, but they are no guarantee of a hearing if criminology is only interested in facts (Presser, 2016).

References

Adichie, C. (2009). Why stories matter. *yes!*, December 9. Retrieved from https://www.yesmagazine.org/people-power/chimamanda-adichie-on-why-stories-matter. Accessed on September 5, 2018.

Alexander, C. (2017). Breaking black: The death of ethnic and racial studies in Britain. *Ethnic and Racial Studies, 41*, 1034–1054.

Alexander, M. (2012). *The new Jim Crow: Mass incarceration in the age of colourblindness*. New York, NY: The New Press.

Aresti, A., Darke, S., & Manlow, D. (2016). Bridging the gap: Giving public voice to prisoners and former prisoners through research activism. *Prison Service Journal, 224*, 3–13.

Back, L., & Tate, M. (2014). Telling about racism: W.E.B. Du Bois, Stuart Hall and sociology's reconstruction. In W. D. Hund & A. Lentin (Eds.), *Racism and sociology*. Zurich: LIT Verlag.

Bakhtin, M. (1981). Discourse in the novel. In M. M. Bakhtin, J. Wright, & M. Holquist (Eds.), *The dialogic imagination. Four essays*. Austin, TX: University of Texas Press.

Bamberg, M., & Andrews, M. (Eds.). (2004). *Considering counter-narratives: Narrating, resisting, making sense*. Amsterdam: John Benjamins Publishing.

Barthes, R. (1975). An introduction to the structural analysis of narrative. *New Literary History*, 6(2), 237–272.

Beck, U. (1992). *Risk society*. Cambridge: Polity.

Berger, R. J., & Quinney, R. (Eds.). (2005). *Storytelling sociology: Narrative as social inquiry*. London: Lynne Rienner.

Best, S., & Hartman, S. (2005). Fugitive justice. *Representations*, 92, 1–15.

Brown, A., & Clare, E. (2005). A history of experience: Exploring prisoners' accounts of incarceration. In C. Emsley (Ed.), *The persistent prison: Problems, images and alternatives*. London: Francis Boutle Publishers.

Butler, J. (2005). *Giving an account of oneself*. New York, NY: Fordham University Press.

Chatterjee, P. (2011). *Lineages of political society – studies in post-colonial democracy*. New York, NY: Columbia University Press.

Couldry, N. (2010). *Why voice matters: Culture and politics after neo-liberalism*. London: SAGE Publications.

Couldry, N. (2012). *Why voice matters: culture and politics after neoliberalism*. London: SAGE Publications.

Craib, I. (2004). Narratives as bad faith. In M. Andrews, S. Day Sclater, M. Rustin, C. Squire, & A. Treacher (Eds.), *The uses of narrative: Explorations in sociology, psychology and cultural studies* (pp. 64–71). New Brunswick, NJ: Transaction Publishers.

Crewe, B. (2009). *The prisoner society: Power, adaptation and social life in an English prison*. Oxford: Oxford University Press.

Davies, W. (2018). Making a convict criminologists: The crooked path. Paper presented to European Society of Criminology, Sarajevo, Bosnia and Herzegovina.

Delgado, R., & Stefanic, J. (2001). *Critical race theory: An introduction*. London: New York University Press.

Drake, D. (2018). Prisons and state building: Promoting 'the fiasco of the prison' in a global context. *International Journal for Crime, Justice and Social Democracy*, 7(4), pp. 1–15.

Drake, D., Earle, R., & Sloan, J. (Eds.). (2014). *The Palgrave handbook of prison ethnography*. Basingstoke: Palgrave Macmillan.

Du Bois, W. E. B. (1994/1903). *The souls of black folk*. New York, NY: Dover Publications.

Earle, R. (2011). Boys' zone stories: Perspectives from a young men's prison. *Criminology and Criminal Justice*, 11(2), 129–143.

Earle, R. (2012). 'Who's the daddy?' – Ideas about fathers from a young men's prison. *The Howard Journal of Criminal Justice*, 51(4), 387–399.

Earle, R. (2016). *Convict criminology: Inside and out*. Bristol: Policy Press.

Earle, R. (2018a). Convict criminology in England: Developments and dilemmas. *British Journal of Criminology*, 58(6), 1499–1516.

Earle, R. (2018b). Being inside: Masculine imaginaries, prison interiors. In M. Maycock & K. Hunt (Eds.), *New perspectives on prison masculinities*. Basingstoke: Palgrave Macmillan.

Earle, R., & Phillips, C. (2013). 'Muslim is the new black': New ethnicities and new essentialisms in the prison. *Race and Justice, 3*(2), 114–129.

Easton, S. (2018). *The politics of the prison and prisoner: Zoon politikon*. London: Routledge.

Ellis, C. (2009). *Revision: Autoethnographic reflections on life and work*. Walnut Creek, CA: Left Coast Press.

Ellis, C., Adams, T., & Bouchner, A. P. (2011). Autoethnography: An overview. *FQS Forum: Qualitative Social Research, 12*(2), 1–13.

Gander, C. (2013). *Muriel Rukeyser and documentary; the poetics of connection*. Edinburgh: Edinburgh University Press.

Geertz, C. (1988). *Works and lives: The anthropologist as author*. Cambridge: Polity Press.

Gillard, S., Turner, K., Lovell, K., & Norton, K. (2010). Staying native: Coproduction in mental health services research. *International Journal of Public Sector Management, 23*(6), 567–577.

Gilroy, P. (1987). *There aint no black in the Union Jack*. London: Routledge.

Gormley, A. (2017). 'Inside' Koestler exhibition, speech at launch event 11/10/17, South Bank Centre, London [personal notes of author].

Haraway, D. (1988). Situated knowledges: The science question in feminism and the privilege of partial perspective. *Feminist Studies, 14*(3), 575–599.

Harding, S. (1987). *Feminism and methodology: Social science issues*. Bloomington, IN: Indiana University Press.

Hesse, B. (2014). Escaping liberty: Western hegemony, black fugitivity. *Political Theory, 42*(3), 288–313.

Honeywell, D. (2013). Doing hard time in the United Kingdom. In S. Richards (Ed.), *Prisoners in solitary confinement: USP Marion and the supermax movement*. Carbondale, IL: Southern Illinois University Press.

Honeywell, D. (2015). Doing time with lifers: A reflective study of life sentence prisoners. *British Journal of Community Justice, 13*(1), 93–104.

Jewkes, Y. (2002). *Captive audience: Media, masculinity and power in prisons*. Cullompton: Willan Publishing.

Kann, M. E. (2005). *Punishment, prisons and patriarchy: Liberty and power in the early American Republic*. New York, NY: New York University Press.

Kierkegaard, S. (1954). *The sickness unto death*. New York, NY: Doubleday.

Larsen, L. (2017). When ex-convicts become criminologists. *Sapiens*, November 22. Retrieved from https://www.sapiens.org/culture/convict-criminology/. Accessed on November 30, 2017.

Law, J. (2000). On the subject of the object: Narrative, technology and interpellation. *Configurations, 8*(1), 1–29.

Leibling, A. (2004). *Prisons and their moral performance: A study of values, quality and prison life*. Oxford: Oxford University Press.

Malinowski, B. (2010). *Argonauts of the western Pacific*. Oxford: Benediction Classics.

Merton, R. K. (1972). Insiders and outsiders: A chapter in the sociology of knowledge. *American Journal of Sociology, 78*(1), 9–47.

Mills, C. W. (1951). *White collar*. New York, NY: Oxford University Press.

Mills, C. W. (1959). *The sociological imagination*. Harmondsworth: Penguin Books.
Mills, C. W. (1979). Mass society and liberal education. In I. L. Horowitz (Ed.), *Collected essays of C.W. Mills*. New York, NY: Oxford University Press.
Morgan, S. (1999). Prison lives: Critical issues in reading prisoner autobiography. *The Howard Journal of Criminal Justice, 38*(3), 328–340.
Phillips, C. (2012). *The multicultural prison: Ethnicity, masculinity and social relations among prisoners*. Oxford: Oxford University Press.
Pratt, J. (2002). *Punishment and civilisation: Penal tolerance and intolerance in modern society*. London: SAGE Publications.
Presser, L. (2009). The narratives of offenders. *Theoretical Criminology, 13*(2), 177–200.
Presser L. (2016). Criminology and the narrative turn. *Crime, Media, Culture, 12*(2), 137–151.
Presser, L., & Sandberg, S. (Eds.). (2015). *Narrative criminology: Understanding stories of crime*. London: New York University Press.
Ricoeur, P. (1984). *Time and narrative*. Chicago, IL: Chicago University Press.
Ricoeur, P. (1995). Fragility and responsibility. *Philosophy & Social Criticism, 21*(5/6), 15–22.
Robertson, S., Carpenter, D., & Donovasn-Hall, M. (2017). From the edge of the abyss to the foot of the rainbow – narrating a journey of mental health recovery', the process of a wounded researcher. *Qualitative Report, 22*(8), 2296–2307.
Ross, I. R., & Richards, S. C. (2003). *Convict criminology*. Belmont, CA: Wadsworth Publishing.
Russell-Brown, K. (1992). Development of a black criminology and the role of the black criminologist. *Justice Quarterly, 9*(4), 667–683.
Said, E. (1993). *Culture and imperialism*. London: Chatto & Windus.
Slade, M. (2009). *Personal recovery and mental illness: A guide for mental health professionals*. New York, NY: Cambridge University Press.
Smith, L. (1963). *Killers of the dream*. London: W. W. Norton & Company.
Squire, C. (2014). *What is narrative research?* London: Bloomsbury Publishing.
Stanley, L. (Ed.). (1990). *Feminist praxis: Research, theory and epistemology in feminist sociology*. London: Routledge.
Sykes, G. (1958). *Society of captives: The study of a maximum security prison*. Princeton, NJ: Princeton University Press.
Wacquant, L. (2002). The curious eclipse of prison ethnography in an age of mass incarceration. *Ethnography, 3*(4), 371–397.
Wakeman, S. (2014). Fieldwork, biography and emotion: Doing criminological autoethnography. *British Journal of Criminology, 54*(5), 705–721.
Warr, J. (2019, January). 'Always gotta be two mans': Lifers, risk, rehabilitation and narrative labour. *Punishment & Society*. doi:10.1177/1462474518822487 (on-line advance).
Williams, R. (2015). *Politics and letters: Interviews with new left review*. London: Verso Books (ebook).

INTERVIEWS

Chapter 5

Reflections after 'Socrates Light': Eliciting and Countering Narratives of Youth Justice Officials

Olga Petintseva

Introduction

The research project discussed in this chapter addresses how narratives about offenders' personalities and backgrounds inform youth justice practice (Petintseva, 2018). I analysed court case files and interviews with youth justice practitioners about their professional experiences with young people with a migration background. I particularly examined how officials narrate instances of youth crime and, accordingly, which interventions they deem appropriate. The underlying sociological discussion concerns the ways in which professionals' interpretations shape practice (Petintseva, 2018). As acknowledged by social constructionist scholars, problematisations indicate solutions to 'the problem' (Bacchi, 2009). As a researcher of institutional discourse and subtle discriminatory processes in particular, it was my working premise that (co-)constructing alternative accounts can potentially help mediate penal harm (Clear, 1994; Presser, 2013).

In the early stages of data collection, I found that professionals' narratives were often generalising, expectations-based and, at times, discriminatory. This was exemplified in different ways, such as using rigid notions of culture, ethnicity and migration; making references to rather vague 'past experiences' and 'cases of colleagues'; anticipating future developments of young people's correctional trajectories; and mobilising disclaimers[1] as a discursive strategy. These stories hinted at silent normative frameworks and reference points against which youth justice professionals assess young migrants. For example, when a social worker elaborates that 'they are not like our children', this implies expectations about what is

---

[1]The use of disclaimers is a discursive strategy whereby the speaker indicates a priori social desirability but goes ahead and says what she/he actually intends to say (e.g. 'I'm not racist, but …') (Machin & Mayr, 2012).

'appropriate' behaviour, attitude and upbringing (see also Petintseva, 2018; Terrio, 2009).

I wanted to unpack such accounts. To an extent, I embarked on this enterprise with the aim of generating alternative understandings of the cases together with the research participants, i.e. hoping that we could 'complicate' some of the stories. After analysing the case file documents and after conducting several 'orthodox' open-ended interviews, I also felt that my analysis of the data was becoming a retrospective commentary on what I was reading and hearing. Therefore, the question arose whether a researcher can become more active and attempt to disrupt what often appeared to be prejudiced institutional discourses and narratives in the process of research. The aim was to exchange thoughts on the collected stories with the respondents, instead of gathering the data and presenting them with my critical reflections afterwards.

This chapter reflects on how I complemented open interviews with 'light' Socratic dialogues, which pressed the informants to justify and even reconsider their statements. Inspired by the work of Brinkmann (2007) and other scholars who have explored different modes of active and agonistic interview styles (Kvale, 2005; Tanggaard, 2007), I decided to enter into discussion with research participants. In these Socratic dialogues discussed in this chapter, the aim was to challenge some of the respondents' assertions. In turn, several of the interviewees eagerly challenged me.

The 'light' Socratic dialogic style implies changing the focus of the interview, in attempts to move the narrator from *doxa*, i.e. the 'common' knowledge and practice by which the world appears as self-evident (Bourdieu, 1977), to episteme, i.e. the foundation for the judgements about concrete situations, actions and broad action-guiding concepts such as, for example, 'justice' or 'protection'. In the interview context, this involves actively challenging the conversation partners to justify their claims and opinions.

This chapter draws on narrative criminological scholarship, which holds that narratives inform action (Presser, 2009; Presser & Sandberg, 2015a, 2015b). Moreover, narrative criminologists consider how we as interviewers co-construct the narrative: for example, Presser (2004, 2005) contends that story-making is a dynamic and collaborative process in which people jointly interpret social problems and identities. If interviews are not only artefacts but also producers of social reality (Holstein & Gubrium, 1995), then an engaged interview – the Socratic dialogue that I present in this chapter – can potentially be a site of the construction of alternative narratives. Moreover, the play of discourse *in* research is as such interesting from an epistemological viewpoint (Presser, 2004).

I first contextualise my research project and situate it within the narrative criminological research tradition. I then discuss the different methodological approaches to 'active' interviewing to substantiate the choice for a particular mode of epistemic (or Socratic) interviewing. Subsequently, I connect with insights from feminist research practice, which entails a strong engagement with participants, attentiveness to the research context, reflexivity and a critical transformative agenda. Finally, I summarise and reflect upon the key principles of *Socrates light*.

The objective of this chapter is not to provide a 'how to' guide, which could never work for complex and context-dependent social actions such as constituting, collecting and analysing narratives. The chapter demonstrates how I used a rather 'intrusive' form of interviewing, in the hope of stimulating methodological discussions within the field of narrative criminology. The proposed interview model provides interesting insights into how narrative performance responds to the interview circumstances and communicative exchanges – in this case, researcher's interventions (Presser, 2005). Moreover, I argue that entering into a debate with the research participants – which includes presenting them researchers' readings of their statements – can be seen as a way of having them participate in the analysis. This joint reconsidering of the narratives can perhaps contribute to the constitution of alternative accounts.

Discourses and Stories About Young Migrants in the Practice of Youth Justice

The main focus of my study was on youth justice officials' narratives about young people in their professional practice. Belgian youth justice, where the data collection took place, is characterised by a relatively informal culture of discretionary exchanges. For example, most of the interactions take place outside of the actual courtroom; magistrates usually do not wear gowns; professionals communicate frequently in the hallways and via phone calls, there is no obligation to convict the minor even if the offence is proven; there is no compulsory sequence of decisions or minimal sentencing; the court imposes 'measures', etc. Youth justice nominally centres on what is 'in the youth's best interests', meaning that not only the offence but also the young person's overall personality, school and family situation need to be taken into account (Franssens, Put, & Deklerck, 2010; Muncie, 2008). One result of this institutional framework is that the social practice of youth justice (Cicourel, 1976) is permeated with meaning making in general and storytelling in particular, in attempts to understand what has occurred and to find a suitable way to react (see also Petintseva, 2015, 2018). This 'suitable way to react' needs to account for the offence, the young person's upbringing and school situation, the interests of people victimised and public order and safety.

My analysis focused on professional narratives about migrant youth, zooming in on two case studies: Roma young people born in Slovakia and Czech Republic and Northern Caucasian migrants (mainly from Chechnya).[2] I foregrounded how

---

[2]Court case files were selected based on the birthplace. The case studies comprised of young people born in the Russian Federal District Northern Caucasus (in practice, predominantly Chechnya) on the one hand, and in Slovakia and Czech Republic (in practice, all cases but one contained at least one reference to 'Roma' in the included documents) on the other hand.

professionals problematise young people's deviant behaviour, agency, family background, educational experiences and socioeconomic and legal position. Despite nuances, the overall tendency was to ascribe deviant behaviour and difficulties in judicial trajectories of Caucasian youth to experiences in their country of origin and to migration as such – i.e. external elements that are in principle eligible for rehabilitation. For Roma youth, professionals often framed problematic behaviour and the course of correctional trajectories as an inherent cultural essence (see Petintseva, 2017, 2018). I argued that these ways in which situations become problematised imply different ways to proceed – say, to offer protection, rehabilitation, responsibilisation and/or sanctioning (Bacchi, 2009).

The research was based on in-depth study of 55 court case files and interviews with 41 youth justice professionals (judges, prosecutors, social workers, educators and psychologists in confinement facilities, consultants involved in mediation and restoration, and intercultural mediators) in two judicial departments in Belgium. After analysing various case file documents, including police reports, communication of the prosecutors, court social services reports, assessments from measure executing facilities, court rulings, input from schools the young people attended, and letters from young people to the judge, I formulated a number of statements that roughly summarised the findings.[3] These statements were deliberately generalised and intended to trigger discussion and further elaboration in interviews. I presented the statements in printed form to the interview participants, introducing them as simplified tendencies of what I was reading in the case files. Throughout the interviews, I asked the informants to what extent these summaries were recognisable to them, and if so, what they meant for their practice, thus probing for the underlying logic of their decision-making. As the case file analysis was based on documents that offer somewhat detached accounts of complex situations, I tried to elicit professionals' experiences with and opinions about particular cases, systematically asking interviewees for examples and counter-examples. Research participants chose which stories they told, but because of the narrow selection of the case studies, I had already encountered, via document analysis, most of the cases of young people they referred to.

Some ethnic stereotypes and tropes about young people (Roma) in particular guided professionals' understandings of the situation and of their (possible) interventions. The following is an example of rather common narratives about young people, told by a youth judge:

> *'Sabina' was also a typical case. That was a gang thing, about 14–15 years old, already having a boyfriend from the gang. A guy*

---

[3] An example, to give the reader an idea of the type of statements discussed during interviews: 'Youth from the Northern Caucasus are rather involved in violent offences and while assessing the underlying causes, youth justice professionals sometimes link those to migration backgrounds of the youth, namely the war situation in their regions of origin. Slovak and Czech Roma youth are frequently involved in property offences and while assessing the underlying causes, youth justice professionals sometimes link those to culture or to the socioeconomic situation (in the countries of origin and in Belgium).'

who was older. [...] She was being used. While the family knew this... they did that themselves as well. You can feel that it's a girl who never knew anything else... [...] And she wanted to get away and you can feel that from the moment that you incarcerate her.... You can feel that if we could work with her for years, from the youth... [justice], she really benefited from this. She has made a major evolution, so that you felt... she is going back to that environment and, in no time, she is integrated in that environment again and we lost her. [...] If she had been more autonomous, then we could've pulled her out of there. 'You know, child, you have all those possibilities, hang out with the right people!' [...] And that's a cultural thing. Those Roma kids are 14, they already live with their in-laws, they are pregnant. Going to school, you don't even have to try. And by the age of 17, they have 2–3 kids at home. [...] It's as if they don't have a life (Interview with a youth judge).

Such narratives (in this case not only ethnicised but also particularly gendered) often frame intrusive judicial interventions as the only possible way to react and, specifically, to pull the young people out of their criminogenic, ethnocultural environment.

Youth justice professionals' narratives varied in the extent to which they were messy or seemingly coherent (Sandberg, 2013). Accounts that came about with little in-person interaction (e.g. relatively minor offences, of in cases when, for various reasons, the young person does not see the judge regularly) appeared especially clear-cut and coherent. Some contained straightforwardly prejudiced statements, whilst others were pitted with mixed messages and nuances (e.g. stories regarding young people from Caucasus contained much less ethnic stereotypes than the stories of crime of Roma youth). Evaluating the narratives for their factual correctness and completeness was not the aim of my research (see also Sandberg, 2010). I do posit that such institutionally produced narratives and the underlying grand discourses are necessarily selective and strategic – given the institutional goals, conventions and the available (re)sources. Throughout youth justice trajectories, such stories of crime and correction are co-constructed by multiple actors. Furthermore, both written and spoken accounts convey a language of authority, conferring legitimacy and entitlement to a certain action (often evoking the vocabulary of powerlessness), while warranting penal harm or restraint from judicial interventions (Presser, 2013, 2016; Presser & Sandberg, 2015a). Hence, regardless of their accuracy, these accounts are performative and real in their effects (see Bacchi, 2009; Bacchi & Bonham, 2014; Petintseva, 2018).

Challenging Institutional Narratives and Penal Harm

Narrative criminology proposes that narratives inform and motivate human action and social life more generally (Presser, 2009; Presser & Sandberg, 2015a).

Put differently, narrative criminology approaches narratives as constitutive of reality, seeing narratives as antecedents of (potentially harmful) action, instead of merely post-factum justifications for decision-making (Fleetwood, 2016; Presser, 2009, 2016). Only having made a link to narrative criminology in the final stages of my project, I was intuitively working from the premise that officials' narratives in themselves instigate or mediate penal harm.

Although conceptually, narrative criminological scholarship foregrounds the narrative constitution of different types of actors and harms (see, for example, Kurtz & Upton, 2017; Presser, 2013; Presser & Sandberg, 2015b), empirical work has been primarily directed at the self-narratives of offenders. The idea of *homo narrativus* (Presser & Sandberg, 2015b) has only to a limited extent been extended to institutional contexts (Presser, 2013). So far, narrative criminologists concerned with understanding institutional actors' stories have mostly, though not exclusively, analysed police narratives. For instance, van Hulst (2013) discusses how police canteen culture produces institutional stories of a particular kind; Kurtz and Upton (2017) theorise how storytelling (re)produces the broader police power. Ugelvik (2016) studied how immigration detention officers legitimise their work through backstage narrative constructions. Beyond the police, Verde, Angelini, Boverini, and Marajana (2006) discern court psychiatric reports as narrative products. Evans (2017) observes that presentence reports for youth courts are coauthored by 'unreliable' narrators (i.e. the defendant and the youth justice worker). This author sees assessments of young people who came in conflict with the law as 'convenient fiction', in which key actors collude. Evans theorises that such reports for sentencing purposes not only explain past deviant behaviour but also shape future sentencing decisions.

In essence, the gap between the 'stories-of-the-self' (be it offenders or officials) and the institutional narratives is not especially significant, considering that, from the symbolic interactionist perspective, we are always constructing selves even as we construct others. Nevertheless, I will argue that critical narrative criminologists must *interrogate* institutional narratives if they produce penal harm. Questioning institutional narratives seems ethically permissible as such stories are not deeply personal accounts of intimate experiences and self-descriptions that participants confide to researchers. Moreover, in institutional contexts, professionals such as those I interviewed have a certain societal responsibility, with commitments to transparency, professional ethos, accountability, impartiality and nondiscrimination. Hence, their accounts not only need to be morally justifiable to the official, they also ought to comply with the existing rules and institutional goals (Cicourel, 1976). To *problematise* officials' narratives does not necessarily entail culpabilisation of individual narrators as prejudiced individuals. It is to convene a critical discussion of societal and institutional structures. Such a discussion requires viewing narratives as embedded within larger discourses and being attentive to their power and the power relations in which they are implicated (Presser & Sandberg, 2015a).

Because of the predominant focus on individuals' self-narratives in the empirical research conducted thus far, research methods that narrative criminologists apply have been attuned to these intimate encounters, mostly involving nonintrusive research interviews, observations and archival inquiry. In this 'orthodox' way of interviewing, the researcher positions herself as an empathetic listener who is somewhat invisible. The intervention from the researcher is then limited to standard prompts (e.g. 'tell me more', the echo probe, silence), not asking leading questions, inviting spontaneous storytelling and assuming a nonevaluative attitude (Presser, 2010). Research under the umbrella of narrative criminology has yet to position the researcher as an active interlocutor who consciously engages in questioning the narratives, and co-constructing counternarratives.

Merging Active Interviewing and Feminist Research Practice

As my goal was to challenge some of the research participants' accounts, I looked for methodological tools that would allow to instigate discussions throughout the process of research. This is where I came across different 'active' interviewing styles, which scholars often use in 'studying up'. I then infused and counterbalanced these methodological insights with some core principles of feminist research interview – both of which I discuss hereafter. The result of this merge is *Socrates light* interviewing style.

'Researching up', actively

Scholars 'researching up' attend to the micro-politics of interpersonal interactions and relationships and relate them to a wider analysis of power (see, for example, Bogner, Littig, & Menz, 2009; Phillips, 1998). Methodological literature on researching the powerful, specifically the so-called elite and expert interviews, explicitly accounts for control in the interview setting (Odendahl & Shaw, 2001): the way that the conversation is structured, what roles both the researcher and the respondent assume, talking about sensitive issues and getting past 'corporate answers'. Driven by a critique of intentional passivity of researchers, a variety of 'active' interviewing styles have been proposed. In so-called 'active interviews', the interview becomes more of a two-way discussion; a confrontation even (Kvale, 2005). Moreover, interviews have been conceptualised as 'discourses crossing swords', where the researcher consciously challenges research participants' views (Tanggaard, 2007). In this model, the interview becomes a scene of productive negotiation of meaning, whereby a 'conversation' can become a 'fight' (Tanggaard, 2007). The so-called agonistic interviews equally focus on conflict and power aspects of the interview and transform the interview interaction into a 'battlefield'. Correspondingly, this entails a more journalistic interviewing style. In 'psychoanalytical interviews', in turn, the interviewer gives critical interpretations and embarks on the enterprise of 'healing the patient'. All of these interviewing styles explicitly account for power relations, conflicts and dissensus (Kvale, 2005).

The particular rationale and mode of 'active' interviewing that appealed to me is a form of Socratic dialogue (or 'epistemic' interviews as Brinkmann (2007) describes). Brinkmann (2007) takes a critical stance towards orthodox qualitative interviews, arguing that they reflect contemporary consumer society in which the 'client' (respondent) is always right. In research process, private beliefs and narratives then become commodities that researchers collect and report upon. Likewise, Reinharz (1992) criticises researchers' opportunism of taking, interpreting and publishing accounts of 'data providers'. Kvale (2005) equally makes sharp statements in this regard, discussing the 'tyranny of intimacy' and production of *the Self*, where open empathetic interviews (but also focus groups that originate from market research) become a social technology in the context of consumer-focused strategies. Some rather radical positions have been taken in this respect also concerning interviews with the 'powerless'. It has, for example, been contended that classical dialogical interviews involve soft, subjectified forms of power exertion, under guise of mutual interests and egalitarianism, while 'faking' rapport or friendship and instrumentalising people's stories and human relationships, hereby skilfully using subtle therapeutic techniques (Kvale, 2005).

Based on such critiques, Brinkmann (2007) proposes moving away from passive listening. His suggested approach entails entering a debate and moving the participant from the state of being opinionated to being capable of questioning and justifying what she/he believes. The emphasis then shifts to civic responsibility and accountability, which is different from personal experience-focused interview and which is particularly applicable to research participants occupying relatively powerful institutional positions. I summarise the differences between classical (doxastic) interviewing and epistemic interviewing (or Socratic dialogues) in Table 5.1.

In epistemic interviews, the 'client' is not necessarily right (nor wrong, for that matter) because opinions and beliefs can be debated, tested and challenged in an open conversation. Socratic dialogues should be understood as a joint search for

Table 5.1. Doxastic Interviews Compared to Epistemic Interviews.

	Doxastic interview	Socratic dialogues (Brinkmann, 2007)
Aim of the interview	Probing into *doxa*	Probing episteme
Researcher's role	Empathic (methodological) listening	Identifying and challenging assumptions and tacit beliefs; can illustrate inadequacies in thinking about ethical problems and abstract notions
Level of intervention on the part of the researcher	Minimal influence from the interviewer; passive mirror (cf. Rogers) or therapeutic analyst (cf. Freud)	Engaging narrator and researcher; dialectical, more talkative researcher
Style of the interview	Psychotherapeutic influences or 'the interviewee is right'	Active and confronting style, the interviewee is challenged and asked for justifications or reflections
Substance of the interview	Life history, self-narratives, intimate experiences	Institutional discourses, tropes, professional practice, moral, ethical, political and philosophical issues

knowledge. Thematically, these research interactions zoom in on conflicts in interpretations, while trying to approximate mutuality and reciprocity within the conversation. Such interviews are chiefly suitable for debating moral and ethical dilemmas (see also Thuesen, 2011).

While seemingly fruitful for discussing institutional accounts, a number of issues arose with these ideas, especially given the fact that my research engaged with narratives. Speaking of 'crossing swords', 'agonistic', 'confrontation' and so on evokes aggression. Some 'active' researchers even make explicit arguments against 'feminisation' and empathy in research (Tanggaard, 2007). These arguments conflict with feminist research principles which are – by training and nature – closer to me as a person and as researcher. I felt a deep commitment to the context that I was researching and believed that it would be beneficial to enter critical but constructive, reflexive and engaged discussions. Also, straightforward confrontation did not align with my research goals, as the underlying stake was not to 'prove' that the stories the respondents were telling were correct or wrong but to nuance and enrich the institutional stories. Finally, in studies of institutional talk, scholars sometimes represent narratives produced by professionals working in (state) institutions as noncreative reflections of grand institutional discourse; professional culture as monolithic (Collins, 1993; Oude Breuil, 2011; Wolfe, 1996); and officials' accounts as detached corporate narratives. However, my lengthy presence in youth courts – during case file research, some observations of court hearings, informal talks and open-ended interviews – made me believe that the emotions of state agent are also highly constitutive of narratives about young people (see also Saarikkomäki, 2015). Youth justice professionals repeatedly expressed compassion, frustration, helplessness and anger. 'Cold' confrontation and attempts at demolishing their arguments would likely trigger these emotions (Thuesen, 2011) and potentially make the respondents shut down, become defensive or produce 'standard' narratives.

Infusing insights from feminist research interviewing

Feminist research pursues liberation without 'teaching' participants in a top-down fashion (Acker, Barry, & Esseveld, 1983). Correspondingly, feminist approaches ought to be nonoppressive, participatory and reflexive. Importantly, feminist researchers have advocated that researchers should not downplay their own position. Instead, they aim to build rapport, be self-reflexive and engage in mutual sharing and self-disclosure (Harding & Norberg, 2005; Reinharz, 1992). The active modes of interviewing discussed in the previous section – whether rightfully so or not – evoked associations with 'tricking' the participants, putting them with their backs against the wall and somehow imposing researcher's own views. Even if I felt that several of the research participants were engaging in discriminatory practices, entering into an open discussion throughout the process of research seemed more constructive than simply confronting or calling them out. In order to understand the social practice of youth justice and to sensibilise (or, if you will, touch) the professionals, shifting between open, narrative interviewing and engaged and respectful discussions seemed necessary.

Whereas most of the 'active' interviewing models that scholars use in elite' or 'expert' interviewing[4] involve somewhat aggressive styles, Briggs (2003) argues that 'researching up' can benefit from the insights of feminist researchers. Specifically, he proposes to reconceptualise those interviews as a reciprocal relationship within the interview context. Arguably, refraining from the rigid distinctions between the subject and the interviewer contributes to more critical and self-reflexive research interactions and outcomes (Kezar, 2003).

Overall, I borrowed three relevant points from feminist research practice while engaging in 'light' Socratic dialogues, discussed hereafter:

(1) Pursuing respectful and engaged encounters with research participants (Reinharz, 1992);
(2) Attentiveness to the research context and interaction, and especially reflexivity on how these might influence the stories told. This entails reporting on the way something is put, body language, emotional reactions, researcher's own experiences and background and so forth (Presser, 2005; Reinharz, 1992);
(3) The pursuit of social justice and a transformative agenda (Harding & Norberg, 2005).

Engaging in 'Light' Socratic Dialogues

Drawing on Brinkmann's (2007) ideas and the core principles of feminist research interviewing discussed above, I engaged in 'light' Socratic dialogue with youth justice professionals. Based on my case file research and open-ended interviewing eliciting specific stories, I attempted to challenge underlying normative frameworks and tropes in interviews with youth justice officials. To be more precise, I invited the research participants to justify, reflect upon or even to reconsider the accounts about the deviancy of young people they provided earlier. Thus, the goal of such an interview is to challenge respondents' accounts, based on specific examples and counternarratives (Briggs, 2003).

What I designate '*Socrates light*' involves active and reflexive interviewing, debating some of the narratives and their rationales. The narrators are conceived as accountable actors given their professional role, status and expertise. What follows are several lessons learnt that could be of relevance to other researchers engaging in coproducing alternative narratives and/or in active interviewing as such. Although I am eager to share numerous experiences and reflections, in the following subsections, I limit myself to four points that notably came to the fore while applying 'Socrates light': (1) in practice, it appeared that during the epistemic interview, a researcher cannot simply 'switch

---

[4]That is, interviewing people in (institutionally) prominent positions. Although such interviews do not necessarily differ from other types of interviews, a large number of methodological accounts in this regard has been produced, particularly accounting for the issues of power and control of the course of the interview (see e.g. Bogner et al., 2009; Petintseva, Faria, & Eski, forthcoming).

hats' and straightforwardly stick to either the doxastic or the epistemic mode. Instead, it is crucial to reflexively shift between emphatic listening and actively questioning the participants' stories. (2) Certain topics or areas are more suitable than others for light Socratic interviewing, which relates to the point made earlier concerning debating self-narratives and institutional narratives. (3) Empathy, openness and respect are important even when assuming an 'active' or critical role. (4) In this type of research, it is particularly important to reflect and report on the course of interaction and see the reactions that the discussion triggers as valuable data.

Shifts and porous distinctions between epistemic and doxastic modes
I found that the step towards Socratic dialogues is best taken after open and 'passive' interviewing (focussing on listening), initially collecting narratives with as little influence on the part of the researcher as possible. This gives the researcher the necessary time to reflect on the narrative and to think about the ways to debate it. In my experience, also some rapport is necessary before the researcher can start to question what the participant is saying. The setting that I was studying was characterised by a certain hierarchical structure and especially the magistrates were very talkative and they often referred to their expertise, experience and independence. An outsider who immediately jumps into discussions would be cut off quickly. In my case, I was at least a decade younger than most of the participants, which made me feel that I needed to sufficiently demonstrate an open attitude *and* some expertise before starting to ask critical questions.

In practice, even when switching to the 'active mode', the distinction between doxastic and epistemic styles was blurry. 'On the spot' adaptations to the interaction on the part of the researcher (i.e. not sticking to either an epistemic or a doxastic interview; being either observing or active) are crucial. In this respect, Thuesen (2011) who has integrated a 'phronetic' approach emphasises the importance of a reflexive attitude. This phronetic approach is rooted in the philosophy of Aristotle, where through discussion, one is trying to stir her/his own and others' actions while reflecting. Such a reflexive attitude entails choosing a suitable course of action in a given situation, understanding the feeling of the moment and, hence, shifting between dialogic and active interview approaches and accounting for reactions and emotions of the participant. Experienced and interaction-sensitive researcher should be able to feel when to become less confronting. Indeed, in most of my cases, the articulate professionals did not seem to be easily intimidated by critical questions. Quite the contrary, they often became more engaged than in the open-ended interviews – becoming more talkative, seeming excited, and stating that discussions were thought-provoking. However, in some encounters, this active style on my part made the respondent shut down. Consider this example of an interaction with a senior social worker:

> O: *And you say that this is a cultural conflict... conflict in what sense and how is this cultural?*

R: *In that case, it was, actually, that was a girl who had very limited mental capacities, type II education, which means a very low IQ... who was enrolled by her mother and she was married to a sixteen-year-old boy, so actually very young. So, this daughter was imported from Slovakia and these people, they just go and sit on the floor, openly breastfeed the baby... These are customs of which we say: 'ok, do this in a private sphere or at least try to cover your breast with the blouse.' You know, sometimes I think that these people have very different habits and conventions and that it is not self-evident for these children, you know, their own customs in the western society.... that this just contradicts with what they see at home. And you know, I also think that a lot of these Roma youth know that their parents were involved in thefts in the past [...] and maybe this has to do with less opportunities and being accustomed to property offences and maybe because of other values and norms patterns that they actually have... But it is our task to make sure that these young people commit fewer offences eventually...*

O: *But in this case, you are speaking of different things, such as family matters, mental capacities and daily customs... and... being brought up with some normalisation of property crime... I don't quite get the link.*

I expect that this is partially so... interconnected [long silence and I notice some discomfort but keep on asking questions].

Yes, but I mean, is all of this culture and to make sure that these young people commit less offences, youth justice needs to intervene in all of this?

Yeah it's complicated... [long silence].

But if you ascribe this to culture, does 'culture' consist of these aspects...? Rather diverse yet negative aspects as you seem to indicate...? And is all of this relevant for [judicial] measures?

I don't know. It depends... *[long silence and starts telling another story that shifts the attention away from this discussion]* (Interview with a court social worker).

During the interview, I clearly read the signs of discomfort in the social worker's body language and her voice starts trembling in the recording. Not only did I make her uncomfortable with rather direct and general questions, this probing made the answers short and evasive. Despite other attempts, I did not succeed in bringing up this narrative and the related discussion again. In this case, it is difficult to assess whether she went on to reconsider the story later on or whether the only effect was an awkward end of the conversation and her discomfort in general.

Obviously, there is no cookbook recipe for when to 'switch' to either a listening or a discussing mode, but experience and sensitivity to interaction is required, as well as being well prepared with a good set of possible types of questions and scenarios. I outline which areas especially lend themselves to discussions in the interview setting next.

Types of topics to discuss during Socratic interviews
The interview style that I propose here is relevant for linking particular narratives to broad ethical, moral and political matters and it can help us get a glimpse of the complexity of normative knowledge. But what topics are suitable for debates and how to start such an interview?

In my experience, complex and fluid notions such as 'culture', 'protection', 'deviancy', etc. lend themselves to in-depth discussions in relation to specific stories. Vice versa, most narratives cannot be isolated from such broad frameworks and concepts, which are often only implied or hinted at in individual narratives. But one needs the story first. It is therefore constructive to elicit the story without intervening too quickly. Moreover, the *Socrates light* style is especially applicable to debates about interpretations, assessments and implications of particular concepts, rather than people's intimate experiences or the factual correctness of their statements.

Discussions can be held at different levels and shifting between these levels is intellectually interesting. For instance, based on a particular story, we would move on to discuss more abstract concepts guiding professionals' practice and common institutional norms and conventions. For example, if a respondent would indicate that she/he took a specific decision to protect the young person, we would go on to discuss what 'protection' means in youth courts practice in general.

The richest discussions came about while discussing norms and convictions based on specific stories, while pressing for details. Questions that I brought up in reply to participants' accounts were, for example: 'Why is being progressive sometime right and sometimes wrong?'; 'Does protection solely consist in this?'; 'How do you define a good family?' 'Is school the only way to acquire the necessary skills?'; 'Could you've interpreted this interaction differently?' A variety of my interventions aimed to raise research participants' awareness of the ways in which they constituted agency in storytelling. I used such strategies because youth justice practitioners often framed young people and their parents as active agents, while they frequently disavowed their own agency and discretionary power.

Overall, to make sure that the participants did not feel threatened and/or led, I found it helpful to introduce the interview approach at length, e.g. 'I'll be asking provoking questions for the sake of the discussion.' This made the respondents interested and eager to discuss: several of them told me how they were used to having researchers ask them questions but that these would merely concern 'dry' matters regarding the rules, practices and decision-making, much more than their frames of reference and interpretations.

While entering such conversations, I realised that when people are pushed to justify their statements, they often tell 'extreme' and 'tell-able' stories in order to make their point. Such narratives are often marked by statements like, for example, 'this case has left a major impression on me', 'this was one of the most difficult trajectories that I've encountered throughout my career', 'I will never forget Ruslan'. Challenging questions provoke quick reactions and invite especially polarising narratives, involving character oppositions, conflict and negativity. For instance, many stories accounted for how order was threatened and then restored by the professionals' intervention. Again, it is helpful to probe for other or 'everyday' examples. Also, responses that seem to indicate the extremes or that might be told in response to challenge need to be accounted for when analysing and reporting: for example, including the interviewer's intervention, or reflecting on how the conversation might have shifted upon such interventions.

Engagement, respect and empathy

In active interviewing I described earlier, trust is merely developed to obtain information. In *Socrates light*, gaining trust and entering a discussion should not be seen as a cunning strategy of leading the respondent to some absolute 'truth' by asking questions (Kvale, 2005). Instead, essential ingredients of *Socrates light* are (1) commitment and engagement; (2) authentic mutual trust; (3) reflexivity; (4) attempts at approaching egalitarianism and (5) ethic of care (Kezar, 2003).

Initiating discussions should not be equated to having a hidden agenda to demagogically 'educate' highly articulate and independent actors, who, in the first place, are rarely susceptible to such practices. Particularly helpful in this regard was sharing my own interpretations and experiences, for example, given the topic, references to my own migration background and cultural ways of interpreting interactions with institutions made the interaction a reflexive two-way exchange. It also made me aware of my own frames of reference and biases. Consider this example when a social worker described 'uninvolved' parents:

> R: *And with the Roma we actually see that the parents succeed in coming here [Community institution] but not ... well, they are not really involved. They come visit and these are mostly very happy visits from which you can see that the parents don't really get the seriousness of ... our son is incarcerated here. [...]*
>
> O: *Ok ... and how can you assess ... well... for example that the parents do not see the seriousness of the offences? Do they say this explicitly?*
>
> R: *Yeah... Of course, from their interactions. [Describes at length that parents and children talk and laugh together but do not talk to professionals]. And they also receive many invitations from us, calls... If they made it here [for the visit], they could also talk to us.*

> O: *I don't quite get why such... laughter.... indicates noninvolvement. Personally, from what you describe, I would interpret this as a warm interaction, which exactly shows warmth or a bond at least. Based on my own experiences, I would read this... not talking to you... as some kind of distrust towards the authorities or perhaps a language barrier as such. Or how do you determine that this is not the case?* (Interview with a social worker in a Community institution)

Later on in this exchange, when I was about to leave, the social worker started asking me about my experiences with the Belgian bureaucratic system in the first years after migrating to Belgium. She eventually shared that because of the experiences of her Albanian husband, she sees herself as somebody who is sensitive to cultural interactional differences. She added that in the course of the interview (referring to my comment in the quote above) it struck her that she maybe nevertheless sometimes 'projects' too quickly.

Admittedly, the two-way exchanges also changed my attitude concerning the rationales and the intentions of youth justice professionals over the course of research. Based on case file documents and even the first interviews, many of the officials came across as simply prejudiced. Asking for their reasoning and reflections on my analysis placed the narratives in a different light, exposing the underlying reference points, concerns and, often, feelings of powerlessness and frustration. At the same time, many of them are easy to (over)sympathise with, as the vast majority were people who are eloquent, passionate and knowledgeable about their professional activities, but who also use their narrative strategically in a number of ways. For example, they would merge different rationales and make their position sound logical; even when pushing a repressive agenda, they would succeed in appearing as a caring professional; sometimes they would anticipate and actively counter my suspicions of discriminatory assumptions.

When the researcher becomes increasingly visible, her/his own position and feelings become more exposed as well. For example, within interview interactions, I sometimes found it challenging to retain a balanced mix of openness, empathy, not making moral judgements, being able to challenge the participants' accounts and (co-)creating an atmosphere in which stories can be scrutinised and, potentially, reconsidered. There were several instances in which I had developed strong feelings and even antipathy towards the participant, for instance:

> *That one has barely an IQ of a houseplant [laughs]. This is of course not very flattering to state it like this. But in many cases, this is the case, that I detect that they [Roma] are very limited.* (Interview with a youth judge)

> *I don't know whether this has to do with bad hygiene or something but I think, personally, but I think that there is lots of incest in that [Roma] community and that's the reason why they actually*

degenerate. It's not nice to say it like this, but I'm afraid that this is true. (Interview with a youth judge)

From a critical perspective, it is vital to uncover and challenge such logics. One way of doing this is by directly instigating debates in the course of research (but equally critique can be embedded in evaluations, recommendations, activism, etc.). Even if only a minority of the participants produces such accounts, they have a very serious impact on young people and their judicial trajectories, especially considering the fact that one judge could have up to 450 young people under her/his supervision. In the interview interaction itself, however, I did not have any easy 'solutions' for such encounters, except for patiently probing and trying to discuss the origins and potential harms of these discourses and reflexively reporting on the discussions held. I tried to avoid directly attacking interviewees for biased or blunt statements but rather to bring up historical deep-seated exclusion of Roma, or – as we were discussing prejudices – to subtly introduce confrontational questions relating to their stance on the fundamental principles of equality and nonpresumptuousness of justice.

Attentiveness to the research context and interaction
I argue that it is important for researchers, especially, those who consciously enter an 'active' mode, to reflect on how the interaction proceeded. For analysis, this implies paying attention to how our words and behaviour affect the participant and how the interaction and even the narrative might shift following researcher's intervention (see also Thuesen, 2011). Narrativists have repeatedly argued that this coproduction should be highlighted in academic writings (De Fina & Georgakopoulou, 2011; Presser, 2004). Specifically, this could involve discussing such things as asking leading questions, encouraging or discouraging of certain accounts, reflecting on the relationship with the respondent and discernible turning points within the conversation (Presser & Sandberg, 2015b). Taking such contexts into consideration accords with the constitutive view of narratives, where analysis should move beyond interpreting de facto narratives to actively reconstructing them, while noting their inherent messiness and variability (Sandberg, 2016).

The difficulties researchers encounter in pushing the boundaries of the naturalised parts of *doxa* and related negotiations (Bourdieu, 1977) are equally relevant to any constructionist research: respondents' responses including evasive, emotional or angry answers become highly valuable empirical material (Thuesen, 2011). In a number of interviews, my participants would display resistance: narrative resistance, resistance to certain questions or statements and resistance to my research as such (see also Vitus, 2008). This resistance tells a great deal about their social practice, institutionally available discursive and nondiscursive resources and agendas (see also Vitus, 2008). Not filtering out colliding views, staying as close as possible to the actual interaction (e.g. elaborating on the narration, genre and function of the story, linguistic aspects of the narrative, the storytelling context) and self-exposure of the researcher allow the reader to understand the choices made and, potentially, to interpret the data in a different fashion than the researcher (see also Presser & Sandberg, 2015b; Tanggaard, 2007). Transparency, including discussions of tensions, ambiguity and reactions to confrontation, and reflexivity are major quality criteria of any qualitative research, which unequivocally applies to narrative-focused 'active' research methods.

Understanding the setting is also important as authenticity may be difficult to achieve if the researcher becomes 'too' active too quickly. In addition to the point I made at the beginning of this section related to shifting between epistemic and doxastic styles, I would argue that active interviewing should ideally proceed within an ethnographic context, not least because rapport can be established so that 'confrontation' becomes more of a 'natural' discussion. It is also in that context that one can understand more comprehensively what effect the researcher has on the participants' performance. I spent significantly more time in one of the two courts where the research was conducted. Discussions with research participants were not out of place in this first court, as I became part of the *décor* in this institutional setting. Also, I could observe the shifts in, or the stability of, the stories between doxastic and epistemic interviews. In the other court, where professionals barely knew me and the interviews proceeded in a much more formal manner, asking critical and perhaps leading questions seemed merely to prompt (temporary?) linguistic restructuring of the participants' responses (see also Presser, 2010).

Discussion: Will Interview(er)s Change the World?

Aside from being an interesting 'methodological experiment', *Socrates light* can be innovative in three respects: (1) as a source of epistemological reflections on how narrative performance gets shaped by the interview context and/or a particular interviewing style; (2) as a means of exchanging ideas during research and thereby somehow involving the participant in the analysis and (3) as a way of potentially coproducing counternarratives and therefore contributing to meaningful social transformations.

First, it is of epistemological interest to discuss what kind of performance researchers get when they intervene and to report on this 'making of' the narratives. As narrative researchers, we've mainly wanted to know the story of the participant (be it a self-narrative or the story of *the* Other), much less the narrative we get when we challenge it. Stories are discontinuous, living and messy products, which get – even without 'active researchers' – coproduced in the research context (Tanggaard, 2007). The ways in which stories are told, circulated and debated tell us a great deal about institutional contexts, such as that of youth justice but also about their changeability and adaptation to the interaction context.

As to the *second* point, after having described the institutional stories and discourses (collected by means of case file research and initial interviews), I felt that my analysis was becoming a one-sided post-factum commentary on officials' accounts (Aspden & Hayward, 2015). Drawing on the work of Latour, Tanggaard (2007) argues that researchers should 'allow the object to object'. In such discussions, respondents can perhaps counter some of the researcher's interpretations or provide further clarifications. Also, if knowledge and subjectivity are discursively produced, it makes sense to become visible as an active questioner in the narrative interview – to an extent, unveiling what the researcher will make of the accounts elicited. The participant then becomes engaged in a dialogue *about* their narrative and in analysis 'on the spot'.

The *third* point on whether adapting the interview style and, potentially, shifting storytelling can bring about meaningful social change, is more difficult to make in a decisive fashion. If narratives are constitutive of action (penal harm, in this case) (Presser, 2009) and institutional 'core stories' reinforce discriminatory practices (Kurtz & Upton, 2017), then uncovering and trying to counter discursive harms that come about in the practice of youth justice can be progressive (Petintseva, 2018). It is my contention that criticising such practices via some sort of 'you're doing it wrong' moralising rhetoric – be it in the interview setting or via recommendations – drives people into defensive modes instead of encouraging them to imagine alternative understandings. In my experience, narratives instigating penal harm can be best countered based on particular examples, drawing the officials' attention to case specifics and nuances. Coproducing alternative narratives can then potentially contribute to transformation through consciousness raising and demystification (Kezar, 2003). This enterprise is closely linked to a critical and social justice-based research agenda, which is also explicitly promoted by feminist researchers. One way of pursuing such a research agenda could be by initiating agonistic debates about counternarratives to the hegemonic modes of reasoning. This implies valuing conflict, pluralism and confrontation (Vitus, 2008) and the underlying goal is disrupting and complicating formula stories (Loseke, 2007; Sandberg, Tutenges, & Copes, 2015). Narratives that are rightfully ambiguous, complex and carve on expanded repertoires will allow people to speak and perhaps to think of alternative accounts that are less underpinned by boundary work. Copes (2016, p. 209) posits: 'the effects that boundaries have on behaviour suggest that tapping into these narratives by countering them or facilitating new ones can alter behaviour for the better'.

Admittedly, *Socrates light* is a 'light' form of resistance through research and, at this stage, there is no way of establishing whether counternarratives have actually been initiated or whether only the interview performance has been influenced in some instances. To put it differently, even if an alternative account is discussed, the question remains whether it is a (temporary) change of style or of substance. One could posit that narrative interventions at the level of institutional performance can at best promote 'imaginary solutions' (McAra, 2016; Petintseva, 2018). The institutional context of youth justice is indeed constrained by self-contradictory models, tight budgets, priorities, high workloads, limited interactions, long waiting lists and insufficient sensitivity to diversity. This structural and organisational context fosters a narrative habitus (Fleetwood, 2016) that shapes the stories produced by individual practitioners. Impacting institutional performance hence cannot be read separately from the context of state institutions and their embodied practices (McAra, 2016).

Conclusions

This chapter reflects on developing 'Socrates light' in my research. A shift from self-stories to institutional narratives that promote penal harm has epistemological and methodological implications. Institutional contexts are settings of storytelling of a particular kind: they are crafted for a specific professional audience, they are guided by legal and institutional genres and registers, they follow conversational conventions and reflect culturally and institutionally available scripts, but equally the agency and emotions of the practitioners. These 'stories of stories' are often impersonalised, impregnated with assumptions and projections, and they are strongly bound to interactional contexts. Drawing on the work of narrative criminologists, the chapter proposed to incorporate narrative, 'active' (confrontational) and feminist interviewing (Fontana & Frey, 2005). The result is a *Socrates light* style of interviewing that suggests a two-way model, in which the researcher enters a discussion and attempts to uncover and challenge tropes and silent interpretative schemata (Reinharz, 1992). Any narrative inquiry presupposes a relational methodology (Clandinin, 2016) and relationships differ. Certainly, important knowledge can develop from challenging respondents to give 'good reasons' and, to an extent, it can have transformative potential if alternative accounts can be constituted throughout the research interactions. Conversely, the researcher can be challenged to provide good epistemic reasons for her/his theoretical beliefs that seem unrecognisable to the respondents, in this way enriching the initial analysis.

I argued that discussions of grand dilemmas based on particular stories, while reflexively adjusting the interviewing style, are relevant in different respects: to reflect on the changing interaction and narrative performance in the interview setting, to engage participants in analysis and to think about counternarratives.

Before engaging in this type of interviews, a researcher needs to answer some questions for herself/himself: can narrators be held accountable and can a researcher challenge them, or is, as Brinkmann (2007) provocatively posited, the narrator always 'right'? Could debating the norm guiding the narratives contribute to counternarratives if such stories justify social harm? Is overcoming nondirective rules of qualitative research and somewhat 'stirring' the research participant necessarily problematic? Given the fact that I was working with powerful actors (at least, in relation to young people) and engaging in issues of public concern with a specific focus on narratives that constitute penal harm, to me, critical questions were justified (see also Thuesen, 2011). Such an approach could potentially contribute to unmasking power and powerlessness, and the ways in which they are interwoven (see Presser, 2013) and provide insights into how narratives become co-constructed in interview settings. In view of narrative criminologists' stance that narratives are intersubjective practices, understanding this narrative negotiation is relevant, even though we cannot yet conclusively uncover whether 'the narrative' has actually changed.

Acknowledgements

This research is funded by Research Foundation – Flanders.

References

Acker, J., Barry, K., & Esseveld, J. (1983). Objectivity and truth: Problems in doing feminist research. *Women's Studies International Forum, 6*(4), 423–435.

Aspden, K., & Hayward, K. (2015). Narrative criminology and cultural criminology. Shared biographies, different lives? In L. Presser & S. Sandberg (Eds.), *Narrative criminology: Understanding stories of crime* (pp. 235–259). New York, NY/London: New York University Press.

Bacchi, C. (2009). *Analysing policy: What's the problem represented to be?* Frenchs Forest: Pearson Australia.

Bacchi, C., & Bonham, J. (2014). Reclaiming discursive practices as an analytic focus: Political implications. *Foucault Studies, 17*, 173–192.

Bogner, A., Littig, B., & Menz, W. (Eds.). (2009). *Interviewing experts*. London: Springer.

Bourdieu, P. (1977). *Outline of a theory of practice*. Cambridge: Cambridge University Press.

Briggs, C. L. (2003). Interviewing, power/knowledge, and social inequality. In J. A. Holstein & J. F. Gubrium (Eds.), *Inside interviewing: New lenses, new concerns* (pp. 495–506). Thousand Oaks, CA: SAGE Publications.

Brinkmann, S. (2007). Could interviews be epistemic? An alternative to qualitative opinion polling. *Qualitative Inquiry, 13*(8), 1116–1138.

Cicourel, A. V. (1976). *The social organization of juvenile justice*. London: Heinemann Educational Books Ltd.

Clandinin, D. J. (2016). *Engaging in narrative inquiry*. London: Routledge.

Clear, T. R. (1994). *Harm in American penology: Offenders, victims, and their communities*. Albany, NY: State University of New York Press.

Collins, P. (1993). Learning for the outsider within: The sociological significance of Black feminist thought. In J. Glazer, E. Bensimon, & B. Townsend (Eds.), *Women in higher education* (pp. 45–65). Needham Heights, MA: Ginn Press.

Copes, H. (2016). A narrative approach to studying symbolic boundaries among drug users: A qualitative meta-analysis. *Crime, Media, Culture, 12*(2), 193–213.

De Fina, A., & Georgakopoulou, A. (2011). *Analyzing narrative: Discourse and sociolinguistic perspectives*. Cambridge: Cambridge University Press.

Evans, J. (2017). Artful dodgers: The role of unreliable narrators in the production of authorized histories and assessments of young people in conflict with the law. *Deviant Behavior, 38*(9), 1042–1058.

Fleetwood, J. (2016). Narrative habitus: Thinking through structure/agency in the narratives of offenders. *Crime, Media, Culture, 12*(2), 173–192.

Fontana, A., & Frey, J. H. (2005). The interview: From neutral stance to political involvement. In N. Denzin & Y. Lincoln (Eds.), *The SAGE handbook of qualitative research* (3rd ed., pp. 695–727). Thousand Oaks, CA: SAGE Publications.

Franssens, M., Put, J., & Deklerck, J. (2010). *Het beleid van de jeugdmagistraat*. Leuven: Universitaire Pers Leuven.

Harding, S., & Norberg, K. (2005). New feminist approaches to social science methodologies. *Signs, 30*(4), 2009–2015.

Holstein, J. A., & Gubrium, J. F. (1995). *The active interview*. Thousand Oaks, CA: SAGE Publications.

van Hulst, M. (2013). Storytelling at the police station. The canteen culture revisited. *British Journal of Criminology*, *53*, 624–642.

Kezar, A. (2003). Transformational elite interviews: Principles and problems. *Qualitative Inquiry*, *9*(3), 395–415.

Kurtz, D. L., & Upton, L. (2017). War stories and occupying soldiers: A narrative approach to understanding police culture and community conflict. *Critical Criminology*, *25*, 539–558.

Kvale, S. (2005). The dominance of dialogical interview research. *Barn*, *3*, 89–105.

Loseke, D. R. (2007). The study of identity as cultural, institutional, organizational, and personal narratives: Theoretical and empirical integrations. *The Sociological Quarterly*, *48*(4), 661–688.

Machin, D., & Mayr, A. (2012). *How to do critical discourse analysis*. London: SAGE Publications.

McAra, L. (2016). Can criminologists change the world? Critical reflections on the politics, performance and effects of criminal justice. *British Journal of Criminology*, *57*(4), 767–788.

Muncie, J. (2008). The punitive turn in juvenile justice: Cultures of control and rights compliance in Western Europe and the USA. *Youth Justice*, *8*(2), 107–121.

Odendahl, T., & Shaw, A. (2001). Interviewing elites. In J. F. Gubrium & J. A. Holstein (Eds.), *Handbook of interview research* (pp. 299–316). Thousand Oaks, CA: SAGE Publications.

Oude Breuil, B. (2011). Alles stroomt…? Over 'cultuur' in de culturele criminologie. *Tijdschrift over Cultuur & Criminaliteit*, *1*, 18–34.

Petintseva, O. (2015). Studying discriminatory practices in youth justice decision-making. In J. Christiaens (Ed.), *It's for your own good: Researching youth justice practices* (pp. 175–193). Brussels: VUB Press.

Petintseva, O. (2017). Selectieve "culturalisering" in de praktijk van de jeugdbescherming in België. *Tijdschrift over Cultuur & Criminaliteit*, *7*(3), 51–73.

Petintseva, O. (2018). *Youth justice and migration. Discursive harms*. London: Palgrave Macmillan.

Petintseva, O., Faria, R., & Eski, Y. (forthcoming). *Interviewing the powerful in crime and crime control*. London: Palgrave Macmillan.

Phillips, R. (1998). The politics of history: Some methodological and ethical dilemmas in elite-based research. *British Educational Research Journal*, *24*(1), 5–19.

Presser, L. (2004). Violent offenders, moral selves: Constructing identities and accounts in the research interview. *Social Problems*, *51*, 82–101.

Presser, L. (2005). Negotiating power and narrative in research: Implications for feminist methodology. *Signs*, *30*(3), 2067–2090.

Presser, L. (2009). The narratives of offenders. *Theoretical Criminology*, *13*(2), 177–200.

Presser, L. (2010). Collecting and analyzing the stories of offenders. *Journal of Criminal Justice Education*, *21*(4), 431–446.

Presser, L. (2013). *Why we harm*. New Brunswick, NJ: Rutgers University Press.

Presser, L. (2016). Criminology and the narrative turn. *Crime, Media, Culture*, *12*(2), 137–151.

Presser, L., & Sandberg, S. (2015a). Introduction. What is the story? In L. Presser & S. Sandberg (Eds.), *Narrative criminology. Understanding stories of crime* (pp. 1–22). New York, NY: NYU Press.

Presser, L., & Sandberg, S. (2015b). Research strategies for narrative criminology. In J. Miller & W. Palacios (Eds.), *Advances in criminological theory: The value of qualitative research for advancing criminological theory* (pp. 85–99). Piscataway, NJ: Transaction Publishers.

Reinharz, S. (1992). *Feminist methods in social research*. New York, NY: Oxford University Press.

Saarikkomäki, E. (2015). Perceptions of procedural justice among young people: Narratives of fair treatment in young people's stories of police and security guard interventions. *British Journal of Criminology*, 56(6), 1253–1271.

Sandberg, S. (2010). What can 'lies' tell us about life? Notes towards a framework of narrative criminology. *Journal of Criminal Justice Education*, 21(4), 447–465.

Sandberg, S. (2013). Are self-narratives strategic or determined, unified or fragmented? Reading Breivik's Manifesto in light of narrative criminology. *Acta Sociologica*, 56(1), 69–83.

Sandberg, S. (2016). The importance of stories untold: Life-story, event-story and trope. *Crime, Media, Culture*, 12, 153–171.

Sandberg, S., Tutenges, S., & Copes, C. (2015). Stories of violence: A narrative criminological study of ambiguity. *British Journal of Criminology*, 55, 1168–1186.

Tanggaard, L. (2007). The research interview as discourses crossing swords. The researcher and apprentice on crossing roads. *Qualitative Inquiry*, 13(1), 160–176.

Terrio, S. (2009). *Judging Mohammed. Juvenile delinquency, immigration, and exclusion at the Paris Palace of justice*. Stanford, CA: Stanford University Press.

Thuesen, F. (2011). Navigating between dialogue and confrontation: Phronesis and emotions in interviewing elites on ethnic discrimination. *Qualitative Inquiry*, 17(7), 613–622.

Ugelvik, T. (2016). Techniques of legitimation: The narrative construction of legitimacy among immigration detention officers. *Crime, Media, Culture*, 12(2), 215–232.

Verde, A., Angelini, F., Boverini, S., & Marajana, M. (2006). The narrative structure of psychiatric reports. *International Journal of Law and Psychiatry*, 29(1), 1–12.

Vitus, K. (2008). The agonistic approach. Reframing resistance in qualitative research. *Qualitative Inquiry*, 14(3), 466–488.

Wolfe, D. (1996). *Feminist dilemma in fieldwork*. Boulder, CO: Westview Press.

Chapter 6

Stories that Are Skyscraper Tall: The Place of 'Tall Tales' in Narrative Criminology

Carmen Wickramagamage and Jody Miller

Introduction

Narrative criminology has no doubt made stories respectable again in a discipline that, given its affiliation with Enlightenment thinking, has long professed a commitment to a positivist notion of truth. Indeed, the embrace of narratives has meant grappling with the place and utility of 'lies.' In doing so, however, we often view the plotlines found in stories credible and insightful specifically when they speak to broader cultural processes and the stories made available by these. Thus Sandberg (2010, p. 455) notes that '[r]esearch participants cannot choose from an infinite pool of language and meaning.... [N]o matter what kinds of stories are told, or whether they are true or false, they tell us something important about values, identities, cultures, and communities.'

In this chapter, we grapple further with this relationship between story, individual and cultural plotline, to offer additional caution about the challenges of verisimilitude and plausibility in making sense of individuals' stories. We draw from a mixed-methods study of women's pathways to incarceration in Sri Lanka, and utilise our encounters with Daya, a transgender inmate trapped in a women's carceral world, to explore the complex relations among 'truth,' 'fiction' and 'lies', and their implications for narrative criminology. If 'narratives are not only *spoken by* individuals but also *spoken through* them' (Sandberg, 2010, p. 458), what do we do with 'tall tales' that have no ready place in available cultural storylines? And what insights can such tales offer as caution against researchers' orientations towards the plausible and familiar? We begin by offering some background on the narrative turn, its relation to positivist science and criminology and its insights about lies. We then explore these theoretical developments further through our interrogation of Daya's stories, and more importantly, of our own struggles to make sense of them.

Narratives, Truth and Lies

In a way, scepticism of stories is understandable: Viewed as an applied science, criminologists may see their mission as focussing on measurable factors that cause criminal behaviour, with the ultimate objectives of aiding crime prevention and intervention. Given that criminologists deal with populations that have fallen foul of the law, and thus have every reason to remain 'under the radar,' it is no surprise that many criminologists view narrative work with some scepticism, often grounded in the assumption that research participants have little interest in or incentive to divulge the truth about their offending behaviours and have every reason instead to distort, if not conceal, the truth of their activities. Indeed, 'the truth may put their free status in jeopardy' (Sandberg, 2010, p. 449) and many reasons exist for impression management when speaking with researchers (Copes & Hochstetler, 2010).

This makes a fundamental scepticism towards and distrust of the accounts of the crime-involved populations that criminologists make their subject or object of study unavoidable (Presser, 2016). The desire to keep participants on the straight and narrow path of truth is often paramount in criminological studies, with methodologies devised intent on doing so. As Sandberg (2010) notes, 'validity' is at the heart of this insistence: 'The question about whether or not research participants are telling the truth is closely linked to concerns about the *validity* of data. When narratives are conceptualised as record, an account has been understood as valid "if it represents accurately those features of the phenomena that it is intended to describe, explain or theorize"' (Hammersley, 1987, p. 69, in Sandberg, 2010, p. 452).

Narrative criminology is different. It does not fight shy of the role of narrative and narration in the study of those who are crime-involved. As Lois Presser – one of its pioneer proponents – puts it, narrative criminology does not see narrative as a postdated attempt to record, rationalise or interpret offending behaviour and action. It sees narrative as antecedent to or even constitutive of experience (Presser, 2009, p. 177). Presser and Sandberg (2015, p. 1) have defined narrative criminology as 'any inquiry based on the view of stories as instigating, sustaining, or effecting desistance from harmful action. We study how narratives inspire and motivate harmful action and how they are used to make sense of harm.' In other words, stories do not simply impose form or shape on inchoate experiences that predate them. They provide roadmaps for or structure action, given that every community, mainstream or marginal, has a repertoire of stories they can draw on. In that sense, there is no world of objective experience outside of narrative (Sandberg, 2010, p. 451).

Presser and Sandberg (2015) go even further: in 'making sense' of offender accounts of experience, researchers, too, respond consciously or unconsciously to its narrative potential, properties or attributes. That is, researchers understand recounted experience in terms of its 'fit' or congruence with a given narrative form. Indeed, '[e]ven events are narrative in structure and the observer's capacities to recognise them are also narrative in form' (Sandberg, 2010, p. 451). Though there can sometimes be a mismatch between what people say they do and what they actually do (Jerolmack & Khan, 2014), narratives are very much a part of self-presentation and are made possible by the social and cultural milieus in which individuals are embedded (Miller & Glassner, 2011). In that sense, the number of narratives at the disposal of study participants is finite, the milieu limiting the number of narratives available for the narrator to make sense of her or his world and experience. If discourse, as Foucault (1972) notes, is 'language in action,' then 'viewing narratives as embedded within larger discourses highlights their power and the power relations in which they are implicated. It also highlights and contextualizes the limits of the individual narrator's agency' (Presser & Sandberg, 2015, p. 3).

But where do lies, or stories that have little affinity with lived experience or life-worlds, fit into this renewed appreciation of narrative in criminology? Are narrative criminologists as ready to embrace obvious 'fibs' that have little or no discernible grounding in 'reality'? What takes the place of the 'real', reality or objective phenomena in a world constituted only by the 'word'? In Jonathan Swift's (1726) eighteenth-century English classic, *Gulliver's Travels*, Gulliver, in the last of his four journeys to distant lands, encounters a species of rational horses among whom lying is unknown and for which there is no word in their lexicon. The culmination of Gulliver's four-part journey with this sobering discovery transmits a truth that is clearly the author's: the extent of the fall of his own human species from an ideal state. Yet transmission of this 'truth' takes the form of a fabrication, thus underscoring the point that invention is not necessarily the opposite of but a means to arrive at truth.

Though criminology deals with 'real-life' offenders, Presser's (2009, pp. 178–179) definition of narrative foregrounds this element of creativity when she defines narrative as a 'temporally ordered statement concerning events experienced by and/or actions of one or more protagonists' that 'draws *selectively* on lived experience' (our emphasis). Nevertheless, she makes an important distinction between the world of make-believe, which is the stuff of fiction, and the role of narrative in narrative criminology. Even as narrative criminology acknowledges that narratives may not faithfully correspond to and bring to life a given reality in all of its myriad detail (see Maruna, 2001), there is still an expectation that the selection is based on *actual* events experienced by and/or actions of the 'real-life' protagonist/study participant. 'Experience,' in other words, is still the necessary corollary of 'expression.' Hence, while there *is* human intervention in the form of selection and arrangement, the narrative must show some affiliation to lived experience. In their introduction to *Narrative Criminology*, Presser and Sandberg (2015, p. 12) admit to as much in pointing to narrative criminology's implicit affiliation with the realist tradition. The realist tradition is implicit, too, in Miller, Carbone-Lopez, and Gunderman's (2015, p. 70) argument that the 'narratives of offenders have assisted criminologists in better understanding the impact of individual, family and situational factors on criminal involvement.'

Literary scholars, among them Eric Auerbach (1953), Ian Watt (1956) and Colin MacCabe (1985), have long questioned the emphasis on the 'real' insisting that 'real' is ultimately a matter of 'effect.' Tracing the antecedents of 'realism' as a mode of representation in nineteenth-century literature and the arts to socio-economic and intellectual trends in post-Enlightenment Europe, scholars of literary history have shown that the interest in 'objective reality' in the arts is inseparable from the focus on verifiable truth in the emergent dispensation of science and laissez-faire capitalism (Abrams et al., 1962). They sever, thus, the link between 'realism of content' and 'realism of presentation,' foregrounding instead the element of representation in every genre of the arts, including the 'realist'. For literary scholars, there are many means to arrive at the truth, the 'realist mode' being just one such. What 'representative realism' aims at is *'vraisemblance'* or 'verisimilitude': 'an appearance of truth' (*Collins' English Dictionary*), a point also stressed by MacCabe (1985). So, Dennis Walder (1995, p. 135) has this to say in his discussion of Charles Dickens' *Great Expectations*, a textbook example of the realist genre of English fiction: '[W]e are viewing the novel as a genre capable of registering in satisfyingly complex ways what we think we know about how the world we live in has come about.'

Where then does verisimilitude reside? According to Nancy K. Miller (1985, p. 341), it is in 'common sense.' For Shoshana Felman (1989, p. 143), therefore, '[r]ealism ... postulates a conception of "nature" and of "reality" which seeks to establish itself, tautologically, as "natural" and as "real"'. Consensus within a community of readers or speakers, thus, determines whether a particular account or representation is probable or plausible. In that sense, for Miller, 'the critical reaction to any given text is hermeneutically bound to another and preexistent text: the *doxa* of socialities. Plausibility, then, is an effect of reading through a grid of concordance' (1985, p. 341). Miller is quick to point out that one cannot demand the same from 'life' 'because in life, unlike in art, anything can happen; hence the constraints of likeness do not apply' (p. 340). For Gérard Genette, quoted in Miller (1985, p. 341), 'extravagance is a privilege of the real'.

Carlo Tognato (2015, p. 264) is one narrative criminologist who moves in this direction, when he posits that offender narratives are ultimately 'not about truth but about verisimilitude'. Presser (2013, 2018) makes a similar point: stories need not be true to cause harm. What matters is that a large enough community, with the power to inflict harm on others, begins to believe the story and to act upon its basis. Nevertheless, while credibility need not be based on 'facts' or the 'truth', a credible story must still be located within a shared repertoire of stories within a community for it to be taken seriously. There seems little room for individuals whose stories are unique to them or uniquely their own.

In 'What Can "Lies" Tell Us About Life?', Sandberg (2010, p. 38) attempts to destabilise this surreptitious link between narrative criminology and realism, quoting Dean and Whyte (1958) to suggest that researchers should not concern themselves with whether research participants are lying. Rather, they should 'seek answers to the question: What does the informant's statement reveal about his feelings and perceptions, and what inferences can be made from them about the actual environment or events he has experienced?' (2010, p. 448). Presser (2009) likewise notes that we need not know if a story is true to recognise its role in promoting criminal behaviour, a point affirmed by Miller (2010, p. 165), who asserts that 'no matter how much we strive to improve the validity of our data... ultimately the interview itself cannot provide authentic access to individuals' "experiences."'

So does this mean that lies have a place in narrative criminology, even when they are obviously fabricated and have no discernible links to what can be verified through fact, background checks or even shared story stock? Sandberg (2010, p. 462) appears to answer yes, asking, 'Why must we necessarily know whether or not a story is true for it to be worth studying? Even obvious lies can be interesting, and the natural inclination to minimize lying may not always be the best approach.' His concluding lines are quite revealing of his stance: 'The most common question in ethnographic research (do research participants lie?) can thus be turned on its head with a more important one: what can "lies" tell us about life?' (2010, pp. 462–463). But would Sandberg's definition of 'lying' include a freefall narrative by a crime-involved storyteller that defies gravity and has no discernible anchor in terra firma?

Sandberg's bold and unequivocal use of 'lie' instead of the euphemism 'story,' to name a tendency in accounts for exaggeration and distortion, opens up new avenues for investigating the place of the 'lie,' allowing us to ask: What can patent lies or tall stories tell us about the underlying belief in and emphasis on plausibility in narrative criminology? We address this issue via one such set of 'tall tales.' Central to our discussion is the story of Daya,[1] the unabashed spinner of 'tall' stories, whom we met during a research project on women's pathways to incarceration at a prison in Sri Lanka.

Encounters with Daya in Context

We met Daya during our visits to the female wing of a prison in Sri Lanka between September and December 2014 in connection with a study of women's pathways to incarceration. The research combined quantitative and qualitative methodologies – life event calendars (LECs) combined with narrative interviews utilising a semistructured interview guide. The goal was to map study participants' pathways to offending and facilitate their reflections on those pathways.

During the period of our research, there were between 80 and 100 women incarcerated at the prison, with the population regularly in flux due to transfers, releases and admissions. While it housed women from various parts of the island, according to prison welfare officials, given the prison's relatively rural location the inmates tended to be 'better' behaved (a coded statement implying that they embodied more stereotypically feminine attributes) because there were fewer 'big-city' women to 'spoil' the local carceral population. We completed interviews with 96 women, a principle reason given by those who declined interviews being their unwillingness to dredge up a painful past. Daya was initially among those who refused to participate. They held themselves aloof at first though making sure we were aware of their presence as well as their influence

---

[1]We use a pseudonym and conceal other identifying facets of Daya's story in an effort to safeguard their confidentiality. Because Daya identified as transgender, and since personal pronouns in (colloquial) Sinhala language are not gender-specific (though grammatical gender operates in formal use) and we are unable to confirm Daya's referential preferences, we use the pronouns they/them/their in telling their story. This is in keeping with GLAAD's Media Reference Guide; see https://www.glaad.org/reference/transgender.

among both the guards and inmates, so much so we worried that they were instigating others not to volunteer for interviews.

Daya was hard not to notice. They did not fit the 'conventional' profile of incarcerated 'women.' They were fluent in English, which is a signifier of elite class status in a country where less than a third of the population self-reports English literacy (Department of Census and Statistics, Sri Lanka, 2012) and fewer still are fluent in spoken English. Daya looked 'different' from the 'typical' Lankan woman in appearance and comportment as well and stood out even before we learnt of their transgender identity. In addition to cropped hair, Daya sported numerous tattoos, a form of body adornment rarely seen among Lankan women. Nor did the regulation-issue female prisoner garb – white cloth and blouse – sit well on Daya. In conversation, they claimed to drink and smoke cigarettes. In that respect, Daya did not qualify for inclusion in local understandings of 'respectable femininity' nor, we should hasten to add, did they desire it. We invoke the local gender norms because of their usefulness in situating our discussion in the culture's expectations for individuals designated female at birth, since this impacted our reactions to both Daya and the cisgender women in our study.

'Respectable femininity' is best connoted by embodying the quality of *lajja-baya* or 'shame-fear,' an outcome of the invention of a new Sinhala (Buddhist) and Tamil femininity during the British colonial period (de Alwis, 1996, pp. 106, 128–129). Embodiment of the ideal requires refraining from alcohol consumption and smoking, though a large portion of incarcerated women are sentenced for offences associated with the production and sale of illicit alcohol (Miller, 2013). The Excise Act of 1951, upheld as recently as 2018 (Rajakarunanayake, 2018), prohibits women from serving or being served alcohol in public and the dominant discourse labels women who drink as 'unfeminine'. *Lajja-baya* also characterises 'respectable' women as those 'whose public movement is circumscribed and who [are] demure and dressed with decorum' while a woman without *lajja-baya* 'moves in public too much and speaks too loudly' (Lynch, 2007, p. 143).

Daya was atypically confident to the point of being brash in the way they addressed the prison authorities – unafraid to talk back to and reprimand officers, presenting themselves as almost their equal. In conversation with the lead author, they noted that most officers were less educated than them. Prison authorities, in turn, adopted an indulgent attitude towards Daya's at times insolent behaviour. Moreover, it was evident that the prison authorities depended on Daya to some degree to maintain order in the female wing. Daya conveyed messages to fellow inmates from the guards, adopting a stentorian voice in relaying those commands. They took charge of the hot water distributed at inmates' teatime and took the lead in arranging the dining area for meals. Though Daya initially refused to speak to us, it was clear they wanted us to acknowledge their presence as someone to reckon with as the inmate leader of the female wing and someone who held special status in the prison officers' eyes.

Having initially acted aloof, Daya gradually began to thaw and, though still refusing to be interviewed, they started exchanging greetings with us and helping to recruit women to participate in the research. For these reasons, they piqued our curiosity. We were keen to know their story. In that sense, Daya demonstrated that interview participants are not always entities passively awaiting information mining by researchers at the latter's initiative. They ensured we would regard them as a unique individual with a story worth hearing. Unexpectedly, Daya eventually volunteered for an interview at a time of their own choosing.

This was not the incarcerated 'woman' we had anticipated. Instead, our research was undergirded by certain assumptions regarding whom we were likely to encounter, and by the more fundamental assumption that all inmates in the prison's female wing would be women. The majority of women incarcerated in Sri Lanka are convicted for 'excise and narcotic drug offences' and those related to sex work (Department of Prisons, Sri Lanka, 2017, which reports statistics only on the sex/gender binary), and we anticipated meeting such women, most notably those with low educational attainment (Department of Prisons, Sri Lanka, 2017), low socioeconomic indices, participation in the illicit liquor, drug, or sex trades via male partners or kin, or participation in such markets as a result of male partners' incarceration, separation, or death. Miller's (2002) research found that sex workers often end up in prison for failure to post bail or pay fines, thus suggesting that they are at the lower end of the socioeconomic spectrum. In Sri Lanka, as elsewhere, it is those without economic means who face the full brunt of the law. Daya did not fit this (stereo)typical profile. Incarcerated for assault, they had a history of multiple assault and fraud charges and multiple incarcerations.

Cultural conditions in Sri Lanka emphasise timidity and submissiveness in Lankan women, so it was unexpected to encounter an individual in the female ward with multiple charges for violent physical assault. Less than 1% of direct female prison admissions are for murder while between 2 and 7% are for 'simple hurt' (Department of Prisons, Sri Lanka, 2017). At the time of our research, only three female inmates were convicted for murder, and these for the murder of spouses or male kin. Among the few others convicted of violent offences was a young unmarried woman charged with infanticide and another convicted of aiding and abetting an assassination plot against a politician during Sri Lanka's recently concluded civil war.

Daya was different. They described having trouble with 'anger management' and had been told by the prison doctor to learn to control their emotions so as to prevent recurrence of the same behaviour. They proved an 'outlier' both in terms of their offences as well as their socioeconomic profile. They thus challenged our assumptions regarding Sri Lankan women's pathways to incarceration *and* our assumption that all individuals in the female ward would be women. Daya was an outlier in another important way: when they spoke with us, they narrated a tale that tested the limits of credibility, and had the researchers scrambling to 'make sense' of their story/ies.

Daya's Tall Tale(s): Looking for the 'Truth' in the 'Fib'

In the course of our study, we had an occasion to interview Daya twice. The first was during a visit by the first author, Carmen, who had decided to encourage

Daya to open up by strategically deploying a presumed shared class identity with Daya – conversance in English – correctly guessing that it would convey to them our recognition of them as exceptional. Asked casually why they were uninterested in participating, Daya had surprisingly expressed a willingness to talk, and their interview had unexpectedly commenced. Unbeknownst to Carmen, they had again volunteered for another interview with two RAs on a subsequent occasion. The extracts below illustrate the 'heights' to which Daya's tall tales could rise:

> *She [sic.[2]] was left at a church...by her mother, who also left a note in very good English. She carries her mother's name, though she does not have any contact with her. The priest found her under a pew in the church late at night.... First she said she is 'angry with' her mother. 'She should have killed me before I was born if she couldn't have me. Why did she leave me in a church to be brought up in a children's home?'* [Lead author's interview notes]

> *At the orphanage, she had lived in a tree-house. She preferred to live in her own world.... One day, on Parents' Day, she waited by the gate of the orphanage for her mother to come [for a visit]. Because her mother did not come, she decided to distance herself from [humans] and to make animals her world.... She had 20 dogs, a cobra and a monkey.... The cobra was rescued by her when it was going to be killed by some people. She had to put some blanket stitches on the cobra's wounds. It was named Blanket for that.... Her cobra slept on her chest every night. It would wake her up in the morning by tapping on her cheek.... She had been very sad when she had to hand over the cobra to the zoo when she joined the army, because they had not permitted her to keep it with her.* [Interview notes from RAs]

> *From age 16 on she was homeless and lived on the streets – literally lived on the railway line. She dressed and looked like a boy and no one therefore took her for a girl.... She studied under street lamps and had only 9 books with her. I asked her whether the principal of the school knew where she lived or what she did. She said 'no,' the principal thought she was living with a friend. I asked her where she left her [school] uniforms if she lived on the streets. She said she left them at the principal's house.* [Lead author's notes]

Daya's story/ies stretched the limits of credulity and challenged us to grapple with how such tales can be put to use in understanding individuals' motivations,

---

[2]Field notes and correspondence that refer to Daya as a woman, and with female pronouns, are preserved in their original form. Daya's interview with the lead author was in English and with the two RAs in Sinhala.

influences and actions. Our own attunement to plausibility was thus revealed. Daya's stories did not draw from a shared stock of available narratives within any particular ethnic or religious community in Sri Lanka though, as we show later, a mix of multiple local and 'Western' cultural influences can be gleaned in Daya's stories when scrutinised more closely, and at least one of their stories speaks to how 'fantastic' stories, whether religious, spiritual or supernatural, play important roles across societies.

One does not have to look too carefully for the 'holes' or inconsistencies in their narratives. For instance, that they lived on the railway track for 3 years while attending an elite girls' school and their unusual relationship with a pet cobra. Also noteworthy is their account of the violent assault that led to their incarceration. Daya insisted that they had used the ancient indigenous technique of *nila sastra* to turn lifeless the arm of a male foreigner who had attempted to sexually harm them. Pointing therapy is the closest equivalent of *nila sastra*, a therapeutic technique found in Sri Lanka, India and China, among other Asian countries, where points are activated in the nerve centres for healing purposes. In Sri Lanka, *nila sastra* is also believed to come in handy to subdue one's opponent in unarmed combat. Daya was obviously referring to the latter although this form of combat, now hardly in use, is one imparted only to men.[3] This story, though, finds some home in the place of sorcery, 'black' magic and exorcism rituals still common, especially in Sri Lanka's rural villages (Kapferer, 1991, 1997), even as it contradicts signifiers of 'Western' privilege in other facets of Daya's account. Daya said that the man they disabled begged them to restore life to his limb every time they encountered each other in court but that they threatened to kill him if they could ever get their hands on him. Daya related the episode with obvious relish; they displayed neither embarrassment nor compunction. There were many more stories of this variety where plausibility, as we defined it, was in short supply.

Yet Daya was a good storyteller. When they spoke, it was hard to imagine they were 'fibbing'. It was when Carmen began to write down and reflect upon what Daya had said that the inconsistencies became palpable. As Carmen wrote up Daya's oral narration, she noted:

> *I find this section a little hard to believe or understand. Though living on the streets or railway line, she continued to attend this leading school and there is no mention of where she kept her books, uniforms, where she took a bath before she went to school and where she changed and so on.*

Yet is it all in the realm of fantasy and fiction? And if so, would it still be of some research value? Excerpts from Carmen and Jody's email exchange in the immediate aftermath of the interview illuminates the 'incredulity' beginning to

---

[3]Personal communication from P. B. Meegaskumbura, Professor Emeritus, Sinhala Literature, Language and Cultural Studies, University of Peradeniya, Sri Lanka.

lace the discussion on what to make of Daya's story/ies and whether to include them in the sample:

> Carmen: *Jody, I think I have been taken for a big, long ride by this woman (or does she herself not know that she's lying?). First, as I started writing up her story, I began to think it sounded quite improbable.... What's the value of her narrative then? If she is not telling the 'truth' about herself or if this is the story she wants to believe or weave of herself and tell others, then what?*
>
> Jody: *Wow. I've read through all of this and looked [at additional information about her]. There are different positions on what to do with interviews where it seems clear that the person told 'tall tales', which I agree with you, seems pretty clear in this instance. In some cases, 'lies' can be put to use. But she's also an outlier with regard to the 'typical' woman in prison too, on a whole host of criteria. And, given [additional information you came across regarding a con scheme], looks like telling tall tales is much of what she does outside of prison too. I guess my inclination in this situation would be to hold onto her materials, but lean toward excluding her from data analysis. We can always decide to revisit.*
>
> Carmen: *I could casually ask one of the welfare officers what her story is. The guards told me to take her story with a grain of salt (looks like it is a ton of salt!) after I spoke to 'Daya' and they were standing behind me, making fun of her while she was speaking to me. She would start smiling and looking away and when I would ask 'why', she would say 'they [prison officers] are making fun of me'. But she told the story with confidence, loud and clear, and did not worry the guards could hear her (one at least understands English and she was listening). So I wonder: from a psychological perspective, what her motives are. Maybe she lives in this make-believe world and keeps fabricating lives for herself as she goes.*
>
> Jody: *It would be interesting to see what the WOs say. Grain of salt, for sure, though you may be right about the psychology of her life, from her POV. I'm also curious about the [other information], and I'm sure there's some truth to [it].* (Email correspondence, October 2–3, 2014)

Though Daya's second interview with the RAs had come subsequent to the correspondence between the first and second authors detailed above, the contents of the second interview, which showed further embellishments, convinced Jody and Carmen to leave Daya out of the sample. For we had decided Daya was telling 'tall stories' and was thus unreliable as narrator and witness to their life and offending.

Despite the initial scepticism regarding Daya's tales that the email correspondence reported above reveals, in subsequent exchanges, Carmen and Jody again started asking each other why Daya's story should be less relevant, and what their patently tall tales have to tell us not just about the quest for 'truth' in criminology but also about the implicit commitment to plausibility in narrative criminology. So even where 'stories' that individuals tell themselves and others are not explicitly based in fact, they are recognised as offering insights on influences and motivations, specifically, *if* there is a link between their stories and the stock of narratives available within the culture or subculture of which they are a part. Sandberg (2010, p. 458) thus cautions against seeing the teller as 'author' and 'authority' of their own narrative: 'Narratives are not only *spoken by* individuals but also *spoken through* them.'

Looked at from such a perspective, Daya's is an interesting case. On the face of it, their stories did not match the repertoire of stories available to or drawn upon by the 'typical' incarcerated woman in Sri Lanka, stories given the seal of authenticity by similar accounts reported in mainstream media. This is of course not surprising given Daya's transgender identity, which garners little visibility in Lankan society and in its shared plotlines. Equally importantly, Daya's stories featuring blanket-stitched cobras and superhuman strength honed through the practice of an ancient therapeutic art often lacked the verisimilitude derived from commonsensical understandings of 'reality,' not just for Lankan women but for men as well. The story of Daya thus challenges some of the fundamental premises of traditional naturalist qualitative research in criminology but offers cautions for narrative criminologists as well by pushing us to consider what to make of lies when they do not readily correspond with available cultural plotlines.

A careful analysis of their story suggests an eclectic mix of fact and fiction which also varied from one telling to the next, a mix where common sense could be invoked to separate and categorise some facets as 'true' and some 'untrue.' Some aspects of their story were built upon available plotlines from popular culture, though, given Daya's status as a 'Westernized' English-speaking postcolonial subject, not necessarily local. A good example is the English name of their pet cobra, Blanket, showing a person straddling dual linguistic-cultural worlds. Among the recognisable popular culture plotlines are the story of being left under a church pew at birth by their mother; and another, that the love of their life – a female soldier – had sacrificed her life trying to deflect a bullet meant for Daya under enemy fire.

To take, for example, the story of abandonment at birth: Is Daya borrowing from a popular 'Western' storyline where Christian churches often become places, because of their status as sanctuaries, to leave unwanted babies? There is no discernibly local flavour to this story. In Sri Lanka, Buddhists comprise 70% of the population, followed by Hindus and Muslims. Buddhist temples are thus the most prevalent places of religious worship and there is no factual or fictional tradition of using temples for this purpose. On the other hand, there is a tradition of left-at-church-at-birth plotlines in British fiction dating as far back as the eighteenth century if Mathew Gregory Lewis's Gothic novel, *The Monk*, is anything to go by.

Or consider the story of Daya's sacrificial soldier girlfriend: this is a familiar, yet melodramatic, storyline from battlefield and war not necessarily local. Daya also details having a badge pinned on them by a prominent female politician during their passing out parade from the military. As they had no mother to do so, here the politician takes the place of Daya's mother, the stuff of a recognisable sentimental storyline. Indeed, popular psychology could be resorted to in making sense of these themes: being left in a basket inside a church, waiting for a mother that never comes, being taken under the wing of a female politician who would become a surrogate mother figure, all carry features of the so-called 'Absent Mother Syndrome' (Henley, 1973) prevalent in pop psychology.

Other details of Daya's story/ies are seemingly grounded in fact. First, the aspects where their stories conform to or touch base with verifiable facts regarding their life. This was not difficult, given that Daya described being brought up in a reputed orphanage and attending a leading private girls' school. In an effort to 'triangulate' Daya's story, one member of the research team made discrete enquiries without divulging any details about Daya's present whereabouts. This enquiry yielded details that in some aspects corresponded Daya's story, confirming that they had indeed been brought up in a leading orphanage that was founded by a foreign woman. However, the children at this orphanage did not attend the elite school mentioned by Daya; instead they were enrolled at a nearby village school although looked up to by the other kids and their parents as *walauwe babala* or 'elite children' because of their connection to a 'white' woman.

At some point, Daya had also joined the army against the advice of the orphanage directors. And Daya's love of animals was also confirmed. We couldn't verify the death of Daya's army girlfriend under tragic circumstances but it was clear that they were mourning some loss that was deeply personal. Prison officials told us that they had been depressed upon arrival and had been under medication for some time. Daya described suffering 'mood swings' and 'anger' issues for which they were under treatment. They even offered to share the journal they kept for therapy. Thus, whatever the source of their loss, Daya had obviously felt it deeply. Many stories Daya narrated thus had some basis in fact and may well have been motivated by the struggles and losses they had experienced in their life as well as the desire for meaning and purpose in a societal context that erases their very existence.

Is Verisimilitude Enough?

Nonetheless, we are left with what to make of those stories with little grounding in available plotlines and for which verisimilitude is a stretch: their elite school attendance while concealing homelessness; their pet cobra Blanket and the blanket stitches for which it was named; their drug-sniffing dog named Kruger hired out to the Army with the fee paid into their account even during incarceration; their use of *nila sastra* to harm a man who sought to harm them. Whether fact-based, fanciful or otherwise, Daya had found use for one such 'fiction,' i.e., the ties they claimed to a prominent female politician. Records show that they had been convicted for fraud, using the politician's name in a criminal operation; indeed, the politician concerned had lodged a complaint with the police. How do we deal with the continuum of 'fact,' 'fantasy' and storytelling in Daya's account? And is it necessary to distinguish the role of 'make-believe' or intentional lies? We struggled with the question of whether Daya was an outlier that we should simply ignore or whether they offer a lesson in narrative criminology that is of use to all involved. We offer two such considerations, one to do with Daya, the other with the many women in our study, both interrelated.

First, digging deeper, Daya's 'tall' tales do have some important relation to their behaviour and experiences, even as these may not be direct or obvious. For example, whether or not Daya has actually mastered the ancient art of *nila sastra* to turn their harasser's limb lifeless, they have obviously grievously hurt him, as their criminal case demonstrates. And Daya's repetition in both the interviews that their 'thoughts are not feminine' could be a plausible explanation for their more (stereo)typically 'masculine' offenses. Hence, their stories were likely shaped by an embodied identity for which there is little validation and support in the society they inhabit. 'I am gay,' Daya announced upon sitting down to talk with Carmen, carrying their sexual orientation as a badge of pride. They also specifically identified as 'transgender,' which is a relatively new and notably 'Western' identity term in Sri Lanka that has both incorporated and displaced existing local terminology for and self-meanings of gender identity (Kuru-Utumpala, 2013; Miller, 2017; Miller & Nichols, 2012; Wijewardene, 2007). In fact, Daya asked Carmen's opinion on transitioning since they 'did not feel feminine' and sometimes adopted a male gender presentation when not incarcerated.

There is little cultural space in Sri Lanka for individuals with Daya's gender and sexual identities. Same-sex sexual practices are criminalised under Sri Lanka's Penal Code, as is 'cheating by personation,' which targets individuals whose gender presentations do not match their assigned sex (Institute for Participatory Action in Development, 2016, p. 17). There is distinct opprobrium, even hostility, directed towards lesbians,[4] given the centrality of 'wedded motherhood' to the normative feminine identity in Sri Lanka (Kuru-Utumpala, 2013). And there appears even less tolerance for transgender people (Nichols, 2010; Wijewardene, 2007).

The 'violence' of the 'sex/gender binary' is manifestly reflected in the prison's two wings: male and female. Despite Daya's masculine identity and articulated sense of being more at home in the company of men, their classification as female thus placed them in the women's wing of the prison. Indeed, one of the prison's Welfare Officers took it upon himself to inform Carmen, with a conspiratorial air, that Daya was a 'homo,' a pejorative term, and that they had been transferred to this prison for an alleged relationship with a female guard at another. Daya

---

[4]Though we use the term lesbian as shorthand here in reference to women with a same-sex sexual orientation, this is a 'Western' term, whose use for women in same-sex relationships in parts of the formerly colonised world has been challenged (Kuru-Utumpala, 2013, pp. 155–156).

rebuffed such punitive sanctions and spoke openly of their many girlfriends, treating these as ordinary topics of conversation in the Sri Lankan sociocultural context. Yet, Daya also noted that people, including other inmates, looked askance at them, declaring, 'I am not a pervert; I am unique.' Drawing from a Sinhala figure of speech, Daya voiced their anger at being labelled deviant: 'A blind man cannot see nor appreciate the gem that he holds in his hand. I am like that gem.' Daya's 'tall' tales invoked such unique and special qualities, which were otherwise routinely undercut.

Notably, even our translations of the English interview guide had failed to accommodate Daya's reality: the gender-neutral *partner* in English had been translated into Sinhala using masculine gender nouns, indicating the deep-rooted heteronormativity or 'compulsory heterosexuality' (Rich, 1980) in conceptualising romantic, sexual and marital relations in Sri Lanka. Study participants were likewise presumed to be women, with no consideration for how a person like Daya might fit. As a consequence, the life history calendar and notes on Daya's interview guide came back with a whole series of blanks. Daya's volunteered narratives thus had to supplement what the LEC failed to capture.

Daya's erasure – in Sri Lankan culture and law, in the carceral setting, and in the research – thus may be consequential in situating them as someone who feels free to tweak the 'facts' of their life to create a world more meaningful to them. Their erasure in fact may necessitate it. Wijewardene's (2007, p. 101) analysis of Sri Lankan transmen's gender identities explores how they 'are continuously thrown back on their own imaginative resources to frame their gender difference. Self-perceptions have served as the only resource in their lives to represent themselves with dignity in a society violently intolerant of gender diversity.' Similarly, Daya's stories cannot be discounted as mere fantasies; they had a bearing on the trajectory of their life path. As Miller et al. (2015, p. 70) suggest, 'people have a tendency to behave in conformity with the self-stories they have created around themselves.' Daya's self-stories bolstered an exceptional identity: they were the gem that Lankan culture was blind to.

Transacting Meaning: Tellers and Listeners

Yet, everyone involved in the research – the principal researchers, research assistants, welfare officers and guards at the prison – displayed far more scepticism towards Daya's story than towards the stories of the other interview participants. Indeed, while Carmen was speaking to Daya, the guards not only hovered around with amused smiles on their faces that conveyed familiarity with Daya's *modus operandi* but later gave Carmen friendly advice on taking their stories with the proverbial grain of salt. Our second consideration, then, is this: Did Daya become an outlier *because* of what they said, or had the study anyway been designed to consign someone like them to the category of the outlier?

There were additional implicit assumptions about women's pathways to incarceration inflecting the study, some located in local gender norms, others drawn from the findings of (mostly American) feminist criminology (Daly, 1992; Gaarder & Belknap, 2002; Simpson, Yahner, & Dugan, 2008). These included the centrality in the LEC and interview guide of intimate relationships, intimate partner control and violence, and childhood neglect and abuse. Such foci framed incarcerated women through a monolithic feminine gender identity which positioned them as recipients – not instigators – of violence (see Allen, 1987). Moreover, some feminist scholars have noted that gendered cultural assumptions, including that 'women have a different relationship to offending than men…[that] crime is almost always stigmatizing for women' (Fleetwood, 2015, p. 44), and that it is 'doubly deviant when engaged in by women and girls' (Miller et al., 2015, p. 72), mean that women who opt for or 'fall into' criminal pursuits must resort to culturally validated narratives as a means of 'gendered repair work' (Fleetwood, 2015, p. 50). This entails fitting their offending/norm-violating trajectories into culturally endorsed narratives that garner understanding, if not sympathy, from the listener.

This is the case in Sri Lanka, as elsewhere. Studying Sri Lankan women migrant workers, Gamburd (2000) devotes a chapter to the role of the 'horror story genre,' which facilitates such women's presentation as self-sacrificing mothers whose migration decisions carry only pain, no gain, for the woman worker. Miller (2002, p. 1055) has highlighted the obverse: *How* the dominant Lankan narrative that equates 'good' women with sexual purity can push young unmarried women, who have been 'duped' into premarital sex through false promises, into sex work.

Considered in light of these insights, Daya patently refused the invitation to 'do gender' in this way and did not engage in feminised repair work in narrating their life of offending. Their violent assault on the man left with a 'lifeless' arm is atypical; and while Daya's account of his attempt to sexually harm them provides what might be termed a typical feminine motivation for retaliation – acts of violence in order to protect one's 'chastity' being not just culturally validated but even demanded in Lankan cultures – Daya nevertheless took pride in having turned his arm 'lifeless,' teaching him a lesson for 'messing with' the wrong person, their explicitly retaliatory stance more akin to the expected performance of masculinity in Sri Lanka.

Now to the question of why the same scepticism did not manifest itself towards the narratives of women in the study. Is it that their stories were congruent with some familiar trajectory into offending for the 'typical' Sri Lankan crime-involved woman? According to French literary theorist Gérard Genette, 'plausibility' and 'propriety,' or *vraisemblance* and *bienseance*, are connected. They are 'wedded to each other; and the precondition of plausibility is the stamp of approval affixed by public opinion' (Miller, 1985, p. 340). So, let us consider the following fact: except for one, none of the other study participants said they would return to a life of offending upon release, all of them describing their present incarceration as marking a turning point in their lives for the better. The one exception was herself noteworthy. Incarcerated for drug sales, she first articulated the normative narrative when asked what advice she had for other women: 'Prison is not the place for women. I would not want something like this to happen to anyone else. I won't go anywhere near drugs hereafter. I will not do this ever.' Yet right after, queried about what she would do upon release, she resorted to a Sinhala figure of speech alluding to her continuation in the drug field: 'I will continue with this. A person who falls into a pit must come through the mouth of that very same pit.'

Even women with previous histories of incarceration said they would desist from offending. They also resolved to be 'good' – either taking to a religious life as *sil maatha* (i.e. an interim status for Buddhist women who are not ordained as nuns but observe 10 precepts rather than the 5 that lay Buddhists are required to observe) or living with family members who would help them stay away from their 'old life.' Most of the women adopted plotlines available to Sri Lankan women to explain their crimes: they were innocent or unwitting victims initiated into a life of offending by men and remaining in it for reasons of poverty. Considering the conventional Sri Lankan gender norms that engender passivity and subordination among women, such stories were credible and plausible. Others claimed ignorance or lack of intent: a woman incarcerated for forgery said she didn't know what she had done; another said she didn't know the value of the gold necklace she had taken and, in any case, meant to return it the next day; yet another convicted of fraud claimed she had not meant to cheat people and intended all along to return the monies but, alas, had been arrested before she could do so. There was no inclination among the researchers to disbelieve or discount these narratives. Yet are they more truthful than Daya's except that we used 'common sense' in deeming them more plausible?

Just one further example would suffice. Two of the RAs were interviewing Maduri, who was narrating a sad tale relating to her life selling drugs. The story had both the teller and the two listeners crying, as witnessed by Carmen who was at the prison on this occasion. Maduri's story contained all the ingredients of a plotline familiar to us in the Sri Lankan context: a first-time offender, led to offending by poverty and a life of deprivation, drawn into crime by the man she loved. As she was in the middle of this very moving story, the guards announced that she was being transferred to another prison in preparation for release. Maduri jumped for joy and got up from the table with alacrity after bidding the RAs goodbye. We were all happy for her. The guards had observed this exchange from afar and were quick to offer their own counternarrative: 'Oh don't worry Miss, she will be back very soon. This is not her first time.' We can only speculate about how many other stories fit neatly the grooves of familiar plotlines and thus were deemed credible, so much so that no similar alarm bells went off in our minds about whether these women were telling the truth or how we might 'triangulate' to verify or understand their stories. Most study participants were happy to present themselves as poor hapless victims, and we were only too happy to accept them as such. In this way, it is perhaps irrelevant whether the participants themselves knew when they were being untruthful or whether it is simply second nature to fit one's story into a popular plotline ready at hand.

Conclusion

We may conclude from the above that not only are study participants fitting their stories into familiar storylines, perhaps giving the researchers what they think the latter wish to hear, but researchers instinctively detect such storylines, are quick to place them in such familiar moulds, and even to give them the status of 'truth,' whether in a more traditional, naturalist way, or in narrative criminology's grounding of stories in the presumed available repertoire of larger storylines available in a given cultural context. Whether conducting interviews or engaged in observation, researchers unavoidably make use of their own cognitive and interpretive schemas to 'make sense' of what we see and hear. There is no 'raw' data that are prior to selection, arrangement and interpretation by the researcher. Indeed, we co-construct stories with our study participants, as they consider and assess what stories we wish to hear based on who we are and how we react to their tellings. This suggests narratives that are obvious lies or plainly inconsistent are no less valid than those that better fit our commonsensical understandings of what is 'probable' or, a la Genette, more appropriate (*bienseance*). Indeed, our notions of the probable are as much influenced by post-Enlightenment emphases on verifiable truths as the 'realist' interest in verisimilitude. Even checking for accuracy to weed out truth from untruth, such as our efforts at triangulating Daya's story, won't do, and our attempt at doing so admittedly shows us falling back on more naturalist assumptions about our data.

Distortions, exaggerations and lies – as much as storylines that uphold verisimilitude – are part of the human effort to 'put order' and make sense of life though 'life' itself should not be perceived as occupying some *a priori* position in relation to narrative. In that sense, the stories we tell ourselves and others, whether factual, coherent or consistent, have validity in understanding pathways to incarceration and, more broadly, the human experience. Daya's story has taught us at least one important insight for narrative criminology: it is necessary to push beyond the seemingly easy 'fit' between stories and familiar cultural plotlines. These, too, would otherwise take on a quality of verisimilitude that may stifle our efforts to understand individuals, their social worlds and the place of narrative within these. Indeed, Jonathan Swift's *Gulliver's Travels* took us there nearly three centuries ago with the insight that human invention is a means of arriving at truth.

References

Abrams, M. H., Adams, R. M., Daiches, D., Donaldson, E. T., Ford, G. H., Lipking, L., ... Smith, H. (Eds.). (1962). Introduction: The restoration and the eighteenth century. In *The Norton Anthology of English literature* (4th ed., Vol. 1). New York, NY: W. W. Norton & Company.

Allen, H. (1987). Rendering them harmless: The professional portrayal of women charged with serious violent crimes. In P. Carlen & A. Worral (Eds.), *Gender, crime and justice* (pp. 81–94). Bristol: Open University Press.

de Alwis, M. (1996). The production and embodiment of respectability: Gendered demeanours in Colonial Ceylon. In M. Roberts (Ed.), *Sri Lanka: Collective identities revisited* (pp. 105–143). Colombo: Marga Institute.

Auerbach, E. (1953). *Mimesis: The representation of reality in Western literature*. Princeton, NJ: Princeton University Press.

Copes, H., & Hochstetler, A. (2010). Interviewing the incarcerated: Pitfalls and promises. In W. Bernasco (Ed.), *Offenders on offending: Learning about crime from criminals* (pp. 49–67). Cullompton, UK: Willan.

Daly, K. (1992). Women's pathways to felony court: Feminist theories of lawbreaking and problems of representation. *Review of Law and Women's Studies, 2*, 11–52.

Dean, J. P., & Whyte, W. F. (1958). How do you know if the informant is telling the truth? *Human Organization, 17*, 34–38.

Department of Census and Statistics, Sri Lanka. (2012). Percentage of population aged 10 years and over in major ethnic groups by district and ability to speak Sinhala, Tamil and English Languages. Retrieved from http://www.statistics.gov.lk/ Accessed on July 3, 2018.

Department of Prisons, Sri Lanka. (2017). Retrieved from http://www.prisons.gov.lk/Statistics/statistic_english.html.

Felman, S. (1989). Woman and madness: The critical phallacy. In C. Belsey & J. Moore (Eds.), *The feminist reader: Essays in gender and the politics of literary criticism* (pp. 133–155). New York, NY: Basil Blackwell.

Fleetwood, J. (2015). In search of respectability: Narrative practice in a women's prison in Quito, Ecuador. In L. Presser & S. Sandberg (Eds.), *Narrative criminology: Understanding stories of crime* (pp. 42–68). New York, NY: New York University Press.

Foucault, M. (1972). *The archaeology of knowledge and the discourse on language.* New York, NY: Pantheon Books.

Gaarder, E., & Belknap, J. (2002). Tenuous borders: Girls transferred to adult court. *Criminology, 40*, 481–517.

Gamburd, M. R. (2000). *The kitchen spoon's handle: Transnationalism and Sri Lanka's migrant housemaids.* Ithaca, NY: Cornell University Press.

Henley, A. (1973). The abandoned child. In C. D. Bryant & J. G. Wells (Eds.), *Deviancy and the family* (pp. 199–208). Philadelphia, PA: F. A. Davis.

Institute for Participatory Interaction in Development. (2016). *Rapid situation assessment of transgender persons in Sri Lanka* Self-published by Institute for Participatory Interaction in Development. Dehiwala, Sri Lanka.

Jerolmack, C., & Khan, S. (2014). Talk is cheap: Ethnography and the attitudinal fallacy. *Sociological Methods & Research, 43*, 178–209.

Kapferer, B. (1991). *A celebration of demons: Exorcism and the aesthetics of healing in Sri Lanka.* Bloomington, IN: Indiana University Press.

Kapferer, B. (1997). *The feast of the sorcerer: Practices of consciousness and power.* Chicago, IL and London: University of Chicago Press.

Kuru-Utumpala, J. (2013). Butching it up: An analysis of same sex masculinity in Sri Lanka. *Culture, Health & Sexuality, 15*, 153–166.

Lynch, C. (2007). *Juki girls, good girls: Gender and cultural politics in Sri Lanka's global garment industry.* Ithaca, NY: Cornell University Press.

MacCabe, C. (1985). *Theoretical essays: Film, linguistics, literature.* Manchester: Manchester University Press.

Maruna, S. (2001). *Making good: How ex-convicts reform and rebuild their lives.* Washington, DC: American Psychological Association.

Miller, J. (2002). Violence and coercion in Sri Lanka's commercial sex industry: Intersections of gender, sexuality, culture, and the law. *Violence Against Women, 8*, 1044–1072.

Miller, J. (2010). The impact of gender when studying 'offenders on offending'. In W. Bernasco & M. Tonry (Eds.), *Offenders on offending: Learning about crime from criminals* (pp. 161–183). London: Willan Publishing.

Miller, J. (2013, June). Women's incarceration in Sri Lanka: Patterns, pathways and contexts. Presentation at the Women in Prison: Risk Factors and Consequences Conference, Phoolan Devi Institute, VU University, Amsterdam, Netherlands.

Miller, J. (2017, June). Sex work, violence, and identity in Sri Lanka: Observations of continuity and change via ethnographic returning. Presentation at the Workshop on Longitudinal Ethnographies of Violence, Netherlands Institute for the Study of Crime and Law Enforcement, Amsterdam, Netherlands.

Miller, J., Carbone-Lopez, K., & Gunderman, M. V. (2015). Gendered narratives of self, addiction, and recovery among women methamphetamine users. In L. Presser & S. Sandberg (Eds.), *Narrative criminology: Understanding stories of crime* (pp. 69–95). New York, NY: New York University Press.

Miller, J., & Glassner, B. (2011). The 'inside' and the 'outside': Finding realities in interviews. In D. Silverman (Ed.), *Qualitative Research: Theory, Method and Practice*, (3rd ed., pp. 131–148). London: Sage Publications.

Miller, J., & Nichols, A. (2012). Identity, sexuality and commercial sex among Sri Lankan nachchi. *Sexualities, 15*, 554–569.

Miller, N. K. (1985). Emphasis added: Plots and plausibilities in women's fiction. In E. Showalter (Ed.), *The new feminist criticism: Essays on women, literature and theory* (pp. 339–361). New York, NY: Random House.

Nichols, A. (2010). 'Dance Ponnaya, dance!' police abuses against transgender sex workers in Sri Lanka. *Feminist Criminology, 5*, 195–222.

Presser, L. (2009). The narratives of offenders. *Theoretical Criminology, 13*, 177–200.

Presser, L. (2013). *Why we harm*. Piscataway, NJ: Rutgers University Press.

Presser L. (2016). Criminology and the narrative turn. *Crime, Media, Culture, 12*, 137–151.

Presser, L. (2018). *Inside story: How narratives drive mass harm*. Berkeley, CA: University of California Press.

Presser, L., & Sandberg, S. (2015). Introduction: What is the story? In L. Presser & S. Sandberg (Eds.), *Narrative criminology: Understanding stories of crime* (pp. 1–20). New York, NY: New York University Press.

Rajakarunanayake, L. (2018). Say 'cheers' to women who raise their glasses. *The Island*, January 20. http://www.island.lk/index.php?page_cat=article-details&page=article-details&code_title=178443. Accessed on January 20, 2018.

Rich, A. (1980). Compulsory heterosexuality and lesbian existence. *Signs, 5*, 631–660.

Sandberg, S. (2010). What can 'lies' tell us about life? Notes towards a framework of narrative criminology. *Journal of Criminal Justice Education, 21*, 447–465.

Simpson, S. S., Yahner, J. L., & Dugan, L. (2008). Understanding women's pathways to jail: Analyzing the lives of incarcerated women. *Australian and New Zealand Journal of Criminology, 41*, 84–108.

Swift, J. (1726/1967). *Gulliver's travels*. London: Penguin Books.

Tognato, C. (2015). Narratives of tax evasion: The cultural legitimacy of harmful behavior. In L. Presser & S. Sandberg (Eds.), *Narrative criminology:*

Understanding stories of crime (pp. 260–286). New York, NY: New York University Press.

Walder, D. (1995). Reading *great expectations*. In D. Walder (Ed.), *The realist novel* (pp. 139–170). London: Routledge.

Watt, I. (1956). *The rise of the novel: Studies in Defoe, Richardson and Fielding.* Berkeley & Los Angeles, CA: University of California Press.

Wijewardene, S. (2007). 'But no one has explained to me who I am now...': 'Trans' self-perceptions in Sri Lanka. In S. E. Wieringa, E. Blackwood, & A. Bhaiya (Eds.), *Women's sexualities and masculinities in a globalizing Asia* (pp. 101–116). New York, NY: Palgrave MacMillan.

TEXTS

Chapter 7

By Terrorists' Own Telling: Using Autobiography for Narrative Criminological Research

Simon Copeland

Introduction

We live in an autobiographical age. Today, individuals from virtually every demographic are choosing to commit their lives to print (Plummer, 2001; Yagoda, 2009). Autobiographies surrounding criminal and other deviant conduct play a special role in accounting for such conduct (Scott & Lyman, 1968). Since modern autobiography's genesis in Jean-Jacques Rousseau's 'transformation of "confession" into a secular, public, and purely literary gesture' (Mendelsohn, 2010), autobiography and criminality have necessarily been entwined. Cultural theorist Michael Mascuch (1997), for example, argues that the contemporary popularity of autobiography can, at least in part, be traced to public demand for the gallows confessions of the notorious 'London hanged'. Today, autobiographical accounts not only influence how the general public understands criminality and crime but also how participants understand themselves and their actions. Criminal autobiographies are now some of the most commonly read works within prisons (James, 2016). This chapter argues that autobiographies present a unique, if underutilised, resource for narrative criminological researchers to access stories that relate to crime and criminality. Whilst practically and theoretically difficult to work with, these texts comprise a mass of smaller stories that relate to the incidents, events, places and characters encountered over the course of a lifetime. I argue that the richness of autobiography, something of obvious interest to narrative criminologists, can be properly exploited with reference to analytic strategies derived from literary criticism.

Whilst traditionally dominated by the accounts of notorious or otherwise exemplary offenders, burgeoning public demand for different kinds of autobiography has encouraged a broader range of individuals to have accounts of their experiences heard (Campbell, 2016; Lawson, 2015). Subgenres of potential interest include the personal accounts of police officers (see, for example, Goddard, 1956); 'hit and tell' memoirs of soccer hooligans (Pennant, 2000); white-collar criminals (Guppy, 1996); gang members (Shakur, 2004); drug users

(Dresner, 2017); those involved in racially, politically and ethnically motivated crimes, including genocide (Balakian, 2010; Ngor, 1988); and prisoners (Senghor, 2017). The prevalence of these texts offers a potentially profitable source of data for researchers interested in virtually all forms of criminality and related behaviours. In light of some observers' contentions that 'life-course criminology...now is criminology' (Cullen, 2011, p. 310), the ability of autobiography to provide a means to explore individuals' criminal trajectories is obvious. As such, existing criminological research has demonstrated how published autobiographies can help explain behavioural change and desistence among offenders (see, for example, Maruna, 1997; Poulton, 2012). Given narrative criminology's focus on the role of stories in instigating, sustaining and effecting changes in individuals' participation in harmful action (Presser, 2009; Presser & Sandberg, 2015), I argue that autobiographies then present an exceptional form of data. Furthermore, as I will explore, narrative criminology's underlying concern with what stories do rather than how authentic or objectively truthful they are (Presser, 2009) negates a central problem that has hampered the use of autobiographies in various research contexts.

As the number and diversity of individuals writing autobiographies increase, so too do opportunities to examine the self-accounts of populations that are either otherwise extremely difficult or impossible for the researcher to access (including those who are deceased). Through autobiography it is possible to examine the accounts of extremely broad demographics of individuals in terms of both context and time period (Altier, Horgan, & Thoroughgood, 2012). Such texts are unique in other ways. For one, they are carefully considered and assembled over a period of time that allows for significant reflection and reworking (Colmer, 1989). Relatedly, this writing process may be undertaken with the assistance of others such as ghost writers or coauthors. The inclusion of additional authors in the production of autobiographical texts has led some to query whether the protagonists at the heart of these accounts retain ownership of these self-narratives (Woodward & Jenkings, 2018, p. 213). Confusingly, some researchers have chosen to exclude coauthored autobiographies from their studies whilst nevertheless including other accounts produced with the help of a ghost writer (Altier, Boyle, Shortland, & Horgan, 2017, p. 314). Authorship in solo-written autobiography is similarly frequently presented as 'unproblematic, singular and personal' (Woodward & Jenkings, 2018, p. 191). Such understanding necessarily belies the co-constructed characteristic of all narratives. Relatedly, autobiographies constitute a literary and physical product as well as text – something that commonly necessitates the input of others rather than the author alone. French literary theorist Gérard Genette coined the term 'paratexts' to refer to those elements of a literary work – titles, subtitles, cover artwork, photographs, prologues, forewords and introductions – that render it comprehensible and consumable to the reader in the form of a book (1997, p. 1). Although paratexts may appear to sit outside of the author's self-narrative, given that they nevertheless inevitably impact on how a text is read, they cannot be discounted from any interrogation of these texts.

This chapter takes issues regarding authorship and paratexts in autobiography as its starting point. Crucially, like many narrative researchers, I argue that all narratives are co-constructed. This not only promotes a more nuanced understanding of self-narratives but also avoids many of the definitional knots that researchers have tied themselves up in in attempting to disaggregate autobiographies by the varying level of external input in their production. In light of this position, I therefore also argue that an autobiography's paratextual components should necessarily be considered part of its narrative. Equally, I hope to demonstrate how paratexts can provide new avenues to further the interrogation of the authors' self-narratives. After considering these theoretical issues this chapter presents an example that demonstrates certain strategies for breaking down, organising and analysing autobiographical texts. Whilst my own research examines a corpus of terrorist authored autobiographies, here, scrutinising a single account provides a more useful example.

In 2006 American citizen, Omar Hammami (also known as Abu Mansuur al-Amriiki) travelled to Somalia to join Islamist militant group al-Shabaab. His 127-page autobiography, *The Story of an American Jihadi: Part One*, uploaded to the internet in 2012, provides a detailed recollection of his life growing up in the US, a drawn-out journey through various countries culminating in jihad and experience as a member of al-Shabaab. Released shortly after he had publically broken away from the group, Hammami was killed by his former comrades before the publication of any subsequent volumes that his title implies he had planned to author (BBC, 2013). Nevertheless, his autobiography is recognised by security analysts and academic researchers as one of the most extensive accounts of a Western jihadist (Anzalone, 2012). However, before addressing how this analysis of Hammami's account may be undertaken, I turn to an overview of autobiography's use in the study of terrorism more generally.

Autobiography and the Study of Terrorism

Public consumption of autobiographies authored by terrorists, similar to other criminal counterparts, dates back to the turn of the twentieth century (see, for example, Berkman, 1912; Savinkov, 1917). More recently, autobiographies written by terrorists have become best sellers (Stone, 2003; O'Callaghan, 1998) and have even been met with critical acclaim (McDonald, 2014). Significantly for counterterrorism practitioners, there also exists a body of accounts by individuals who have turned back from the path of extremism (Husain, 2007; Kaddouri, 2011). Whilst autobiographical texts have been fruitfully explored by a limited number of academics and researchers who seek to understand the ideological or psychological milieu in which individuals engage in militancy (Holbrook, 2017; della Porta, 2013, 2006; Ramsay, 2013; Youngman, 2016),[1] for the most part they have received less than systematic analysis despite a long-standing recognition of their potential as a source of detailed information (Altier et al., 2012; Cordes, 1987; Rapoport, 1987). Within terrorism studies, the most prominent approach

---

[1]Here autobiographies provide important primary source material and form one part of a wider corpus of information about militant movements, especially when read alongside manifestos and other interviews and statements.

towards the analysis of terrorist autobiographies has focused on identifying and coding the occurrence of incidents and episodes for the purpose of both quantitative (see, for example, Altier et al., 2012; Gill, 2015; Shapiro & Siegel, 2012) and qualitative (Acharya & Muldoon, 2017) analysis.

These methodological shortcomings are to be expected given that, for all the recent interest in countering extremist narratives in terrorism studies, the discipline is generally characterised by a limited understanding of narrative that rests solely on a small body of psychological literature (Copeland, 2018; Glazzard, 2017).[2] Relatedly, in treating narrative accounts as either subjective or objective records of events, researchers in this area are hamstrung by perennial questions of authenticity and truthfulness when working with terrorist autobiographies. Narrative criminologists, by contrast, have already demonstrated how research underpinned by a different theoretical paradigm, that holds that the relationship between narrative and experience is dynamic and inextricable and that stories are constitutive antecedents to harm, can significantly increase our understanding of individuals' engagement in political violence (Colvin & Pisoiu, 2018; Cottee & Hayward, 2011; Joosse, Bucerius, & Thompson, 2015). Included are insights gained through the analysis of autobiographical texts (Berntzen & Sandberg, 2014; Sandberg, 2013; Sandberg, Oksanen, Berntzen, & Kiilakoski, 2014). Such research holds obvious relevance for practitioners responsible for countering violent extremism – many of whom state that their aim is to counter, provide alternatives to, and/or develop resilience against, extremist narratives (Copeland, 2018; Glazzard, 2017).

Defining Autobiography

Recognised as a distinctive literary genre since the late eighteenth century, autobiography has become the publically recognised mode for individuals to provide and present an account of their life (Smith & Watson, 2010, p. 4). According to literary theorist Philippe Lejeune's classic definition, autobiography comprises a 'retrospective prose narrative written by a real person concerning his own existence, where the focus is his individual life, in particular the story of his personality' (1989, p. 4). In its common usage, the term 'autobiography' is often taken as synonymous and employed interchangeably with 'memoir' and 'memoirs'. However, analysts of life writing commonly draw a terminological division here. Typically inward facing and self-reflective, autobiography focusses on the development of the self over time, usually the course of one's life (Yagoda, 2009, p. 1). By contrast, the term 'memoir' has historically been associated with recollections of a narrower scope that focus primarily on the deeds and accomplishments, rather than the lives in their entirety, of prominent public figures (Smith & Watson, 2010, p. 3). An early choice for the analyst then is to decide

---

[2]Commonly this research relies heavily on the work of psychologist Dan McAdams (1988, 1993). However, unlike other psychologists who work on narrative, such as Jerome Bruner (1990) or Donald Polkinghorne (1988), McAdams makes little reference to any literary theory of narrative, instead drawing on Erik H. Erikson's work on identity (1968, 1975).

whether to include both memoir and autobiography in their research. In particular, memoir may prove useful for the close examination of certain events or behaviours, whilst autobiography also reveals the integration of these events into individuals' understandings of their whole lives as lived.

This initial consideration aside, the process of defining autobiography/memoirs then appears fairly straightforward. However, one issue has dogged the genre – accusations that the self-narratives contained within autobiographies are not the author's own but rather are someone else's reading and assemblage of their life story. Woodward and Jenkings in their study of military autobiographies, for example, note the common criticism made of these texts which dismisses them as 'only the product of slick publishing machines and competent ghostwriters' (2018, p. 213). In a similar manner to Polletta's assertion that who it is telling their story impacts on how it is received (2006, p. 3), such accusations are levelled at some individuals or demographics more than others. For example, celebrities are frequently questioned as to their level of input in their own autobiographies (Mendelsohn, 2010). Even within the same genre, authors of different standings are met with different levels of suspicion. For example, generals and officers are commonly given more ownership and credit for the production of their autobiographical narratives than are supposedly less educated, lower ranking members of the military (Woodward & Jenkings, 2018, p. 191). Significantly, criminal and terrorist autobiographies, especially those published in commercial settings, are frequently met with charges that ghost writers and coauthors exercised undue control over the writing of these texts (Hopkins, 2013, p. 69).

Lejeune approaches issues of authorship by arguing that 'in order for there to be autobiography … the author, the narrator, and the protagonist must be identical' (1989, p.5). An 'autobiographical pact' is entered into whereby the autobiographer affirms to the reader that they alone occupy all three of these roles – or in other words, that it is their narrative voice explaining events that (to some extent at least) really happened. The signature of the author's name appearing on the cover page forms the most vivid symbol of this pact in making reference to a world that exists beyond the text. In the case of fictional autobiography, this pact is incomplete because the protagonist differs from the author and is a character who exists only within the world of the text. However, a fundamental challenge to the autobiographical pact comes in the form of texts that present themselves as autobiography whilst simultaneously bearing the name of an additional author as well as that of the protagonist. Relatedly, texts that do not include the name of another writer often nevertheless reveal the concerted input of such a person in their paratexts.

Within literary studies Sandra Lindemann has explored texts that encompass a 'written account of a subject's life produced by a writer, on the basis of an oral account produced by the subject, over the course of a series of interviews' (2017, p. 1). Others have referred to such works as 'dictated autobiography' (Sanders, 1994), 'as-told-to autobiography' (Couser, 2004) or in Lejeune's terms 'the autobiography of those who do not write' (1989). These critics recognise that a middle ground between individual autobiography (wherein the author, narrator and subject are one and the same) and biography exists where a professional writer offers assistance to the protagonist in telling their story (Couser, 2004, pp. 34–35). However, for the most part researchers who seek to use autobiography as a means of accessing individuals' self-narratives do not engage in any more than a superficial consideration of the construction of such works. Instead, a false dichotomy exists in the approach to these texts; the self-narratives in single-authored autobiographies are taken as entirely the authors' own whilst, by contrast, those from accounts that openly acknowledge the input of an additional author are given short order because of a perception that they cannot be attributed to one individual alone. The result in some research has been arbitrary distinctions as to which texts merit exclusion that do not hold up under closer scrutiny (Altier et al., 2017).

Efforts to disaggregate autobiographies by authorial input quickly collapse in practice given the sheer diversity of how these texts are composed. The idea that the self-narratives contained within such accounts can be attributed to a single individual is unsustainable for a number of reasons. First, in the production of virtually every autobiography, editors, proofreaders and an array of individuals asked to provide feedback on the text exercise a degree of input over the final text. More importantly, the premise that any narrative, even those that relate entirely to ourselves, are the possession of any single individual has been rejected by many scholars of narrative. Mikhail Bakhtin, for example, argues that language in itself is fundamentally pervaded by the words of others – those who have come before the speaker and have shaped it usage (1981, 1986). In this sense, 'every word, expression, utterance, or narrative bear the traces of all subjects, possible and real, who ever used or will use this word, expression, utterance, or narrative' (Brockmeier & Harré, 2001, p. 46). Culture also fundamentally impacts not only the stories we tell about ourselves but how we tell them. As Jerome Bruner argues, in writing our autobiographies we necessarily 'become variants of the culture's canonical forms' (Bruner, 1987, p. 15). Without seeking to delve too far into discussions of narrative's fundamentally co-constructed nature, it should be recognised that all stories are never entirely our own. Autobiographies, even those that list only a single author, should then be recognised as collaborative social activities. A case can be made to include texts that satisfy Lejune's autobiographical pact to the extent that the narrator, and the protagonist and at least one of the authors are all the same. Crucially, all such texts, even those that include significant collaboration in their production, nevertheless reveal more about the self-narratives of the protagonist and the behaviours they engage in than initially apparent.

Paratexts

When approaching an autobiography, a reader or analyst is not met by an unadorned textual account of the author's life. Rather, this self-account is subsumed within a collection of paratexts, at a minimum usually a front cover (with title and artwork) and some form of introduction or foreword to the work. These apparently supplementary elements make an autobiography a physical and broadly cultural product as well as a text. Here the literary designs of the author meet the social and commercial expectations that relate to the process of publishing a text (Genette, 1997). Given that paratexts exist and present as something of a transitional space between the inside and outside of a text, how then should these elements be incorporated into the analysis?

Whilst paratexts may appear as tangential to the text they accompany, they are always a constituent, if somewhat subordinate, element of a text's narrative (Genette, 1997, p. 12). They perform a significant role in signalling that texts should be read in a certain way, i.e. as autobiography. In particular, prologues, forewords, quotations and introductions as well as photographs of the protagonist at different stages of their life are all paratextual conventions associated with autobiography. The importance of this paratextual function is seen in the considerable lengths terrorists who publish their own autobiographies go to mimic this form. American domestic terrorist and Olympic Park bomber Eric Rudolph, for example, includes an effusive 'about the author' section in his self-published account that mimics both the form and language of promotional material seen on conventional autobiographies in proclaiming that 'Rudolph has never before spoken about his case' (2013, p. 235). Paratexts can be broken down into those that relate to either the written or visual presentation of a text. Addressing each of these elements in turn, I then seek to demonstrate both how paratexts may be incorporated into the analysis of autobiographies and what they reveal about the authors' self-narratives.

Written Introductions to the Text

Autobiographies typically contain an array of dedications, acknowledgements, prefaces, prologues, forewords, introductions, author's notes, publisher's notes that precede and offer some form of written introduction to the main text. Significantly, prologues and introductions allow authors and analysts to explore the processes of remembering and forgetting and how new meanings and explanations emerged during the production of these texts. It is rare for autobiographies to not contain some form of introspective assessment regarding the process of their production within paratextual components. The introductions or prologues of a number of terrorists' autobiographies speak directly to the dynamic and inseparable relationship of narrative and experience. Former M-19 guerrilla María Eugenia Vásquez Perdomo, for example, describes how she discovered meaning in the process of recalling her life in the preface to her autobiography. She recalls how:

> Meaning is granted by the purpose of narrated memory. In the autobiography a memory is unfurled for something or someone. In this respect there are no naïve memories…the written words and I influenced each other, we affected each other always. Thanks to this exercise, I found meanings and explanations that had been invisible to me (2005, pp. xxxiii–xxxiiv).

The introductions found in autobiographies are then unique in providing a space for individuals to explicitly discuss the process of recounting one's life and how such undertaking impacted upon their understandings of their own experiences. These explanations provide valuable insight into why individuals comprehend and tell their lives in certain ways.

Introductions also provide space for authors to explore the considerable undertaking that producing an autobiographical account of one's life entails. For active or former terrorists, writing such text can also be a dangerous act. Terrorists who have published revelatory or critical accounts of the groups they were once part of have been murdered by their former comrades (*Irish Times*, 1999; O'Kane, 1999). An interesting question to ask then is how does the act of producing an autobiography fit into the authors' self-narratives? The written introduction to the text provides space for authors to explore this question in discussing why they have chosen to produce an autobiography. However, it is this area more than any contained within autobiography that appears susceptible to trope – or commonly recurring literary and rhetorical devices, motifs or clichés. Numerous terrorists conform to the 'humility topos' that is a fixture of modern autobiography more generally (Sutton, 2015, p. 211), in affirming that after many requests, and much resistance on their part, they have only now begrudgingly accepted to author such an account of their life.

Relatedly, many present their intentions in publishing an account of their life as selfless – something that they hope can discourage others from following a similar troubled path to their own (see, for example, Black, 2017; al-Bahri, 2013). The understanding that one's own experiences and life story may impact in a positive way then becomes an important part of the evolving story that individuals tell about themselves and their life – or their narrative identity (see also Presser, 2004, 2008). David Hamilton, a former combatant from Northern Ireland, for example, states 'I pray god may use this book to reach other "hopeless cases"' (1997). Given that his personal narrative is ultimately redemptive, encompassing his own descent into violence and depravity before finding god at his lowest point in prison and turning his life around, the act of writing an autobiography performs a number of functions in integrating his past, present and future selves. In particular, it transforms his past experience and transgressions into something good that relates to how he understands himself now (as an example to others) and his future (in helping save others as his religious adherence dictates).

Covers

Another subset of paratexts relate to the visual presentation of a work. The most obvious of these elements is the artwork found on their covers. However, whilst there has been interest amongst literary critics regarding the photographs that are frequently included within autobiographical texts, there remains relatively little analysis of the significance of these texts' front matter (Rambsy, 2009, p. 71). Nevertheless, as the first element of a text that a reader will encounter, the book covers are arguably more important to the reception of a text than has been recognised (Rambsy, 2009, p. 71; Woodward & Jenkings, 2012).

First, these covers visibly highlight the dynamic relationship between the personal and the social contained within all narratives. In the terrorist case, such images expose public narratives as pertaining to what terrorists and terrorism are expected to look like, something which terrorists' autobiographies then also reflect back in an effort to appeal to potential audiences. Unsurprisingly, the covers of terrorist autobiographies are dominated by visual symbols of violence. Many feature bullets (Giorgio, 2003) or guns (many of which such as the iconic AK-47 assault rifle also have revolutionary connotations in their own right – see, for example, O'Doherty, 2011; al-Bahri, 2013). Masked figures also feature prominently (Black, 2017; Conway, 2014). Obscuring the face serves to dehumanise these individuals and present them as 'others' who sit outside the bounds of normal society by way of their heinous acts. Relatedly, a common visual convention regards arranging the front cover so that a militant appears to be aiming a gun directly at the reader (Hamilton, 1997; Leslie, 2014; de Soyza, 2011), which stresses the threat such individuals pose to readers and the public more widely. Readers then expect that books with images of violent and dangerous men on the outside will contain narratives that speak to similar themes on the inside. However, often between text and cover a tension exists. For example, in their study of military autobiographies, Woodward and Jenkings argue that in regard to the masculine gendering of war 'covers of memoirs are complicit in promoting this model, even when the text problematises and destabilises this model' (2018, p. 364). Similarly, the autobiography of a number of terrorists from the conflict in Northern Ireland are a lot more revealing, and less violent, than the images of masked men on their covers suggest (Black, 2017; Collins, 1997). The researcher may then interrogate incongruities in how the image and the central text sit together – for example, in the case given above, the contradictions of tough masculinity in presenting an introspective account of necessarily violent lives.

A number of terrorist autobiographies have covers that chime with or attempt to reflect the textual accounts of the author. Closeup images of the author's face are used on the front covers of a number of accounts that ultimately seek to humanise celebrated or notorious terrorists (see, for example, Khaled, 1973; Stone, 2003; Yousef, 2010). Similarly, the cover of Alastair Little's *Give a Boy a Gun* (2009) subverts the image of a militant pointing a weapon towards the reader replacing this figure with that of young boy aiming a toy gun at the camera. Behind him soldiers interact with women and children in a scene that juxtaposes everyday life with the abnormality brought about by the ongoing conflict. Crucially, the image (and the book's title no less) speaks to the dominant narrative of Little's account – the innocence lost to the circumstances of his upbringing in conflict-torn Northern Ireland.

The imagery that adorns front covers also holds multiple layers of meaning. Omar Hammami's self-published autobiography (2012) centres around an image of the sun setting above the sea in what appears to be America. In the foreground a pier juts out towards the horizon. The narrative of the image may be read in many ways. It immediately conjures metaphorical notions of a long-distant goal or enlightenment – something that will require a journey to realise. Given that the path the pier provides quickly drops away, leaving only a mass of dark ocean, such a journey will require a leap into the unknown. This image therefore conforms to Hammami's self-narrative regarding the importance of his own spiritual, ideological and physical journey on the path for jihad (something I will return to later in greater detail). This main photograph is also overlaid with two smaller images. The top left-hand corner features an image of the black flag adorned with a white shahada (an Islamic creed) that has been commonly adopted by Islamist militant groups and has been used by al-Shabaab since 2006 (Jarle Hansen, 2013, p. 145). In the opposing bottom right corner, a box and segment of text, that appears to mimic the font and style of the 'breaking news' features of US news broadcasters, reads: 'Exclusive: US JIHADIST UNVEILED'. Hammami's chosen nom de guerre sits in the middle. Such a layout then juxtaposes the two worlds that he finds himself straddling as someone who grew up in America and whose outlook is firmly couched in Western sensibilities but who has nevertheless chosen to embrace a new world. His employment of a more abstract choice of cover than those used in the vast majority terrorist autobiographies also speaks to Hammami's egotistical self-narrative of himself as someone rendered an outsider because of his great intelligence. As this example demonstrates, interrogating the composition of the covers of autobiographies can help shed light on how their authors seek to present themselves and their influences in doing so.

Analysis in Practice

Autobiographies by their very nature present unruly texts to work with. They contain a mass of smaller stories, incidents, events, characters, places, cultural norms and expectations that their authors have encountered over their lifetime and thought salient enough to include in the telling of their lives. The scene that initially confronts the researcher can therefore be overwhelming, especially when working with a corpus of autobiographical texts. Strategies for breaking down, interrogating and managing the analysis of these detailed texts are therefore critical. Existing work within narrative criminology has demonstrated approaches that exploit the richness of autobiographical texts. For example, in his analysis of the autobiographical components of Anders Breivik's sprawling manifesto/compendium, Sandberg (2013) demonstrates a means for identifying and analysing the 'several, sometimes competing, self-narratives or characters' that the author utilises throughout (p. 75; see also Frank, 2012). However, in-depth descriptions of the methodological processes for organising the analysis of autobiographical texts are often missing from research.

To demonstrate how a number of strategies for analysing the different components found in autobiographical texts I again return to the account of American jihadist Omar Hammami. My aim here is to show how approaches drawn primarily from literary studies can be utilised to both analyse, and importantly systematically manage, the process of working with such detailed and unruly texts. Crucially, for narrative criminological research, these approaches also highlight the place of certain types of stories and storytelling in how individuals construct their autobiographies, and by extension understand their actions.

Constituent and Supplementary Events

Literary theorists have developed a number of means to break down and organise the events contained within a story. Roland Barthes and Seymour Chatman argue that a distinction can be made between constituent and supplementary events (Barthes uses the terms 'nuclei' and 'catalyzers' (1982, pp. 295–296) whilst Chatman refers to them as 'kernels' and 'satellites' (1978)). Constituent events are those that cannot be removed without fundamentally changing the story; they are the key turning points and events driving the story forward (Barthes, 1982, p. 267). Supplementary events, by contrast, can be taken away and whilst leaving the story, on the face of it at least, intact. Such understanding typically induces a hierarchy of events with constituent ones considered the more salient. However, as Barthes and Chatman both argue, the inclusion of additional and supposedly supplementary incidents raises a crucial question; since they are not necessary to the progress of the story why did the author feel obliged to include them in their account? Asking this question is often useful in the interpretation of autobiographical texts, especially given that these works are contrived and carefully assembled rather than spontaneously pulled together (Colmer, 1989).

Analysis of Omar Hammami's account has focused on key incidents and 'turning points' – in other words, constituent events – that appear to account for his deepening ideological commitment and sense of marginalisation in the US (see, for example, Mastors & Siers, 2014). However, inclusions in his account that may at first appear supplementary nevertheless prove important. At the beginning of his autobiography Hammami includes a long, rambling and often contradictory family history. In particular, he goes off on something of a tangent in an effort to paint a picture of his mother's side of the family as being characterised by delinquency – variously describing relatives as 'bootleggers' and 'known to be rowdy' (2012, p. 4) – despite admitting that he has little knowledge of and has met few of these characters. In describing these supplementary events Hammami also makes the rather outlandish claim that 'I think having the IRA on one side of my family tree and al-Qaacidah on the other might have given me a bit of a bad temperament' (2012, p. 8). The 'IRA' side of his family is a reference to his mother's family, whom he states are of 'Irish decent' (2012, p. 4) whilst the Syrian heritage of his father is presumably his 'al-Qaacidah' side – though there is nothing to suggest that either side have any link with these terrorist groups (he is also either unaware or unconcerned that their Protestant background would prohibit their membership or support of the predominantly Catholic IRA).

Nevertheless, his refashioning of his family is important for how he understands his own move towards and engagement in terrorism. In particular, he draws on a narrative that involvement in political struggle, much like criminality or other forms of deviancy, runs in certain families and somehow accounts for his own confrontational nature. In this sense, he understands and gives meaning to the idea that his own involvement was preordained. Supplementary events then often carry a significant burden of meaning, something which may commonly be overlooked in the search for key moments or incidents. Analysts should bear this in mind when breaking texts down. In Hammami's case they provide new insight into how he understands himself, his actions and the impact of his family upon his engagement in political violence.

Genre

Presser and Sandberg have highlighted how offenders' self-narratives draw upon standard types or genres of stories (2015, p. 93). In their production, autobiographies also consciously or unconsciously conform to and take on the shape and characteristics of common literary genres such as epic, drama or tragedy. The genre to which a text conforms is usually identifiable not only through its content but also through the tone of the narration. The autobiographies of Palestinian terrorists, for example, frequently draw from the collective narratives of their social group and kin in being rooted in the genre of tragedy (see, for example, Khaled, 1973). Local storytelling conventions and features also condition how autobiographical narratives are told (Moore, 2010). Colombian revolutionary María Eugenia Vásquez Perdomo's autobiography (2005) is shaped, at least in part, by South American, and specifically Colombian, traditions of magical realism, a genre of narrative fiction and art that merges realistic depictions of the world with elements of magic and the supernatural (see, for example, the works of Luis Borges, Alberto Manguel and Gabriel García Márquez). Thus, in explaining conflicting aspects of her identity as a female militant and later a mother, Vásquez Perdomo makes reference to the idea that she is surrounded and inhabited by ghosts – something that she eventually ends up becoming herself.

Genres can also be further broken down into subgenres and narrative templates. For example, bildungsroman, or the 'coming of age' story that focuses on the psychological and moral growth of the protagonist from youth to adulthood, is a template frequently drawn upon by terrorists in narrating their physical and ideological moves to extremist positions (Deary, 2010, p. 81). Unsurprisingly, structures that frame the author as an embattled, lone hero are also popular among terrorists (cf. Aspden & Hayward, 2015, p. 253). Whilst drawing on both of these templates, Omar Hammami's light-hearted but egotistical narration also often resembles that of a picaresque novel – a genre of fiction that depicts a series of loosely connected episodes or adventures of a roguish but likable protagonist who survives a corrupt and hostile society by living on their wits (Kent & Gaunt, 1979). However, in their episodic telling, such tales are usually lacking a larger plot. Hammami's account by contrast employs a more rigid, and recognisable, narrative structures. In his classic work, *The Hero with a Thousand Faces* (1949), Joseph Campbell argues that all myths conform to the same underlying template that he terms the 'Hero's Journey'. Although Hammami's narration does not include all of the 17 different stages that every hero passes through in Campbell's original conceptualisation, it does draw on many of them, along with the same overarching structure.

Crucially, peers and family occupy a central role in how Hammami deploys this template. His description of outgrowing his hometown Salafi friends who, unlike him, were not prepared to embrace and travel abroad for jihad, speaks directly to the 'call to adventure' – a phase suggesting that the protagonist's initial ideals and settings are challenged when they become aware of a new and forbidden world (Campbell, 1949, p. 49). Similarly, he reframes his struggle to overcome the efforts of his family and friends to prevent him from travelling for jihad as merely the first test on the 'road of trials' that he, the protagonist, must surmount to achieve his goal, at times explicitly referencing the 'future trials' he would face (2012, p. 100). His declaration that he would 'walk from the south of Somalia to the north by foot if it would help matters' (2012, p. 42) with his wife, who wanted him to leave the battlefield, also speaks directly to the notion that those around him were subjecting him to tests to endure and another stage of the hero's journey, with 'the woman as temptress' who would derail it (Campbell, 1949, p. 120).

Crafting his account as a hero's journey performs a number of important tasks for Hammami, not least helping to repair to the rupture in his narrative identity brought about by his disillusionment and break from al-Shabaab. Having ultimately found being a member of a militant group disappointing and not what he had envisioned, he reframes the act of actually making it to Somalia and jihad as more important than any ends he achieves there. He states 'my biggest personal achievement is to have performed Hijrah [emigration] and to have engaged in Jihaad' (2012, p. 121). Talking up the challenges he had to overcome and the significance of what he has already achieved then smooths the crisis or lack of direction he faces at failing to achieve the goal he has pursued and focussed his life around.

For Hammami the presentation of one's life to an external audience carries a discernible goal: to inspire others. Although having broken from al-Shabaab at the time of his autobiography's publication, he nevertheless remained committed to the idea of jihad as a necessarily violent struggle. Relatedly, he is clearly conscious of his personal capacity to reach, and potentially inspire, individuals in the West given his background; 'I haven't seen too many middle class "white" guys from Alabama in Jihaad these days. Hopefully others will say to themselves: "I can do that too!"' (2012, p. 124). Along with a light-hearted narrative voice and pop culture references, the heroic framing of his self-narrative makes his example accessible and appealing to potential imitators. Additionally, recasting his family and friends' efforts to intervene as merely trials or temptations that must be endured provides an easily replicable narrative template for those who wish to follow in his footsteps to steel themselves against any similar challenges they encounter. Genre then presents as a set of constraints that individuals adopt and bristle against in how they recount their experiences, something that in turn influences not only their understanding of them but also what narrating them in this way might also accomplish.

Collected Stories

Upon inspection it quickly becomes apparent that autobiographical accounts contain within them a mass of smaller stories. These smaller stories contribute to the larger point of 'the' autobiography. An analytical strategy for the narrative criminologist then may be to examine both where these micro-stories are gathered from and how they become part of the author's articulation and understanding of their experiences and the world around them (see also Sandberg, 2010). In their analysis of how and why shared stories become part of individuals' life narratives, Schiff, Noy and Cohler focus on the idea of 'collected stories' or the 'individualized articulation of stories that were not discovered through direct experience but were, rather, vicariously encountered. They are the stories of others' (2001, p. 160). Here the narrator was neither participant nor witness to the events they nevertheless include in their accounts. Unlike collective memories that 'are the property of social groups who talk about, and reconfigure, defining moments of group history through the frame of present day concerns' (Schiff et al., 2001, p. 161 – see also Halbwach, 1952; Moore, 2010, p. 46), collected stories are not necessarily shared by all members of such social groups. Instead, these stories may be dyadic or shared between as few as two persons. Here, one individual may provide the other with an account of their own experiences or instead a story that relates to those of a third party.

Like all autobiographies, Omar Hammami's account is replete with collected stories – the most prominent being those that related to his uncle Rafiiq and his time spent in a Syrian prison as a suspected member of the Muslim Brotherhood. Linguistic demarcations, particularly the emotive tone, of Hammami's detailed retelling of stories of the '20 years in a tormenting hell of a prison' (2012, p. 4), demonstrate an 'intimacy with the narrative in ways that are more than just someone recounting someone else's story' (Azarian-Ceccato, 2010, p. 116). Collected stories are more than the repetition of encountered stories; they are 'used to complete details in a life history, to demonstrate authorial intentions, and to show dearly held meanings' (Schiff et al., 2001, p. 187). For Hammami, stories of how the guards from the (largely) secular Syrian regime punished his uncle and fellow prisoners for outwardly displaying their religiosity are taken as indicative of the subjugation Muslims endure across the world and strengthen his 'hatred for the disbelieving rulers of the Muslim countries' (2012, p. 23).

The stories of his uncle also provide a cultural script as to the idealised behaviours and bond between members of group engaged in a shared ideological struggle and their willingness to endure extreme hardship for one another. Hammami recalls his uncle telling him 'how the brothers would take turns sacrificing for the weak, by standing in front when the guards came in to beat them. Those brothers would cry if they were refused their turn' (2012, p. 23). Crucially, Hammami faces an 'unexpected reality' (2012, p. 109) when he is met with petty theft, dishonesty, selfishness and bullying (of which he is sometimes the victim) upon joining al-Shabaab. Here his expectations of what it entails to be a member of a group engaged in shared political struggle are intrinsically shaped by the collected stories of his uncle, something that conflicts and nags away at him throughout his own differing experience and eventual decision to leave al-Shabaab (2012, p. 91).

In addition to examining how the stories of others are deployed within autobiographical texts, a profitable strategy for analysis may be to focus on whose stories are collected and retold. All stories are not equally encounterable by all persons, and, as a result, therefore tell us something about individuals' social contexts. Whilst the majority of the collected stories in Hammami's account were told to him by the protagonist directly, he nevertheless reveals that his uncle was someone he had 'heard about for my entire life' (2012, p. 22). Other family members were then, at least in part, somewhere he collected stories of his uncle's actions from – something that he fails to mention elsewhere. Given that collected stories must resonate with the narrator in some way to be personally salient enough to be told as part of their autobiography, this resonance may, at least in part, be derived from the significance they afford to the teller or the relationship that they share with them. Terrorists frequently repeat instances of harm perpetrated against close family members that they were not witness to but nevertheless elicit an emotional reaction on their behalf (see, for example, Collins, 1997, p. 32). In Hammami's case the collected stories of his uncle are afforded greater significance in his narration than the actual relationship the two of them share. Nevertheless, acquiring knowledge about one's ancestry influences identity at a personal level (Strathern, 1999, p. 78). In this sense, then such familial link makes the stories of his uncle available to Hammami to interweave into that he tells about himself.

Of course, some collected stories appear in autobiographical accounts without reference to where or through whom they were encountered. The stories that circulate within peer networks, for example, are often included without reference to their origin. However, this absence is significant in illuminating social contexts. As existing work in narrative criminology has demonstrated, certain stories are so ubiquitous in certain settings that explaining them becomes unnecessary and illogical (Sandberg, 2016). For the authors of autobiographical accounts then, some stories are so well known by those around them that they cannot, or in any case do not, relate where they encountered them. Examining a corpus of autobiographical texts often reveals how certain stories are shaped, refashioned and/or spurned in various contexts and settings. In the course of analysing the autobiographies of different, sometimes opposing, participants in the same conflicts I have found their accounts to frequently include versions of the same stories. Here the capacity of stories to transcend geographical, temporal and political divides is highlighted. Autobiography may then provide an opportunity for narrative criminologists to answer Presser and Sandberg's call for the study of the flow of narratives in social spaces (2014, p. 9).

Interrogating collected stories represents a fruitful strategy for understanding autobiographical narratives. Through collected stories individuals extend their knowledge of the world beyond merely the circumstances they personally encounter (Schiff et al., 2001, p. 167). In doing so, the line between the authors' story and the stories of others they collect becomes permeable (Bakhtin, 1981, 1986). The stories collected from the authors' family, friends and local settings become a fundamental part of their own self-narratives.

Conclusion

Narrative criminology posits that stories shape action. This chapter has sought to demonstrate that autobiographies present a unique opportunity for narrative criminologists to 'get at' a whole host of stories, storied actions and by extension the social self. My aim here has been to highlight how the complex and cluttered mass of stories that autobiographical texts necessarily comprise – including those that pertain to the writing or contained within paratextual elements of such accounts – can be broken down, managed and analysed. For narrative criminology, certain analytical approaches, notably those derived from literary criticism, provide new avenues to explore how in writing their life stories individuals necessarily shape their understandings of them. First, events that might otherwise be dismissed as supplementary, unimportant or analytical dead ends are always in some way revelatory when it comes to autobiographical writing. Having been selected from the vast array of events that make up a life, these inclusions disclose meanings, often including those that the author themselves does not fully appreciate. Similarly, others have long identified genre and narrative templates as useful lenses to explore individuals' self-narratives. I hope that the example of how such systems can be mapped directly onto elements of individuals' autobiographical accounts may spark further discussions and innovations regarding the application of this approach. Finally, as demonstrated, collected stories – or those encountered via others – are not merely retold in autobiographical accounts but are included for distinct purposes and therefore constitute essential rather than tangential elements of these texts. What these stories do and from where they are collected then become pertinent questions for understanding individuals' accounts of their lives. These strategies then present viable options for harnessing autobiography in the 'doing' of narrative criminology.

Acknowledgements

This work was partly funded by the Centre for Research and Evidence on Security Threats (ESRC Award: ES/N009614/1).

References

Acharya, K., & Muldoon, O. (2017). Why "I" became a combatant: A study of memoirs written by Nepali Maoist combatants. *Terrorism and Political Violence*, 29(6), 1006–1025.

Altier, M., Boyle, E., Shortland, N., & Horgan, J. (2017). Why they leave: An analysis of terrorist disengagement events from eighty-seven autobiographical accounts. *Security Studies*, 26(2), 305–332.

Altier, M., Horgan, J., & Thoroughgood, C. (2012). In their own words? Methodological considerations in the analysis of terrorist autobiographies. *Journal of Strategic Security*, 5(4), 85–98.

Anzalone, C. (2012). The evolution of an American jihadi: The case of Omar Hammami. *CTC*, June. Retrieved from https://ctc.usma.edu/the-evolution-of-an-american-jihadi-the-case-of-omar-hammami/. Accessed on July 13, 2019.

Aspden, K., & Hayward, K. (2015). Narrative criminology and cultural criminology: Shared biographies, different lives? In L. Presser & S. Sandberg (Eds.), *Narrative criminology: Understanding stories of crime* (pp. 235–259). New York, NY and London: New York University Press.

Azarian-Ceccato, N. (2010). Reverberations of the Armenian Genocide: Narrative's intergenerational transmission and the task of not forgetting. *Narrative Inquiry*, *20*(1), 106–123.

al-Bahri, N. (2013). *Guarding bin Laden: My life in al-Qaeda*. London: Thin Man Press.

Bakhtin, M. (1981). In M. Holquist (Ed.), C. Emerson & M. Holquist (Trans.), *The dialogic imagination: Four essays*. Austin, TX: University of Texas Press.

Bakhtin, M. (1986). In C. Emerson & M. Holquist (Eds.), V. W. McGee (Trans.), *Speech genres and other late essays*. Austin, TX: University of Texas Press.

Balakian, G. (2010). *Armenian Golgotha: A memoir of the Armenian genocide, 1915–1918*. New York, NY: Vintage Books.

Barthes, R. (1982). In S. Sontag (Ed.), A. Barthes Reader (Trans.), *Introduction to the structural analysis of narratives* (pp. 251–252). New York, NY: Hill & Wang.

BBC. (2013). Al-Amriki and al-Britani: Militants 'killed' in Somalia. *BBC News*, September 12. Retrieved from https://www.bbc.co.uk/news/world-africa-24060558. Accessed on August 12, 2019.

Berkman, A. (1912). *Prison memoirs of an anarchist*. New York, NY: Mother Earth Publishing Association.

Berntzen, L., & Sandberg, S. (2014). The collective nature of lone wolf terrorism: Anders Behring Breivik and the anti-islamic social movement. *Terrorism and Political Violence*, *26*(5), 759–779.

Black, J. (2017). *Killing for Britain*. Edinburgh: Frontline Noir.

Brockmeier, J., & Harré, R. (2001). Narrative: Problems and promises of an alternative paradigm. In J. Brockmeier & D. Carbaugh (Eds.), *Narrative and identity: Studies in autobiography, self and culture*. Philadelphia, PA: John Benjamins Publishing Company.

Bruner, J. (1987). Life as narrative. *Social Research*, *54*(1), 11–32.

Bruner, J. (1990). *Acts of meaning*. Cambridge, MA: Harvard University Press.

Campbell, D. (2016). Police memoirs: How officers are making crime pay. *The Guardian*, December 16. Retrieved from https://www.theguardian.com/books/2016/dec/16/police-memoirs-officers-crime-pay-rereading. Accessed on April 8, 2018.

Campbell, J. (1949). *The hero with a thousand faces*. New York, NY: Pantheon Books.

Chatman, S. (1978). *Story and discourse: Narrative structure in fiction and film*. Ithaca, NY: Cornell University Press.

Collins, E. (1997). *Killing rage*. London: Granta Books.

Colmer, J. (1989). *Australian autobiography: The personal quest*. Melbourne: Oxford University Press.

Colvin, S., & Pisoiu, D. (2018). When being bad is good? Bringing neutralization theory to subcultural narratives of right-wing violence. *Studies in Conflict & Terrorism*. doi:10.1080/1057610X.2018.1452754

Conway, K. (2014). *Southside provisional: From freedom fighter to the four courts*. Dublin: Orpen Press.

Copeland, S. (2018). Telling stories of terrorism: A framework for applying narrative approaches to the study of militant's self-accounts. *Behavioral Sciences of Terrorism and Political Aggression*. doi:10.1080/19434472.2018.1525417

Cordes, B. (1987). When terrorists do the talking: Reflections on terrorist literature. In D. Rapoport (Ed.), *Inside terrorist organizations* (pp. 150–171). London: Frank Cass.

Cottee, S., & Hayward, K. (2011). Terrorist (E)motives: The existential attractions of terrorism. *Studies in Conflict & Terrorism*, *34*(12), 963–986.

Couser, T. (2004). Making, taking and faking lives: Voice and vulnerability in collaborative life writing. In T. Couser (Ed.), *Vulnerable subjects: Ethics and life writing* (pp. 34–55). Ithaca, NY: Cornell University Press.

Cullen, F. (2011). Beyond adolescence-limited criminology: Choosing our future. *Criminology*, *49*, 287–330.

Deary, M. (2010). *Radicalization: The life writings of political prisoners*. Oxford: Routledge.

Dresner, A. (2017). *My fair junkie: A memoir of getting dirty and staying clean*. New York, NY: Hachette Books.

Erikson, E. (1968). *Identity: Youth and crisis*. London: W. W. Norton & Company.

Erikson, E. (1975). *Life history and the historical moment*. London: W. W. Norton & Company.

Frank, A. (2012). Practicing dialogical narrative analysis. In J. Holstein & J. Gubrium (Eds.), *Varieties of narrative analysis* (pp. 33–52). Los Angeles, CA: SAGE Publications.

Genette, G. (1997). In J. Lewin (Trans.), *Paratexts: Thresholds of interpretation*. Cambridge: Cambridge University Press.

Gill, P. (2015). *Lone-actor terrorists: A behavioural analysis*. Abingdon: Routledge.

Giorgio (2003). *Memoirs of an Italian terrorist*. New York, NY: Carroll & Graf Publishers.

Glazzard, A. (2017). Losing the plot: Narrative, counter-narrative and violent extremism. International Centre for Counter-Terrorism Research Paper. Retrieved from https://icct.nl/wp-content/uploads/2017/05/ICCT-Glazzard-Losing-the-Plot-May-2017.pdf. Accessed on July 7, 2019.

Goddard, H. (1956). *Memoirs of a bow street runner*. New York, NY: William Morrow and Company.

Guppy, D. (1996). *Roll the dice*. London: Blake Publishing.

Halbwachs, M. (1952). In L. Coser (Trans.), *On collective memory*. Chicago, IL: The University of Chicago Press.

Hamilton, D. (1997). *A cause worth living for: My journey out of terrorism*. Godalming: Highland Books.

Hammami, O. (2012). The story of an American jihaadi: Part One. Retrieved from https://azelin.files.wordpress.com/2012/05/omar-hammami-abc5ab-man-e1b9a3c5abr-al-amrc4abkc4ab-22the-story-of-an-american-jihc481dc4ab-part-122.pdf. Accessed on April 4, 2017.

Holbrook, D. (2017). What types of media do terrorists collect? An analysis of religious, political, and ideological publications found in terrorism investigations in the UK. International Centre for Counter-Terrorism Research Paper. Retrieved from https://icct.nl/publication/what-types-of-media-do-terrorists-collect-an-analysis-of-religious-political-and-ideological-publications-found-in-terrorism-investigations-in-the-uk/. Accessed on October 20, 2018.

Hopkins, S. (2013). *The politics of memoir and the Northern Ireland conflict*. Liverpool: Liverpool University Press.

Husain, E. (2007). *The Islamist: Why I joined radical Islam in Britain, what I saw inside and why I left*. London: Penguin Books.

Irish Times (1999). 'Killing rage' caught up on Collins. *Irish Times*, January 30. Retrieved from https://www.irishtimes.com/news/killing-rage-caught-up-on-collins-1.1258683

James, E. (2016). Books behind bars: Five of the best stories about prison life. *The Guardian*, April 11. Retrieved from https://www.theguardian.com/books/booksblog/2016/apr/11/books-behind-bars-five-best-stories-prison-life-alan-sillitoe-erwin-james. Accessed on April 8, 2018.

Jarle Hansen, S. (2013). *Al Shabaab in Somalia: The history and ideology of a militant islamist group, 2005–2012*. Oxford: Oxford University Press.

Joosse, P., Bucerius, S., & Thompson, S. (2015). Narratives and counternarratives: Somali-Canadians on recruitment as foreign fighters to Al-Shabaab. *British Journal of Criminology*, 55(4), 811–832.

Kaddouri, Y. (2011). *Lach met de duivel: Autobiografie van een 'rotte appel'-Marokkaan*. Amsterdam: Uitgeverij Van Gennep.

Kent, J., & Gaunt, J. (1979). Picaresque fiction: A bibliographic essay. *College Literature*, 6(3), 245.

Khaled, L. (1973). *My people shall live: The autobiography of a revolutionary*. London: Hodder & Stoughton.

Lawson, M. (2015). Serial thrillers: Why true crime is popular culture's most wanted. *The Guardian*, December 12. Retrieved from https://www.theguardian.com/culture/2015/dec/12/serial-thrillers-why-true-is-popular-cultures-most-wanted. Accessed on April 8, 2018.

Lejeune, P. (1989). *On autobiography*. Minneapolis, MN: University of Minnesota Press.

Leslie, D. (2014). *Lighting candles: A paramilitary's war with death, drugs and demons*. Edinburgh: Black and White Publishing.

Lindemann, S. (2017). As-told-to life writing: A topic for scholarship. *Life Writing*, 15(4), 523–535.

Little, A. (2009). *Give a boy a gun*. London: Darton Longman & Todd Ltd.

Maruna, S. (1997). Going straight: Desistance from crime and life narratives of reform. In A. Lieblich & R. Josselson (Eds.), *The narrative study of lives* (pp. 59–93). Thousand Oaks, CA: SAGE Publications.

Mascuch, M. (1997). *The origins of the individualist self: Autobiography and self-identity in England, 1591–1791*. Hoboken, NJ: JOhn Wiley & Sons.

Mastors, E., & Siers, R. (2014). Omar al-Hammami: A case study in radicalization. *Behavioral Sciences & the Law*, 32, 377–388.

McAdams, D. (1988). *Power, intimacy, and the life story: Personological inquiries into identity*. London: The Guilford Press.

McAdams, D. (1993). *The stories we live by: Personal myths and the making of the self*. New York, NY: William Morrow and Company.

McDonald, H. (2014). Eamon Collins murder: Police arrest man in South Armagh. *The Guardian*, February 26. Retrieved from https://www.theguardian.com/uk-news/2014/feb/26/eamon-collins-murder-police-arrest-man. Accessed on October 11, 2018.

Mendelsohn, D. (2010). But enough about me: What does the popularity of memoirs tell us about ourselves? *The New Yorker*, January 17. Retrieved from https://www.newyorker.com/magazine/2010/01/25/but-enough-about-me-2. Accessed on March 24, 2019.

Moore, C. (2010). *Contemporary Violence: postmodern war in Kosovo and Chechnya*. Manchester, UK: Manchester University Press.

Ngor, H. (1988). *Surviving the killing fields: Cambodian Odyssey*. London: Chatto & Windus.

O'Callaghan, S. (1998). *The informer*. London: Bantam Press.

O'Doherty, S. (2011). *The volunteer: A former IRA man's true story*. Durham, CT: Strategic Book Group.

O'Kane, M. (1999). Body of IRA 'traitor' was mutilated. *The Guardian*, January 28. Retrieved from https://www.theguardian.com/uk/1999/jan/29/northernireland.maggieokane. Accessed on April 20, 2018.

Pennant, C. (2000). *Cass*. London: John Blake.

Plummer, K. (2001). *Documents of life 2: An invitation to a critical realism*. London: SAGE Publications.

Polkinghorne, D. (1988). *Narrative knowing and the human sciences*. Albany, NY: State University of New York Press.

Polletta, F. (2006). *It was like a fever: Storytelling in protest and politics*. Chicago, IL: University of Chicago Press.

della Porta, D. (2006). *Social movements, political violence, and the state: A comparative analysis of Italy and Germany*. Cambridge: Cambridge University Press.

della Porta, D. (2013). *Clandestine political violence*. Cambridge: Cambridge University Press.

Poulton, E. (2012). 'Not another football hooligan story'? Learning from narratives of 'true crime' and desistance. *Internet Journal of Criminology, 2012*, 1–20.

Presser, L. (2004). Violent offenders, moral selves: Constructing identities and accounts in the research interview. *Social Problems, 51*(1), 82–101.

Presser, L. (2008). *Been a heavy life: Stories of violent men*. Champaign, IL: University of Illinois Press.

Presser, L. (2009). The narratives of offenders. *Theoretical Criminology, 13*(2), 177–200.

Presser, L., & Sandberg, S. (2014). Narrative criminology for these times. *British Society of Criminology Newsletter, 75*(Winter), 7–10.

Presser, L., & Sandberg, S. (2015). Research strategies for narrative criminology. In J. Miller & W. Palacios (Eds.), *Advances in criminological theory: The value of qualitative research for advancing criminological theory* (pp. 85–100). Piscataway, NJ: Transaction Publishers.

Rambsy, H. (2009). Re-presenting Black Boy: The evolving packaging history of Richard Wright's autobiography. *Southern Quarterly, 46*(2), 71–83.

Ramsay, G. (2013). *Jihadi culture on the World Wide Web*. London: Bloomsbury Publishing.

Rapoport, D. (1987). The international world as some terrorists have seen it: A look at a century of memoirs. In D. Rapoport (Ed.), *Inside terrorist organizations* (pp. 32–58). London: Frank Cass.

Rudolph, E. (2013). *Between the lines of drift: The memoirs of a militant* (3rd ed.). Retrieved from http://www.armyofgod.com/EricLinesOfDrift%201_18_15 Opened.pdf. Accessed on June 7, 2019.

Sandberg, S. (2010). What can "lies" tell us about life? Notes towards a framework of narrative criminology. *Journal of Criminal Justice Education, 21*(4), 447–465.

Sandberg, S. (2013). Are self-narratives strategic or determined, unified or fragmented? Reading Breivik's Manifesto in light of narrative criminology. *Acta Sociologica, 56*(1), 69–83.

Sandberg, S. (2016). The importance of stories untold: Life-story, event-story and trope. *Crime, Media, Culture, 12*(2), 153–171.

Sanders, M. (1994). Theorizing the collaborative self: The dynamics of contour and content in the dictated autobiography. *New Literary History, 25*(2), 445–458.

Sandberg, S., Oksanen, A., Berntzen, L., & Kiilakoski, T. (2014). Stories in action: The cultural influences of school shootings on the terrorist attacks in Norway. *Critical Studies on Terrorism, 7*(2), 277–296.

Savinkov, B. (1917). *Memoirs of a terrorist.* New York, NY: A. & C. Boni.

Schiff, B., Noy, C., & Cohler, B. (2001). Collected stories in the life narratives of holocaust survivors. *Narrative Inquiry, 11*(1), 159–194.

Scott, M., & Lyman, S. (1968). Accounts. *American Sociological Review, 33*(1), 46–62.

Senghor, S. (2017). *Writing my wrongs: Life, death, and redemption in an American prison.* New York, NY: Convergent Books.

Shakur, S. (2004). *Monster: The autobiography of an L.A. Gang member.* New York, NY: Grove Press.

Shapiro, J., & Siegel, D. (2012). Moral hazard, discipline, and the management of terrorist organizations. *World Politics, 64*(1), 39–78.

Smith, S., & Watson, J. (2010). *Reading autobiography: A guide for interpreting life narratives.* Minnesota, MN: University of Minnesota Press.

de Soyza, N. (2011). *Tamil tigress: My story as a child soldier in Sri Lanka's bloody civil war.* Sydney: Allen & Unwin.

Stone, M. (2003). *None shall divide us.* London: Blake Publishing.

Strathern, M. (1999). *Property, substance, and effect: Anthropological essays on persons and things.* London: Athlone Press.

Sutton, S. (2015). Amplifying the text: Paratext in popular musicians' autobiographies. *Popular Music and Society, 38*(2), 208–223.

Vásquez Perdomo, M. (2005). *My life as a Colombian revolutionary: Reflections of a former guerrillera.* Philadelphia, PA: Temple University Press.

Woodward, R., & Jenkings, K. (2012). Military memoirs, their covers and the reproduction of public narratives of war. *Journal of War and Culture Studies, 5*(3), 349–369.

Woodward, R., & Jenkings, K. N. (2018). *Bringing war to book: Writing and producing the military memoir.* Basingstoke: Palgrave Macmillan.

Yagoda, B. (2009). *Memoir: A history.* New York, NY: Riverhead Books.

Youngman, M. (2016). Broader, vaguer, weaker: The evolving ideology of the Caucasus Emirate leadership. *Terrorism and Political Violence, 31*(2), 367–389.

Yousef, M. (2010). *Son of hamas.* Carol Stream, IL: SaltRiver.

Chapter 8

Stories of Environmental Crime, Harm and Protection: Narrative Criminology and Green Cultural Criminology

Avi Brisman

Introduction and Background on Green Cultural Criminology

Green criminology refers to the study of acts and omissions that adversely affect human and nonhuman life, ecosystems and the biosphere (or ecosphere). More specifically, green criminologists explore and analyse the causes, consequences and prevalence of environmental crime and harm; the responses to and prevention of environmental crime and harm by the legal system (civil, criminal, regulatory), by nongovernmental entities, and by individuals and social movements; and the meaning of mediated representations of environmental crime and harm.

Green criminology connects the local to the global – and the micro to the meso to the macro – from research on individual-level environmental crimes to business/corporate violations to state transgressions. With a wide range of interests and ecophilosophical orientations (see Halsey & White, 1998; White, 2013), green criminologists have undertaken research on, inter alia, agriculture and food; animal abuse/animal rights; air pollution and water pollution; climate change and deforestation; poaching and trafficking of flora and fauna; and the trade, transfer and disposal of waste, including e-waste (e.g. Beirne & South, 2007; Lynch et al., 2017; Sollund, 2008; South & Brisman, 2013; White & Heckenberg, 2014).

As Ruggiero and South (2013, p. 360) note, green criminology 'does not set out any one particular theory.' Rather, green criminologists have engaged in both intradisciplinary theoretical engagement (drawing on both mainstream and critical theoretical orientations within the larger field of criminology) and extra-disciplinary theoretical engagement (interfacing with theories and ideas outside criminology) (Brisman, 2014, p. 25). One example of the former is green cultural criminology – an emergent array of perspectives linked by sensitivities to image, meaning and representation in the study of environmental crime and environmental crime control – an orientation designed especially for critical engagement with the politics of meaning surrounding environmental crime and environmental crime control, and for critical intervention into those politics. Accordingly, green cultural criminology (1) considers the way(s) in which environmental crime, harm and disaster are constructed, represented and envisioned by the news media (online, print, etc.) and in popular cultural forms (e.g. books, films); (2) dedicates increased attention to patterns of consumption, constructed consumerism, commodification of nature and related market processes and (3) devotes heightened concern to the contestation of space, transgression and resistance, in order to analyse the ways in which environmental harms are opposed in/on the streets and in day-to-day living.[1] Put another way, green cultural criminology concentrates on representations of two particular types of behaviour that have animated much cultural criminological study and thought – consumption and consumerism, on the one hand, and transgression and resistance on the other.

This chapter focuses on the first of these three areas, with a particular interest in narratives of environmental crime and/or harm. In so doing, it identifies instances in which green cultural criminology has engaged with another criminological perspective – narrative criminology – as well as to offer possibilities for how it might do so. That green cultural criminology has not hitherto (or has not adequately) sought connections with narrative criminology is not, by itself, a satisfactory reason for such an undertaking. Nor is the inverse of this proposition – that narrative criminology should probe stories of environmental crime and/or harm because it has not yet (or has not sufficiently) done so, is not, alone, a suitable rationale. There are, to be sure, other criminological perspectives with which green cultural criminology might seek integration – other constructions and representations of environmental crime and harm besides narrative. So, why *narrative criminology*? Correspondingly, given that there are many types of crime and harm that narrative criminology might explore, why should narrative criminology contemplate environmental ones?

With respect to the second of these two questions, the answer should be axiomatic: the environment is important, even when society is faced with economic crises, religious conflict and war, and unending social problems and inequalities, because the Earth is our only home; it provides living beings – humans' and nonhuman animals' – only source of air, food and shelter. Thus, narrative criminology (like criminology, more generally) should study environmental crime and harm because without the environment, there is no crime, no criminology, no narrative, no narrative criminology – no humans, no nonhuman animals, no life as we know it.

The answer to the first of these questions – why green cultural criminology should probe environmental narratives – rests with the broader significance of 'cultural narratives.' As Craig (2016, pp. 352–353) explains, '[c]ultural narratives are deeply embedded social stories that frame and contextualise events within a particular culture to help give them meaning.' Cultural narratives, which include

---

[1]See, e.g. Brisman (2014, 2015, 2017a, 2017b, 2017c), Brisman, McClanahan, and South (2014), Brisman and South (2012, 2013, 2014, 2015, 2017a, 2017b, 2017c, 2018), Di Ronco et al. (2019), Mazurek (2017), McClanahan (2014), McClanahan, Brisman, and South (2017), Redmon (2018) and Schally (2018).

narratives about our relationship to the environment, not only reflect and thus reveal individual and cultural identity, but *construct* and *inform* such identities (and our sense of 'what counts as good and bad' (Copes et al., 2015, p. 34)), giving meaning to events, perpetuating and inculcating social norms, and helping to orient action (Autessere, 2012, p. 209; Craig, 2016, p. 353). Because cultural narratives, in general, can assist members of a particular group or culture to contextualise, frame and understand their group's or culture's place in the world, and can help instill value systems into group or cultural members, those narratives regarding the environment can impart moral principles and reasoning with respect to the Earth, thereby making them a vital area of study for green cultural criminology.

This chapter begins by offering some defining features of narrative criminology, before turning to two examples of narrative criminological work focused on environmental crime and/or harm. One analyses a corporate (offender's) website; the other examines attorneys' stories of environmental wrongdoing. Together, they depict a cultural narrative in the US of the causes, consequences, punishments (or lack thereof) and corporate representations of environmental harm. Next, this chapter turns to a discussion of examples of depictions or representations of environmental harm and protection in literature. Here, the focus is on *fictional* works that are explicitly environmental – where the subject, plot and message centre on one or more environmental issues, such as a particular harm, its cause or causes and possible responses thereto.

The focus on fiction – the focus on fictional expressions of cultural narratives regarding the environment – is, for purposes of this chapter, twofold. First, fiction not only *reflects* the world (Smith & Waite, 2018, p. 15) – as it is, or 'how we got here' (Bonneuil, 2015, p. 18) – but how or what it might be (Newitz, 2019; see generally; Dickinson & Wright, 2017; Sandberg & Ugelvik, 2016). Thus, fiction about the environment hints at our far and not-too-distant future. Second, fiction, in Colvin's (2015, p. 215) words 'provides a world of "fewer risks", enabling readers to "consider the experiences of others without facing the potentially threatening consequences of that engagement"' (Kidd & Castano, 2013, p. 378). In this way, fiction offers the prospects of a 'cultural reset button, inviting us to imagine how we might redo' (Newitz, 2019) what we have done to the Earth, as well as the possibility of a 'dry run' or 'dress rehearsal,' so to speak, for different options available to us.

Finally, this chapter considers what might be called 'allegories of environmental harm.' In the section with this name, I examine literature that is less overtly environmental, noting Ruggiero's (2002) rereading of Herman Melville's *Moby Dick* to illuminate points and issues of interest to green criminologists regarding acceptable and unacceptable economic practices, as well as my allegorising of the fable of *The Three Little Pigs* (and various permutations thereof) as a story of climate change migration (Brisman, 2019). This section, 'Allegories of Environmental Harm,' then suggests an interpretation of the American children's story *Muncus Agruncus: A Bad Little Mouse* (Watson, 1976) as a cautionary tale of Western hubris in the face of environmental catastrophe. The goal of this section is to demonstrate how green criminologists working in this area ('allegories of environmental harm') have attempted to identify environmental lessons and messages in works with ostensibly other or broader messages. Again following Craig (2016), the intent is to acknowledge both that cultural narratives (and our interpretation of them) change and to demonstrate (the importance of) human agency to transform those narratives (and our interpretation thereof).

Narrating Environmental Harm: Corporate Offenders and Attorney Stories

Narrative criminology is a theoretical and methodological paradigm centred on the perspective that stories can influence (promote, curb or prevent) action, including harmful action (e.g. Presser, 2009; Presser & Sandberg, 2017).[2] Whereas 'criminologists have long mined personal narratives for evidence of social forces that shape lawbreakers' attitudes, values, and behavior' (Page & Goodman, 2018, p. 3) or 'as vehicles for data on the factors that promote criminal behavior' (Presser & Sandberg, 2015, p. 1), narrative criminologists argue that stories *themselves* can instigate or prompt, sustain, or effect desistance from criminal behaviour and/or harmful action not proscribed by law. In other words, that stories are *constitutive* of crime and harm (including desistance from crime and harm), rather than just organising, ordering and relaying information about specific crimes or criminal events, is what distinguishes narrative criminology from conventional criminological accounts involving stories.

To date, most scholarship in narrative criminology has entailed crimes or harms pertaining to drug use, property crimes, violence or some combination thereof – committed by *individual offenders* – a reflection of the interests of criminology more generally.[3] In an exciting departure from previous narrative criminological work on street crimes committed by individual offenders, Schally (2018) has investigated the discursive construction of harm and 'business-as-usual' approach of Tyson Foods, Inc. ('Tyson') – the US agribusiness. Utilising critical discourse analysis, Schally has examined the ways in which the 'corporate behemoth' (2018, p. 2) legitimised harm-doing through use of discourses on the company's website. As Schally (2018, pp. 78–79) explains,

> The stories told on the website – stories of humble beginnings and hard work building to success – reinforce dominant normative logics of capitalism…Tyson's discourses, particularly the origin story, consistently construct them as 'good,' allowing them to benefit from the binary codes of good and evil – because if you are one, then you surely cannot be the other.

---

[2] Following Presser (2010, p. 432), Presser and Sandberg (2015, p. 16n.1) and Sandberg and Tutenges (2015, p. 158) – and in an attempt to maintain consistency with my prior work – I use the terms 'narrative' and 'story' interchangeably. For a discussion of my approach, see Brisman (2017b, pp. 71–72n.2).

[3] See, e.g. Copes (2016), Copes et al. (2014), Dollinger (2018), Miller, Carbone-Lopez, and Gunderman (2015), Presser (2012), Sandberg and Tutenges (2015), Sandberg, Oksansen, Berntzen, and Kiilakoski (2014) and Sandberg, Tutenges, and Copes (2015); cf. Presser (2013).

Schally (2018) observes that 'Tyson's origin story may not necessarily be an instigator of action in the first instance, but rather allows the harm inflicted by their practices to continue' (2018, p. 78). So long as the public absorbs Tyson's story and message about being part of 'a decent whole and a benign presence in society,' Schally continues, 'then their harmful actions can be tolerated' (2018, pp. 78–79).

What is particularly compelling about Schally's research is her study of Tyson's corporate website – the 'contemporary conduit par excellence' of corporate public relations or 'spin' (2018, p. 40). As Schally (2018, p. 49) points out, 'the corporate website has become an important tool for communicating the corporate identity and corporate social responsibility as interest in ethical consumerism has increased…[and it is] a good point of entry for researching how corporations discursively construct their identities and their actions.' Schally's observations are instructive given 'the particularly modern "need" for companies to project social responsibility' (2018, p. 40), but they become even more insightful when one considers the admission (or boast, depending on one's perspective) of then-candidate Donald J. Trump that 'All I know is what's on the Internet' (quoted in Savransky, 2016). Essentially, given that agribusiness, in general, corporations, more generally, and those in or with power, even more generally, rely on the internet for dissemination of information (or as sources thereof), a green cultural criminology oriented towards narrative could consider not just the way(s) in which environmental crime, harm and disaster are constructed, represented and envisioned online, but the ways in which such crime, harm and disaster are normalised through (dominant) online discourse.

While Schally's work may, on the surface, appear to be a sharp turn from previous narrative criminological inquiry, in many respects, it has remained quite faithful – looking to the way that an *offender* has described their[4] ongoing engagement with harm. To be sure, Schally's 'offender' – Tyson – does not acknowledge perpetration of wrongdoing: quite the contrary. And thus Schally's work seems more of an effort at understanding how an offender *justifies* their actions (which they do not see as harmful) than how an offender continues with or desists from behavior that they know is damaging or injurious. But her focus on the offender is consistent with prior narrative criminological work, even if she

---

[4]Early in *Legitimizing Corporate Harm: The Discourse of Contemporary Agribusiness*, Schally (2018, p. 12n.3) states that she uses the pronouns, 'they,' 'them' and 'their,' throughout her book when referring to Tyson and other corporations. While Schally recognises that 'these pronouns personify the corporation,' she finds referring to the corporations as 'it' more problematic because 'it discursively constructs the company as a nonagent (see Korten, 1995).' While using the pronouns 'they,' 'them' and 'their' could be interpreted as an endorsement of the notion of 'corporate personhood' or the holding of *Citizens United v. Federal Election Commission*, 558 U.S. 310 (2010), in order to maintain consistency with Schally, I will employ her locution and refrain from using 'it' or 'its' to refer to corporations.

does broaden narrative criminology's gaze to include (a) a corporate offender; (b) whose denial of *environmental* harm and justifications for ongoing practices; (c) is expressed on a company website (thereby expanding what narrative criminologists might consider a 'story').

Like Schally, Ningard (2018) seeks to extend the narrative criminological project with a consideration of environmental crimes and harms. But instead of looking at (corporate) offenders, as Schally does, or at 'factors of criminalisation or the causing of criminality' (Dollinger, 2018, p. 478), as other narrative criminologists might, Ningard (2018) examines attorney constructions of environmental crime and harm.

In 'Attorney Stories of Environmental Crime: Harms, Agents, and Ideal Cases,' Ningard notes that environmental harms result, in part, from 'structural and institutional arrangements founded on particular constructions of the meaning of environment, right living, and conventional lifestyles in the modern era' (p. 6). Ningard focuses on the 'cultural configurations' of attorneys working in the area of environmental law. Accepting that definitions of crime and harm are produced by institutions and actors via stories, which can influence our expectations of what 'crime' is or 'ought to look like' – and subsequently our reactions when confronted with potential criminal acts – Ningard asks: 'How do lawyers describe a strong legal case against an actor that has caused environmental harm? Who are the victims and offenders in such a case? What actions are involved?'

Ningard's examination of attorney constructions of environmental crime leads to a three-prong typology: (1) 'low-hanging fruit cases' – obvious and straightforward stories of environmental crime, where offenders have engaged in flagrant violation of environmental laws in order to save time or money (or both), and where they often lie or otherwise misrepresent their behavior; (2) 'Davids and Goliaths' – where the state, as an 'enforcement giant,' is viewed as the 'agent of harm,' as opposed to the individual or organisation, which violated the environmental law in the first place; and (3) 'agentless harms' or 'the collectivisation of environmental harm.' In this third category, as Ningard (2018, p. 111) explains,

> Harm done to the environment is constructed in a passive sense, meaning that while we still have great environmental harms to address, there are no harmers with which to attribute blame...[T]his means that...we cannot easily decide just by looking at a case who is in the right and who is in the wrong. The cases have become more difficult, and who is the offender and who is the victim is not easily discerned.

It is in this third category of cases, Ningard continues, 'where the utility of not only criminal law, but environmental law as a whole, is brought into question,' leaving us to ask: 'can law respond to the everyday behaviors which contribute to massive environmental harm? Does cultural change begin with passing more laws?' (p. 112)

Throughout Ningard's study, questions as to the existence of an 'ideal victim,' à la Christie (1986), and to what constitutes 'sympathy-worthy *or* blame-worthy perpetrators' (p. 24) abound, leading Ningard (2018, p. 116) to conclude:

> In my conversations with attorneys, the primary offender discussed overall was the state. Low-hanging fruit cases...were mostly described as things of the past. Today, environmental conditions are allegedly much better, and an increase in knowledge of environmental laws and regulations as well as a changing cultural attitude favorable to sustainability has driven most would-be offenders to attempt to remain in compliance. However, such efforts are often thwarted by an overly authoritative regulatory agency that has set the bar too high. Punishments for environmental violations often exceed what attorneys thought to be fair...By constructing the state as the offender, these stories allow those who violate environmental law to escape scrutiny and attention, as the violations themselves are hardly focused on. This may allow for corporations to escape the label of *criminal*, even when they violate criminal law.

Weaving these three types of stories together, Ningard proposes a 'meta-narrative...that frames the history of environmental harm in the United States' (2018, p. 118). According to Ningard (2018, p. 118),

> [The meta-narrative begins] in an environmental Wild West, where individuals were flagrantly violating environmental law, prompting the passage of criminal statutes and a wave of prosecutions going after the low-hanging fruits. Then we began to see a shift away from these low-hanging fruits...[E]nforcement agencies such as the EPA become the harm-doers, unjustly punishing industry and overexerting their authority. Still, attorneys were hesitant to commit to the notion...that the environment as a whole was getting better. Instead, we have shifted to...where harm exists without a nameable offender, where we are collectively implicated in the harms we face today. The meta-narrative incapacitates. For what shall we do without a clear culprit, especially when we wish to avoid the alleged overreach of the past?

Ningard's study reveals how attorneys, 'who embody the realpolitik of environmental law and regulation,' help shape courtroom narratives or decide sanctioning outcome, thereby illuminating the logic that attorneys apply when conducting their work and demonstrating how, following Fleetwood (2016), habitual, quotidian narratives uphold the status quo – maintaining social structures and inequalities. In this way, Ningard not only continues Schally's attempts to extend the narrative criminological project with a consideration of environmental crimes and harms, but takes matters a step further, studying, in her words 'the (nonfictive) stories of *attorneys*' (p. 114, emphasis added), rather than those of *offenders* (or *an offender*), as expressed on their website(s).

What is particularly intriguing about Ningard's research and conclusion is her insistence that the stories of attorneys are 'nonfictive' (p. 114) – and, indeed, the supermajority of narrative criminological work has focused on *nonfictional* narratives. In other words, one could interpret her work to suggest stories as 'reflect[ing] the world' or 'represent[ing] reality in some objective way,' when, as Smith and Waite (2018, p. 2) suggest, it might be more accurate to suggest that narratives 'and how we use them, construct how we understand and make sense of lived realities.' Whether attorneys' stories are, indeed, 'nonfictive,' is a debate for another day (and one perhaps complicated by the fact that judges issue 'opinions'). For the purposes of this chapter, it provides the occasion to consider works labelled as fiction.

Fictionalised Depictions and Representations of Environmental Harm and Protection in Literature

As Presser (2016, p. 146) observes, '[n]arrative suggests fiction as opposed to hard facts.' One of the reasons that criminology 'came to narrative years later than sociology,' Presser continues, is that 'criminology is especially "wedded to facticity" given that [its] ultimate referent is the wily offender.' While a perspective tied too closely to offenders' stories might seem questionable, narrative criminologists place '*the story* about experience, not the experience as such, at the centre of analysis' (Houge, 2018, p. 4 (emphasis in original)). As such, 'stories about harms in the past, whether individual, institutional, political and/or cultural' become interesting for narrative criminologists 'primarily because they can motivate, maintain or restrain harmful action in the *future* (Sandberg, 2016)' (Houge, 2018, p. 4 (emphasis in original)). Accordingly, Houge (2018, p. 4) explains, 'the influence or animating powers of a story are not conditioned on it being true or not…a story need not be true in relation to the past for it to do work in the present and for the future' (footnoted omitted) – or, as Presser & Sandberg (2015, p. 6) put it, 'from the perspective of narrative criminology narratives are never erroneous.'

With this in mind – and liberated from the matrimonial shackles of facticity – a number of criminologists have sought to explore the constitutive possibilities of overtly fictional work. For example, Page and Goodman (2018), argue for the criminological value of fiction through an exploration of Edward Bunker's semiautobiographical novels. As Page and Goodman (2018, p. 3) explain,

> [d]espite myriad differences, one commonality between conventional and narrative criminological accounts of stories is a concentration on *non-fictional* narratives. This focus allows scholars working in the relatively young tradition of narrative criminology to speak directly to colleagues experienced in viewing stories as providing data for evaluating why people commit crime (and/or why they stop); yet it comes with the obvious cost of largely overlooking the power of fiction to shape people's lives and how they make sense of their past and present [emphasis in original].

While Page and Goodman make clear that they do not consider fiction or 'other creative sources' to be '"data" per se, or that reading fiction is a fitting substitute for conducting empirical research,' they assert that 'fiction can challenge basic assumptions that shape how we elicit, hear, interpret, and present stories (including those collected as data during empirical research' (2018, pp. 2, 3). Focussing on two of Bunker's novels in particular, *The Animal Factory* (1977) and *Little Boy Blue* (1981), Page and Goodman demonstrate how Bunker's fiction enhances our understandings of 'prisonization' and the complex ways in which incarceration transforms people, altering individuals' minds and bodies, affecting how they act, feel and think. For Page and Goodman (2018, p. 14), 'Bunker's writings (and fiction more generally) are not substitutes for systematic research on lawbreaking and penal institutions. Unlike rigorous scholarship, fiction does not (nor should it) attempt to produce valid and generalisable findings.' Actually, Page and Goodman (2018, p. 14) continue, 'novelists, seeking to stir emotions and draw in readers, may – purposely or not – exaggerate and distort social process and reach conclusions based on selective impression and personal experiences...' Because 'life outside of fictional universes (including life inside carceral institutions) is often routine and quite dull' (Crewe, 2009), writers of fiction, especially that related to crime and punishment, may – and, at times, must – resort to overemphasising or overembellishing conflict, violence and the excitement thereof (Page & Goodman, 2018, p. 14). As such, Page and Goodman (2018, p. 14) caution, '[f]or analysts who draw from fiction...there is a danger of mistaking the "fast life" with all aspects of the "real life".' Despite such caveats, Page and Goodman (2018, pp. 2, 3) remain committed to the possible ways in which fiction can 'complement[] the criminological enterprise,' spurring criminologists 'to scrutinise commonsense, opening up new and different questions and alternative approaches to investigating the social world, as well as novel means of communicating findings and arguments.'

Page and Goodman (2018, p. 15) conclude by calling for an appreciation of 'the ability of stories to affect those who read, see, or hear them – not just those who tell them.' Thus, what is innovative about Page and Goodman's work is not just their attention to fiction and fictional devices, but their shift in focus 'from storytellers to their listeners (see also Colvin, 2015)' (2018, p. 3). In a similar way, Brisman (2017a, 2017b, 2017c) has attempted to shift the focus of narrative criminological study from storytellers to their *listeners*, highlighting the potential of fictional narratives to affect the environmental consciousness of those who read, listen to or otherwise engage with them.

In 'On Narrative and Green Cultural Criminology,' Brisman (2017b) asserted – consistent with Ningard's (2018) work above – that narrative criminology need not limit itself to the study of *offenders*, given that in the context of environmental crime and harm, the same individuals and groups may be perpetrators, victims or bystanders – at the same juncture or at different times.[5]

---

[5]That the same individuals and groups may be perpetrators, victims or bystanders (at the same juncture or at different times is not peculiar to environmental crime and harm. 'Classical' or 'ordinary' offenders also – and often – drift in and out of offender-victim-bystander roles. I am grateful to Thomas Ugelvik for this reminder.

Brisman's (2017b) article also maintained that if it is not necessary to confirm the accuracy of a story for it to merit study under the narrative criminological framework, as noted at the outset of this section and as suggested by Colvin (2015) and Sandberg (2010) – and Page and Goodman (2018) more forcefully – that if 'narratives have explanatory power regardless of their veracity' (Kurtz & Upton, 2017) – then disregarding fictional representations becomes little more than sophistry. Brisman's (2017b) work, then, combines the shift in subject matter of Schally (2018) and Ningard (2018) from street crimes (e.g. drug use, property crimes, violence) with the movement of Page and Goodman (2018, p. 3) from 'what stories *do* to and for those who tell them (Presser, 2016, p. 42)' to the power of fiction (especially stories about crime, punishment and related topics) to 'affect those who read, hear, or see them' (Page & Goodman, 2018, p. 15).

As an illustration of the type of twinned narrative criminology and green cultural criminology that I envision – one centred on fiction – and one that has begun to gain traction – I turn to a discussion of children's stories. I highlight the ways in which children's stories tend to individualise environmental degradation and/or emphasise personal actions with respect to conserving nature and protecting the environment, rather than demanding a role for state or corporate entities.

Children's Stories that Individualise Environmental Degradation and Protection

Victoria Perla's (2007) children's book, *When Santa Turned Green*, begins as follows:

> It was just November, but Santa's factory was already in full gear. The elves could feel each day getting busier and busier. Mail was stacking up with notes from good girls and boys. The buzz of Christmas was starting to build. That's when something really crazy happened. Was it a jam in the die-cast car cranker? A sprung sprocket in the minidoll maker? Nope. It was a drop. A simple, solitary drop of water. Plop! From the ceiling onto Santa's nose.

Readers soon learn that the snow is melting on the North Pole – that '[t]he land of permanent freeze [is] getting soggier by the minute,' that 'ice caps [are] shrinking in size,' and that '[g]laciers [are] slipping into the sea.' In an effort to determine why these changes are occurring, Santa hops into his sleigh. He soon discovers that the melting is due to human activities that have been transpiring for quite some time:

> Over the years, we Earthlings have been chopping down our forests. And lumping something called carbon dioxide into the sky. It comes from our cars ... our planes ... our factories ... even our chopped-down trees. And now there's so much of it floating

around Earth's atmosphere it's acting like a big blanket holding in the heat of our planet – which makes temperatures go up, up, up. Scientists call it global warming. And when temperatures go up, our ice caps melt down.

Santa ponders whether global warming is 'a task too big for even him to tackle.' But because the future of the planet is at stake – and Christmas, too! – Santa delivers an early message in lieu of bringing presents: 'that they need[] to take action.' Children around the world respond by making 'lots of little changes, which ma[ke] a world of difference.' For example, some kids start walking to school, thereby saving fuel, while others start composting and recycling. Readers learn about kids who turn off lights when they leave rooms, about children who pick toys made closer to home so that they do not have to be shipped from far away, and about other young people who replace their disposable lunch containers with reusable ones. Santa, himself, makes changes too: 'from energy efficient lighting to wind and solar power for his factory.'

Through these collective efforts – and after years of patience and persistence – '[t]he Earth's heat [is] finally able to slip off into space, giving the glaciers, trees, oceans and environment a much needed breath of fresh air.' In addition, Santa's roof no longer leaks. 'Thanks to the help of almost two billion children,' conditions improve and the story ends.

In an analysis of *When Santa Turned Green*, Brisman (2013, pp. 267–268) explains, that similar messages of child empowerment appear in stories such as *The Magic School Bus and the Climate Challenge* (Cole, 2010) and *The Berenstain Bears Go Green* (Berenstain & Berenstain, 2013). *The Magic School Bus and the Climate Challenge* offers a more in-depth, technical description of climate science and global warming, as well as overviews of alternative energies. With the exception of the suggestion to phone one's mayor, email one's senator or write the president, however, the emphasis is on individual actions to conserve and recycle. In *The Berenstain Bears Go Green*, the anthropomorphised family of Papa Bear, Mama Bear, Brother Bear, Sister Bear and Honey Bear are troubled not by climate change, but by the town dump, which is leaking oil into the creek. The family engages the political process with other residents of 'Bear Country': they complain at the town meeting. The mayor responds, but does so by urging individual efforts on behalf of the public good: he recommends a cleanup and then asks for volunteers. The residents clean up trash and haul away oil drums, and the story ends with the family deciding to carpool, compost, recycle and waste less energy and water. Only in Alyssa Crowne's *Green Princess Saves the Day* (2010) does the story revolve around political action aimed at *preventing* the state from abdicating its regulatory function and facilitating the transformation of public commons to private space: the protagonist, a little girl named Holly Greenwood, organises a march and picnic and circulates a petition to stop Peterson Park from being converted into a shopping centre.

Admittedly, the suggestions put forth in all of these books – walking instead of driving, composting, recycling, turning off lights when not in use, buying locally, replacing disposable/single-use items with reusable ones, participating in cleanups of public commons – are good, and such steps are important. But the disturbing pattern that emerges is one in which environmental degradation is individualised: global warming, for example, is attributed to personal transportation choices; any reference to the role of corporate entities or the state is missing. Such a practice, Brisman (2013, 2017b, 2019) and Brisman & South (2017c) argues, doubles down on the neoliberal logic that it is the duty and responsibility of *individuals*, not corporations or nation-states, to preserve, protect and repair (once damaged) nature, our planet and its ecosystems.

Indeed, many of such stories place the onus on young people and discharge adults of any accountability for the future of the biosphere: these stories ask the next generation (current young people) to instruct the present generation (of adults) how to act in the interests of future generations of humans. Although such stories avoid the 'adultism' ('the perception that children are not capable of providing accurate and constructive accounts of their lived experiences' (Stafford, 2017, p. 602; see also Dunkley & Smith, 2018, p. 6)) that some have criticised, they veer too far in the opposite direction: they 'adultify' young people prematurely, while at the same time, encourage 'adult regression, hoping to rekindle in grown-ups the tastes and habits of children' (Hayward, 2012, pp. 217, 216).

Essentially, in such stories, individuals are to blame for seemingly any and all environmental harm, and thus, individuals – and only individuals – can rectify the problems. Just as Ningard found some attorneys to be critical of 'overly authoritative regulatory agenc[ies]…unjustly punishing industry,' we see in these stories how corporate entities are never at fault and how there is no role for local, state and national governments (except to, once again, encourage personal action) to address ecological despoliation.

To be sure, while the theme of individualisation of causes, consequences and responses/solutions to environmental harm seems to run consistently throughout many children's stories, there has yet to be a systematic study of children's literature – a potential avenue for future green cultural criminological research. And, indeed, not all works fall into this restrictive category of neoliberal moralising. In fact, as Brisman (2017b) has submitted, if narratives can 'shape, inspire, and uphold crime' (Copes et al., 2015, p. 34) – if they can convey 'culturally relevant information' that 'shapes interpretations of the past and guides future action' (Keeton, 2015, p. 126) or 'motivate[s] and shape[s] practices' (Sandberg, 2016, p. 158) more generally, then narratives can influence future action (or can stimulate thought regarding future action) in both negative and positive ways with respect to *the natural world*, its *ecosystems* and the *biosphere as a whole*. Stories such as *The Peaceable Forest: India's Tale of Kindness to Animals* (Ely, 2012) and *Just a Dream* (Van Allsburg, 1990) reveal our capacity for changing for the better our attitudes, behaviours, patterns and practices with respect to the environment.

Of course, human faculty for adverse and affirmative change is quite variable – and what might go wrong in the process has been the subject of a wide range of literature (such as in *Solar*, the 2010 novel by Ian McEwan). The next section considers a different genre of literature for the narratively oriented green cultural criminologist to consider – allegories of environmental harm.

Allegories of Environmental Harm

Kennedy, Gioia, and Bauerlein (2005, pp. 4–5) put forth the following definition of *allegory*:

> A narrative in verse or prose in which the literal elements (characters, settings, actions) consistently point to a parallel sequence of ideas, values, realities, virtues, or other recognizable things. Allegory is often used to dramatize moral principles, historical events, religious systems, or political issues, often for didactic or satiric purposes. An allegory has two levels of meaning: a literal level that tells a surface story and a symbolic level in which the abstractions unfold.

Whether in the form of prose or verse, fable or epic, '[a]llegories turn abstract concepts or features into characters' or 'transform people and places into conceptual entities' (Mikics, 2007, p. 8). The only real requirement for allegory is that 'two or more levels of meaning must be sustained consistently and that the abstract meaning be, more or less, conventional' (Kennedy et al., 2005, p. 5). Put simply, 'Allegory wants us to know that it is being allegorical. It is always saying: watch me, I *mean* something. *I* mean something; I am being allegorical' (Wood, 1999, p. 185 (emphasis in original)).

Some consider allegory to be an 'inferior creation' in that involves 'a mechanical conversion of preexisting materials – for instance, a political situation – into fanciful narratives' (Kennedy et al., 2005, p. 5). As Kennedy et al. (2005, p. 5) explain, with allegory, '[t]he abstract meaning – for instance, a moral precept – exists independently of the work, the latter being a mere illustration of it.' A 'higher art,' according to critics of allegory, entails 'exercise[ing] the imagination upon reality and produc[ing] a new vision of things, not just a figurative version of them' (Kennedy et al., 2005, p. 5). Or, to return to Wood, allegory 'is very different from fiction. (It resembles bad fiction.)' (1999, p. 185)

The green criminologist has – or should have – no truck with the debate over allegory's worth as a literary technique. His or her primary concern is – or should be – with the (environmental) message, not the form or genre or method of conveyance. If anything, because '[a]llegory means' – because with allegory 'there is always something for everybody to translate' – because 'the shapes and extent of its meanings, the high narrow views and the broad low ones, the richly layered levels and the clean thin ones-these are hard to control, and demand an uncommon balance of knowledge, imagination, and restraint' (Stein, 1958, p. 329) – allegory should appeal to the green criminologist. In fact, because allegory has 'endured [the] vicissitude[s] of times, tribunals, religions, cultures' and 'has had a long practice in adapting itself to changing times' (Stein, 1958, pp. 324, 325), green criminologists may be especially interested in the ways in which human–environment relationships have been represented through allegory over the years, how they have (been) transformed and the meanings thereof.

To date, green criminologists have not examined allegories of environmental harm, although Ruggiero (2002) has reread Herman Melville's *Moby Dick* to illuminate points and issues of interest to green criminologists regarding acceptable and unacceptable economic practices. More recently, Brisman (2019) has allegorised the fable of *The Three Little Pigs* (and various permutations thereof) as a story of climate change migration. Because *The Three Little Pigs* is not ostensibly a story of environmental crime and harm, the exercise of reading it as a climate change narrative – one that dramatises human weakness and illustrates a moral with respect to climate-induced migration and injustice – is the opposite kind of endeavour to Brisman (2017b) and other green cultural criminological attempts to examine the dynamics of causation and response to environmental problems described in fiction and science fiction (including children's literature and young adult fiction) and discussed in the previous section. Nevertheless, in allegorising *The Three Little Pigs* as a story about climate change, Brisman (2019) argues that 'we can see visions of our ecocidal tendencies and an array of our potential responses to distributional differences – allowing us to decide *who we want to be* and *what we want to do*: be people that assist those more vulnerable and less fortunate than ourselves or be people that build fortresses of bricks to exclude those forced from their homes.'

Such an undertaking need not be a one-off. To illustrate, *Muncus Agruncus: A Bad Little Mouse* (Watson, 1976), tells the story of Muncus Agruncus, an adventure-loving mouse. Muncus is a master mischief-maker and we sense from the American author, Nancy Dingman Watson, that Muncus is frequently up to no good. On this particular escapade, Muncus enters the house of someone's (some *human*'s) house and proceeds to step in the flour, swing on the clock hands ('thus altering the hour' (p. 8)), tastes turkey, tromps in pies, dribbles ice cream on lace pillows, floods the bathroom, 'decorates' the top of a birthday cake and, barely escaping the swinging broom of a heavy-set woman, escapes to the home in his walls to plot his next bit of naughtiness.

With Watson's dactylic rhymes (such as 'Then up the broad staircase he jousted with pickles,/And danced on the down puff to see how it tickles' and 'Using a sliver of soap for a paddle/He sculled to the curtains and then, Skedaddle!' (pp. 11, 24)), the urge to regard Muncus as a romantic rebel is compelling, as is the hope that he will avoid apprehension. But we might also contemplate *Muncus Agruncus* as an allegory of human profligacy, wherein Muncus's gluttony in the kitchen – 'He tasted the turkey and tromped in the pies,/And gobbled his stomach full up to his eyes' (p. 9) – seems less like a discreet midnight snack, but a perverse championing of Western (excess) consumption.

In the bathroom, Muncus 'run[s] the bathwater full to the brim' (p. 13), pours in some bubbles, sets five small baby boats afloat, but forgets to 'turn off the tide' (p. 18). We might read this maritime excursion, then, less as a heroic triumph over adversity – recall that he uses the soap to row to safety – than a warning of rising tides due to anthropogenic climate change. Muncus's narrow escape ('All round the house he was chased with a broom/Till he found the back door, and none too soon' (p. 30)), as well as his subsequent plans for more mischief ('Muncus Agruncus was tired that night,/But he had fully recovered from fright./And on his desk were the maps and plans/For the next time he might find some time on his hands' (pp. 30–31)) can be seen not as a cause for celebration, but as an unfortunate case of humanity (still) not learning its lesson, despite its brushes with disaster. And while a child might view Muncus's fooling with the clock hands, noted above, as a clever idea for how to stay up past one's bedtime or miss the bus and be late for school, the contemporary (adult) reader might understand this as representative of the perils of toying dangerously with the Doomsday Clock, bringing us closer to human-made catastrophe.

To be clear, we read and tell stories – and *Muncus Agruncus* is no different – 'to entertain, pass the time, and arouse emotions' (Copes, 2016, p. 193). But, as Copes (2016, p. 193) makes clear, stories also serve other purposes and perform other functions. In fact, storytelling may be the way through which we, as human beings, make sense of our own lives and the lives of other people (Copes, 2016; McAdams, 1995). Indeed, by relaying exciting tales about the conquests or the failing of others – and Muncus is a good example – we 'shape social expectations of right and wrong behavior' (Copes, 2016, p. 193). And thus green criminologists might be particularly interested not just in the ways in which stories help us 'to know who we are and how we should behave' (Copes, 2016, p. 193 (citing Holstein & Gubrium, 2000)), but how, with a rereading of *Muncus Agruncus*, we might – or should – behave with respect to the environment. In other words, by allegorising existing tales, such as *Muncus Agruncus* or *The Three Little Pigs* or other such works, we can move from the role of passive analysis of cultural texts to active and creative interpretation that infuses current and prevailing stories with heightened consciousness of environmental harm.

Conclusion

This chapter has considered two examples of narrative criminological work focused on environmental crime and/or harm – an analysis of a corporate (offender's) website and an examination of attorneys' stories of environmental wrongdoing – which, taken together, depict a cultural narrative in the US of the causes, consequences, punishments (or lack thereof) and corporate representations of environmental harm. This chapter has also discussed examples of representations of environmental harm and protection in literature, focussing on *fictional* works that are explicitly environmental – where the subject, plot and message centre on one or more environmental issues, such as a particular harm, its cause or causes and possible responses thereto. Focussing on fiction, this chapter has argued, enables green criminologists to evaluate depictions of our near and distant future, as well as to imagine how we might reconfigure our relationship to the Earth – a trial run for the different options available to us. Finally, this chapter has explored 'allegories of environmental harm,' demonstrating how green criminologists have attempted to identify environmental lessons and messages in fictional works with ostensibly other or broader messages. Following Craig (2016), the intent has been to acknowledge both that cultural narratives (and our interpretation thereof) change and to demonstrate human agency to transform those narratives (and our interpretation thereof). For if anything is clear from green criminological study of environmental crimes, harms and risks, it is the need for dramatic transformations in the attitudes, behaviours, ideas, patterns, practices, structures and systems that have enabled the degradation of the Earth. A criminology attuned to environmental stories may well befit these present and emerging challenging dynamics.

References

Autesserre, S. (2012). Dangerous tales: Dominant narratives on the Congo and their unintended consequences. *African Affairs*, *111*(443), 202–222.

Beirne, P., & South, N. (Eds.). (2007). *Issues in Green Criminology: Confronting harms against environments, humanity and other animals*. Cullompton: Willan Publishing.

Berenstain, J., & Berenstain, M. (2013). *The Berenstain Bears go green*. New York: HarperCollins.

Bonneuil, C. (2015). The geological turn: narratives of the Anthropocene. In Clive Hamilton, Christophe Bonneuil, & François Gemmene (Eds.), *The Anthropocene and the Global Environmental Crisis: Rethinking modernity in a new epoch* (pp. 17–31). London and New York: Routledge.

Brisman, A. (2013). Not a Bedtime Story: Climate Change, Neoliberalism, and the Future of the Arctic. *Michigan State International Law Review*, *22*(1), 241–289.

Brisman, A. (2014). Of theory and meaning in green criminology. *International Journal for Crime, Justice and Social Democracy*, *3*(2), 22–35. doi:10.5204/ijcjsd.v3i2.173

Brisman, A. (2017a). An epilogue to the book, not an elegy for the Earth. In D. R. Goyes, H. Mol, A. Brisman, & N. South (Eds.), *Environmental crime in Latin America: The theft of nature and the poisoning of the land* (pp. 297–301). London: Palgrave Macmillan.

Brisman, A. (2017b). On narrative and green cultural criminology. *International Journal for Crime, Justice and Social Democracy*, *6*(2), 64–77. doi:10.5204/ijcjsd.v6i2.347

Brisman, A. (2017c). Representations of environmental crime and harm: A green-cultural criminological perspective on human-altered landscapes. In M. Brown & E. Carrabine (Eds.) *The Routledge international handbook of visual criminology* (pp. 523–539). London and New York: Routledge.

Brisman, A. (2019). The fable of the three little pigs, climate change and green cultural criminology. *International Journal for Crime, Justice and Social Democracy*, *8*(1), 46–69. doi:10.5204/ijcjsd.v8i1.470

Brisman, A., McClanahan, B., & South, N. (2014). Toward a green-cultural criminology of "the rural". *Critical Criminology: An International Journal*, *22*(4), 479–494. doi:10.1007/s10612-014-9250-7

Brisman, A., & South, N. (2012). Proposing a green-cultural criminology: A new perspective for 21st century criminology. [Predlog ekološko-kulturne kriminologije: nov pogled za kriminologijo 21 stoletja.]. In G. Meško, A. Sotlar, & K. Eman (Eds.), *Ecological crime and environmental protection—multidisciplinary perspectives*. [*Ekološka kriminaliteta in varovanje okolja – multidisciplinarne*

perspektive.] (pp. 17–35). Llubljana: Faculty of Criminal Justice, University of Maribor.
Brisman, A., & South, N. (2013). A green-cultural criminology: An exploratory outline. *Crime Media Culture*, 9(2), 115–135. doi:10.1177/1741659012467026
Brisman, A., & South, N. (2014). *Green cultural criminology: Constructions of environmental harm, consumerism, and resistance to ecocide.* London and New York: Routledge.
Brisman, A., & South, N. (2015). 'Life stage dissolution', infantilization and anti-social consumption: Implications for de-responsibilization, denial and environmental harm. *Young – Nordic Journal of Youth Research*, 23(3), 209–221. doi: 10.1177/1103308815584876
Brisman, A., & South, S. (2017a). Consumer technologies, crime and environmental implications. In M. R. McGuire & T. J. Holt (Eds.), *The Routledge handbook of technology, crime and justice* (pp. 310–324). London and New York: Routledge.
Brisman, A., & South, N. (2017b). Criminología verde cultural. In H. Mol, D. R. Goyes, N. South, & A. Brisman (Eds.), *Introducción a la criminología verde. Conceptos para nuevos horizontes y diálogos socioambientales* (pp. 97–127). [*Introduction to Green Criminology: Concepts for new horizons and socio-environmental dialogues.*] Bogotá: Editorial Temis S.A. and Universidad Antonio Nariño, Fondo Editorial.
Brisman, A., & South, N. (2017c). Green cultural criminology, intergenerational (in) equity and "life stage dissolution" In M. Hall, J. Maher, A. Nurse, G. Potter, N. South, & T. Wyatt (Eds.), *Greening criminology in the 21st century: Contemporary debates and future directions in the study of environmental harm* (pp. 219–232). Surrey: Ashgate.
Brisman, A., South, N., & White, R., (Eds.). (2015). *Environmental crime and social conflict: Contemporary and emerging issues.* Surrey: Ashgate.
Bunker, E. (1977). *The animal factory.* New York: Viking Press.
Bunker, E. (1981). *Little boy blue.* New York: St Martin's Griffin.
Christie, N. (1986). The ideal victim. In E. A. Fattah (Ed.), *From crime policy to victim policy* (pp. 17–30, chapter 1). London: Palgrave Macmillan.
Cole, J. (2010). *The magic school bus and the climate challenge.* New York: Scholastic Press.
Colvin, S. (2015). Why Should Criminology Care About Literary Fiction? Literature, Life Narratives and Telling Untellable Stories. *Punishment & Society*, 17(2), 211–229.
Copes, H. (2016). A narrative approach to studying symbolic boundaries among drug users: A qualitative meta-synthesis. *Crime Media Culture*, 12(2), 193–313.
Copes, H., Hochstetler, A., & Sandberg, S. (2014). Using a narrative framework to understand the drugs and violence nexus. *Criminal Justice Review*, 40(1), 32–46.
Copes, H., Hochstetler, A., & Sandberg, S. (2015). Using a narrative framework to understand the drugs and violence nexus. *Criminal Justice Review*, 40(1), 32–46.
Craig, R. K. (2016). Learning to live with the trickster: Narrating climate change and the value of resilience thinking. *Pace Environmental Law Review*, 33(3), 351–396.
Crewe, B. (2009). *The prisoner society: Power, adaptation, and social life in an English prison.* Oxford: Oxford University Press.
Crowne, A. (2010). *Green princess saves the day.* New York: Scholastic Press.

Dickinson, T., & Richard (2017). The Funny Side of Drug Dealing: Risk, Humor, and Narrative Identity. *Criminology, 55*(3), 691–720.

Di Ronco, A., Allen-Robertson, J., & South, N. (2019). Representing environmental harm and resistance on Twitter: The case of the TAP pipeline. *Crime Media Culture, 15*(1), 143–168. doi: 10.1177/1741659018760106

Dollinger, B. (2018). Subjects in criminality discourse: On the narrative positioning of young defendants. *Punishment & Society, 20*(4), 477–497.

Dunkley, R. A., & Smith, T. A. (2018). By-standing memories of curious observations: children's storied landscapes of ecological encounter. *Cultural Geographies*, 1–19. doi:10.1177/1474474018792652

Ely, K. (2012). *The Peaceable Forest: India's Tale of Kindness to Animals*. San Rafael, California: Insight Kids.

Fleetwood, J. (2016). Narrative habitus: Thinking through structure/agency in the narratives of offenders. *Crime Media Culture, 12*(2), 173–192.

Halsey, M., & White, R. (1998). Crime, ecophilosophy and environmental harm. *Theoretical Criminology, 2*(3), 345–371.

Hayward, K. (2012). Pantomime justice: A cultural criminological analysis of 'life stage dissolution'. *Crime Media Culture, 8*(2), 213–229. doi:10.1177/1741659012444443

Holstein, J. A., & Gubrium, J. F. (2000). *The self we live by: Narrative identity in a postmodern world*. New York: Oxford University Press.

Houge, A. B. (2018). Narrative expressivism: A criminological approach to the expressive function of international criminal justice. *Criminology and Criminal Justice, 19*, 1–17. doi:10.1177/1748895818787009

Keeton, R. M. (2015). "The race of pale men should increase and multiply": Religious narratives and Indian removal. In L. Presser & S. Sandberg (Eds.), *Narrative criminology: Understanding stories of crime* (pp. 125–149). New York: New York University Press.

Kennedy, X. J., Gioia, D., & Bauerlein, M. (2005). *Handbook of literary terms*. New York: Pearson.

Kidd, D. C., & Castano, E. (2013). Reading literary fiction improves theory of mind. *Science, 342*, 377–380.

Korten, D. C. (1995). *When corporations rule the world*. Bloomfield, IA: Kumarian Press.

Kurtz, D. L., & Upton, L. L. (2017). War stories and occupying soldiers: A narrative approach to understanding police culture and community conflict. *Critical Criminology: An International Journal, 25*(4), 539–558. doi: 10.1007/s10612-017-9369-4.

Lynch, M. J., Long, M. A., Stretesky, P. B., & Barrett, K. L. (2017). *Green Criminology: Crime, Justice and the Environment*. Oakland, CA: University of California Press.

Mazurek, J. E. (2017). Nemo's plight: Aquariums and animal abuse. In J. Maher, P. Beirne, & H. Peirpoint (Eds.), *The Palgrave international handbook of animal abuse studies* (pp. 313–336). Basingstoke: Palgrave Macmillan.

McAdams, D. P. (1995). Introductory commentary. *Journal of Narrative and Life History, 5*, 207–211.

McClanahan, B. (2014). Green and grey: Water justice, criminalization, and resistance. *Critical Criminology: An International Journal, 22*(4), 403–418. doi:10.1007/s10612-014-9241-8

McClanahan, B., Brisman, A., & South, N. (2017). Green criminology, culture, and cinema. In M. Brown & E. Carbine (Eds.), *The Oxford Encyclopedia of Crime, Media, and Popular Culture* Oxford: Oxford University Press. doi: 10.1093/acrefore/9780190264079.013.151.

Mikics, D. (2007). *A new handbook of literary terms*. New Haven, CT and London: Yale University Press.

Miller, J., Carbone-Lopez, K., & Gunderman, M. V. (2015). Gendered narratives of self, addiction, and recovery among women methamphetamine users. In L. Presser & S. Sandberg (Eds.), *Narrative criminology: Understanding stories of crime* (pp. 69–95). New York: New York University Press.

Newitz, A. (2019). We need 'Game of Thrones'. *The New York Times*, April 11, A31. Published online as "Why we need 'Game of Thrones'" on April 10, 2019. Retrieved from https://www.nytimes.com/2019/04/10/opinion/game-of-thrones.html?action=click&module=Opinion&pgtype=Homepage. Accessed on July 15, 2019.

Ningard, H. B. (2018). *Attorney stories of environmental crime: Harms, agents, and ideal cases*. PhD dissertation, Department of Sociology, University of Tennessee, Knoxville, TN, USA (defended August 1, 2018).

Page, J., & Goodman, P. (2018). Creative disruption: Edward Bunker, carceral habitus, and the criminological value of fiction. *Theoretical Criminology*, 1–18. doi: 10.1177/1362480618769866

Perla, V. (2007). *When Santa Turned Green*. Kantarevic, M. Illus. Nashville, TN: Thomas Nelson.

Presser, L. (2009). The narratives of offenders. *Theoretical Criminology*, *13*(2), 177–200.

Presser, L. (2010). Collecting and analyzing the stories of offenders. *Journal of Criminal Justice Education*, *21*(4), 431–446.

Presser, L. (2012). Getting on top through mass murder: Narrative, metaphor, and violence. *Crime Media Culture*, *8*(1), 3–21.

Presser, L. (2013). *Why we harm*. New Brunswick, NJ and London: Rutgers University Press.

Presser, L. (2016). Criminology and the narrative turn. *Crime Media Culture*, *12*(2), 137–151.

Presser, L., & Sandberg, S. (2015). Introduction: What is the story? In L. Presser & S. Sandberg (Eds.), *Narrative criminology: Understanding stories of crime* (pp. 1–20). New York: New York University Press.

Presser, L., & Sandberg, S. (2017). Narrative criminology. In A. Brisman, E. Carrabine, & N. South (Eds.), *The Routledge companion to criminological theory and concepts* (pp. 325–328, chapter 4.22). London and New York: Routledge.

Redmon, D. (2018). Video methods, green cultural criminology, and the anthropocene: SANCTUARY as a case study. *Deviant Behavior*, *39*(4), 495–511. doi: 10.1080/01639625.2017.1407110. Epub ahead of print January 10, 2018.

Ruggiero, V. (2002). Moby Dick and the crimes of the economy. *The British Journal of Criminology*, *42*(1), 96–108. doi:10.1093/bjc/42.1.96

Ruggiero, V., & South, N. (2013). Green criminology and crimes of the economy: Theory, research and praxis. *Critical Criminology: International Journal*, *21*(3), 359–373.

Sandberg, S. (2010). What can 'lies' tell us about life? Notes towards a framework of narrative criminology. *Journal of Criminal Justice Education, 21*(4), 447–465.

Sandberg, S. (2016). The importance of stories untold: Life-story, event-story and trope. *Crime Media Culture, 12*(2), 153–171.

Sandberg, S., Oksansen, A., Berntzen, L. E., & Kiilakoski, T. (2014). Stories in action: The cultural influences of school shootings on the terrorist attacks in Norway. *Critical Studies on Terrorism, 7*(2), 277–296.

Sandberg, S., & Tutenges, S. (2015). Meeting the Djinn: Stories of drug use, bad trips, and addiction. In L. Presser & S. Sandberg (Eds.), *Narrative criminology: Understanding stories of crime* (pp. 150–173). New York: New York University Press.

Sandberg, S., Tutenges, S., & Copes, H. (2015). Stories of violence: A narrative criminological study of ambiguity. *The British Journal of Criminology, 55*(6), 1168–1186.

Sandberg, S., & Ugelvik, T. (2016). The past, present, and future of narrative criminology: A review and an invitation. *Crime Media Culture, 12*(2), 129–136.

Savransky, R. (2016). Trump: 'All I know is what's on the internet'. *The Hill*, March 13. Retrieved from https://thehill.com/blogs/ballot-box/presidential-races/272824-trump-all-i-know-is-whats-on-the-internet. Accessed on July 15, 2019.

Schally, J. (2018). *Legitimizing corporate harm: The discourse of contemporary agribusiness*. London: Palgrave Macmillan.

Smith, K., & Waite, L. (2018). New and enduring narratives of vulnerability: Rethinking stories about the figure of the refugee. *Journal of Ethnic and Migration Studies*. doi:10.1080/1369183X.2018.1496816

Sollund, R. (Ed.). (2008). *Global harms: Ecological crime and speciesism*. New York: Nova Science Publishers, Inc.

South, N., & Brisman, A. (Eds.). (2013). *Routledge international handbook of green criminology*. London and New York: Routledge.

Stafford, L. (2017). 'What about my voice': emancipating the voices of children with disabilities through participant-centred methods. *Children's Geographies, 15*(5), 600–613.

Stein, A. (1958). Review: The criticism of allegory. (Reviewed work: The allegorical temper: Vision and reality in Book II of Spenser's "Faerie Queene" by H. Berger, Jr.) *Kenyon Review, 20*(2) (Spring), 322, 324–326, 328–330.

Van Allsburg, C. (1990). *Just a Dream*. New York: Houghton Mifflin.

Watson, N. D. (1976). In W. Watson (Illus.), *Muncus Agruncus: A bad little mouse*. New York: Golden Press/Western Publishing Company, Inc.

White, R. (2013). *Environmental harm: An eco-justice perspective*. Bristol: Policy Press.

White, R., & Heckenberg, D. (2014). *Green criminology: An introduction to the study of environmental harm*. London and New York: Routledge.

Wood, J. (1999). *The broken estate: Essays on literature and belief*. New York: Picador.

BEYOND 'TEXTS': IMAGES AND OBJECTS

Chapter 9

The Stories in Images: The Value of the Visual for Narrative Criminology

Heith Copes, Andy Hochstetler and Jared Ragland

Narratives are situated at the centre of social identities. By telling stories, we narrate who we believe we are and how we want others to see us. Needless to say, investigators have focussed the study of narratives predominantly on the oral stories people tell. Most agree that the style of the story, the depictions of the major characters and larger moral tales both shape and are shaped by perceptions of self. These components of narratives also influence the interpretations imposed by listeners and analysts. Oral stories are certainly vital to narrative identity, but so too are visual stories. The symbols of recognisable stories within images that people create, use and distribute can be powerful tools for identity (Copes & Ragland, 2016). People can mobilise symbols of known cultural types (e.g. rebels, Christians, drug users) in images in similar ways that storytellers mobilise them through verbal archetypes. People use these acculturated symbolic understandings to visually portray and personify how they would like to be seen. Indeed, the communication extends beyond what is said and heard and includes what can be seen. Consider the profile pictures professors published on university web sites, with backgrounds of books that are designed to communicate their stoic, undifferentiated, professional personae.

Our aim here is to demonstrate the value of the visual for narrative criminology in two ways. First, we illustrate how narrative scholars can incorporate images created by others into their analyses. We do this by focussing on how one long-time methamphetamine user (Chico) creates narratives through the use of visual and artistic expressions. Through images on his body, in his yard and on his home, Chico uses art and symbols to construct his identities. Second, we show how investigators can use images during interviews to facilitate participant narratives. The inclusion of images created by participants (or photographs of images) can be a powerful tool in eliciting narrative responses. Ultimately, we illustrate the value of incorporating images and symbols into both narrative analyses and interview settings for narrative criminology.

The Emerald Handbook of Narrative Criminology, 175–195
Copyright © 2019 Heith Copes, Andy Hochstetler and Jared Ragland
All rights of reproduction in any form reserved
doi:10.1108/978-1-78769-005-920191017

Narrative Criminology and Social Identity

Storytelling is the primary way that people construct personal identities (Gubrium & Holstein, 2000). The stories people tell are important for both explaining past behaviour (e.g. as retrospective excuses and justifications) and as possible guides for future behaviour (Presser & Sandberg, 2015). Those using a narrative criminology framework 'seek to explain crime and other harmful action as a function of the stories that actors and bystanders tell about themselves' (Presser, 2012, p. 5). Within this framework, stories are essential elements of culture that people use to interpret and justify behaviour. In addition, stories shape, inspire and uphold behaviour. Within this perspective, people are thought to act out cultural stories when committing acts of crime (Presser, 2009). Narrative criminology encompasses a variety of perspectives to study narratives and their importance for behaviour. Here we rely on a strain of narrative thought that focusses on the role of narratives in creating personal and social identities (Loseke, 2007).

According to Loseke (2007), narrative identity occurs at three levels: macro-level (cultural identities), meso-level (institutional and organisational identities) and micro-level (personal identities). Narratives at the macro-level shape cultural identities, which include 'the imagined characteristics of disembodied types of people that simplify a complex world and construct symbolic boundaries around types of social actors' (Loseke, 2007, p. 663). The groups created with cultural narratives are broad social classifications of abstract actors who represent generic social types. When referring to people who use drugs, cultural narratives reflect the larger cultural assumptions about these people. For instance, in the US terms such as junkies, crack moms, stoners and dope fiends reflect cultural narratives of people who use drugs. Such negative labels impart society's assumption that drug addiction is due to personal failure. Of course, there also are drug-related cultural identities that impart positive qualities to large numbers of people such as 'partier', 'wild child', 'motorhead', 'hippy', 'club kid' and 'outlaw'.

Narratives at the meso-level are those that produce organisational identities. Organisations that seek to bring about change in people's lives (e.g. drug courts, rehabilitation centres and hallway houses) create narratives of ideal clients or those thought to be at the highest chance of obtaining successful change. Those who work within the organisations then use these narratives when interacting with clients. Clients learn these organisational narratives (e.g. medical models vs criminal models of addiction) and this shapes how they manage their recovery. Organisational narratives can both aid or constrain people's attempts at change. For example, organisational narratives in prison rehabilitation groups tend to emphasise the importance of personal responsibility. This leads to staff forcing (through threats of kicking out of group) participants to forgo excuses of any kind for their crimes, which creates difficulties for those who wish to hold on to their accounts for why their crimes occurred (Fox, 1999).

Identity narratives at the micro-level are those that help shape personal identities. They are the specific ways that people construct personal self-understandings and present themselves publically (Loseke, 2007). Personal narratives are created by taking abstract, depersonalised narratives (i.e. cultural and organisational narratives) and adding complexity and personal perspective to the narratives to make them specific to themselves (Sandberg, 2013). The details and specificity added to larger narratives allow people to create a coherent self that is unique yet connected to a more abstract group. These narratives then provide a formula for action in specific situations.

An important aspect of narrative identity is the formation of symbolic boundaries that make clear distinctions among types of people. Symbolic boundaries are 'conceptual distinctions made by social actors to categorise objects, people, practices, and even time and space' (Lamont & Molnár, 2002, p. 168). Symbolic boundaries allow people to create informal dichotomies of people and behaviours. When developing and maintaining symbolic boundaries, people rely on shared narratives or storylines to situate their actions and selves within larger structures. These pre-existing stories are referred to as formula stories (which exist at cultural and organisational levels) and are essential for the construction and representation of personal identities (Loseke, 2007). Formula stories refer to 'narratives of typical actors engaging in typical behaviours within typical plots leading to expectable moral evaluations' (Loseke, 2007, p. 664). These stories seldom provide adequate descriptions of the practical experiences or unique characteristics of embodied people. Rather, they tend to have high drama, one-dimensional characters and ignore real life complexity. By using formula stories as frameworks, actors link personal experiences and behaviours with culturally meaningful groups (ones that listeners understand) for effective communication. The out-groups remain vague, whilst personal stories are plotted with specifics. Symbols, images and other visuals can represent these cultural understandings.

Self-portrayal and storytelling extend beyond linguistics. Katz (1988), for example, observed that street offenders dress with intention to communicate stylistically that they can acquire material goods but have not done so through arduous labour. They might, for example, wear name-brand exercise gear, squeaky clean construction boots or Yeezys depending on local fashions and their subcultural adherence. Some dress to communicate they are ready for a fight by eschewing comfortable clothing in favour of more fight-ready wear. Images on T-shirts may be selected to impart that one is not to be trifled with by presenting brass knuckles, inflammatory images or name brands associated with badness. Such representations are present not only in dress but also in demeanour. Katz (1988) notes that in certain circles people affect the demeanour of heroin users in the interest of looking cool or cold. Gambetta (2011) argues that because criminals face the risk of apprehension but need like-minded associates, they have more or less subtle ways of communicating who they are and their capabilities in the stylistic images of self they present in dress, demeanour and language. Those who frequently engage in street crime are attuned to identifying the authentic and the inauthentic and often have an idea who they are dealing with before any risky conversation occurs. In short, visuals impart meaning and aid in narrative identities.

In the case study that follows we show how Chico[1] used images (on his home, property and body) to construct narrative identities: as antiauthority rebel and as a kind, empathetic and generous friend. Specifically, we show how he develops identities that are in opposition to those valued in conventional society. He desires to be feared but not repugnant, especially among those who are close to him. He exists in worlds that can be dangerous and where one's material conditions are precarious and unpredictable, places where a few friends can be critical for survival. Therefore, the capacity for loyalty and empathy and willingness to help friends is an important and essential mark of his character. Communicating this to those who are close to him is easily as important as being tough and dangerous. Thus, he also portrays himself as a wise and compassionate helper, an elder who has seen it all and who aids others who are on a similar path.

Contextualising Photographs and Interviews

The photo-ethnography began in the summer of 2015 and lasted for approximately 18 months. All photographs included here were taken by Jared Ragland.[2] Data collection consisted of formal interviews (with 52 participants), informal observations and photography (of 29 participants). All participants were actively using meth and were living in rural, north Alabama at the time of the interviews; however, some did stop using over of the course of the project.

Jared Ragland, a photojournalist, and Heith Copes, a sociologist and criminologist, engaged in what some call 'appointment ethnography' (Lindegaard, 2018). Jared and Heith did the field work. Andy Hochstetler, another sociologist, contributed to analysis, and served as a neutral set of eyes in interpreting images and text. We, the former two ethnographers, made plans to meet people in advance of showing up. Meetings were initially arranged through a trusted recruiter or through snowball sampling. Early in the project we relied more heavily on the initial recruiter to set up the appointments with participants. As familiarity in the area was established, we were able to set up our own meetings with participants. After the initial interview with a participant, we asked if they could refer others who may be interested in participating. Jared took photographs of participants (with their consent) and we asked some participants to send photographs that they themselves had taken. (Chico did not send additional photographs.)

Whilst we draw on insights gained from our experiences from the project as a whole, here we focus on one participant – Chico – to illustrate the value of using photographs and images for narrative criminology. He, more than any other participant, boldly used symbols and imagery to represent himself. Thus, he was an ideal participant to highlight the value of studying images for narrative criminology. Chico became a participant who opened his home to us and who helped recruit other people. During the project (and even at the time of the

---

[1]All names included are aliases. We gave participants the power to choose their own aliases to give them a sense of agency in the project (Burgess-Proctor, 2015).
[2]More photographs from the project can be found at https://jaredragland.com.

writing), we were able to see multiple sides of him and see the changing symbols he created and used.

Chico participated in two formal interviews and many casual conversations. The interviews with Chico took place in his home, but we also interacted with him at local restaurants and other public places. The initial interview we conducted occurred on the night we first met him at his home and focused on his life history using drugs. The second interview was a photo/image elicitation interview. Photo-elicitation is a qualitative interview technique where researchers solicit responses, reactions and insights from participants by using photographs or other images as stimuli (Collier, 1957; Collier & Collier, 1986; Harper, 2002). For this interview, we created a photograph interview kit consisting of nine photographs of Chico, his home and the symbols he created. We then showed digital copies of these images and asked him what they meant to him and why he created them. We also asked him about images that we did not photograph (e.g. tattoos on nonvisible parts of his body). We did give Chico digital copies of the images; however, he seemed indifferent towards them and it does not appear that he has displayed them publically.

The analysis presented here is similar to other analyses of narrative identity with the exception that we include an analysis of the physical images he created and that we provide photographs here to better illustrate the ways Chico presented himself through these images. Whilst it was not always possible to get photographs of his identity performances, we include several here that we believe are representative of two of these performances. We include photographs here as a means to provide context to the stories and to draw readers into Chico's worlds. Thus, the analysis is on the images that Chico creates and his accounts of them and his life, rather than on the photographs taken by Ragland.

Our use of photographs is consistent with documentary photography (Copes, Tchoula, Kim, & Ragland, 2018; Schonberg & Bourgois, 2002), but it does have limitations. A key one, also faced by those selecting passages of text, is that presentation demands that investigators select only a few photographs. They must do so using a combination of artistic criteria, generalisability and selecting images that best communicate the categories the authors witnessed and intended (Copes et al., 2018). There are great advantages to including images by comparison to only text. Even when presenting the words of participants exactly as spoken, scholarly work is often abstract and detached from those whose lives are being studied. The photographs not only give insights into the ways that Chico narratively defines himself, but they also aid in humanising him. Human communication and self-presentation, after all, rely heavily on their visual components.

We recognise that care must be taken when using these types of images in research. Decontextualized images may reinforce negative cultural stereotypes more than counter them (Becker, 2007). This is because photographs can prompt multiple meanings in the viewing process (Becker, 2007; Schwartz, 1989). As such, we cannot control how others interpret the images included here; however, we hope that readers will interpret the images within the context of the data presented and our intentions. A goal is to complicate criminology that tends to portray criminality as an essential, intractable, singular trait. Interacting with people (including those who use drugs) in multiple parts of their lives reveals greater complexity and contradictions. We chose photographs that we think represent the experiences and beliefs of Chico and reflect the various ways that he tells his story.

Analysis of the symbols Chico created occurred later in the project. Our initial aim was to focus on the photographs that we took and that select participants sent to us. As the project progressed, we recognised the value in documenting the various images participants created, including art, the arrangement of home and yard and personal style. We began documenting images in the environment for later analysis. During the analysis of field notes and interview transcripts, we would look at the documented images to determine implicit and explicit meaning and consider how these images matched with the stories and narratives of the participants. We would also ask participants what the images meant and why they created them. In what follows, we illustrate Chico's narrative identities through our experiences with him, including direct quotes and photographs of the images he created.

Chico's Visual Narratives

Chico is a 50-year-old Hispanic man who has been using meth for nearly three decades. He lived in a trailer on property that his family owned on Sand Mountain, Alabama. The area is a sandstone plateau in northeast Alabama known for poverty, poultry processing plants, Pentecostal snake handlers, and methamphetamine use. Chico seldom worked – at least not at conventional workplaces. Rather, he cooked and sold methamphetamine and carried out various hustles for money to supplement a disability check he received. He was clear that these hustles do not usually involve 'serious crimes', albeit he openly acknowledged his capacity for violence against those he considers enemies. When asked how he supported his drug use he said, 'I am not robbing, I'm not stealing, I'm not killing. I could, and I may, but I'm not. I pray to the meth God and everything falls into place. It does'. His hustles involved scrapping metal, selling stuff on the internet and facilitating meth sells and taking a commission in either cash or drugs. Such activities often brought him in contact with legal authorities. In the time that we have known Chico, he has been to jail at least four times. For his most recent incarceration he served 1 year in state prison for marijuana possession.

Chico had frequent health problems, likely related to poverty, drug use and self-neglect. Most visible among these are his missing teeth, which has become synonymous with rural poverty and chronic meth use (Murakawa, 2011). Perhaps his most severe health issue (at least that he told us about) is being hepatitis C positive. Despite being aware of the treatment, he refused care. As he said, 'I got hepatitis C. They got a cure for it, fuck, I don't even want it. I am good'.

The people we interacted with during the project typically fell into one of two groups when discussing their meth use. One group was ashamed of their chronic use and their continuance caused them great anxiety and guilt. They hid their use as best as they could from family members and loved ones and often used alone so even their using partners did not know the full extent of what they consumed. They frequently made attempts at going clean, and although they fell short on this goal, their desire was real, if intermittent. The other group celebrated meth and were unrepentant users. Meth was fun and exciting. It gave them a sense of experiential superiority. They often believed that meth was dangerous, but they had the grit to indulge and stay in control. Not all could manage their use, but this group believed they could. Chico fit squarely among this latter group. In fact, Chico used meth daily. When asked how often he used meth he said, 'I do dope every day. I get high every single day'. He was a strong supporter and advocate for using meth, even though he believed strongly that 'dope is mean. It's mean'. Selling, cooking and using meth shaped his daily routines. In fact, he had no reservations about smoking meth in front of us, even on the first day that we met him. In short, Chico was one of the unrepentant.

> *What we call Methamphetamine is a problem. We know that. I'm thankful for the problem – Thank you problem! My god is a meth god, you know what I'm saying? Fuck the other God, fuck him, we don't need him. We need this meth god, that's all we need.*

When asked if meth was his drug of choice, Chico said, 'Is it my first love? Not by far. Is it my last love? I hope so – as far as chemical go'.

By all measures, Chico is marginalised. In many regards he fits the stereotypical image of the rural meth user (Linnemann & Wall, 2013). It would be easy to portray him as someone who fits this narrative. But he, like all of us, is more complex than this simple caricature. He also sees himself as a friend to many, a caring son and hopeful father. He is resourceful when he needs to be. He has a quick wit that makes interacting with him fun and interesting. When looking at the benevolent and charismatic parts of him it is easy to see him as a sympathetic character being shaped by structural and cultural conditions. Although, he would rather portray his own life as being freely selected by him.

In response to this economic and social marginalisation, Chico presented two dominant identities: a rebellious, antiauthority menace to outsiders (see Image 9.1) and a caring, generous friend to insiders (see Image 9.2). He displayed these identities through visible symbols (on his home and his body) and through his stories and his actions. It is in these contexts that we seek to show how he frames his life and creates meaningful identities, through his personal storytelling and his use of images. Our aim is to (1) show how the symbols Chico creates can be used in narrative analyses and (2) illustrate the value of introducing these images (either the actual image or photographs of the images) into interviews to elicit narratives.

Meeting Chico

The value of the visual for Chico's presentation of self was apparent when we first met him. In fact, the images on his home and his body set the tone for the initial interview and highlighted core aspects of his identity – the menacing rebel and outlaw, yet caring friend. Several months into the project we (Copes and Ragland) decided to stay the night in one of the local towns. Doing so would allow us to be around to interact with people at night, when they were more likely

182   Heith Copes et al.

Image 9.1.   Chico Stands in the Doorway of His Trailer, Sand Mountain, Marshall County, Ala. *Source:* Photo by Jared Ragland.

Image 9.2.   Chico in His Yard, Sand Mountain, Marshall County, Ala. *Source:* Photo by Jared Ragland.

to use meth. We got a call from a participant late that evening to connect us with someone we should meet. The participant said this new person was a long-time user, dealer and manufacturer of meth. The description led us to believe that this person would be a good contact and source for the project. We got his address and headed out. After driving a considerable distance down winding roads and through swaths of farmland, we finally found the new participant's home. It was so remote that we lost cell phone coverage. His place was a house trailer set on hilly open land lined by pine trees. As we pulled in we noticed a swastika nailed to the telephone pole in the front yard. As the lights of our truck shined on the trailer a large swastika painted on one side and an anarchy symbol on the other became visible. A tattered American flag, flown upside down, and a Confederate flag were attached to a flag pole. Hanging from one of the pine trees lining the front yard was what looked to be a noose. There was a large hand painted sign facing the road. One side read: 'Not all are welcome'. The other side read: 'Don't get caught being stupid' (see Image 9.3).

As we got out of the car, a shirtless man holding a machete appeared in the doorway of the trailer. He jumped down over the makeshift stairs and began walking quickly towards us, yelling incoherently. After checking us out and verifying that we were alone he invited us into his home. Despite this display, Chico was open and available for questions and conversation for the remainder of the night. Such openness and helpfulness from him continued throughout the project.

Image 9.3. Chico Stands in His Yard, Sand Mountain, Marshall County, Ala. Nearby a Hand-painted Sign Reads, 'DON'T GET CAUGHT BEING STUPID'. *Source:* Photo by Jared Ragland.

This initial meeting highlighted the way Chico used symbols and imagery to present himself to the world. The shocking symbols on the trailer, the carrying of a machete and his exposed, tattooed torso all helped to tell his story (at least parts of his story that he intended to be the first impression). It was clear that the initial identity he presented to us, and anyone who approached, was that of a menacing figure. However, as we got to know Chico and he came to see us as friends, he revealed other sides of himself.

Chico the Menacing Rebel

Perhaps the main identity Chico performed was that of a man who has given up on society and who should be seen as a menacing rebel. This character was at war with authority and polite society. He was against government interference in the lives of people, especially concerning drug use. He was very much opposed to the police. As he said, 'First and foremost the police hate me and I hate them. I got no love for 'em'. He was resistant to authority of any kind, which is one reason that he did not want to get treated for his hepatitis C. He was critical of the correctional system, and believed that in its current state it was too oppressive and strikingly similar to indentured servitude. He actively attempted to complicate the lives of those in authority, especially police. One day when we came to Chico's house he advised us not to park in a certain area because it was covered in broken glass. When we asked why there was broken glass, he said that he did that so police would have to park and walk in the glass when they came to his house. He would also intentionally alter the height of the deck and stairs into his home with the hopes of having an officer trip when coming in the house.

One way that Chico visually showed his resistance to authority was by publicly displaying symbols designed to offend. This is best illustrated by the way he decorated his home and yard (see Image 9.4). He regularly decorated his trailer with racist, antigovernment and general antipeople symbols. On one visit, Chico was on the run from police and was rarely home – it was just too risky to be in his house. But that did not prevent him from adding a bit of extra artwork before leaving. He said this artwork was yet another way to annoy local police. The symbols '100% 24/7' were meant to convey that he is always real and clearly the inference is that his character is all outlaw, and that he would never back down from his beliefs. FTW is an acronym for 'Fuck the World'.

Chico also created signs to convey his menacing personae. The signs gave a clear message – you are not welcome. When asked about the 'Don't get caught being stupid' sign he said, 'When people pull up that's what they see so people will be more aware of themselves'. His response was ominous in that the meaning was clearly threatening but still ambiguous. Was it a reminder for his friends to avoid being caught? Was it a warning for strangers to not come to his home and get harmed doing something foolish? Did it pertain only to potential robbers or thieves or was it a threat to any who were not invited or who did something deemed offensive? During one conversation he referenced this sign. He pointed to a bat in the room and said:

Image 9.4. Chico's Trailer, Sand Mountain, Marshall County, Ala.
Source: Photo by Jared Ragland.

That bat's for everybody. If you're in my house and somebody's fuckin' with you, get the bat and handle it. At the same time, if you're fuckin' with somebody you might get the bat put on you. The bat is real. I had to use it on a few people. I will hit you with a bat if you get caught being stupid, I promise you will meet the bat.

In this passage, he made a claim to the sincerity of the implicit threat and presented his menacing identity. In the same interview, he joked about the sign and how it might be interpreted when he said, 'that's how you know you're in the South'. He seldom gave clear answers to questions about what certain signs meant as he preferred to leave things vague, uncertain and difficult to predict. Such added mystique was part of the appeal of being dangerous. On one visit, we saw that he had stolen and displayed a Drug Free Zone sign on a tree (see Image 9.5). When asked to describe why he put it up he said, 'The police, man, they come to my house so many times this year it's unreal. Two in the morning, nine in morning, it didn't matter. Me and a buddy of mine went where the sign was at. I put that up for the police. Just to piss them off. And, maybe they won't bother me as much, but that didn't work [laughter]'. He found great humour in putting up this sign as he believed it mocked police and made ironic the notion that he could be controlled by a government statement.

Perhaps the most offensive yard displays were the noose and the effigy of a man hanging from his tree. During our first visit to Chico's home, we saw a noose hanging from one of the large pine trees that lined the property facing the road. It

186   Heith Copes et al.

Image 9.5. A 'DRUG FREE ZONE' Sign Is Posted to a Tree in Chico's Front Yard, Sand Mountain, Marshall County, Ala. *Source:* Photo by Jared Ragland.

disappeared for a time. Then one day it reappeared, but this time it included an effigy of a man, who he called 'hanging man' (see Image 9.6). We asked him about hanging man and told him that this was racist. He countered by saying:

> It ain't no different than if you ride by someone's house and they got those lawn ornaments, black people fishing, Mexican man with sombrero, or a fat lady bending over. If I was a fat lady I might be offended. It's not against the law. You can hang anything you want in the tree.

He would not accept that a hanging figure (with a brown bottle as face) was racist. Regardless, passers-by would not know the backstory to the effigy or know that he related it to representations of ethnic minorities found in conventional places. Whilst he was aware of the historic implications of a representation of a hanging person of colour, the offence was at least in part intentional.

Chico also used his body as a way to convey his antiauthority beliefs. Chico had numerous tattoos, many were memorials to loved ones, but not all. Image 9.6 shows many of his tattoos. His chest has two large Aryan style subjects; both are depictions of Viking warriors. The largest one is a portrait of a Viking with a large scar across his eye, perhaps Odin. The other is a warrior with sword and shield. The connotations of raiders and menacing figures were not lost on him, and the time he spent incarcerated means that he knew these images are associated with

Image 9.6. An Effigy Is Attached to a Noose in Chico's Front Yard, Sand Mountain, Marshall County, Ala. *Source:* Photo by Jared Ragland.

white pride by some even if they are common tattoo themes. On his arm was a large anarchy symbol. Image 9.7 shows his hands with the words 'Hell Fire' tattooed across his fingers. These words reflected both his willingness to fight (i.e. to bring hell to others) and his acceptance that he had experienced hell himself (i.e. hell fire was within him).

His unrepentant use and love for meth can be a shock for conventional others. The public expects people who use meth to be ashamed and guilt-ridden for their choices. This shock was part of the appeal for Chico. It likely was part of the decision to tattoo drug symbols on visible parts of his body. These include large images on his arms and hands. One theme of these tattoos is his fondness of drugs. On his left arm, in the midst of a numerous others, is a large marijuana leaf. A smaller marijuana leaf is on his right arm. He did say that he was not interested in getting any meth-related tattoos though.

Many of our earlier encounters with Chico included repeated attempts to shock us: from coming at us with a machete, to wearing a *dia de los muertos* mask (see Image 9.8) as he sat in his yard, to blatantly displaying and mentioning weapons in his home. He very much relished in the offence he caused to conventional sensibilities. Indeed, offending the conventional was a strong drive in much of his action and thought. He saw himself as a rebel and was intent on fighting the system and those who may condemn him, no matter how small the victory. His use of symbols on his home and body exemplified this identity narrative. It also was a recurrent theme in his verbally narrated story.

Image 9.7. Chico Holds a Propane Torch between Taking Hits of Meth and Smoking Marijuana Inside His Home on Sand Mountain, Marshall County, Ala. *Source:* Photo by Jared Ragland.

Image 9.8. Chico Wearing a Dia de los Muertos Masks, Sits in His Living Room Underneath a Swastika, Copy of the US Constitution and a Confederate Battle Flag. *Source:* Photo by Jared Ragland.

Chico the Friend

In addition to his menacing identity, Chico also presented himself as a good friend who sacrificed to help others. Chico saw himself as someone who would help friends in need and to look out for others. He said he was loyal and all in for those he considered friends. Such presentations of self were less visual than his menacing personae. Nevertheless, he did include a few visual representations of this part of his identity. On his skin, there were praying hands, several non-sexualized women and a few loved ones' names. On his arm he has 'Love Hurts' with the name of his ex-wife. Image 9.3 shows the name of his ex-wife with a rose over his chest.

The caring side of Chico was revealed to us one day when we visited him after his girlfriend left him. The details surrounding the event were complicated and we were given contradicting stories from him, his girlfriend and the man with whom she left. On this day Chico was sad and had been crying because not only had his girlfriend left him, but he believed she was a part of a plot to frame him for a crime. He carried around a letter that she wrote to him, and showed it to us as evidence that at least she cared for him at one time.

Women lived with Chico on two occasions over the time that we knew him. He recognised that there is much hassle that comes with painting shocking symbols on his trailer, and that this affects others. Neighbours heed warnings and are unavailable for help or even simple company to those residing with him. Police were suspicious of him and kept an eye on his place for suspicious activities. Thus, both times when women lived with him he painted over the antagonistic symbols so that the women would not have to deal with the consequences of them (see Image 9.9). As he described:

> *The police know what I do. I don't got to worry about nobody tellin' – they already know. They go by here pretty regular and slow roll. I did have a swastika painted on my trailer on the outside. I had a big anarchy symbol painted on this side. I just had covered it up a couple weeks ago. I got people in my house that I am concerned with and I don't want to see them get in no trouble. My little girlfriend ain't but 21. I don't want to see her get in no trouble, so I thought the law might stay away. They might take some of the folks off me, 'cause people would ride by here taking pictures and putting them on Facebook just amazed like, 'Oh a swastika and Hitler blah blah blah'. Y'all ain't Jewish by the way, are ya?*

Whilst this last sentence may sound ominous, he later explained that he did not subscribe to the racist ideology associated with Nazism. Rather, for him the symbols were merely used as displays to offend police and others in authority.

Chico was also generous with his belongings. He frequently let people down on their luck (either homeless or running from police) stay at his home. On one occasion he stayed with a friend who was on the run so he would not be by

Image 9.9. Chico and Alice Sit in the Front Yard of Chico's Trailer on Sand Mountain, Marshall County, Ala. *Source:* Photo by Jared Ragland.

himself – they were eventually both arrested. Another day when we were visiting him his cousin brought him a pickup truck load of alcohol that had been salvaged from a burned convenience store. He later told us that he gave almost all of it away. He even shared his meth, though not as frequently as other belongings. He repeatedly offered meth to us, which we always refused. His asking us if we wanted meth became a running joke – we interpreted it as his way of showing us that we were a part of his group through humour. On at least one occasion, Chico often asked us rhetorically, 'I'm not such a bad guy, right?'

The rebel image Chico displayed was primarily for outsiders, especially those in authority or those set to condemn him. The friend identity was more often presented for those closer to him and who spent time in his presence. Accordingly, it is the rebel identity that is more vigorously told through the visual. First impressions are important, and the intent was to look menacing. Whilst these two dimensions make up part of Chico's story, they certainly do not tell his whole story. There is much more to Chico.

Photo-elicitation and Narratives

Stories are the predominant way we construct personal identities, but images can be valuable tools to aid in eliciting narratives (Collier, 1957; Collier & Collier, 1986; Harper, 2002). Photo-elicitation interviews (PEIs) rely on selecting images that garner reactions, emotional responses and meanings that may not have been accessible using verbal methods alone (Suchar, 1989).[3] This is because images have the power to bring forth memories, emotions and reactions that words alone cannot. Whether the images are provided by the researchers or by the participants, images can connect concepts in ways that verbal communication cannot because images can 'mine deeper shafts into a different part of human consciousness than do words-alone interviews' (Harper, 2002, p. 23).

By asking participants about the images they create, researchers can engage participants by focussing on aspects of their lives that they find important. One reason it is important to use images to elicit interviews is because decontextualised images (whether images created by participants or photographs taken by researchers) can be interpreted in numerous ways. We really cannot know what a person is thinking or attempting to accomplish with the images they create unless we ask (Ferrell, 2001). Further, what participants physically create may be subject to even wider interpretation. For him, the swastikas on his home were not symbols of racial hatred or white pride. Rather, they were merely ways to annoy those in authority.

Linguistic and visual methods are not mutually exclusive; incorporating images into the standard interview process enhances each. Photo-elicitation is used to acquire insights that cannot be tapped into when relying strictly on oral interview methods or by simply looking at an image created by participants. PEIs can act as a trigger to memory, provide meaning or clarity to a situation and can evoke an emotional, multi-layered response in participants (Gariglio, 2016; Schwartz, 1989). When we showed Chico photographs of his trailer over the years (Images 9.4, 9.5 and 9.9) he was brought back to the circumstances that led him to paint the offensive signs or paint over them. He recalled fondly of the time Alice (a young woman he truly liked) lived with him. But he also remembered perceived betrayals. Indeed, he pointed out that 'hanging man' was wearing the clothes of a friend who had crossed him in a love triangle. Thus, people may have more detailed and emotional responses when photographs or other visual stimuli are included in the interview. When we showed Chico a portrait of himself from 2 years prior (Image 9.2) he became quiet and contemplative, until he broke the silence by saying, 'I must have been high there!' In short, one of the strengths of PEIs that involve the images participants create is that they help participants tell their personal identity narratives.

Interestingly, images and selected photographs designed to reflect how a person lives also give a participant a chance to see how they look through others eyes. During the PEI we said that some viewers may see a mean, scary racist when they look at the photograph in Image 9.1. He said, 'They don't know me. I'm not a racist. Do you tell them that I'm Mexican?' But he continued, 'That person, sometimes I have to be him'. His implication was that at times it is necessary to be seen as a scary person so that others do not try to take advantage of him.

---

[3]Whilst we use the term photo-elicitation interview we also mean the verbal introduction of any image into the interview to elicit responses.

Whether narrative criminologists are interested in studying offenders, victims, criminal justice agents or particular events, the use of photo-elicitation techniques offers a powerful addition to the more standard data collection of semi-structured interviews. The use of photographs and other images enhances the retrieval of memories, helps participants to demarcate change over time (in self-identity, lifestyle or personal circumstances) and allows for the more active participation of the researched in the research process. Indeed, our PEI interview with Chico helped to bring to focus his multi-layered experiential reality of his life – in both narrative and visual form. Just as narrative researchers strive to capture the multilingual in offenders' accounts, visual ethnographers can capture the multifocal.

Conclusion

As the study of narratives becomes increasingly important for understanding how people make sense of the past and how narratives direct future behaviour, it is important to recognise that not all narratives are spoken. It is true that narrative identity is performed primarily through language and verbal stories, but much communication is not verbal. People are not just the writers of their life stories, they are also the artists of them. Anthropologists have traditionally incorporated presentations in space and place, including people's homes, into their analyses. Space does not just shape passive recipients, rather people create their surroundings to convey personal narratives. We should not ignore the importance of created environments, images and symbols in constructing personal identity narratives. Symbols put on people's homes, clothing and bodies can shed light on their identities without requiring verbal interactions. It is probably safe to assume that these images not only reflect culturally situated understandings and resources, but they also are purposive and often imbued with messages. Our aim here was to add to the methodological study of narrative criminology by illustrating the value of analysing images created by participants and the power of using images to elicit narratives during interviews. To do this, we focussed on the way people (specifically Chico) used visual imagery to tell their stories. Chico's stories give some insights into how narrative criminologists can use the symbols people present as a means to examine their narrative identities. Simply driving by Chico's home tells a story of who lives there. Passers-by see the story of a man who opposes conventional expectations of appropriate behaviour, but they do not get the whole story. Getting the full story requires knowing Chico and hearing his interpretation of the symbols and how they fit into his narrative identity. Interacting with him and applying a theoretical lens can show how his identities are shaped by his marginalisation and accompanying refusal to acknowledge state authority. They also show that some of his intentions in presentation are not worked out completely or intended for outsiders to completely understand; perhaps part of the fun is in the abstraction as in art generally.

Two of our observations will be familiar to cultural criminologists. One is that images are created and selected for presentation by both the subject and the analyst (Ferrell, 2001; Hayward, 2010). Both have interpretations in mind during the stages of image production and presentation. The second is that outsiders can best interpret images with the help of those who originally produced them. Only by examining what producers say and by spending enough time with them to understand nuance can some of an images' meanings beyond the superficial be discerned. Only Chico knew some of the intentions of his projects before explaining them, and outsiders might not have expected some of the less obvious ones. He intended to play with and resist authority in much of his life and images, including by prodding authorities and the potentially judgemental wherever he could. He also intended to outrage and look dangerous to those who might threaten or bring trouble to him. He believed a strong intimidating front could prevent others from trying to take advantage of him. He resisted his circumstances by proudly proclaiming personal autonomy and how little he cared for the world and all conventional living in many images. At the same time, he indicated at times that his image production was partially a strategic ruse to keep those people he did not care about away and inconvenienced on the approach. Strangers seldom are benevolent for him, and do him little good. On our visits, his friends paid little attention to the menacing images around them, however. Chico wants others that know him to see that he is approachable, can be compassionate and will assist them; he also desires to be seen as a complex, person with a sense of humour by those that matter. Some intentions in his presentation were private, until someone asked and, of course, some may remain that way. Our aim here was to show the value of including images into the study of narratives, specifically narrative identity. It was not to make a determination whether Chico truly was a menacing figure or a caring friend. He probably is both depending on the situation. Rather, we simply described the ways that Chico variously presented himself through stories and artefacts (i.e. painting on home and signs).

People are autobiographical producers capable of improvising conversationally within frameworks and motifs shaped by cultures, structures and personal histories but with layers of dimension. We consider the past, present and future in deciding what aspects to present to which audiences. Whilst critics of photographs in analysis of those who use drugs or commit crime may loathe that photographs tend to be themed and therefore appear stereotypical at a glance, analysis and discussion on meaning with image producers is likely to reveal nuance, and judging by the current case a surprising amount of complex intention. We know that narrative criminology can gain much by including images in data collection and in analyses (as well as in the final products).

References

Becker, H. (2007). *Telling about society*. Chicago, IL: University of Chicago Press.

Burgess-Proctor, A. (2015). Methodological and ethical issues in feminist research with abused women: Reflections on participants' vulnerability and empowerment. *Women's Studies International Forum, 48,* 124–134.

Collier, J. (1957). Photography in anthropology: A report on two experiments. *American Anthropologist, 59*, 843–859.

Collier, J., & Collier, M. (1986). *Visual anthropology: Photography as a research method*. Albuquerque, NM: University of New Mexico Press.

Copes, H., & Ragland, J. (2016). Considering the implicit meanings in photographs in narrative criminology. *Crime, Media, Culture, 12*(2), 271.

Copes, H., Tchoula, W., Kim, J., & Ragland, J. (2018). Symbolic perceptions of methamphetamine: Differentiating between ice and shake. *International Journal of Drug Policy, 51*, 87–94.

Ferrell, J. (2001). *Tearing down the streets: Adventures in Urban Anarchy*. New York, NY: Palgrave Macmillan.

Fox, K. J. (1999). Changing violent minds: Discursive correction and resistance in the cognitive treatment of violent offenders in prison. *Social Problems, 46*, 88–103.

Gambetta, D. (2011). *Codes of the underworld: How criminals communicate*. Princeton, NJ and Oxford: Princeton University Press.

Gariglio, L. (2016). Photo-elicitation in prison ethnography: Breaking the ice in the field and unpacking prison officers' use of force. *Crime, Media, Culture, 12*(3), 367–379.

Gubrium, J. F., & Holstein, J. A. (2000). The self in a world of going concerns. *Symbolic Interaction, 23*(2), 95–115.

Harper, D. (2002). Talking about pictures: A case for photo elicitation. *Visual Studies, 17*(1), 13–26.

Hayward, K. (2010). Opening the lens: Cultural criminology and the image. In K. Hayward & M. Presdee (Eds.), *Framing crime: Cultural criminology and the image*. Abingdon: Routledge Cavendish.

Katz, J. (1988). *Seductions of crime: Moral and sensual attractions in doing evil*. New York, NY: Basic Books.

Lamont, M., & Molnár, V. (2002). The study of boundaries in the social sciences. *Annual Review of Sociology, 28*(1), 167–195.

Lindegaard, M. (2018). *Surviving gangs, violence and racism in Cape Town: Ghetto chameleons*. London: Routledge.

Linnemann, T., & Wall, T. (2013). 'This is your face on meth': The punitive spectacle of 'white trash'in the rural war on drugs. *Theoretical Criminology, 17*(3), 315–334.

Loseke, D. R. (2007). The study of identity as cultural, institutional, organizational, and personal narratives: Theoretical and empirical integrations. *The Sociological Quarterly, 48*(4), 661–688.

Murakawa, N. (2011). Toothless: The methamphetamine "epidemic," "meth mouth," and the racial construction of drug scares. *Du Bois Review: Social Science Research on Race, 8*(1), 219–228.

Presser, L. (2009). The narratives of offenders. *Theoretical Criminology, 13*(2), 177–200.

Presser, L. (2012). Getting on top through mass murder: Narrative, metaphor, and violence. *Crime, Media, Culture, 8*(1), 3–21.

Presser, L., & Sandberg, S. (Eds.). (2015). *Narrative criminology: Understanding stories of crime*. New York, NY: New York University Press.

Sandberg, S. (2013). Are self-narratives united or fragmented, strategic or determined? Reading Breivik's Manifesto in light of narrative criminology. *Acta Sociologica, 56*, 69–83.

Schonberg, J., & Bourgois, P. (2002). The politics of photographic aesthetics: Critically documenting the HIV epidemic among heroin injectors in Russia and the United States. *International Journal of Drug Policy, 13*, 387–392.

Schwartz, D. (1989). Visual ethnography: Using photography in qualitative research. *Qualitative Sociology, 12*, 119–154.

Suchar, C. S. (1989). The sociological imagination and documentary still photography: The interrogatory stance. *Visual Studies, 4*(2), 51–62.

Chapter 10

Reading Pictures: Piranesi and Carceral Landscapes

Eamonn Carrabine

Giovanni Battista Piranesi's disturbing images of fantasy prisons set out in his *Carceri d'Invenzione*, published in the middle decades of the eighteenth century, have had a profound impact on cultural sensibilities. In his own day, Piranesi had achieved acclaim for his images of the decaying architecture of ancient Rome and it was the scale of this 'melancholy dilapidation' (Scott, 1975, p. 20) that also informed the awesome imagery contained in the *Carceri*. The chapter explores Piranesi's distinctive visual language and situates it in an eighteenth-century penchant for ruins and what they might signify. The macabre fantasy structures bear little relation to actual, existing prison buildings, but they do herald a new aesthetic combining both terror and beauty to sublime effect. This chapter is the latest step in my ongoing effort to indicate how punishment has an art history and the project is one tracing forms of representation from the 1500s up to the present day (Carrabine, 2016, 2018a, 2018b). In this regard Piranesi's art is pivotal and his disturbing compositions demand detailed analysis, as they offer insight into the rich complexity of the relation between past and present.

The overall ambition is to indicate how punishment has an art history and by studying it as such the suggestion is that the gap between the disciplines might be bridged. It is driven by the premise that the history of punishment and the history of art are linked in ways that have yet to be fully recognised. For instance, studying the visual culture of punishment is a way of recovering a body of thought about how the poor 'saw' in eighteenth-century Britain, not least since one of the many slang terms for the gallows was the 'the sheriff's picture frame' (Gamer, 2015). Just under two decades ago it could be claimed that 'visual representations... have been largely ignored in the social sciences', which is indicative of a 'deep mistrust' of images (Holliday, 2000, pp. 503–504) in disciplines like anthropology, economics, geography and sociology, where the uses of visual material in social research has long been marginalised. Yet since then there has been a striking resurgence of interest in visual methods across the social sciences, which has been accompanied by a rise in scholarship on visual culture that has now established itself as an exciting and expanding intellectual field.

Visual criminology is one instance of this development (see Brown & Carrabine, 2017, for a range of examples, and McClanahan, 2019, for an account of the ways that rurality has been imagined and visualised as a landscape of horror), but the challenge remains one of constructing a framework that can do justice to both the power of images in social life and their place in social research. It is possible to see a distinctive form of 'visual narrative analysis' developing and covering a broad range of approaches: where some social scientists 'tell a story *with* images, others tell a story *about* images that themselves tell a story' (Riessman, 2008, pp. 140–141, emphasis in original). In this chapter I will be concentrating on the latter, but it is important to recognise the tensions between 'word' and 'image', where the word is associated with 'law, literacy, and the rule of elites', while the image is equated 'with popular superstition, illiteracy, and licentiousness' (Mitchell, 2015, p. 13). Especially since they are long-standing and concern a certain privileging of textual narrative over visual description, even in disciplines like art history where one would expect this not to be so. I begin by setting out these deep-seated tensions in a little more detail, as both visual and narrative approaches in criminology are still in their infancy and have much to learn from these disputes.

Image and Narrative

In his introduction to a ground-breaking collection of essays on art by leading French thinkers (including Barthes, Baudrillard, Foucault, Kristeva and Serres) Norman Bryson makes the point that so much Anglo-American art history 'reacts to the image by seeking documentation: that is where it does its reading – in documents' and he occasionally has the 'sense that patronage studies, in particular, will read *anything* rather than read the painting' (1988, p. xvi, emphasis in original). The collection was explicitly designed to address this audience and highlighted the importance of reading a painting as a semiotic sign and opened up this world to the then contemporary currents in 'critical theory', which had become the umbrella term to cover feminism, Marxism, psychoanalysis, postcolonialism and poststructuralism. This movement transformed art history as an academic discipline and was foundational to the 'new' art history that had begun to invade and challenge the tranquil domains of the visual arts. Scholars from various disciplines, most notably from literary studies and philosophy, have migrated to the field and revitalised art history, suggesting there is much to be gained from pursuing interdisciplinary strategies and crossing disciplinary borders.

The relationships between 'art history' and 'history' are also telling, and much can be gleaned from Hayden White's humorous intervention at a conference in the late 1980s, where he reportedly 'chided art historians with tongue-in-cheek comments about his "coming from the side of campus where *real history* is taught", which he distinguished from the "slide shows to young men and women ripe for a European tour"' (in Harris, 2001, p. 22, emphasis in original). This kind of scepticism towards art history's procedures as a form of historical enquiry was certainly significant in the critique of the discipline mounted from other radical quarters. White is an influential historian and his *Metahistory* (1973) provided a narrative analysis of classic historical texts, focussing on such nineteenth-century luminaries as Jules Michelet, Leopold Ranke, Alexis de Tocqueville and Jacob Burckhardt. He maintained that each modelled his narrative (or 'emplotted' to use White's own term) on a distinct literary genre – Michelet wrote his histories in the form of romance, Ranke in that of comedy, Tocqueville deployed tragedy and satire prevails in Burckhardt. Of course, this also poses the question of what is 'real' history and it has been said that White's own position sits on the border between two propositions: 'the conventional view that historians construct their texts and interpretations, and the unconventional view that they construct the past itself' (Burke, 2008, p. 83).

The chapter examines the relationships between narrative and visual methods by considering that scholarship in art history which has sought to address the relationships between 'word' and 'image'. Much of it belongs to the 'new art history' in the 1980s, and which had become critical of how conventional approaches in the discipline had tended to see art as the visualisation of narrative. For example, Bryson's (1981) study of French painting in the Ancien Régime explored the relationships between 'word' and 'image' by examining the kind of stories pictures tell, drawing a distinction between the 'discursive' aspects of an image (posing questions on visual art's language-like qualities and relationships to written text) and those 'figural' features that place the image as primarily a visual experience – it's 'being-as-image' – that is entirely independent of language. The tension between words and images was later explored by Mieke Bal (1991) in her *Reading Rembrandt* where she strives to reconcile a semiotics of visual art with a 'narratology' of it; drawing on her background in literary studies she studied the interplay of verbal and visual elements to understand the role of narrative in pictures. In particular, she examines how a still image tells a dynamic story unfolding in time, identifying 'how textuality determines the rhetorical effect of paintings' (Bal, 1991, p. 31).

Svetlana Alpers, in contrast, situates herself much more explicitly in opposition to the 'old art history' and its iconographic methods. Her *Art of Describing* (1983) insists that Italian Renaissance art, which preoccupied much of the writing of art history, is invested in narrative, while seventeenth-century Dutch art was concerned rather with 'picturing'. Dutch painting depicts or reconstructs the process of seeing itself as a central function of a visual culture where meaning is not so much 'read', but is instead 'seen'. Her essay 'Interpretation without Representation, or, The Viewing of Las Meninas' (1983/1995) takes Foucault's extraordinary reading of the enigmatic painting by the Spanish artist Velasquez, which completely bypassed art historical methods altogether in his discourse analysis of the picture, as the basis for articulating her own discontent with traditional art history methods. She acknowledges the strength of his analysis, which is carefully attuned to pictorial surface and his ambition to 'keep the relation of language to vision open' (Foucault, 1966/2002, p. 10). Foucault focused on the artwork itself, as if it were before him, and described in meticulous detail what he saw to prompt questions about the nature of representation itself. His analysis highlights how the picture works as a discourse by describing how the complex arrangement of visual exchanges in it speaks to various subject positions in complex and uncertain ways. It depicts Velasquez in the act of creating a portrait of Philip IV and his second wife Mariá Anna by placing the viewer in the positions that the sitters would have occupied – and they are shown only reflected in a distant mirror at the back of the painting – so that the spectator becomes Sovereign. The significance of the painting, Foucault maintains, rests in its self-reflexive awareness of what it means to represent the world.

It is here that Alpers suggests that the strength of Foucault's interpretation lies, as she goes on to argue that the picture oscillates between two contrasting modes of representation that are central to Western art. One mode, typically Italian, treats painting as like 'a window on the perceived world', where the artist and the viewer look from the 'same side of the picture surface' through the use of linear perspective, while the second mode 'is not a window but rather a surface onto which an image of the world casts itself' and is more Dutch, detached and descriptive (Alpers, 1983/1995, pp. 288–289). It treats the painterly surface as a fragment of the world, with no regard to human scale or viewer. The power of Las Meninas, Alpers argues, inheres in its dazzling embrace of these conflicting tactics of representation. This conclusion could not be reached through the then conventional art history methods, which have sought meaning through narrative plot, rather than close attention to visual representation. The force of her critique then resides in the need to see what is actually before our eyes, rather than rely purely on texts, to address 'fundamental questions about the nature of representation, meaning and interpretation' (Greslé, 2006, p. 227).

These remain important arguments and they indicate that one of the defining features of the 'new' art history was an 'interest in image/text relations' (Harris, 2001, p. 175), which have considerable importance as visual and narrative criminologies take shape. The focus on language is symptomatic of the 'linguistic turn' that has had such a profound influence on intellectual thought since the 1960s and this chapter will concentrate on one strand in it. In particular, it will introduce the approach Jacques Derrida developed and defined as 'deconstruction', which in some important respects revealed the limitations of language, and seeks to create the effects of 'decentring' by highlighting how signification is a complex, often duplicitous, process. The chapter then situates Piranesi's images in an account of landscape, not least since he was a leading exponent of the veduta (a faithful representation of an actual urban or rural view) that had achieved the status of a distinctive and popular genre by the eighteenth century. Yet it was only really from the 1500s that the first independent landscapes in the history of European art began to appear, and it is here we begin.

The Origins of Landscape

The emergence of landscape as a distinct, independent genre occurred during the sixteenth century and offered densely textured depictions of that quintessentially German place – the forest. In eerie scenes that create a mood of disorder these radical experiments in representation wrestled landscape away from its subsidiary role as pictorial setting for biblical or historical subjects. These were remarkable pictures that told 'no stories', mostly devoid of living creatures, human or animal, but 'which nevertheless make a powerful impression of incompleteness and silence' (Wood, 1993/2014, p. 9). Crucially, they originated in northern Europe, where the relationship of landscape place-setting to narrative storytelling was frequently different from the artistic output associated with the Italian Renaissance and particularly in Florence, Venice and Rome. Of course, there are some astonishing and complex landscape vistas in the great works from the period, but with only a handful of controversial exceptions do empty landscapes (that is without a human or religious subject) appear in finished, formal paintings. Nor do they yet exist as an independent, full-fledged genre. According to Christopher Wood (1993/2014) the origins of the tradition can be traced to the German painter Albrecht Altdorfer (c.1480–1538), a contemporary of Lucas Cranach and leading light of the Danube School of painters. Altdorfer's innovation was to prise 'landscape out of a merely supplementary relationship to subject matter' (Wood, 1993/2014, p. 41) and nothing like his enigmatic landscape paintings would be seen again until the end of the sixteenth century.

Wood's use of the term 'supplementary' here is deliberately designed to invoke Jacques Derrida's understanding of the 'supplement' to a work. Although Derrida mainly concentrated on philosophical and literary texts, he also deconstructed works of art – most notably in his *The Truth in Painting* (Derrida, 1978/1987) to explore the importance of the decorative, marginal elements that accompany the main theme of the picture. In much medieval and Renaissance painting the landscape is subordinate to the principal motif, the mere backdrop to the focal point of the action. The organising force of 'Argument used to be seen in opposition to 'by-work' or parergon, the accessory element' (Andrews, 1999, p. 7), and it was Derrida who challenged the conventional assumptions about the marginal status of the 'mere' supplement, emphasising mutual dependency rather than strict hierarchy. Instead, he questions the terms of the opposition, where par is taken to mean 'alongside' or 'against', and ergon is defined as 'work', so 'by-work' is regarded as a reasonable translation of parergon. The terms are deployed in Immanuel Kant's (1790/1992) *Critique of Judgement*, and Derrida (1979, p. 18) maintains that Kant's 'recourse to archaic, scholarly' language (Greek in this instance) is to confer 'something approximating conceptual dignity on the notion of the hors d'ouevre which does not remain simply outside of the work, acting from the sidelines, next to the work (ergon)'. Derrida emphasises that the pargeron, for Kant and philosophical thought generally, is a way of relegating marginal elements and operates against the main work (the ergon).

The process can be seen in a contemporary account where the term parerga is used in this supplementary sense, in a comment made by Bishop Paolo Giovio (a historian and art collector) in 1527 on the Ferrarese court painter Dosso Dossi, where he states:

> The elegant talent of Dosso of Ferrara is proven in his proper works, but most of all in those that are called parerga. For in pursuing with pleasurable labour the delightful diversions of painting, he used to depict jagged rocks, green groves, the firm

banks of traversing rivers, the flourishing work of the countryside, the joyful and fervid toil of the peasants, and also the distant prospects of land and sea, fleets, fowling, hunting, and all those sorts of things so agreeable to the eyes in an agreeable and festive manner. (Giovio in Wood, 1993/2014, pp. 64–65).

In the passage a clear distinction is drawn between 'proper' painting, which we can assume would refer to portraits, historical and religious subjects, and those diversionary elements indulged in simply for pleasure.

It is striking that landscape painting had a somewhat 'deferred development' in the West, and that in other parts of the world (as in China, for example) 'landscape painting was an advanced art by the time of the Dark Ages in Europe' (Casey, 2002, p. 5). The question of why it took so long for an independent landscape tradition to emerge is a complex question to answer, not least since many medieval and Renaissance artists could certainly depict landscapes exceptionally well. The promotion of landscape from periphery to centre was accomplished initially by giving landscape a 'name, and thus an invisible and virtual frame' and then 'by sealing it off from texts and other pictures with a physical frame' (Wood, 1993/2014, p. 51). In Derrida the ambition is to demonstrate how porous the boundaries are between the ergon (the 'work') and parergon (the 'bywork'), and he draws on examples in Kant (1790/1992) to indicate how the drapery on near-nude statues, columns on a building and the frames for paintings are transitional elements, troubling what constitutes the 'inside' and 'outside', and are types of pargera (accessory, ornament, decoration).

In a characteristic move Derrida deploys the idea of parergon to deconstruct the theoretical apparatus structuring Kant's argument and he cites such paintings as Lucas Cranach's (1532) *Lucretia*, depicting a nude woman wearing a transparent veil, to disturb the neat categories Kant tries to impose. Derrida's argument has been helpfully summarised as follows:

> In the first instance the ergon is the nude (literally as well as figuratively in the 'body') and the drapery is the ornamental extra. But the body as 'nude' is partly constituted by the co-presence of the drapery. The nude needs the pargeron drapery to reinforce the sense of nudity; so it is dependent upon, and collaborative with, the so-called ornamental extra, and that ornamental extra loses its status as independent, dispensable supplement. (Andrews, 1999, p. 7).

Indeed, the supplement is most definitely not incidental, rather it highlights the internal 'lack in the system it augments' (Derrida, 1979, p. 22). The process of signification is radically decentred here, and his method of deconstruction delights in exposing how philosophical texts (like Kant's in this example) attempt to suppress the unsettling effects of their own use of language. Such manoeuvres often involve forms of conceptual violence or exclusion and are tempered by an anxious sense of their own instability, as revealed in his analysis of Kant's distinction between the picture and it's frame, the 'inside' and 'outside' of a work, an opposition that once questioned undermines the entire thrust of Kant's *Critique of Judgement*.

It was Derrida's contention that both visual and verbal practices never exist in any pure or unmediated form, while an 'otherness' always haunts a work. By illustrating how the parergon pollutes the purity of the ergon he invites us to reconsider the conventionally low status of landscape in art and rethink the significance of the marginal. It complicates the relationship between the inside and outside of an art object, so that the frame becomes the focus of his essay, expanding what we think frames are and what they do. In Wood's (1993/2014, p. 73) account of how the trifling by-work came to trouble the main subject matter he notes how it was the German Renaissance that 'contributed to the broader process of centring the supplement by aggressively converting portions or aspects of the picture that had once been accessory to its purpose, landscape in particular, into the most conspicuous theatres for pictorial ingenuity and inventiveness'.

During the seventeenth century a self-conscious tradition of landscape art and painting became firmly established and was accompanied by generic (paysage in French, paesaggio in Italian) and subgeneric codification, with a system of rules and conventions seeking to aesthetically process the terrestrial environment. The geographer Yi-Fu Tuan has noted how in late sixteenth-century England the concept of landscape 'shed its earthbound roots' and 'became fully integrated with the world of make-believe' (cited in Kelsey, 2008, p. 205). Under this singular term lurk two rather different ideas, one of 'domain' and the other of 'scenery', are encapsulated in Dr Johnson's classic 1755 dictionary definition of landscape: (1) 'A region, the prospect of a country'; (2) 'A picture, representing an extent of space, with the various objects in it' (cited in Olwig, 2008, p. 159). It is the play between these meanings that accounts for how landscape works as a cultural practice, as a medium naturalising deep-seated political agendas (see also Mitchell, 2002, for an influential discussion of this point).

Dark Visions

Once this fictional quality of landscape is recognised, it is not difficult to see how the genre could be deployed with such versatility and speak to so many imagined communities. It is this flexible duplicity that is largely responsible for its ensuing durability:

> adapted as it was to classical idioms (the paysage historique à la Poussin); the homely rural scene (as in Dutch seventeenth-century art, or in the work of British artists such as Constable and Turner); the Romantic sublime (as in the work of the German Caspar David Friedrich or the British John Martin); the 'realist' and regionally specific landscapes of nineteenth-century artists (including those of the Impressionists), and the many varieties of the picturesque purveyed in both elite and mass cultural forms, from grandiose painting to modest lithograph. (Solomon-Godeau, 2010/2017, p. 108).

The passage gives a sense of the range of ways the world has been portrayed. Of course, it cannot convey all the developments and conventions associated with how we come to view land as a landscape, let alone our place in it, but it does point to when and why certain cherished images of 'nature' began to take centre stage. Landscape art, consequently, has been understood as a key site for articulating class relations, a means of forging national identity, a vital mechanism in the exercise of colonial power, and a web of gendered values embedding processes of subjugation (see also Carrabine, 2018c, for further elaboration on these different dynamics).

Representations of landscape convey certain mythologies; as the eco-feminist Carolyn Merchant (1996, p. 43) put it, the 'narrative of frontier expansion is a story of male energy subduing female Nature, taming the wild, plowing the land, recreating the garden lost by Eve' and this civilising mission made 'the land safe for capitalism and commodity production'. More recently Bill McClanahan (2019, p. 2) has drawn on ideas from ecocriticism to enliven a green criminological imagination through an analysis of horror cinema's representations of rural landscapes, urging us to 'recognize what we might think of as ecologies of horror and the horror of ecology'. Many commentators have gone beyond simply regarding landscape as a category of imagery, acknowledging instead that it is a category of perception and a historical force. Here, the landscape genre is subjected to a process of 'reading' in which real and imagined spaces are conceived as 'texts', visual and verbal modes of representation, containing traces of contemporary political and social relations.

The essays in Simon Pugh's (1990b) *Reading Landscape: Country-City-Capital* provide a now classic intervention, which were inspired by the cultural critic Raymond Williams, and explore the passage from rural to metropolitan capitalism in the genre. This re-visioning of landscape is an important step towards a fuller understanding of Piranesi's artistic achievements and innovations. His vast output, which combined with remarkable flights of fantasy, created a new and lasting poetics of representation. The *Carceri*, or Prisons, are hailed as his most celebrated work today, yet the acclaim is out of all proportion to their modest position within Piranesi's immense oeuvre and they were initially intended as a private work, thought to be of only minor appeal to the young artist's public and rarely purchased. Their first appearance was around 1745, under the title *Invenzioni capric di carceri*, which were later substantially reworked and republished the 14 plates with two additional compositions under the title *Carceri d'invenzione* in 1761, when Piranesi was 41 and at a critical stage in his career.

If seen the *Carceri* series is seldom forgotten. Fig. 10.1 is one of the menacing images from it, depicting a macabre fantasy structure where carceral space is expanded to the point of dizziness. The sinister subterranean scene deploys a fragmented perspective in which shadowy human figures as well as the viewer's gaze become lost. The multiplication of staircases, suspended beams, grates, chains and ropes combined with the haunting presence of silhouettes gives of the impression of an entrapment in hell. It has been said that such 'arresting details' are like the 'focussed moments in a confused dream, confused because there is no narrative to follow, because it is never clear what exactly the figures are doing and

Fig. 10.1. Giovanni Battista Piranesi, *Carceri*, pl X, First State, c.1745. *Source:* © The Trustees of the British Museum.

because it is not even at all clear what manner of prisons these are' (Penny, 1988, p. 11). A question that immediately arises is where did these nightmare visions come from? One response is to say that the series creatively combines various artistic trends of the eighteenth century. A key influence is a Baroque tradition of theatrical stage design that is largely lost to us now (they have long since crumbled away). Those drawings and designs that have survived are associated with the work of Ferdinando and Francesco Galli, known as Bibiena after their home town, and their family who devised ingenious sets that were widely imitated across Europe from the end of the seventeenth century onwards. Their innovation was to produce a scene per angolo (a way of looking at things at an angle) that appeared to deepen the stage and gave quite extravagant illusions of perspective. Ferdinando Bibiena expounded on the principles in his major treatise Architettura Civile, of 1711, which carefully set out how to achieve the dynamism of this new concept, where the traditional centre viewpoint was dispensed with in favour of several diagonal axes, creating rich spatial vistas (see Fig. 10.2) stimulating the vision of spectators.

None of these designers, however, relished the qualities of stone masonry quite as much as Piranesi. In this regard it is worth emphasising that pivotal to understanding Piranesi's 'strange originality lies in his insistence on being styled architeto veneziano' (Wilton-Ely, 1978a, p. 11). Although he remains one of the

Fig. 10.2. Ferdinando Galli de Bibiena, Illustration of a Scene Design from *Direzioni della Prospettiva Teorica*, c.1711. *Source:* McNay Art Museum/Art Resource, NY. © Photo SCALA, Florence.

greatest topographical engravers of all time, his proud and rather eccentrically assumed title of Venetian architect reveals a lifelong passion for architecture throughout a prolific and varied career. He built very little, yet the lack of practical architectural commissions obliged him to sharpen his skills in etching souvenir views for the flourishing Grand Tour market in Rome. It was in 1740 that he first arrived in the Eternal City, as a 20-year-old draftsman attached to the Venetian ambassador, which became his subject and home for the rest of his life – virtually inventing the idea of Rome's 'tragic beauty' (Yourcenar, 1962/1984, p. 88) in over a thousand or so haunting engravings of the city.

Shortly after his first visit to Rome he would memorably write, 'Speaking ruins have filled my spirit with images that accurate drawings could never have succeeded in conveying' (cited in Pinto, 2015, p. 1), which conveys his enthusiasm for the expressive quality of ruins and architectural fantasy. Yet the importance of his Venetian origins and training in architecture and stage design are regarded as the most potent of influences. Especially since Venice, with its many opera houses and theatres, offered numerous opportunities for imaginative designers, and its lively traditions of spectacle in state ceremonies, processions and festivals were particularly open to the world of the stage, illusion and fantasy. The city itself was the most densely urban of environments, providing a sensual theatre of architectural experiences and changing perspectives, intensified by varying atmospheric effects of light and colour. In Venetian art there is a long tradition of introspection and subtle awareness of the city's vulnerability that is manifest in the topographical details included in the religious pictures and background settings of early Renaissance portraits. This tradition was given fresh impetus at the time of Piranesi's birth and was one he was later to explore across his work.

Fascinating Ruins

It is no accident that Venice was the birthplace of the veduta, which translates as 'view' and refers to the faithful representation of an actual urban or rural landscape that is largely topographical in conception. The earliest exponents came from northern Europe, where topography in the art of the cartographer and the painter had been preoccupied with observed fact, stretching back to the fifteenth century. Landscape views and maps were often combined here in diverse and elaborate ways, so that when the Dutch artist Gaspar van Wittel (later famous as Van Vitelli) arrived in Venice around 1697 and painted panoramic views of the city, he was drawing on this tradition while initiating a school of view painting that became a phenomenon in the eighteenth century. Canaletto was the most celebrated practitioner of it and patronage by the 'milordi inglesi' was to make the veduta the most popular contemporary art form (alongside the commemorative portrait), quickly spreading to other important centres on the peninsula, including Rome, Florence and Naples. His immense success was almost completely dependent on the admiration of wealthy foreign travellers, mostly British, for whom the picturesqueness of Venice held a special attraction. These works include the Grand Canal looking West towards the Carità (see Fig. 10.3), which displays his extraordinary ability to render the light, life, buildings, and expanse of Venice in carefully crafted compositions. The semblance of realism and precise observation is highly contrived, requiring considerable skill and using theatrical effects to enliven the scene, compressing a formidable amount of topographical detail into the setting.

The popularity of these images is bound up with the Grand Tour, which was seen in European aristocratic and intellectual circles as a mandatory trip dedicated to completing one's cultural education. It reached a peak in the eighteenth century, becoming a social and socialising form of travel, with an established set of conventions and itinerary. Italy became the preferred destination of wealthy Northern Europeans who came for sojourns lasting months or years, creating a

Fig. 10.3. Canaletto *The Mouth of the Grand Canal Looking West towards the Carità*, c.1729–1730. *Source:* Royal Collection Trust/© Her Majesty Queen Elizabeth II 2019.

demand for paintings, drawings and etchings to be purchased as souvenirs of their foreign travels. Coinciding with this fashion was a taste for ruins; especially the remains of ancient buildings that were thought to bear witness to a noble past that was irretrievably lost. Thus, a genre developed that sought to represent ideal landscapes in a purely decorative way. These became known as capriccios, or caprice, defined as 'whimsical fantasises', where imaginary elements are added to real landscapes. Giovanni Paolo Panini developed the art form in Rome in paintings such as *Roman Capriccio: The Pantheon and Other Monuments* (see Fig. 10.4), which collects an array of ancient monuments and deposits them in a fanciful rural setting with scant regard for topographical fidelity. The ruin becomes a fiction, transitioning from margin to centre:

> The caprice represents the move of the ruin in painting from the background to the status of subject. We can speak of the poetics of a representation when it has become the subject of invention and thus a work of art unto itself. In the case of the caprice painting, ruined architecture has become the focal point of the artist's invention. (Augustyn, 2000, p. 433).

The ruin's earlier condition as periphery to, and setting for, the main subject is analogous to the very status of landscape in relation to the religious subjects of painting, as discussed at the beginning of this chapter, where the shifting emphasis on the supplementary, decorative and ornamental cautions against underplaying the significance of its function.

Fig. 10.4. Giovanni Paolo Panini, *Roman Capriccio: The Pantheon and Other Monuments*, 1735. *Source:* © Indianapolis Museum of Art.

Rome was the city most visited on the Grand Tour and had become the Mecca for travellers by the time Piranesi arrived. Shortly after he was producing veduta and adopting the etched view as a means of securing a livelihood, identifying what would sell in this dynamic market, which in turn became much sought-after mementoes by wealthy foreign visitors. In this initial work 'ruins are shown in their surroundings more or less correctly, without being oversized, later they became huge in comparison with their setting and with the unnaturally dwarfed figures that populate them' (Lehman, 1961, p. 91). Fig. 10.5 is an example anticipating this increasing sense of the histrionic, where the towering ruins of antiquity (in this example it is the remains of an aqueduct system) stand aloof from the mundane activity below, where the inclusion of a clothes-line adds a humorous, yet humbling detail to the scene and is characteristic of his earlier work. It has been said that the 'souvenir is the relic secularised, but whereas the relic derives from the corpse, a presence, the souvenir is 'dead' experience' (Pugh, 1990a, p. 145). There is a sense in which souvenirs, ruins, monuments and emblems revived earlier memento mori – mediations on the transience of life on earth – in more secular forms of vanitas.

In Piranesi's etchings of decaying architecture we can see how the scale of this slow destruction informed the extraordinary imagery contained in the *Carceri*, which blends architectural fantasy with a powerful and unsettling vision of confinement. These are the 'only works in which Piranesi abandons himself to

Fig. 10.5. Giovanni Battista Piranesi, *Vedute di Roma: the Fontana dell' Acqua Giulia*, c.1753. Source: © National Galleries of Scotland.

what he called his caprice, or to put it better, to his obsessions and to his hallucinations' (Yourcenar, 1962/1984, p. 105). It seems that his main creative energies were focussed on these capriccios, as a vehicle for architectural experimentation and improvisation, organised around a certain set of themes. Indeed, another reading insists that the compositions reveal 'a highly controlled discipline at work, exploiting the mechanics of baroque illusionism through perspective and lighting to explore new dimensions of architectural expression' (Wilton-Ely, 1978b, p. 72). The penchant for ruins spoke not only to nostalgia, of fallen majesty, but they also have a tragic quality and the sociologist Georg Simmel managed to convey this feeling when he wrote in a 1911 essay on the ruin that 'what strikes us is not, to be sure, that human beings destroy the work of man – this is indeed achieved by nature – but that men *let it decay*' (Simmel, 1911/1958, p. 380, emphasis in original). What is unsettling is that such 'places, sinking from life, still strike us as settings of a life' and that it is human will that 'has led the building upward'; while 'what gives it its present appearance is the brute, downward-dragging, corroding, crumbling power of nature' (1911/1958, p. 381). The wilderness of nature and how we are all at the mercy of dark forces beyond our control would become crucial to the revival of the Gothic imagination in the late eighteenth and nineteenth centuries. Piranesi's imaginary prisons bear little relation to existing prison buildings or any traditional images of them, but they do herald a new aesthetic combining both terror and power to sublime effect.

Sublime Effects

As an aesthetic concept, which originated in classical Greece, the sublime was the subject of considerable debate in the eighteenth century, not least since the experience of it was the antithesis of all the values associated with the Age of Reason in which it was so enthusiastically embraced. The concept was most influentially developed by the English thinker Edmund Burke, whose *Philosophical Inquiry into the Origin of our Ideas of the Sublime and Beautiful*, was originally published in 1757. Although many thinkers had addressed 'the beautiful' by identifying it with classical ideals of harmony, grace and proportion, others thought it eluded a universally comprehensive definition, Burke's unique contribution was to identify 'the sublime' as all-consuming force beyond beauty that mixes pleasure with pain and fear in all who behold it. Many of the chapter headings in the Inquiry could just as easily be titles for Piranesi's prison drawings: 'Terror', 'Privation', 'Vastness', 'Infinity', 'Difficulty' and so forth. Here there is an attempt to explain why ancient ruins, dark forests, inaccessible castles, dank dungeons and raging thunderstorms (amongst other elemental forces) were becoming attractive to a new artistic and literary sensibility developing in the eighteenth century. The sublime signals the limits of rationality and Burke's *Enquiry* was the first text to realise and systematise this profound change in aesthetic values.

The re-publication in 1761 of the *Carceri* involved a substantial reworking of the plates with stronger tonal contrasts, while architectural immensity and spatial ambiguity were further amplified (see Fig. 10.6 for an example). This version is regarded as definitive and was the one destined to achieve European influence. The overall tone is more sinister, where vast new structures recede to infinity and exemplify Burke's understanding of the sublime. For some commentators the major thematic change is one veering towards melodrama to achieve this effect:

> With few exceptions, the physical horror of prisons was now rendered explicit in terms of their structural immensity and spatial complexity...Also now inserted is a complete repertoire of penal apparatus in the form of chains, cables, gallows and sinisterly indistinct instruments of torture, many of them infused with a sense of decay through endless use. Animating this punitory hell is an increased number of figures, together with certain episodes of punishment being enacted. Although this latter feature already appears once in the original version with plate X [Fig. 10.1], there the group of bound prisoners thrust forward on a cantilevered slab possesses the effect of sculpture in the mode of Michaelangelo's Slaves rather than that of the pathetic huddles of oppressed humanity in the later version of the plates. (Wilton-Ely, 1978b, p. 85).

Others have noted how a 'suggestion of torment floats in the air of the Prisons' but it is almost always a 'vague' suggestion. As Marguerite Yourcenar

Fig. 10.6. Giovanni Battista Piranesi, *Carceri*, pl XIII, Second State, c.1761. *Source:* © The Trustees of the British Museum.

(1962/1984, pp. 117–118) goes on to write, the 'true horror of the Prisons is less in their few mysterious scenes of torture than in the indifference of these human ants roaming through enormous spaces, whose various groups seem almost never to communicate amongst themselves or even to take not of their respective presences, and still less to realise that in some dim corner a prisoner is being tortured'. For me the crucial question, and one which ties visual and narrative criminologies, is why did he call these spectacular architectural hallucinations Prisons?

Already in Piranesi's time the later *Carceri* images spoke to fresh themes and offered striking visual analogies of disturbing experiences. They are certainly among the first and most enigmatic indications of the obsession with torture and incarceration that comes increasingly to the fore in the last decades of the eighteenth century. Horace Walpole saw them as 'chaotic and incoherent scenes where death sneers in the darkness' (cited in Yourcenar, 1962/1984, p. 125) and these dark images appear in his novel *The Castle of Otranto*, published in 1764 and set in an imaginary Italian dungeon. Likewise, William Beckford's novel *Vathek*, published in 1786, traces a disturbing journey through vast subterranean halls that are strongly influenced by Piranesi's Prisons. Both Walpole and Beckford are regarded as pioneers of the gothic novel, while allusions to Piranesi feature prominently in Victor Hugo, and the image of confinement is a metaphor put to a wide range of uses in literary sensibility. Such settings reveal much about the structuring principles of the Romantic imagination, and the tensions betrayed in the appeal of raw despotic power. Fictional metaphors and social critique are interwoven:

> arbitrary arrests (lettres de cachet) and the state prisons of the Ancien Regime, the symbolism of the Bastille and of its epic fall, the revolutionary jails, the political detentions throughout Metternich's Europe...the police repressions of popular uprisings – all conspired to dramatize and poeticize the prison image...The eighteenth century is known to be the age of 'reason'; but it is also – especially as the century came to a close – an age that delighted in horror, and was fascinated by all the manifestations of coercion. The obsession with walls, crypts, forced religious vocations, inquisitorial procedures, parallels the beginnings of a revolt against arbitrariness. (Brombert, 1978, pp. 7–8).

I have argued elsewhere (Carrabine, 2012) that this fascination with horror could very easily fall into hammy melodrama (a tone wonderfully sent up in Jane Austen's *Northanger Abbey*, written in the 1790s), but the creeping unease generated by Franz Kafka's modernist fiction is hugely indebted to the Gothic. In his novels *The Trial* (1914) and *The Castle* (1922) and shorter stories like 'Before the Law', 'In the Penal Colony' and 'The Metamorphosis' they each take up the theme of an innocent victim caught up in relentless machinations well beyond their control.

From Josef K.'s arrest for a nameless crime in *The Trial* (with no hope of acquittal) to Gregor Samsa's grotesque metamorphosis (into a giant insect) Kafka's stories explore the question of confinement with immensely unsettling results. In the latter story the horror derives not so much from the description of the bizarre transformation, but the indifferent way his family react to the event, suggesting that the tale is really 'about our acquiescence in the face of the evil that surrounds us' (Eco, 2007, p. 323). The theme of confinement and doomed flights from imprisonment are crucial Gothic conventions, yet for Burke the pleasures deriving from horror arise when we are at a safe distance from the causes of fear. Otherwise the experience would be simply terrifying.

Conclusion

To return to the question why Piranesi called these nightmare fantasies Prisons, one answer is to look forward and see how they have had such a grim resonance on our own times. Another response is to look backwards and explore a concept which has especially preoccupied the Italian imagination and that is visions of the Last Judgement, of Hell, and the descent into Dante's inferno. So, a fruitful line of enquiry would be to explore the ties between Piranesi's 'entirely secular Prisons and the old sacred conceptions of an Immanent Justice' (Yourcenar, 1962/1984, p. 120) in medieval other worlds. I want to finish then with some thoughts on where the approach outlined here might lead. Some time ago Foucault criticised historians for what he called their 'impoverished idea of the real' (cited in

Burke, 2008, p. 64), as they left no space for what is imagined. French historians have since responded to this accusation in significant ways.

One example is Jacques Le Goff's (1981/1984) *The Birth of Purgatory*, which traces the origins of the idea of a netherworld in the Middle Ages by connecting it to changing conceptions of space and time. He argued that the idea of a 'third place' in the afterlife, along with heaven and hell, came into full bloom as a formal Catholic belief and doctrine rather late – in the twelfth century. It was gradually established as an intermediate space in which some lost souls were subjected to a trial that could be reduced through the prayers of perishable mortals. A distinct geography of the other world took shape in a detailed theology of retribution, sacrifice, penalties, pardons and spiritual exchange between the living and the dead. Le Goff was also one of the first scholars to examine the history of dreams, so that studies of visions, ghosts and the supernatural have become central to the new concern in cultural history with the active role of the imagination. Such studies have explored 'apparitions of the ordinary dead, of everyday ghosts' and those occasions when the departed might return from the grave (Schmitt, 1994/1999, p. 2).

My overall point then is that Piranesi's images have offered powerful metaphors for understanding social relations, and that the methods of both narrative and visual criminology can draw on studies in the history of representation, whether these be literary, visual or mental that have flourished in recent decades and from which critical counter-languages can emerge. In this regard, Derrida's method of deconstruction where the strategy is to focus on a repressed theme, pursue its textual traces and indicate how they subvert the apparatus striving to hold them in place. By challenging conventional assumptions his approach can be characterised as critical (rather than purely nihilistic, as his detractors maintain), so that when he addresses the systems of painting and language, he describes the 'parasitizing' of systems, their flowing into one another and how they create a 'partition of the edge' (Derrida, 1987, p. 7). He plays on this inside and outside of a work through a consideration of the transitional position of the frame and the idea of a supplement, as we saw earlier in this chapter, opening up new ways of thinking about them.

In Derrida all texts are a 'play of presence and absence, a place of the effaced trace' (Spivak, 1976, p. lvii) and he deliberately deploys a strategy of re-contextualising concepts by moving them from one system or discipline to another. Later he would introduce the idea of 'haunting into the very construction of a concept' (Derrida, 1994, p. 161) in a book preoccupied with the 'death' of communism and how Marxism would continue to haunt capitalist societies long after its supposed demise. His concept of 'hauntology' is a pun on the more traditional concept of ontology, the philosophical study of what can be said to exist. Yet it brings into focus the question of time 'in a way that had not quite been the case with the trace or différance' and is more than an 'attempt to revive the supernatural' or 'just a figure of speech' (Fisher, 2014, p. 18). Instead, it is a crucial addition to the project of deconstruction and can help enlarge our understanding of the real, the symbolic and the imaginary. Piranesi's Prisons pitch us straight into extraordinary landscapes and the aim of this chapter has been to mobilise some conceptual resources to engage with them.

Acknowledgement

This work was supported by a Leverhulme Trust Major Research Fellowship, MRF-2014-052.

References

Alpers, S. (1983/1995). Interpretation without representation, or, the viewing of *Las Meninas*. In E. Fernie (Ed.), *Art history and its methods: A critical anthology* (pp. 281–290). London: Phaidon Press.
Alpers, S. (1983). *The arts of describing: Dutch art in the seventeenth century*. London: Penguin Books.
Andrews, M. (1999). *Landscape and Western art*. Oxford: Oxford University Press.
Augustyn, J. (2000). Subjectivity in the fictional ruin: The caprice genre. *The Romantic Review*, 91(4), 433–457.
Bal, M. (1991). *Reading Rembrandt: Beyond the word-image opposition*. Cambridge: Cambridge University Press.
Brombert, V. (1978). *The romantic prison*. Princeton, NJ: Princeton University Press.
Brown, M., & Carrabine, E. (Eds.). (2017). *The Routledge international handbook of visual criminology*. London: Routledge.
Bryson, N. (1981). *Word and image: French painting of the Ancien Régime*. Cambridge: Cambridge University Press.
Bryson, N. (1988). Introduction. In N. Bryson (Ed.), *Calligram: Essays in new art history from France* (pp. xiii–xxix). Cambridge: Cambridge University Press.
Burke, P. (2008). *What is cultural history?* Cambridge: Polity.
Carrabine, E. (2012). Telling prison stories: The spectacle of punishment and the criminological imagination. In L. Cheliotis (Ed.), *The arts of imprisonment: Essays on control, resistance and empowerment* (pp. 47–72). Dartmouth, NH: Ashgate Publishing.
Carrabine, E. (2016). Picture this: Criminology, image and narrative. *Crime, Media, Culture*, 12(2), 253–270.
Carrabine, E. (2018a). Punishment in the frame: Rethinking the history and sociology of art. *The Sociological Review*, 66(3), 559–576.
Carrabine, E. (2018b). Reading a "Titian": Visual methods and the limits of interpretation. *Deviant Behavior*, 39(4), 525–538.
Carrabine, E. (2018c). Geographies of landscape: Representation, power and meaning. *Theoretical Criminology*, 22(3), 445–467.
Casey, E. S. (2002). *Representing place: Landscape painting & maps*. Minneapolis, MN: University of Minnesota Press.
Derrida, J. (1979). The Parergon. *October*, 9(Summer), 3–41.
Derrida, J. (1978/1987). *The truth in painting*. Chicago, IL: University of Chicago Press.
Derrida, J. (1994). *Specters of Marx: The state of the debt, the work of mourning, & the new international*. London: Routledge.
Eco, U. (2007). *On ugliness*. London: Harvill Secker.
Fisher, M. (2014). *Ghosts of my life: Writings on depression, hauntology and lost future*. Hants: Zero Books.
Foucault, M. (1966/2002). *The order of things*. London: Routledge.

Gamer, M. (2015). *The Sheriff's picture frame: Art and execution in eighteenth-century Britain*. Unpublished PhD thesis, Yale University.
Greslé, Y. (2006). Foucault's *Las Meninas* and art-historical methods. *Journal of Literary Studies*, 22(3/4), 211–228.
Harris, J. (2001). *The new art history*. London: Routledge.
Holliday, R. (2000). We've been framed: visualising methodology. *Sociological Review*, 48(4), 503–521.
Kant, I. (1790/1992). *Critique of judgement*. Oxford: Oxford University Press.
Kelsey, R. (2008). Landscape as not belonging. In R. DeLue & J. Elkins (Eds.), *Landscape theory* (pp. 203–213). London: Routledge.
Le Goff, J. (1984). *The birth of purgatory*. London: Scolar Press.
Lehman, K. (1961). Piranesi as interpreter of Roman architecture. In R. Parks (Ed.), *Piranesi* (pp. 88–98). Northampton, MA: Smith College Museum of Art.
McClanahan, B. (2019). Earth–world–planet: Rural ecologies of horror and dark green criminology. *Theoretical Criminology*. doi:10.1177/1362480618819813
Merchant, C. (1996). *Earthcare: Women and the environment*. London: Routledge.
Mitchell, W. J. T. (2002). Imperial landscape. In W. J. T. Mitchell (Ed.), *Landscape and power* (2nd ed., pp. 5–34). Chicago, IL: University of Chicago Press.
Mitchell, W. J. T. (2015). *Image science: Iconology, visual culture, and media aesthetics*. Chicago, IL: University of Chicago Press.
Olwig, K. (2008). The "actual landscape," or actual landscapes. In R. DeLue & J. Elkins (Eds.), *Landscape theory* (pp. 158–177). London: Routledge.
Penny, N. (1988). *Piranesi*. London: Bloomsbury Publishing.
Pinto, J. (2015). *Speaking ruins: Piranesi, architects, and antiquity in eighteenth-century Rome*. Ann Arbor, MI: University of Michigan Press.
Pugh, S. (1990a). Loitering with intent: From Arcadia to the arcades. In S. Pugh (Ed.), *Reading landscape: Country-city-capital* (pp. 145–160). Manchester: Manchester University Press.
Pugh, S. (Ed.). (1990b). *Reading landscape: Country-city-capital*. Manchester: Manchester University Press.
Riessman, C. (2008). *Narrative methods for the human sciences*. London: Sage.
Schmitt, J.-C. (1994/1999). *Ghosts in the middle ages: The living and the dead in medieval society*. Chicago, IL: University of Chicago Press.
Scott, R. (1975). *Piranesi*. London: St. Martins Press.
Simmel, G. (1911/1958). Two essays: "The handle" and "the ruin". *Hudson Review*, 11(3), 371–385.
Solomon-Godeau, A. (2010/2017). Framing landscape photography. In S. Parsons (Ed.), *Photography after photography: Gender, genre, history* (pp. 107–122). Durham, NC: Duke University Press.
Spivak, G. C. (1976). Translator's preface. In *Of grammatology* (J. Derrida) pp. ix–lxxxvii. Baltimore, MD: The Johns Hopkins University Press.
Wilton-Ely, J. (1978a). *Piranesi*. London: Lund Humpries.
Wilton-Ely, J. (1978b). *The mind and art of Giovanni Battista Piranesi*. London: Thames & Hudson.
Wood, C. (1993/2014). *Albrecht Altdorfer and the origins of landscape* (2nd ed.). London: Reaktion Books.
Yourcenar, M. (1962/1984). *The dark brain of Piranesi and other essays*. Oxon: Aiden Ellis.

Chapter 11

The Tales Things Tell: Narrative Analysis, Materiality and my Wife's Old Nazi Rifle

Thomas Ugelvik

Introduction: Material Culture Studies Meets Narrative Analysis

The discipline of criminology was slow to take up narrative analysis (Presser, 2016; Presser & Sandberg, 2015; Sandberg & Ugelvik, 2016). In the last decade, however, a growing number of scholars have started collectively to explore the potential of narrative analysis in criminology. The discipline has, however, been even less eager to incorporate ideas and insights from material culture studies, understood by Miller (2008, 2010) as a field of inquiry that is concerned with deconstructing and transcending the usual dualism between subjects and objects and to study how social relations and identities are created through production, acquisition and consumption of 'stuff'. Of course, there are examples of studies of phenomena as diverse as art fraud (Polk, 2016), police officer body cameras (Ariel, 2016) and hostile architecture (Petty, 2016), where scholars explore the way human beings in practice relate to and interact with specific material objects, but they rarely seem interested in the material culture aspects. In other studies, material objects such as human DNA and fingerprints are foregrounded (Cole, 2005), but they are frequently dealt with due to their practical properties, rather than their cultural significance or the role they play in identity construction. Criminology has also recently witnessed something of a 'spatial turn', which has included an increased focus on the world of material objects (Hayward, 2012). These examples notwithstanding, studies that could feasibly be labelled as material culture criminology are still quite rare.

On reflection, this seems strange because material culture studies could be a particularly relevant addition to the discipline. Objects can be used as weapons, they can be stolen and they can be used to solve crimes and apprehend and control offenders. In Norway, for instance, nine out of ten reported crimes are automobile related, yet criminologists are not interested in cars. Objects like doors, locks and walls are intrinsic to the practice of punishment as we know it. Keys are not just important tools that prison officers use and carry around in their belts; they are symbolically and culturally loaded objects that are vital to the construction of prison officer as well as prisoner subjectivity. And when it comes to money, the acquisition of which is the goal of much criminal activity, it still has a material dimension (plastic cards, key pads) even if actual metal and paper money may seem anachronistic. Based on such examples, one might even argue that material culture studies should be at the core of criminology. Material objects are, after all, part of almost all crimes, as well as crime control in any shape, way or form. Yet criminologists are only rarely interested in either the material or even the cultural dimension of cars, locks, keys or money. Material objects are ubiquitous to crime and punishment, but only very rarely has criminology taken them seriously as objects of analysis in their own right.

The goal of this chapter is to explore the overlap between objects and stories, and the possible connections between narrative criminology and material culture, using a single specific object – my wife's hunting rifle – as an extended example. I will explore the many connections between the stories we tell and the objects that surround us. I will discuss the stories that objects represent, the stories they may prompt us to tell, the stories we tell each other and ourselves using objects as props and the stories our things tell about both us, their owners or users, and the wider sociocultural context we are part of. Finally, I will ask whether some narratively loaded objects may anticipate or perhaps even precipitate certain actions. Is it true that objects sometimes ask us to or even demand that we put them to use? In what ways can objects be seen as actors in their own right?

Objects, Bodies, Narratives

Objects can be grasped from a great many different perspectives. They can be understood from the perspective of physics, as material objects in the world with a shape, size and mass. They may be seen from the point of view of practical use. Objects can be more or less well suited to perform a specific function. Objects are also frequently inscribed in human meaning-making processes and in human cultures. As culturally inscribed, they signify in ways that may impact individuals deeply; things may be objects of veneration, desire or disgust. They may have a symbolic and ritualistic function, in the sense that the use of cloaks and wigs can be said to materialise state power in and through the courtroom ritual. Finally, we understand and construct the world around us, and our position in that world, at least partially through objects. From what we might call a phenomenological-existential perspective, objects may be seen as vital to our understanding of ourselves. An object, then, is never 'just a thing'. This chapter is based on the idea that the link between objects, bodies and the world can fruitfully be seen through the lens of narrative theory.

There is a famous part of *Being and Time* where Heidegger (2010, p. 15) discusses the relationship between a carpenter and his hammer. The hammer as an object gets meaning through its relation to other related objects, like nails, planks, a saw and so on, and through its inscription in human meaningful activity. The hammer understands the carpenter as someone who is actually grasping it with the plans to use it in a specific way and for a specific purpose. As a piece of equipment, the hammer is understood first by the hand, only later by the carpenter and then only after the hammer has contributed to turning him or her into a carpenter. Material objects continuously shape our understanding of ourselves, and the relationship we have with the world around us. The material quality of things means that they take up space. An object with mass and weight can be said to impose itself on our field of possible actions. We may have to step over or walk around big objects. Smaller objects may be picked up if they are not securely fastened to something bigger. However, when they are part of our everyday lives, this material quality of things often disappears. When we are caught up in using objects, when everything is functioning smoothly, we are not consciously aware of the equipment we are using because we are already absorbed in the activity and in the meaningful context as a whole, which, to us, in a sense is one and the same. Things may be inscribed in the field of ongoing human meaning-making even when we are not really paying attention.

Merleau-Ponty (2002) builds on Heidegger. For him, the world is not first and foremost a geometrical space or the sum of all objects out there, but a phenomenal field where meaning is created through our situated embodied interaction with the world around us, including other people as well as objects. Against the view that objects and bodies are clearly delimited things that exist independently of and exterior to each other, *partes extra partes*, he argues that bodies should be seen as always overlapping with the world of objects and other bodies, and as intentionally directed at this world as a field of possible (and impossible) actions. Such a perspective rejects both traditional realist and idealist accounts by arguing that in our ordinary experiences as human beings there is no separation between 'inner' and 'outer', between subject and object. We are all continuously in the process of becoming at the interface between our bodies and the world of objects that surrounds them.

Building on Merleau-Ponty, Young (2005) describes how this embodied and situated process of becoming is gendered. She shows how men and women inhabit space differently and how they relate to objects and use objects differently. Gendered expectations directed at men and women, as men and women, shape how they make use of various objects. The act of throwing a ball 'like a girl' makes the ball an intrinsic part of becoming a girl according to Young. The experience of not mastering the act of throwing and of having other people (boys) out-throwing you as a matter of course is constitutive of female identity. When the female body and the ball together, as one, enact a cultural script that tells people that girls should be bad a throwing, girls in practice limit the movement of their own bodies and the actions they are able and willing to perform.

Miller (2010) also follows Merleau-Ponty when he argues that our commonsense opposition between persons and things, between subjects and objects, should be disrupted. Objects do not merely represent us. They should not be seen just as mere signs that say something about us in the way that, say, an expensive Italian bicycle may be said to communicate something about its owner to other cognoscenti. Things also construct us and we construct each other and ourselves through them. Subjects create and consume and use objects, but objects also create subjects. Miller shows this through a number of analyses of specific objects. One example is his analysis of how it is the sari that wears and creates the Indian woman, and not the other way around. According to Miller (2010), the sari contributes to make its wearer what she is, i.e. both woman and Indian at the same time. The act of wearing a sari, which is quite difficult at first, shapes her body and the way she moves, and once she is comfortable with wearing one, it gives her a tool that allows her to express a variety of subtle emotions. At this stage, the sari becomes an instrument of power. Much more than just a piece of clothing that represents the wearer and her or his personal taste, a sari constitutes the wearer as a specific person. According to Miller, people create themselves through the medium of objects.

This interesting claim brings us back to narrative theory and the reason for including a chapter about material objects in a book about narrative criminology. Narrative criminology, for its part, is based on the premise that people create themselves through the medium of not objects, but stories. The two perspectives may look mutually exclusive, but they need not be. For both claims to be true, however, there needs to be a field of conceptual overlap between the world of material objects and the world of narratives. According to Frank (2010), stories and material objects may sometimes work together, each informing the other. Stories, like objects, can guide perceptions and actions. Objects, like stories, employ lives and give structure and plan to individual biographies. Objects can be used to give stories a tangible presence. According to Law (2000), effective stories always perform themselves into the material world, in the form of social relations, but also in the form of machines, architectural arrangements and bodies. Law (2000, p. 2) even argues that 'there is no important difference between stories and materials'. That may be a statement too radical for some, but at any rate it is true that stories inevitably have a material dimension the moment they are told, either in the form of ink on paper, pixels on a screen or, less tangible but equally material, sound waves moving through matter. Material objects, on the other hand, may act like stories in certain respects. We might not all agree that stories and objects are more or less the same, but at least it seems clear that there may exist a field of conceptual overlap between the two. And this is where we turn to the narratively loaded material object.

The Gun: The Mauser 98K Rifle

Following the capitulation of the German occupation forces in May 1945, substantial stocks of all kinds of military equipment were transferred to the reinstated Norwegian government. Among the spoils of war were a large number of Mauser 98K rifles. The Mauser rifle was, at the time, considered among the most reliable infantry weapons in the world. In its time, 30 different countries used it for their armed forces, and an estimated 102 million units were manufactured between 1898 and 1945, during which it was employed in both world wars by the German Army. It was the standard issue weapon of German soldiers throughout the Second World War. It is safe to use, robust and reasonably accurate. According to gun historian Robert W. D. Ball (2011), it is 'the best bolt-action rifle ever made'. So naturally, the German Mauser rifles that were transferred to Norway were soon put to good use by the Norwegian armed forces, complete with German Wehrmacht symbols still stamped into the steel (Images 11.1–11.3).

In the 1950s and 1960s, however, the postwar arms race meant that the Mauser very soon was outdated from a military perspective (Chivers, 2010). When your enemy has an automatic assault rifle, even a very good bolt-action rifle like the

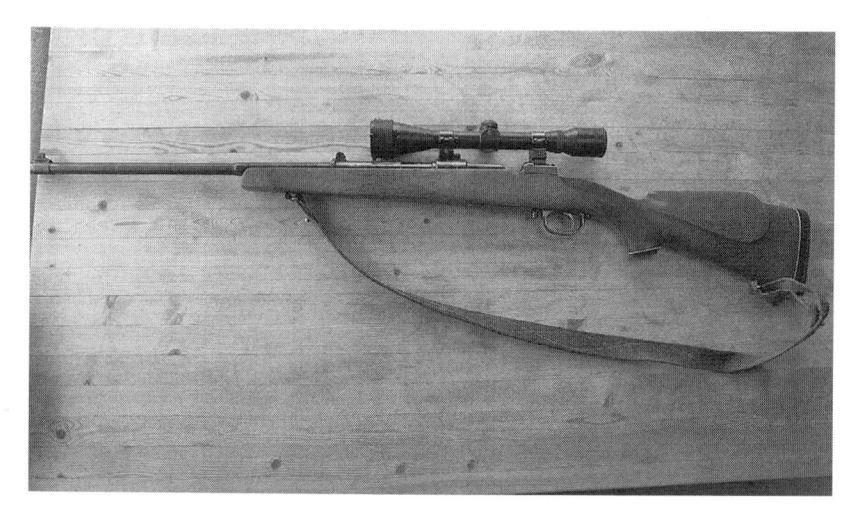

Image 11.1. Ugelvik Family Mauser Rifle. *Source:* Photo by Thomas Ugelvik.

Image 11.2. Ugelvik Family Mauser Rifle; Detail with Wehrmacht Symbols. *Source:* Photo by Thomas Ugelvik.

Image 11.3. Ugelvik Family Mauser; Detail with Wehrmacht symbols.

Mauser K98 is a liability. As in many other countries, the Norwegian Mausers were gradually decommissioned and sold off as civilian hunting rifles. They are still used by hunters to this day, not just in Norway, but all over the world. My father-in-law, an army reserves lieutenant at the time, bought one of these rifles. He added a new stock and a telescopic sight, and used it for many years to hunt reindeer in the Norwegian mountains. Ten years ago, that tradition was taken up by his youngest daughter, my wife. I usually go with her on these hunting trips. On our last trip, I lay right next to her on the rocky ground when she shot a beautiful white reindeer calf, close enough to feel the pressure from the gunpowder exploding in the cartridge. The physical impact and the fatigue we both felt after following the herd for 7 days straight combined with the general tension of the situation to create an unforgettable story.

Connections between Objects and Stories

Using this one particular object as a leitmotif, in what follows, I will explore six different kinds of connections that may be said to exist between objects and stories. For researchers, these connections may be used as empirical and theoretical perspectives. That is, each of these connections may give rise to research questions researchers may ask when faced with specific objects in research settings. They may guide fieldwork and interview protocols. They may bring new ideas to data analysis.

An Object May Be Used as a Storytelling Prop

The first kind of connection between stories and objects is the kind I have just established in regard to the Mauser. I have shown a specific object (or rather two images of a specific object), and I have told a story about the past involving that object, weaving the two together. If this was a conference presentation and not a book chapter, I might have considered bringing the physical object along to use it as a sort of theatrical prop to aid my storytelling, although with regard to the specific object in this case, that might not have been such a good idea. Theatrical props may have various different functions. A prop may be used as a truth confirmation device, to add realism and verisimilitude to a story. They may also have emotional relevance. An object may give a certain 'tone' to a scene and thus lead audiences in the direction of a specific emotional state to further the actor's performance and the director's aim with the scene. Perhaps the most famous theatrical prop in the history of theatre, the skull of Yorick's the court jester held by Hamlet in the pivotal graveyard scene, may be said to do several things at once. It acts as a *memento mori* that puts Hamlet face to face – literally – with both his own mortality and the changes in Denmark during his absence. In a sense, it can be said to stand in for an imaginary mirror that, thrust before the Danish prince, he cannot help but look at himself in. The skull, which in a surprising number of productions is actually a real skull (Williamson, 2011), may be said to have layers of meaning for different audience members and actors. This insight, that objects mean different things for different people, adds complexity to the use of props. Even an object that is more or less unambiguous may spark different emotions and connotations in different observers. When an object is as loaded with multiple and complex meanings, such as an old Wehrmacht Mauser, or the skull of a human being for that matter, it can be very difficult for the user of the prop to control the part it ends up playing in the production. Focus on this kind of connection between objects and stories leads to questions of how the use of a prop may impact storytelling and how physical objects and stories interact in specific narrative settings.

A Material Object Tells a Story About Its Past

The second kind of connection between stories and objects that I would highlight is the story an object may be said to tell as a specific material object in the world. From this perspective, a thing tells a story about how it has been treated and used. When you pick up my wife's Mauser and look closely at it, you will see that there are numerous small marks, probably from its use as a hunting rifle rather than from its military days. It smells of gun oil and spent cordite. The telescopic sight, obviously retrofitted much later, looks anachronistic. The Mauser looks old and worn, but not like a museum piece. Because of its modifications, it probably has no value to collectors. It is a piece of history, but not in the way collectors want it to be. So if one looks closely and knows what to look for, the gun itself, as a material object with a history, can tell us how it has been treated and perhaps what it has been used for. The material quality of things means that an object always has narrative potential if one knows what to look for.

When we look at this kind of connection between stories and things, we inscribe an object in a temporal sequence where we acknowledge its past, present and future. A human-made object has been created and used. That creation process and the use it has been put to can be interpreted from looking closely at it or feeling its weight in one's hand. If you know about wood and metal-working, you can probably tell, just by looking at my wife's gun, which tools were used in its production and whether it is mass produced or handcrafted by an artisan. Connoisseurs can apparently tell, just by looking at a Mauser, whether it was made before or after 1941. The material object in your hand also presents itself as a carrier of potential. It may point towards future use. I will return to this aspect below. Focus on this kind of connection between objects and stories will lead researchers to look very closely at an object to try to re-create its past lives. It may lead to detailed study of materials and construction processes.

An Object Can Tell a Story About Its Intended Purpose

Third, the gun tells a story about its intended purpose, what the designer meant it to do. Originally a military weapon, the Mauser was made to endure punishing conditions and to work in all temperatures and even after extended exposure to harsh field conditions. It is built for robustness rather than elegance. The designer also had to find a compromise between firepower and portability. Much like reindeer hunters, soldiers need to be able to carry their gun as well as a reasonable amount of ammunition with them for long days of walking. So the Mauser was made for reliability and ease of use as much as accuracy. Anyone with a little knowledge of how firearms work can pick one up and fire it within seconds with a good chance of hitting something, at least at a relatively short distance. One does not have to be a specialist to use it, a fact that is both impressive and chilling.

This kind of functional perspective is very common. We use it all the time when we understand and interact with the world around us. A frying pan is a metal pan made for frying food. There are a limited number of other potential uses – it can be used to collect water coming though a leaky roof, or it can be turned upside down and used as an impromptu drum – but it has a clear intended primary purpose. In the case of the Mauser, however, things get a bit more complicated because different observers might look at an object and see different stories about intended use. What is the purpose of a gun? Shooting, perhaps, but shooting what, for what purpose and in what context? Some people might look at the Mauser and see a story about war, death and the senseless slaughter of the Holocaust. Others will see a hunting weapon that tells a story about tradition, nationality and a certain relationship between human beings and nature. During the Second World War, most Norwegian Mausers were never actually used for anything else than target practice. Was the purpose of these guns, then, in fact not to kill enemy troops, but to communicate the believable potential for killing? After the war this Mauser has seen its fair share of killing. The design team, however, probably did not consider the Mauser's use in reindeer hunting in the design process. It might make sense to say that the function of an object, its intended use and purpose, is dynamic. It may not be identical to the explicit goal of the designers. Privileging this kind of connection between stories and objects may lead researchers to ask how human beings and (especially) man-made objects interact with specific purposes. It might lead us to study how objects tell stories about how they are made and how they have been used, in practice in accordance or in conflict with stated aims and functions.

An Object Tells a Story About Its Sociocultural Context

This leads us to a fourth kind of connection between objects and stories. Once we start to move away from the material object itself, an object, as a cultural artefact, may be said to tell a story, or probably in most cases several different stories, about the sociocultural context of which it is part. Take the flag of Mozambique. It is one of three UN member states' national flags that feature a firearm, along with Guatemala and Haiti. The Mozambique flag includes the image of an AK-47 Kalashnikov assault rifle with a bayonet attached to the barrel (Chivers, 2010). Flags are highly symbolic objects. Colours are frequently significant. In this case, the colour green stands for the riches of the land, black represents the African continent, yellow symbolises the country's minerals and so on. There is also an open book, symbolising the importance of education, and a hoe, which represents agriculture. And then there's the AK-47, according to Chivers the human-made object responsible for the largest number of human deaths. The design of the flag has been wrapped up in political controversy since it was adopted in 1983. A 2005 competition saw almost 200 new designs proposed yet the flag remains the same to this day. Critics have claimed that a peace-loving nation cannot and should not have an assault rifle in its flag. Defenders of the flag claim that the rifle represents the liberation struggle, anti-colonialism and ultimately a guarantee of peace. The use of its silhouette in a national flag invokes a tapestry of different but interconnected stories – multiple meanings that may only make sense from a particular sociocultural point of view.

The same is, albeit perhaps to a more limited degree, true of my wife's Mauser. It can be understood as connected to a wider sociocultural context in different ways. The Mauser might, for instance, be understood with reference to gendered cultural norms. Of course, even in Norway, one of the most gender-equal societies in the world, hunting is still predominantly a man's game. I would conservatively estimate that 98 out of a 100 hunters we meet following the herds are men. According to Miller (2010), a power drill is the most conspicuously gendered object in the home, but I would argue that a hunting rifle, when present, is equally, if not more, gendered. The kitchen may be seen as a feminine space in many contexts, but the activity of bringing meat into the kitchen is a decidedly masculine one. Of course, there are rifles on the market that are manufactured specifically for female hunters (Blair & Hyatt, 1995), but this just means that the vast majority of rifles, including old Mausers, are implicitly built for and marketed at men. You have rifles, and you have women's rifles, which means that my wife regularly is seen as someone who goes against received gender scripts when she carries her Mauser around the mountains looking for reindeer. Other hunters frequently seem surprised and slightly bemused when we meet and stop, as one does, for a little chat. In many cases, she receives respect when she successfully shows that she knows what she is doing. Sometimes she is ignored by men who insist on talking to me about hunting related stuff, even though she is clearly carrying the rifle. Many incorrectly assume, they end up telling us after we have chatted for a while, that I have already filled my hunting quota and that we continue hunting together until she has filled hers. In short, the Mauser is loaded with sociocultural meaning. That means that the objects and the reactions they are met with can be used to empirically access the relevant sociocultural context. This insight may lead researchers to ask what meanings specific objects have for different actors in different contexts, with what consequences. Particularly significant and culturally loaded objects can be used to study the wider sociocultural context more generally.

An Object Tells a Story About Its Owner/User

Which leads us to the fifth kind of connection between object and storytelling: An object may tell a story about its owner. Differently put, we more or less explicitly and self-consciously tell stories about ourselves through objects all the time. Clothing may be the most obvious example. People often want to communicate a certain style or tailor their dress to a specific context when they choose what to wear (Hebdidge, 1979). Even resistance against the fashion industry and gendered clothing expectations directed at men and women frequently follow certain informal codes. It is very difficult to dress in an unmarked way that would communicate nothing about you. In a sense, we are what we wear.

The weapons industry has been willing to capitalise on the connection between objects and their stories about their users/owners for a very long time. The Thompson submachine gun, better known as the Tommy gun, for instance, a favourite of gangsters since it was launched in 1921, was nicknamed 'the annihilator' in order to appeal to customers and thus increase its sales. Closer to the present day, the movie character 'Dirty' Harry Callahan and his famous catchphrase ('Go ahead, make my day.') sparked an impractically large handgun craze, where bigger is better, which has continued to this day. In an ongoing battle of technological one-upmanship, gun manufacturers are competing to attract customers who are looking for the biggest and 'baddest' gun out there.

As a military weapon, the Mauser has not been the focus of an active marketing campaign in quite the same way. That is not to say that Mausers do not tell stories about the people using them. In what we might call hunting culture, a Mauser is not just any old rifle; in fact, 'generic rifles' may not exist within this culture. The historical connection to the Second World War seems to appeal to many people, but more than that, the age of the weapon and the materials it is made from position the owner as a specific kind of hunter, and even a specific kind of person. The Mauser is a kind of material object that needs care and applied knowledge to work properly. It tells a story of its owner as someone who values old objects and who manages to take care of what could essentially be a museum piece and keep it in working order.

To some, the Mauser is also given significance and worth by not being a modern maintenance-free stainless steel rifle. In the process of writing this chapter, I have been sneaking around open online hunting discussion forums. In the following example taken from the outdoorsdirectory.com, a person who calls himself Murphy puts it very nicely in response to a post by someone who calls themself Mauserboy:

> *I'm like Mauserboy. I don't mind cleaning a gun. It is what I call bonding with my rifle. It shows appreciation and gratitude, no, not to the inanimate object but to the many people who contributed to it and to the craft and skill that went into it. It also shows an appreciation and respect to those who will own it after I'm gone, or the new owner if I decide to sell it. The same way I enjoy seeing a rifle that is 40 plus years old and showing signs of honest wear with care, but not abuse. ... Maybe I am stuck in the 20th or even the 19th century, but it was that era when men relied so heavily on their firearms for their very existence, that gives me my deep appreciation for them today.*

According to Marcel Mauss (1954), objects, when they are given to someone as a gift, are imbued with a special essence or spirit. This essence, which Mauss gives the Maori name Hau, works to bind the gift giver and the recipient together in a relationship of reciprocity where the gift creates an imbalance that must be addressed. Something similar seems to be happening when Murphy is cleaning his gun. They are bound together and in the process the object is filled with a spirit or an essence that gives it unique significance. It is clearly a simple hunting weapon no longer; Murphy's description is filled with a sense of nostalgia and reverence. His gun is almost like an old friend. Furthermore, it is part of his own self-narrative, the story of what kind of person he is. Recall Miller's (2010) claim that our common-sense opposition between persons and things, and between subjects and objects, should be disrupted. Objects do not merely represent us, according to Miller, they also construct us and we construct each other and ourselves through them. In the case of Murphy, an object and a story about an object seamlessly combine to aid him in his online self-narrative.

People create themselves through the medium of things (Miller, 2010). This goes for any object, but guns are perhaps more narratively loaded than many other objects. According to Fagan and Wilkinson (1998), handguns are symbols of respect, power, identity and masculinity to young people in the US. In some inner cities, using a gun has become a rite of passage into manhood, or at least into one accessible respected social identity in this context. Being familiar with handguns means being an adult man in this setting. Different guns can signify different kinds of masculinity. For generations of Norwegian men who, like myself, did mandatory military service, army assault rifles did something similar. We competed in dismantling and reassembling our personal assault rifles – at the time, we were issued Heckler and Koch G3 rifles – while blindfolded. We were told to keep it in spotless condition, to sleep with it inside our sleeping bags at night while in the field and we were expected to know its serial number both forwards and backwards by heart. Recall Merleau-Ponty's (2002) claim that as human beings, we are continuously in the process of becoming at the interface between our bodies and the world of objects that surrounds them. The cultivation of an almost symbiotic relationship with this object was a vital part of the process of becoming a good soldier. These insights might lead researchers to study connections between objects and identity construction. They might look at how individuals and groups understand themselves and each other through the medium of objects, and the stories things tell about the people associated with them.

Objects Can Tell Their Own Story

Finally, the sixth kind of connection between stories and objects that I want to address in this chapter. Narrative criminology has, so far, to a large extent been preoccupied with the connection between narratives and action (Presser & Sandberg, 2015; Sandberg & Ugelvik, 2016). The central premise is that the way we talk about and narratively construct the world has consequences for our actions. Narrative criminologists have argued that some stories make some harmful actions more likely. The question is whether the same can be said about some objects. Objects have traditionally been studied as part of this world distinct from human agency; as real, but passive. This has been challenged in recent years by the idea, sometimes referred to as agential realism (Rosiek & Snyder, 2018), posthumanism or new materialism (Conty, 2018), that objects may in some ways themselves be seen as actors (Rosenberger, 2014). This idea is perhaps most famously linked to Bruno Latour (1993, 1994) and his actor–network theory. According to this view, the world of objects does not simply passively await our use; it actively responds to and mediates our actions. Interestingly, Latour (1994, p. 31) uses the gun advocacy dictum that it is human beings, and not guns, that kill to unpack the relationship between actions and objects:

> No materialist claims that guns kill by themselves. What the materialist claims is that the good citizen is transformed by carrying the gun. A good citizen who, without a gun, might simply be angry may become a criminal if he is holding a gun – as if the gun had the power to change Dr. Jekyll into Mr. Hyde. Materialists thus make the intriguing suggestion that our quality as subjects, our competences, our personalities, depend on what we hold in our hands.

He concludes that it is neither people nor guns that kill by themselves, and that responsibility for actions must be shared among humans and objects.

When an object is inserted into a specific situation, it may evoke a shared narrative script (Wilkinson & Fagan, 1996). According to Goffman (1971), individual behaviour is scripted in the sense that a person's definition of and understanding of a situation makes some scripts or action patterns available and more probable than others. Scripts are ways of organising behavioural repertoires that are more or less appropriate for different situations. From this perspective, material objects may affect what people are able to see as real and possible, and as worth doing or best avoided. Following Frank (2010), stories have the same quality; they lead us forward in the direction of certain fitting actions. They offer a plot that makes some particular future not only plausible, but compelling (Presser, 2018). Like stories, objects may contribute to organising actions into sequences, one following logically after the other. In this way, stories and material objects may work together, each informing the other, each one acting on our understanding of a situation and the options that are seen as open to us. People do not absolutely have to follow these scripts, but if they choose not to, they have to live with being seen as someone who failed to live up to the expectations that the script carries for the subject positions involved. If you choose to not act according to the script, you may lose control of your own narrative. In some situations, it might seem like the object-story has a will of its own.

Just by being there, in my hand, an object may be said to try to persuade me to use it. As any carpenter (and Heidegger) would tell you, if you own a hammer, it seems only natural to solve many problems with nails. The tools and other objects we own structure our way of seeing and being in the world, and therefore our actions. In the case of my wife's rifle, the Mauser changing hands was co-constitutive of the father–daughter relationship. It allowed one daughter to walk in her father's footsteps, and marked her as different from her two older sisters, who do not hunt. At the same time, the rifle seems to want to go hunting. If it is not used, it turns into a dead artefact hidden away in our attic. Gathering dust, it could even conceivably threaten the stability of the father–daughter relationship. When I took the Mauser out to photograph it for this chapter, it immediately seemed to tell my wife in no uncertain terms that she should feel bad about not going hunting this year.

Developing the idea of non-human agency further, and admittedly moving some distance away from my wife's rifle, in the US, gun rights advocacy groups stubbornly repeat the apparent truism that 'guns don't kill people, people kill people.' The gun is seen as but a passive tool, manipulated by human actors. Of course one might (as opposing activists do) interject that humans would not be killing each other quite as often if they did not have easy access to handguns, but one could go even further and give the guns themselves a say in the matter. Some objects, by simply being present and available in certain situations, may activate specific action scripts that seem to increase the likelihood of certain kinds of actions. The very presence of a gun may create fear and panic, but also excitement. Following, Katz (1988), we might say that they are objects that have a seductive quality. The feel of a handgun might certainly be said to be a sensual experience. If one is unaccustomed to being around weapons, they are surprisingly heavy, yet easy to use. Even most beginners can pick up a modern handgun and be able to hit a target with reasonable accuracy after just minutes of practice. They feel like power materialised. In some situations, individuals thus empowered may choose to act on that feeling. According to Fagan and Wilkinson (Fagan & Wilkinson, 1998; Wilkinson & Fagan, 1996), once a gun is brought into a discussion, it raises the conflict level. It blocks off some alternative responses and makes other actions more probable. It does this by activating cultural scripts that agents may choose to follow or resist, but that they cannot simply ignore. Fagan and Wilkinsons' respondents say that showing a gun is disrespectful, a violation of the others' physical space. Guns also change the calculus of a dispute, raising the stakes both in terms of status and strategy. It changes the situation from a regular conflict into a potential life-and-death situation. Following this show of disrespect, the 'victim' is expected to retaliate by getting out a gun of his own. Both parties may soon feel compelled to move forward and actually use their guns. Sometimes, our actions are caught up in a situation that fits a pre-existing plot, and that plot may lead you onward, making some actions more likely. Through its position in the overall narrative structure and the available plots for these situations, the gun may even be said to conduct the actors' actions. The gun itself, once it is no longer hidden in an inner pocket, seems like an agent in its own right.

On the other hand, in some cases, a handgun seems to ask to be used, but in a specific way that can be said to limit the damage potential for all parties. The so-called 'side grip' way of firing a pistol has been associated with US inner city gang culture. Turning a pistol so its grip is horizontal rather than vertical is not a very efficient way of using a gun, at least not if the goal is to actually hit what you are aiming at. Normally, recoil lifts the barrel against gravity. When firing in this manner, recoil pulls the gun sideways instead. The sights are also much less useful. The 'side grip' style makes up what it lacks in accuracy by adding a certain narrative and even cinematic quality to the shooter, however. In this case, we might even call it cinematic quite literally, as one of its advantages is said to be that it makes it easier to get both the gun and the gun wielder's face into the same tight camera shot at the same time. The 'side grip' style, then, is generally quite useless as a marksmanship technique, but it is efficient from a storytelling perspective. One might ask how many lives have actually been saved because this incredibly impractical way of wielding a firearm – conjoined to a particular story being told – has been fashionable in some contexts. Has this way of shooting at someone actually contributed to keep the murder rate lower than it would be if people used weapons in the manner in which the designer intended them to be used? It is possible to speculate that it might be easier to get a handgun out and fire it at someone, if both parties tacitly agree to lower the potential to actually hit someone substantially. 'Side grip' might give people the opportunity to look cool and act forcefully but at the same time lower the risk of injury to self and others. It has increased narrative potential with less damage.

A gun clearly is an object that is loaded with both narrative and damage potential. In specific situations, it can be used to tell a story about valour, righteous anger and masculinity, but also one about cowardice and spoilt identity (Goffman, 1963). Based on these insights, researchers may choose to study how objects shape individuals' actions and the role objects play in specific chain of events. We might focus on how the interplay between objects and stories may make some actions more or less probable, and how objects sometimes may be said to even take over the storytelling situation and lead their owners/users down certain unwanted paths.

Conclusion

The six different kinds of connections between stories and objects highlighted in this chapter can be seen as separate but to some extent overlapping perspectives on the different connections between the world of stories and the world of objects. Researchers may want to focus on (1) how objects are used as part of storytelling; (2) how material objects may tell stories about their past; (3) how human-made objects tell stories about their intended purpose; (4) how objects are inscribed with and can tell stories about a wider sociocultural context; (5) how people construct themselves through the medium of objects and (6) how some objects sometimes actively seem to participate in storytelling themselves. These perspectives may lead to diverse methodological approaches. One might want to interview owners, users, designers or manufacturers of objects. These interviews can focus on how people more or less actively, more or less explicitly, tell stories about themselves using objects. Or one might decide to study an object itself; its construction, current state and future uses. We might look closely at how identities are crafted and relationships formed at the intersection of things and tales. Such interviews may look like standard semi-structural qualitative interviews, or they may be guided by actual hands-on access to the object in question in the interview setting. Researchers may also want to observe the use of objects in real-life practice and look at how things may trigger and animate storytelling among users. Researchers may even want to learn to use and even master objects themselves as part of the research process. A phenomenological ethnographic approach might start with a researcher acquiring an object and, as a novice, slowly learning how it works. She/he might carry it around for some time, becoming familiar with its weight and the reaction it may inspire in other people. She/he could even note how the new object impacts on her/his field of perception, action and narration, and how it in turn might lead to new self-identities. The various perspectives on the connections between stories and objects may each, in short, lead to different kinds of studies using different kinds of data in different ways. So far, the analytical surface has barely been scratched.

Human beings interact with objects. We produce them and consume them; we avoid some objects and desperately crave others. From a material culture perspective, our relationships with physical objects structure our lives and make us who we are. When we relate to objects, the wider cultural context they are part (e.g. the received cultural gender scripts connected to a gendered object) of become relevant to us and part of us. I have shown that objects and stories can be seen as connected in several ways. I have highlighted six possible perspectives in this chapter. The difference between them is first and foremost analytic. In practice, in everyday life, these things are all happening simultaneously.

The storytelling potential of material objects is regularly employed by museums, filmmakers and advertisers, but it is also a general feature of human life. Objects are part of what Husserl called the lebenswelt (Ihde, 1990), the lifeworld, the barely noticed social, historical and physical context in which all our actions take place, but which is frequently just taken for granted. The point of this paper has been to argue that as a discipline, criminology would do well to pay close attention to the world of material objects and in particular to the multiple connections between narratives and objects. According to Rosiek and Snyder (2018, p. 1), objects in this world are 'simultaneously real, constituted in part by our activity, and also protean in a way that responds to our inquiry practices and evades any effort to capture them in a single representation'. Human beings are dependent upon a web of material conditions and relations as much as they are dependent on the field of storytelling. The ongoing interaction between the world of narratives and the world of objects is always happening; as human beings we are always immersed in the continual interchange between stuff and stories.

References

Ariel, B. (2016). Wearing body cameras increases assaults against officers and does not reduce police use of force: Results from a global multi-site experiment. *European Journal of Criminology*, *13*(6), 744–755.

Ball, R. W. D. (2011). *Mauser military rifles of the world*. Iola, WI: Gun Digest Books.

Blair, M. E., & Hyatt, E. M. (1995). The marketing of guns to women: Factors influencing gun-related attitutes and gun ownership by women. *Journal of Public Policy & Marketing*, *14*(1), 117–127.

Chivers, C. J. (2010). *The gun: The story of the AK-47*. London: Penguin Books.

Cole, S. A. (2005). More than zero: Accounting for error in latent fingerprint identification. *Journal of Criminal Law and Criminology*, *95*(3), 985–1078.

Conty, A. F. (2018). The politics of nature: New materialist responses to the anthroposcene. *Theory, Culture & Society*. *35*(7–8), 73–96.

Fagan, J., & Wilkinson, D. L. (1998). Guns, youth violence, and social identity in inner cities. *Crime and Justice*, *24*, 105–188.

Frank, A. W. (2010). *Letting stories breathe: A socio-narratology*. Chicago, IL and London: University of Chicago Press.

Goffman, E. (1963). *Stigma: Notes on the management of spoiled identity*. Englewood Cliffs, NJ: Prentice Hall.

Goffman, E. (1971). *The presentation of self in everyday life*. Harmondsworth: Penguin Books.

Hayward, K. (2012). Five spaces of cultural criminology. *British Journal of Criminology*, *52*(3), 441–462.

Hebdidge, D. (1979). *Subculture: The meaning of style*. London: Routledge.
Heidegger, M. (2010). *Being and time*. Albany, NY: State University of New York Press.
Ihde, D. (1990). *Technology and the lifeworld: From garden to Earth*. Bloomington, IN and Indianapolis, IN: Indiana University Press.
Katz, J. (1988). *Seductions of crime: Moral and sensual attractions in doing evil*. New York, NY: Basic Books.
Latour, B. (1993). *We have never been modern*. Cambridge, MA: Harvard University Press.
Latour, B. (1994). On technical mediation: Philosophy, sociology, geneaology. *Common Knowledge*, *3*(2), 29–64.
Law, J. (2000). On the subject of the object: Narrative, technology, and interpellation. *Configurations*, *8*(1), 1–29.
Mauss, M. (1954). *The gift: Forms and functions of exchange in archaic societies*. London: Cohen & West.
Merleau-Ponty, M. (2002). *Phenomenology of perception*. London: Routledge.
Miller, D. (2008). *The comfort of things*. Cambridge: Polity.
Miller, D. (2010). *Stuff*. Cambridge: Polity.
Petty, J. (2016). The London spikes controversy: Homelessness, urban securitisation and the question of 'hostile architecture'. *International Journal for Crime, Justice and Social Democracy*, *5*(1), 67–81.
Polk, K. (2016). Fakes and forgeries in art, and the more specific term 'art fraud': A criminological perspective. *Criminology and Criminal Justice*. doi:10.1093/acrefore/9780190264079.013.280
Presser, L. (2016). Criminology and the narrative turn. *Crime, Media, Culture*, *12*(2), 137–151.
Presser, L. (2018). *Inside story: How narratives drive mass harm*. Oakland, CA: University of California Press.
Presser, L., & Sandberg, S. (2015). Introduction: What is the story? In L. Presser & S. Sandberg (Eds.), *Narrative criminology: Understanding stories of crime*. New York, NY and London: New York University Press.
Rosenberger, R. (2014). Multistability and the agency of mundane artefacts: From speed bumps to subway benches. *Human Studies*, *37*, 369–392.
Rosiek, J. L., & Snyder, J. (2018). Narrative inquiry and new materialism: Stories as (not necessarily benign) agents. *Qualitative Inquiry*, 1–12. DOI: https://doi.org/10.1177/1077800418784326
Sandberg, S., & Ugelvik, T. (2016). The past, present, and future of narrative criminology: A review and an invitation. *Crime, Media, Culture*, *12*(2), 129–136.
Wilkinson, D. L., & Fagan, J. (1996). The role of firearms in violence 'scripts': The dynamics of gun events among adolescents. *Law and Contemporary Problems*, *59*(1), 55–89.
Williamson, E. (2011). Yorick's afterlives: Skull properties in performance. *Borrowers and Lenders: The Journal of Shakespeare and Appropriation*, *6*(1), 1–21.
Young, I. M. (2005). *On female body experience: 'Throwing like a girl' and other essays*. Oxford: Oxford University Press.

PART II: ANALYSING STORIES

STUDYING THE VICTIM

Chapter 12

Excavating Victim Stories: Making Sense of Agency, Suffering and Redemption

Elizabeth A. Cook and Sandra Walklate

Introduction

Victims' stories have for some time been the essence of much victimological research, surfacing in the form of autobiographies, witness testimonies and photography, and every so often finding their way into policy and practice. With the rise of a formally organised victims' movement, stories of harm, suffering and injustices have steadily gained currency with the launch of policies such as victim impact statements, and victims' panels, charters and codes signalling a 'formalisation' of victims' voices in criminal justice policy internationally (McGarry & Walklate, 2015, p. 104). A number of high-profile victim lobby groups have now gained the attention of a curious public of onlookers, who have become increasingly invested in the private lives of these public figures and the 'public display of private affairs' (Bauman, 2000, p. 37). Thus victims' stories have consequences for those who tell, hear and read them and promise a rich insight into understanding victims' experiences, particularly in the aftermath of violence.

Despite the wealth of stories now broadcast across different platforms, they remain a relatively untapped resource across the competing positivist, radical and critical victimological traditions. Simultaneously, the priorities of positivist victimology have remained an enduring influence on measuring and documenting victimisation. This approach has focused on identifying patterns and typologies of victims through the use of criminal victimisation surveys and has been subjected to ongoing critique by critical victimologists for its tendency to overlook the lived realities of victims' experiences in favour of aggregated data on victimisation (see inter alia Walklate & Spencer, 2016). An emergent cultural victimology is now taking shape which aims to 'foreground[s] suffering, our exposure to it, how it is presented to us, and what sense we make of it' (McGarry & Walklate, 2015, p. 18). This turn to the 'cultural' in victimology, alongside the renewed public interest in victims, and the recent revival of interest in stories from cultural, psychosocial, feminist and visual criminologies, offers a timely opportunity for victimology to further develop a narrative approach to understanding victim experiences of all kinds.

The Emerald Handbook of Narrative Criminology, 239–257
Copyright © 2019 Elizabeth A. Cook and Sandra Walklate
All rights of reproduction in any form reserved
doi:10.1108/978-1-78769-005-920191023

The narrative 'turn' in criminology has proliferated in recent years, emphasising the value of narrative texts for better understanding criminal behaviour, actions and motivations. However, despite this rising interest, a similar narrative 'turn' in victimology has only recently materialised shifting the focus from how moral transgressions are accomplished to how these moral transgressions are experienced by others (see, for example, Pemberton, Mulder, & Aarten, 2018a, 2018b; Walklate, Maher, McCulloch, Fitz-Gibbon, & Beavis, 2018). As Pemberton et al. (2018b, p. 2) highlight, while narrative criminology has endeavoured to answer 'why we harm', a narrative victimology is perhaps more keenly focused on 'what it is to be harmed'. The potential for a 'narrative turn' in victimology carries with it all kinds of possibilities and problems in adding detailed and nuanced understandings to the victim experience which are often smoothed out and sometimes erased from the vision of victimhood provided by criminal victimisation data. Using data from a case study, this chapter explores the implications of such an approach for victimology, with particular reference to the experience of lethal violence and its aftermath (McGarry & Walklate, 2015; Pemberton et al., 2018a, 2018b; Walklate et al., 2018).

The chapter falls into four parts. First we discuss the promise of a narrative turn for victimology and what the narrative approach might reveal about victims' experiences that criminal victimisation surveys and large-scale studies have previously neglected. Considering the constellation of practices employed in narrative research across the disciplines, the second part of this chapter presents an account of doing narrative research with victims to highlight the practicalities and ethics of listening to victims' stories. To illustrate the methodological and theoretical questions posed by such a narrative turn, the third part presents the story of June: a mother bereaved by the gun violence that unfolded in the community of inner-city Manchester nearly two decades ago. June's story intimately tells the loss of her son, the role of faith in dealing with the aftermath of this violence and the prospect of redemptive suffering. Here we consider the purposes this story served for her personal recovery in the aftermath of this violence and the wider political consequences of storytelling for victims in the public sphere. The final part considers the practical challenges of doing narrative research with victims. This focusses in particular on the ethics of misreading unfamiliar stories and the need to avoid academic provincialism when engaging with issues of faith, religion and suffering. In the conclusion we hope to give some sense of the experience of doing narrative research with victims and its ramifications for both narrative work and victimology more generally. However, first it will be of value to consider why the turn to narrative for victimology.

Why Narrative Victimology?

Victims' stories have maintained a long-standing presence in criminal justice policy and practice, gaining public, political and media sympathies particularly in the past 40 years. With a growing number of spectators, the sentiments of fear, danger and jeopardy relayed in stories of lethal violence hold not only personal consequence for victims but moral significance for a wider community of policy-makers, criminal justice professionals and activists (Meyers, 2016). Victims' stories therefore promise a rich terrain of exploration, revealing valuable insights into experiences of harm, injustice as well as resilience and recovery. Such experiential understandings of violence were absent from early victimological work which for the most part displayed a preference for notions of victim precipitation (Wolfgang, 1958) and/or victim proneness (Hindelang, Gottfredson, & Garofalo, 1978), victim typologies (Von Hentig, 1948) and other such concepts. The discipline has long since come under critique for its focus on understanding lifestyle as a mediating factor contributing to exposure to personal violence and being too far removed from more contemporary concerns with the effects of such violence.

A nascent cultural victimology has emerged, taking particular note of the recent movement from 'victim narratives' to 'trauma narratives' which has become preoccupied with how experiences of violence are represented rather than how they are lived and embodied (McGarry & Walklate, 2015). The concept of narrative therefore has become of increasing interest in understanding who, how, where and why some stories are told and gain traction in the public (and policy) domain and others are not. Narrative focusses attention not on the measurable nature and extent of violence but upon how violence is experienced and lived from the point of view of the victim (qua Rock, 1998). Recognising the promise of narrative for victimology not only affords a space to challenge the theoretical assumptions associated with which 'variables' matter under such circumstances but also provides the space in which the voice of the victim can be heard in their own terms. In this space theoretical assumptions may not only be challenged, and refined, but can also be disrupted and transformed.

Victims' experiences of lethal violence, the focus of this discussion, are characterised by disorder and uncertainty and threaten to unsettle relationship upon which assumptions are based. As Crossley (2000, p. 528) summarises, traumatising experiences 'throw into relief our routine and taken-for-granted expectations, highlighting the way in which a lived sense of coherence, unity and meaning normally prevails'. However, the practice of storytelling in suffering provides an opportunity for coherence to experiences of violence which are unthinkable and unimaginable to those not party to such events. Narrative is therefore perhaps ever more important in stories of lethal violence as the act of narrativising experience lends a coherence and comprehensibility through which victims can make sense of traumatic events over time (Pemberton, 2015; Pemberton et al., 2018b). Continuing, Crossley (2000, p. 528) therefore highlights that 'the importance of narratives again comes into effect, as the individual attempts to "reconfigure" a sense of order, meaningfulness and coherent identity'. Narrative interviewing also afford victims a space to reassert control and agency over experiences which have been previously disempowering and isolating. A narrative victimology minimises the risk of, as Fraser (2004, p. 185) writes, 'hijacking' the stories of victims and encourages victims to regain a sense of control from powerlessness. More importantly, while narrative research provides the discursive space to discuss, if desired, the experience and effects of lethal violence upon victims, it also affords victims a means of drawing upon other aspects of their life stories that they themselves have deemed important.

The sentiments of pain, injustice and loss are, however, similar scripts in the narratives of offenders as a rapidly developing field of narrative criminology has demonstrated. Of course it is important to note that viewing victims and offenders in dichotomous terms has long been challenged within criminology more generally. The route into crime as a consequence of victimisation, that which Chesney-Lind and Pasko (2004) have called the 'the continuity of abuse' (running away from home because of abuse, being returned to home by caring professionals to experience more abuse etc.), has been well documented for both male and female offenders (see inter alia Hubbard & Pratt, 2002; Rumgay, 2004). Thus it would be surprising not to find within narrative criminology some evidences of stories documenting such 'hard lives' (Fleetwood & Sandberg, 2017). Similar connections may be seen in Maruna's (2001) *Making Good* which explores the importance of narrative for offenders in the desistance process and how such narratives help to make sense of the past and move towards redemption and recovery. However, the story unfolding below is one in which it is the mother of the victim of lethal violence whose pain and suffering is the focus of attention. In more conventional victimological terms she is a secondary victim, yet the voices of such victims, as intimated above, have become a powerful influence in the policy domain. Before this discussion is taken further it will be useful to say a few words on method.

Doing Narrative Research with Victims of Lethal Violence

To illustrate the methodological and theoretical questions posed by such a narrative turn for victimology, this chapter draws upon narrative interviews conducted with bereaved families of gun violence involved in a local grassroots campaign, Mothers Against Violence. Fifteen interviews were undertaken during the course of the research, varying between 45 minutes to over 3 hours in length. These interviews formed a part of a broadly ethnographic approach designed to foreground suffering, encourage cultural immersion (on the part of the researcher) and gain an understanding of the value and meaning that victims give to these experiences. Interviewees were asked to recount their lives as a stream of narration rather than a series of single experiences, and were typically engaged within an informal, conversational manner so not to stifle discussion. Interviews were audio-recorded with the consent of participants, transcribed first-hand by the researcher and accompanied by fieldwork reflections evaluating each exchange and noting any points for further analysis. In contrast to the rigid format of an interview schedule with prearranged questions, these narrative interviews were guided by a short aide-memoire which allowed for consistency as well as room for flexibility and development as the discussions progressed. As more was learnt about the everyday routines of Mothers Against Violence, interview questions were refined and developed.

This narrative interviewing technique aimed to elicit a 'whole which is more than the sum of its parts, an order or hidden agenda' in order to establish connections between experiences (Hollway & Jefferson, 2000, p. 34). The narrative interviews adopted in this research provided an understanding of the 'connection among experiences, actions, and aspirations' and how experiences of lethal violence might inform people's engagement in Mothers Against Violence (Presser & Sandberg, 2015, p. 1). Open questions were used to begin the interview, such as: Could you begin by telling me your personal story? Beginning the interview with this more exploratory, open-ended question encouraged a natural flow of conversation where answers could be provided at the interviewee's own pace and tone. For example, a number of respondents avoided the terminology of 'victim' when describing their experiences and therefore a concerted effort was made to avoid this language during the interview. Questions were rephrased in the participant's own words and language and followed the order of events that the interviewee had initially identified as significant to them. Stories elicited from these open questions generally followed a chronological format beginning with early experiences, such as childhood and growing up, but typically came to revolve around the experience of violent bereavement in a coherent manner as they were told.

Further exploratory questions such as: Can you tell me about the story of your involvement in Mothers Against Violence? prompted interviewees to reflect on their experiences of violent bereavement in light of their involvement in Mothers Against Violence. Interviewees were prompted only for clarification in order to allow them to independently identify events of significance in their story and to avoid the risk of upsetting the flow of narration. The researcher made minimal use of prompts and, although against many first instincts, moments of silence were allowed for reflection and to provide more space for participants to explain and elaborate in their own time. Presser (2010, p. 436) pays particular attention to this strategy in her research with offenders noting that using minimal prompts allows for more 'spontaneous storytelling' before she moves to actively soliciting stories from participants.

This approach to narrative practice seems particularly significant for the purpose of developing a narrative victimology. Victims are routinely required to share their stories within the constraints of criminal justice institutions, through courts, in police interviews and in victim impact statements. Stauffer (2015, p. 111) explores this through her concept of 'ethical loneliness', highlighting the cruel irony that arises when 'an institution designed for hearing fails to listen'. However, opening up a discursive space in which victims could relay their stories in their own time and language provides an opportunity for harms to be confronted. Participants in the research with Mothers Against Violence could make their own choices over where the story begins and ends, what to conceal and how to gain control and ownership over what has happened.

Stories of lethal violence were recounted vividly and victims narrated detailed accounts attending closely to the details of the day, what they had been doing at the time they received the news of the event and their immediate responses to it. Participants narrated the events leading up to the moment that they heard the news, paying particular attention to their final moments with the victim often with remarkable detail. For those who had suffered in the aftermath of lethal violence, these stories represented a powerful means of animating experiences, marking out key events and humanising those involved to those who would listen. Intricate details, such as the final conversations they shared with the victim and the ordinariness of the activities they were carrying out at the time, acted as aids to walk listeners through the story. These discursive strategies are used to give a sense of who that person is and to recognise the choices, sentiments and situations that have unfolded in this story of lethal violence. However, they also invite us to imagine ourselves in the situation of others. The following section presents the story of June as a means of realising the promise of stories in victimology for understanding how victims experience the moral transgressions of others and what influence they have upon victims' narratives.

June's Story

To read and recognise the story shared by June, the story must first be situated within the specific historical context of post-industrial Manchester and the discourses of gun and gang violence that emerged at the time. Despite a rich cultural history of migration, music and art, Moss Side and the neighbouring community of Hulme has for a long while struggled to detach itself from the label of gun violence that appeared during the 1980s and 1990s in Manchester. Amid tensions of unemployment, poverty, social exclusion, 'environmental degradation', police distrust and the eventual emergence of gangs, widespread fear and moral panic of the 'gang' problem during these decades fuelled media fictions about Moss Side and Hulme as dangerous, disorderly suburban 'problem' areas besieged by gang rivalries and turf wars (Fraser, 1996; Peck & Ward, 2002). Manchester's branding as 'Madchester', a city renowned for its vibrant music and nightlife, quickly dissipated and transformed into 'Gunchester', the nation's archetype problem area. In August 1999, at the height of gun and knife violence in Manchester, the community was witness to four shootings leading to the deaths of three young men. In the aftermath, dozens of women gathered together to discuss the impact of these events on the community. Mothers Against Violence was established shortly after with the aim of raising public awareness of gun and knife crime, promoting positive lifestyles for young people and campaigning for the end of violence. At the time of writing, Mothers Against Violence had been campaigning on these issues for two decades, becoming a rendezvous for a diversity of experiences, identities and histories within this community.

At the forefront of Mothers Against Violence is June, a charismatic matriarch who helped to found the charity following the loss of her son to gun violence. June is a reserved but quietly confident woman and a long-standing member of the organisation, sharing one of the most intimate relationships with Mothers Against Violence. Located in a leafy residential area, their offices can be found in a local community centre: the building is worn, well lived in and host to a number of other community and social care services often found bustling around together. On the day of our meeting, I[1] found June in her office, a small but cosy room lined

---

[1]This chapter is based upon data collected by the first author during doctoral research.

with leaflets and information about services and photos of young people who have passed away. One of these photos was that of June's son, a tall, young man sitting on a white sandy beach. June greeted me in her usual way, throwing her arms around me and then welcoming me into the office. Over the next three and a half hours, our interview elicits a rich, in-depth and uninterrupted story spanning across her childhood, the loss of her son and the importance of faith in dealing with the aftermath of his death.

Practising Faith as 'Preparation' for Violent Bereavement

During our interview, June discussed her practise of Christianity and would often draw upon passages from the Bible to tell her story, highlighting the significance of faith-based understandings of justice, suffering and agency. June had attended Church since childhood, firstly with her mother as a child and continued her relationship with her faith after being baptised in a Methodist Church. From conversations in the Church community and regular attendance at prayer meetings, June noted the importance of 'meditating' and 'studying' these lessons about her faith. Reflecting on this over time, June had come to recognise that these lessons were in fact preparation for what was to follow. Nearly 20 years ago, after returning home from teaching on a Summer Vacation Bible School, June answered to a knock at her door from a friend of her son who had invited him out that evening. June describes her son as a 'tall and handsome', friendly young man, 'he had friends from all over the place'. Following his friend, June's son left the house that evening to play basketball and later that night was shot dead. Reflecting on this episode two decades later, June retold me the story of her experience, recognising the renewed importance of her conversations with God:

> *And that was the last time I saw my son. He left the house and the amazing thing about that, when my son was coming down the stairs – this is what I'll talk about in relation to – because I wasn't that familiar at that time with God's voice. I thought I was hearing his voice you get what I'm saying. But there was nothing that I could pin my hat onto kind of to prove it in the sense you know what I mean. But as my son was coming down the stairs I believe that God spoke to me and he said tell him not to go out. And I thought tell him not to go out? This is me now thinking tell him not go out? He's twenty. You [can't] tell a twenty-year-old boy not go out? But I believe if I had obeyed he wouldn't have gone. I believe that with all my heart because he was that type of person. So I thought I can't tell him that – not to go. Y'know. And it came...the voice came and it kind of shook me a little bit inside because I wasn't expecting that – how can you tell a twenty-year-old boy not to go out with his friend...And he brought the car, and he took him in the car and they went in the car and never came back. He never came back, yeah? And every time I think about that I think you know something June if you had obeyed,*

> *your son would have been still alive. But again, because the bible tells me all things are working together for my good...*
>
> *So, I believe I was being prepared as well for what happened to me you get what I'm saying? Even though I didn't fully understand everything, now I know more now than I did then. I know more now than I did then before my son...*

Lethal violence confronts victims with a moment of crisis. Indeed, our interview involved candid accounts of the pains of bereavement which was intimately connected to a maternal suffering. However, faith was an important anchor during this time. Read from the perspective of a narrative victimology, prayers and readings which she had reflected earlier on in life were able to lend coherence to her painful experience, constructing a meaningful narrative around her experience. Recounting this story, she drew a distinction between 'then' and 'now', explaining how her familiarity with God's voice had developed since the death of her son. June describes hearing a voice or impulse telling her to stop her son from leaving the house, one which she now recognises clearly as part of her conversation with God. June consistently returned to the phrase, 'all things are working together for my good' throughout the interview, remaining faithful to the notion that her son's death held purpose and consequence and placing trust in a higher power. The death of her son was realised as forming part of a greater 'calling' and 'purpose'. Rather than becoming a 'spiritual challenge', as Balk (1999, p. 487) has argued, these experiences are recounted as providing confirmation of 'what she had read' and consolation and validation of 'what she believed':

> *And, all of a sudden, one day I just thought I heard him come in and when I looked back 'round he wasn't there...And he came to my mind and he wasn't there and a kind of sadness came upon me and then all of a sudden I heard his voice. He said, 'Mummy why are you so sad?' And I looked 'round and there was nobody there [laughs] and I said, 'because I miss you'. And he said to me 'I'm alright. I'm alright'. And that took my life in another turn because it was confirming for me what I believe and what I read. Not only just what I believe because I had to read it first to believe it... And I remember that never happened to me again after that. I was quite calm and normal with that. It's like it settled me. That he was alright and he was telling me that he was alright do you get what I'm saying? So, I think well if he's alright why am I worried? [laughs]*
>
> *...So that's where I am and I think by the time my son was killed I was ready for what God had called me to do.*

She often came to describe her experience through expressions of 'destiny', 'vision', 'journey' and 'sacrifice' which spoke to the notion of fate, finding purpose and restoring meaning in, as Rock (2004, p. 444) writes, an 'otherwise meaningless act'. The story had become a blend of memories of past uncertainties and painful experiences, her understanding of her purpose in the present day and her hopes for Mothers Against Violence in the future.

Finding a 'Calling' in the Aftermath of Violence

During our afternoon of discussion, June remained confident of the significance and consequence of her son's death, returning often to the passage 'all things are working together for my good'. Reconciling the death of her son with the birth of Mothers Against Violence, she described how her son represented the 'seed' for change:

> ...*my son was the seed that was sown into the earth to bring it about... My son's life was never a waste. Even when he died I never saw it as a waste. I believed that something good was coming out of it do you get what I'm saying. So that's how the change has come about it.*
>
> *Why's he dead, Lord? You know what I mean – but now I can see the why him. And because of the way I think that he is in a better place and his life was for a purpose, the life that he lived, the 20 years that he lived, was for a purpose and that purpose was being fulfilled by the things that I did do you get what I'm saying?*

Rather than challenging her commitment to faith, this confrontation with lethal violence provided affirmation of the lessons she had only just started to understand in her early life. June made assertive connections between the pains of bereavement and the purpose that these pains gained through the emergence of Mothers Against Violence. She was not alone in this line of thought as a number of other bereaved relatives made references to the notion of violent bereavement as 'transformative' or 'catalysts' for change. Describing this, June refers to her engagement in Mothers Against Violence as an act of fate: on the one hand, her 'calling' to become a 'vessel' and, on the other hand, encouraged and reassured by the confidence that this 'calling' instilled:

> *He was just using me as his vessel to speak to people and to tell them the truth and I knew he was with me and I knew that he held me together to tell you the truth. Otherwise, I think I would have gone under myself.*

Referring to her own part as a mere 'vessel', June might be referring the Mothers Against Violence as a greater project with a greater purpose. Describing the emergence of Mothers Against Violence as a 'calling' also perhaps reflects the notion of vocation within Christianity: the invitation to being summoned to carry out God's work. Here, June's reference to becoming a 'vessel' to carry out 'God's work' or to a 'calling' infers an alternative understanding of agency to those established in victimology. In her faith-based understanding of agency, agency is construed in the literal sense whereby June represents an agent. Our tendencies in the past have been to equate agency with action, voice and speaking out, whereas a lack of agency has been equated to silence, shame and fear. However, in this context, June exerts agency by denying it and adopting an identity of agent for something else: her faith. This concept of agency still captures the sense of voice and act of speaking but does so with the principles of another power in mind. In this way, Mothers Against Violence is perhaps seen as part of June's conversation with God.

This illustrates the way in which narrative research represents a valuable opportunity for a victimological engagement with religion, faith and spirituality. Rather than focus on the truthfulness or the historical accuracy of this story, the narrative approach emphasises the meanings and significance of the story for the storytellers. The story is real in its consequences for June. She discusses this in the following passage:

> *Whatever I'm doing now, I can continue to do until my last breath because I believe it's what I was called to do. I was called to do it. The circumstances that led me to here wasn't a very pleasant one but after the unpleasantness came the joy. The satisfaction, the amazing tingle in my body, in my mind.*
>
> *For me, I've lived so much more than I've died. You get what I'm saying. And it's just so amazing you know what I mean. Yeah. But I don't really know. I think of where my son and where he brought me to, I wouldn't have it any different....*

Rather than undermining her sense of self-identity, lethal violence provided clarification and confirmation – much like Denzin's (1989, p. 34) notion of 'epiphany': moments that 'leave marks on people's lives [and] have the potential to create transformational experiences'. Epiphany moments, such as the sudden loss of a son, are defined by the subject and lend significance to other elements of the life story: between the strengthening and practice of faith and role as a bereaved mother on a public campaign. June became a visible and distinguished figure of leadership in Mothers Against Violence and her story took on a public life long after the problem it was originally voiced in response to had diminished. This story provided a source of motivation, inspiration and understanding within the community in which it was read and heard, reinforcing it and drawing acknowledgement from a wide public audience. Victims' stories, such as June's, can bridge divides and encourage identification across groups of people, offering a platform for understanding, reworking and learning about otherwise dissimilar individuals. Reflecting on this legacy of her son's death, June voiced the sense of fulfilment that she feels today:

> *And because I'm satisfied with where I am at this present moment, because of my son's death, I usually tell people if I had to live again I*

will do the same thing. My son's death because it has brought me into a place that I'd never been before and it's taken me beyond what I ever thought or imagined. I'm thinking who would have been phoning me up and sending me emails like that and asking my opinion of things you get what I'm saying [laughs] – who would have been doing that?

Therefore, whilst it is the case that victimology has had suffering as its focus since its inception (McGarry & Walklate, 2015), this story adds some considerable nuance to how such suffering might be experienced and understood over and through time from the 'victim's' perspective. One way of making sense of these experiences is through the concept of redemption.

Redemptive Suffering

The significance of stories of suffering lies not only in what they 'reveal' about the storytellers but in what they 'do' for others and how they might encourage recovery from harm (Presser, 2016, p. 139). Green and Pemberton (2017, p. 93) make the case for the power of understanding experiences in the victim's own terms and the power of narratives to enable victimology to do this. This is a focus which has been further endorsed by Pemberton et al. (2018b) and Walklate et al. (2018). To date, however, much of this narrative work has been conducted on offenders' stories of desistance from crime and Maruna's (2001) work has made a significant contribution to this. His work resisted the temptation to look for significant points of desistance for offenders but was concerned to embrace the desistance process as part and parcel of an offender's redemption narrative. This holistic approach to understanding desistance led Maruna (2001) to identify a number of themes in stories of redemption and Stone (2016, p. 957) has gone on to suggests that 'Redemption stories cast past negative experiences as necessary for the positive present and future: "If I hadn't gone through that, I wouldn't be the person I am today".'

This kind of narrative of redemptive suffering runs through the story of June as presented above. June's faith afforded her a way of making sense of her own suffering and its purpose for informing her life now. This story is not too dissimilar from that of Kim Phuc (often referred to as 'The Girl in the Photograph' or 'The Napalm Girl') whose rediscovery of Christianity also seems to have enabled her to make sense of her past, present and future, as a whole (see Walklate, 2019).

This search for making sense of one's past, present and future is not confined to those who have experienced 'extreme' suffering as in the two examples cited above. For example, Zehr (2001) presents the stories of a more 'ordinary' kind in which the people who were the subject of them found a way to come to terms with the effects of violent crime which were extraordinary and exceptional for them. All of Zehr's (2001) respondents voice the full range of feelings any individual might have to challenging events from revenge to forgiveness, but rather like June and Kim Phuc they do not talk of themselves as victims or survivors. Zehr (2001) struggled to find a word that would encompass these experiences so he settled for 'transcending'. In a similar vein, June found a way of making sense of her painful past and giving a meaning to her future through a transcendental commitment to faith. Thus she has resisted being frozen in the moment of a bereaved mother. Through her faith she set on a path to redemption in which making sense of her past, present and future come together as a whole. Importantly this path is hers and hers alone: she has been the agent acting on her own choices (Green & Pemberton, 2017). So her son might have been in the wrong place at the wrong time but, for her, the pain associated with this has been reconciled by her belief in a bigger purpose behind this event for her and her son. In her terms they are now both at peace.

Other stories of reconciliation as a way of dealing with the impact of lethal violence touch on similar processes of redemption. For example, Colin and Wendy Parry established the Warrington Foundation4Peace in memory of their son, Tim, and fellow victim, three-year-old Johnathan Ball, victims of the IRA bomb planted in Warrington in 1993. As time has evolved their story of redemptive suffering has been widely reported in local and national media in the UK. In a letter to his son published in the Huffington Post on 20 March 2018, 25 years on from the 1993 bomb, Colin Parry writes: 'So you see, Tim, that your life and memory is a beacon to so many others.' Thus it is possible to suggest Colin and Wendy Parry found a way to transcend their experiences creating a life with a meaningful whole for themselves rather than staying locked in a past ruptured by violence. Similarly, Walklate et al.'s (2018) case study of Rosie Batty and her influence on policies addressing violence against women in Australia in the aftermath of the brutal murder of her son Luke hints at a desire to create something good out of the bad. Taken together all of these stories hint at redemption. Importantly this redemption is not a simple and/or measurable moment, but it is a process of coming to terms with the impact of the different violence(s) in different lives in their own way for those subjected to them. However, importantly many of these stories are not only private ones, they are also public ones. Brison (2002, p. 51) states:

> In order to construct self-narratives we need not only the words with which to tell our stories, but also an audience able and willing to hear us and to understand our words as we intend them. This aspect of remaking a self in the aftermath of trauma highlights the dependency of the self on others and helps to explain why it is so difficult for survivors to recover when others are unwilling to listen to what they endured.

Thus the role of the audience, in whatever shape and form that takes, enables the avoidance of 'ethical loneliness' (Stauffer, 2015). In avoiding such loneliness, victims of any kind, but of lethal violence in particular, are able to engage in the kind of repair work essential to their sense of self as well as avoiding the stigma of blame so easily associated with the experience of victimisation. As Pemberton et al. (2018a, p. 12) point out:

> The damage of victimisation can be understood as a narrative rupture, which endangers a sense of control and continuity of one's life story throughout time and with the social surroundings. The way victims attempt to make sense and meaning of their ordeal occurs in narrative modes of reasoning, while they adopt narrative means to regain agency and re-establish communion with their social context.

Such stories have particular importance in reinforcing and strengthening dialogue between communities: they 'gather people around them' and can voice demand for changes (Plummer, 1995, p. 174). Most importantly, these stories return the prospect of ownership to victims which criminal justice agencies have historically attempted to retain for themselves. Recognition of this has significant methodological and theoretical implications for victimology.

For June's dialogue with faith and bereavement to come to the fore, there needed to be not simply a qualitative orientation to gathering 'data' about her and her experiences. There also needed to be a conceptual openness to hearing what she was saying. There are different ways this might have been achieved. For example, McGarry (2017) makes a compelling case for victimology to dig deeper into biographical methods in order to better appreciate when 'typical victims' have 'no story to tell and no one to tell it to'. Here he is alluding to the ways in which positivist victimology erases some victim experiences more than others. For him it is the inability of such a victimology to envision the young, white, male soldier as a victim. Yet this victim too has a story to tell which has its own narrative and epiphany moments (McGarry, 2017, p. 114) which put this soldier on the road to recovery. Whether through the biographical method embraced by McGarry (2017) or the in-depth interviews deployed with June, both approaches facilitate an appreciation of living in time and through time. In other words, the importance of lives lived both diachronically and synchronically is centred. The narrative method that facilitates the ability to take the long view (in time) simultaneously reveals so much more about victimhood and how to make sense of it.

One of the consequences of the contemporary desire to see the world through the prism of pain (Fassin, 2012) is that we are also drawn into assuming individuals become defined by that moment of pain. This is patently not the case for June or the other examples cited here. People can and do change. Experiences of lethal violence can become 'turning points' or junctures in the life stories of victims, prompting new ways of thinking, changes in meaning or renewed purpose. Importantly for June, this is not a story of conversion and/or the way in which religion might contribute to desistance from crime (qua Maruna, Wilson, & Curran, 2006). This is a story about how to continue living in the face of demanding circumstances. Nonetheless these moments can also hold transformative potential and come to punctuate, lend significance to and make life stories coherent. Thus the kind of narrative analysis proffered here assists in appreciating this. However, this excursion into making sense of June's story through the lens of redemptive suffering also raises important theoretical challenges for narrative victimology.

The Challenges for a Narrative Victimology

The story presented in this chapter was a rich, uninterrupted story and a consequence of a series of open-ended, conversational questions that asked respondents to recount their life stories. However, narrative research is not without its difficulties. Narrative does not merely represent a 'more or less transparent and neutral medium for conveying something that lies beyond language and the story' (Bruner, 1987; Hydén, 1997, p. 50). The nature of this relationship is uncertain and therefore the translation of experience into narrative is not necessarily linear (Presser & Sandberg, 2015). Rather, as Riessman (2008, p. 3) explains, '... transforming a lived experience into language and constructing a story about it is not straightforward, but invariably mediated and regulated by controlling vocabularies'. This problem prompted some to question whether the researcher may ever be able to 'fully know' the subjects of their research (Hollway & Jefferson, 2000; Mauthner & Doucet, 2008). Indeed, even as Bruner (1987, p. 14) contends that narrative offers the only means for communicating experience, he concedes that narrative is nonetheless very 'unstable'.

The conceptual openness embraced in the narrative approach adopted here gave space for thinking through June's story through a relatively underdeveloped conceptual agenda for victimology more generally. This story highlighted the importance of providing faith-based understandings of suffering, agency and injustice but also raised concerns of reading the unfamiliar in the 'wrong' lens. The import of faith and spirituality to people's lives has been increasingly marginalised through the twentieth and twenty-first centuries and this process of marginalisation is as evident in criminology and victimology as it is in other social sciences (Spalek & Imtoul, 2008). Akers (2010) offers a review of the available criminological work that has focused on the relationship between religion and crime which has since been noted by Cottee (2014) who has argued that much of this work pays attention to the deterrent effects of religious belief. However, when religious belief is seen to encourage violent actions replete with transcendental rewards, this relationship not only becomes more complicated, criminology also becomes mute (Routledge & Arndt, 2008). As Cottee (2014) argues, criminology has indeed been remarkably quiet in understanding these interconnections in relation to violence, and the same remains true in the parallel discipline of victimology.

Arguably, this highlights the other side to Fassin's (2012) concern with seeing the world through the prism of pain. Most of the time, human beings do not choose pain as their way of life. Importantly, understanding the gap between when victims embrace a victim identity and when they do not (pointed out some time ago by Rock, 2002) is still a prescient concern for this area of investigation. June did not embrace a victim identity focussing on her pain. She found redemption from her suffering through her faith, which was made visible by an open conceptual agenda and methodological approach. Importantly she had a story to tell and someone to tell it to. As McGarry (2017) alludes to, there may be considerable more mileage in unpacking what and who is made visible and invisible in the secular assumptions in the dominance of positivist victimology and the discipline of criminology more broadly.

Stories of suffering are shaped not only by the storyteller but mediated by the audiences by which they are 'heard' or 'read'. Reading nonsecular stories with a secular lens also raises ethical and political questions over the professional use of victims' stories, whether in the context of media platforms, truth commissions or academic scholarship. For example, Yazir Henri (2003) has commented on the dangers of appropriating victims' life stories outside of the setting in which they were originally exchanged. Reflecting on his personal experiences of providing testimony at the South African Truth and Reconciliation Commission in 1996, Henri (2003, p. 266) stresses that:

> Serious thought needs to be given to the ethics of appropriating testimony for poetic licence, media freedom, academic commentary and discourse analysis. Arguing these lines and 'It's on the public record' are too easy positions to take since they do not address the rights of self-authorship and the intention of the speaker, the reclamation of one's voice and one's agency.

As researchers, when we read the stories of victims, a degree of distance is almost inevitably created between the lived experience and narrative. Rather than simple recitals of experience, researchers are intimately involved in the coproduction of stories, helping to tell the story and later to read it. In this sense, it is important to acknowledge that this 'reading' of June's story is a product of criminological analysis which has its own established frameworks and assumptions rooted in secularism. Unfamiliarity with matters of faith and spirituality in criminology creates a danger that such stories might be over-attributed to social forces and concepts. It is therefore essential to remember that this analysis is a secular criminological reading of a nonsecular story. As Orsi (2016, p. 42) discusses in his critique, studies of modern religion have come to replace the 'presence' of Gods which now 'appear as tropes, metaphors, and distortions of language'. Reducing Christianity to a 'narrative' of coping and comfort upon which victims draw upon diminishes their understandings to outer world views rather than inner-world, existential, intrinsic ways of actually being in the world.

The ethical responsibility to read June's story is therefore in a sense a methodological dilemma, as Henri writes, and requires attention to the 'interpretive conflicts' in storytelling, writing and reading (Borland, 1991). Many different actors are invested in the creation of stories aside from the storyteller and, as Polletta (2006, p. 1) writes, 'we battle over storytelling as well as celebrating'. Narratives are characterised by ambiguity, uncertainty and contradiction, and are subject to subsequent mediation by the audience by which they are 'heard' or 'read' (Stauffer, 2015). June's story served the purpose of personal recovery but also held wider political consequences and a social life for victims in the public sphere, providing inspiration and motivation for others in the community. Therefore, while narrative research with victims can provide a platform for rediscovering agency, researchers must be sensitive to issues of ownership and authenticity and consider whether the act of interpretation risks diluting experiences rather than remaining faithful to them. As Henri (2003) asserts, victims must find a space in which their stories can be heard without compromising the dignity of victims outside of these exchanges.

Conclusion

As Walklate and Spencer (2016, p. 191) state tracing the victim and victimological 'story' is '……fraught with difficulties: where to start geographically, where to start historically, whose story is to be listened to and so on'. However, making sense of victims and victimhood is also fraught with conceptual, methodological and ethical difficulties. June's story raised several questions concerning the professional uses of victims' stories, the ethics and issues of authenticity in reading stories which are unfamiliar and the condition of victimology more broadly in making sense of matters of faith and spirituality. However, it also highlighted the promise of narrative research for adding nuance to understandings of victims' experiences. The narrative approach has become the subject of numerous disciplines in the social sciences where some have argued that 'specificity has been lost with popularisation' (Riessman, 2008, p. 5). Narrative has emerged in various forms in criminology, very often with the assumption that we are talking about the same thing, using it in the same way and achieving the same outcomes. However, as the emergence of a narrative victimology has demonstrated, narrative serves different purposes.

Narrative victimology has a long way to travel to fully realise the applications of narrative in understanding what it means to be harmed and to learn the lessons (and from the mistakes) of narrative criminology. This chapter has endeavoured to outline some of these difficulties as they emerged as part of the process of doing narrative research. This 'doing' comprised all of these challenges and posed some new ones for those who might claim to speak on behalf of victims as a means of influencing criminal justice policy. It also poses some challenges for those victims who might use their voice to make claims for all victims. Of course living through the disruption of experiences thrust upon individuals unexpectedly is challenging and a narrative victimology offers some deep sense of those challenges. However, a narrative victimology as presented here also serves as a reminder that human beings sometimes stay frozen in and with the events that have affected them, and sometimes do not. This is equally important to recognise for a victimology still wedded to the policy domain.

References

Akers, R. (2010). Religion and crime. *Criminologist*, *36*(6), 1–6.
Balk, D. E. (1999). Bereavement and spiritual change. *Death Studies*, *23*(6), 485–493.
Bauman, Z. (2000). *Liquid modernity*. London: Polity Press.
Borland, K. (1991). "That's not what I said": Interpretive conflict in oral narrative research. In S. B. Gluck & D. Patai (Eds.), *Women's words: The feminist practice of oral history*. London: Routledge.

Brison, S. (2002). *Aftermath; violence and the remaking of the self.* Princeton, NJ: Princeton University Press.

Bruner, J. (1987). Life as narrative. *Social Research, 54*(1), 11–32.

Chesney-Lind, M., & Pasko, L. (2004). *The female offender: Girls, women and crime.* London: SAGE Publications.

Cottee, S. (2014). We need to talk about Mohammad: Criminology, theistic violence and the murder of Theo Van Gogh. *British Journal of Criminology, 54*(6), 981–1001.

Crossley, M. (2000). Narrative psychology, trauma and the study of self/identity. *Theory & Psychology, 10*(4), 527–546.

Denzin, N. (1989). *Interpretive interactionism.* London: SAGE Publications.

Fassin, D. (2012). *Humanitarian reason: A moral history of the present.* Berkeley and Los Angeles, CA: University of California Press.

Fleetwood, J., & Sandberg, S. (2017). Street talk and Bourdieusian criminology: Bringing narrative to field theory. *Criminology and Criminal Justice, 17*(4), 365–381.

Fraser, H. (2004). Doing narrative research: Analysing personal stories line by line. *Qualitative Social Work, 3*(2), 179–201.

Fraser, P. (1996). Social and spatial relationships and the "problem" inner city: Mossside in manchester. *Critical Social Policy, 16*(49), 43–65.

Green, S., & Pemberton, A. (2017). The impact of crime: Victimisation, harm and resilience. In S. Walklate (Ed.), *The handbook of victims and victimology* (2nd ed.). Abingdon: Routledge.

Henri, Y. (2003). Reconciling reconciliation: A personal and public journey of testifying before the South African truth and reconciliation commission. In P. Gready (Ed.), *Political transition: Politics and cultures.* London: Pluto Press.

Hindelang, M., Gottfredson, M., & Garofalo, J. (1978). *Victims of personal crime: An empirical foundation for a theory of personal victimisation.* Cambridge, MA: Ballinger.

Hollway, W., & Jefferson, T. (2000). *Doing qualitative research differently: Free association, narrative and the interview method.* London: SAGE Publications.

Hubbard, D., & Pratt, T. (2002). A meta-analysis of the predictors of delinquency among girls. *Journal of Offender Rehabilitation, 34*(3), 1–13.

Hydén, L.-C. (1997). Illness and narrative. *Sociology of Health & Illness, 19*(1), 48–69.

Maruna, S. (2001). *Making good: How ex-convicts reform and rebuild their lives.* Washington, DC: American Psychological Association.

Maruna, S., Wilson, L., & Curran, K. (2006). Why god is often found behind bars: Prison conversions and the crisis of self-narrative. *Research in Human Development, 3*(2–3), 161–184.

Mauthner, N. S., & Doucet, A. (2008). What can be known and how? Narrated subjects and the listening guide. *Qualitative Research, 8*(3), 399–409.

McGarry, R. (2017). The "typical victim": No story to tell and no one to tell it to. In S. Walklate & M. Hviid-Jacobsen (Eds.), *Liquid criminology: Doing imaginative criminological research.* London: Routledge.

McGarry, R., & Walklate, S. (2015). *Victims: Trauma, testimony and justice.* London: Routledge.

Meyers, D. (2016). *Victims' stories and the advancement of human rights.* Oxford: Oxford University Press.

Orsi, R. (2016). *History and presence.* Cambridge, MA: Harvard University Press.
Peck, J., & Ward, K. (2002). Placing manchester. In J. Peck & K. Ward (Eds.), *City of revolution: Restructuring manchester.* Manchester: Manchester University Press.
Pemberton, A. (2015). *Victimology with a hammer: The challenge of victimology.* Tilburg: Tilburg University.
Pemberton, A., Aarten, P. G. M., & Mulder, E. (2018a). Stories as property: Narrative ownership as a key concept in victims' experiences with criminal justice. *Criminology and Criminal Justice, 0*(0), 1–17.
Pemberton, A., Aarten, P. G. M., & Mulder, E. (2018b). Stories of injustice: Towards a narrative victimology. *European Journal of Criminology, 16*(4), 391–412.
Plummer, K. (1995). *Telling sexual stories: Power, change and social worlds.* London: SAGE Publications.
Polletta, F. (2006). *It was like a fever: Storytelling in protest and politics.* Chicago, IL: University of Chicago Press.
Presser, L. (2010). Collecting and analyzing the stories of offenders. *Journal of Criminal Justice Education, 21*(4), 431–446.
Presser, L. (2016). Criminology and the narrative turn. *Crime, Media, Culture, 12*(2), 137–151.
Presser, L., & Sandberg, S. (2015). What is the story?. In L. Presser & S. Sandberg (Eds.), *Narrative criminology: Understanding stories of crime.* New York, NY: New York Press.
Riessman, C. (2008). *Narrative methods for the human sciences.* London: SAGE Publications.
Rock, P. (1998). *After homicide: Practical and political responses to bereavement.* Oxford: Clarendon Press.
Rock, P. (2002). On becoming a victim. In C. Hoyle & R. Young (Eds.), *New visions of crime victims.* Oxford: Hart Publishing.
Rock, P. (2004). *Constructing victims' rights: The home office, new labour, and victims.* Oxford: Oxford University Press.
Routledge, C., & Arndt, J. (2008). Self-sacrifice as self-defence: Mortality salience increases efforts to affirm a symbolic immortal self at the expense of the physical. *European Journal of Social Psychology, 38*(3), 531–541.
Rumgay, J. (2004). *When victims become offenders; searching for coherence in policy and practice.* London: The Fawcett Society.
Spalek, B., & Imtoul, A. (2008). *Religion, spirituality and the social sciences.* Bristol: Policy Press.
Stauffer, J. (2015). *Ethical loneliness: The injustices of not being heard.* New York, NY: Columbia University Press.
Stone, R. (2016). Desistance and identity repair; redemption narratives as resistance to stigma. *British Journal of Criminology, 56*(5), 956–975.
Von Hentig, H. (1948). *The criminal and his victim.* New Haven, CT: Yale University Press.
Walklate, S. (2019). Images of atrocity: From victimhood to redemption and the implications for a (narrative) victimology. In E. Murray & R. Lippens (Eds.), *Visualising atrocity.* London: Palgrave Macmillan.
Walklate, S., Maher, J., McCulloch, J., Fitz-Gibbon, K., & Beavis, K. (2018). Victim stories and victim policy: Is there a case for a narrative victimology? *Crime, Media, Culture: International Journal, 00*(0), 1–17.

Walklate, S., & Spencer, D. (2016). Conclusion: Critical victimology beyond academe; engaging publics and practices. In S. Walklate & D. Spencer (Eds.), *Reconceptualizing critical victimology: Interventions and possibilities*. Lanham, MD: Lexington Books.

Wolfgang, M. (1958). *Patterns of criminal homicide*. Philadelphia, PA: University of Philadelphia Press.

Zehr, H. (2001). *Transcending: Reflections of crime victims*. Intercourse, PA: Good Books.

Chapter 13

Narrative Victimology: Speaker, Audience, Timing

Kristen Lee Hourigan

Introduction

Just as offenders compose narratives about themselves, their crimes and their victims, so do victims construct narratives about offenders, their own victimisation and its effects. Therefore, just as storytelling plays a role in crime and criminal justice, storytelling also plays a role in survival, healing and resilience in the aftermath of crime. When investigating the stories of offenders, Presser notes that narrative criminologists are not focussed upon uncovering an objective truth (2016). Rather, they seek to uncover how offenders understand and create meaning from events, how they justify or judge actions and where they see themselves fitting into their social worlds. Likewise, the value of studying the victim narrative is not in determining its objective veracity. Rather, its primary aim is to uncover the meaning-making processes underneath and behind the story, its construction, delivery, effects and connection to one's identity and social world.

By considering the narratives of crime victims, this chapter develops method in the subfield of narrative victimology. Drawing upon my research investigating narratives of individuals who have lost loved ones to homicide (co-victims), I argue that narrative victimologists must examine victims' narratives with sensitivity towards their fluid, co-constructed, purposeful and situated nature. The value of such sensitivity has been demonstrated by narrative criminologists (for example, see Brookman, 2015; Sandberg, 2013). Such work indicates that our level of understanding can be greatly increased by recognising and appreciating the conditional nature of offender narratives. This is equally true of the narratives constructed by victims in the wake of crime.

Situating Narrative Victimology

Within criminology, both the narrative approach and the subfield of victimology are relatively new. Pemberton, Mulder, and Aarten (2018) recently advanced a strong claim for the value of narrative victimology, pointing out that such a subfield would be a valuable complement to narrative criminology. The victim experience is particularly ripe for a narrative approach for several reasons. First, the offence is cognitively structured as a historical event within the victim's life story, shaping how the victim sees the self, specific others and the social world in general (Crossley, 2000). Second, criminal victimisation often causes disruption to the life story (Crossley, 2000), which can have a direct and lasting effect upon the victimised party, including effects to identity. This is especially true in cases of serious, unexpected crime that upsets the individual's sense of order and predictability in the world. Such disruption can involve a sense of severance of the past from the present which may be 'bridged' narratively (Brison, 2002). Finally, victim narratives are often focussed upon actors' intention and have an inherent moral quality (Pemberton et al., 2018). Therefore, because we make moral choices based on the narratives we construct, share and reflect upon (Sarbin, 1986), victim narrative provides insight into the motivation behind actions that follow victimisation. For these reasons, a narrative approach is especially useful when exploring the victim experience.

Approaching the crime victim experience through narrative is also reasonable because it is through the construction of narrative that many of the effects of victimisation are dealt with. Victimisation may call into question the most fundamental assumptions of life (Janoff-Bulman, 1992). After a criminal offence, victims are likely to feel increased levels of vulnerability (Janoff-Bulman, 1992) and a sense of uncertainty about, and severance from, the social world (Strang, 2002; Zehr, 2001). What was once viewed as knowable and ordered is now volatile, fragile and unstable. This is especially true when the victimisation is intentional (Brison, 2002) and for those victimised within 'unanticipated incidents in familiar or benign settings' and victims of highly intrusive crimes (Strang, 2002, pp. 18–19).

After trauma, the construction of narrative may restore one's sense of order and social connection (Crossley, 2000). Since identity is constructed upon social connection, coherence and continuity, the trauma and disruption that result from criminal victimisation can jolt one's identity or sense of self into a state of uncertainty or flux. As Zehr eloquently noted, '(v)ictimization represents a profound crisis of identity and meaning, an attack on oneself as an autonomous but related individual in an orderly world… so we must recover a redeeming narrative which reconstructs a sense of meaning and identity' (2001, pp. 189–190). Identity processes can alleviate some of this unease by allowing for increased predictability, order and control. By categorising self and others, one can anticipate attitudes, emotions and behaviours likely to occur in social interaction (Burke & Stets, 2009). This allows individuals to effectively navigate their social worlds by reducing uncertainty. In some cases, the effects of trauma can even spur positive change or growth, including changes to self-perception or evaluation (Calhoun & Tedeschi, 2001). The connection between narrativization and identity construction makes narrative analysis an ideal means to exploring how victims of crime establish meaning following victimisation as well as how they mend a damaged sense of control or order. Furthermore, by understanding the identities victims construct in the wake of crime, we can begin to generate meaningful theories surrounding criminal victimisation.

Narrative analysts have fruitfully drawn from the insights of symbolic interactionism (Cooley, 1902; Mead, 1934; Stryker, 1980 [2002]). The symbolic interactionist perspective provides much insight into factors that influence one's identity. Through symbolic interaction, identities are products of language. Therefore, investigation of narrated experience is inherently well suited for investigations into identity processes. It is through the telling of one's story (to both self and others) that the self is created in that the speaker makes meaningful decisions about the way to construct narrative in order to convey a certain identity or impression of oneself to the listener, selectively omitting or adding emphasis, for example (Presser, 2008). By investigating narrative, we can uncover how individuals interpret events in their lives, learning how they view themselves, and the social world, in the aftermath of those events (McAdams, 2006). Whilst narrative criminologists often draw on interviews, studies observing storytelling in situ are able to explore what stories do in those social settings and for the people that tell them. Storytelling itself can be viewed as a sort of performance (see Goffman, 1974) and, as such, during the telling of the story the speaker is essentially attempting to convince the listener, who was absent at the original event, of their interpretation of that event. Therefore, the story does more than recount objective history. It gives meaning to experience and connects it to other aspects of one's story. This selective reconstruction is especially relevant when individuals are recounting particularly complex, troubling or traumatic events, such as criminal victimisation.

Finally, the study of narrative allows the researcher insight into aspects of the victim's social world of which he or she may not be consciously aware. For example, analysing the language crime victims use to describe offenders allows for insight into the victims' attitudes towards the offender and the crime, as well as information about what groups the victim views the offenders and the self as falling within. Victims may be averse to acknowledging commonality between the self and offenders. Also, people are not necessarily aware of the groups with which they identify, since identities function at both conscious and unconscious levels (Burke & Stets, 2009). Narrative therefore provides insight into identity and social connection by negating the need for conscious awareness or acceptance of similarities that would be necessary if the participant were responding to direct questions in interviews or surveys. Crossley (2000) highlights the importance of considering language in understanding experience, as it is through language and discursive structuring that we are constantly creating and negotiating meaning. Therefore, in order to fully understand why some people touched by crime embrace their victimhood while others use the trauma as fuel for agentic action, we must turn to the victim narrative.

Although the subfield of narrative victimology is in its infancy, victims' narratives have been utilised in studies across a variety of topics and disciplines. These include studies of violent loss (for example, see Janoff-Bulman, 1992), trauma (for example, see Crossley, 2000; McGarry & Walklate, 2015; Walklate,

2016), policy development (for example, see Elias, 1993; Walklate, Maher, McCulloch, Fitz-Gibbon, & Beavis, 2018), restorative justice processes (for example, see Strang, 2002), meaning-making and the reconstruction of self (for example, see Brison, 2002), victim impact statements (for example, see Roberts, 2009), forgiveness (Hourigan, 2018), deauthorization of victims (for example, see Trinch, 2007, 2014), media depictions of victimisation (for example, see Wright, 2016) and political protests (for example, see Polletta, 2006), as well as specific types of victimisation, including rape (for example, see Sebold, 1999; Trinch, 2014), intimate partner violence (for example, see Trinch, 2007) and mass atrocities, such as the Holocaust (for example, see Delbo, 1995; Langer, 1991).

In the sections that follow, I will demonstrate the process of narrative victimological research by reflecting upon the methodological strategies undertaken in a large research project conducted in the northeastern US (see Hourigan, forthcoming). Over the course of over 3 years, I engaged in participant observation, attending 96 victim-centred events, including monthly meetings of three co-victim self-help groups; local charity events and fundraisers surrounding issues of victimisation; private and public memorials; advocacy and community outreach events; and holiday and celebratory family gatherings. I also completed 36 intensive, face-to-face interviews with co-victims, most of whom were also present at victim-centred events I observed. This pairing of methods allowed me to compare participants' stories as shared in multiple social settings with differing levels of privacy, from one-on-one interviews to live, televised speeches prepared in advance and delivered to large audiences of gathered strangers. Such narratives were supplemented by content analysis of a variety of forms of written narratives, given to me by participants. My focus was upon the narratives participants constructed, communicated and reflected upon. These methods allowed me to observe narratives both verbal and written and delivered in interaction with myself and others, including participants' loved ones, neighbours, strangers, fellow co-victims, imprisoned offenders, at-risk youth, policy-makers and advocates. Using these, I sought to better understand the effects of loss to homicide upon one's identity and emotions.

Through this work, I noted three different types of narratives that emerge as individuals construct their new realities in the wake of violent loss. In response to the level of disruption caused by extreme trauma, these narratives function to establish what many participants referred to as a 'new normal'. I have termed these the *victim*, *survivor* and *transcender* narratives.[1] These three narrative

---

[1] It should be noted that although many co-victims use the terms 'victim' or 'survivor' to refer to themselves and others who have lost to homicide, as do many advocates, policy-makers, support persons, criminal justice personnel and researchers, these terms are not accepted by all co-victims. Some feel the term 'victim' implies a direct victimisation and therefore reserve use of the term for the person killed in the homicide. Others feel 'victim' has negative connotations, implying a vulnerability and weakness that they do not identify with. The term 'survivor' engenders similar criticism from some co-victims. Some feel it implies that someone survived the incident, indicating that a homicide attempt was unsuccessful and there was, therefore, a survivor of the attempted homicide.

types are discussed at length elsewhere (Hourigan, forthcoming). It suffices to say here that the narratives of co-victims of homicide fit into three broad categories. The main differentiating feature between them is each narrative's focus. The focus of a *victim* narrative is inward, directed at self and the crime's effects upon the self. In my sample, such storytellers often referred to themselves as 'victims', and the main points in the story related to the trauma, devastation and persistent anguish felt by the storyteller. By contrast, a *survivor* narrative portrays the storyteller's personal tragedy as a catalyst for action towards healing the trauma that follows criminal victimisation. In my work, *survivor* narratives depicted murder as motivation for helping others who had lost loved ones in similar events. Finally, *transcender* narratives are even more broadly focussed. The original crime is only discussed as the impetus for subsequent action, and the offender, the criminal act and the direct victim are peripheral or secondary within the plot of the narrative. Such *transcender* narratives in my sample focussed upon the storyteller's strong desire to 'do good' in the future and to help society at large by confronting grand social problems which lead to crime.

In what follows, I will endorse two fundamental methodological strategies, persistent observation and prolonged engagement, highlighting the benefit of these for a narrative approach to victimology. I will draw upon the research project discussed above to demonstrate the value of these strategies in criminal victimology. In doing so I will emphasise three key features of crime victims' narratives: speaker, audience and timing.

Researching Victim Narratives

As I will show, crime victims' narratives can be dynamic and purposeful. As narrative victimologists we therefore must seek out narratives in a variety of contexts, co-constructed within differing social settings, and we must pay attention to how the narratives may (or may not) change across time, place and situation. Doing so will offer the best opportunity to uncover meaning created in the wake of crime and the effects of the construction of such meaning.

Persistent Observation of Stories and Prolonged Engagement with Storytellers

Victim narratives can be observed in a wide array of settings, with a variety of intended audiences, and may be spoken or written. And, while some victim narratives are spontaneous, delivered in front of news cameras, in one-one-one interviews or during self-help or support group meetings, others are painstakingly practiced and/or edited to most effectively deliver the intended message to the audience. This might include letters addressed to offenders, parole board members or policy-makers; victim impact statements, whether written or spoken in court or left undelivered; self-published books; and speeches constructed for audiences consisting of at-risk youth, governmental decision-makers or loved ones at a memorial service or dedication. Victims may also tell their stories within myriad group settings including anticrime or at-risk youth programs, restorative justice initiatives, charity events, rallies, lobbying events, memorials, victims' rights events and advocacy or community outreach events. These are just a sampling of the various locations victim narratives can be observed, as my intention here is to raise the reader's awareness as to the variety of victim narratives, not to provide an exhaustive list.

As narrative victimologists, we must remain mindful of the differences between narrative formats, settings and audiences, and attempt to gather stories from disparate contexts in order to generate the most comprehensive data possible. As Pemberton et al. (2018) note, narratives and their interpretations 'can vary not only between victims but also at different points in time from the perspective of the same person... Fully understanding the meaning of the victimisation event and the possibilities, difficulties and barriers in coping with its aftermath then requires the inclusion of this multitude of different narratives' (pp. 8, 16). For these reasons, a robust methodological strategy for narrative victimologists would involve persistent observation of stories and prolonged engagement with storytellers.

Persistent observation also allows for exploration of the influence of narratives upon the listener and the listener's subsequent narratives. Such influence is especially apparent in groups that meet on a regular, frequent basis and consist of many of the same attendees, such as planning committees, fundraising groups, victims' rights or advocacy coalitions and self-help or support groups. Regular group meetings allow not only for prolonged contact between narrator and audience but also for anticipation of continued interaction, making it the ideal circumstance for narrative ethnography (for a variety of examples of narrative ethnographic work, see Holstein & Gubrium, 2012). Regular members seek to form mutually respecting bonds and to make positive impressions upon others in the group in anticipation of future mutual social support.

Finally, making ourselves present for the narration of participants' stories on multiple occasions and circumstances increases the validity of our interpretations by providing the opportunity to build deeper levels of trust and a stronger rapport with participants than is possible in research relying solely upon single interviews. Such methods also facilitate understanding and appreciation for the uniqueness of each narrative. For example, in many cases, through extended engagement, I became viewed as a member of the group or community in which my research took place. My presence was no longer questioned and co-victims became very comfortable with me. This increased the likelihood that their social interactions in my presence were truer to their typical behaviour than would have been the case in the presence of someone viewed as a stranger or outsider. The richness and depth of the resulting data demonstrate the value of persistent observation and prolonged engagement in narrative victimology specifically, as well as narrative analysis more generally.

Below, I will explore three key features of narrative that highlight its fluid and purposeful nature as it relates to criminal victimology. In doing so, I will demonstrate the value of engaging in persistent observation of stories and prolonged engagement with storytellers when conducting narrative victimological research.

Key Features of Crime Victims' Narratives

There are several features of narrative that are especially useful in uncovering the nature, power and potential of crime victims' stories. Of particular importance are the effects of the speaker, the audience and the timing of the narrative's delivery or use. In this section, I will highlight the relevance of these features based on my work exploring co-victims' narratives.

Speaker

Walklate et al. (2018) stress the factors that result in some victim storytellers being listened to while others are silenced. Such factors include the characteristics of the storyteller and the audience's judgement of the storyteller. Also impactful is whether the victim in the story is perceived as worthy of sympathy based upon his or her portrayal as a moral and blameless character (Christie, 1986). If the victim is perceived as what Meyers (2016) refers to as an 'impure victim', his or her story is likely to be unheard, misunderstood or distorted. On the contrary, if victims are perceived as what Meyers refers to as 'heroic', their narratives can have widespread and lasting effects. Some speakers are capable of delivering the narrative in such a way that the audience feels a connection to the speaker, whether this ability stems from the storyteller's charisma and authenticity, skill in public speaking or perceived innocence and unpardonable suffering. In such cases, the narrative becomes a sort of shared story and can have very powerful consequences (for example, see Walklate et al., 2018).

In my work, I asked co-victims of homicide to reflect upon their storytelling experiences. Carol[2] discussed how her story was deeply impactful when she shared it with at-risk youths each year. She told me that she did not hold back the rawness of her pain, as she felt that witnessing her anguish, even 20 years after her loss, helped the youths to see the potential impact of their choices. As a speaker, Carol had great power to influence because she was perceived as both innocent and heroic in her survival. Tanya had a very different experience when sharing her story. She explained that she refused to return to self-help group meetings after her first visit. Given her late son's status as a young, black male in the inner city, she believed that the other group members, who hailed from white, middle-class suburbia, saw her as 'part of the problem'. She felt that her story of sorrow and loss was not given space in these groups because of the shadow that was cast upon her by the stereotype that young, black, male homicide victims were in some way responsible for their own demise and that she had failed as a mother to steer her son towards a path of relative safety and morality. Though both women's stories focussed upon having lost a teenage son to gun violence, the outcome of each remains drastically different due to the way the speaker is perceived by the audience. The disparity illustrates why, as narrative victimologists, we must remain mindful of who is delivering a story and how they are perceived by the listener.

---

[2]Participants' names have been altered to protect confidentiality.

In order to best understand the effects of crime on victims, we should seek out the stories of those who are likely to be perceived as 'ideal' victims as well as those who are not. This is no easy feat, as building rapport with a wide array of storytellers can be difficult and time-consuming, as my work can attest to. Gaining trust can be especially challenging in cases in which the storyteller feels his or her story was previously misunderstood or misused and in instances in which the narrator has been outcast or attacked after the telling of his or her story. In my work, I built relationships over the course of several years and relied heavily upon word of mouth to build my reputation in the community as a person deserving of trust. This led me to connect to many individuals I would not have otherwise come into contact with and whose confidence I may not have been able to gain.

Although my process of gaining entrée spanned several years' time, the rapport-building that took place early on was not in anticipation of the creation of such a project. Through previous volunteer work with a local commission focussed on justice, I became well acquainted with several individuals who eventually fostered my entrée into social circles of co-victims. These connections proved invaluable, especially in cases in which I was attempting to connect with individuals who were not a part of any formalised victim support network or those who were of generations, racial/ethnic groups and religions different from those I was seen as falling within. My previous connections were also advantageous when seeking folks who had different social experiences and upbringings than myself and who lived and worked in areas beyond the boundaries of those I had frequented. One woman with whom I volunteered, Diane, was highly active in a variety of victim-related groups and regularly attended relevant events. Diane went to great lengths to support the development of my sample, connecting me to individuals she had come to know well through these community events. One of these contacts, Sandra, was heavily involved in a network of individuals in the inner city who advocate for antiviolence. I had crossed paths with Sandra several times, having attended many of the same local events over the year prior, but I had never been directly introduced to her. Given the enthusiasm with which Diane supported my work, Sandra came to trust my motivations and intentions. Not only did Sandra take part in an interview, but she also connected me to several other individuals who had lost loved ones to violence, including J.R., the director of an antiviolence program situated in an impoverished, urban area nearby. I spoke to J.R. about my need to diversify my sample to include more individuals unaffiliated with co-victim self-help groups, men and people of colour. Since J.R. fit these characteristics, he volunteered to take part in an interview and invited me to his office to discuss my work in more detail. This meeting led to my inclusion in a community outreach event on the street outside J.R.'s office. While there, he introduced me to several individuals who either worked for, volunteered with or utilised services of the program, and several asked to be a part of my research. Most of these co-victims were men of colour who had had experience within gangs, had engaged in drug trafficking or had been previously incarcerated for violent offences.

The resultant diversity within my sample allowed me to not only witness the stories of those who were seen by the world as blameless victims but also those who were less likely to fit neatly into notions of 'ideal' victimhood (Christie, 1986). As narrative victimologists, such breadth in our collection of narratives is invaluable. For example, particularly telling were those stories in my sample gathered from homebound elderly folks and individuals who were previously incarcerated. In many cases, once I had gained the trust of these storytellers and proved myself as genuine in my intent, I was viewed as a part of an inner circle. Participants connected me to friends and neighbours, offering their support as proof of my perceived authenticity, and shared detailed stories that often lasted several hours. A handful of participants told me that the stories they shared with me were ones they had never shared previously or had only shared with their most closely trusted others, such as spouses or siblings. Such narrations held particular value for participants, as they felt unrestrained in their telling and therefore heard in ways they had not previously. The opportunity to share their stories in this fashion fostered within them a sense of the story having great importance and purpose.

Audience

Often, narratives take a prominent position within victim-centred events and the audience to which they are delivered is of central concern to the storyteller. Victims' stories open self-help group meetings, give heart to fundraising and advocacy events, create a sense of common purpose or experience and add a raw emotional quality to events, re-empowering those who had been disempowered and fostering a sense of urgency, vulnerability and empathy that aid in securing the attention of funders, policy-makers, offenders or at-risk youth.

In my own work, the pairing of face-to-face interviews, participant observation and content analysis of written narratives provided the opportunity to gather a spectrum of narratives delivered for a variety of audiences and purposes. Some narratives I observed at regular events, happening monthly or annually, others at singular events. Each event had its own composition of attendees, some solely consisting of co-victims (and myself), others incorporating other types of victims of crime. Some involved individuals who had never been directly touched by crime, such as advocates, local at-risk youth, governmental figures, social workers and members of local religious institutions. The purpose of various events also differed. Some were designed to support co-victims in particular, others had more broad goals. Some were memorials, others were meant to raise awareness or funds. While most maintained a consistent focus upon those previously impacted by crime, some aimed to positively impact current or future offenders, thereby reducing the risk of future criminal harm to potential victims.

Observations during two of the three self-help groups I attended regularly became particularly valuable because meetings open with the sharing of each attendee's story. There is a sense of meaning-making within these repeated stories. Each month, a member's story helps to situate the speaker with relation to the original event, his or her healing processes and the audience. I found that long-standing group members have a substantial amount of influence over newer members because of an implicit authority related to having lived through similar trauma and having 'made it out' or 'survived'. Newer members listen intently to those who are further along in their healing processes to gain knowledge, understanding and to be validated in their own sense of trauma and loss of control. After criminal victimisation, such peer support or mutual aid groups fill a need within the victim to feel understood by others who have endured similar life experiences (see Rappaport, 1993).

My persistent observation of such group meetings was especially informative, as it allowed me to witness participants with varied experiences and social positions tell, and retell, their stories within a variety of meaningful social contexts. This allowed me to follow the narrative as it was shaped, and reshaped, in context. In many cases, these observations were then followed by one-on-one interviews within which I was able to enquire about stories I had heard.

The continual reflection upon one's own narrative in the company of influential others sometimes led to a reconstruction of the speaker's narrative. One co-victim in particular stood out as exemplary of this reconstruction process. When she shared her story with me in private, it was a much different story than the one I had heard her share at self-help group meetings, which had the features of a *victim* narrative. The story she shared in private was a *transcender* narrative, highlighting the process she underwent to forgive the man who killed her son and focussing upon her efforts to help him, as well as local youthful offenders, to shift their thinking and 'lead a good life'. After she had detailed her story, I asked, 'Have you told your story often?' She replied that she only shared certain aspects of her story at self-help group meetings. She said, 'For a long time I wouldn't even talk about (forgiveness), because I thought I was gonna be thrown out or something'. She found solace being surrounded by others who had experienced similar tragedy and pain, so the prospect of rejection led her to reconstruct her public narrative to better align with the narratives of other group members, most of whom shared *victim* narratives, rich with strong, negative, offender-directed emotion. Although she did not falsify her story or add qualities to her public narrative that were untrue, in such social contexts she offered a version of her story for which she anticipated a better reception, omitting aspects of her story that she depicted as fundamental in other company. Both narratives were authentic expressions of her experiences, but each captured different aspects of her reality. Hers is a prime example of the value of utilising methods that allow the researcher to witness multiple rehearsals of one's narrative, in juxtaposition to one another and as delivered in situ.

Through selective affiliation, crime victims may seek out others with a shared experience of victimisation. Within such social circles, victims are able to find acknowledgement for their stories that they cannot find elsewhere, including with biological family members and close friends. Crime victims often indicate that they feel others who have not experienced a similar event could not possibly understand their experiences, regardless of good intentions or strong emotional bonds. In my research, participants who regularly attended monthly self-help group meetings indicated that these social circles took on qualities of a primary reference group (Cooley, 1909). Their commitment to such groups was strong and the bonds between members were often immediate. Participants regularly referred to other members as 'family' and they often spoke of such groups being the only spaces within which they could be open and true to the full range of their emotions and experiences. In this way, crime victims will often surround themselves with others who view them the way they view themselves and who expect from them attitudes and behaviour they expect from themselves. For these reasons, narratives that victims construct for such audiences may be especially useful in illuminating the way one is changed by criminal victimisation. Even outside of the formalised victim support networks, or in cases of relatively new members, there is often a sense of shared experience between those similarly victimised. This shared experience bonds individuals and gives influential power to the narratives of each.

Hurvitz (1970) showed that members of self-help groups often become significant others for one another, and the group becomes a new reference group for members. This is not surprising given that individuals drawn together by personal tragedy and the resultant struggles are dealing with trauma that can be all-consuming. Which groups are most influential in any given situation depends on several factors, 'most important of which is the relevance of the group to the perceived problematic situation at hand' (Matsueda, 1992, p. 1584). Therefore, victims' self-help groups are likely to be viewed as quite relevant to the situation. New or struggling members are likely to feel that such groups consist of others who have knowledge, life experience and tools that could prove invaluable as they structure their experience, construct meaning and heal in the aftermath of criminal victimisation. For this reason, witnessing the construction and use of narrative within victim-related social networks is a valuable method for investigating the effects of crime on victims.

If we are to explore narrative as it is constructed, used and perceived within groups, it is important that we remain mindful of the differences between groups. For example, despite their similarities, each self-help group has a unique ideology, structure, style of interaction and demographic composition. For this reason, the self-help group is a valuable location to explore the interaction between narrative and audience, especially if the researcher has the opportunity to witness the same participant's narrative delivered in multiple groups. In my work, I witnessed co-victims sharing their narratives with a variety of audiences and had the opportunity to bear witness to the way the audience affected the narration. Just as Riessman (2002) points out, if the listener was a different person, one's story may have been told differently. At times, I observed the same narratives being embellished while addressing offenders, decision-makers or potential funders and cut back when shared with college students or newly traumatised co-victims. Such observations allowed for deeper insight into the purpose of the narration process and the mutable nature of co-victims' narratives. Ideally, narrative victimologists would gather narratives constructed for different audiences in a variety of environments, bringing to light the differing effects of perceived audience engagement (for more on the role of the audience, see Berlant, 2004; Polletta, 2006; Meyers, 2016).

Gloria and Jeanne's cases are exemplary because of the wide range of people with whom they regularly share their stories, in a broad spectrum of social contexts. Throughout the 3 years I was engaged with this research project, I was present while Gloria, who lost her daughter in an incident of intimate partner violence, shared her story at intimate holiday dinners, meetings of two different self-help groups, fundraisers for victims of intimate partner violence, homicide memorial events and various public Crime Victims' Rights Week programs. I witnessed Jeanne narrating her story in six separate contexts: her interview; annual homicide victim memorial events; a panel discussion for at-risk teens and three different contexts of self-help group meetings, those at which only regular members were in attendance, those with new attendees and those during which local college students had come to supplement their educations in studies of grief or justice. Depending upon the audience and associated purpose of their narration, Gloria and Jeanne shifted focus, utilised different language, emphasised emotion differently and included differing levels of detail. Witnessing these co-victims' narratives situated within multiple contexts and with varied audiences provided much greater insight into their meaning-making processes than would have been possible through only the use of interviews.

For a narrative to be effective, the story must be delivered to an audience that is 'able and willing to hear us and to understand our words as we intend them' (Brison, 2002, p. 51). Furthermore, this audience must become 'caught up in' the narrative in order for the speaker to truly feel as if they have been heard (Stauffer, 2015). As narrative victimologists, we are poised to be such an engaged audience for crime victims. On several occasions, I became fully engrossed in my participants' stories. I learnt early on that I needed to set an alarm if my interviewee had a commitment to attend to after our time together, as the process of storytelling would enthrall us both into such a state of immersion that hours would pass without notice. There was no doubt that my captivation left many interviewees feeling heard, as several expressed their gratitude afterwards, indicating that this instance of telling their story was particularly meaningful and fulfilling.

Given our role as audience, as narrative researchers we must remain reflexive (Bordieu & Wacquant, 1992). Reflexivity is particularly important when considering victim narratives spoken in interaction with the researcher, such as during face-to-face interviews. Such interviews offer a simple yet effective way for narrative victimologists to gather data. However, researchers must remain mindful of the co-constructed nature of such narrative (see Presser, 2005). In the context of an interview, how participants relate to the researcher and what they choose to disclose is influenced by how they see the researcher within the interaction, what role they see him/her taking and how they feel they relate, or do not relate, to the researcher personally and/or professionally. Those who have been victimised may be especially likely to assume disingenuous motivations or question how their stories will ultimately be used. For these reasons, narrative victimologists must remain mindful and reflective as they engage in interactions with crime victims so that they can eliminate as many potential barriers as possible and establish research relationships that are trusting and forthright. We must be transparent in our motivations and be vigilant for signals from participants that uncertainty exists, or is increasing, so that we can reaffirm our intentions. Through continued self-reflection, we can remain attuned to our own biases, perspectives and influence upon the construction of respondents' narratives, as well as our interpretations of these.

Timing

Another feature of the victim narrative that cannot be overlooked is that of timing, both cultural and personal. A narrative delivered at two different moments in time may result in dramatically different outcomes, whether those be directly related to the narrator or more broadly impactful, as in the case of policy change or the establishment of new laws. For example, when conditions are ripe within the culture and political climate of a country, new laws may be spurred by the narratives constructed around a single case, ultimately being named after specific victims, for example Clare's Law in the UK and Megan's Law in the US (Walklate et al., 2018). At different moments in time, audiences are more or less sensitised to various issues surrounding victimisation, so we must always situate the narratives we are exploring within the broader socio-political context.

We must also be mindful of the timing of the narrative's delivery within the storyteller's personal journey. Just as with regard to cultural timing, the same narrative can hold different meanings and result in different outcomes if delivered at different times within the storyteller's life. At times, crime victim's narratives are intentionally constructed as a means to influence others, including policy-makers, jurors, judges, offenders, funders or fellow sufferers. The same narrative may then take on new forms and purposes at a different time. For example, a victim impact statement may become a valuable part of a scrapbook of a murdered loved one, as I found on multiple occasions within my sample. As they are being constructed and initially delivered, such narratives may have a very different purpose than when they are reflected upon retrospectively. Therefore, it is crucial that we preserve the context within which the narrative is observed. The meaning associated with it, the purpose behind its delivery and its effects may shift significantly from context to context.

One co-victim in particular demonstrated this point nicely. She showed me her typed victim impact statement, preserved for over 20 years within a large, detailed scrapbook created to memorialise her son. This scrapbook had become so tattered over the years that it was literally falling apart at the seams. It had grown so worn because she had shared it with countless young men and women who were a part of the at-risk teen divergence program at which she shared her story. Within this book, her victim impact statement had taken on a new purpose. It began as a means to illuminate the full effect of the crime to the sentencing judge. Over time, it signified a time long past, when this co-victim was still in the grip of raw, unchecked emotion. Now, she shared it with wayward teens to open their hearts to the anguish that their actions were capable of causing. It sat alongside pictures, newspaper clippings and poetry expressing the love and depth of loss felt for her son, taken when he was the same age as the audience she now placed herself, and her narrative, in front of. If taken out of context, we lose sight of the dynamic nature of this victim impact statement. It was originally constructed and delivered as a *victim* narrative, crisp and neat, clutched in sweaty palms as this co-victim addressed the court and displayed her raw emotion. In its current form, this single sheet of paper had taken on new meaning and importance. It had become a small part of a much longer story, a *transcender* narrative, with a much broader reach. Now, it is used as a reminder of what once was, as an agent of connection, fostering empathy and making the victim role more palpable and powerful for audiences of would-be offenders. This example speaks to the flexibility of narrative and reminds us of the value of analysing narrative as situated within a larger social context.

Conclusions

In the wake of crime, victims use narrative to make sense of their victimisation and its aftermath, impose order, re-establish a sense of control and persuade the listener (and the self) of the authenticity of the story. Victims may spend time sharing their stories, reflecting, learning from other victims' narratives and both constructing and verifying their identities as crime victims through narrative. Studying victims' narratives as used within participants' natural settings, especially observing group interactions, enables deep appreciation for the significance of context, including the speaker, audience and timing.

Rather than being bound by a single, objective and verifiable 'truth', narrative allows us to value individual subjective experience and its nuance. Therefore, in order to understand how crime effects victims differently, we should seek out the stories of crime victims with various social histories and demographic classifications as well as those who are likely to be perceived as 'heroic' and 'impure' (Meyers, 2016). Due to the feelings of vulnerability and distrust that often follow criminal victimisation, gathering such stories may be unusually challenging. However, the level of insight that can be garnered from such work is worth the effort and time required to develop rapport and establish trust with crime victims. Victim accounts enrich our understanding of how victimisation is repeatedly made sense of, over time, and through multiple tellings. Through such stories, we become privy to a more vivid and complete record of the effects of crime. As victims of crime narrate their stories, the aftermath of victimisation (the healing process, how the experience shapes identity, etc.) become as important, if not more important, than the original event.

The greatest strength of a narrative victimological methodology is undoubtedly the wealth of complex and multilayered data that can be drawn from within narrative. Because narrative is both fluid and contextual, it is important for victimological researchers to appreciate it as such, following the narrative as it changes shape. The objective of a victim narrative, its tone and the story itself may change as it is presented by varied speakers, in different company and at various points in time. Therefore, for the most comprehensive understanding of crime we should compare victim narratives built and delivered at different times and with different purposes in order to more fully understand the many forms such narratives take and the capacity that exists in each to create meaning, bridge difference, bond parties and spark change.

Here, I advocate for persistent observation of stories and prolonged engagement with storytellers in order to capture the shifting and contextual nature of the victim narrative. It is through such methods that we can understand how narratives are assembled, conveyed and interpreted in context. Such work complements aggregate data and facilitates the investigation of wide variation in cases that other methods disallow. Focussing upon narrative allows researchers to avoid the constraint of preformed answer options, as are used with standardised surveys. Though they have clear value, criminal victimisation surveys decontextualize. By investigating narrative through persistent observation and prolonged engagement, we can deepen our understanding by reconnecting stories to the conditions within which they are constructed and delivered.

Observation of storytelling is an established approach to studying the narratives of offenders. Among other crimes, such methods have been successfully used to understand the nature and power of stories about murder (Presser, 2012), rape (Trinch, 2014; Ugelvik, 2015), illegal drug production (Hammersvik, Sandberg, & Pedersen, 2012), drug dealing (Sandberg & Pedersen, 2011), theft (Copes, 2003) and tax evasion (Tognato, 2015). Other work has examined offender narratives with a broader lens, investigating how stories are constructed and used by offenders during criminal action (for example, see Presser, 2008), while imprisoned (for example, see Fleetwood, 2015) and while reintegrating back into society after release from prison (Maruna, 2001). The research project described here serves as evidence of the value of expanding the scope of our investigations to include engagement with the victim narrative. Victims are a central aspect of the criminal process, including in relation to understanding how and why crime is committed, as well as the scope and complexity of the effects of criminal acts. Therefore, in order to truly understand crime, we must understand the victim experience.

Observation of the narratives of crime victims is uniquely valuable, as the development and delivery of narrative can be a crucial aspect of the healing process following victimisation. Criminal victimisation can cause victims to feel uncertain of, and severed from, a social world that is no longer knowable or relatable, as it once was (Strang, 2002; Zehr, 2001). Sharing narrative in circles of similarly victimised individuals allows victims to construct new meaning, establish order and reconnect socially (Crossley, 2000). Criminal victimisation also disrupts one's life story, and the construction of narrative in the aftermath of that trauma allows victims to 'bridge' the past and present (Brison, 2002). Therefore, not only studying victim narrative but also capturing it in a variety of social contexts, times and forms allows researchers to best understand the effects of crime. For example, participating in such a wide variety of events related to the co-victim experience allowed me to hear many participants narrate their stories at multiple times, in varying contexts or circumstances and in the company of fluctuating groups of people. Without doing so, I would not have been able to witness the way *victim*, *survivor* and *transcender* narratives emerge in the wake of violent loss. Such methods allowed me to uncover the various ways meaning is constructed in the wake of crime. Despite the devastation accompanying participants' losses to homicide, through narrative storytellers were afforded the opportunity for both negative and positive outcomes, each with a direct connection back to the original loss. *Victim*, *survivor* and *transcender* narratives offer co-victims different ways of making sense of loss of a loved one to violence. These kinds of narrative point to the fact that meaning is not settled and continues to be remade in different settings and to diverse ends, including as an impetus for efforts towards communion, empathy and determination to bring about positive change in the self, others and society as a whole.

The methods discussed here (the coupling of intensive interviews, participant observation and content analysis) are not the sole methodological strategy through which we can achieve persistent observation of stories and prolonged engagement with storytellers. For example, to illustrate the power and contextual nature of narrative, some may successfully engage in persistent observation of stories by exploring a single case from a variety of angles (for example, see Walklate et al., 2018). Others may effectively accomplish prolonged engagement with storytellers by utilising life story interviewing (as proposed by McAdams, 2008) or by engaging in autobiographical or autoethnographic processes (for example, see Brison, 2002; Sebold, 1999). Despite the method used, what is most important is our awareness and transparency about the fluid and contextual nature of the victim narratives we engage with.

As criminologists, it is crucial that we increase our level of understanding of the experiences of those most directly affected by criminal events: the victims. Through narrative victimology, we decrease the likelihood that crime victims will be misunderstood, ignored, misrepresented or left further disenfranchised and traumatised by empathic failure (Neimeyer & Jordan, 2002). In doing so, we can support and understand innumerable individuals as they seek to re-establish a sense of normalcy and predictability in their social worlds following criminal victimisation. We can develop more sensitive policies and practices, revealing more about their true impact upon crime victims. By studying victim narratives, we can better understand the depth and breadth of the effects of crime, including effects occurring within the self, in close social circles and on more grand scales, such as those related to the criminal justice process or media coverage of the crime and its aftermath. Over time, the budding subfield of narrative victimology will allow us to better understand the various forms of victim narrative, as well as the consequences of such stories, including effects upon the speaker, the audience and the social institutions in which they are communicated.

Acknowledgements

The study was supported by the Larry J. Siegel Graduate Fellowship, American Society of Criminology, Division of Victimology.

References

Berlant, L. (2004). Compassion and withholding. In L. Berlant (Ed.), *Compassion: The culture and politics of an emotion* (pp. 1–14). London: Routledge.

Bordieu, P., & Wacquant, L. (1992). *An invitation to reflexive sociology*. Chicago, IL: University of Chicago Press.

Brison, S. J. (2002). *Aftermath: Violence and the remaking of the self*. Princeton, NJ: Princeton University Press.

Brookman, F. (2015). The shifting narratives of violent offenders. In L. Presser & S. Sandberg (Eds.), *Narrative criminology: Understanding stories of crime* (pp. 207–234). New York, NY: New York University Press.

Burke, P., & Stets, J. (2009). *Identity theory*. New York, NY: Oxford University Press.

Calhoun, L. G., & Tedeschi, R. G. (2001). Posttraumatic growth: The positive lessons of loss. In R. A. Neimeyer (Ed.), *Meaning reconstruction & the experience of loss* (pp. 157–172). Washington, DC: American Psychological Association.

Christie, N. (1986). The ideal victim. In E. A. Fattah (Ed.), *From crime policy to victim policy*. New York, NY: St. Martin's Press.

Cooley, C. H. (1902). *Human nature and the social order*. New York, NY: Scribner Publishing.

Cooley, C. H. (1963 [1909]). *Social organizations: A study of the larger mind*. New York, NY: Schocken Books.

Copes, H. (2003). Streetlife and the rewards of auto theft. *Deviant Behavior, 24*, 309–332.

Crossley, M. L. (2000). Narrative psychology, trauma and the study of self/identity. *Theory & Psychology, 10*, 527–546.

Delbo, C. (1995). *Auschwitz and after*. New Haven, CT: Yale University Press.

Elias, R. (1993). *Victims still. The political manipulation of crime victims*. Newbury Park, CA: SAGE Publications.

Fleetwood, J. (2015). In search of respectability: Narrative practice in a women's prison in Quito, Ecuador. In L. Presser & S. Sandberg (Eds.), *Narrative criminology: Understanding stories of crime* (pp. 42–68). New York, NY: New York University Press.

Goffman, E. (1974). *Frame analysis*. New York, NY: Harper & Row.

Hammersvik, E., Sandberg, S., & Pedersen, W. (2012). Why small-scale cannabis growers stay small: Five mechanisms that prevent small-scale growers from going large scale. *International Journal of Drug Policy, 23*, 458–464.

Holstein, J. A., & Gubrium, J. F. (2012). *Varieties of narrative analysis*. London: SAGE Publications.

Hourigan, K. L. (2018). Forgiving the unforgivable: An exploration of contradictions between forgiveness-related feeling rules and lived experience of forgiveness of extreme harm. *Humanity and Society, 43*(3), 270–294.

Hourigan, K. L. (forthcoming). *Redefining Murder, Transforming Emotion: An exploration of forgiveness after loss due to homicide*. London: Routledge.

Hurvitz, N. (1970). Peer self-help psychotherapy groups and their implications for psychotherapy. *Psychotherapy: Theory Research and Practice, 7*, 41–49.

Janoff-Bulman, R. (1992). *Shattered assumptions*. New York, NY: Free Press.

Langer, L. L. (1991). *Holocaust testimonies: The ruins of memory*. New Haven, CT, and London: Yale University Press.

Maruna, S. (2001). *Making good: How ex-convicts reform and rebuild their lives*. Washington, DC: American Psychological Association.

Matsueda, R. L. (1992). Reflected appraisals, parental labeling, and delinquency: Specifying a symbolic interactionist theory. *American Journal of Sociology, 6*, 1577–1611.

McAdams, D. (2006). *The redemptive self: Stories Americans live by*. New York, NY: Oxford University Press.

McAdams, D. (2008). Personal narratives and the life story. In O. P. John, R. W. Robins, & L. A. Pervin (Eds.), *Handbook of personality: Theory and research* (pp. 242–262). New York, NY: Guildford Press.

McGarry, R., & Walklate, S. (2015). *Victims: Trauma, testimony and justice*. Abingdon: Routledge.

Mead, G. H. (1934). *Mind, self and society*. Chicago, IL: University of Chicago Press.

Meyers, D. T. (2016). *Victims' stories and the advancement of human rights*. New York, NY: Oxford University Press.

Neimeyer, R. A., & Jordan, J. R. (2002). Disenfranchisement of empathic failure: Grief therapy and the co-construction of meaning. In K. Doka (Ed.), *Disenfranchisement grief: New directions, challenges, and strategies for practice*. Champaign, IL: Research Press.

Pemberton, A., Mulder, E., & Aarten, P. (2018). Stories of injustice: Towards a narrative victimology. *European Journal of Criminology, 16*(4), 391–412.

Polletta, F. (2006). *It was like a fever. Storytelling in protest and politics*. Chicago, IL: University of Chicago Press.

Presser, L. (2005). Negotiating power and narrative in research: Implications for feminist methodology. *Signs, 30*, 2067–2090.

Presser, L. (2008). *Been a heavy life: Stories of violent men*. Chicago, IL: University of Illinois Press.

Presser, L. (2012). Getting on top through mass murder: Narrative, metaphor, and violence. *Crime, Media, Culture, 8*, 3–21.

Presser, L. (2016). Criminology and the narrative turn. *Crime, Media, Culture: International Journal, 12*, 137–151.

Rappaport, J. (1993). Narrative studies, personal stories, and identity transformation in the mutual help context. *The Journal of Applied Behavioral Science, 29*, 239–256.

Riessman, C. K. (2002). Narrative analysis. In A. M. Huberman & M. B. Miles (Eds.), *The qualitative researcher's companion* (pp. 217–270). Thousand Oaks, CA: SAGE Publications.

Roberts, J. V. (2009). Listening to the crime victim: Evaluating victim input at sentencing and parole. In M. Tonry (Ed.), *Crime, punishment, and politics in comparative perspective*. Crime and Justice: A review of research (*Vol. 38*). Chicago, IL: Chicago University Press.

Sandberg, S. (2013). Are self-narratives strategic or determined, unified or fragmented? Reading Breivik's Manifesto in light of narrative criminology. *Acta Sociologica, 56*, 69–83.

Sandberg, S., & Pedersen, W. (2011). *Street capital: Black cannabis dealers in a white welfare state*. Bristol: Policy Press.

Sarbin, T. R. (1986). The narrative as a root metaphor for psychology. In T. R. Sarbin (Ed.), *Narrative psychology: The storied nature of human conduct*. New York, NY: Praeger.

Sebold, A. (1999). *Lucky*. New York, NY: Scribner Publishing.

Stauffer, J. (2015). *Ethical loneliness: The injustice of not being heard*. New York, Columbia: Columbia University Press.

Strang, H. (2002). *Repair or revenge: Victims and restorative justice.* New York, NY: Oxford University Press.

Stryker, S. (1980 [2002]). *Symbolic interactionism: A social structured version.* Caldwell, NJ: Blackburn Press.

Tognato, C. (2015). Narratives of tax evasion: The cultural legitimacy of harmful behavior. In L. Presser & S. Sandberg (Eds.), *Narrative criminology: Understanding stories of crime* (pp. 260–286). New York, NY: New York University Press.

Trinch, S. (2007). Deconstructing the 'stakes' in high stakes gatekeeping interviews: Battered women and narration. *Journal of Pragmatics, 39,* 1895–1918.

Trinch, S. (2014). De-authorizing rape narratives: Stance, taboo and privatizing the public secret. *Journal of Language Aggression and Conflict, 2,* 204–225.

Ugelvik, T. (2015) The rapist and the proper criminal: The exclusion of immoral others as narrative work on the self. In L. Presser & S. Sandberg (Eds.), *Narrative criminology: Understanding stories of crime* (pp. 23–41). New York, NY: New York University Press.

Walklate, S. (2016). The metamorphosis of victimology: From crime to culture. *International Journal of Crime, Justice and Social Democracy, 5,* 4–16.

Walklate, S., Maher, J., McCulloch, J., Fitz-Gibbon, K., & Beavis, K. (2018). Victim stories and victim policy: Is there a case for a narrative victimology? *Crime, Media, Culture, 00,* 1–17.

Wright, S. (2016.) 'Ah…the power of mothers': Bereaved mothers as victim-heroes in media enacted crusades for justice. *Crime, Media, Culture, 12,* 327–343.

Zehr, H. (2001). *Transcending: Reflections of crime victims.* Brattleboro, VT: Good Books.

Chapter 14

Finding Victims in the Narratives of Men Imprisoned for Sex Offences

Alice Ievins

> *How would you feel if you met these lot and heard their story and then you met their victims?* (Prison officer)

Those who provide psychological treatment to men convicted of sex offences have historically spent a lot of time identifying and correcting cognitive distortions, although as Maruna and Mann (2006) point out, analysts do not agree on the meaning of 'cognitive distortions'. The term is variously used to describe the attitudes, excuses or justifications which *precede* and may cause sexual offending, as well as those which *follow from* it and constitute an attempt to manage the shame, and may even lead to the offending continuing. In any case, the term is used to describe ways of thinking which are considered dangerous and factually incorrect, and thus as morally and epistemologically distorted. Because of the term's slipperiness, it is often overused, and can be confused in clinical practice 'with any causal explanation for offending given by offenders, no matter how valid the explanation might be' (Maruna & Mann, 2006, p. 161). Explaining the offence thus risks being seen as justifying or excusing it, and becomes something which practitioners should seek out and quash.

The weight given to the idea of cognitive distortions has led researchers to be cautious when working with men convicted of sex offences. Researchers have urged their peers to be careful not to reinforce denial and cognitive distortions when conducting interviews (e.g. Cowburn, 2005; Waldram, 2007); others have highlighted the purported risks of 'passive collusion' (Digard, 2014, p. 215) with participants. Blagden and Pemberton, for instance, argue that researchers 'must be constantly mindful of not subscribing to participants' views' (2010, p. 277), and suggest that carelessly conducted research risks undoing the work of psychological interventions:

> One may even, at times, be confronted with the question: 'do you think I'm innocent?', or the confirmatory phrase: 'you know what I mean?'. It is vital here that the researcher does not confirm or acquiesce to these verbalisations.

This way of thinking about interviews is unfamiliar to mainstream qualitative researchers (Crewe & Ievins, 2015), who normally adhere to a more 'appreciative' vision (Matza, 1969), and it is heretical to narrative criminologists, for whom what matters is not the historical or moral truth of an account, but *what the narrative is doing*. They consider narratives to have a constitutive power – to be a form of action in the world – and thus their interest is in what narratives and narrators try to achieve, what narratives tell us about who the narrator is or wants to be, or about the narrative structures which are available in a particular community (Sandberg, 2010).

Narrative criminology's contention that stories are an instrument for doing is supported by growing evidence among psychological researchers that the perhaps 'distorted' narratives of men convicted of sex offences are heavily influenced by what they are trying to achieve with them. For instance, researchers have suggested that they maintain that they are innocent of their offences in order to retain relationships with families and friends (Lord & Willmot, 2004), remain safe in an institution in which identification as a 'sex offender' could lead to violence (Mann, 2016) and most importantly, to manage feelings of shame. Blagden, Winder, Thorne, and Gregson (2011) conducted an analysis of the accounts of men who used to deny their sex offences but then came to admit them. These men said that their earlier insistence that they had not committed the offence was a conscious and deliberate attempt to cope with the self-disgust and fear it induced. Imagined in this way, the narratives of men convicted of sex offences are a way of 'pushing back' against the stigma and shame of their conviction.

Other, more critical researchers have explored the way power intervenes in the narratives of men convicted of sex offences, considering their stories to be both an object of power and a site of resistance. Lacombe (2008), for instance, conducted an ethnography of a Canadian treatment programme for men convicted of sex offences. Those participating in the programme were encouraged to develop their understanding of their 'crime cycle', the sequence of events, thoughts and emotions which led up to their crime, and then to write a 'relapse prevention plan' which would help them to cope with things more helpfully in the future. Lacombe showed that the programme deliverers used various techniques to shape the way the participants told their stories, reconstructing them into narratives which inevitably led to the offence and which communicated that the men were irrevocably dangerous. Waldram's (2012) ethnography of a similar Canadian treatment programme further highlighted the intersection of issues of truth and power. He argued that prisoners used narratives as ways of making sense of themselves as morally acceptable beings, and that this clashed with the judicial-correctional 'truth discourse' (p. 13) and scientific ways of thinking which dominated the programme. In order to succeed in the course, the men needed to learn how to tell their stories the 'right' way, one attuned to the programme's demands for consistency, abstraction and factual evidence, although some continued to resist these demands.

In Waldram's and Lacombe's accounts, men convicted of sex offences have to balance their attempts to narratively imbue their lives with moral meaning with a countervailing force exerted by juridical and therapeutic 'truth'. In this chapter, I show how the narratives of men convicted of sex offences have to push against another countervailing force: that exerted by the idea of their victim. Ugelvik has described prisoners' victims as 'painful reminders of the fact that they have hurt another' (2012, pp. 264–265), as well of the fact that they are seen by wider society as the sort of ethically unacceptable person who is able to hurt another, and thus who deserves to be excluded. He has outlined some of the narrative strategies prisoners use in order to construct themselves as ethical subjects despite these reminders. In this chapter, I argue that these techniques are only partially successful, and that the silent figure of the victim retains a communicative power.

The Study

In the summer of 2015, I conducted my PhD fieldwork at an English medium-security prison which only held men convicted of sex offences (Ievins, 2017). The research aimed to understand how these men experienced imprisonment, with a particular focus on how it affected their sense of identity, their social relationships with other prisoners and their relationships with prison staff. I focused primarily on two prison wings and conducted 42 semi-structured interviews with prisoners, most of whom were randomly selected; these interviews had a mean length of four hours, and were often conducted over several sessions. Twelve much shorter interviews were conducted with prison officers. The interviews did not explicitly seek to gather narratives, but they nevertheless contained them: my interview participants described actions and their effects over time, sought to present themselves as a particular type of person and made a point (see Presser & Sandberg, 2015). Prisoners were given consent forms and interview schedules before the interview began, and interviews were conducted in a private room. All but two interviews were audio-recorded and transcribed verbatim, and I took close-to-verbatim notes on interviews with the two prisoners who felt uncomfortable being recorded. I also spent a significant amount of unstructured time in the prison, engaging in participant observation, getting to know people and watching life as it was lived.

It was clear from my prior reading, and immediately clear when talking to prisoners on the wing, that how prisoners experienced the prison was profoundly affected by the moral connotations of their conviction. I therefore asked interview participants what they were convicted of, whether they thought their conviction was fair, how their conviction made them feel about who they were and how the 'sex offender' label affected their lives. I never explicitly asked participants what they had done, fearing that this question might alienate or upset people unnecessarily. I considered the narratives that I was offered to be forms of identity work: whether prisoners maintained that they were innocent, or said that they were guilty but they had changed, I judged that they were trying to resist the totalising implications of the 'sex offender' label imposed by their conviction and imprisonment. In line with the conventions of narrative research,

I never challenged the stories which interviewees told, and I used the same language as they used: if they described themselves as 'innocent', for instance, I also referred to them as 'innocent'. My motives were epistemological, moral and practical: I wanted an appreciative understanding of people's worlds, I doubted my right to question people's perspectives and I wanted to build trust and rapport.

Over time, I began to fear that I had not been told the full story, and thus that the story my research was telling was partial (in both senses of the word). On my last day of fieldwork, I looked up the records of participants who had consented and took note of their charges and sentence lengths. In some cases, I googled them: I was interested in shame and stigmatisation, and knowing what had been publicly said about people helped me understand what they faced. I found out that a couple of men whom I had liked and trusted (and still do) had offended against very young children in their families. (They had told me in the interviews that they were guilty, but had not said what they were guilty of.) Learning who their victims were was upsetting, and while I by no means think that their offending belied the reality of their kindness and decency towards me or even their moral integrity at the time that I knew them, I struggled to integrate their offending into my understanding of who they were.

Over time, my guilt and confusion grew, nurtured by my participation in a new project involving ethnographies of imprisonment for men convicted of sex offences.[1] The week the fieldwork began, I watched *Three Girls*, a BBC television programme based on the stories of the victims of the Rochdale child grooming case. I was profoundly moved, and started worrying if I was on 'the wrong side': I had interviewed men convicted of similar offences, and had sympathised with the damage their convictions had done to them, without thinking much about other people who had been harmed by the same events. At the same time, the public conversation about sexual harassment and abuse following the accusations against Harvey Weinstein had forced me to think more seriously about the relationship between my feminism and my work.[2] I went back to my PhD transcripts to see what role, if any, the 'other side' – the men's victims – played in the narratives these transcripts recorded. My quest was not purely empirical, however: I wanted to see if these transcripts offered a way of thinking about harm and justice that moved beyond 'sides', that made it easier to take everyone's pain seriously without feeling that sympathising with one character in the story was a betrayal of another.

My experience of guilt and discomfort was similar to that of a haunting, a term used by Gordon to describe 'how that which appears to be not there is often a seething presence, acting on and often meddling with taken-for-granted realities' (2008, p. 8). The sign of a haunting is a ghost, and ghosts merge 'the

---

[1] The project was funded by the European Research Council and led by Ben Crewe. For more details, see https://www.compen.crim.cam.ac.uk/Ourresearch.
[2] Harvey Weinstein was a famous Hollywood producer who has been accused of dozens of cases of sexual assault.

visible and the invisible, the dead and the living, the past and present' (p. 24). They often reach out to us, calling us to peer into the spaces where they seem absent, and they have a profound effect on those who recognise them. As Gordon puts it, '[b]eing haunted draws us affectively, sometimes against our will and always a bit magically, into the structure of feeling of a reality we come to experience, not as cold knowledge, but as transformative recognition' (p. 8).

It is perhaps unsurprising that researching 'offenders' led me to a preoccupation with 'victims'. Christie (1986) convincingly argues that the two character types are co-constitutive of each other: you can't have an offender without a victim, and vice versa. Christie's argument is narratological in its shape, although it precedes narrative criminology. He shows how real experiences of harm and damage get flattened as they are retold for criminal justice processes. They become a sort of formula story, a rigid yet pervasive way of thinking and talking about stereotyped characters and their actions towards each other (Loseke, 2001). He argues that whether someone is granted victim status is essentially perspectival, and that there is a dyadic relationship between ideal victims and ideal offenders. Ideal victims can only have been hurt by distant, malicious, and often foreign, monsters. The same is true in reverse: to see someone as a monster, they must have hurt a pure and defenceless victim. The offender–victim dyad shapes both how we interpret the stories we hear ('if he hurt someone that weak, he must be evil') and delegitimises the stories which cannot be made to fit into its frame ('if he's a good guy, she must be lying', or 'if she's impure, he must be innocent').

In the remainder of this chapter, I show that victims did not just haunt me, they also haunted the prison. The ghosts of victims walked the wings of the prison, where they shaped the judgements made about prisoners by their peers and by prison staff. They also lurked in the narratives the men themselves told. I conclude by arguing that the context of the prison is much of what made victims ghostly, and that narrative criminology has a lot to say about the relationship between stories and justice.

Victims in the Prison

Victims were very rarely explicitly mentioned in the prison, whether as individuals or as a category. Nevertheless, they haunted the wings, and were present in the prison as both a memory and as a tool. It was the harm that had been done to victims which led to prisoners' incarceration, and prisoners and staff, prisoners and staff repeated the mantra that the aim of imprisonment was to 'prevent another victim'. At times, the idea that all prisoners had 'created' victims was used as an equaliser; as one man put it, 'there's always a victim in whatever you are doing'. More often, though, victims were used as a tool of categorisation: the victim 'made' the offender. Notably, in the prisoner hierarchy, those who had been convicted of offences against children were considered to be less morally and socially worthy than those who were convicted of offences against adults

(Ugelvik, 2015). The significance of the victim's identity was clear in the language prisoners used to talk about their peers, whom they defined more by whom they had harmed than by what the specific harm was:

> *Sex offenders, I think broadly speaking you've got paedophiles who offend against children. You have, like...they call them 'surfers', like, internet downloaders. ... You have the guys who I class not as chancers, but who've been convicted by their ex-wife or something like that, or girlfriends, so there's that sort of thing, which is not classed as bad as the other offences. ... There's a sliding scale, yeah. So you've got your top ones, like your streetwalkers, that take women off the streets and that sort of thing, right? And the paedophiles are up there as well. The paedophiles and then surfers and then the guys who offend against someone they know, like a date rape or something like that.*

Significantly, prisoners did not always know what their peers had been convicted of, or whom they had harmed, and so they often made judgements about the identity of the victim based on prisoners' appearances:

> *Inmates stereotype other inmates. You can tell with the way certain people behave and the way they are, the way they look and the way they act. You can use a bit of initiative and you think, well he's not a serial paedophile or a convicted paedophile. He's having regrets totally.*
>
> *Interviewer: How can you tell that? What sort of person looks like a person that isn't a paedophile? [Laughs]*
>
> *Well, for instance, say if you look at... like my padmate [cell mate] for instance, he's young, he's only 22, you can tell that he doesn't have a problem with attracting the opposite sex. Me, personally, I'm a good judge of character. Then you look at some of these people, they are like in their sixties, seventies and eighties, it's quite obvious what they are in for.*

The co-constitutive relationship between the identities of victims and the identities of offenders was so strong that how a prisoner looked was enough for their victim to be imagined.

Victims were sometimes used as a tool by prison staff and prisoners, who conjured victims punitively to justify lack of sympathy and poor treatment:

> *If you spoke to the families of their victims and told them they have TVs and PS2s [PlayStation Twos], what would they say?* (Prison officer)

> *I've had a go at someone, for telling about their offence, and they were saying about how the courts had fucked their lives up and probation had screwed them over by putting them in a hostel and that, and I had to say 'Have you ever thought about how your family might feel? Or your victim or her family? I don't know what you've done but you need to pack that shit in. I don't want to hear all that.'* (Prisoner)

The implication of these claims was that the delivery of punishment, and the prisoner's suffering, were in the service of the victim. The ghost of the victim thus played a role in different facets of the prisoner's punishment, particularly those which were intended to be punitive.

Victims were also conjured in psychological interventions. Victim empathy had formed a significant part of the Sex Offender Treatment Programme, the standardised cognitive-behavioural treatment programme which ran throughout England and Wales, although this part of the course was later dropped as it was not found to have an effect on reoffending (Mann & Barnett, 2013). Many prisoners described the value of being asked to imagine their victims:

> *I'm learning from my mistakes. I want to understand why I'm here. I want to understand how the victims feel. I've already done a victim [engaged in victim empathy work in my treatment group], I sat in a chair and pretended to be the victim on the web cam, talking about it, so I can understand how she might be feeling. I did that yesterday, no, Friday.*
>
> *Interviewer: Did you find that helpful?*
>
> *Yeah definitely. It was a bit upsetting, like, thinking about what I asked her to do and that, and I shouldn't have. I can understand why it's gonna affect her, and I've already wrote a letter to her. It's not gonna get sent to her, it's just that the course…saying how sorry I am and that and that I'm never gonna do anything like this again to anyone and I hope you understand, that you can move on now you know I've said sorry. But I know it's not gonna be sent to her.*
>
> *Interviewer: Did it make you feel better though, being able to write it?*
>
> *Yeah definitely. And I said 'Don't worry, I'm being punished, I'm in prison.'*

The empathy prisoners were asked to practice was *imaginary*: it was about how they (and the treatment provider) thought a victim would feel, and was not about empathising with a real person. Such therapeutic interventions were powerful because they were cathartic, but they were also intensely depersonalising. The idea of the victim was used as a tool, a way of shaping how prisoners told their stories, but the real victim had no capacity to speak for themselves. The victim was simply a figure to be deployed in the service of the prison's narrative goals. This aspect of the technique becomes clearer as well when we consider how the men sought to make sense of their own stories and reckon both with their real victim and the mythic victim created by the prison.

Narratives of Offenders and Victims

In the narratives that my interview participants told to make sense of themselves and their lives, they all reckoned with their victims. The nature of this reckoning varied: in some cases, the men were highly aware of having hurt someone they knew well and expressed significant guilt; in some, they were conscious of the victim as an abstract figure; in others, they maintained that there was no victim, and so their narratives argued against the idea that they were an offender. I describe these stories typologically, as there were clear patterns in the narrative forms which participants deployed, and in the role that victims played in them. I acknowledge, however, that grouping the stories together unavoidably simplifies them, and there was more variation than can be adequately represented here.[3]

The Real Victim and the Penitent Offender

Nine men presented their victim as a real, and really damaged, person. All of these men admitted guilt for their offences, all but one of them knew their victim prior to the offence, and for at least four men, the victim was their daughter or stepdaughter. They often referred to their victim either using their name or by the relationship they had with them (as 'my stepdaughter' or 'my neighbour'), and they, unprompted, expressed their belief that they had hurt their victims: 'I just did a stupid thing. Messed my stepdaughter's life up, really, just at the time when she's doing all her school and college and everything.' The men who told these stories knew the people they had hurt, they knew their ages and hopes and interests, and as such it was easier for them to picture the effects of what they had done. Several said that they worried that their traumatised victim might now struggle to pursue their desired employment, for example. The men who told these stories also tended to have quite a broad understanding of who the real victim was, often emphasising that their own families had suffered too, but generally this was because they had been hurt by the offence itself and not by the resulting imprisonment. The man quoted above, for instance, believed that his wife was 'the main victim'. However, this did not stop him from seeing his stepdaughter as a victim, and, crucially, he considered his wife to have been hurt by what he had done and not by how he had been punished. This pain thus remained something for which he was personally responsible.

---

[3]Relatedly, I have excluded from the typology the narratives of four men who maintained that they were convicted of nonsexual offences, and of one man who had dementia and struggled to recount why he was in prison.

Finding Victims in the Narratives of Men Imprisoned for Sex Offences **287**

In many cases, prisoners engaged in a conscious process of imagining their victims; it was not something that automatically spilt over from their prior knowledge of the victim, but it was instead a deliberate ethical practice. One participant, who was convicted of raping his adult neighbour, purposefully focused his mind on the suffering of his victim, and he gave shape to this by thinking about his family suffering in similar ways:

> *Interviewer: How does your conviction make you feel about who you are?*
>
> *Like I said, I think I said earlier, angry. Regret. But I have to own it. It's taking ownership. It's only over the last, you know, quite recently actually, I think because of the SOTP [Sex Offender Treatment Programme facilitators] coming over to see me, I've started thinking about it a bit, like the impact I've had, the impact I've had on the victim, I should say. Because a lot of it – I know people say – there's so many emotions that go on at the time of the sentencing then trying to deal with the sentence after, a lot of it was dealing with the loss. A lot of it was self-centred as well – I'm just being honest – you're trying to adapt to it, the effect on your family and all these sorts of things, and although I did think of the victim, like 'Fuck, it's a shame' sort of thing, it's only recently that you start thinking. You start comparing it, because I've got little nieces growing up now. I've got my mum, my sister, and if something happened to them…my blood runs cold, sort of thing. I suppose the realisation's starting to seep through now, now I'm starting to settle into my sentence, it's like 'Now, this is what you've done.'*

This man reported that when he was first sentenced and imprisoned, he was too focused on the suffering of himself and his family to think about the way his actions had made his victim suffer. As time progressed, though, and as he adapted to his sentence, he was able to think about the moral meaning of his offence. This reflection stirred feelings of guilt, and made him more willing to engage in treatment programmes. Other participants invested their remembering with rehabilitative meaning, and insisted that it stopped them from slipping into their old ways:

> *Obviously many nights – I still do it now, I think it's good and healthy – I still think about what I've done, I still sit there with regret. Not in a damaging way, in a healthy way.*
>
> *Interviewer: What's healthy about it particularly, do you think?*
>
> *I think it's healthy because it helps me move forward because I realised that although I have to remember, as part of the tools I learnt on the course, to make sure I don't reoffend, also I've got to have remorse, good healthy remorse where I realise how damaging, disgusting, terrible [it was].*

These prisoners wanted to build a better future, and to do so they felt that they had to reflect on their pasts. This reflection was encouraged by their participation in cognitive-behavioural treatment programmes which required them to identify the thought processes which had enabled their offending, in the hope that they would be able to manage them better in the future.

Excessive remembering carried dangers, though, and allowing the victim to be too present in the prison risked reinforcing prisoners' statuses as offenders. The men who shared these stories felt guilty about their offences and they wanted to acknowledge their pasts, but they believed that they deserved the opportunity to move on:

> *It's happened, it's happened. I can't change it. I can't do nothing about the past, Alice. I can try and make my future a bit better. See what I mean? And I know that's what I'm going to do. But as I say, I won't forget what I've done, it's always on my mind. And I hope this woman has a better life. Yeah. Yeah. Because no one deserves that, no one.*

It was as though they wanted to be able to remember their victims but also to exorcise them, allowing them to 'knife off' (Maruna & Roy, 2007) their pasts and build a new, better self.

In some cases, the men believed that institutional attempts to induce 'victim empathy' hindered their more authentic attempts to think about what they had done. One interview participant, who was convicted of several offences against a young child he knew, disclosed extreme feelings of self-hatred and self-disgust, and said that he was angry and upset when he was sentenced: 'I would have been a lot happier serving much longer, not only because I thought I deserved it but [because of] the thought that justice was actually being done and she would have had more peace of mind knowing that I am locked away and can't do it again.' He wanted to do what was possible to make amends and to ensure that he never did anything similar again. He was given a 'Victim Awareness booklet' while he waited to be assessed for his suitability for programmes, but he considered it 'completely inappropriate to what I have done':

> *Everything seems to be thrown in. Rather than being specific to one person, they've covered all the crimes, and if you accidentally tick the wrong box, you are kind of admitting to something you haven't done. ... And it's how is this specific to my crime or supposed to be oriented towards my crime if I'm having to answer questions that aren't suitable to what I've done? 'Who is the victim?' I know who the victim is. 'What did you steal?' How is that appropriate to the question at hand? ...*
>
> *Interviewer: And is it an assessment for you to do so they can work out what [programmes] you should go on, or is it just, like, a personal-*

> *It's supposed to increase your empathy towards your victim and possibly open up an avenue to reconciliation and further... Technically, I think it's to pick apart...You are having to self-analyse what you did and it's to try and give you a kick up the backside to realise what you are in for and why you are in for it and see it from the victim's point of view. But there is that many questions in there that you shouldn't have to be answering because they are not appropriate to the situation. It's kind of contradictory because it confuses the issue in the same process.*

It is common for prisoners to complain of 'tick-box' approaches to rehabilitation (Crewe, 2009); here this literally extends to how victims are imagined by the prison. This tick-box approach clearly did not support this man's attempts at reckoning. He was being asked to consider a mythological victim, and as he tried to picture the real person he had hurt, this abstracted figure kept blocking his view.

The guilt that these men expressed had a fundamentally interpersonal dimension: it was about having hurt a particular person (or people), by doing a particular thing (or things). The stories they told, and their conception of the pain they had caused, were real and complex. They broke out of the constraining boxes that criminal justice categories ('victim' and 'offender') placed them in, and these men faced challenges when their version of what they had done rubbed up against other, more official versions. In some cases, this tension emerged at trial, and several of these men disputed the details of their charges (because they insisted that they started abusing their victim when she was older than she said in court, for instance). In others, the tension developed after their conviction, when they had to start dealing with treatment and probation staff. One participant, for instance, said that he pled guilty to rape, but he nevertheless disputed the account of his offence given on his pre-sentence report. In particular he disagreed with the claim that he had planned to commit the offence. When he was in court to be sentenced, he had felt unable to challenge this version: 'I was looking at a life sentence and there's no way you could go up there and start picking fault with it, saying "Look at this, blah blah blah", because it looks like you're taking it away from the victim who was in court on the day.' This version of the story had an afterlife in the prison, however, and formed the basis of the account of the offence on his Offender Assessment System (OASys) report, a risk assessment tool which played a significant role in planning his sentence. He was engaged in strained discussions with his probation officer about this:

> *The thing with mine is, like I'm saying with my OASys, I'm not saying I didn't do this offence. Pretty much mine and my victim's story are aligned with each other, there's just a few little discrepancies because obviously you've got two different points of view. My problem is with the wording that my probation officer is*

using; I'm not saying I didn't do it. So you could say I'm just being a bit pedantic, whatever, but what I say is, let's just get it sorted from the off so it's all correct and, you know, good, and then there's no problems later on.

Despite – or perhaps because of – the authenticity of these men's guilt, they were unwilling to surrender their stories to the state. They had done what they had done, to real people and in real ways. They wanted to hold on to the truth of what had happened, using language which felt genuine to them. In presenting their victim as a real person, then, they sought to hold on to their own reality; neither they nor the person they had hurt could be placed easily into a box.

As narrative criminologists have stressed, stories are often acts of ethical self-construction (Ugelvik, 2012). Through telling these stories, these men sought to present themselves as reformed people (Presser, 2008) whose decency was reflected in their capacity to fully imagine their victim. At the same time, they presented their stories as both more complete and more authentic than those implied by the limiting categories of 'victim' and 'offender' which had been imposed by the criminal justice system.

The Missing Victim and the Punished Offender

Fourteen men told stories of greater narrative complexity. They admitted at least some guilt, but they described their offence as technically against the law but not something they held particular moral responsibility for, for instance because the victim consented but was underage. One participant offered an extreme example of this. He had drunkenly left a party and the next thing he remembered was waking up in a police cell and being told he had tried to rape someone on the way home:

To be fair, on my part it's always been hard because obviously the whole situation was…I'd been drinking anyways, with my friends, went and bought some alcohol and just drinking. Anyway, the whole situation was one of my friends lives in a certain area and it was just close by, so I'd been drinking obviously, I was drunk, drunk out of my head, and I just thought 'I want to go'. Earlier I tried to go home, but obviously I can't remember the situation, scenario.

Interviewer: Oh, so you can't remember what happened?

No. That's where the biggest problem is.

Interviewer: Ok. I've also spoken to a couple of other people who… OK. So you don't know if you did it, basically?

Yeah. And it was hard because obviously when you say that, you know, at the same time I'm not scrutinising anyone but at the same

> time it's like it gives an open – how can I say this? – it gives a blank page, I guess, for the police and everyone else to fill in whatever they want, I guess like they can put their own details on it, so for me it felt like they never told the whole truth, do you know what I'm saying?

Perhaps unsurprisingly, since he was unable to remember it, he described himself as somewhat alienated from his offence. Throughout the interview, he described the events on the walk home using the noun 'the situation'. It was not something that he *did*, an event that requires a verb; it was just a thing that happened, that *was*. Since he could not remember what happened, he worried that the official account of that night might not be the 'whole truth', and thus that he might be being punished for more than he did. Like many other men's narratives, his described quite an arbitrary charging process, one which affected the punishment he received but which did not clarify what he had done: 'It was... attempted...well, at first they said sexual assault, and then they said it was attempted rape'.

The victim did not feature at all in this man's narrative. She was neither an agent who held some responsibility for what happened, nor someone whose life was affected by what happened. This is perhaps unsurprising: he did not remember what happened, he did not know her and he was not even entirely sure of his guilt. In other stories, victims were less dramatically missing, but they were nevertheless presented as insignificant characters. In most cases, this was because the interviewees believed them to be willing participants and thus did not believe that they had been hurt. One participant, for instance, was convicted of inciting prostitution for financial gain, saying that he had set up and run a website to help two women sell sex. He felt very little guilt as the women in question were already selling sex when he got involved:

> *I'm not gonna say I'm glad I committed it but I don't have any remorse. I don't have any remorse whatsoever. I had no victim. They can chat this shit to me about 'Well, everyone's a victim, the community are victims.' Well, yeah, I've been a victim then. There was a car crash at the end of my road, so suddenly I was a victim then, because it kept me up at night. We're all victims, then. Every single one of us.*

Because he did not believe that his victims were 'true' victims, he struggled to see himself as a 'true' offender. He repeatedly said that he had 'fallen through the sex offender net' and did not morally deserve the label. Nevertheless, he was profoundly ashamed of being in prison, and wept when he spoke about missing the first year of his daughter's life.

The men who told these stories were similarly focussed on what had happened to them and to their families as a result of their offending, and they expressed particular shame at the weight of the 'sex offender' label, a label which they did not feel that they deserved. One participant, for instance, described the offence as something *he* would have to carry:

> *One of the big regrets of my life is probably to have offended, but at the end of the day I've got to carry it for a long time now, because at the end of the day I've got a criminal record that I can't get rid of. And that word, 'sex offender', it's not a nice word, is it, it's a thing you've got to carry with you for the rest of your life really.*

The way this man experienced his punishment – as something removing him from his family and his obligations, and exposing him to lasting shame and stigmatisation – meant that his mind was focused on his own sufferings, although he did consider himself to be responsible for his punishment. The treatment programmes which were available in the prison had encouraged him to consider his victim, which he maintained he found valuable, but his descriptions indicate that his victim remained a theoretical figure to him:

> *It put me in the victim's point of view, and the role-plays that I did, acting as a victim, and you can see then what position he or she could be in after the event, especially [with] friends, that person could be teased! They cover that, after it's all come out and they say what's happened. You get that side of it, what that person could go through, being teased about it. It's all that, you know. One of the questions I got was about after the event and the family and all that.*
>
> *Interviewer: And did you find that experience changed how you thought about the whole thing?*
>
> *Yeah it did. It makes you think 'Was it worth it? Why did it happen?' My family, their family, you know. Although it was consenting, I should have said no. It was a no, I understand that, and why pursue it? But you don't think of the consequences, that's the main thing, of that person's friends, the friendships, the mental effect on the family, my family, all that sort of thing. They've got to struggle. While I'm in prison, they've got to do all the work [looking after his elderly mother]. Because I know I'm in prison, I've still got to have stuff shipped in and sort my finances out and all that, and they've got their own lives to live as well, and you don't think about that, do you? You can't take them for granted. And my mother as well, not seeing her. And when she says 'Who are you?' [She had dementia]. It's a weird feeling.*

The programmes he undertook might have encouraged him to empathise with the victim, but he nevertheless referred to them abstractly – as 'he or she', 'that person' and 'the victim', but never by name. He described the concrete suffering of his own family much more vividly and tangibly, and he demonstrated more concrete awareness of the harm he had done to them than the harm he had done to his abstract, and abstracted, victim.

These men offered a different narrative of ethical self-construction, one with similarities to the 'stability narratives' described by Presser (2008). They presented themselves as ultimately moral people whose overriding decency could not be undermined by the sexual harm they were convicted of committing. They reckoned with the moral pressure exerted by their mythic victim by either ignoring or failing to individualise them. If their victim was barely present, they could not be truly bad.

The Victim as the Offender and the Offender as the Victim

Fourteen interview participants described themselves as the victims of profound injustice. They had been convicted of different offences, including sexually abusing children in their families and raping their adult partners, but they rarely described the charges in detail. They never mentioned their victims by name, and seldom described in detail their relationship to them prior to the offence. Instead, the victim featured in the background of these stories as the dissembler whose false accusations had kicked off the plot. When they were mentioned, it was with evident hostility:

> *My so-called ex-partner reckoned I raped her on numerous occasions without her knowledge. [Laughs]*
>
> *Interviewer: When she was asleep?*
>
> *She reckons when she was sleeping, I raped her, she's woke up and felt like I've been inside her.*

Their bitter insistence on their innocence percolated through the interviews, shaping what they wanted to talk about, the words they used to talk about it and the inflections they used when speaking. When describing the events that led them to prison, they made liberal use of audible scare quotes, referring pointedly to 'the *alleged* offences', for instance. They talked at length about the pain of being referred to and seen as a 'sex offender', a label which hurt because it was inaccurate. This pain reverberated throughout the prison: they were regularly referred to using this term, and their very presence in this type of prison implied that this was who they were. This research project also reinforced this injustice:

> *Like, when you gave me that form [the consent form] to fill in, and it said 'Life in prison of a sex offender'. If it was 'Life in prison as a sex offender', I would have filled it in, but it says 'Life in prison of a sex offender'. Something like that.*

> *Interviewer: It was 'The social experiences of sex offenders in prison'.*
>
> *Of a sex offender. If it was as a sex offender, I might have [signed it]. Of a sex offender, which means you were calling me a sex offender.*

These men fundamentally disagreed with the roles which had been officially distributed by the courts (and in this case the research): there was no victim, they insisted – the victim had claimed that identity by lying – and thus they could not be an offender. They had been unjustly hurt, and blamed their victims, the courts and the prison for this.

Several men actively contested their officially assigned role, vocally disagreeing with staff members who referred to them as 'sex offenders'. In some cases, this challenge came at significant personal cost. One participant, for example, was a compliant prisoner, but he consistently challenged anyone who implied that he was guilty:

> *Interviewer: How would you say you see yourself?*
>
> *Victim. [Laughs] How do I see myself?*
>
> *Interviewer: I mean, victim is a response.*
>
> *My probation officer, I've never met her face to face, but we just do not get on. I think it's because I'm maintaining my innocence, she doesn't like it. She's made some threats to me which I know she can't do because I've read all the PSIs [Prison Service Instructions] and what have you. She said 'Have you got no compassion for your victims?' and I said 'I am the victim', which started her off again.*

He worried that his confrontational relationship with his probation officer would have an adverse effect on the nature of his post-release probation supervision, and his insistence on his innocence had affected his risk level in the prison, stopping him, for a time, from accessing his desired job in the gardens. Despite these repercussions, he refused to say he was guilty:

> *Interviewer: Given that maintaining innocence makes things harder for you, what is it that stops you from just saying – not that I think you did – but just saying to them 'Yeah alright, you got me'?*
>
> *I see what you're saying. ... What stops me from saying [it], although it could make my life inside and outside prison a lot easier, I didn't do it. I didn't do it. And I cannot – I can't think of a word so I'll use confess, I don't mean confess – but I can't confess to something I have not done. Everything, I mean, some of the lads have said to me 'Why are you doing this? You'll make your life so much easier if you say "Yeah, I'm a dirty bastard, I did it"' – sorry,*

> sorry [for swearing]. But I can't. I just can't. I can't. I can't. I didn't do it and as much as they're gonna punish me for it, I can't say I did it because it never happened.

He thus presented himself as an honourable martyr, acting with dignity in an environment that promoted dishonesty.

In order to reinforce their positive identities, these men presented a counter-narrative (Bamberg & Andrews, 2004) to the official narrative initiated by the victim and endorsed by the state. Rather than focussing on the details of the false accusation, they typically described the injustice of what the criminal justice system had done to them. Significant portions of the interview were dedicated to angry, sometimes inaccurate, descriptions of legal procedures, many relating to which evidence was disclosed, admitted or believed. This was partly related to the focus of the interviews – I specifically asked questions about the fairness of the conviction and not about what had actually happened – but procedural and evidentiary concerns played a similarly weighty role in the more ad hoc stories of injustice prisoners would tell me, unprompted, when I chatted with them during the participant observation phase of the research. There was a clearly gendered aspect to this critique, and it was common for these men to insist that the courts 'always go on the woman's side', and to criticise anyone who said that women should be automatically believed. Mostly, though, their critique was epistemological. In particular, prisoners complained about the injustice of being convicted solely on the basis of the victim's testimony without any corroborating physical proof. They delegitimised such testimony by referring to it as 'hearsay', and insisted that it was wrong to convict someone purely on the basis of one person's story. What was needed was 'evidence':

> *I know I didn't touch that lass [girl], I know that for a flying fact, but to have so many members of a jury say 'Yes, you did it', and they don't even know you and they don't even know the person that's accused you, that's really annoying because even the lass's family members all said 'He didn't do that'. ...*
>
> *Interviewer: And the thing that annoys you about it is the fact that it's unfair?*
>
> *It's not that it's unfair, it's the fact that it's hearsay. There was no other evidence. It was word against word. And the fact of it being is that they can't turn round and say 'Oh well, we didn't have any evidence bar hearsay'. It's like, well, you need definitive facts.*

They also questioned the value of these stories because they believed they had been elicited in ways which distorted their veracity:

> *Because the conviction itself, the process, the legal system itself, is more legal rangling dangling than knowing the truth. It starts with the police and their target is not to resolve the case, their target is*

> to get the conviction. That, for them, is resolving it. .,. If there's a proof of it, if there's DNA, if there's fingerprints, if there's consistencies, I can understand that. Yeah? But if that allegation is made and there's a different allegation made and then there's a different second statement and the victim is saying [in her interview at the police station] 'I don't know which hole it was' and if the victim if saying 'Oh, officers, I'll tell you this bit'. I have the documents so I can show you. ... I listened to this police interview, and officer says 'OK, tell me about when he was doing it.' 'Yeah he did it.' 'Any pain?' She goes 'Yeah, I went to hospital.' So the officer got excited, 'Oh yeah, went to hospital, that's good.' She went 'Oh yeah, I was at school, I went to hospital. My leg started hurting.' Officer said 'No, tell me about [when] he was doing it.'

These men insisted that the official stories, those which had first been drawn out of their accusers and then validated by the courts, were untrue and thus unfair, and they were unwilling to let them be the only ones to be told. Instead, they resisted them by telling their own narratives of injustice, and in some cases, by reinforcing their narratives by suggesting alternative readings of legal documents. In the quotation above, for instance, the participant suggests that I read the transcript of the police interview with the victim – 'I have the documents so I can show you' – to help me to understand how unfair the process was. Another man said something similar: 'Sometimes I just want to scream at these people [probation officers and treatment professionals] and say "For God's sake, read the trial transcript, look at it!" but they don't care. All they look at is the verdict.'

On other occasions, they maintained that their good character was proof of their innocence, and insisted that the people who really knew them knew that they were not guilty. Generally, the resulting implication – that the victim was lying – was left tacit, although the connection was clearer in one interview:

> In my family, everybody who knows me all know me as innocent. They've all said 'You're innocent, we know you are.' Even one of my best friends, she's a bisexual woman, and even she said, she said 'Listen, I've known you since we were kids and there's no way.' There was points where I was actually scared of kids, 11, 12, 13, 14 and 15 year olds because they can come out with anything and they can be dangerous.

This participant's insistence on his own innocence prompted him to discuss children's propensity to lie; he went on to discuss in detail the circumstances of the child who accused him. In his mind, at least, there was a connection between his own character and the falsity of the accusations against him. He, and other men whose stories followed this pattern, thus attacked the way roles had been distributed by the courts on two reciprocal fronts. There was no victim – the victim had lied and the court had incorrectly allowed them to lie – and so they could not be offenders. But at the same time, they were not offenders – they were solid, decent, family men – so there could not have been a victim.

The ethical self-construction engaged in by these men took a different form to that of the men who told different stories. Their task was not to imply that there was more to the truth than was implied by the official story, either by showing the depth of their true empathy or by arguing that the official story was incomplete or irrelevant. Rather, their goal was to discredit the official story and to establish their own as more authentic. This was narrative as active resistance – to the state, and to the stories told by their victims.

Conclusion: Stories and Justice

Prisons ask prisoners to take responsibility for the pain they have caused while also making them experience pain themselves. They physically separate prisoners from the people they have hurt, while binding them to each other by the fact of their conviction. In this context, it is unsurprising that there were commonalities among the stories prisoners told about their victims. Almost all of them said they had been assigned a category – 'sex offender' – that did not reflect the complexity of what had happened, and they all offered more nuanced versions in response. Many of them critiqued the legal system as a producer of stories, whether because of its reliance on unfair testimonial evidence or because it made charging decisions which obscured as much as they illuminated. Their frustration with the system continued into the prison, and the suffering prisoners and their families experienced meant that, in almost all cases, their affective attention was focused on those closest to them. As a result, they had less imaginative space for their victims. When the effort to think about their victims was imposed by the prison in its deliberate attempts to induce empathy, it was at best ineffective in promoting genuine engagement, and at worst stood in the way of it.

One way of exploring these narratives would be to argue that they offer straightforward examples of ethical self-construction (Ugelvik, 2012). Within such an analysis, we would argue that victims constitute a 'problem to be managed' in order for prisoners to continue to see themselves as morally upright human beings. In this chapter, I have outlined three techniques participants used to do this. Some displayed penitence and reform by telling stories which indicated that there was more to them and the person they hurt than was implied by the simple categories of 'victim' and 'offender'. Others presented stories of moral stability, and attempted to evade the ethical consequences of being labelled an 'offender' by telling stories which overlooked the fact of having hurt a 'victim'. A third group actively defied both the version of the story presented by the state and the victim, and the consequences of this story for their moral identity – they were simply not an 'offender'. These techniques were only ever partially successful, however, and their victims retained a communicative power, and existed in prisoners' narratives as haunting but incomplete reminders of the unstoried pain hiding in the shadows.

There is an additional way of understanding these stories, however. They are not simply techniques for constructing an ethical self within the shaming context of the prison; they are also *outputs* of that context, and as such they are phenomena which take us closer to or further from justice. Stauffer (2015) has argued that the stories which we tell about harm affect our capacity to heal from it, both as individuals and as societies, and she shows that most criminal trials (and, more controversially, many restorative justice processes) only allow limited and stunted versions of the true story to emerge. The stories told by the men interviewed for this project had been similarly shaped by the institutions which were punishing them. The conditions of their imprisonment made it hard for prisoners to engage fully with what they had done, let alone to produce an account which fully made room for the people they had hurt. If victims were ghosts in the narratives of the imprisoned men, the prison, as well as the prisoners, had written them that way.

Thinking about the relationship between stories and justice pushes us to think evaluatively about stories – to think not just about what they do in the world but also about how 'good' they are, whether they promote healing, and whether they are the type of stories we want our criminal justice system to produce. This should be a form of evaluation which is sympathetic, and which moves us out of the impasse created by trying to pick a side. It involves looking out for the stories hidden in the shadows, and thinking with sympathy about what it means to silence, what it means to be silenced and what structural conditions might make silencing more likely. It also involves thinking imaginatively about institutional forms which might promote the telling of better, more just stories. Narrative criminology, with its commitment to understanding the relationship between stories and structures (Presser & Sandberg, 2015), as well as its interest in 'what is not said' (Presser, 2019), is ideally placed to engage in these discussions.

References

Bamberg, M. G. W., & Andrews, M. (2004). *Considering counter narratives: Narrating, resisting, making sense*. Amsterdam: John Benjamins Publishing Company.

Blagden, N., & Pemberton, S. (2010). The challenge in conducting qualitative research with convicted sex offenders. *The Howard Journal of Criminal Justice*, *49*(3), 269–281. doi:10.1111/j.1468-2311.2010.00615.x

Blagden, N., Winder, B., Thorne, K., & Gregson, M. (2011). 'No-one in the world would ever wanna speak to me again': An interpretative phenomenological analysis into convicted sexual offenders' accounts and experiences of maintaining and leaving denial. *Psychology, Crime and Law*, *17*(7), 563–585. doi:10.1080/10683160903397532

Christie, N. (1986). The ideal victim. In E. A. Fattah (Ed.), *From crime policy to victim policy: Reorienting the justice system* (pp. 17–30). Houndmills: Macmillan.

Cowburn, M. (2005). Hegemony and discourse: Reconstructing the male sex offender and sexual coercion by men. *Sexualities, Evolution & Gender, 7*(3), 215–231. doi: 10.1080/14616660500231665

Crewe, B. (2009). *The prisoner society: Power, adaptation, and social life in an English prison*. Oxford: Oxford University Press.

Crewe, B., & Ievins, A. (2015). Closeness, distance and honesty in prison ethnography. In D. H. Drake, R. Earle, & J. Sloan (Eds.), *The Palgrave handbook of prison ethnography* (pp. 124–142). Houndmills: Palgrave Macmillan.

Digard, L. (2014). Encoding risk: Probation work and sex offenders' narrative identities. *Punishment & Society, 16*(4), 428–447. doi:10.1177/1462474514539536

Gordon, A. F. (2008). *Ghostly matters: Haunting and the sociological imagination* (2nd ed.). Minneapolis, MN: University of Minnesota Press.

Ievins, A. (2017). *Adaptation, moral community and power in a prison for men convicted of sex offences*. Ph.D. dissertation, Cambridge: University of Cambridge.

Lacombe, D. (2008). Consumed with sex: The treatment of sex offenders in risk society. *British Journal of Criminology, 48*(1), 55–74. doi:10.1093/bjc/azm051

Lord, A., & Willmot, P. (2004). The process of overcoming denial in sexual offenders. *Journal of Sexual Aggression, 10*(1), 51–61. doi:10.1080/13552600410001670937

Loseke, D. R. (2001). Lived realities and formula stories of 'battered women'. In J. F. Gubrium & J. A. Holstein (Eds.), *Institutional selves: Troubled identities in a postmodern world* (pp. 107–126). New York: Oxford University Press.

Mann, R. E. (2016). Sex offenders in prison. In Y. Jewkes, J. Bennett, & B. Crewe (Eds.), *Handbook on prisons* (2nd ed., pp. 246–264). Abingdon: Routledge.

Mann, R. E., & Barnett, G. D. (2013). Victim empathy intervention with sexual offenders: Rehabilitation, punishment or correctional quackery?. *Sexual Abuse, 25*(3), 282–301. doi:10.1177/1079063212455669

Maruna, S., & Mann, R. E. (2006). A fundamental attribution error? Rethinking cognitive distortions. *Legal and Criminological Psychology, 11*(2), 155–177. doi: 10.1348/135532506X114608

Maruna, S., & Roy, K. (2007). Amputation or reconstruction? Notes on the concept of 'knifing off' and desistance from crime. *Journal of Contemporary Criminal Justice, 23*(1), 104–124. doi:10.1177/1043986206298951

Matza, D. (1969). *Becoming deviant*. Englewood Cliffs, NJ: Prentice-Hall.

Presser, L. (2008). *Been a heavy life: Stories of violent men*. Urbana, IL: University of Chicago Press.

Presser, L. (2019). The story of antisociality: Determining what goes unsaid in dominant narratives. In J. Fleetwood, L. Presser, S. Sandberg & T. Ugelvik (Eds.), *The Handbook of Narrative Criminology* (pp. 409–424). Bingley: Emerald.

Presser, L., & Sandberg, S. (2015). Introduction: What is the story? In L. Presser & S. Sandberg (Eds.), *Narrative criminology: Understanding stories of crime* (pp. 1–20). New York: New York University Press.

Sandberg, S. (2010). What can 'lies' tell us about life? Notes towards a framework of narrative criminology. *Journal of Criminal Justice Education, 21*(4), 447–465. doi: 10.1080/10511253.2010.516564

Stauffer, J. (2015). *Ethical loneliness: The injustice of not being heard*. New York: Columbia University Press.

Ugelvik, T. (2012). Prisoners and their victims: Techniques of neutralization, techniques of the self. *Ethnography, 13*(3), 259–277. doi:10.1177/1466138111435447

Ugelvik, T. (2015). The rapist and the proper criminal: The exclusion of immoral others as narrative work on the self. In L. Presser & S. Sandberg (Eds.), *Narrative criminology: Understanding stories of crime* (pp. 23–41). New York: New York University Press.

Waldram, J. B. (2007). Everybody has a story: Listening to imprisoned sexual offenders. *Qualitative Health Research, 17*(7), 963–970. doi:10.1177/1049732307306014

Waldram, J. B. (2012). *Hound pound narrative: Sexual offender habilitation and the anthropology of therapeutic intervention.* Berkeley, CA: University of California Press.

CATEGORISATIONS, PLOTS AND ROLES

Chapter 15

Narratives of Conviction and the Re-storying of 'Offenders'

Bernd Dollinger and Selina Heppchen

Introduction

Narrative criminology does not regard crime as something simply given. Crime does not exist as an objectively describable event, but is produced as a communicative reality. Without stories with a particular form and content, crime could not be spoken of. According to Presser (2009, p. 186), the question of a noncommunicated reality can be bracketed here because narrative criminology is dealing with the question of how narratives constitute and plausibly present a crime reality. Narratives are seen as a special form of communication. Presser (2016, p. 138) points out that narratives are often defined as 'a temporally ordered, morally suggestive statement about events and/or actions in the life of one or more protagonists'. A narrative thus implies the assumption that 'protagonists' act or are affected by actions, that this takes place over time and, as crime is involved, that an event or course of events is usually assessed negatively.

Many studies to date show that the central concern of narrative criminology is very fruitful and can be realised through different empirical approaches (Presser & Sandberg, 2015). In our view, however, the empirical analysis of the interactive work which is necessary to make crime stories plausible should be emphasised even more as a supplement to these studies. One cannot simply attribute criminality to individual events, and one cannot easily attest to individual persons as offenders. If someone is to be identified as an offender, it is above all (and beyond purely legal arguments) necessary to have a story at hand that convincingly and compellingly justifies this attribution (e.g. von Arnauld & Martini, 2015; Gubrium & Holstein, 2009; Scheppele, 1994). An offender must be produced interactively as an 'offender'. Irrespective of the particular characteristics, penchants, interests, ways of acting, etc. that may characterise a person, in the case of a crime story, he or she must be identified as a member of the category 'offender'. Categories are the basis on which specific people can be spoken of in everyday life and in institutional contexts (Hall, Slembrouck, & Sarangi, 2006, p. 25). Categories provide information about who a person 'really' is – how they are socially evaluated and classified – and how they should be treated. And we assume that categories are a core component of crime stories. It therefore makes an important contribution to narrative criminology to focus on categorisations more precisely than before because categorisations are actually made in every story about crime.

To substantiate this assumption in the following, we use the ethnomethodological research method of 'Membership Categorisation Analysis' (MCA). We choose this method because the analysis of categorisations is its characteristic feature. In the words of Housley and Fitzgerald (2015, p. 1): 'Categories are central to social life and experience and an empirical understanding of their actual use in real-time at the situated and granular level can generate insights into a wide spectrum of social behaviours and problems.' MCA's methodological recommendations are useful to meticulously trace how individual categories are used and how, in disputes over the validity of different categories, one category is enforced against another. We describe the methodological implications of MCA in more detail below and then apply them to the case study 'Dave'.

Dave is a youth who has been charged with sexual offences and is threatened with imprisonment. His example shows an instructive double focus of juvenile criminal proceedings: on the one hand, the question is what 'really' happened. On the other hand, the question is what kind of person he is, for the sake of determining how to deal with him. This dual focus on an offence and on character is typical of proceedings against young people (Dünkel, Grzywa, Pruin, & Selih, 2010; Emerson, 1969). In the course of proceedings, a certain narrative turns out to be 'true'. Komter (2012) speaks of the temporal 'career' of statements in these proceedings, starting with police investigations up to negotiations in court: statements take place in certain contexts and are brought into new contexts via criminal proceedings. Here they get 'a life of their own', they gain new meanings and can be used in new ways.

For defendants in criminal proceedings, how individual events ('crimes') are presented and how the defendants are portrayed as persons are of the utmost importance. Even small changes in the meaning of the way in which events and persons are presented can lead to a modified assessment of stories and the responsibility of individual persons (Ask, 2018). If, for example, persons ('offenders') are intentional actors who have caused great damage, it is likely that they will experience little sympathy in a trial and will be punished harshly. On the other hand, they can get sympathy if they were influenced by negative external circumstances and did not act in bad faith (Loseke, 2003).

Given the importance of such attributions, it is not surprising that defendants are not simply passive objects towards them. Rather, through certain forms of self-presentation, they try to influence the way in which they are judged in court (Dollinger & Fröschle, 2017; Emerson, 1969; Komter, 1998). Defendants often structure their stories in such a way to increase the story's credibility and to minimise the extent to which they present themselves as 'punishable'. This may not always be successful and in the case of sexual offences, i.e. especially stigmatised offences (Gavin, 2005; Waldram, 2007, 2009), there are particular challenges to the aspiration to positive self-presentation (Victor & Waldram,

2015). Yet defendants have an interest in influencing the interactions during a court hearing in their favour. Ultimately, the judge decides and legal guidelines structure to a large degree the chances of articulating oneself during a trial (Atkinson & Drew, 1979; Hall & Matarese, 2014, p. 86; Polletta, Chen, Gardner, & Motes, 2011). Nevertheless, defendants have room for manoeuvre, which they seek to use in order to present themselves to court in a manner suitable for them and to obtain a favourable judgement. We describe this kind of agency in detail by tracing how Dave categorised himself and how he was categorised by others in the context of his trial.

Methodological Approach: Membership Categorisation Analysis

The case study 'Dave' comes from a research project with young men who were threatened with imprisonment based on the German Youth Courts Act. We interviewed a total of 15 young male defendants between the ages of 15 and 21 years before and after their trials, and also attended the main hearing[1] as observers (Dollinger & Fröschle, 2017). The interviews were structured openly so that the interviewees could express themselves freely and comprehensively. All interviews were recorded and transcribed in their entirety. We established contact with the young men through various professional actors, such as social workers in educational institutions or correctional facilities, public prosecutors and judges. It was particularly challenging to obtain the necessary permits from the pertinent authorities, institutions and, if necessary, legal guardians in order to contact the defendants and to observe their main hearings. It was finally possible to obtain the permits, and incentives in the form of vouchers for the defendants proved helpful in motivating them to participate in the study. The interviews took place in the locations where the interviewees were accommodated, i.e. in educational institutions, in pre-trial detention or in prison.

The objective of the interviews before trial was to gather narratives of the interviewees about themselves, their families, their offences and other agents, such as friends, social workers, police officers, etc. In the second set of interviews (after the trials), our interlocutors reflected on how the trials had gone, the outcome, their personal conduct and those involved. Field protocols of the court hearings we observed were a further source of information for our study. A comparison of the narratives before, during and after the trial allows for a reconstruction of two

---

[1]In Germany, most proceedings against young people end with diversion; in 2015 the figure was 75.9% (Heinz, 2017, p. 93). The significance of a main hearing for the remaining cases is therefore all the greater (with the possibility of discontinuation even after the start of a hearing). Trials against youths (aged 14 to 17 years at the time of the offence) are not public, trials against adolescents (aged 18 to 20 years at the time of the offence) are public. The defendant must be present during the main hearing. At the end of the main hearing, the verdict is delivered, if the proceedings are not terminated. The verdict contains, among other things, the sanctions imposed if the court considers sanctions to be necessary (Laubenthal, Baier, & Nestler, 2015).

aspects: the time-related transformation of the narratives used by the defendants (what we call 're-storying');[2] and the narratives, which crystallised during the trial as the 'real' story about the defendants and the events in question.

For the analysis of our data we use the ethnomethodological research method of MCA.[3] Based on an early elaboration by Sacks (1995), MCA focuses on the way how categories are used in conversations and how they are negotiated between interacting participants. Categories do not have to be named explicitly; they can only be hinted at (Rapley, 2012). Yet, it is crucial that interlocutors – e.g. in the course of an interview – indicate that they are oriented towards categories in order to assign a certain meaning to people (or places, institutions or others). Categories must therefore not be assigned externally by the researchers, but MCA demands that researchers reconstruct how categories are established interactively by associating characteristics and activities with categories in concrete conversations.

A story used by Sacks (1995) conveys a meaningful example: 'The baby cried. The mommy picked it up.' The example shows various important aspects of categorisations, which we can only briefly name here:[4]

- First, people in the story *are each identified by a single category*. Categorisation is, as it were, economical; Sacks (1995, p. 246) speaks of an 'economy rule'. It states that a single category can suffice communicatively to characterise a person. Admittedly, many statements could be made about any person, but information can be unnecessary in conversations. For a concrete conversation, it can be irrelevant whether a baby is generally quiet or often cries, how old it is exactly, whether it is male or female and so on. The categorisation as 'baby' can be sufficient.

---

[2]In their analysis of the narratives of sex offenders, Victor and Waldram (2015) also discuss 're-storying'. According to Victor and Waldram, sex offenders face the difficult challenge of having to reconcile serious and highly stigmatised crimes with their identity. They must align their own actions, possible contradictions with their previous identity and social rejection through appropriate narratives. Victor and Waldram (2015, p. 119) assume that a constructive 're-storying' of one's past and present entails the possibility of a future life without crime. We use the term differently because we do not assume that narratives and delinquent actions could be separated (see also Dollinger, 2020).

[3]Sacks (1995, I, p. 238) spoke of an MCD ('Membership Categorisation Device') as being a collection of categories, including rules of their application. The name MCA was proposed by Eglin and Hester (1992), not just to emphasise collections of categories but also the relevance of individual categories, and to cover 'the full range of categorisation practices' (Eglin & Francis, 2016, pp. 7–8).

[4]We only describe aspects of the MCA which are directly relevant to the subject matter of this chapter. For further important basics of MCA, recommendations on the methodical procedure and the relevant terminology of MCA, we strongly recommend the following: Lepper (2000), Silverman (1998) and Stokoe (2012). On the controversial relationship between MCA and conversation analysis, see, for example, Benwell and Stokoe (2006), Silverman (1998) and Watson (2015).

- A second point concerns *the linking of individual categories*. Without being explicitly linked in the story, the two actors are connected: the baby and mother seem to belong together. They belong to a 'collection of categories' (Silverman, 1998, p. 79), here a family. Sacks calls this collection a 'membership categorisation device'. According to common sense, particular categories belong together and form a unit. Where there is a mother, there is a child, and vice versa, so that a person listening to the above story is able to perceive a course of interactions, in which persons act in relation to one another who belong together. If categories are closely connected, listeners of a story would notice if a category is not mentioned or they would supplement it implicitly (Silverman, 1998, p. 82). The category 'baby' refers to a 'mommy' or to parents, and if the latter would not be mentioned when talking about a baby, a listener wonders where the mother or parents of the baby are.
- A third point relates to *the linking of categories with activities and characteristics*. Children cry. The fact that they do so fits with common expectations, as does the attention and support of the mother who responds to the crying. The mother behaves 'correctly' in terms of the 'category-bound activities' (Sacks, 1995, I, p. 241) which are attributed to a 'mommy'. In addition to activities, characteristics are associated with categories (Eglin & Hester, 1992), such as mothers being concerned about their children, being older than the children, etc.
- Fourth, these connections are often *normatively qualified*, as normative standards apply to members of a particular category (Eglin & Hester, 1992; Jayyusi, 1984). For example, in the absence of very good reasons for such behaviour, a mother who leaves her crying child alone and walks away would be perceived as irresponsible. In this respect, categories are relationally interwoven with other categories, thereby implying typical activities and communicating normative behavioural expectations. Members of categories have category-specific rights and duties and, like the mother and the child, they can have a hierarchical relationship with each other (Silverman, 1998, pp. 81–85).
- Fifth, MCA attaches particular importance to the fact that communication is strictly related to the concrete contexts in which it occurs. Categories (such as baby or mother) are culturally widespread, but it is still necessary for people to justify and render intelligible in concrete contexts when and why certain categories are appropriate. Categorisations make sense for specific people in specific contexts; they are an 'occasioned accomplishment' (Garfinkel & Sacks, 1970, p. 345), i.e. people use categories on a context-specific basis in the scope of interactions (Watson, 2015).

These five points show that a story depends on categorisations. The two sentences 'The baby cried. The mommy picked it up.' are not explicitly connected in content, for example by a causal construction ('*therefore* the mommy picked it up') or by a temporal course ('*then* the mommy picked it up'). But such connections can be heard. According to common sense as a resource through which conversation is interpreted (Sacks, 1995), it is plausible for a listener to hear more than is actually said. Baby and mother belong together (as a family); they exhibit expectable activities and behave normatively properly. When people hear the two sentences in a concrete situation, they can therefore be expected to hear a story in which a mother picks up *her* baby *because and after she/he cries*.

In the context of crime, there are special categories with particular qualities and category-bound activities. Terms like 'thief', 'murderer', 'rapist', 'repeat offender', 'victim' depict incumbents of categories, each with typecast activities and characteristics that 'explain' why it is appropriate to identify a person as a (particular) offender or involved in crime in a special way (Watson, 1976). For example, a person who commits an act of violence is a violent offender, and a violent offender is a person who commits an act of violence. The category-bound activity defines the member of a category and vice versa. And where there is a violent offender, there is a victim of violence. In this regard, categories form collections (or 'membership categorisation devices'). Because categories are 'inference rich', i.e. knowledge about people in a society is often tied to categories (Sacks, 1995, I, pp. 40–41), it is generally known that offenders are actively harming others, that victims suffer passively and so forth (Loseke, 2003; Tabbert, 2015). The activities and characteristics of members of categories are matched, e.g. in that the actions of an offender 'fit' the suffering of a victim, so that a narrative emerges: an offender acts violently, a victim gets hurt and this connection forms a crime story.

In an analysis of crime narratives, the relevant categories and evaluations must be related to concrete interactions. It is necessary to convey reasons why a single act (or omission) can *correctly* be identified as criminal conduct in a particular context: 'Unless persons are able to produce recognisable references to crime, and unless those who interact with them can recognise them as references to crime, then intelligible talk about and action in relation to crime would be impossible' (Hester & Eglin, 2017, p. 22). In order to constitute crime, it is necessary to describe a violation of a norm in a situation, to attribute motives, to establish a damage, etc (Francis & Hester, 2004; Watson, 1997). In the respective communication, categories of crime are adapted to the situation and made comprehensible to the participants in this very communication (i.e. to listeners of a story, to readers of a newspaper, etc.).[5]

Before we apply these principles to the case study 'Dave', we would like to point out that we use *research interviews* in the context of Dave's trial as the form of communication within which we reconstruct categorisations. As far as possible, the categories revolving around crime should not be determined by

---

[5]This corresponds to a central concern of ethnomethodology, which aims at exploring how people, as members of social interactions, practically produce social order by mutually indicating that they orient themselves to certain events, categories and meanings (Garfinkel, 1967). They make events 'observable-and-reportable, that is, available to members as situated practices of looking-and-telling' (Garfinkel, 1967, p. 1).

research because the central object of MCA is the mutual negotiation of a (crime or other) reality by actors and the methods they use to produce such a reality. In an open interview, the special situation occurs that there is no 'natural' conversation. This special circumstance makes it all the more necessary to identify and substantiate categories that are not predetermined by research, but are important for the interviewee. Researchers have to 'put aside their preoccupations about what might intuitively or commonsensically be happening in interaction and focus instead on the detail of members' concerns and orientations' (Benwell & Stokoe, 2006, p. 68). Research interviews are social interactions in which a kind of crime reality can emerge. Interviews do not entail simply obtaining information from the interviewee, but the establishment and processing of an interaction between the participants (Atkinson & Delamont, 2006). In this way, the interview situation shapes the stories that are told, and interviews, especially those of an open nature, provide the interviewee with an opportunity to qualify themselves as a particular person (Halsey, 2017; Presser, 2004). The subsequent analysis *must therefore focus on how an interviewee describes his or her view* in the interaction of an interview.

'Dave' and the Category-bound Construction of an Offender

Dave is a German minor charged with sex offences. At the beginning of his first interview, he explains how he was left in a foster home only a few months after his birth. In the following years, he always lived in social welfare institutions away from his family. Like the majority of our interviewees (Dollinger, Fröschle, Gilde, & Vietig, 2016), he relates the story of a life that has had numerous problems and is a far cry from a 'normal' childhood. Dave's story is a 'sad story' (Goffman, 1991), in which one negative event follows from another. At the time of his first interview, Dave was staying at an educational social welfare institution. There he was awaiting his trial.

Between Psychiatry and Criminal Law

Once Dave has described the problems he has experienced in his life, at the beginning of the first interview, the following interaction emerges:

> I: *[…] and how did that come that it came to court? That's the way it is, with police or charges. It's important to us.*
>
> Dave: *I ended up harassing some girls-*
>
> I: *Mmm.*
>
> (..)
>
> Dave: *Erm […] girls, at my residential college. And they didn't dare tell anyone about it at first because I, erm, threatened them, and said that if they told anyone what had happened, they'd have problems.*

> *So they didn't tell anyone about it. And then (..) they gradually told on me. After that I went to a psychiatric hospital (..) (city in western Germany) (.), voluntarily, to work on things. Then (.) I was thrown out of that.*[6]

Referring to the offences in question, Dave provides a narrative that does not include any details or an explicit agent. He admits to behaviour that violates norms, but only passively refers to himself as having 'ended up harassing' ('übergriffig geworden', passive voice in the German original) 'some girls'. The term 'übergriffig' refers broadly to sexual offences but does not denote a specific kind of action or crime. Dave does not disclose to the interviewer exactly what offence(s) he has been charged with. In this way, he categorises himself as a sex offender, but only implicitly, by mentioning an activity that indicates sexual offences. This category-bound activity identifies him as a member of the category 'offender', so that the interviewer can perceive him as such.

In the main hearing in the German judicial system, it is of great importance how defendants come across (see footnote 1). For example, are they perceived as having acted particularly brutally? Or having been persuaded to commit the offence by others? Or are defendants seen as having acted out of an emergency? These assessments influence judgements. In the passage quoted above, Dave provides a passive description (as is often the case in narratives of (alleged) offenders; O'Connor, 2000, 2015). Dave does not say, 'I committed X offence', but says he 'ended up' being an offender. Accordingly, he did not act according to personal volition because of sexual desire, out of a lust for power or another reason, but rather, an unspecified course of events made him behave that way. He admits to an offence without explaining what exactly happened, why it happened and without exposing himself as an active offender. Throughout the two interviews, he presents himself as a victim of adverse circumstances in the context of a sad story. Listeners to his narratives can interpret his harassment as the result of a troubled life story. Dave is a special kind of offender, one who was driven into illegal action ('ended up') by external influences. *He is a subcategory of offender as he himself is a victim of negative circumstances.*

---

[6]We used the following transcription conventions:
(.) Pause (1 second)
(..) Pause (2 seconds)
(...) Pause (3 seconds)
(Number) (Pause in seconds)
[Text] Commentary regarding voice quality; ensuing italics indicate duration
- Abruption
[...] Omission
(Text) Omission to protect anonymity and explanation of content
((Text)) Non-verbal feature

Dave also describes agency in relation to the victims of his deeds. Dave categorises them as victims of his behaviour, and at this point, he explicitly highlights his personal agency ('because I, erm, threatened them'). Although he does not describe himself as a wilful agent in terms of the actual offence, he does relate agency by explaining how he tried to hide the offence by threatening the 'girls': he told them not to say anything about what had happened. He therefore confirms the categorical dichotomy of offender and victim and admits to wrongdoing (thus again categorising himself as an offender). However, the explicit admission of this misconduct only relates to the context of criminal prosecution. His personal conduct in terms of the alleged offence itself still remains unclear.

So far, it is evident that Dave admits to being a sex offender. Sex offences are highly stigmatised, and sex offenders face high penalties (Sack & Schlepper, 2011). However, defendants usually want to avoid imprisonment with a long prison sentence. They often present themselves in such a way that harsh sentences do not seem to make much sense or are not necessary (Komter, 1998). This interest also seems to apply to Dave, but this assumption must be reconstructed empirically. For this purpose it is helpful to analyse the *categories of places* in the interview passage quoted above (for categorisations of places, Dollinger & Fröschle, 2017; Lepper, 2000, pp. 25–29). Dave refers to two places at which he spent time: the 'residential college' and the 'psychiatric hospital'. The residential college is where the offences were committed. Residential colleges are not just places where children and/or adolescents go to school, they are also places where they live. The residential college therefore indicates a biographical continuity in Dave's life, following from his stays in foster homes and at other places away from his family. The residential college furthermore reveals that Dave was attending school when he committed his offences. Despite living away from home, in this respect, he seems to have been a 'normal' adolescent who went to school regularly.

The second place, the psychiatric hospital, is different: it does not suggest (relative) normality, but rather the provision of special treatment because of mental health problems. By referring to his time at the psychiatric hospital, Dave categorises himself as abnormal and in need of treatment. Here, he describes his personal behaviour once again, explaining how he went to the psychiatric hospital 'voluntarily'. It remains unclear as to why exactly he did that; a possible mental illness is only vaguely alluded to, with his description of going there 'to work on things'. In terms of his narrative self-presentation, however, he categorises himself as a person who recognises his own problems and is prepared to work on them and take responsibility.

Punishment seems unnecessary because Dave himself wants to be a better person. He categorises himself as a sex offender, but as one who acknowledges his mistakes and appears hardly 'punishable'. A sex offender could be categorised as a serious criminal who, out of sexual desire, injures others and who has to be 'locked away' for a long time. Dave implicitly rejects such a categorisation, which would be highly disadvantageous for him, by presenting himself in the way described as insightful and ready to work on himself. The readiness, 'to work on things', fits little into the category of a serious offender, but rather indicates characteristics of an offender who is capable of and willing to become a better person.

In the further course of the first interview, Dave reinforces this impression of an offender who is not 'worthy of punishment'. He categorises himself as an adolescent with problems who is aware that he needs to change, but he does not primarily categorise himself as a serious offender. Despite this self-categorisation, Dave could not avoid facing the criminal justice system. His actual trial was imminent at the time of the first interview. The following passage illustrates how he assessed his trial and the criminal dimension of his behaviour.

> Dave: *And now I've been charged, but I'm a first-time offender. So my solicitor told me (..): 'Don't worry, we'll just take things as they come.' ((clears throat)) That's the way it is (.), I'll come away with a suspended sentence.*

This passage contains an assessment, which Dave makes regarding the criminal dimension of his case. Corroborated by a direct reported speech by his solicitor (see Griswold, 2016), he categorises himself here as a 'first-time offender', i.e. he again belongs to a special subcategory of offenders. According to this subcategory, he had not committed any other crimes before the sexual harassment. Membership in this subcategory is, according to the solicitor's expertise, no reason to be concerned. Dave (or the lawyer in Dave's story) associates the subcategory 'first-time offender' with the quality of being unproblematic, as they will 'just take things as they come' ('kochen wir alles auf niedriger Flamme', German idiom that metaphorically refers to something that can be dealt with largely unproblematically). 'Persistent offenders' have been widely discussed in recent years as a key problem and became the target of tough criminal penalties both in Germany and elsewhere (Clear & Frost, 2015; Hofinger, 2015; Reiner, 2007). In contrast, a 'first-time offender' belongs to a subcategory of delinquents who seem to warrant diversion or, at the most, only lenient punishment. Therefore, Dave's case appears unspectacular. He belongs to the subcategory 'first-time offender' who has no particular need for punishment.

Between Social Work and Criminal Law

If one summarises the previous analyses, it is clear that Dave has relativised the (alleged) offences in terms of criminal law, which he has countered by categorising himself as a largely unspectacular offender. He avoids making his own role in the commission of the sexual offence in question transparent, although he demonstrates that he is willing to work on himself and to improve. But there is a problem: As he describes in an interview passage quoted above, he was 'thrown out of' the psychiatric hospital. He does not say why this happened, but the problem remains that during the first interview he finds himself in a situation where a harsh verdict is imminent and he could be categorised as a serious criminal by the judge. Being thrown out of a supportive institution does not provide a credible story to contrast the category 'serious offender'. Even for a 'first-time offender' it is a serious matter to be effectively expelled from psychiatry and charged with sexual offences.

Another passage from the first interview can show how Dave categorises himself in this situation and how this self-categorisation relates to the threat of punishment. During the first interview, he is staying at a welfare institution, which is firstly home to young people with a special need for socio-educational support. Secondly, the institution is home to adolescents who are also in need of socio-educational support, but also on the basis that this support will serve to prevent them from being imprisoned on remand while awaiting trial. Dave makes a clear distinction between the two groups:

> Dave: *I'm in the 'SGB eighter' section. Everything is pretty nice.*
>
> I: *What do you mean by the 'SGB eighter' section?*
>
> Dave: *Well there's a partition wall, a partition door to the stairway.*
>
> I: *A partition door that separates you from whom?*
>
> Dave: *The others here.*
>
> I: *The other–*
>
> Dave: *Well we kind of have our own apartment.*
>
> I: *The others are the, erm–*
>
> Dave: *R-inmates.*

Adolescents in need of help but without a criminal background are accommodated in the facility on the basis of volume VIII of the German Social Code (SGB), which Dave refers to as the 'SGB-eighters'. Dave describes the other adolescents who are avoiding imprisonment on remand as the 'R-inmates'. He separates the two groups into 'sections' by a symbolically relevant dividing line.

Dave identifies himself as being among the adolescents with a need for socio-educational support. He is a member of the 'SGB-eighter' category, which he evaluates positively because 'everything is pretty nice'. When asked by the interviewer what it means to be in such an 'SGB-eighter section', Dave again does not provide a detailed description, but first refers to the spatial differentiation in the institution between the 'SGB-eighters' and the other adolescents who have a criminal background. Only then does his further qualification follow, that he has his 'own apartment', which the other youths do not appear to have. He is therefore an adolescent who has it 'nice', who has his 'own apartment' and is different from the offenders. He is a relatively 'normal' adolescent who belongs to a group he refers to as 'we' that has privileges, making the group different from the one categorised as (more) criminal.

Since the institution assigns him to the 'normal' group, Dave implicitly states that the professionals working in the institution categorise him as a 'normal youth'. Dave communicates an external categorisation of himself by the professionals working in the institution, and this implicit categorisation supports his assumption that he is not a serious offender. There seem to be good institutional reasons for considering him to be largely normal. Such institutional and professional action is usually deemed 'reasonable' (Scott & Lyman, 1968, p. 55) and can make a favourable impression on a judge. If the judge would severely punish Dave by categorising him as 'serious offender', he would have to argue against Dave's self-categorisation as 'normal youth' and the – according to Dave – identical categorisation of Dave by professionals.

The Verdict and Its Consequences

The court sentenced Dave to a few weeks of juvenile detention, which he for all intents and purposes interprets as an 'acquittal'. He describes the verdict in the second interview in the following way:

> Dave: *It's pretty good really. I mean, after the (.) detention, it'll all be over.*
>
> I: *Uh-huh.*
>
> Dave: *That means NO (.) no more thoughts of prison in the back of my mind. ((voices in the background)) (.) And then I'll actually just- and then I'll actually be a normal adolescent again, just with youth welfare status, and nothing else.*

The penalties for sexual offences, in Germany as elsewhere, can be severe. Dave does not receive a harsh punishment, however, and is only sentenced to a relatively short period of juvenile detention, which according to the legal situation in Germany is not considered imprisonment, and in official terms, is not even a criminal penalty (Section 13 of the German Youth Courts Act). Dave explains that the risk of imprisonment had been 'in the back of his mind', so from his point of view, it was unclear whether he might have been categorised as a serious offender by the court after all, and given a tough sentence. He finds the verdict 'pretty good'. *It solves the decisive categorisation conflict in his favour*: the conflict between *a serious offender* responsible for a particularly stigmatised act, or as a *(more or less) normal adolescent*. The question of whether Dave is a case for psychiatric help or social work does not play any role here; the fact that Dave admits to crime as a 'first-time offender' is not relevant here either. The primary conflict is between prison, i.e. categorisation as a serious offender, and youth welfare status, i.e. a socio-educational categorisation which indicates from Dave's point of view, by and large, a normal adolescent.

According to Dave, the verdict resolves this conflict: he will only spend a brief period in juvenile detention, before 'it'll all be over'. The fact that he will be cared for by the youth welfare services after his detention is something he portrays as an attribution of normality ('a normal adolescent'). Accordingly, he is not a serious offender or a person worthy of condemnation, but a normal adolescent who has problems that can be handled by social work. The attributed need for support from the youth welfare service could potentially also be interpreted as an abnormality. Yet, this potential meaning does not matter to Dave because from his perspective, 'youth welfare status' is simply ('actually just' or 'actually [...] again') associated with the characteristic of being a normal adolescent. Normality and youth welfare status do not contradict each other, but belong together, and they can even be associated with privileges ('own apartment', see above).

Dave is aware of the risk he faced of being categorised as a sex offender and of going to prison for a long time. In the second interview, he explains that many people had expressed their support for a tough penalty. Dave states that even some of the social workers at the socio-educational institution in which he was living at the time of the interviews were disappointed with the leniency of the verdict. He also says the following:

> Dave: *I mean, you know, the parents of the victims, (.) they would definitely have preferred me to get ten years, or to see me locked up forever.*
>
> I: *OK.*
>
> (5)
>
> Dave: *Yes. But I'm really glad that I came away with a, well, with a black eye.*
>
> I: *OK.*
>
> Dave: *And that I was really lucky.*

The desire that someone should be severely punished categorises this person as a serious offender. According to Dave, parents thought he should be punished severely. Although a certain punishment was imposed on him, Dave, however, does not consider it to be serious, as expressed by his description of coming away 'with a black eye'. The contrast between the wish expressed by the parents of the victims on the one hand to see him locked up 'forever', and his coming away 'with a black eye' on the other, could hardly be greater. In this context, the relatively long 5-second break is telling (Jefferson, 1989). Dave does not directly speak after the interviewer's brief remark ('OK'). Through the resulting silence, the parents' desire for hard punishment is in the air and gains special weight. During this pause, the option of harsh punishment remains unchallenged. Only after the unusually long conversational pause does Dave continue by describing himself as someone, who came away from his trial very well indeed. Things could have been different, and Dave appears to be very pleased with the outcome of the trial. He implicitly conveys that he is aware of the seriousness of his crime. He is someone who was 'really lucky', i.e. with less luck he would have been harshly punished. Dave does not say here that as a largely normal youth he was given a fair and mild sentence, but that he only got away with a 'black eye'. Such a 'black eye' would also fit to a serious offender, who deserved a hard punishment, but was lucky to escape it. Dave's categorisation as a 'normal youth' was therefore uncertain. Also from his point of view the 'serious offender' was a threateningly realistic categorisation for him. It was only with the judgement that it was averted.

In fact, Dave's self-categorisation as a (largely) normal youth was always profoundly precarious. Given that sexual offences are highly stigmatised, it would be impossible for a sex offender to describe himself simply as being normal. A person must be authorised to make such an imputation (Sacks, 1984). The commission of sexual offences – to which Dave admits – is the opposite of a 'normal' activity, whether in terms of common sense or criminal law. The demand for harsh punishment by the victims' parents makes this very clear. A youth who admits to serious offences but nonetheless categorises himself as being a 'normal youth' would run the risk of being considered a defiant offender who is worthy of particular condemnation (Dollinger & Fröschle, 2017). In this case, however, the judge reiterates Dave's account, and such affirmations by institutional authority figures are of key importance to lending credibility to stories (Scott & Lyman, 1968). Dave's narrative, which was given in the first interview, is therefore supported: he *is* a normal young person with certain problems, but he is not a serious offender.

In the second interview, Dave uses the ruling issued by the judge as a source of confirmation to finally reject the category of a serious offender. He portrays himself as a person who is determined to develop on a positive basis in the future:

> I: *Do you feel that the verdict benefits you in any way?*
>
> (.)
>
> Dave: *Yes. (.) I can start all over again now and do better things, (.) instead of being worried about something like that.*

Dave dismisses the risk of harsh punishment as 'something like that'; it appears to be a source of annoyance from the past, which contrasts with his intention of starting 'all over again now'. Dave recounts himself as being a young person with a high degree of motivation and the intention to do 'better things' than before. In this respect, the judicial verdict seems to have been correct because Dave attests to the personal characteristics of wanting to behave well and to move forward. He has the characteristics to be motivated and to want to lead a better life. He is a normal youth with normal desires. The judge was right and the precarious categorisation conflict between 'normal youth' and 'serious offender' is solved.

Re-storying, Categorisation and Narrative Criminology

We do not know whether Dave 'actually' returned to criminal offending after the verdict – or whether he ever 'really' committed an offence. In our view, this is irrelevant to our study and perhaps a question like this is even of subordinate importance to narrative criminology. If Dave were to become suspected of further crimes, revised stories would emerge about him. In this process of re-storying, Dave would be categorised as a recidivist, and his earlier accounts would take on a new meaning. The earlier verdict would probably appear to be a mistake, as 'too soft'. His life story would become the life story of a long-term criminal, while his insistence on normality would be understood as a mere 'chess move', which he made in order to receive as lenient a verdict as possible, while 'in reality' he had been predisposed to a sustained pattern of criminal behaviour. Ultimately, however, this would be nothing more than a particular narrative about Dave.

Stories are often reworked; they are an achievement in which many people are involved. Narratives take place on an interactive basis and are embedded in particular contexts, and the contexts themselves are shaped by the narratives (Mandelbaum, 2014). Narratives change and gradually become stabilised during the various stages of a criminal investigation and trial. The analysis of categorisations makes it possible for narrative criminology to trace these often subtle processes. It becomes apparent that different categories compete to determine the truth about a defendant. It is particularly important for narrative criminology in this context to bracket a (possibly) extranarrative reality. Narrative criminologists should not presuppose that a particular version of a story is right or wrong. Rather, in order to fathom the processing of crime narratives it is highly insightful to reconstruct in detail how reality claims related to crime are substantiated and interactively stabilised (von Arnauld & Martini, 2015; Atkinson & Drew, 1979; Komter, 1998; O'Connor, 2000). MCA makes an important contribution here in establishing that crime stories are told by using categories and subcategories of offenders, victims and others involved in a crime case. These categories can be varied during a conversation or interview; they can contradict each other and they often remain vague (Komter, 1998; Sandberg, 2016). Nevertheless, categorisations fulfil important communicative functions by providing information about who a person 'really' is and what 'really' happened when crime (or a candidate event which may become 'crime' in a conversation) is discussed. As our case study shows, narratives always vary with their communicative context and they constitute the truth about crime through often inconspicuous forms and contents of categorisations. Narrative criminology can benefit from exploring the respective subtle communicative processes in detail.[7]

As a final point, we would like to stress that the constitution of a crime reality often takes place *in the competition of different narratives*. Although the final decision on a case is left to a judge (or a jury or a public prosecutor), there are

---

[7]This exploration can also be done by associating MCA with conversation analysis, as is often demanded (Stokoe, 2012).

often – as in Dave's case – witnesses, experts, the police, a public prosecutor, socio-educational institutions, victims, victims' parents, the defendants' lawyers and parents, etc. The many different participants each have their own interests and personal perspectives. The truthfulness of narratives and offender categorisations is negotiated in this polyphony (Emerson, 1969; Komter, 1998). In the context of criminal justice, individual narratives are embedded in power asymmetries in which the person in the centre – a potential 'offender' – can only partially determine how he or she is perceived. From our perspective, an important task of narrative criminology is to reconstruct very precisely and in detail how people deal with this situation, how they are treated institutionally and how they are ultimately identified as a particular person who deserves (or does not deserve) punishment.

References

von Arnauld, A., & Martini, S. (2015). Unreliable narration in law courts. In V. Nünning (Ed.), *Unreliable narration and trustworthiness* (pp. 347–370). Berlin: Walter de Gruyter.

Ask, S. (2018). 'She had it coming?': An experimental study of text interpretation in a police classroom setting. *Nordic Journal of Linguistics*, *41*(2), 133–153.

Atkinson, J. M., & Drew, P. (1979). *Order in court: The organisation of verbal interaction in judicial settings*. London: Macmillan Publishers.

Atkinson, P., & Delamont, S. (2006). Rescuing narrative from qualitative research. *Narrative Inquiry*, *16*(1), 164–172.

Benwell, B., & Stokoe, E. (2006). *Discourse and identity*. Edinburgh: Edinburgh University Press.

Clear, T. R., & Frost, N. (2015). *The punishment imperative*. New York, NY: New York University Press.

Dollinger, B. (2020). *Changing narratives of youth crime: From social causes to threats to the social*. London: Routledge.

Dollinger, B., & Fröschle, T. (2017). Me and my custodial sentence: A case study on categorization work of young defendants. *Narrative Inquiry*, *27*(1), 66–84.

Dollinger, B., Fröschle, T., Gilde, L., & Vietig, J. (2016). Junge Menschen vor Gericht: Fallstudien zum subjektiven Erleben von Verhandlungen durch das Jugendgericht. *Monatsschrift für Kriminologie und Strafrechtsreform*, *99*(5), 325–341.

Dünkel, F., Grzywa, J., Pruin, I., & Šelih, A. (2010). Juvenile justice in Europe. In F. Dünkel, J. Grzywa, P. Horsfield, & I. Pruin (Eds.), *Juvenile justice systems in Europe* (*Vol. 4*, pp. 1813–1870). Mönchengladbach: Forum Verlag Godesberg.

Eglin, P., & Francis, D. (2016). Editors' introduction. In S. Hester, *Descriptions of deviance* (pp. 6–9). University of Southern Denmark. Retrieved from http://emca-legacy.info/files/Descriptions_of_Deviance.pdf. Accessed on July 2, 2017.

Eglin, P., & Hester, S. (1992). Category, predicate and task: The pragmatics of practical action. *Semiotica*, *88*(3/4), 243–268.

Emerson, R. M. (1969). *Judging delinquents*. Chicago, IL: Aldine Transaction.

Francis, D., & Hester, S. (2004). *An invitation to ethnomethodology*. London, Thousand Oaks, CA, New Delhi: SAGE Publications.

Garfinkel, H. (1967). *Studies in ethnomethodology*. Cambridge: Polity Press.
Garfinkel, H., & Sacks, H. (1970). On formal structures of practical action. In J. C. McKinney & E. A. Tiryakian (Eds.), *Theoretical sociology* (pp. 337–366). New York, NY: Appleton-Century-Crofts.
Gavin, H. (2005). The social construction of the child sex offender explored by narrative. *Qualitative Report, 10*(3), 395–415.
Goffman, E. (1991). *Asylums*. London: Penguin Books.
Griswold, O. (2016). Center stage: Direct and indirect reported speech in conversational storytelling. *Issues in Applied Linguistics, 20*(1), 73–89.
Gubrium, J. F., & Holstein, J. A. (2009). *Analyzing narrative reality*. London: SAGE Publications.
Hall, C., & Matarese, M. (2014). Narrative. In C. Hall, K. Juhila, M. Matarese, & C. van Nijnatten (Eds.), *Analysing social work communication* (pp. 79–97). London: Routledge.
Hall, C., Slembrouck, S., & Sarangi, S. (2006). *Language practices in social work*. London: Routledge.
Halsey, M. (2017). Narrative criminology. In A. Deckert & R. Sarre (Eds.), *The Palgrave handbook of Australian and New Zealand criminology, crime and justice* (pp. 633–647). Cham: Palgrave Macmillan.
Heinz, W. (2017). *Kriminalität und Kriminalitätskontrolle in Deutschland – Berichtsstand 2015*; Version 1/2017. Retrieved from http://www.unikonstanz.de/rtf/kis/Kriminalitaet_und_Kriminalitaetskontrolle_in_Deutschland_Stand_2015.pdf. Accessed on May 17, 2019.
Hester, S., & Eglin, P. (2017). *A sociology of crime* (2nd ed.). Abingdon: Routledge.
Hofinger, V. (2015). *Die Konstruktion des Rückfalltäters*. Weinheim: Beltz Juventa.
Housley, W., & Fitzgerald, R. (2015). Introduction to membership categorisation analysis. In R. Fitzgerald & W. Housley (Eds.), *Advances in membership categorisation analysis* (pp. 1–22). London: SAGE Publications.
Jayyusi, L. (1984). *Categorization and the moral order*. Boston, MA: Routledge.
Jefferson, G. (1989). Preliminary notes on a possible metric which provides for a 'standard maximum' silence of approximately one second in conversation. In D. Roger & P. Bull (Eds.), *Conversation: An interdisciplinary perspective* (pp. 166–196). Clevedon: Multilingual Matters Ltd.
Komter, M. (1998). *Dilemmas in the courtroom*. London: Routledge.
Komter, M. (2012). The career of a suspect's statement. *Discourse Studies, 14*(6), 731–752.
Laubenthal, K., Baier, H., & Nestler, N. (2015). *Jugendstrafrecht*. Berlin: Springer.
Lepper, G. (2000). *Categories in text and talk*. London: SAGE Publications.
Loseke, D. R. (2003). *Thinking about social problems* (2nd ed.). New York, NY: Aldine Transaction.
Mandelbaum, J. (2014). Storytelling in conversation. In J. Sidnell & T. Stivers (Eds.), *The handbook of conversation analysis* (pp. 492–507). Chichester: Wiley-Blackwell.
O'Connor, P. E. (2000). *Narratives of prisoners*. Lincoln, NE: University of Nebraska Press.
O'Connor, P. E. (2015). Telling moments: Narrative hot spots in accounts of criminal acts. In L. Presser & S. Sandberg (Eds.), *Narrative criminology* (pp. 174–203). New York, NY: New York University Press.

Polletta, F., Chen, P. C. B., Gardner, B., & Motes, A. (2011). The sociology of storytelling. *Annual Review of Sociology, 37*, 109–130.

Presser, L. (2004). Violent offenders, moral selves: Constructing identities and accounts in the research interview. *Social Problems, 51*(1), 82–101.

Presser, L. (2009). The narratives of offenders. *Theoretical Criminology, 13*(2), 177–200.

Presser, L. (2016). Criminology and the narrative turn. *Crime, Media, Culture, 12*(2), 137–151.

Presser, L., & Sandberg, S. (Eds.). (2015). *Narrative criminology.* New York, NY: New York University Press.

Rapley, T. (2012). Order, order: A 'modest' response to Stokoe. *Discourse Studies, 14*(3), 321–328.

Reiner, R. (2007). *Law and order.* Oxford: Polity Press.

Sack, F., & Schlepper, C. (2011). Das Sexualstrafrecht als Motor der Kriminalpolitik. *Kriminologisches Journal, 43*, 247–268.

Sacks, H. (1984). On doing "being ordinary". In J. M. Atkinson & J. Heritage (Eds.), *Structures of social action* (pp. 413–429). Cambridge: Cambridge University Press.

Sacks, H. (1995). *Lectures on conversation (Vols. 1 and 2).* Oxford: Blackwell.

Sandberg, S. (2016). The importance of stories untold. *Crime, Media, Culture, 12*(2), 153–171.

Scheppele, K. L. (1994). Practices of truth-finding in a court of law: The case of revised stories. In T. R. Sarbin & J. I. Kitsuse (Eds.), *Constructing the social* (pp. 84–100). London: SAGE Publications.

Scott, M. B., & Lyman, S. M. (1968). Accounts. *American Sociological Review, 33*(1), 46–62.

Silverman, D. (1998). *Harvey Sacks. Social science and conversation analysis.* Cambridge: Oxford University Press.

Stokoe, E. (2012). Moving forward with membership categorization analysis: Methods for systematic analysis. *Discourse Studies, 14*(3), 277–303.

Tabbert, U. (2015). *Crime and corpus.* Amsterdam: John Benjamins Publishing Company.

Victor, J., & Waldram, J. B. (2015). Moral habilitation and the new normal: Sexual offender narratives of posttreatment community integration. In L. Presser & S. Sandberg (Eds.), *Narrative criminology* (pp. 96–121). New York, NY: New York University Press.

Waldram, J. B. (2007). Everybody has a story: Listening to imprisoned sexual offenders. *Qualitative Health Research, 17*(7), 963–970.

Waldram, J. B. (2009). "It's just you and Satan, hanging out at a pre-school": Notions of evil and the rehabilitation of sexual offenders. *Anthropology and Humanism, 34*(2), 219–234.

Watson, D. R. (1976). Some conceptual issues in the social identification of victims and offenders. In E. C. Viano (Ed.), *Victims and society* (pp. 60–71). Washington, DC: Visage Press.

Watson, R. (1997). The presentation of victim and motive in discourse: The case of police interrogations and interviews. In M. Travers & J. F. Manzo (Eds.), *Law in action* (pp. 77–97). Aldershot: Ashgate Publishing.

Watson, R. (2015). Re-reifying categories. In R. Fitzgerald & W. Housley (Eds.), *Advances in membership categorisation analysis* (pp. 23–49). London: SAGE Publications.

Chapter 16

Police Narratives as Allegories that Shape Police Culture and Behaviour

Don L. Kurtz and Alayna Colburn

The Narratives of Police Culture

The American criminal justice system, at its core, is a collection of stories, and much of our societal understanding of crime, criminal justice and policing is grounded in the narratives of workers or those found in popular culture. Narrative analysis, as a growing approach to understanding human behaviour, has expanded in the last two decades. This method is now firmly entrenched in a number of fields including anthropology, psychology and criminology (Briggs, 1996; Garro & Mattingly, 2000; Gubrium & Holstein, 2009; Reissman, 2008; Presser, 2009, 2010). The vast majority of narrative criminology research is applied to understanding criminal behaviour and/or desistance from criminal offending (Maruna, 2001; Stevens, 2012; Youngs & Canter, 2012). Others explore media accounts of criminal identity or situational constructions of crime narratives (Linnemann, 2010; Peelo, 2006; Peelo & Soothill, 2000). A limited subset of narrative criminology has focused on state actors in the criminal justice system and how narrative processes shape their identity, behaviours and serve as a source of legitimation (Katz, 2016; Kurtz & Upton, 2017a; Kurtz & Upton, 2017b; Ugelvik, 2016).

Ian Loader argues that policing is an important way society tells stories about itself (Loader, 1997). This chapter extols the value of applying narrative criminology as a framework for analysing police culture and for understanding police storytelling and shared narratives as an essential element of the identity-making and behavioural process found among those employed in law enforcement. Through a narrative analysis, we argue researchers can illuminate important facets of how police stories, popular cultural narratives of law enforcement and organizational oral histories shape ideological frames, fortify police culture and influence police decision-making and behaviour (Fielding, 1994; van Hulst, 2013). Specifically, we argue that narrative methods – applied to law enforcement – are potentially transformative to our understating of police culture and offers particular value in clarifying the transition from shared perceptions and values to the specific actions and behaviours of officers. For example, this approach provides a unique lens for understanding perspectives held by officers involved in the shootings of unarmed suspects. 'I'd rather be judged by 12 than carried by 6' is a popular mantra in police circles, and while it is generally offered as simple quip, it reflects deep narratives of perceived risk, management of threats and clearly contends that officers should take certain, even deadly, actions when facing ambiguous but threatening situations. This is just one unsophisticated example that illustrates how shared narratives in law enforcement may translate from police culture into decision-making and officer behavioural choices.

Prior research establishes that 'informal ideologies' structure police culture and influence the working environment and climate of police organizations (Loftus, 2008). Furthermore, Ugelvik (2016) argues that narratives allow actors in the criminal justice system to construct 'techniques of legitimation' and 'backstage self-legitimation work may be important for government representatives in general' (p. 229). Ugelvik's observation of narratives among detention workers showed how these stories allowed offers to attach responsibility to offenders, developed cautionary tales to structure action and construct shared ideas about professionalism.

We argue that police narratives likely play a significant role in the production of contemporary police culture and that theoretical and methodological exploration of police narratives and storytelling are an important connective tissue to existing literature on law enforcement culture and officer behaviour. Thus, police stories are an essential part of the 'meaning-making structure' in policing and often convey particular power well beyond the limitations of enacted organizational or agency policies and help officers believe their actions as legitimate (Ugelvik, 2016).

Police narratives and stories also offer some unique methodological challenges for narrative scholars as analysis of police stories must focus on the underlying plot details while still analysing the themes or metaphors provided by the narrative. This may require specific attention to the role stories play in police culture, training and development of organizational cohesion beyond surface elements or presented details. Furthermore, narrative researchers must explore the shared narratives distinct to the profession, while still examining divergent meanings that stories convey to different departments and even specialized units within a department. By examining police narratives, we propose that scholars can gain considerable insight into the production and maintenance of police authority. We believe that police culture is primarily accomplished through shared narratives and that law enforcement offers an innovative research population for narrative criminology.

This chapter offers several arguments for expanding the application of narrative theory and methods to law enforcement and possibly other criminal justice professions. In this chapter, we will contemplate the importance of police storytelling and narratives through four interrelated applications of narrative criminology: (1) by examining the role of storytelling as an important cultural production in policing, (2) by assessing the potential theoretical role of popular culture stories and images of law enforcement officers as a source that may structure police narratives and self-image, (3) the role of police organizational and officer narratives in defining social problems and community decay as arbiters of 'truth' that shapes conceptions of police legitimacy and (4) an examination of unique methodological applications and challenges of employing narrative methods to studying law enforcement.

Narrative Development and Storytelling in Police Culture

Perhaps no other profession in criminal justice, or even American society, is more appropriate for a detailed narrative analysis than policing, and narrative criminology provides an important theoretical connection to existing literature on police culture. Previous scholars (Campeau, 2015; Reiner, 1985; Skolnick, 1966) examined the concept of police culture as a guiding force for the individual behaviours and decision-making of officers – even arguing that deviance and undesirable actions of individual officers is best understood as reflective of the negative aspects of this shared police culture. In other words, scholars like Skolnick rejected the 'bad apple' hypothesis favouring a belief in a strong connection between negative individual behaviour of officers and a shared professional culture widely observed in policing. Other researchers expanded police culture and identified specific characteristics that included views of officers as hyper-masculine, action focused, politically and socially conservative, socially isolated, cynical and marked by extreme loyalty among officers (Campeau, 2015; Reiner, 1985). Loftus (2008) notes that even amidst changing social structures towards greater equality in policing and beyond, law enforcement culture remains male dominated, white and heterocentric. Furthermore, Loftus (2008) argues that police culture displays signs of developing resentment towards efforts to change this prevailing culture through organizational recruitment of women and other efforts to diversify the profession. We contend that narrative criminological theory and methods offer a meaningful approach to understanding the informal mechanisms found in police culture and police narratives represent a mostly uncultivated area of police research.

While little attention has focused on unique narratives in law enforcement, some research previously investigated the concept of police storytelling as a crucial element of police culture and training (Fletcher, 1996; Ford, 2003; van Hulst, 2013; Schaefer & Tewksbury, 2018; Waddington, 1999). For example, Fletcher (1996) posits that storytelling serves an important role in police organizations and that the sharing of stories may continue training from police academies, promote organizational unity, empower police cultural values and/or provide acceptable venues to manage work stressors. Fletcher further argues that police organizations likely benefit from many of the functions of storytelling, and she envisions organizational stories as an integral part of police culture. Conversely, in some cases storytelling may undesirably shape organizational behaviours in ways that potentially challenge or outright reject formal policy or established organizational policy practices. In these instances, the storytelling process likely reproduces many negative aspects of police culture, including gender inequality and contentious police–community relations. Merlijn van Hulst

(2013, p. 636) argues that storytelling is powerful for understanding the informal mechanisms of police culture, and the evaluation of stories should focus on their content, setting and purpose, among other aspects of analysis.

Several scholars suggest that police storytelling is an essential, but unofficial, feature of police training and the informal activity of retelling stories imparts professional knowledge to new officers including specific tactics needed for professional practice (Ford, 2003; van Hulst, 2013; Shearing & Ericson, 1991). Shearing and Ericson (1991, p. 487) argue that storytelling is an essential part of how officers learnt the 'craft' of policing and direct the development of decision-making skills because stories allow officers to advance guiding principles for action rather than reduce the job to simplistic practices. In this process, stories become parables that shape beliefs, values and decision-making. Others contend that storytelling presents a distraction from the often mundane aspect of day-to-day police work and the multitude of stories may allow officers to construct professional identities more aligned with popular culture representations of police work as dangerous or exciting (van Hulst, 2013). Rantatalo and Karp (2018) argue that stories often focus on the rare, extreme and the usual.

The idea of police parables corresponds seamlessly with narrative criminology and supports the value of this type of analysis to police culture. Parables are narratives established to teach a greater truth or to promote a higher moral principle and certainly fits with narrative analysis. Consequently, parables provide a broader meaning and often include stories passed intergenerationally through a shared community. As a community, law enforcement appears to have a number of unique examples of these narrative devices and viewing police storytelling as parables, not factual accounts, further highlights the importance of how narratives transmit values, shape beliefs and inform police decision-making. These stories then allow new officers to assimilate to police culture and acquire expected commonsense knowledge not available in official training or codified in organizational policy manuals (Fletcher, 1996; Ford, 2003; McNulty, 1994; Rantatalo & Karp, 2017; Shearing & Ericson, 1991).

While police parables and other storytelling may serve many important functions, such as organizational cohesion, they also bound police culture in a way that effectively 'shuts out outsiders' (Fletcher, 1996, p. 41). Fletcher (1996, p. 40) offers the conception of the 'core story' as an ideal example of police folklore – a clear illustration of how police values and behaviours are reinforced by such parables. Fletcher's (1996) oral history of the '250-pound man in the alley' indicates that women were specifically questioned about how they would react if they found themselves cornered in an alley by a violent perpetrator with limited protection or ability to call for backup. This parable apparently only applies to women, and of the 106 women Fletcher interviewed only 5 had not faced the story. The main issue with such a narrative concerns the extreme focus on the vulnerable female officer without any consideration to how anyone, man or woman, would fare against a large adversary with no real means of protecting themselves. Fletcher contends that the 'core story' provides a specific example of how gendered arraignments of policing are, in part, the result of parables that paint the profession as only appropriate for men. The core story further fits with a number of masculinised stories that highlight the potential for physical violence as the defining characteristic of good policing.

The many adaptations of the core story serve to reject suitability of women for law enforcement because these narratives construct masculine heroes and envision women officers primarily as victims or observers of these heroics. The core story parallels with research on the importance of storytelling for the transition of police values and behaviours because stories and organizational narratives help maintain power structures by reifying certain behaviours and beliefs as 'real' practices in law enforcement (Humphreys & Brown, 2002). Certain stories also likely prevent organization change because they restrict the range of shared organizational values and actions (Murgia & Poggio, 2009). Näslund and Pemer (2012, p. 91) argue that 'dominate stories exercise power by fixing meaning… giving words and concepts a certain, local meaning, which restricts the storytelling possibilities in that organization'. However, Näslund and Pemer note that dominate stories are not unchangeable and entail an 'ongoing process whereby meaning attributed to past and present organizational events is defined and redefined' (p. 90).

One area of police storytelling that garnered more attention is the so-called 'war stories', and similar to other narrative processes in policing, the function of war stories remains debatable. Some explanations for the purpose of war stories include the development of the police working personality (Ford, 2003), to reinforce policing as solely a masculine occupation (Fletcher, 1996), and to familiarize officers with the communities they serve (van Hulst, 2013, p. 13). Some research focuses on the embellished nature of war stories and notes that war stories frequently use dark humour to remove negative emotional responses (Fletcher, 1996; Ford, 2003; Kurtz, 2006; Kurtz & Upton, 2017b; Van Maanen, 1972). Ford (2003, p. 3) describes war stories as 'a recounting of idealized events, entertaining humour, or police-related social commentary. They carry a message celebrating police values or techniques…War stories deal with the heroic, the extreme, and the cynically humorous'. Van Maanen (1972) argues that war stories may more effectively capture the attention of new recruits than many elements of standard police trainings, suggesting they offer an officer-to-officer training tool.

Previous research has examined the role of war stories, jokes and legends as a means for cultural transmission in policing (Ford, 2003; McNulty, 1994). Additionally, some training places a particular emphasis on the heroic police archetype with a 'warrior heart', and this ideal was consistently restated throughout police training as an important narrative (Conti, 2011). Staff would frequently discuss the type of heart needed for police work while also talking about the solidary that exists among officers as they run towards danger. Recruits in this study were also encouraged to shed their civilian characteristics throughout academy training in favour of gaining the characteristics of the idealized cop (Conti, 2011). Some observers even posit that successful officers must abandon the book smarts associated with formal academy training in favour of informal, commonsense wisdom that comes from 'the street' (Fletcher, 1990; Hunt, 1985; Rubinstein, 1973). Rantatalo and Karp (2017) argue that stories allow those new to law enforcement to develop an insider role while also increasing knowledge shared within the police community. Fletcher (1996) stresses, however, that storytelling can support some officers while excluding others, which may be part of a larger effort to socialize officers into the practice of telling stories. Police stories often focus around the officer being in control, or being the hero of a situation and controlling the enemy thugs, dirtbags and criminals of society.

Some, albeit, limited research directly connects narrative theory to police storytelling, cultural development and officer behaviours. Kurtz and Upton (2017a) applied narrative analysis to 65 interviews with police officers from six Midwest departments of various sizes, and these authors noted that language and narrative beliefs shaped much of the ways officers viewed their profession, understood their interactions with community members and articulated the daily risk of the job. One type of narrative device – the occupying soldier account – was apparent in many of the interviews with officers. The essence of this narrative focused on the differences between officers and the communities they patrol, with particular attention on defining certain portions of town as particularly dangerous. In essence, officers believed they frequently patrol 'war zones' in an attempt to control a criminal insurrection without much trust from the general public. Furthermore, these interviews indicated officers' struggle, at times, to differentiate between the average citizen and those perceived enemy combatants. The occupying solider narrative is also linked with the growing literature of police militarization, particularly through expanded use of military language and tactics. The occupying soldier narrative fits with Ugelvik's findings that many narratives are designed to 'attribute legal or moral responsibility', and in this case, the aggressive and broken windows police techniques are necessitated by community action.

In another application of narrative criminology to police culture, Kurtz and Upton (2017b) assessed how gender represented an important element for police stories and likely structured the moral meaning behind these accounts. The research included interviews with 28 officers, and findings indicated that women were frequently viewed through a gendered lens and that various types of police storytelling played an important role for police culture. The authors indicated that flow of action stories, war stories and gender narratives each provided a unique context for understanding the construction of masculinity in policing. In particular, the authors found examples of Fletcher's core story and other gendered narratives commonly focused on the hypothetical failures of women which connected to previous application of the 'doing gender' process in policing (Chan, Doran, & Marel, 2010; Garcia, 2003; Kurtz, 2006; Morash & Haarr, 2012; Rabe-Hemp, 2008). Officers frequently and uncritically rehashed stories that construct male heroes or linked to the perceived failures of women. Many of these stories were not fully connected to factual events; however, officers freely retold stories because they 'heard of it happening'. Additionally, the authors concluded that the situational context of storytelling may represent an important aspect for understanding the culture making process because these informal settings could exclude and define gender dynamics more freely than 'flow-of-action' and other stories that occurred at work. While some scholarship exists on police storytelling, it appears narrative criminology could further expand this limited research.

Through a complex interaction, media depictions probably shape officer narratives, influence the way officers interpret their job, structure the content of war stories and direct other police behaviours and values. We therefore conclude that cultural level narratives appear to be an important and particularly interesting focal point for future application of narrative criminological to police culture.

Police Narratives Conceived from Popular Culture

Officers undoubtedly arrive to the profession of law enforcement with preconceived notions of the job. American popular culture for the last century is filled with narrative scripts and cultural tropes that surely reach those seeking employment in criminal justice, and these images of policing may even entice officers to this profession (Huey & Broll, 2015). Thus, their entrance into policing is likely influenced by popular culture images of officers before ever putting on a uniform. Popular culture representations in movies, television and even fiction and nonfiction literature create some pre-established narratives for officers, which likely influence individual officers and the broader profession. Due to the universality of these popular culture references, when one chooses to become a police officer, one is choosing to embrace at least some of these popular cultural connotations and beliefs about the job. What happens to these popular narratives when one becomes an officer? Do they disappear? Of course not, so we must conclude that some of the beliefs and depictions appearing in police narratives and through storytelling are born from pre-packaged popular culture assumptions about criminal justice in general and the specifics of policing appearing in popular culture. The role of popular culture in shaping the shared narratives of actual law enforcement officers is a potentially fertile, but not fully analysed, question for narrative scholars.

In many ways, police narratives mirror the process of offender narratives and thus the narrative process of offender identity is applicable law enforcement. Youngs and Canter's (2012) research on offender narratives applied to predicting criminal action seems applicable to the potential role of police narratives on officer actions. These authors specifically argued that within any given culture, only a few narratives exist, thus limiting the storylines and roles a person can assume. Their work connected cultural narratives and cognitive psychology by exposing processes that occur between criminal identity, emotional development and cognitive distortions. Youngs and Canter further argued that 'particular narratives operating through offence roles, act positively to drive specific criminal action patterns; that different offending styles are underpinned by different narrative processes' (p. 247). Certainly a belief that narratives shape and limit offence roles should indicate that police narratives – both in organizations and within popular culture – also sculpt and/or limit the available roles officers can assume and likely direct officer 'action patterns'. Indeed one can easily identify several police narratives and corresponding behaviour patterns (such as the rogue and frustrated officer), and scholars indicate that the state of American cop shows are reflective of a broader culture narratives consisting of racial prejudice, disappointment in the criminal justice system and general suspicion of others (Nichols-Pethick, 2012; Oliver, 1994; Rosenberg, 2016a, 2016b, 2016c).

By their obvious visibility in movies, television, video games and other media, it is not difficult to notice the cultural significance of the police (Young, 2011). Long-running police procedurals, like the Law and Order and CSI franchises as well as litany of popular movies, paint particular and highly visual pictures of daily law enforcement. As such, television often condenses and limits understandings of police work. Most reality television edits hours of footage to find the most entertaining moments to air, 'true crime' accounts of policing. For example, the television series *Cops* focusses on the most entertaining and dramatic aspects of policing. *Cops* would not be nearly as successful without offering the entertaining aspects viewers want to see: the police chase, foot pursuits of perpetrators and the apprehension that is guaranteed to follow. The show becomes much less appealing if producers chose to include footage of officers filling out the stack of paperwork or completing common service calls. As one author critically argued (Linnemann, 2017), certain television shows depict police officers as 'the good guys', seemingly regardless of their actual behaviour, chosen to hold back the ever-looming threat of murder and corruption. They are perceived as the guardians of society regardless of their shortcoming – the final protective line for humanity.

Due to this, television shows and movies have the capability of communicating to a society beliefs of right or wrong (Smolej, 2010), and portrayals of crime are essential parts of social control because they define what is condemnable in society and how deviants should be punished for their misconduct (Ericson, Baranek, & Chan, 1987). While some may discredit or ignore the significance of criminal behaviour provided by popular culture representations, doing so overlooks the 'largest public domain in which thought about crime occurs' (Paul, 2017, p. 2). Furthermore, the extreme nature of criminal behaviour depicted in popular culture likely aids in visions of nearly all police action as appropriate. Officers themselves may utilize these stories to help construct techniques of legitimation (Ugelvik, 2016). By missing the realistic portrayals of police work, including serving community needs and order maintenance, popular culture images envision 'real police work' as only associated with the violent use of force (Martin, 1999; Sherman, 1982; Whitaker, 1982).

Violence as a tool of policing is a popular theme in television and cinema with depictions of brutish officers portrayed as heroes. Yet there are co-occurring messages being fed to viewers when officers recklessly utilise violence (Anker, 2014; Braudy, 2016; Thacker, 2015). 'Police stories suggest that even in its most violent and corrupt forms – as inseparable from security, law and order – the police are never beyond redemption' (Linnemann, 2017, p. 4). Such messages of violence and coercion in television and beyond indicate that police violence is necessary, if not appropriate. The link between popular culture and actual behaviour is clear considering police violence is often viewed with impunity (Linnemann, 2017; Weber, 1946) as is the case in fictional television shows and movies, as well as in multiple police-perpetrated shootings of unarmed citizens (Tate, Jenkins, & Rich, 2018).

We argue that any application of narrative criminology must examine the contributions of broader cultural scripts and popular cultural images to understanding the production of police culture. An analysis of movie representations by Aiello (2013) found the portrayals of police as hyper-masculine 'hotshot' cops was a common character in both dramatic and comedy policing portrayals. These hotshot officers shared a number of traits including physical strength, a willingness to use violence, a flippant recklessness personality and indifference to due process and procedure in pursuit of justice among a number of other shared traits. Clearly, these characteristics mirror the ideal vision of police officers glamorized through war story sessions, and media representations may influence why and how officers tell such stories. Thus many of the storylines told in police organizations are partially built from pre-packaged social narratives and 'fictionalized knowledge' garnered from popular culture similar to the process Peelo and Soothill (2000) observed with newspaper accounts of crimes.

Narratives presented through popular cultural media may also reinforce and shape actual officer and organizational views of women in policing. The police profession exists on a masculine frontier and considered an exemplar of stereotypical gender performance (Aiello, 2013). While American crime dramas are becoming more diverse in depicting female characters in powerful positions (Heidensohn & Brown, 2012), they are still falling behind portrayals from other countries (Paul, 2017). Reality seems to mirror media as women have consistently held lesser positions in law enforcement than men. According to a 2007 survey among American police departments with over 100 sworn officers, 85% identified as male, with small departments recording even higher percentages of male officers (Bureau of Justice, 2010, p. 2). What is worse, Martin (1999) argues female officers 'may act as police officers, but the job tasks and service styles remain gendered' (p. 117). Even though there are growing pop culture displays of women in law enforcement, women still dominate in special victims units and lead cases pertaining to sex offences (Kurtz, Linnemann, & Williams, 2012; Martin & Jurik, 2007), essentially reducing women's advancement in policing back to the historically devalued position of police matron (Westmarland, 2001).

The narratives appearing in television, movies and other media then represent a particular focus ripe for narrative analysis. This analysis could explore among many topics how officers use popular culture to make sense of their job and role within the community, how popular images influence beliefs about the acceptability of violence or even excessive force and how officers articulate frustrations with the criminal justice system.

The Thin Blue Line

One can discount popular cultural narratives as works of fiction building upon the rare and extreme; however, actual police narratives are frequently born and/or reflect elements of popular culture. Consider the viewpoint of law enforcement that visually depicts the profession as 'the thin blue line', the metaphoric position as society's last line of defence from the craven and criminal underclass. The thin blue line is so strongly engrained in law enforcement and American culture that the symbol is associated with fallen officers. Interestingly, the thin blue line is born uniquely of popular culture. It was first credited to a British military standoff (thin red line) and then a poem by Nels Dickmann Anderson that used the term to reference the US Army. Later the term was linked to policing in television and as the title of a 1988 documentary. The popularity of this conception is so strongly engrained in American culture that several organizations and websites produce 'thin blue line' items, marketing products like T-shirts, wristbands, speciality blue line American flags and even gun skins. The thin blue line narrative also highlights the assumed differences between officers and citizens and further progresses an 'us versus them' mentality among officers.

The thin blue line narrative directly accentuates tensions between officers and the communities they serve and may influence how officers interpret interactions with community members. In prior work, the lead writer (Kurtz & Upton, 2017a) found several examples of the thin blue line narrative displayed via community distrust represented in officer interviews. Officers in this research discussed a belief that they were under the ever 'watchful' eyes of community members that often had ill intent. An officer described this concern by stating that 'I mean you're constantly mindful that you're being watched. If you're on a quick trip getting a cup of coffee, people are sizing you up...'. Another patrol officer discussed this concern directly related to tensions with the community and stated 'I work in a largely minority community. I think they expect the worst. They expect harassment, racial profiling'. In a clear example of the thin blue line narrative, one officer acknowledged how, over time, the differentiation between law enforcement and community members can foster this divisiveness in officers. This officer stated 'I think that it's almost an us against them, and it turns into the officers against the public, and it's really hard to straddle that line. When they get into that mentality it's sorta like every regular person who is not an officer is a criminal' (Kurtz & Upton, 2017a, 2017b). In maintaining the imagined or real distance between officers and the communities they serve, a bitterness or distrust between the two could develop in many communities, and this conflict is an integral part of the thin blue line narrative.

An additional concern with the narratives associated with 'the thin blue line' relates to the idea that death surrounds officers as they go about their daily job. Statistics suggest that as compared to other occupations, policing is not particularly dangerous (United States Department of Labor, 2016). However, it seems that civilians arrive at this occupation having already accepted the 'danger' narrative as fact, which likely shapes who they become as officers and how they perform daily tasks. This narrative pushes a limited subset of society into seeking the profession – people that are more likely to be conservative, justify physical violence and deadly force, are distrustful of the community, and generally suspicious of those outside of law enforcement. Such notions surely play a role in the recounting of situational stories shared between officers. The shared and assorted types of stories may influence officer perceptions of right and wrong, particularly in reference to decision-making and expected support of others employed in law enforcement. Depending on the situation, this support becomes more complete. In a field study of officers in a metropolitan area, Schaefer and Tewksbury (2018) found that officers would support another officer shooting a juvenile, given the juvenile in question shot at the officer first, then dropped their weapon. The authors even note one respondent said they 'could articulate all day that we feared for our life once that shot was fired. If it wasn't for our experience he would have been dead' (p. 288). Objections to the story's explanation of use of force are not voiced, and it is expected that officers will support each other regardless of the details of the situation.

Dating back to the 1950s, the prototypical police television shows and films depict officers as the stereotypical crime fighters who maintain society and civility against violent criminal offenders (Maguire, Sandage, & Weatherby, 1999), an artistic rendition of the 'thin blue line'. As one author noted, crime programming creates a responsive cycle of fear and retaliation within the viewer that first includes a sense of fear from seemingly random violent crime, followed by the narrative resolution with a sense of vengeance that may include a dead or otherwise roughed up offender (Sparks, 1992). American crime narratives engage audiences in a continuous cycle of unease, crisis, punishment and resolution (Paul, 2017). With such examples of the rogue cop Harry Callahan from the 1970s hit *Dirty Harry*, we observed a shift from the sober depictions of unsophisticated beat cops to the conservative 'tough on crime' community protectors taking back the city thought lost (King, 2013). It should not come as much of a surprise that most American crime dramas primarily focus on violent street crime (Jenner, 2016) because viewers are fascinated with the particular narratives produced by these crime dramas and the emotional reaction they can produce.

By perpetuating the 'thin blue line' narrative, officers are reinforcing the questionable level of physical risk commonly associated with their job, in addition to alienating themselves within their community by convincing themselves everyone not associated with law enforcement is a criminal. It is important to take these points into consideration in future research, as both are common within policing circles and narratives.

Police Narratives as 'Truth'

An interesting aspect of exploring police narratives is that officers are just one potential voice among many to explain many elements of society. Yet, more so than most community actors, police narratives shape our collective understandings of the nature of social problems and community decay. As an important and ever-growing institution, criminal justice in general, and law enforcement more explicitly, produces a number of cultural scripts about the purpose and legitimacy of state power and the extent and causes of various social problems. As noted by Loader, police are an important way society tells its story (1997), and therefore narrative criminology provides a remarkable interpretation of the processes that police use to describe social problems and define communities. In this case, broader police powers are situated in narratives produced by the police themselves and interconnected within various social contexts over time and place. Rantatalo and Karp (2018) note that this sense-making of occupational experience begins as early as police academy training, and as such, these narratives function to organize students' experiences in educational contexts (Clandinin & Connelly, 2000; Worth, 2008).

Whereas previous narrative scholarship examined narratives in the construction of commonsense knowledge – for example, the media studies outlined above – narrative criminology offers potential research to explain how department-level stories shape communities. While the narrative process of officers shares much with the process developed by offenders, it certainly appears that police narratives are born of unique departmental and community context and that officers' views of their community can often differ from the broader community's understanding of crime and/or social problems. Through this process, officers construct identities that may reject parts of communities they serve. Some note that 'policemen generally view themselves as performing society's dirty work. Today's patrolman often feels cut off from the mainstream culture and stigmatized unfairly' (Van Maanen, 1973b, p. 3). Others find that aggressive police practices like 'broken windows' policing are frequently perceived as abusive and unfair by community members (Green, 1999). Consequently, a gap exists between the police and the public. This difference can result in discourse often reproducing and magnifying 'us versus them' rhetoric and practices found in policing. The narratives born of police culture are unique because of the structural positioning of law enforcement within society further affixes power not assigned to the majority of other social actors within a community. Consequently, narrative approaches to understanding law enforcement could focus on the agreement and divergence between community and police officer narratives particularly related to conceptions of crime and disorder.

A recent American example of the disconnection between community narratives and those offered by law enforcement was illuminated after the flashpoint events involving the death of African American teenager Michael Brown in Ferguson, Missouri, in August 2014. Following the shooting death of Brown by a Ferguson police officer, Darren Wilson, the community responded with multiple days of civil unrest and outcries for officer Wilson's arrest. Officers on the other hand, described Ferguson as crime-ridden and violently aggressive towards law enforcement (see *Missouri* v. *Brown*). Community reports that followed the incident offered an alternative narrative – that of police hyper-aggression. Eventually, the US Department of Justice (USDOJ, 2015) conducted a comprehensive investigation of Ferguson Police Department (FPD) and findings supported community beliefs that FPD developed a culture of harassment and hyper-aggression towards many of the citizens of Ferguson. The report (USDOJ, 2015) stated that 'This culture within FPD influences officer activities in all areas of policing, beyond just ticketing...They are inclined to interpret the exercise of free-speech rights as unlawful disobedience, innocent movements as physical threats, indications of mental or physical illness as belligerence'. The example of Ferguson underscores the value of the narrative approach, as it appears that the behaviour of officers within the department was significantly shaped by police narratives about the violent and criminal nature of the Ferguson community. More interesting, citizens and officers seemly possessed alternative versions of reality based on their structural position in society; however, the power affixed to law enforcement allowed the narratives born from the FPD to dominate and suppress community viewpoints for decades. In essence, the officers had a monopoly on the 'truth' and the ability to constrict community narratives about officer aggression and abuse.

Ferguson offers another interesting example of police narratives that arise from the disconnections between community and law enforcement with the so-called 'Ferguson effect'. The Ferguson effect is the, mostly discredited, idea that increased scrutiny directed on police practices that followed the high-profile deaths of Brown and others that resulted in increased crime, particularly murder in urban areas. This entire theory appears a narrative born from police responses to criticism of aggressive police practices. The term is frequently credited to St. Louis Police Chief Doyle Sam Dotson III, although it was widely circulated among pro-police groups and conservative circles. The concept appears to lack credibility and is widely panned by academics and many politicians, yet the narrative remains a prime example of how the power affixed to law enforcement can shape viewpoints of social problems. While the 'Ferguson effect' could be dismissed as an extreme example, using a narrative analysis allows researchers to view police as important cultural producers and critically appraise their beliefs about crime and social decay. Prior research indicates officers dismissed political, social and economic causes of crime and believed that most social problems boil down to rational choice and hedonistic drives of a criminal underclass (Linnemann & Kurtz, 2014).

Interestingly, certain segments of society also seem more readily prepared to take on law enforcement narratives as truth especially in our current social and political climate. Those segments of society may correspond to demographic characteristics or personal connections to policing. Quite simply, many trust what officers promote because they may have limited or no negative connections with police and view officers have always protecting community interests. Regardless of the relationship or reason, many messages pertaining to the work of policing, the communities' officers serve and the perpetration of crime are accepted and touted as truth. Narrative criminology then provides a remarkable interpretation of the processes employed by police that define social problems and community need and characterize broader conceptions of truth.

Methodological Challenges and Growth Areas

From a methodological standpoint, Presser and Sandberg (2015, p. 86) proposed many areas of possible analysis appropriate to narrative criminology including the parts of a narrative, the word choices and use of particularly verbs, the specific genre, the narrative coherence and the context of storytelling. While the majority of current narrative literature focuses on offenders, Presser's and Sandberg's analysis points are quite appropriate to police storytelling and narratives and represent a logical step from offender narratives to those of other actors in the criminal justice system; however, stories born in law enforcement culture present several unique methodological challenges for narrative criminology.

An examination of police stories must focus on the underlying plot details while still analysing the themes or metaphors present in the narrative. This may require specific attention to the role the stories play in police culture, training and development of organizational cohesion beyond on the provided surface meaning or the details. Furthermore, narrative researchers must explore the shared narratives distinct to the profession while also examining unique meanings that stories convey to different departments and even specialized units. Language and story choices, like ethnographies, can also 'display the intricate ways individuals and groups understand, accommodate, and resist a presumably shared order. These portraits emerge from global constraints among nations, societies, native histories, subsistence patterns, religions, language groups, and the like' (Van Maanen, 2011, p. xviii).

An analysis of officer stories, particularly war stories, should not regard them as factual accounts and instead focus of the importance of the story beyond the truth. As previously noted, war stories likely deliver a moral lesson similar to those provided by parables and are not factual accounts. One particular value of narrative criminology is the usefulness of examining embellished or misleading accounts. In fact, Sandberg (2010, p. 462) states, 'instead of always searching for "the truth" one should appreciate the multitude of stories present in social context'. Sandberg (2010) further argues that even 'obvious lies' can reveal much about the complexity of social situations or subcultures. Within the scope of narrative criminology, focussing on the types of police narratives could demonstrate the importance of these accounts to police culture and the behaviour of individual officers or even departments. This is similar to the narrative process for offenders but applied for the unique subculture of policing. We argue that narrative methodology allows for particular appreciation of these stories and more significantly an understanding of the role of officer narratives in shaping enforcement culture and behaviours.

While narratives are conceptualized in many ways (Presser, 2010), we believe interpretive narratives are a particularly important context that should allow researchers to capture the potential sense-making practices associated with police stories. As such, these sense-making and informal narratives provide a theoretical model for understanding how different types of stories shape police identity and likely situated within different units, police organizations or communities. Storytelling then emerges as an important aspect of police culture, and research could further illicit information regarding the role attached to police as social actors in these narratives or the underlying moral lesion the narratives may espouse. These simple stories told by officers as parables or allegories offer valuable territory for understanding the intense elements of police culture because these stories attach meaning to the behaviours of community members, bystanders and officers themselves. The stories add coherence to police culture, and collective stories 'help a group of people to know itself as a group' (Presser & Sandberg, 2015, p. 94).

Possibly the most interesting future application of narrative criminology is research on 'action' elements of police stories and narratives. Do officer stories detailing the extreme and daily risk in policing – like the occupying soldier narrative – shape future actions? These narratives indicate that officers often negatively interpret the behaviour of others or assign criminal motives to citizens. Surely ascribing sinister meanings to many individuals or even areas of a community will inform officer reactions. So researchers must focus on how shared stories lock police values by further reinforcing organizational beliefs and behavioural practices (Murgia & Poggio, 2009). For example, stories that envision the community as a war zone surely influence officer interaction with community members and a general perception of risk. Kraska (2001) argued that defining crime in terms of an 'insurgency' by its nature requires police to envision their role as a 'counterinsurgency'. As previously noted, officers' risk of felonious death have essentially declined over the past few decades despite the highly visual nature of police deaths. For narrative criminologists, these stories and parables tend to explain officer behaviours, such as the shootings of unarmed citizens, as always justified because the level of fear officers acquire related to community aggression. The militaristic narrative supports numerous other order and control behaviours while similarly minimizing the importance of community service aspects of policing.

Despite some indication that stories lend towards the extreme or the rare, stories could also shape police action in a positive manner and increase professionalism. Ugelvik (2016) found a subset of narratives in his research that focused professionalism among detention workers. This type of story highlighted officers who displayed excellent decision-making skills and good judgement when dealing with difficult situations. Such stories seemed designed to highlight how good decision-making can 'save the day' and on the unique qualities required for the job. The idea that storytelling could increase professionalism also fits with some research arguing that storytelling as an important aspect of police training (Ford, 2003; van Hulst, 2013; Shearing & Ericson, 1991). At any rate, this remains an important focus area of future research.

The language used in specific narratives represents the least studied aspect of the role of storytelling in contemporary police culture. Therefore, future research should pay close attention to the role of language and cultural accomplishment through certain terminology. We argue that language offers particular insight into the production and maintenance of police authority and culture and the unique language used in officer narratives offers additional meaning and story coherence. Take the simple term 'war stories' that is frequently used in police culture and extensively found in the literature. Labelling this type of storytelling as 'war stories' may seem unimportant, but upon further analysis, this term links with the expansion of military tactics and language in policing. While officers are not at war, policing is becoming more warlike in ideology, technology and discourse (Kraska, 2001). Thus, the simple use of war-related terms in such stories likely contributes to existing police militarization, and narrative researchers could explore such language and discourse in police culture.

An important area of narrative analysis for policing may be the social content or setting in which officers share stories and develop narratives. For example, war story exchanges often occur during binge drinking and other social settings removed from formal police situations and thus the setting becomes an important analysis point for war stories as they most frequently occur during nonduty hours primarily attended by men. Therefore, war storytelling and the narratives developed and supported in these social settings may represent an understudied ingredient that explains the stronghold of masculinity in police culture. The informal nature of war storytelling settings may also produce a safe haven for officers to construct narratives of resentment and in-group grievance which buttresses resistance to formal efforts at changing police organizations (Loftus, 2008). We argue that when using a narrative framework, we can further detail the influential role of police storytelling found beyond the police station (van Hulst, 2013), but also note that access to such settings may be difficult.

Finally, research on police narratives are likely to face several limitations and concerns specific to law enforcement as a research population. First, peer cohesion is a noted element of police culture which could limit the willingness of officers to share aspects of stories, to detail informal professional values or to share certain narratives. In fact, some narratives like the 'thin blue line' indicate intense secrecy and solidarity among officers which could limit their willingness to discuss the identity-making aspects of shared narratives. Prior research indicates that officers fear reprisal from others within their department if they violate expected norms of secrecy (Cancino & Enriquez, 2004), and certainly this should impact willingness to participate in research.

Second, officers learn specific language through organizational narratives that allow them to define behaviours, like excessive and deadly force, in language that reduces their negative connotations and may justify extreme behaviour. In fact, several examples point to officers developing particular language to rationalize violent and even deadly force. For example, Dave Grossman teaches popular classes on how to justify lethal force and the aptly named 'Force Science Institute' instructs officers on how to define their actions as appropriate. Much of this involves learning and applying legalistic terms to officer decision points and behaviours. In another example, Betty Shelby, an officer who killed an unarmed subject in Oklahoma, recently began teaching a class on 'surviving the aftermath' of the use of deadly force. For this reason, exact wording should remain an important aspect when constructing questions and analysing specific language of officers. While these and other limitations may restrict some access to understanding law enforcement culture, the potential power of narrative analysis for illuminating police culture cannot be understated.

Conclusion

By and large, it is worthwhile to acknowledge the important role police occupy within society; however, it is equally important to gain a more complete understanding of how this role is shaped by narratives passed down and replicated through popular culture or departmental mentors relaying the job's history. In this chapter, we have contemplated the importance of police storytelling and narratives through four interrelated applications of narrative criminology by first examining the role of storytelling as an important cultural production in policing. Secondly, we assessed the potential theoretical role of popular culture stories and images of law enforcement officers as a source that may structure police narratives and self-image. Thirdly, we established the role of police organizational and officer narratives in defining social problems and community decay as arbiters of 'truth' that shape conceptions of police legitimacy, and lastly examined the unique methodological applications and challenges of employing narrative methods to studying law enforcement. We hope this chapter serves as an important resource for future narrative scholars seeking to better understand the narratives that help shape police culture.

References

Aiello, M. F. (2013). Policing the masculine frontier: Cultural criminological analysis of the gendered performance of policing. *Crime, Media, Culture, 10*(1), 1–21.

Anker, E. (2014). The liberalism of horror. *Social Research: International Quarterly, 81*(4), 795–823.

Braudy, L. (2016). *Haunted: On ghosts, witches, vampires, zombies, and other monsters of the natural and supernatural worlds*. New Haven, CT: Yale University Press.

Briggs, C. L. (1996). *Disorderly discourse: Narrative, conflict, & inequality*. New York, NY and Oxford: Oxford University Press.

Bureau of Justice. (2010, June). *Women in law enforcement, 1987–2008*. Washington, DC: Bureau of Justice Statistics. Retrieved from https://www.bjs.gov/content/pub/pdf/wle8708.pdf. Accessed on July 15, 2019.

Campeau, H. (2015). 'Police culture' at work: Making sense of police oversight. *British Journal of Criminology, 55*, 669–687.

Cancino, J. M., & Enriquez, R. (2004). A qualitative analysis of officer peer retaliation: Preserving the police culture. *Policing: An International Journal of Police Strategies & Management, 27*(3), 320–340.

Chan, J., Doran, S., & Marel, C. (2010). Doing and undoing gender in policing. *Theoretical Criminology, 14*(4), 425–446.

Clandinin, D. J., & Connelly, F. M. (2000). *Narrative inquiry: Experience in story in qualitative research*. San Francisco, CA: Jossey-Bass.

Conti, N. (2011). Weak links and warrior hearts: A framework for judging self and others in police training. *Police Practice and Research, 12*(5), 410–423.

Ericson, R. V., Baranek, P. M., & Chan, J. B. L. (1987). *Visualizing deviance: A study of news organization*. Milton Keyes: Open University Press.

Fielding, N. (1994). Cop canteen culture. In T. Newburn & E. A. Stanko (Eds.), *Just boys doing business* (pp. 46–63). London and New York, NY: Routledge.

Fletcher, C. (1990). *What cops know*. New York, NY: Pocket Books.

Fletcher, C. (1996). 'The 250 lb man in an alley': Police storytelling. *Journal of Organizational Change Management, 9*(5), 36–42.

Ford, R. E. (2003). Saying one thing, meaning another: The role of parables in police training. *Police Quarterly, 6*(1), 84–110.

Garcia, V. (2003). "Difference" in the police department: Women, policing, and "doing gender". *Journal of Contemporary Criminal Justice, 19*, 330–344.

Garro, L. C., & Mattingly, C. (2000). Narrative as construct and construction. In C. Mattingly & L. C. Garro (Eds.), *Narrative and the cultural construction of illness and healing* (pp. 1–49). Brekeley and Los Angeles, CA: University of California Press.

Green, J. A. (1999). Zero tolerance: A case study of police policies and practices in New York City. *Crime & Delinquency, 45*, 171–187.

Gubrium, J. F., & Holstein, J. A. (2009). *Analyzing narrative reality*. Los Angeles, CA; London; New Delhi: SAGE Publications.

Heidensohn, F., & Brown, J. (2012). From Juliet to Jane: Women police in TV cop shows, reality, rank, and careers. In T. Newburn & J. Peay (Eds.), *Policing: Politics, culture, and control*. Portland, OR: Bloomsbury Publishing.

Huey, L., & Broll, R. (2015). I don't find it sexy at all': Criminal investigators' views of media glamorization of police 'dirty work'. *Policing and Society, 25*(2), 236–247.

van Hulst, M. (2013). Storytelling at the police station the canteen culture revisited. *British Journal of Criminology, 53*, 624–642.

Humphreys, M., & Brown, A. D. (2002). Narratives of organizational identity and identification: A case study of hegemony and resistance. *Organization Studies, 23*(3), 421–447.

Hunt, J. (1985). Police accounts of normal force. *Urban Life, 13*(4), 315–341.

Jenner, M. (2016). *American TV detective dramas: Serial investigations*. New York, NY: Palgrave Macmillan.

Katz, J. (2016). Culture within and culture about crime: The case of the "Rodney King riots". *Crime, media, culture, 12*(2), 233–251.

King, N. (2013). Calling Dirty Harry a liar: A critique of displacement theories of popular criminology. *New Review of Film and Television Studies, 11*(2), 171–190.

Kraska, P. B. (2001). *Militarizing the American criminal justice system: The changing roles of the armed forces and the police*. Boston, MA: Northeastern University Press.

Kurtz, D. (2006). *Controlled burn: The gendering of stress, burnout, and violence in policing*. Dissertation, ProQuest.

Kurtz, D. L., Linnemann, T., & Williams, L. S. (2012). Reinventing the matron: The continued importance of gendered images and division of labor in modern policing. *Women & Criminal Justice, 22*(3), 239–263.

Kurtz, D. L., & Upton, L. (2017a). War stories and occupying soldiers: A narrative approach to understanding police culture and community conflict. *Critical Criminology, 25*(4), 539–558.

Kurtz, D. L., & Upton, L. L. (2017b). The gender in stories: How war stories and police narratives shape masculine police culture. *Women & Criminal Justice, 28*(4), 1–19.

Linnemann, T. (2010). Mad men, meth moms, moral panic: Gendering meth crimes in the Midwest. *Critical Criminology, 18*(2), 95–110.

Linnemann, T., & Kurtz, D. L. (2014). Beyond the ghetto: Police power, methamphetamine and the rural war on drugs. *Critical Criminology, 22*, 339–355.

Linnemann, T. (2017). Bad cops and true detectives: The horror of police and the unthinkable world. *Theoretical Criminology, 23*(3), 355–374. doi:10.1177/1362480617737761.

Loader, I. (1997). Policing and the social: Questions of symbolic power. *British Journal of Sociology, 48*(1), 1–18.

Loftus, B. (2008). Dominant culture interrupted recognition, resentment and the politics of change in an English police force. *British Journal of Criminology, 48*(6), 756–777.

Maguire, B., Sandage, D., & Weatherby, G. A. (1999). Television news coverage of the police. *Journal of Contemporary Criminal Justice*, *15*(2), 117–190.

Martin, S. E. (1999). Police force or police service? Gender and emotional labor. *The Annals of the American Academy of Political and Social Science*, *561*(1), 111–126.

Martin, S. E., & Jurik, N. C. (2007). *Doing justice, doing gender: Women in legal and criminal justice occupations*. Thousand Oaks, CA: SAGE Publications.

Maruna, S. (2001). *Making good: How ex-convicts reform and rebuild their lives*. Washington, DC: American Psychological Association.

McNulty, E. W. (1994). Generating common sense knowledge among police officers. *Symbolic Interaction*, *17*(3), 281–294.

Morash, M., & Haarr, R. N. (2012). Doing, redoing, and undoing gender: Variation in gender identities of women working as police officers. *Feminist Criminology*, *7*(1), 3–23.

Murgia, A., & Poggio, B. (2009). Challenging hegemonic masculinities: Men's stories on gender culture in organizations. *Organization*, *16*(3), 407–423.

Näslund, L., & Pemer, F. (2012). The appropriated language: Dominant stories as a source of organizational inertia. *Human Relations*, *65*(1), 89–110.

Nichols-Pethick, J. (2012). *TV cops: The contemporary American television police drama*. New York, NY: Routledge.

Oliver, M. B. (1994). Portrayals of crime, race, and aggression in 'reality-based' police shows: A content analysis. *Journal of Broadcasting & Electronic Media*, *38*(2), 179–192.

Paul, J. (2017). An analysis of portrayals of crime, criminals, and cops in Icelandic television. *Sociation Today*, *15*(1), 1–20.

Peelo, M. (2006). Framing homicide narratives in newspapers: Mediated witness and the construction of virtual victimhood. *Crime, Media, Culture*, *2*(2), 159–175.

Peelo, M., & Soothill, K. (2000). The place of public narratives in reproducing social order. *Theoretical Criminology*, *4*(2), 131–148.

Presser, L. (2009). The narratives of offenders. *Theoretical Criminology*, *13*(2), 177–200.

Presser, L. (2010). Collecting and analyzing the stories of offenders. *Journal of Criminal Justice Education*, *21*(4), 431–446.

Presser, L., & Sandberg, S. (2015). Research strategies for narrative criminology. In J. Miller & W. R. Palacios (Eds.), *Qualitative research in criminology* (p. 85). Piscataway, NJ: Transaction Publishers.

Rabe-Hemp, C. E. (2008). Female officers and the ethic of care: Does officer gender impact police behaviors? *Journal of Criminal Justice*, *36*(5), 426–434.

Rantatalo, O., & Karp, S. (2018). Stories of policing: The role of storytelling in police students' sensemaking of early work-based experiences. *Vocations and Learning*, *11*(1), 161–177.

Reiner, R. (1985). *The politics of policing*. Brighton: Wheatsheaf Books.

Reissman, C. K. (2008). *Narrative methods for the human sciences*. Thousand Oaks, CA: SAGE Publications.

Rosenberg, A. (2016a). How police censorship shaped Hollywood. *The Washington Post*, October 24. Retrieved from http://www.washingtonpost.com/sf/opinions/2016/10/24/how-police-censorship-shaped-hollywood/?utm_term=.64aa12dfe725. Accessed on July 15, 2019.

Rosenberg, A. (2016b). How pop culture's cops turned on their communities. *The Washington Post*, October 25. Retrieved from http://www.washingtonpost.com/sf/opinions/2016/10/25/how-pop-cultures-cops-turned-on-their-communities/?utm_term=.58f90add5199. Accessed on July 15, 2019.

Rosenberg, A. (2016c). In pop culture, there are no bad police shootings. *The Washington Post*, October 26. Retrieved from http://www.washingtonpost.com/sf/opinions/2016/10/26/in-pop-culture-there-are-no-bad-police-shootings/?utm_term=.ab584a788857. Accessed on July 15, 2019.

Rubinstein, P. (1973). *City police*. New York, NY: Farrar, Straus and Giroux.

Sandberg, S. (2010). What can "lies" tell us about life? Notes towards a framework of narrative criminology. *Journal of Criminal Justice Education*, *21*(4), 447–465.

Schaefer, B. P., & Tewksbury, R. (2018). The tellability of police use-of-force: How police tell stories of critical incidents in different contexts. *British Journal of Criminology*, *58*(1), 37–53.

Shearing, C. D., & Ericson, R. (1991). Culture as figurative action. *British Journal of Sociology*, *42*(4), 481–506.

Sherman, L. (1982). Learning police ethics. *Criminal Justice Ethics*, *1*(1), 10–19.

Skolnick, J. H. (1966). *Justice without trial: Law enforcement in a democratic society*. New York, NY: John Wiley & Sons.

Smolej, M. (2010). Constructing ideal victims? Violence narratives in Finnish crime-appealing programming. *Crime, Media, Culture*, *6*(1), 69–85.

Sparks, R. (1992). *Television and the drama of crime: Moral tales of the places of crime in public life*. Buckingham: Open University Press.

Stevens, A. (2012). 'I am the person now I was always meant to be': Identity reconstruction and narrative reframing in therapeutic community prisons. *Criminology and Criminal Justice*, *12*(5), 527–547.

Tate, J., Jenkins, J., Rich, S., & Muyskens, J. (2018). Fatal force: 2018 police shootings database. [Data file]. *The Washington Post*. Retrieved from https://www.washingtonpost.com/graphics/2018/national/police-shootings-2018/?noredirect5on&utm_term=.7ca785012007&utm_term5.55f31eb7bee3. Accessed on July 15, 2019.

Thacker, E. (2015). *Tentacles longer than night: Horror of philosophy (Vol. 3)*. Alresford: Zero John Hunt Publishing.

Ugelvik, T. (2016). Techniques of legitimation: The narrative construction of legitimacy among immigration detention officers. *Crime, Media, Culture*, *12*(2), 215–232.

United States Department of Justice. (2015). Civil Rights Division: 'Investigation of the Ferguson Police Department' Retrieved from www.justice.gov/crt/about/spl/documents/ferguson_findings_3-4-15.pdf-741k-2015-03-04. Accessed on June 3, 2015.

United States Department of Labor, Bureau of Labor Statistics, Census of Fatal Occupational Injuries. (2016). *Fatal occupational injuries by industry and event or exposure, all United States, 2014* [Data file]. Washington, DC: United States Department of Labor. Retrieved from https://www.bls.gov/iif/oshwc/cfoi/cftb0286.pdf. Accessed on July 15, 2019.

Van Maanen, J. (1972). *'Pledging the police': A study of selected aspects of recruit socialization in a large, urban police department*. Doctoral dissertation, University of California, Irvine.

Van Maanen, J. (2011). *Tales of the field: On writing ethnography*. University of Chicago Press.
Waddington, P. A. J. (1999). Police (canteen) sub-culture. *British Journal of Criminology, 39*(2), 287–309.
Weber, M. (1946). Politics as a vocation. In H. H. Gerth & C. W. Mills (Eds.), *From Max Weber: Essays in sociology* (pp. 77–128). New York, NY: Oxford University Press.
Westmarland, L. (2001). *Gender and policing: Sex, power and police culture*. Portland, OR: Willan Publishing.
Whitaker, G. P. (1982). What is patrol work? *Police Studies: International Review of Police Development, 4*(4), 13–22.
Worth, S. E. (2008). Storytelling and narrative knowing: An examination of the epistemic benefits of well-told stories. *Journal of Aesthetic Education, 42*(3), 42–56.
Young, J. (2011). Moral panics and the transgressive other. *Crime, Media, Culture, 7*(3), 245–258.
Youngs, D., & Canter, D. V. (2012). Narrative roles in criminal action: An integrative framework for differentiating offenders. *Legal and Criminological Psychology, 17*(2), 233–249.

Chapter 17

Revealing Criminal Narratives: The Narrative Roles Questionnaire and the Life as a Film Procedure

David Canter, Donna Youngs and David Rowlands

A Psychological Approach to Narrative Criminology

As Sandberg and Ugelvik (2016) have clearly argued 'narrative research should be seen as a multidisciplinary collection of supplementary perspectives and methods that may generate very different insights and conclusions' (p. 131). This is particularly relevant to the study of offenders' activities because it demonstrates that by exploring the stories that are the basis of many different forms of criminality, from being a drug mule to committing mass murder, it is possible to reveal the underlying processes that facilitate crime and criminality that are not accessible by other means. This is compatible with a parallel (and epistemologically related) development in psychology that seeks perspectives on human agency beyond organic or social determinism.

Bruner (e.g. Bruner, 1991) was one of the first psychologists in recent times to develop an account of how personal narratives contribute to an individual's experience of reality. McAdams (1993), being one of the clearest and most prolific advocates in psychology for the value of the study of personal narratives, took this idea further. He has demonstrated for over a quarter of a century that personal myths can be fruitfully seen as organised according to two themes that he terms Agency and Communion, where Agency is concerned with power and achievement and Communion with love and intimacy (McAdams, 1993; McAdams, 2016). The combination of the extremes of these two dimensions gives rise to four narrative forms: high agency and high communion, high agency and low communion, low agency and high communion, and low agency and low communion. Interestingly, it is possible to relate these to the idea that there are four basic plots throughout the literary tradition. These are described in detail most directly in Frye's (1957) seminal book. He calls these plots – Tragedy, Romance, Adventure and Irony.

Frye (1957) is at pains to emphasise that real life is not as tidy as literature. It is therefore noteworthy that there is some possibility of an overlap between the dominant narrative forms in personal life stories, derived from combinations of agency and communion, and Frye's (1957) basic plots. The relationship between McAdams (2016) model and Frye's (1957) basic plots in the criminal context is consequently a rather subtle one that is considered in more detail with the help of case studies below and in Youngs and Canter (2011).

McAdams' two primary psychological dimensions differentiate human functioning, as revealed through personal life stories, across a range of areas of psychological study. Thus, although the psychological narrative approach is rooted in models of human beings as active agents or protagonists in their own storyline, other perspectives that use a different vocabulary nonetheless relate to similar issues. For instance, when Leary (1958) considered interpersonal aspects of personality he proposed two dimensions, which he described in terms of Dominance/Submission and Love/Hate. Other examples that emphasise distinct psychological dimensions are those revealed in the analysis of Schutz's widely used FIRO theory of interpersonal tendency (Schutz, 1958). They suggest that his original three dimensions of behavioural orientation may be better conceptualised as the two dimensions of Control and Openness/Inclusion, also echoing Leary's personality dimensions. In other words, many researchers starting from different points and using different methodologies give added weight to McAdams framework even if they describe the two key dimensions with slightly different terminologies. Hermans' (1996) ideas on the self, its strivings and meaning in life, also provide powerful further support for the two similar motivational trends. These distinguish between 'S' motives, which are strivings for superiority, power and expansion and 'O' motives, which are strivings for contact and intimacy with others (Hermans, 1996). Taken together all of the studies cited above support the conclusion that it is reasonable to assume these same dimensions will underlie all individuals' life stories, including those of criminals. This is likely to be the case whether considering differences in how a person relates to others or how an individual finds meaning in life.

The psychological perspective which foregrounds the role of personal narratives as dominant aspects of how people make sense of their lives complements many aspects of narrative criminology. This perspective assists the building of more general theories and models that have theoretical and practical significance. It provides a contribution to Presser's (2009) argument that an offender's narrative is an immediate antecedent of offending and thus has a direct impact as a 'key instigator of action' (Presser, 2009, p. 177). She implies, as Toch (1992) argued in relation to the violent men's stories he studied, that offending is the enactment of a narrative rather than the narrative being an interpretation of the context out of which the offence has emerged. Although within the current argument both the enactment and the interpretation are inevitably related.

This utilisation of narrative ideas is consistent with Presser's conceptualisation of narrative as one '…that effectively blurs the distinction between narrative and experience by suggesting that experience is always known and acted upon as it has been interpreted symbolically' (p. 184). This is distinct from a narrative operating as a post hoc, interpretative device that provides insight into an individual's subjective understanding of the nonnarrative factors that motivated behaviour. Understood in this way, the narrative framework has the potential to explain what Presser calls 'dynamic factors at the point of behaviour'.

The value of this perspective can be seen both for understanding the instigation of crime and desistance from it. Maruna (2001), for instance, suggests that different self-narratives are themselves implicated in whether or not offenders reconstruct their identities so that criminality is not part of them. Furthermore, Horgan (2009) shows the significance of changes in personal narratives for 'walking away from terrorism'. These reconstructions of identities through changed personal narratives are also reflected in McAuley's (1997) studies of what supports or inhibits paramilitary activity in Northern Ireland. Such narratives may represent the mechanisms that Ward (2010) discusses in his analysis of sexual offenders' specific cognitive distortions. In Ward's (2010) argument the cognitive distortions reflected in the justifications for and belittling of the actual sexual offence are seen as aspects of the role the offender is taking in his personal narrative. For instance, claiming that the offender had a relationship with his accuser and he is thus a victim of the account, not the aggressor.

Maruna and Mann (2006) argue against a causal role for narratives as post hoc rationalisations, claiming that narratives represent a potential form of the alternative, positive causal processes. Yet, it is clear that giving an account of a personal life story, or even a crucial episode in that story, may be both an interpretation that encompasses rationalisations for criminal acts as well as providing the basis for future actions. A crucial aspect of the narrative perspective is that narratives are dynamic. They are shaped by the person but also shape their actions.

From a psychological point of view the narrative framework offers a causal process that assigns the offender personal agency, informing understanding of why offenders engage in (as well as desist from) crime. This point of view eschews a positivist emphasis on the individual as an organism. As Canter (2011) shows, considering offenders' narratives treats them as active persons rather than merely sociobiological organisms. Self-narratives invoke personal meaning, purpose and personal roles that direct future actions. Thus, the individual is positioned firmly in the driver's seat (Bruner, 1987; Singer, 2004). It also allows a consideration of the proximal antecedents to crimes, informing understanding of the immediate precursors to offending actions. These are what Presser calls the neglected 'here and now of crime' (Presser, 2009, p. 179).

Others, such as Fleetwood (2016), caution the assignation of agency within the context of narrative, arguing that stories are social constructions, referencing Presser's (2009) study in which violent men morally justified their actions by deploying a plotline of heroic struggle, reflecting a culturally available story. Brookman and colleagues concur, contending that narratives have a cultural rather than psychological etiology (Brookman et al., 2011). Though the key here could lie with the idea of 'moral justification', a proposition that shares more ground with cognitive distortions (Bandura, 1990; Matza & Sykes, 1957) and choice than social moorings. Recognising the cultural underpinning of narrative forms does not negate a protagonist's position as an active agent in embracing and acting out a given role or story. Individual proclivity and prevailing culture exert interactive influences upon narratives and behaviour. Canter and colleagues explicitly recognise the influence of culture in governing available narrative forms (see Youngs & Canter, 2012); however, self-agency is accorded in the choice of interpretation among those available, and that facilitates action (Youngs & Canter, 2012).

Systematic Methodologies

The psychological approach developed here helps to extend the potential of narrative criminology through its development of standardised procedures that allow replicable examination of the form and content of offender narratives that emerge in different contexts. Two procedures in particular illustrate the substantive contributions that have been made to date in articulating the form and structure of criminals' personal narratives.

A number of studies have revealed that for any type of offences, be it rape, murder, burglary or arson, for example, there are different styles of how that type of offence can be carried out. These styles have been revealed through considering what actions tend to co-occur. These considerations elucidate the distinct patterns of criminal actions that distinguish different subsets within any crime type. For example, a rape can be a violent attack or use of verbal threats. A burglary can leave the property untouched except for what is stolen or in complete disarray. As long ago as 1994, Canter argued that the best way to make sense of these different patterns of activity was in terms of an underlying story or narrative that the offender was bringing to bear. For Canter (1994), the empirical patterns of offence actions – how the victim was controlled, the nature of the violence, the style of interaction with the victim, for example, could be made sense of not in terms of a personality trait, such as psychopathy, but by understanding the narrative the offender is living.

Roles as the Essence of Episodic Narratives

The Concept of an Offence Role

When considering criminality as well as the overall life narrative, the crime episodes themselves are of particular interest. These can be encapsulated in the role the offender considers themselves to have played. To explore these roles, Youngs and Canter (2011) draw upon an extensive psychological and criminological literature, developing the idea that the roles admitted to by an offender when describing a crime are useful proxy for the narrative any given role is part of. This concept of the 'role' extends previous thinking on cognitively focused scripts of actions and reactions in violent scenarios. More generally, roles and role-taking are at the heart of the symbolic interactionist perspective on criminality (e.g. Matsueda, 1992).

Furthermore, one of the key processes implied by Mead's (1927/1982) influential espousal of symbolic interactionism is the claim that 'delinquent behaviour can occur in the absence of reflective thought, via habitual or scripted responses established through previous experiences' (Heimer & Matsueda, 1994, p. 368). The idea that individuals take on externally imposed roles that shape their continued involvement in criminality is also central to labelling perspectives (Becker, 1963; Lemert, 1951; Tannenbaum, 1938). Tannenbaum, in particular, discusses the dramatisation of evil, drawing attention to a storied understanding of crime within which role-taking is central. Other authors discuss criminal desistance in terms of role transition (Massoglia & Uggen, 2010). For example, Maruna, Immarigeon, and LeBel (2004) define a secondary level of desistance that is 'the assumption of the role...of the changed person' (p. 19). The idea that narrative processes may be activated as offence roles builds then on a diverse range of previous perspectives on crime.

Of course, considering the declaration of which role a person remembers to have been salient when committing a crime raises the possibility of the roles being shaped as justification. They also are likely to be influenced by the context of eliciting the roles, as all story telling is understood as shaped by who the audience is. The influence of the processes of rationalisations and context always needs to be borne in mind when interpreting the results of studies using this approach. However, the impact of these processes was reduced in the studies drawn on here (Youngs & Canter, 2011) by presenting respondents with a number of possible roles and asking them how much each one described the experience they remember. This reduces the generation of any particular role as the obvious dominant one. It also allows for a more subtle analysis of the themes that bring together different role selections for any individual as considered further below.

The Narrative Roles Questionnaire

Following Presser (2009), it is argued that a particular crime narrative may have the following components:

- The offender's interpretation of the event and his/her actions within that event
- The offender's self-awareness or identity in the interpersonal crime event
- The emotional and other experiential qualities of the event for the offender

In order to develop a standard procedure to explore these components, open-ended pilot interviews with 30 offenders were held. The imprisoned offenders had been convicted of a variety of offences, covering the full range from burglary to murder. During these interviews they were asked to describe their feelings and experiences when committing a recent offence. Each interview was transcribed verbatim and content analysed. This consisted of deriving categories from the transcriptions and establishing clear definitions for each category. The reliability of the assignment of material to categories was checked by having more than one person use the defined categories and establishing that the same material was assigned to the same categories by different people. The three components were used to guide the derivation of categories. The categories were then grouped into themes and a representative verbatim statement from the interviews selected to capture each theme.

The resulting set of 33 statements capture, in a typical set of words as might be used by an offender. The key descriptions of their experience of the event (e.g. It was the only thing to do; I was doing it because I had to; I found I couldn't help myself; I was doing a job), the offender's self-awareness/identity (e.g. I was a victim; I was like a professional; I was in control; It was a manly thing to do) and emotional state during the offence (e.g. It was fun; It was like I wasn't part of it; I just wanted to get it over with). These statements comprised the first version of a Narrative Roles Questionnaire (NRQ).

These statements are used in the study of the offenders' roles in a crime through asking them to consider a particular crime they had committed, which they remember well (Youngs & Canter, 2011). Offenders are asked to describe the activity itself in detail. They are then asked to complete a questionnaire that lists the 33 role statements in order to indicate on a 5-point Likert scale the extent to which they agree/disagree that each role statement described their experience. The offenders' responses are then related to a given criminal context enabling the qualities of the agency and communion that are underpinning the action in that event.

Different Offence Narrative Roles

To identify the underlying themes inherent within the 33 different roles possible during offending, Youngs and Canter (2011) collected responses from 71 offenders. They then conducted a multivariate analysis on the responses, identifying the structure presented in Fig. 17.1. This analysis represents the degree of co-occurrence of any pair of roles as a relative distances in a two dimensional space. So, for example, roles that co-occur often such as 'being on a mission' and 'looking for recognition' are closer in the configuration than 'I was confused' and 'it all went to plan', which never were selected by the same person, are far apart.

The resulting configuration of the 33 role statements is open to interpretation that reflects the two facets of agency and communion (McAdams, 1993) reviewed above. Agency is reflected in the distinction between narratives of power and potency, such as being a professional or seeking revenge. This contrasts with those accounts in which the individual is a weak victim pushed by the fates. Communion is illustrated by the contrasts in intimacy between those experiences that are ego-involved in the process such as 'getting one's own back' rather than taking a risk that kept the experience independent of the person.

Combining these dichotomies generates the four narrative role themes:

- The Professional (Adventure narrative) role is one of calmness, competency and mastery of the environment that contrasts with
- the Revenger (Tragedy) role of distress and blame.

- The Victim (Irony) role is one of disconnectedness and despair that contrasts with
- the Hero (Quest) role of hubris, of taking on and overcoming challenges.

Items capturing each of these thematic roles are given in Table 17.1. The items comprising the four roles are related to the three components of narratives proposed by Presser (2009), namely Identity, Cognitive distortions and Affective components, reflecting the distinctions presented in Table 17.2.

Case Study Exemplars of Narrative Role Themes

Example A (Canter & Youngs, 2012): *A Revengeful Mission* narrative role; this shows the significance of not being able to stop whilst on a mission. He was convicted of Grievous Bodily Harm with intent, and was 24 years old.

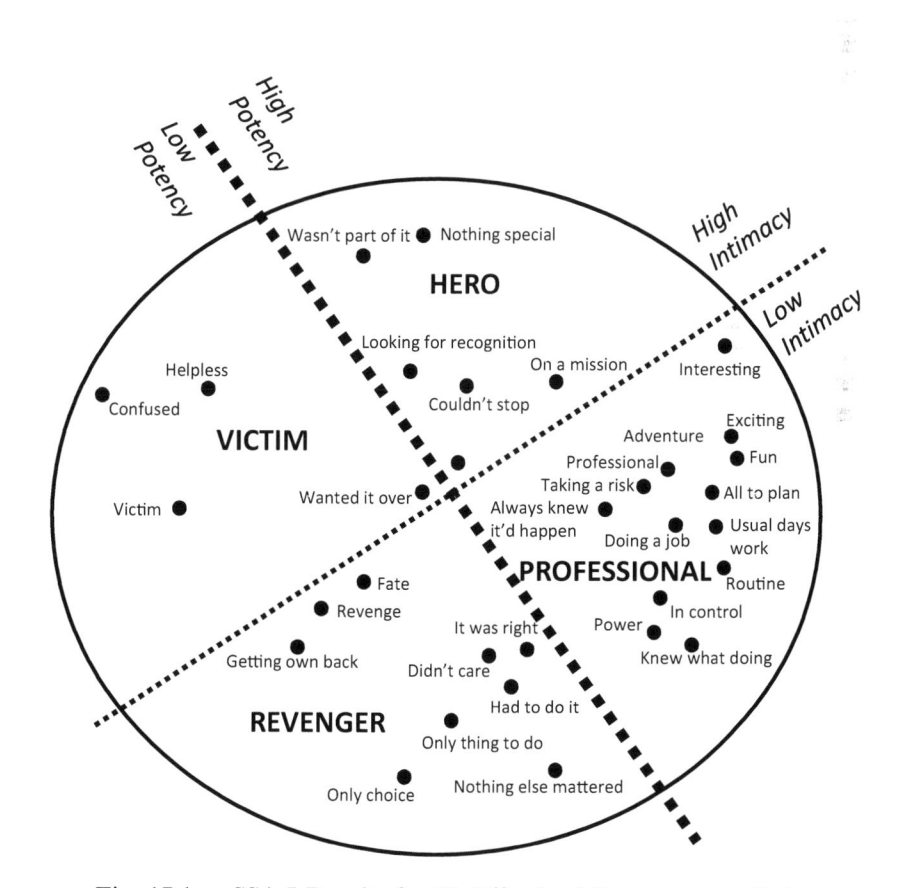

Fig. 17.1. SSA-I Results for 71 Offenders' Responses on Roles Questionnaire.

Table 17.1. Indicative Statements that Define Themes of Narrative Roles Taken from Narrative Roles Questionnaire.

Professional	'I was like a professional'
	'For me, it was like a usual day's work'
	'I was doing a job'
	'It was routine'
Hero	'I was looking for recognition'
	'I couldn't stop myself'
	'It was like I wasn't part of it'
	'It was a manly thing to do'
Victim	'I was a victim'
	'I was helpless'
	'I was confused about what was happening'
	'I just wanted to get it over with'
Revenger	'I was trying to get revenge'
	'I didn't care what would happen'
	'It was my only choice'
	'I had to do it'

My mum had a grievance with this fella next door, he was putting pressure on her and bullying her. I used to think he was a family friend but he kept knocking on her door with bottles of brandy and stuff hassling her to have a drink with him. I used to play football for him when I was a kid. My mum told me what he had been doing and I vowed to front him, something had to be done. I didn't make any preparations as was not really a vendetta. On the night it happened I had been taking coke for 6 hours and had been drinking all day. He came into my local with his mate. It was all in good spirits until he came in. He said, 'your mum is just a slut anyway'. I told my friend that he was getting it, he snapped a cue in half and I put 2 snooker balls in my sock, we waited outside in my mate's car. I knew I wanted to hurt him, I was going to run at him when they came out. Whatever happened, happened. There was a scuffle on the floor and my victim tried to run away. I got up before him and hit him 5 or 6 times. I saw all the blood and stopped hitting. He got up and said I was getting killed, I started to chase him again but he ran in through his flat door. I was fuming. I realized what I had done and was caked in blood.

I was given life with a three and a half year tariff. The alternative to this would have been to just not do it. It did no good anyway, I am in here and my kids have got no dad there. I know how it feels to have no dad around and I promised myself that I would be there for my kids, that's the biggest thing that's done my head in. I had to eat my words, they have no dad, well only once a week when they come and visit me in here.

Table 17.2. Narrative Integration of Affective, Cognitive and Offence-specific Identity Components of Offending.

Narrative Role	Offence Identity	Cognitive Distortions	Emotional State
Quest narrative The proposed hero role that emerges from a quest narrative is comprised of the following:	Strong; others significant	Present own alternative evaluations of actions; refocus impact in terms offender's own objectives	Calm; displeasurable
Tragedy narrative The proposed revenger role hypothesised to emerge from the tragedy narrative, is further hypothesised to have the following components:	Weak; others not significant	Responsibility attributed to others; minimise impact	Aroused; neutral
Adventure narrative The proposed professional role, rooted in an adventure narrative, is hypothesised to emerge out of the following:	Strong; others not significant	Present own alternative evaluations of actions; minimise impact	Calm; neutral
Irony narrative The proposed victim role is hypothesised to emerge out of the irony narrative and to comprise following:	Weak; others significant	Responsibility attributed to others; refocus impact in terms of offender's own objectives	Aroused; displeasurable

The proposed Revengeful Mission role was hypothesised to emerge out of the following of offence identity, cognitive and emotional components:

Offence identity: Strong; Others Significant
Cognitive Distortions: Present Own Alternative Evaluations of Actions; Avoid/ Refocus Impact in terms Offender's Own Objectives.
Emotional State: Calm; Displeasurable

They reflect the underlying combination of High Potency and High Intimacy psychological processes. The potency is revealed in the very direct violent action that was initiated by the respondent and the intimacy by how he argues that was a reaction to a significant personal relationship.

Although A had been given a life sentence for a very violent assault he describes the assault he committed almost like a 'Gunfight at OK Corral'. This has an almost frivolous, fantasy-like quality to it rather than the serious endeavour it actually was. To restore his manly pride, wounded in the insult to his mother, he waited for his victim and then attacked him. The sense of potency and the offender's determination to impose his will characteristic of the Revengeful Mission role is clear in the statement 'I knew I wanted to hurt him'. He claims he felt there were demands on him to do it and that he 'had to do it'. So, although he was exerting his authority, he implicitly exonerates himself by reference to 'higher powers'. This builds on the story line of his being part of a social context that required these actions from him. It is that context of the narrative that provides this justification.

He implies that 'whatever happened, happened' as though it was part of a bigger mission. This is a clear example of the forms of cognitive distortion expected within the Revengeful Mission offender's interpretations: There is no attempt to deny responsibility or minimise the harm rather the offender supersedes other judgements, asserting his own evaluation of the incident. The significance of the victim playing a role in the offender's narrative is also clear, illustrating the criminal aspects of high levels of 'intimacy' hypothesised within this role.

He did claim it 'was not really a vendetta', but it is clear from his account that there was a history to his anger and that despite his claim that he 'didn't make any preparations' he did indeed create a vicious weapon and wait for his victim. This speaks of the relatively calm, controlled emotional state that drives a Revengeful Mission. The statement 'I was fuming' describes a cold fury that is consistent with the negative feelings associated with this role without suggesting any loss of this control. He seemed to think that he could assuage the insult and return from the violence, but now realises what a weak storyline that was to follow.

Example B: *A Tragic Hero* narrative role in which the offender can see no other way of acting and the act was everything, nothing else mattered. He was convicted of murder, and was 26 years of age.

> *'I am in here for murder; there are other little crimes with it as well, like assault and sexual assault.*
>
> *I walked into this house and was having a drink and my victim was slagging one of my mate's girlfriends off* ['slagging off' means to insult]. *I thought 'that's not right' The lad whose girlfriend it was there. I said 'you better say something to him'. He didn't and so I got up and just started laying into him while he was on the chair. There are parts of the incident I just don't remember. After beating him up for a bit, I took him to the bathroom, filled the bath and told him he would either die by drowning or I was going to fucking kill him. I was stabbing him for an hour or so. I didn't take any weapons with me, I was not out to cause trouble, that's not my lifestyle, I try and avoid trouble. I can't remember where I got these knives from.*
>
> *The reason I did it was just because of what he said about my mates, to let him know he just couldn't do that.*

Afterwards I went and got a wheelie bin from outside and brought it in the house. I told him to climb in it from the bath but he fell on the floor. He was there for about 20 minutes, I thought he was dead. I stabbed him in the back of the neck again when I realised he wasn't and he got in the bin. I threw white spirit all over it set it on fire and took him in this bin down to the canal. I kicked it over and he fell in the water, he was screaming so I picked up a brick and hit him over the head to shut him up.

I went back to the flat, borrowed clothes and went out on my own then, that was my night ruined. I seen a bouncer at this club that all bouncers go to when they are not working. This one I saw had broken my leg before, I got into a fight with him and hit him over the head with a piece of scaffolding and kicked him a few times. I can't remember where I slept that night. I handed myself in 2 days later and what I was in police custody I was all black and blue. They had the police doctor look at me and they found a tooth in my knee, it was not my victims or the bouncers, so it could be anyone's.

The proposed Tragic Hero role was hypothesised to emerge out of the following of offence, cognitive and emotional components:

Offence identity: he has only a Weak idea of what his distinct identity is; Others are Not Significant in his life

Cognitive Distortions: Responsibility Attributed to Others rather than accepting the blame himself; Minimise the Impact of the offence on the victim

Emotional State: although he was Aroused, he dose not express positive or negative emotion. His state seems to be Neutral

The role of a Tragic Hero reflects the underlying combination of Low Potency and Low Intimacy psychological processes.

As Frye (1957) makes clear the essence of tragedy is that of a heroic figure overpowered by the fates. In Tragedy, there are wrathful gods or hypocritical villains who attempt to manipulate the tragic hero to evil ends. The protagonist is generally pessimistic and ambivalent as he has to avoid the dangers and absurdities of life, in which he finds that pain and pleasure, happiness and sadness are always mixed. The recurring emotions are sadness and fear. He is perceived as powerless at the hands of his nemesis. In the Tragedy, the 'extraordinary victim' confronts inescapable dangers pursued by life's doom. Common tragedies are stories of 'the fall', dying gods and heroes, violent death, sacrifice and isolation. In the classic tragedy, the hero finds himself (as it is usually male) separated in some fundamental way from the natural order of things. The separation makes for an imbalance of nature, and the righting of the balance is the tragic hero's downfall. Like Oedipus, the tragic hero may be supremely proud, passionate and of soaring mind; yet, these extraordinary attributes are exactly what separate him from common people and bring about his eventual demise. Frye (1957) remarks that tragedy evokes in the listener 'a paradoxical combination of a fearful sense of rightness (the hero must fall) and a pitying sense of wrongness (it is too bad that he falls)' (Frye, 1957, p. 214).

The offense role that this narrative produces is that of the Tragic Hero. Consistent with this role, the offender attributes responsibility for his actions to others, including the victim: 'The reason I did it was just because of what he said about my mates...'. The protagonist thinks he has no choice. He indicates that it is the only option available to him. He believes it is 'fate' that shapes his experiences rather than anything he does himself. He eventually 'heroically' hands himself in. This role captures the individual's egotistical sense of his own significance. While, in line with the low intimacy associated with this role, the others involved are merely foil for his actions. The consequence for them means nothing to him, as his comment 'that was my night ruined' reveals so clearly.

The account given by B shows the justification which is the hallmark of a tragedy. The offender saw his actions as being the right thing to do 'to let him know he just couldn't do that', although it ultimately leads to disaster. The commitment to violence that is chillingly portrayed in this narrative is emphasised by the killer having an unknown person's tooth in his knee. Yet, as the offender's comment here that 'I try and avoid trouble' reveals, the horror of the violence he perpetrates is set against a weak self-identity, producing the Tragic Hero role. Many people would actually describe this man as on a tragic life course from his early years or as 'a disaster waiting to happen'.

Example C: *A Professional* narrative role showing the contribution of being in control and how they relate to the excitement. The offender was convicted of theft and robbery at age 23 years.

> *Going into a shop and picking a rack of watches worth £5K-£10K. I ask the sales man to see the watch I put it on and just walk out. I would sell it for money but not for drugs, but to buy nice clothes. Sometimes I go out with the intention of doing it but sometimes I'll just do it then and there if it looks nice, or I'd go back the next time. If I go on my own I'll stay local but if I'm with someone else than I'll go out of town like to London or York.*

> *The planning is done in the car, we'll discuss where they'll wait for me, have the car parked and which way I'll run. They'll never chase you.*

> *I feel excited when talking about it, preparing to do it and thinking about when you get the money and where you'll go and what clothes you'll buy. It is an adrenaline rush. I always laugh when I run it's a nervous thing, the buzz. When there are no customers in the shop I'll run out but if there are customers then I'll walk and then run. In the car you think is it going to happen and then afterwards you have it. Park the car out of the way and plan a route. They don't expect you to be in a car but on foot. Feel safe when I get in the car.*

> *I usually go for small things that are high value, something you can conceal and run with. I split the money with my mate and we party for the weekend. I've only been caught for the little things and not for the big things.*
>
> *It takes 5 minutes to plan the theft because we go there and have a look around, then do it and leave...if you walk around town then you get yourself on CCTV.*

The proposed Professional role was hypothesised to emerge out of the following of offence identity, cognitive and emotional components:

Offence identity: Strong sense of who he is; Others are Not Significant in his personal narrative
Cognitive Distortions: Presents Own Alternative Evaluations of his actions, ignoring how others may see them; Minimise Impact on the victims
Emotional State: Calm; Neutral

This reflects the underlying combination of High Potency and Low Intimacy psychological processes.

Example C is typical of adventure narratives, which in our respondents were most often provided by burglars and robbers. Here, the confident feeling and 'strong' self-identity of being a 'professional' is clearly expressed. He is pleased to point out his expertise, mentioning how he thwarts the expectations of the authorities and his awareness of the need to avoid CCTV cameras. Indeed, his account is dominated by details of the technicalities of the offending, the 'tricks of the trade'. The excitement produced out of this adventure is mentioned directly, to the extent that he even feels 'excited when talking about it'. But typical of the Professional, the role he adopts during the actual commission of the offence is a less aroused one of calm competency ('I put it on and just walk out'). The offence produces pleasure which comes from the power he feels in what he considers to be the success of his actions. In line with the low intimacy levels underpinning this offense role, the offender highlights the irrelevance of the consequences of his actions for others by simply not mentioning the victim or nature of the target at all.

Characteristic of the Professional offense role, the offender makes no attempt to disown or attribute responsibility for his actions to others. Rather, he entirely owns his actions (indeed boasts of them) but presents his own alternative framework for the evaluation of them ('I would sell it for money but not for drugs, but to buy nice clothes').

Frye (1957) calls this type of narrative a 'Romance' in reference to such archetypal stories as *Ulysses*, which he compares with the sun's zenith, summer and triumph. Stories of the hero's great exploits, of apotheosis and of entering into paradise are manifestations of this mythic archetype. In the Romance, an aspect of life is configured as a successful hunt, or a pilgrimage to some desired end, consisting of three stages: a perilous journey with preliminary minor adventures, then usually some kind of battle in which either the hero or his foe, or both, must die and finally exaltation of the hero. The protagonist is an ever-moving adventurer who tries to overcome adversity and take control of the new challenges in order to emerge victorious throughout life's journey. He or she embarks on a long and difficult journey in life in which circumstances constantly change and new challenges continually arise. In the criminal context, this accords with offending being seen as an opportunity to gain satisfaction and pleasure from mastery of the environment that is facilitated by the adoption of a Professional offence role.

Example D: *A Victim* narrative in which the offender expresses helpless confusion. He was 46 years old at the time.

> *I was supposed to drive my stepson to the scrap yard but he wanted to stop at the bet shop. I drove to the bet shop and waited in the car. He comes running out with a bat and money bags, he'd done an armed robbery. He got in the car and I drove away. I was screaming, 'what have you done' and he was screaming, 'drive Dad drive'. As I'm driving I'm screaming and the money is going everywhere. The police were chasing us in their cars and the helicopter was following us as well. Chasing and sirens. It was a 25 minute chase, everywhere I went they were chasing me, I was going the wrong way on the roads. I crashed into a bollard and ran away. Police caught me. I got 7 years and my son got 5 years. My son pleaded guilty and I didn't know it was happening so I pleaded innocent and got 2 years extra.*
>
> *I would not have gone to the bet shop. He had a bat up his sleeve so I didn't know what he was planning to do. I should have drove off, but I couldn't as I would have got a hard time from the mother, but I got a hard time anyway. He apologises for what he'd done. He did it and got out before me. But he's done it to me again. I had my own flat and he had hidden drugs in there. He got 5 years and I got 4 years and he got out before me again! This isn't me, armed robbery and drug possession. I usually get charged for driving offences. I don't touch drugs and don't go to bet shops.*

The proposed Victim role was hypothesised to emerge out of the following offence identity, cognitive and emotional components:

Offence identity: Weak; Others Significant
Cognitive Distortions: Responsibility Attributed to Others; Avoid/Refocus Impact in terms of offender's own objectives
Emotional State: Aroused; Displeasurable

This reflects the underlying combination of Low Potency and High Intimacy psychological processes.

This role emerges from a life story in which nothing makes much sense; it is almost as if there are no rules and nothing matters. The term refers equally to a genre or a style of film characterising 'a dark, corrupt and violent world'. The seemingly tough characters often found in Film Noir seem to represent Frye's idea of Irony. His definition of Irony is rooted in Socrates as an *eiron* or self-deprecator (Frye, 1957, p. 172). This general framework for life would produce offender accounts of the roles they were playing in terms of confusion and powerlessness. An extension of this sense of powerlessness, given a world view where normal social and moral codes do not apply, will be the inverted notion that it is in fact the offender that is the main victim in the event. This is the generalised sense of impotence characteristic of Irony rather than the angry conviction that one has been wronged seen in Example A. Being a victim is essentially associated with negative emotions. They point to endings that just dissipate into nothingness and are certainly not happy ones.

Example D is the account of an individual who has indisputably adopted a Victim offending role. He saw himself totally at the mercy of his stepson's misdemeanor, clearly revealing the hypothesised tendency to attribute responsibility to others that is characteristic of this role. He suggests this all came out of a confused, helpless lack of understanding of what he was involved in that reveals the weak self-identity associated with the Victim role. The hallmarks of the victim narrative are strongly indicated also by the comment the offender makes that the person he thought was to blame, his son, got out of prison before he did.

The significance of others within his story is clear, both in the general positioning of his account and plight relative to his son as well as in specific references throughout to others (e.g. 'I should have drove off, but I couldn't as I would have got a hard time from the mother'). The predicted negative and aroused emotional state associated with the adoption of the Victim role during an offence is neatly captured in this account with the offender's description, 'As I'm driving, I'm screaming...'

Summary of the Four Narrative Roles Themes

Connecting cognitive, affective and narrative perspectives on criminality we propose that four dominant themes can be seen to underlie roles that characterise the narratives of offenders who participated in our studies.

The Revengeful Mission role in which the offender who sees himself as strong and powerful is seeking a particular impact on another person (s). This often is part of a Romantic Quest narrative underpinned by high levels of the two fundamental psychological dimensions of potency and intimacy. This role is further revealed in distorted cognitions about the ends or consequences of their actions, while accepting responsibility for the means. The adoption of this role is associated with a calm, nonaroused but negative emotional state.

In the Tragic Hero role, the respondent regards the offence as an inevitable, justified response. One which the offender is powerless to avoid. The commission of the crime is entirely about the enactment of the offender's Tragedy; the victim is irrelevant. Underpinned by low levels of potency and intimacy, this role is further revealed in cognitive attributions of the responsibility to others as well as the dismissal of the harm done. Adoption of this role is associated with an aroused but not entirely negative emotional state.

The Professional role is one in which the offence is an opportunity to demonstrate strength and expertise as part of an unfolding adventure. The focus is on this mastery of the environment in pursuit of the gains the protagonist seeks rather than the victim or target. The role features high levels of potency but low levels of criminal intimacy. The hallmark cognitive distortions are produced by a combination of ignoring the victim, yet owning responsibility for the offense actions but reinterpreting the end consequences in one's own terms. The emotional state that facilitates the adoption of this role during the commission of the offence is one of calm neutrality.

When acting out the Victim role, the offender regards the offence as a consequence of his powerlessness at the hands of others, within a generalised Irony narrative. Within this role, responsibility is attributed to others and the offender is in an aroused, negative emotional state. The crime is interpreted by the offender as happening as a result of his confusion, helplessness, and sense of alienation.

The Life As A Film (LAAF) Approach to Criminal Narratives

In contrast to the episodic focus of the NRQ, a standard procedure for exploring how offenders see their own overall life trajectory was developed, building on life narrative accounts that McAdams (1993) explored in his Life as a Book procedure. This procedure was developed with effective individuals leading constructive lives. It relies on a fluency and an understanding of themselves and their lives that are rare in an offending population. These intensive procedures also orient to concrete accounts of life events and episodes rather than an overarching perspective that emphasises identity and the dynamics of an unfolding story.

However, it was found in initial explorations that many convicted people did not understand the notion of their life as a book. Often also, their conceptualisations of their life are limited in coherence, either because their life has been so dysfunctional or because of limited intelligence and/or education. The generally low literacy of people in prison (cf., for example, Greenberg, Dunleavy, & Kutner, 2007) also greatly limits their ability to articulate accounts of themselves with reference to literary models.

Beyond the practical challenges that require a direct, engaging process with potentially reluctant participants, there are also the conceptual, psychological demands of finding a mechanism that allows offenders to generate content/ material, which reveal the dynamic processes of an unfolding story; but not any plausible story, one that elucidates the ways in which their narratives indicate perspectives on their past and aspirations, or beliefs, about their future. This is a requirement for a procedure that indicates naturally unfolding events that lead forward in time.

The 'life as book' (McAdams, 1993) tends to generate a historical, 'autobiography' style account, structured by social milestones (e.g. leaving school, getting married) rather than by significant events that are intrinsic to a personal perspective on their life story. These challenges to obtaining offender life narratives when taken together with benefits of exploring such narrative as indicated by Toch (1987), Agnew (2006), Maruna (2001) Presser (2009, 2010) and Youngs and Canter (2011, 2012) indicate there would be value in a methodology that complements earlier procedures, developing a shorter, less threatening, yet engaging process to which convicted men and women would respond readily.

With this objective a procedure based on a modification of the techniques used by McAdams (1993, 2001) for the derivation of constructive life stories has been developed. This is the LAAF (Life as a Film) procedure (Canter & Youngs, 2015). Unlike the life as a book or other life story interviews, the film framework elicits a future orientation. It requires some sort of conclusion or outcome rather than only emphasising what has happened in the past. This assists in exploring the respondents' understanding of what their life trajectory might be which contributes further to indicating their self-concepts.

It is also possible to derive a number of essential components that are present for any film, giving a rich source of psychological insights. This includes aspects of the dominant characters, inevitably including a representation of the self. It reveals interpersonal interactions, change over time, and of course some kind of plot, with a beginning and an ending. There are also structural issues that relate directly to the developing narrative model put forward by Canter and Youngs (2012), which are revealed by asking the respondent what sort of film (genre) is being described.

The LAAF Procedure

The general LAAF technique used to elicit narrative-relevant content is presented below. A short version (section a) of the procedure using an open-ended prompt and four key prompts can be used alone. When time and sample characteristics allow, a longer version with a range of additional prompts can be used in addition (sections A and B).

Instructions for a LAAF elicitation interview
Section A
If your life were to be made into a film, what type of film would it be?

Basic Prompts

- What would happen?
- Who would the main characters be?
- What would the main events that might happen in the film be?
- How do you think it might end?

Section B
The Main Scene of the Film

- What happens in the most exciting scene in the film?
- Where is it?

- What is going on?
- Who else is there? What are they doing?
- How are you acting?
- How do you feel?
- How does the Film open?
- When does the film start?
- What is going on?
- What are you like then?

Now tell us in as much detail as you can what happens between this opening scene and the main scene.

- Are you in the film?
- What sort of person are you?
- Who do you have good feelings about and why?
- Who do you have bad feelings about and why?
- What do other people think about you?
- What mistakes do you make?
- How do you change during the film?

The content analysis framework was developed from a number of sources. Existing narrative psychology theories and frameworks were considered. A range of psychological concepts identified as pertinent to the nature of an individual's agency in relation to criminal action were also drawn upon. Responses are subjected to a detailed interpretation procedure to derive an understanding of the substantive content in terms of four classes of issue, as follows.

Remit: implicit psychological content
Narratives are coded in terms of what the individuals talk about. Given the open-ended nature of the procedure, one level of interpretation considers the way in which the individual understands the LAAF task in terms of what to talk about.

Explicit processes used to organise content
Narratives are examined for their psychologically active components. These are the psychological processes by which the content is structured to produce the substantive connections and movement between the components, the storyline. A range of psychological structuring processes identified in McAdams' (1993) general narrative psychology as well as the offense-specific narrative roles identified by Canter and Youngs (2009, 2012) and Youngs and Canter (2011, 2012) are assessed.

Psychological complexity
The richness of the narratives is explored. This is considered on a substantive basis (e.g. number of distinct people; number of distinct psychological ideas)

and a formal basis (e.g. account length-number of words; presence of contingent type sequences).

Nature of agency vis-à-vis others and the world
The form and nature of the self's agency is studied. This assesses variations in the descriptions of how the individual deals with the world. An important aspect of this that is considered is how the individual describes the way in which they relate to others within the narrative.

An Example of a LAAF Response from a Man Who Had Committed Burglary

It would be something like *Shameless* and *Bread* with the scouse and the manc. There would be convicts and working families with the odd person doing crime on the side. *Significant person?* I had a good friend before 1998 but since then I've been by myself as our friendship got chucked back in my face. I was nicked on charges that I wouldn't have been and since then I find it hard to trust people and now I only have acquaintances. But there is my younger sister. *Main events?* When my family broke up when I was 3–7 years old then 7–13 my family was back together but there were lots of drinkers and it was always disrupted. My stepfather would send me out to play and would sexually abuse my sisters. He was always having a crack at me too. I was always trying to get my family back together but I ended up in care. I got back in touch with my dad at 16 but he died in 1997 and my ma died in 1998. I ended up cutting my wrists and every relationship since has been chaotic. I'm still in touch with my little sister but she doesn't come to see me. At home I stay with friends but they are all drug users so it's back to stage 1, I've asked for some help with drugs but I haven't heard anything yet and I'm out in 4 weeks. My sister is drug free but she is married to a drug dealer which surprised me because I didn't think she was like that. *Audience reaction?* I am an honest person, but if someone did something to me I would retaliate but not violently.

Example of a LAAF Response from a Man Who Had Committed Murder

It would probably be a film like *Brave Heart* or *Rob Roy*, standing up for what I believe in. I would be dishing out my own punishment for wrongdoings. The audience would probably think of the film in both positive and negative ways. I would punish myself for some of the things I did but it would all be better afterwards. Don't know if the audience would like me, I don't even like myself sometimes. I think maybe they would; there are a lot of people who like me. The significant people would be my family and friends; I have 1 brother, 1 sister, and 1 or 2 mates that I really love. My Granddad would be the most significant person; he has always singled me out – but in a good way. He has got 20 grandkids and I'm his favourite, I spend most of my time with him. The ending would be like snakes on a plane – crap, I dunno how it will end.

Conclusions and Developments

The standardised procedures summarised consist of an episodic exploration of roles when committing a crime: the NRQ. The potential of this has even been demonstrated with mentally disordered patients (Spruin, Canter, Young, & Coulsten, 2014). Analysis of the NRQ within various groups has revealed the consistent occurrence of four narrative themes, encapsulated in dominant roles that can be summarised as Victim, Revenger, Hero, Professional.

Complementing this, the consideration of offenders' view of their life trajectory, as revealed through the LAAF, has also produced rich results. The details of this procedure are given in Canter and Youngs (2015). Recent studies are showing the real potential of the practical significance of this approach. For example, Rowlands, Youngs, and Canter (2018) have used the LAAF to demonstrate that the transformation from a low agency/communion substance-using identity towards a high agency/communion recovery identity parallels the movement away from drug addiction. This offers the prospect for interventions that explore the way a substance misuser sees her/his life story unfolding and how that can be reconstructed. A comparison of offenders and nonoffenders using the LAAF also revealed an interesting distinction not readily available by other means (Youngs, Canter, & Carthy, 2016). An unresolved dissonance in offenders is not usually present in those who did not commit crimes.

The next stage of the research will be the thematic integration across the four content categories to explore the identification of distinct overall life narratives. The competing hypotheses being tested are that these will reflect either the narrative role themes as they relate to full life accounts rather than one-off events, or particular combinations of these roles that interact to produce new life story forms. This relating of episodic to overall narratives may inform debate around the multiplicity and ambiguity of an individual's narrative forms (e.g. Brookman, 2015).

References

Agnew, R. (2006). Storylines as neglected causes of crime. *Journal of Research in Crime and Delinquency*, *43*, 119–147. doi:10.1177/0022427805280052

Bandura, A. (1990). Mechanisms of moral disengagement. In A. Reich (Ed.), *Origins of terrorism; psychologies, ideologies, theologies, sates of mind* (pp. 161–191). New York, NY: Cambridge University Press.

Becker, H. (1963). *Outsiders*. New York, NY: Free Press.

Brookman, F. (2015). The shifting narratives of violent offenders. In L. Pressed & S. Sandberg (Eds.), *Narrative criminology*. New York, NY: New York University Press.

Brookman, C. H., & Hochstetler, A. (2011). Street codes as formula stories: How inmates recount violence. *Journal of Contemporary Ethnography*, *40*(4), 397–424. doi:10.1177/0891241611408307

Bruner, J. (1987). Life as narrative. *Social Research*, *54*(1), 11–32.

Bruner, J. S. (1991). The narrative construction of reality. *Critical Inquiry*, *18*(1), 1–21.

Canter, D. (1994). *Criminal shadows: Inside the mind of the serial killer.* London: HarperCollins.

Canter, D., & Youngs, D. (2012). Sexual and violent offender' victim role assignment: A general model of offending style. *Journal of Forensic Psychiatry and Psychology, 23*(3), 297–326. doi:10.1080/14789949.2012.690102

Canter, D., & Youngs, D. (2015). The LAAF procedure for exploring offenders' narrative. *The Howard Journal of Criminal Justice, 54*(3), 219–236.

Canter, D. V., & Youngs, D. E. (2009). *Investigative psychology: Offender profiling and the analysis of criminal action.* Chichester: John Wiley & Sons.

Canter, D. V., & Youngs, D. E. (2011). Narratives of criminal action and forensic psychology. *Legal and Criminological Psychology, 17*(2), 262–275.

Fleetwood, J. (2016). Narrative habitus: Thinking through structure/agency in the narratives of offenders. *Crime, Media, Culture, 12*(2), 173–192.

Frye, N. (1957). *Anatomy of criticism: Four essays.* Princeton, NJ: Princeton University Press.

Greenberg, E., Dunleavy, E., & Kutner, M. (2007). *Literacy behind bars: Results from the 2003 National Assessment of Adult Literacy Prison Survey.* NCES 2007-473. National Center for Education Statistics. Retrieved from http://nces.ed.gov/help/orderinfo.asp

Heimer, K., & Matsueda, R. L. (1994). Role-taking, role commitment, and delinquency: A theory of differential social control. *American Sociological Review, 59*(3), 365–390. doi:10.2307/2095939

Hermans, H. J. M. (1996). Voicing the self: From information processing to dialogical interchange. *Psychological Bulletin, 119*(1), 31–50. doi:10.1037/0033-2909.119.1.31

Horgan, J. G. (2009). *Walking away from terrorism.* London: Routledge.

Leary, T. (1957). *The interpersonal theory of personality.* New York, NY: Ronald Press.

Lemert, E. M. (1951). *Social pathology.* New York, NY: McGraw-Hill.

Maruna, S. (2001). *Making good: How ex-convicts reform and rebuild their lives.* Washington, DC: American Psychological Association.

Maruna, S., & Immarigeon, R. (2004). Ex-offender reintegration: Theory and practice. In S. Maruna (Ed.), *After crime and punishment: Pathways to offender reintegration* (pp. 1–25). Cullompton: Willan Publishing.

Maruna, S., & Mann, R. E. (2006). A fundamental attribution error? Rethinking cognitive distortions. *Legal and Criminological Psychology, 11*(2), 155–177. doi: 10.1348/135532506X114608

Massoglia, M., & Uggen, G. (2010). Interactionist theory of desistance and the transition to adulthood. *American Journal of Sociology, 116*(2), 543–582.

Matsueda, R. L. (1992). Reflected appraisals, parental labeling, and delinquency: Specifying a symbolic interactionist theory. *American Journal of Sociology, 97*(6), 1577–1611.

McAdams, D. P. (1993). *The stories we live by: Personal myths and the making of the self.* New York, NY: Willam Morrow and Company.

McAdams, D. P. (2001). The psychology of life stories. *Review of General Psychology, 5,* 100–122.

McAdams, D. P. (2016). *The redemptive self: Stories Americans live by.* New York, NY: Oxford University Press.

McAuley, J. W. (1997). The Ulster loyalist political parties: Towards a new respectability. In *Études irlandaises, n°22-2, 1997. Le processus de paix en Irlande du Nord, sous la direction de Pierre Joannon* (pp. 117–131). doi:10.3406/irlan.1997.1407

Mead, G. H. (1927/1982). The objective reality of perspectives. In *Proceedings of the sixth international congress of philosophy* (pp. 75–85). doi:10.5840/wcp6192726

Presser, L. (2009). The narratives of offenders. *Theoretical Criminology, 13*, 177–200. doi:10.1177/1362480609102878

Presser, L. (2010). Collecting and analysing the stories of offenders. *Journal of Criminal Justice Education, 21*(4), 431–446.

Rowlands, D., Youngs, D., & Canter, D. (2018). Exploring an agency-communion model of identity transformation in recovery from substance misuse. *Journal of Substance Use, 24*, 265–272. doi:10.1080/14659891.2018.155273

Sandberg, S., & Ugelvik, T. (2016). The past, present, and future of narrative criminology: A review and an invitation. *Crime, Media, Culture: International Journal, 12*(2), 129–136. doi:10.1177/1741659016663558

Schutz, W. C. (1958). *FIRO: A three-dimensional theory of interpersonal behavior*. New York, NY: Rinehart.

Singer, J. A. (2004). Narrative identity and meaning-making across the adult lifespan: An introduction. *Journal of Personality, 72*(3), 437–459.

Spruin, E., Canter, D., Young, D., & Coulsten, B. (2014). Criminal narratives of mentally disordered offenders: An exploratory study. *Journal of Forensic Psychology Practice, 14*, 438–455. doi:10.1080/15228932.2014.965987

Sykes, G., & Matza, D. (1957). Techniques of neutralization: A theory of delinquency. *American Sociological Review, 22*(6), 664–670. Retrieved from http://www.jstor.org/stable/2089195

Tannenbaum, F. (1938). *Crime and community*. London and New York, NY: Columbia University Press.

Toch, H. (1987). Supplementing the positivist approach. In M. Gottfredson & T. Hirschi (Eds.), *Positive criminology* (pp. 138–153). Beverly Hills, CA: SAGE Publications.

Toch, H. (1992). *Violent men: An inquiry into the psychology of violence* (revised. ed.). Washington, DC: American Psychological Association. doi:10.1037/10135-000

Ward, T. (2010). The good lives model of offender rehabilitation: Basic assumptions, etiological commitments, and practical implications. In F. McNeil, P. Raynor, & C. Trotter (Eds.), *Offender supervision: New directions in theory, research and practice* (pp. 41–64). Cullompton: Willan Publishing.

Youngs, D. E., & Canter, D. V. (2011). Narrative roles in criminal action: An integrative framework for differentiating offenders. *Legal and Criminological Psychology, 17*, 1–17. doi:10.1111/j.2044-8333.2011.0201

Youngs, D. E., & Canter, D. V. (2012). Offenders crime narratives as revealed by the Narrative Roles Questionnaire. *International Journal of Offender Therapy and Comparative Criminology, 57*, 1–23. doi:10.1177/0306624X11434577

Youngs, D. E., Canter, D. V., & Carthy, N. (2016). The offender's narrative: Unresolved dissonance in life as a film (LAAF) responses. *Legal and Criminological Psychology, 21*(2), 251–265.

NARRATIVE DIALOGUE, THE UNCONSCIOUS AND ABSENCES

Chapter 18

Doing Dialogical Narrative Analysis: Implications for Narrative Criminology

Dan Jerome S. Barrera

Introduction

Dialogical narrative analysis (DNA) is a recent addition to the plethora of methods in narrative analysis. It seeks to provide a balance to the *whats* and *hows* of stories (see Gubrium & Holstein, 2009) and their material effects on storytellers and listeners. That is, it focusses not only on the *content* but also on the *effects* of stories (Frank, 2010). While DNA has received considerable attention from researchers, it has not gained much ground compared to other methods such as those outlined by Riessman (2008). Foremost of the reasons is its heuristic nature. Arthur Frank, its proponent, did not intend it to have a step-by-step procedure. Its approach is criticism that fosters a 'movement of thought' through dialogical questions (Frank, 2010, 2012).

But its nature may slow down its diffusion to various fields (as discussed below). For example, in criminology, I know of only three published studies that have used or at are least inspired by DNA (see Barrera, 2017; Brookman, 2015; Sandberg, Tutenges, & Copes, 2015). Moreover, some researchers use DNA's theoretical bases, but use other methods to analyse their data. For instance, Chadwick (2014) complains that 'Frank (2010) does not give us many clues as to how we would go about such a project as part of the concrete and practical work of doing analysis,' and proceeds to use the listening guide or voice-centred relational method (Gilligan, Spencer, Weinberg, & Bertsch, 2003). Nevertheless, some scholars have recently picked up the theoretical and methodological foundations that Frank (2010, 2012) provided as the point of departure in providing a clearer heuristic guide for DNA. Together, Brett Smith (2016) and Nick Caddick (2016) illustrated how to use DNA on research interview data. But research interview data are not the sole source of stories; others include autobiographies, literature, news reports and everyday conversations. Frank (2010, p. 15) treats these genres of storytelling as a 'continuum'; that is, each depends on the others.

In this chapter, I will provide an illustration of DNA on stories in the media reports about the drug war in the Philippines. I will show how such stories affect drug policy implementation. I will also provide a brief review of the diffusion of

DNA in other fields as well as some of DNA's implications to the emerging field of narrative criminology. In doing these, I hold firmly to the basic tenets of socio-narratology and DNA which will be provided in detail in the next section. This study offers additional contribution to narrative criminology which has so far granted less attention to state-level narratives, and, therefore, misses how cultural, institutional, organisational and individual stories are linked (Loseke, 2007).

Nevertheless, a handful of narrative criminologists have initiated this task. For example, Tognato (2015) studied how cultural narratives about tax evasion were performed through public sphere telling and how this performance affected responses to tax evasion. Keeton (2015), on the other hand, focussed on Biblical narratives on how these were used by North American colonisers to remove indigenous tribes from their lands. Keeton emphasises more on the '*whats*' of storytelling, while Tognato on the '*hows*'. Socio-narratology focusses on both of these aspects of storytelling, and answers Keeton's call for criminologists to 'develop theoretical understandings' (p. 145) about the stories' effects on policies.

Socio-narratology and Dialogical Narrative Analysis

In his book, *Letting Stories Breathe: A Socio-narratology*, Frank (2010) initially provided the theoretical (socio-narratology) and methodological (DNA) components of his approach in analysing stories, which build upon his own rich work on illness and narratives (e.g. Frank, 1995) and others' works in folklore, philosophy and psychological and social research, among others. His theoretical propositions are as dialogical as his methodological approach, which is much influenced by the philosophy of Mikhail Bakhtin (1984). His approach, however, does not limit stories as mere representations of events but as enablers of actions.

This view coheres much with that of the proponents of narrative criminology. Presser (2009, p. 177), for instance, calls an offender's story as an 'explanatory variable..., a key instigator of action' (see Presser & Sandberg, 2015a, 2015b also). Sandberg (2010; see Sandberg, 2013 also), moreover, acknowledges the plurivocality of stories within one's account of an experience as opposed to Presser's (2008) former emphasis on a unified life story. However, socio-narratology offers additional theoretical and methodological tools to narrative criminologists, especially with the former's focus on Bakhtin's concepts of *polyphony* and *heteroglossia*. Polyphony suggests that stories are always resonant with others' stories and cultural narratives; while heteroglossia shows how stories are always 'assembled from multiple codes of language usage and genre... governing which genres are appropriate to represent which situations' (Frank, 2012, p. 35). And, actions, for example crime or harm in general, can be considered as polyphonic and hetoreglossic interpellations of stories because they themselves are stories (Carr, 1986).

Socio-narratology

Frank (2010, p. 202) defines socio-narratology as the 'inquiry into our ways of mirroring – and improving – our lives' and quotes Rabih Alameddine

(2009, p. 450) who said: 'Events matter little, only stories of those events affect us.' Stories not just mirror actions retrospectively but also prospectively. Here, Frank reverses the more common perspective on stories as mere (sometimes faulty) record of the past, or what Presser (2009) calls as 'narrative as record' view. As Sandberg (2010) notes, it is not important whether the story is true; what is important are its effects on identities and crime. Supporting narrative criminologists, Frank (2010, p. 3) believes that 'Stories animate human life... [They] work with people, for people, and always stories work *on* people, affecting what people are able to see as real, as possible, and as worth doing or best avoided' (emphasis in original). He adds that 'human life depends on the stories we tell: the sense of self that those stories impart, the relationships constructed around shared stories, and the sense of purpose that stories both propose and foreclose.' He sees the relationship between life and story, however, as a reciprocal process, as neither of them has temporal precedence of the other. With this view, he agrees with the perspectives of Bruner (1987) and Ricoeur (1984).

The *social* part of socio-narratology views stories as actors and as selection/evaluation systems which interpellate actions (Frank, 2010, 2012). This is so because stories provide models for identities and connect or disconnect people. Somers (1994) provides the same view that actions are contingent upon identities narratives provide. This view is also endorsed by Presser (2009). As Frank (2012, p. 45) states, stories provide a 'space in which people can claim identities, reject identities, and experiment with identities.' He borrows from Louis Althusser the term 'interpellation,' suggesting that stories interpellate or hail people to assume identities. Similar mechanism works when stories connect or disconnect people. Stories interpellate people on who to associate with or disconnect from. They make life social. Frank (2010) treats stories as *fabrication mechanism*, a term from Bruno Latour. Stories are so good at this that people with different interests can rally behind a single cause laid down by a story. He attributes this to the stories' interpretive openness or ambiguity in Polletta's (2006) terms.

But not all stories are successful interpellators. Interpellation is dependent upon one's *narrative habitus*, a term he adapted from Pierre Bourdieu's habitus. Narrative habitus is the 'collection of stories' hailing a person to assume identities. It is a 'disposition to hear some stories as those that one ought to listen to, ought to repeat on appropriate occasions and ought to be guided by' (Frank, 2010, p. 53). And narrative habitus is organised in what Frank, adapting Pierre Bayard, calls the *inner library*. Just like in a physical library, stories one has heard are arranged psychologically, and stories that are not familiar or not resonant with what is already in the library or cannot be easily located in this library are most likely put off. Therefore, stories are seen as 'unchosen forces' (p. 53) and decisions as 'unchosen choices' (p. 25). However, contrary to what narrative criminologist Fleetwood (2016) suggests, this does not preclude agency on the part of the actor because people are responsive to new stories. Frank (2010) calls this process *narrative ambush*: 'stories that have no place in people's inner library still teach those people who they can be.' He concludes that 'humans are the sum of perpetually *accumulating* stories, because often enough stories break into the inner library, reshaping the new accumulation' (p. 60).

Moreover, the *narratology* part of socio-narratology studies the capacities of stories that enable them to do things *for* and on *people*. Frank (2010) emphasises that stories are about bringing humans trouble, are character-driven, bracket a particular point of view, bring suspense, have interpretive openness, are out of control, are inherently moral, resonate with other stories, are symbiotic with humans and shape-shift, tell the truth and arouse people's imaginations. He concludes that a story is any narration that has these capacities aside from its Labovian structure. Stories, therefore, are material semiotic companions – they are semiotic in nature but material in their effects. This leads us to the narrative/story distinction that Frank (1995, 2010, 2012) has long been pointing out. Socio-narratology views stories as local and specific; while narratives are resources (templates) from which storytellers tell their stories.

Dialogical Narrative Analysis

Frank (2010, p. 73), instead of calling DNA as a method, calls it as a 'movement of thought... [implying] movement, reciprocity, and constant flux.' DNA is a heuristic guide rather than a step-by-step procedure in the prescriptive model of methodology. DNA is an act of criticism that uses questions to move our thought forward. It also promotes an interpretive scheme that is dialogical in nature. And it provides exemplars as tentative models of presenting the results. Hinged on socio-narratology, DNA 'studies the mirroring between what is told in the story – the story's content – and what happens as a result of telling that story – its effects' (pp. 71–72). Some analysis may foreground content more than the effects or vice versa. But a balance between the two is also possible. DNA also uses the analytical techniques illustrated by Presser and Sandberg (2015b), but it proceeds beyond them by answering some dialogical questions which shall be discussed below.

Preparation for dialogical narrative analysis

Before embarking on practicing DNA, one must first be familiar and be equipped with DNA's interpretive assumptions and techniques that make DNA *dialogical*. First, the researcher should acknowledge that no story is ever original (Frank, 2010, 2012). A story is a dialogue of multiple stories, heard or imagined. One should bear in mind that as the storyteller is caught up in a collection of stories so is the researcher with his narrative habitus, too (Frank, 2010). Thus, dialogical interpretation must begin with the researcher's recognition that he/she is caught up with stories that may or not overlap with that of the storyteller, and thus may require a shift in horizon on the part of the researcher. Next, Bakhtin's principle of human's *nonfinalizability* should be kept in mind. No story and no life are ever final. The researcher does not have the last word. Thus, research should invite dialogue and not finalise the characters of people (Frank, 2005, 2010, 2012). Equally important is another principle of thinking *with* and not *about* the character. Analysis in a dialogical way is having a dialogue *with* the character and not *about him/her.*

Moreover, Frank (2010) suggests the following as actual acts of interpretation. The analyst must *go into the story* by translating them into mental images. Next is to *go into the point of view* of the marginalised character (e.g. antagonist). Another is *attention to omissions* – what details that might be expected but omitted by the teller. Also, the analyst must *foreground differences* between him/her and the storyteller. Further, interpretation should take *slowly*: it takes time to immerse with the data and their sources and relevant contexts to fully appreciate what is being analysed. Finally, in keeping up with the dialogical nature of the analysis, the researcher must *appreciate* the story and the storyteller.

Animating interest, data collection and preparation, and story selection
DNA starts with *animating interest* (Frank, 2012). Frank shares this question that animates his interest and acts as his analytical compass every time he is confused or lost: '*Medical treatment too often increases patients' suffering rather than reducing this suffering; why is this, and how could it change?*' (p. 37) Then, *data collection* and *data preparation* can proceed from fieldwork (if applicable) to the collection of stories. But the collection of stories presupposes the *identification of stories* in a text. Frank suggests that stories have horizontal and vertical dimensions. Horizontally, Labov and Waletzky's (1967) structural model of a story, with complicating action and resolution as the minimum parts, can be used for such purpose. Vertically, Frank (2012) suggests that stories must have the capacities he has outlined such as characters, suspense and imagination. Next, the researcher can then proceed to *story selection*, wherein practical wisdom gained from experience is used 'in an iterative process of hearing stories speak to the original research interest, then representing those stories in writing, revising story selections as the writing develops its arguments, and revising the writing as those stories require' (Frank, 2012, p. 43). Here, stories are taken as wholes and few exemplars will be analysed thoroughly and presented in a report. Note further that analysis occurs during attempts to write the report.

Questions for movement of thought
Although DNA is a heuristic guide and can become cumbersome at times, its analysis must start somewhere. In *Letting stories breathe*, Frank (2010, pp. 75–85) provides (nonexhaustive) dialogical questions to open up analysis (although not all will be applicable to any given project). These questions include: 'What does the story make narratable? Who is holding their own in the story, but also, is the story making it more difficult for other people to hold their own? What is the effect of people being caught up in their own stories while living with people caught up in other stories? What is the force of fear in the story, and what animates desire? How does a story help people, individually and collectively, to remember who they are? How does a story do the work of memory?' (pp. 75–85).

In a later chapter on DNA, Frank (2012, pp. 44–46) refines these questions and categorises them into resource questions, circulation questions, affiliation questions, identity questions and 'what is at stake?' questions. *Resource questions* include: 'What resources shape how the story is being told? What resources shape how listeners comprehend the story? How are narrative resources distributed between different groups? Who has access to which resources? Who is under what form of constraint in the resources they utilise?' *Circulation questions* can be used by asking, 'Who tells which stories to whom? Who would immediately understand that story and who wouldn't? Are there some people whom [the teller] wouldn't tell that story to, and why not?' Some *affiliation questions* include: 'Who will be affiliated into a group of those who share a common understanding of a particular story? Whom does the story render external or other to that group? Who is excluded from the "we" who share the story?' Next, *identity questions* include: 'How does the story teach people who they are, and how do people tell stories to explore whom they might become?' Lastly, *what is at stake questions* can be asked such as 'How does the storyteller holding his or her own in the act of telling that particular story, in that way? How do the stories that some people have available convince them of what they have to do and to be in order to hold their own?'

Forms of dialogical narrative analysis

Frank (2010) suggests that DNA is best learnt through exemplars. As a heuristic guide, DNA does not prescribe a step-by-step guideline. The researcher can learn how to conduct DNA by learning how previous studies worked with their data. This does not mean, however, that creativity is lost. DNA is not about mimicking what has been done. The *dialogical* component of DNA maintains that the present analysis must also be in dialogue with previous ones. Thus, just like a story which is composed of fragments from previous stories, an analysis must also be composed of fragments of previous dialogical analysis. Frank proposes five (nonexhaustive) forms that DNA can take. A research report can take the form of any or a combination of these.

Organisation through an analytic interest. As stated above, there must be an overarching analytic interest that a researcher should possess even before the study begins. Frank (2010) uses Williams' (1984) paper as an exemplar for this form of DNA. Williams' analytic interest was the genesis of chronic illness in the words of the participants. And the participants provided their genesis accounts through their stories. Frank observes that Williams used genesis as his device to organise the different stories told by the participants.

Building narrative typology. Frank (1995) is most popular in building typologies due to his work on illness narratives which he categorises into restitution, quest and chaos. Narrative types are 'the most general storyline[s] that can be recognised underlying the plot and tensions of particular stories' (p. 75). Typology building recognises the dialogical nature of stories which are drawn from narrative resources (Frank, 2010, 2012). Typologies can be developed around (a) stories' content and/or the storytelling event, (b) researcher's analytic interest/s like participants' solution to problems in a continuum or a matrix, (c) capacities of stories or (d) DNA's dialogical questions. The work of Sandberg et al. (2015) is a good example for this in narrative criminology. They outlined four main stories of violence among drug dealers: business, intimidation, moral and survivor narratives.

Documenting an event's effect through stories. An analysis could also be structured by presenting stories as an event's effects. Frank (2010) uses Erikson (1976) study that documents the effects of a flood of about 132 million gallons of black water containing mining by-products to the villages in Buffalo Creek, West Virginia. The stories are organised around the flood's effects on morale and morality, disorientation, loss of connection, illness and identity, and illusion of safety. Although narrative criminology puts much emphasis on the stories' prospective role in instigating crime and harm, it also acknowledges the reciprocal relationship[1] between stories and harm (Presser & Sandberg, 2015a, 2015b). A particular harmful action generates stories and partly those who committed it sought for such stories to tell. Katz (2016) illustrated this when he studied the stories generated from the Rodney King riots. One should note that the veracity of these stories is not important, only their effects are (Sandberg, 2010). To rehearse Alameddine (2009, p. 450), 'Events matter little, only stories of those events affect us.'

How stories assemble groups. This form of DNA focusses on one type of work that stories do for and on people – group assembling. Stories as noted above make life social by connecting or disconnecting people. Frank (2010) uses as an exemplar the work of Polletta (2006) in social movements. Polletta observes that social movement stories are fabrications. Groups planned activities that could be storied later in a predetermined story. Then, these groups reconstruct their activities using stories. Perhaps, one curious question could be asked on why people with differing interests assemble and relegate their differences away. Polletta answers that it is *narrative ambiguity* that could summon people to align their own story and actions with the overarching one.

Storytelling as institutional emplotment. Institutions have their own preferred narratives. DNA can explore institutional settings and their narratives that oftentimes force people therein to adapt to the preferred and accepted narratives. Frank (2010) uses as exemplars studies on institutions for support groups of relatives of persons with Alzheimer's disease, codependents anonymous, and occupational therapists. All of these groups impose or emplot a certain narrative type that group members should take. DNA could show not only what these narrative types are but also the process of emplotment that the group does and the reactions of both members who are ready to fashion their stories based on the preferred plot and those who are not.

Action as an effect of stories. This is the heart of narrative criminology: Stories, because of their capacities, effect actions (Presser, 2009). A DNA can provide a case comparative organisation of stories and their effects for this purpose. Frank (2010) highlights the work of Philip Smith (2005) on why war occurs. Smith's answer is *stories*. Smith proposed a structural model of genre and argued that stories in apocalyptic mode drive war. He then surveyed the civil sphere stories in the US, UK, France and Spain relevant to the war over the Suez Canal, Gulf War and War in Iraq. He found that countries in which apocalyptic genres

---

[1]Ricoeur (1984) sees this relationship as a spiral not circular and tautological.

predominated engaged highly in war, while those wherein low mimetic stories predominate did not. A report therefore can be structured according to which story affects which actions.

Diffusion of Dialogical Narrative Analysis

Since Frank's (2010, 2012) introduction of socio-narratology and DNA, DNA has been used by several researchers in analysing stories in different fields. However, as noted above, some have difficulties in using DNA due to its heuristic nature (e.g. Chadwick, 2014) and instead used other methods to complement (implement) the propositions of socio-narratology. This has I think affected the diffusion of DNA to various fields. Apart from the heuristic nature of DNA, a possible reason for its poor diffusion in criminology is the preoccupation of researchers towards the 'truth' of one's stories and also to one's single unified story (Sandberg, 2010).

Nevertheless, Brett Smith (2016) and Nick Caddick (2016) in health and sport psychology have provided a clearer heuristic guide in doing DNA built upon Frank's work. Smith (2016) emphasises the cyclical and iterative process of doing DNA that is faithful to Frank's ideals. Researchers can therefore jump between strategies – moving back and forth as the analysis requires. In *getting the story phase*, the analyst must (a) decide what a story and/or narrative is, then (b) collect big and/or small stories and (c) transcribe the data, writing the report as an active and iterative process. Next, in the *getting to grips with stories phase*, the research should conduct (a) indwelling with the data by reading or listening several times, (b) identification of stories, (c) identification of narrative themes and thematic relationships and (d) identification of the structure of the stories. Then, in the *opening up analytical dialogue phase*, an analyst could pose dialogical questions from Frank and Smith's own work such as resource, circulation, connection, identity, body and function questions. Finally, in the *pulling the analysis together phase*, the analysis can use the five forms of DNA that Frank proposed to structure the report. This guide was demonstrated by Caddick (2016) successfully.

DNA has been used primarily on interview and participant observation data in texts. DNA is least popular in other genres of storytelling, for example in media studies where texts are used in combination with photographs and videos to create stories in the civil sphere. In this chapter, I draw upon Frank's socio-narratology and DNA and Brett Smith's (2016) adaptation of DNA to demonstrate how I analysed civil sphere stories relevant to the war on drugs in the Philippines. I show that the media reports in newspapers and TV are told in stories that have an impact on the implementation of the drug policy in the country.

An Illustration of Dialogical Narrative Analysis

The analytic interest that guided my study is: '*Despite of the mounting criticisms from local as well as international political and media figures and human rights groups, why has it been so easy for President Rodrigo Duterte to declare his war on drugs? Why does the war on drugs continue to be popular among Filipinos?*

Importantly, why has Duterte's war on drugs implementation so malleable – it was launched in June 2016, suspended in January 2017, resumed in March 2017, then for the second time suspended in October 2017 but again resumed in December 2018?' My initial guess was that stories in the civil sphere are instrumental, and the results of my study support this.

Getting the Story

Data used in this study[2] were gathered from news reports on TV and in newspapers relevant to the drug situation. Google Advanced Search Tools and YouTube.com were explored using keyword searches, covering 2015–2017.[3] Each data (in text or video) was then downloaded and arranged in preparation for the data analysis. Some news reports that were used as illustration in the study were transcribed in full or in part.[4] Overall, 1,743 news items were collected and analysed. These news items describe 1,864 stories (Table 18.1).[5]

Table 18.1. Profile of the Data Analysed.

News Type	News Agency	Number of News Reports	%	Number of Stories	%
Television	ABS-CBN (*TV Patrol*)	701	40.22	745	39.97
	GMA (24 Oras)	293	16.81	307	16.47
	Subtotal	**994**	**57.03**	**1,052**	**56.44**
Newspaper	*Manila Bulletin*	131	7.52	140	7.51
	Philippine Daily Inquirer	389	22.32	407	21.83
	Philippine Star	229	13.14	265	14.22
	Subtotal	**749**	**42.97**	**812**	**43.56**
Overall Total		**1,743**	**100.00**	**1,864**	**100.00**

---

[2] This study is part of my completed unpublished doctoral dissertation at the University of Cebu, Philippines.
[3] I used search terms containing the name of the media program or outlet (e.g. *TV Patrol* or *Philippine Daily Inquirer*) and the drug situation key terms such as 'drugs,' 'droga,' 'war on drugs,' 'shabu,' 'addict,' 'adik' and the like.
[4] The author, as a native speaker of Cebuano (dialect of Duterte) and fluent speaker of Filipino, translated some statements in dialect to English.
[5] Note that the units of analysis in this study are independent stories, not a single news report which could report more than one story. Nevertheless, most news items just reported one story each.

Getting to Grips with Stories

I read and watched all newspaper and TV news reports several times as an indwelling with the data (Smith, 2016). I used the Labovian model of a story in identifying stories, with the minimum component of complicating action and resolution. Since the news reports used photographs and videos, I used the guidelines provided by Robertson (2017) and Graddol (1993) in identifying visual stories. I also used the works in photography and cinematography (e.g. Thompson & Bowen, 2009) as my guide in how photographers/cameramen used angles, lighting and sound to create stories in photographs and videos. Also, on the process rereading the news stories, I identified narrative themes and structures. I used Philip Smith's (2005) structural model of genre as my guide in building the typologies of narrative structure underlying each story. While doing all of these, I marked what stories I would use as exemplars in my research report. Some of the details of this part of the analysis are presented in the next subsection showing the narrative types and the details of the apocalypse narrative type.

Narrative types of the news stories

Based on Smith's (2005) four genres, I have extracted seven drug war stories from the data. Genres are templates from which storytellers base their stories. These major stories are apocalypse, romance, tragedy, low mimesis, inverted tragedy, inverted romance and inverted apocalypse. The first four types of stories were adapted from Smith; however, I have added the last three as additional types as gleaned from the data. As shown in Table 18.2, the most dominant stories are romantic and apocalyptic, and this is fairly consistent across the time periods, except in 2017 when inverted apocalypse ranked second next to romantic stories.

Table 18.2. The Stories that Occupy the Civil Sphere in the Philippines from 2015 to 2017.

Genre	2015 f	2015 %	2016 f	2016 %	2017 f	2017 %	Total	%
Apocalypse	19	16.24	109	12.11	67	7.91	195	10.46
Romance	89	76.07	532	59.11	357	42.15	978	52.47
Tragedy	2	1.71	72	8.00	131	15.47	205	11.00
Low Mimesis	2	1.71	27	3.00	16	1.89	45	2.41
Inverted Tragedy	1	0.85	70	7.78	57	6.73	128	6.87
Inverted Romance	3	2.56	73	8.11	61	7.20	137	7.35
Inverted Apocalypse	1	0.85	17	1.89	158	18.65	176	9.44
All Stories	**117**	**100**	**900**	**100**	**847**	**100**	**1,864**	**100**

Importantly, these stories and their characteristics have implications on how drug offenders are treated, especially in terms of the *use of force* against them. A direct relationship between genres and the use of force against drug offenders can be inferred from the structural model of genres. As one moves from inverted apocalypse to apocalypse, the desire to use force against offenders also increases. At the extreme, for instance, apocalyptic stories prescribe extreme, and even lethal, force against drug offenders. These stories are primarily storied by Duterte and his police chief in the civil sphere.

Apocalypse: 'Drugs, drugs, drugs. Kill, kill, kill.'
Although, there are seven genres of stories in this study, I will concentrate on just one – apocalypse – to demonstrate how I went on the analysis. I chose apocalypse since this is what currently drives the violent war on drugs in the country. The main protagonists of this story are Duterte and the police, and the antagonists are the drug personalities. Although the most common stories are in romantic mode, Duterte built upon and elevated these stories and moved towards an apocalyptic tone. This then would make it easy for him to 'get away with murder,' as one commentator suggests (Syjuco, 2016). I will show its dialogical nature after showing its structure.

Apocalyptic stories are the third most common type of drug war stories in the data. As described in the preceding section, it tends to place an extreme gap between the protagonists and antagonists. In these stories, drug offenders (both drug pushers and users) are seen as exceedingly evil such that they deserve not only to be apprehended but preferably destroyed, in this case, killed. Such stories have this typical structure: *Drugs proliferate and endanger the country, and drug pushers and users are extremely evil because drug is the root cause of all evil. Therefore, drugs and drug offenders must be destroyed to preserve the country.*

One newspaper report captures such apocalyptic stories from Duterte in a forum at the De La Salle University on 20 January 2016 before the 2016 presidential elections (Corrales, 2016). Transcript No. 1 shows the narrative structure of the *Philippine Daily Inquirer* news item.

Duterte: There Will Be Blood in 'Cleansing' this Country

(1) PDP-LABAN presidential candidate Rodrigo Duterte means business when it comes to fighting crime, and there will be blood.
(2) 'If I become president, there would be no such thing as bloodless cleansing,' Duterte said in a speech during a forum at the De La Salle University in Manila on Wednesday.
(3) Duterte was referring to criminals in the Philippines who carry out robberies and murders with seeming impunity that leave people feeling helpless.

(Continued)

Duterte: There Will Be Blood in 'Cleansing' this Country

(4) Asked to elaborate his statement during an interview after the forum, he said 'there could be no cleansing that is bloodless.'
(5) He cited the rising criminality in the country; some, he said, were perpetrated by drug addicts.
(6) 'My God, I hate drugs. And I have to kill people because I hate drugs,' he said.
(7) He said he would return peace and order within the 3 to 6 months of his term as president if elected.
(8) 'I would return to you the right to walk out at night safe and ride a jeepney without being held up,' he said.
(9) With his iron-fist approach to restore peace and order, the tough-talking Duterte explained that his fight against criminality and drug addiction 'would always be in accordance with the law.'
(10) 'I do not execute people kneeling down with hands tied at their back. It will be a confrontation,' he said.
(11) He said 'the obedience to law is almost optional,' citing the rising criminality and drug problems in the country.
(12) He vowed to deliver his promise of fighting criminals and bring peace and order to the country 'even if it would cost me my life, my honour, and even my liberty.'

The core of this news item is a set of narrative clauses serving as complicating actions (Paragraphs 4–8). As complicating actions, they serve to breach the current condition (i.e. crime situation in the country). Here, Duterte tells the public apocalyptic stories. One of such small stories is the now famous narrative clause in Paragraph 6, 'My God, I hate drugs. And I have to kill people because I hate drugs.'

This is the simplest form of narrative, but in a prospective form (i.e. storying the future). Since crimes, drugs and offenders have become so evil, he hates drugs and thus will kill drug offenders. Aside from the orientation and complication action, the evaluation portion of the news article also reinforces the apocalyptic tone of the article. Paragraphs 9–11 show the binary coding of Duterte and his antagonists. Paragraphs 9–10 depicts Duterte as a law-abiding law enforcer; on the other hand, drug offenders are the complete opposite whose 'obedience to law is almost optional.' Moreover, Duterte here is storied as one who is motivated by higher ideals, not mundane ones: He is motivated by the desire to 'bring peace and order to the country "even if it would cost [his] life … honour, and even … liberty."'

It should be noted that this is not the only apocalyptic story that Duterte has shared in the civil sphere. Almost all of his stories relevant to the drug problem in

2015 and in subsequent years had an apocalyptic tone. Also, Duterte was not alone in spewing apocalyptic stories in the civil sphere. Some politicians, law enforcers and commentators were also apocalyptic in seeing the drug problem. For instance, as reported by *The Philippine Star* on 2 February 2016, one of the presidentiables, Sen. Grace Poe, apocalyptically sees the drug problem in the country (Sy, 2016):

> Maybe one of the reservations of people would be because I'm female, I might not be tough on drugs. One of the first things I would do is to declare drugs a national security threat and a menace to society. Let's make it public who the pushers are.

Seeing the drug problem as a 'national security threat and a menace to society' is very apocalyptic. She also stressed she was also thinking about the revival of the death penalty against heinous criminals including drug offenders as a way to 'scare away criminals.'

In reporting these apocalyptic stories, news media also reinforces such a tone in accompanying photographs. The narrative structure of these photos can be discerned and will now be discussed.[6] A photo of Duterte inspecting a seized firearm in Davao City was inserted in a *Philippine Daily Inquirer* news story bearing his apocalyptic stories on 14 April 2016, entitled 'Duterte bares plan to wage war versus drugs if elected President' (Carvajal, 2016). The photo was used probably to suggest that Duterte would use extreme force to the point of killing drug offenders in his drug war. Also, in the news item about Grace Poe above (Sy, 2016), Poe is portrayed as tough suggestively against drugs and drug offenders. She is shown in the act of boxing in the middle of 'tough-looking' basketball players, suggesting that she has some of the 'masculinity' associated with fighting drugs and crimes.

Also, the PNP Chief Ronald dela Rosa had storied the drug problem in the apocalyptic tone. The apocalyptic narrative could also be seen in TV news reports. For instance, in an interview as reported in an ABS-CBN's *TV Patrol* news report (Davila, 2016) on 9 June 2016, dela Rosa said that 'Yes... they have the right to remain silent... forever' when asked regarding the right to due process of suspected drug offenders. And, when asked whether he had summarily executed someone before, he said 'Do not force me to lie... Oh. I don't want to tell a lie.' And similar to newspaper reports, TV news uses visual aids to create a story. In the interview (at least what is shown in the report) dela Rosa did not explicitly state what consequences of which those who would not heed the request to surrender shall suffer. But the visual story tells it. As the reporter narrates,

---

[6]Due to copyright issues, this photo and other succeeding ones will not be shown in this chapter. The reader can follow the link accompanying the Reference list entry for each of the source cited in the text.

dela Rosa said that the *Oplan Tokhang* of Davao City will be implemented in the whole country where police officers will plead before small-time drug pushers to surrender. But if the request is not heeded, the pushers will suffer the consequences.

a sequence of shots are shown. This sequence shows dela Rosa and fellow officers appearing to be calling one by one the persons facing their back to the camera (suggestive of being surrenderees), with a banner bearing the name 'OPLAN TOKHANG[7]' as backdrop. The shots that coincided with the sentence, 'But if the request is not heeded, the pushers will suffer the consequences' suggest what kind of consequences these are. The first shows that police officers will conduct a tactical operation against those who failed to surrender. The next shows a dead body (blurred) in the midst of onlookers and a crime scene investigator. This is followed by another shot which appears to be a continuation of the previous shot. Then, another shot shows a revolver with an evidence marker. And then the next shot shows a group of crime scene investigators inspecting what appears to be a dead body and documenting the evidence. This sequence of shots tells a story that police officers will conduct an operation against drug offenders and if they resist they will be killed by the police officers.

Finally, news media use camera techniques to reinforce the textual story in a TV news report. In an ABS-CBN *TV Patrol* report on 27 June 2016, the newscaster provides an abstract of the news, then PNP Chief dela Rosa's statement about the President-elect's only order for him was inserted (Santos, 2016),

> News reporter:
> *President-elect Rodrigo Duterte's promise to eradicate crime, illegal drugs, and corruption immediately was clearer than sunlight. Duterte gave the task to his close friend incoming Philippine National Police Chief Ronald 'Bato' dela Rosa to lead the fight.*
>
> PNP Chief:
> *He has no other orders for me: Drugs, drugs, drugs. Kill, kill, kill. Kill drugs.*

Firstly, dela Rosa's line, 'Drugs, drugs, drugs. Kill, kill, kill,' is a small story. A small story 'covers a gamut of under-represented narrative activities, such as tellings of ongoing events, future or hypothetical events, shared (known) events, but also allusions to tellings, deferrals of tellings, and refusals to tell' (Georgakopoulou, 2006, p. 123). The first part on 'drugs' tells us that drugs

---

[7]Oplan Tokhang is a Philippine police operation. Tokhang is a combination of two Cebuano words – *toktok* and *hangyo*. *Toktok* means 'knock'; *hangyo* means 'plead'. Police officers in this operation go to and knock the houses of known drug personalities and plead with them to surrender.

proliferate and is a big problem as signified by the repetitions. The second part is the 'needed' response: 'kill,' which is repeated twice as well. The repetition signals that Duterte and dela Rosa's response would involve killings, numerous killings.

In the same news report, it is equally interesting to note how the camera narratively works immediately before and after dela Rosa's statement. When the reporter mentioned, 'to lead the fight,' dela Rosa is shown in a medium long shot, facing the reporter, and thumps his lap. When he says, 'Drugs, drugs, drugs,' he appears nearer with medium shots. He appears much nearer and more intense with a medium close-up shot while saying the first 'kill'. This is further intensified with a close-up shot – the closest he appears before us – while stating the second 'kill'. Then, the intensity gradually decreases starting with dela Rosa saying the last 'kill'. The camera returns to a medium shot while dela Rosa sums his statement up: 'kill drugs'. Finally, the sequence ends up by returning to a medium long shot.

Opening up Analytical Dialogue

The preceding analyses are just preliminaries which borrow some techniques from other narrative methods like thematic, structural and visual narrative analyses. What sets DNA apart from these methods is its use of dialogical questions towards the narrative types identified. Some of these questions are resource, circulation, connection, identity and function questions, as discussed above. I will use some of these questions to open up the dialogue with the apocalyptic narrative just described, but only on Duterte's stories due to space constraints.

Resource and identity questions
Resource questions deal with narrative resources which include plots and narratives which are culturally available to us. We draw from these resources to tell our stories. It can be said then that Duterte, Sen. Poe and dela Rosa all drew from such resources to tell their drug war stories. *Polyphony* and *heteroglossia* characterise their stories, and this contributes to the ambiguity of such stories.

To make sense of the apocalyptic stories, we need to go back to Smith's (2005) discussion of his structural genre of war. Apocalyptic stories do not just come from nowhere because people cannot tell any story they like anytime. The most common stories in the Philippine civil sphere about drugs are in the romantic mode. This is an excellent resource for Duterte and those whose stories are apocalyptic in tone. They performed *narrative inflation* (Smith, 2005). They made the romantic stories as a stepping stone to launch an apocalyptic one. The latter are just extensions of the former. They took advantage of narrative's interpretative openness (Frank, 2010) or ambiguity (Polletta, 2006). Ambiguity allows one to make a story resonate with another one, although the two are different in nature (e.g. example romance and apocalypse).

For instance, romance is the template for the news article about Duterte above. It is written as a romantic quest. Majority of Duterte's statements here are in romantic mode, for example: fighting crimes and drugs 'would always be in accordance with the law'; 'I do not execute people kneeling down with hands tied at their back. It will be a confrontation'; 'the obedience to law is almost optional.' The theme is observance with the law in fighting against crime and drugs. This is the heart of romantic mode resonating well with what the majority of the Filipinos like. National surveys show that most of the Filipinos (94%) do not want the drug suspects to be killed but be captured alive and they worry (78%) about becoming extrajudicial killing victims (SWS, 2016a, 2016b; see also SWS, 2019). But the trickster's power is to take advantage of narrative's ambiguity. Duterte peppered this romantic quest with apocalyptic tone statements such as 'My God, I hate drugs. And I have to kill people because I hate drugs' and 'If I become president, there would be no such thing as bloodless cleansing.' Duterte has upped the ante from romance to apocalypse and has got away with it, especially that he and his war on drugs got favourable satisfaction and trust ratings from the Filipinos.

This narrative in turn has hailed Duterte to 'claim identities, reject identities, and experiment with identities' (Frank, 2012, p. 45). And in the same way, ambiguity is apparent in the identity he assumes. He said: 'I would return to you the right to walk out at night safe and ride a jeepney without being held up' and he vowed to fight crimes and drugs 'even if it would cost me my life, my honour, and even my liberty.' This is a heroic identity interpellated by a romantic narrative, especially that he emphasised observance of the law. However, ironically, this hero would 'kill' to do it, to 'cleanse' the country of the evils he sees. This is a contradiction to the heroic narrative and identity; however, going back to Smith (2005), such is the case when one uses ambiguity to perform narrative inflation. He poses to be a hero but is in fact more closely like a dirty harry. He assumes a heroic identity within an apocalyptic genre (Barrera, 2017).

Duterte used multiple codes in doing this. His stories are just fragments loaned to him, as Frank (2010, 2012) would suggest. He seemed to have summoned the language of law and justice and the code of self-defence. The latter resonates with the *nanlaban* (suspects fought back) narrative[8] in the police nomenclature in the country (Flores, 2019). In this way, he is walking on a tightrope, a thin line through which romance transforms to apocalypse. In Philippine criminal law, the use of force against suspects is permissible as long as the force used is equal or lesser than that of these suspects. The problem, however, is that stories are out of control (Frank, 2010). The *nanlaban* narrative is pregnant with ambiguity; and it could be invoked even in times where self-defence rules are violated and some observers are thinking that this is occurring (Johnson & Fernsquest, 2018). Duterte is also invoking human rights and Philippine national heroes' language. He wants to bring back to Filipinos the 'right to walk out at night safe and ride a jeepney without being held up' and would do it 'even if it would cost me my life, my honour, and even my liberty.' This latter line is also borrowed heavily from previous narratives of Philippine heroes and presidents. For example, former

---

[8]This is a very popular narrative in the Philippines. This is virtually used as a justification every time police officers have killed a suspect.

President Diosdado Macapagal (1962) said in his speech a similar line that the country 'asserts its natural right to liberty and is ready to defend it with blood, life and honour.'

It can be said then that even a seemingly clear-cut apocalyptic narrative is plurivocal. Such narrative is *polyphonic* and *heteroglossic*, borrowed from multiple narratives and codes of language usage (Frank, 2012). A storyteller, like Duterte, does not own such a narrative. His stories were just constructed through 'fragments on loan' to him (Frank, 2010, p. 14). This is faithful to Bakhtin's (1984) notion of the dialogical nature of life and texts. 'Two voices is the minimum for life,' he said; and likewise, two voices is the minimum for a story.

Effects of the stories on the war on drugs policy

I will demonstrate the power of stories in influencing policy choices, especially in terms of drug policy implementation. I argue that apocalyptic and romantic stories would keep the war on drugs approach going, while the tragic, low mimetic, inverted tragedy, inverted romance, and inverted apocalypse would stop or at least alter it. In saying this, I am starting to show empirical material to back the structural genre of drug war stories in the earlier part of this section that genres are associated with the extent of use of force towards drug offenders. In this model, apocalyptic genre is at the extreme of the continuum by espousing lethal force against drug offenders, while inverted apocalypse is the complete opposite – no force should be used against offenders and war on drugs policy should be 'destroyed.'

Fig. 18.1 shows that graphical representation of the frequency of the types of drug war stories that occupy the civil sphere in the country from 2015 to 2017. Overall, drug war stories steeply increased after Duterte won the presidential elections in May 2016. This indicates that the drug issue had become an important national issue that demands storytelling. The most common stories are those that are prowar on drugs: apocalyptic, romantic and tragic. However, there are also spikes of those that are against this policy following significant events in the war on drugs in January 2017 and August 2017.

Fig. 18.1 also shows significant alterations in the drug policy in the country. First, Duterte's apocalyptic toned war on drugs approach was formally implemented in July 2016. After about 6 months it was suspended in January 2017, but later resumed in March 2017. It was again suspended in October 2017, but resumed in December 2017. What could have influenced these alterations in the drug policy? I argue that stories are responsible for these changes. As seen from Fig. 18.1, most of the stories that proliferated before Duterte launched his apocalyptic war on drugs were in romantic and apocalyptic mode. That is why it was so easy for him to launch his own version of war on drugs in spite of great opposition from several sectors. But when inverted apocalyptic stories dominated the civil sphere due to the alleged killing of Jee Ick Joo by the police in January 2017, Duterte suspended his Project Double Barrel policy on drug offenders. But when the proportion of romantic and apocalyptic stories began to increase more than the antiwar on drugs stories, the

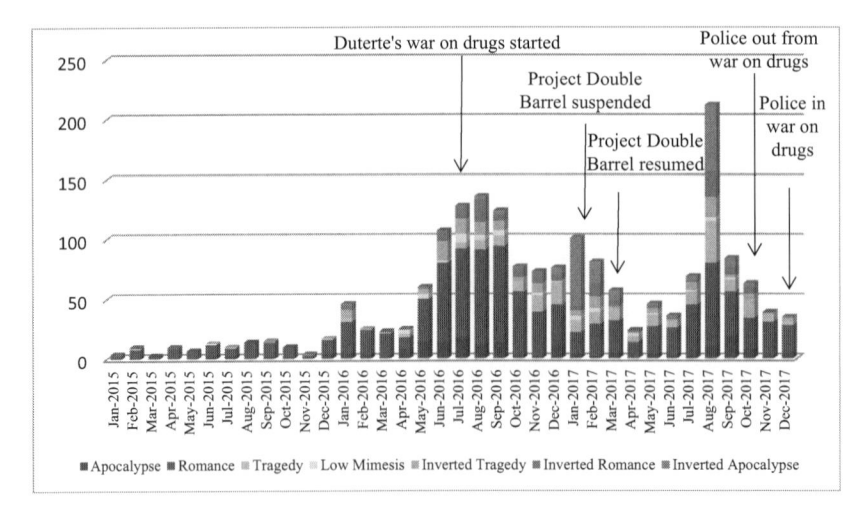

Fig. 18.1. Types of Drug War Stories that Proliferated in the Philippine Civil Sphere, 2015–2017.

project was resumed. For the second time, however, the project was suspended when antiwar on drugs stories proliferated due to the alleged killing of Kian delos Santos by the police. But the Project Double Barrel project was resumed again when prowar on drugs stories proliferated more than antiwar on drugs stories.

Seeing that policies respond to dominant stories in the civil sphere strengthens the arguments of narrative criminology and socio-narratology that stories effect actions. Not only individual actions are affected by stories but also state-level actions, in term of policies. State-level actors, therefore, are also under a 'hypnotic spell' (Frank, 2010, p. 81) that stories cast to those caught in them.

Implications

The analysis that has just been shown is a form of DNA that involves the mirroring between the story's contents and the story's effects (Frank, 2010). In the story content part, I showed the narrative types and their detailed structures in texts, photographs and videos. As seen, news stories are in storied form, too. Also, I have shown how stories in the civil sphere are related to the drug policy implementation in the Philippines. It is the hope of this chapter that DNA will be diffused more in various fields, and most especially in criminology and criminal justice.

As narrative criminologists attempt to make 'narrative criminology as the new mainstream' (Maruna, 2015, p. vii), there is a need for methodological plurality, and DNA can partly fill this gap. But Frank (2010, 2012) has only provided a heuristic guide. This likely contributed to the slow diffusion of DNA to various fields, including narrative criminology. Although Brett Smith (2016) has provided a clearer DNA guide and Nick Caddick (2016) has illustrated such a guide, still a DNA for media texts, photos and videos is still lacking. The current work can be an exemplar for future ones in narrative criminology, but not a template but at best as a fragment that could add up to the dialogical nature of future analyses. Each analysis is a dialogue of several previous analyses. A research is not a singular work. It looks like a chapter of a larger book, which is composed of several studies forming a bigger story.

The extant studies of Barrera (2017), Brookman (2015) and Sandberg et al. (2015) that used DNA in narrative criminology are a good point of departure for future DNA studies in the field. These are good exemplars, but more studies are needed that use other forms of DNA such as storytelling as an institutional emplotment and stories as a means of assembling groups. Noteworthy, is the lack of attention from narrative criminologists on narratives in criminal justice institutions (Ugelvik, 2016). The DNA of storytelling as institutional emplotment can be used to explore such institution. Much work is needed in exploring how criminal justice institutions 'force' its clients (e.g. suspects, victims, community members) to adhere to institutional narratives, to the point of disregarding noninstitutional stories by the clients. Additionally, other forms of DNA and dialogical questions that have not yet been explored can be used for such purpose.

Narrative criminology can also benefit from the theoretical armature of socio-narratology (Frank, 2010). Much is to be learnt from socio-narratology's tenets on the dialogical nature of stories and the *unfinalizability* of humans. As Brookman (2015) shows, the narratives of violent offenders are dialogical and therefore shape-shifting. One's story may be of a particular narrative at a particular point of time, but may shift at another. Also, one's narrative at a point of time is also a dialogue of fragments of other stories. More importantly, criminal justice actors as well as researchers should acknowledge and respect the unfinalizability of suspects, offenders and criminal justice actors themselves.

Conclusion

In this chapter, I have reviewed socio-narratology and its methodological component – DNA. I have shown that DNA has differentially diffused to various fields and much of its aspects are yet to be explored thoroughly in many fields, including narrative criminology. Narrative criminology can learn much from the theoretical and methodological propositions of DNA. Thus, I illustrated how I performed DNA on the drug war stories in the Philippines. I showed the narratological component of the stories that majority are prowar on drugs – romantic and apocalyptic – and that these paved the way for Duterte to launch his apocalyptic style of war on drugs. But as antiwar on drugs stories proliferated as some points, the apocalyptic war on drugs was suspended but later resumed when favourable stories began to spread again. This analysis shows how stories effect changes in the drug policy implementation which has since been so malleable in relation to stories.

References

Alameddine, R. (2009). *The hakawati*. New York, NY: Anchor Books.

Bakhtin, M. (1984). *Problems of Dostoevsky's poetics*. Minneapolis, MN: University of Minnesota Press.

Barrera, D. J. (2017). Drug war stories and the Philippine President. *Asian Journal of Criminology, 12*(4), 341–359.

Brookman, F. (2015). The shifting narratives of violent offenders. In L. Presser & S. Sandberg (Eds.), *Narrative criminology: Understanding stories of crime*. New York, NY: New York University Press.

Bruner, J. (1987). Life as narrative. *Social Research, 54*(1), 11–32.

Caddick, N. (2016). Doing narrative analysis. In E. Lyons & A. Coyle (Eds.), *Analysing qualitative data in psychology*. London: SAGE Publications.

Carr, D. (1986). *Time, narrative, and history*. Bloomington, IN: Indiana University Press.

Carvajal, N. C. (2016). Duterte bares plan to wage war vs drugs if elected President. *Philippine Daily Inquirer*, April 14. Retrieved from https://goo.gl/8921HW. Accessed on January 4, 2018.

Chadwick, R. (2014). Bodies talk: On the challenges of hearing childbirth counter-stories. In S. Mckenzie-Mohr & M. Lafrance (Eds.), *Women voicing resistance: Discursive and narrative explorations*. London: Routledge.

Corrales, N. (2016). Duterte: There will be blood in 'cleansing' this country. *Philippine Daily Inquirer*, January 20. Retrieved from https://goo.gl/pvb8pV. Accessed on January 4, 2018.

Davila, K. (2016). TV Patrol Patong sa ulo nina Duterte, Bato umakyat sa P50-M. *ABS-CBN News*, June 9. Retrieved from https://goo.gl/oMKQt9. Accessed on January 4, 2018.

Erikson, K. (1976). *Everything in its path: Destruction of community in the Buffalo Creek flood*. New York, NY: Simon & Schuster.

Fleetwood, J. (2016). Narrative habitus: Thinking through structure/agency in the narratives of offenders. *Crime, Media, Culture, 12*(2), 173–192.

Flores, H. (2019). Social Weather Stations: Filipinos divided on believing 'nanlaban' stories. *The Philippine Star*, March 1. Retrieved from https://www.philstar.com/headlines/2019/03/01/1897748/social-weather-stations-filipinos-divided-believing-nanlaban-stories. Accessed on April 5, 2019.

Frank, A. W. (1995). *The wounded storyteller: Body, illness, and ethics*. Chicago, IL: University of Chicago Press.

Frank, A. W. (2005). What is dialogical research, and why should we do it? *Qualitative Health Research, 15*(7), 964–974.

Frank, A. W. (2010). *Letting stories breathe: A socio-narratology*. Chicago, IL: The University of Chicago Press.

Frank, A. W. (2012). Practicing dialogical narrative analysis. In J. Holstein & J. Gubrium (Eds.), *Varieties of narrative analysis*. London: SAGE Publications.

Georgakopoulou, A. (2006). Thinking big with small stories in narrative and identity analysis. *Narrative Inquiry, 16*(1), 122–130.

Gilligan, C., Spencer, R., Weinberg, K., & Bertsch, T. (2003). On the listening guide: A voice-centred relational method. In P. Camic, J. Rhodes, & L. Yardley (Eds.),

Qualitative research in psychology: Expounding perspectives in methodology and design. Washington, DC: American Psychological Association.

Graddol, D. (1993). The visual accomplishment of factuality. In D. Graddol & B. Barrett (Eds.), *Media texts: Authors and readers*. Clevedon: Multilingual Matters.

Gubrium, J. F., & Holstein, J. A. (2009). *Analyzing narrative reality*. Thousand Oaks, CA: SAGE Publications.

Johnson, D. T., & Fernsquest, J. (2018). Governing through killing: The war on drugs in the Philippines. *Asian Journal of Law and Society*, *5*, 359–390. doi:10.1017/als.2018.12

Katz, J. (2016). Culture within and culture about crime: The case of the "Rodney King Riots". *Crime, Media, Culture*, *12*(2), 233–251.

Keeton, R. M. (2015). 'The race of pale men should increase and multiply': Religious narratives and Indian removal. In L. Presser & S. Sandberg (Eds.), *Narrative criminology: Understanding stories of crime*. New York, NY: New York University Press.

Labov, W., & Waletzky, J. (1967). Narrative analysis: Oral versions of personal experience. In J. Helm (Ed.), *Essays on the verbal and visual arts*. Seattle, WA: University of Washington Press.

Loseke, D. R. (2007). The study of identity as cultural, institutional, organizational, and personal narratives: Theoretical and empirical integrations. *The Sociological Quarterly*, *48*(4), 661–688.

Macapagal, D. (1962). Address of President Macapagal on independence day. *Official Gazette*, June 12. Retrieved from https://www.officialgazette.gov.ph/1962/06/12/address-of-president-macapagal-on-independence-day/. Accessed on April 5, 2019.

Maruna, S. (2015). Foreword: Narrative criminology as the new mainstream. In L. Presser & S. Sandberg (Eds.), *Narrative criminology: Understanding stories of crime*. New York, NY: New York University Press.

Polletta, F. (2006). *It was like a fever: Storytelling in protest and politics*. Chicago, IL: University of Chicago Press.

Presser, L. (2008). *Been a heavy life: Stories of violent men*. Urbana, IL: University of Illinois Press.

Presser, L. (2009). The narratives of offenders. *Theoretical Criminology*, *13*(2), 177–200.

Presser, L., & Sandberg, S. (Eds.). (2015a). *Narrative criminology: Understanding stories of crime*. New York, NY: New York University Press.

Presser, L., & Sandberg, S. (2015b). Research strategies for narrative criminology. In J. Miller & W. Palacios (Eds.), *Advances in criminological theory: The value of qualitative research for advancing criminological theory*. Piscataway, NJ: Transaction Publishers.

Ricoeur, P. (1984). *Time and narrative* (Vol. 1). Chicago, IL: University of Chicago Press.

Riessman, C. K. (2008). *Narrative methods for the human sciences*. New York, NY: SAGE Publications.

Robertson, A. (2017). Narrative analysis. In G. Bergström & K. Boréus (Eds.), *Analyzing text and discourse in the social sciences*. London: SAGE Publications.

Sandberg, S. (2010). What can "lies" tell us about life? Notes towards a framework of narrative criminology. *Journal of Criminal Justice Education*, *21*(4), 447–465.

Sandberg, S. (2013). Are self-narratives strategic or determined, unified or fragmented? Reading Breivik's Manifesto in light of narrative criminology. *Acta Sociologica, 56*(1), 69–83.

Sandberg, S., Tutenges, S., & Copes, H. (2015). Stories of violence: A narrative criminological study of ambiguity. *British Journal of Criminology, 55*(6), 1168–1186.

Santos, R. (2016). Pagpuksa sa ilegal na droga, krimen sa 3-6 buwan, posible ba. *ABS-CBN News*, June 27. Retrieved from https://goo.gl/h7ZVkz. Accessed on November 30, 2017.

Smith, B. (2016). Narrative analysis. In E. Lyons & A. Coyle (Eds.), *Analysing qualitative data in psychology*. London: SAGE Publications.

Smith, P. (2005). *Why war? The cultural logic of Iraq, the Gulf war, and Suez*. Chicago, IL: The University of Chicago Press.

Social Weather Stations. (2016a).Fourth Quarter 2016 Social Weather Survey: 78% of Pinoys worry about becoming victims of EJK; 94% say it is important that drug suspects be captured alive. Social Weather Stations. Retrieved from https://www.sws.org.ph/swsmain/artcldisppage/?artcsyscode=ART-20161219110734. Accessed on November 30, 2017.

Social Weather Stations. (2016b). Fourth Quarter Social Weather Survey: 66% of Filipinos say the number of illegal drug users in their area has decreased. Social Weather Stations. Retrieved from https://www.sws.org.ph/swsmain/artcldisppage/?artcsyscode=ART-20190216095842. Accessed on November 30, 2017.

Social Weather Stations. (2019). Fourth quarter social weather survey: 66% of Filipinos say the number of illegal drug users in their area has decreased. Social Weather Stations. Retrieved on April 5, 2019 from https://www.sws.org.ph/swsmain/artcldisppage/?artcsyscode=ART-20190216095842.

Somers, M. R. (1994). The narrative constitution of identity: A relational and network approach. *Theory and Society, 23*(5), 605–649.

Sy, M. (2016). Poll bets raising funds through drugs – Grace. *Philippine Star*, February 2. Retrieved from https://goo.gl/Jixe1c. Accessed on November 30, 2017.

Syjuco, M. (2016). This is why Philippine President Rodrigo Duterte will get away with murder. *Time*, August 16. Retrieved from http://time.com/4453587/philippines-rodrigo-duterte-dictator-impunity-marcos/. Accessed on November 30, 2017.

Thompson, R., & Bowen, C. J. (2009). *Grammar or the shot*. Oxford: Elsevier.

Tognato, C. (2015). Narratives of tax evasion: The cultural legitimacy of harmful behavior. In L. Presser & S. Sandberg (Eds.), *Narrative criminology: Understanding stories of crime*. New York, NY: York University Press.

Ugelvik, T. (2016). Techniques of legitimation: The narrative construction of legitimacy among immigration detention officers. *Crime, Media, Culture, 12*(2), 215–232.

Williams, G. (1984). The genesis of chronic illness: Narrative re-construction. *Sociology of Health & Illness, 6*(2), 175–200.

Chapter 19

'Protecting and Defending Mummy': Narrative Criminology and Psychosocial Criminology

Alfredo Verde and Nicolò Knechtlin

> *Just like robots: all regimented, dressed the same, acting in the same way, all chanting together. But then you explain everything that's behind it, and maybe with time it's not all this... It's not only this; there are other things in life. But it seems like you do it because you've got nothing else in your life... That's not true!*
>
> Gianluca

> *Oh Sampdoria, you are my mum – Give us a goal under the North (Terrace)...*
>
> Choir of Sampdoria supporters

Narrative criminology (NC) studies the narratives of offenders, approaching them from a sociological and linguistic perspective. Psychosocial criminology (PSC), by contrast, applies the discoveries of psychoanalysis to criminology, following the British tradition of psychosocial studies, which approach social problems and crime as connected to the dimension of the unconscious.

While both NC and PSC share an interest in crime narratives, they differ in the way in which they conceptualise the relationship between the subject and the stories told. In order to evaluate the possibility of using both approaches, we will try to highlight the differences and similarities between the two. From a sociological standpoint, NC strictly refers to what is narrated, arguing that narratives often precede and produce crime (Presser, 2009). The criminological concepts to which NC refers are neutralisations, thinking errors, identities and situational representations. More broadly, NC draws on insights from narrative psychology, ethnomethodology, cultural structuralism and postmodernism (Presser & Sandberg, 2015). According to Presser (2009), NC should, on the other hand, *not* explore the psychological realities... such a strong position is not necessary for the constitutive view of narrative, and hence for a narrative criminology. A narrative criminology need only bracket non-communicated realities, perhaps positing them as stimulating or conditioning the effects of narrative on human action (Presser, 2009, p. 186).

By contrast, PSC has not explicitly considered narratives as such but has implicitly referred to them, in that it considers offenders' talk about themselves as both revealing and concealing a 'truth' which, from a psychoanalytical perspective, is often unknown to the subject. As Francia and Verde (2015) note, the term 'narrative' rarely appears in the papers of its exponents (Gadd & Jefferson, 2007; Jefferson, 2010), notwithstanding the fact that their research instrument is called 'free association narrative interview', referring to the typical instrument used in psychoanalysis – the free and consciously uncontrolled speech of the analysand (Gadd, 2011; Hollway & Jefferson, 2013). Even in recent contributions (Gadd & Corr, 2015; Harris, 2017), PSC does not attach any importance to narratives as such and to the way in which they have been constructed and staged.

Despite this apparent distance, we want to show that NC and PSC can be fruitfully combined. The goal of this chapter is to develop a sophisticated theoretical combined approach that can help us understand and clearly interpret what people who violate legal norms say about themselves and how they narratively connect their deeds to their identities, both before and after the commission of deviant acts. We have chosen the case of Gianluca, a soccer 'ultras' (the Italian version of hooligans), to test our claim that the subject's self-narratives are the main pathway to understanding her or his actions.

Narrative Criminology and Psychosocial Criminology: Five Points of Contact

In order to explore the possibility of mixing NC and PSC, we will in the following try to highlight the differences and similarities between the two. A first bit of common ground can be found in the study of neutralisation techniques. In their review of 50 years of neutralisation literature, Maruna and Copes (2005) explicitly mention the debt recognised by Sykes and Matza (1957) to psychoanalytic thinking, particularly to the work of Anna Freud (1936) and Fritz Redl (Redl & Wineman, 1951). According to Maruna and Copes (2004, p. 236), psychoanalytical research '"locates" neutralizations securely outside conscious thought', and if one interprets neutralisations (but also, we would add, the subjects' narrations generally) 'as purely conscious and deliberate maneuvers... neutralizations lose something important'. In other words, neutralisations and defence mechanisms share the characteristic of not being thoroughly known by the subject. This reconnects the field of neutralisation to the psychoanalytic concept of the subject.

The second point of contact lies in the fact that NC has portrayed the image of the offender as multifaceted. Self-narratives are sometimes incoherent (Presser, 2008).

This lack of coherence expresses agency as well as determination by social structure (Brookman, 2015; Sandberg, 2009, 2013) and cultural variables and discourses (Fleetwood, 2016; Sandberg & Fleetwood, 2016). Furthermore, NC has not limited itself to the 'said'; it also examines the 'not said' through a focus on ellipses, tropes and formula stories (Brookman, Copes, & Hochstetler, 2011; Sandberg, 2016). PSC, on the other hand, obviously refers to the unconscious. As they share such assumption, a complementarity could be postulated. Presser seems to open to such a possibility:

> My formulation... (...) might be taken to presuppose some foundational desire – to harm, to satisfy one's needs (Maslow, 1954) or to achieve a coherent identity. Just such a presupposition is highlighted in psychoanalytically informed criminology (see Jefferson, 1996) and general strain theory (Agnew, 1992). My proposal does not preclude the possibility of originating desire, but simply takes as its starting point the rhetoric itself (Presser, 2012, p. 18).

Going further than NC, PSC tries to understand the nature of this 'foundational desire', relating it to some particular previous experience. Referring to the discovery of a 'hidden' part of the subject, recent psychoanalytical approaches (e.g. the interpersonal or the Lacanian) have amply recognised that 'depth' is only a metaphor and that the 'new' meaning flashes like lightning in the conversation between two persons. Meaning may result from a sudden filling of a lacuna in the text, or from an unexpected parapraxia that modifies what the speaker is saying.

A third point of contact resides in the commonly held opinion of the importance of the co-construction of the stories between the narrator and narratee. It is true that the interpersonal and Lacanian psychoanalytic subfields have not yet been addressed by PSC, but this can be traced to the contingencies of its birth. PSC is an English baby belonging to the Kleinian lineage in psychoanalysis. It is therefore very traditional in its faith in the existence of one, and only one, 'truth' hidden to the patient and discoverable by the analyst. Conversely, other psychoanalytical approaches, mainly American, developed narrative analyses even before psychology and sociology, in the early 1980s, calling into question the concept of 'one and only truth' (Schafer, 1980; Spence, 1982). At the same time, psychoanalysis has increasingly become a two-person investigation; this places emphasis on the interpersonal and relational (Mitchell, 1988; Stern, 2017) and positions it rather close to NC, which theorises the co-construction of the narrator's 'truth' via the relationship between the interviewer and the subject (Presser, 2009).

A fourth point of contact can be seen in the characteristics of the offenders' narratives: from a psychoanalytical point of view, in both Freud's and Klein's views, the subject constitutes himself as 'good', by using projective mechanisms (Freud S., 1915; Segal, 1979), in order to deal with inner and outer tensions; NC has, on its part, discovered that subjects frequently depict themselves as good, even at the price of incoherence (the so-called 'elastic narratives') (Presser, 2008). Moreover, PSC also has explicitly taken into account the defensive use of commonly shared discourses expressing cultural values and 'producing' the subject's positioning in the social world, explicitly with reference to Foucault

(Hollway, 1984); according to Gadd and Jefferson (2007), the subject makes use of the social discourses he is immersed in as a defence mechanism. In referring to a commonly held discourse, to a proverb, to a commonsense or to a belief shared by the group (all objects of study for NC), the subject can escape anxiety and the sense of guilt and gain self-confidence (Gadd & Jefferson, 2007).

A fifth point is methodological: NC and PSC tend to use small samples. Some studies are even based on the lowest possible sample size: the single case (Maruna & Matravers, 2007), considering that the uniqueness of the subject can allow the discovery of subtle, complex mechanisms. According to Sandberg (2010, p. 451), 'the more data you have, (...), the harder it will be to discover the nuances of narratives. If analyses are detailed, and emphasize semiotics or sociolinguistics, one interview, conversation, or fragment of text can be enough to make an interesting observation'.

As for PSC, Gadd and Jefferson (2007) claim that results obtained by the analysis of one subject can be applied to subsequent cases, in order to ascertain whether the hypotheses formulated 'hold'. Moreover, both traditions use similar tools. NC employs open interviews, observation and even ethnography (Verde, 2018); PSC uses the free association narrative interview – FANI (Hollway & Jefferson, 2013), an open interview technique in which the interviewee is requested to share his thoughts with the researcher, much in the same way as the classic psychoanalytical method. She or he is free to include even lateral and apparently unconnected issues. Moreover, as already mentioned, both approaches argue that the story is constructed in the interaction between the narrator and the narratee; psychosocial criminology also reflects on what might not be said, for defensive purposes.

Similarities notwithstanding, the differences between NC and PSC do not vanish: the most important difference remains the emphasis given by NC to structural and cultural determinations on the one hand and by PSC to the role of anxiety in its different forms as a factor motivating defences on the other.

From such considerations, we will try to mix the approaches, choosing as the object of our study the narrative interview of a soccer hooligan. The choice of such an example is motivated by the mainly sociological nature of the research in the field, which both emphasises class factors (Dunning, Murphy, & Williams, 1988; Taylor, 1971) and debates about the 'real' or 'enacted' nature of hooligans' violence (Marsh, 1978; Marsh, Rosser, & Harré, 1978). Strictly psychological studies in the field have been scarce and refer to a rather simple and mechanical conceptualisation of emotions (Kerr, 1994). With regard to the Italian 'ultras', we have found only one example of a thorough psychological interview with one of them, which, although based on a cognitive-behavioural point of view, advocates a study of 'unconscious feelings, motivations, and psychodynamics, such as defenses, which are very important...' (Maniglio, 2007, p. 207). On their part, psychosocial studies have never approached the hooligan phenomenon, mainly focussing on the relations between supporters and clubs (Harvey & Piotrowska, 2013) and the relations between violence and tourism (Uriely, Ram, & Malach-Pines, 2011).

The present paper tries to fill this gap by analysing the life story of an 'ultras' leader, seeking the subject's conscious and hidden motivations to join the group and their roots in the past and investigating the nature of his connections to the deviant group, his narrative justification of violence, his construction of identity and the possibility of social integration.

Methods

In this project, the main problem was how to recruit participants. Fortunately, the interviewer (the second author) was an insider, a graduate student who had himself been an ultras, and was still regarded as a member of the group. Thus, as a (former) participant observer, he was able to contact the first (Genoese) participants in the project. He then implemented snowball sampling of other subjects belonging to ultras' groups from other cities by tracing the friendships produced by the groups' twinnings. In this way, he was able to gather 15 interviews of ultras in 'key' positions in their groups, mainly group leaders or older members.

His inside knowledge of the ultras' world also helped him to break the ice with the subjects, to put them at ease and to allow them to reveal important aspects of their relationship with violence and to illustrate the narrative justifications of it (DeWalt & DeWalt, 2011).

The interviews were based on free associations (FANI: Hollway & Jefferson, 2013) concerning themes such as family and social relationships (relationships with parents, siblings and peers; sentimental relationships; relationships in the workplace; free-time activities); the history of contacts with the world of soccer and the involvement and relationships with the ultras' group; the subject's position vis-à-vis the ultras' media image and public opinion of them; his view of the role and the causes of ultras' violence; the meaning and the values of the cultural belonging to the ultras' group. The subjects were told that what the interviewer needed was the simple verbalisation of his thoughts, even if they seemed irrelevant, trivial or stupid and particularly if the subject was not inclined to refer them. Given such premises, one should not expect a structured story from the interviewees. Rather, what emerges is a sort of stream of ideas and concepts, sometimes illustrated by a short narrative example, more similar to the musical model of theme and variations.

In this chapter, we will analyse in depth one of the interviews which can be considered, for the characteristics of the subject (a Bangladeshi man, supporter of the Sampdoria team, living in Italy), a good example for the study of the possible connection between the two traditions. From the sociocultural standpoint, the interview reproduces the peculiarity of the world of Italian ultras, with its typical features: strong group bonds, relationships interaction among members during the week, the preparation of chants and banners, charitable activities and social commitment and friendships and rivalries (Doidge, 2015).

The interview was analysed through a first reading and a careful rereading by the first author, followed by annotation of the main characters and themes, the narrative strategies, the neutralisation techniques and defence mechanisms identified. In this way, it became possible to write another story, 'our' co-constructed story of Gianluca as told jointly by the subject and the researchers.

Gianluca's Life Story

Gianluca, a 27-year-old man, is the only child of an Italian mother and a Muslim Bangladeshi father. Both parents instilled in him their passion for the Sampdoria soccer club. Since the age of 11 years, he has been attending matches at the local stadium, and he began to frequent his team's 'own' terrace when he was 17 years old. In his youth, however, his attendance was not always regular, as his father's work required the family to move house frequently. His childhood was spent in Bangladesh, other Islamic countries, England and finally Genoa (they kept a second home in Genoa throughout, however).

After taking a BA in Business Marketing in London, Gianluca did several different jobs, including some where '*you have to get your hands dirty*', because he wanted to start at the bottom, he says, and not do a '*shirt and tie*' job straightaway. He is one of the 'elders' of the ultras' group, while the newcomers are in their teens or early 20s.

The interview took place in an open air space of the Genoa University and lasted 2 hours, during which time the interviewer rarely interrupted the flow of speech. Time passed very quickly and Gianluca, after some initial reluctance to open up, became very eloquent and also very assertive. In our analysis, we want to show how the NC and PSC approaches can be mixed, mentioning in brackets which approach we are using.

> I: *Tell me about when you were a child. About your family...*
>
> G: *I was a fairly quiet kid. I mean everything was normal; I used to go to school; I never had any trouble with my parents. I was a good kid. Well, maybe a bit lively, a bit restless, like all kids...*
>
> I: *What sort of relationship did you have with your father?*
>
> G: *Shit, when he'd had a few, he was like, you know, a right pain in the ass. He had some trouble at wo... work as well, but after a while he managed to get over it. So, no real problems, but not at all a happy childhood. But you might say I saw the mistakes he made and I hope I learned something from them... You know, my father is from Bangladesh and a Muslim, which seems a bit strange because he drinks. But there, those who respect this commandment are... and he is a classic father; he never says no; he has never denied me anything, never said no to me, always bent over backwards for me. But he always demanded total respect; he never raised his hand to me, though: never, never. As I said, he always bent over backwards for me; he had an awful lot of love for me. But even now, I mean, even if I really get into the shit, he'll never turn his back on me; he just sulks, but I don't think he'd ever turn his back on me. So we've got a good relationship; I mean, I can talk to him easily now about more or less anything...*

If we analyse Gianluca's account from an NC standpoint, we are struck by the number of idioms and the frequent contradictions, which he resolves either through empathic repetitions of concepts or by showing that he is aware of them. From a PSC standpoint, Gianluca moves from denying any problems in the family (in reality dramatically present) to admitting them through a series of 'specifications' and 'distinctions', not least because the interviewer immediately prompts him with regard to his relationship with his father. As can be seen, Gianluca immediately says that his father is a 'pain in the ass' when he has been drinking and that his childhood was 'not at all happy'.

The father is described through pairs of antithetical terms, in oxymora: He '*is from Bangladesh and a Muslim, which seems a bit strange because he drinks*'; '*he is a classic father*', but '*he never says no*'; he '*always demanded total respect*', but '*never raised his hand to me, though: never, never*' (NC). Here, the iteration has a function of denial: we must therefore presume the presence of an interior narration – of which he is certainly aware, but which cannot be told – of a father who is both inconsistent and demanding, in short, somewhat confusing (PSC), and who does not fulfil Gianluca's need to transform incoherence into some superior coherence. From a Meadian point of view, we might call it an incomplete 'generalised other' (NC), or, from a Freudian perspective, an incoherent superego (PSC). There is a marked contrast between the previous description of 'normality' and this description. From the point of view of defence mechanisms, we can discern the use of intellectualisation, connected with the minimisation of pain and the denial of psychic suffering (PSC), while the emphatic repetitions and the use of tropes (NC) serve to 'reinforce' his assertions through the mechanism of suppression (PSC). It is noteworthy that Gianluca does not tell anything about his mother during the interview, and this absence is analytically very significant. It is true that the interviewer did not explicitly ask about her, but the fact is still noteworthy.

The interviewer then asks Gianluca to talk about his friends and about girls. Fortunately, the 'internal thread' works, and he returns to his childhood and to the countries in which he has lived, describing his arrival in Italy:

> G: *Then we went to London (…) and then back to Genoa, more or less back to the friends I've more or less had since the middle school; my friends from the primary school are all in far away countries. But from the middle school up to university, they are all people I'm in touch with, now and then. And then there are the friends from my hometown, Camogli, because I'm from Camogli. We grew up, because anyway our real home [Italian 'casa casa', iteration] was here in Genoa, even though we lived abroad; our fixed home was the one in Genoa.*

Here, Gianluca's identity is reinforced through his attachment to a territory (PSC), and the oxymoron is implicit: 'the Bangladeshi boy from Camogli' (NC), who has his 'real home' there. Again, the repetitions are many (NC). Moreover, he obviously says he did not like to move around so often: they had been on the move since the days of his infant school, and each time, he had to leave his friends behind. At this point, however, soccer is mentioned for the first time.

> G: *As a kid at school, though, I noticed that if you can play soccer, you make lots of friends; it's incredible. A kid who's not incapable or useless, maybe a bit... I mean, when you go out and you're in the playground, what you do? You play soccer. And when they pick the teams, you say 'I'll have him', and then you become the one who... That's how I always made friends quickly, wherever I went...*

Soccer appears as a magical remedy, since it is a factor of social integration and harmonisation of the boy's interior world – a veritable balm that enables him to face separation by providing a symbolic filiation that allows him to 'play at home' (indeed, we might say that Gianluca's life was a continuous 'away match') (PSC). Moreover, soccer leads to friendships and social relationships through the choice of players for the respective teams. Thus, it functions as a great attenuator of the experience of separation and loss (PSC). The same holds with regard to sentimental losses; girls come and go, but Sampdoria will always be there: *'maybe I've been lucky to put Sampdoria, the stadium, before all the rest. I mean, when you split up, it's not like that was the only thing I had, because I've still got my companions and the match; that's always soothed it a bit...'*. Thus, Sampdoria and soccer occupy a veritable 'transitional space', in Winnicott's meaning (1953), a space which, however, has to be harmonised with the subject's social life and relationships with the opposite sex (PSC). These are all examples of how the two approaches – NC and PSC – can support each other. The fact that the interviewer has been an 'ultras' helps Gianluca to reveal himself, but his narrative is ambiguous (NC), and ambiguities are resolved via iteration and repetition. A psychodynamic explanation may explain his embarrassment (PSC).

Here, the first reference to the ultras 'ideology' emerges when Gianluca reports explaining to a girl who opposed his membership of the ultras that, when you are a member, *'you're not a delinquent, a run-of-the-mill dick-head'*, that there are reasons and values underlying your choice and goes on to explain what he said to the girl. By contrast, the general public, represented by the girl, sees the ultras as *'all regimented, with no brain'*:

> I: *So it's a choice...*
>
> G: *Yes, it's a conscious choice; a lot of people have to give up other things, other things that they could do. What annoys me is when you hear people talking about letting off...; you do it because you want to let off steam one day a week, because you are repressed, because your life is empty, so you go and do that. But it's not like you have to do these things to shrug off mediocrity. No. Maybe there are some whose minds work like that, but all the guys I know, if they hadn't joined the ultras, they would have been people who got their satisfaction from other things in life... in different fields.*

Here, it emerges that Gianluca is aware of the equalising, conformist nature of the group, albeit projected onto others, and can look at himself from the outside.

In such cases, he justifies himself through complex narratives, resorting to the group's ideology and in some way harmonising individuality and collective identity, autonomy and dependence on the group (NC). However, Gianluca expresses a great desire to try new experiences; this, he reports, prompted him to do various manual jobs, despite having a BA in business marketing (to assert his independence from an overbearing father?) (PSC). What also emerges from this part of the interview is Gianluca's marked spirit of solidarity with his fellow workmates, combined with an equally strong sense of independence (which indicates maturity and a capacity for self-determination) (PSC). The defences of intellectualisation and denial enable Gianluca to construct personal opinions, his sense of the self and the capacity of agency (PSC). One example concerns his free time, which includes a passion for travelling – not as a 'tourist', but as a 'traveller': the tourist has an external relationship with his journey; he sees it from the outside, while the traveller *'tries to become part of the environment'*, without relying on what the guidebooks say. Travelling may also represent the agentic choice to reproduce, from an active point of view, what he was obliged to suffer as a child, i.e. the series of moves (PSC). Acutely, the interviewer connects this topic with that of soccer, comparing the normal fan to the tourist and the ultras to the traveller, who *'lives the experience to the full'*.

The interview then moves on to Gianluca's memory of how he first became involved with the world of soccer fans. His interest was first aroused during childhood and, as we will see, within the family setting. Over time, however, Gianluca migrated from the 'quieter' sectors to the terraces occupied by the 'ultras'. As he himself says: *'...people who more or less, no not more or less, think like you! A lot of times, 99% of things, when someone says something, you've got nothing to add, because he's already said it all'*. Thus, paradoxically, Gianluca's need for autonomy is counterbalanced by his desire to fit into the group (PSC):

> G: *...but you know, with time, you feel yourself getting involved; and the more you get involved, the more you want to be there at times when you know something has to be done. I mean, you feel you're more responsible as well; if something goes wrong, you stop being an outsider and you start to be...; if the choreography doesn't work or if during the match something goes wrong, you feel bad about it; you feel bad about it and you say to yourself 'it made me look bad, as well'.*

Thus, the group becomes an inflated expression of the self and of the subject's identity. Kohut (1971) has described the grandiose Self, defining it as the heir to infantile omnipotence (in Freudian terms, the magic nature of the infant's own will, since, for the baby, desire and its realisation coincide). Following Freud (Freud S., 1921), the grandiose Self incorporates the team, a veritable collective Ego Ideal of the group (PSC).

But membership of the ultras group also serves to fulfil the need to support the team and, consequently, to support oneself as dependent on it (PSC). Once again,

Gianluca makes a distinction, this time between the ultras and the ordinary fans of Sampdoria (the 'Doriani'):

> G: *I've always seen the Ultras as, how should I say, the finest example of Sampdoria supporters; there is no one else like them... I've got the greatest respect for the clubs, for the Doriani. I mean, nobody forces you to be Doriano; maybe someone who is Doriano is just the same as one of the ultras, maybe even more...But, when it comes to supporting Sampdoria, defending her and always standing by her side on any ground; being there, not whistling, booing, criticizing – I mean, shit, working for the good of Sampdoria – like I said, at one time, and even now, it's an overwhelming passion: the colors, being a Sampdoria supporter... being a Sampdoria supporter means carrying the team, living the experience 100%, my team is Sampdoria, my passion is Sampdoria, I'm in love with her, I want to support her, I want to support her 100%..., who can give me this possibility? Who can teach me to do it? Who can I work with to do it? The Ultras. When things are going badly, instead of whistling, like most people, they make an effort to... It's like saying, if you've got a kid, and he's going through a bad time, what you do? Do you insult him or do you give him a hand?*

Several themes emerge in this extract. First of all, Sampdoria is compared to a girl; the image is female (maternal) (PSC). This notion fits in with a reference in the literature on ultras; indeed, with regard to South American soccer fans, Giulianotti (2002, p. 33) claims that they 'talk of their respective clubs as "mothers", whereas they are its "sons" or "children". More routinely, while the players at the club may change, the ground is always "home". Renouncing support or switching allegiances to a rival club is impossible; traditional supporters are culturally contracted to their clubs'.

This image also has a narcissistic connotation ('*I'm in love...*'): the image of the team as a weak mother, needing support, conceals the image of a weak, defenceless child in need of support. Here, we find a projective identification of the subject's own weakness, i.e. 'if I support Mummy and she supports me, in the end I'm supporting myself' (PSC). The reason is immediately traced back, through associative links, to the traumatic situation of Gianluca's childhood, the difficulties connected with his family's frequent moves, with an inconsistent father and a mother who is never significantly mentioned in his narrative (PSC):

> ...*living in Bangladesh, my mum and my father being so far from home, they wanted me to grow up with a sense of identity of where I came from, my origins. The idea they hit on was this thing of Sampdoria, so every Sunday I was on the phone to my uncle, who told me about the match.*

Thus, Sampdoria was actually proposed by Gianluca's parents as a 'transitional object', a link to the homeland (PSC). This process was made possible by the presence of a transgenerational tradition of support for Sampdoria on the mother's side, reconnected in memory to his grandfather and his place of birth, Sampierdarena. Gianluca remembers the stories told by his uncle, who had frequented the South Terrace since his boyhood, and mentions the presents he received as a child (team gadgets, key-rings, T-shirts). However, he splits and denies the sentiments of depression and inadequacy, projecting them onto the ever-hated rival club, Genoa, culturally older and more closely identified with the cultural context of the city (while Sampdoria has always drawn its supporters from outside the urban area) (PSC): 'Luckily, when I was a kid, my folks didn't say "they're bastards; they're shits", but they did somehow let me know it. In short... they're ... poor unlucky bastards; and we're the lucky ones'.

Gianluca goes on reiterating his fusional identification with the group and with the team in the usual narrative style, a sort of psalm-like singsong with sermonising tones, almost befitting a mantra (NC), which conveys powerful emotions in order to convince and justify – himself, first of all – and especially to deny separation and interior poverty (PSC):

> G: *You feel the group; in the end, you, with the other guys, you are the group, and there you risk your good name, and then it's one of those things you care most about, and you bend over backwards to defend that name, you put yourself on the line, you put your life on the line, I mean, Sampdoria becomes your girl, your mum, your family, your... It's everything...*

Thus expressed, and felt, this belonging gives rise to a desire for fatherhood: the wish to take up his place in the chain of the generations, so that he can pass on the values of the group and of life to a new stock of young fans (PSC):

> G: *Well, at least for what I'm like, I see myself carrying the group forward, carrying forward a form of aggregation, giving a possibility to future lads who we hope will be drawn to this world, giving them the same possibility that you've had, the luck you've had to be able to live certain experiences, to make friends, to see how you match up, to grow, what you feel this experience has given you; so it's right to give others this possibility, and it's up to you to carry forward; you like the idea because you know you're doing something for someone else...*

However, Gianluca did not find it easy to become a member:

> G: *When you're the youngest, or one of the youngest, you get picked on; you get slapped around and stuff like that, but with time...; it's the usual sort of apprenticeship; at the beginning you hate it, but after a while you appreciate it more and more. Anyway, the people who picked on you at the beginning were the first to..., if there was anything; they took care of you, they took you with them; in fact, the more slaps you took, the more they took care of you.*

The violence suffered is therefore justified through rationalisation, expressed in the usual iterative way (NC). We will see that Gianluca will adopt the same strategy in order to rationalise the policy of violent clashes with opposing groups of ultras (NC):

> G: *It's obvious, from one generation to the next; it's obvious that gratuitous violence like this ... But that stuff wasn't really violence... It's a sort of rite... Like at school with the new boys, like in the army with new recruits, with cadets... I mean, it's something that, I think, you want to strengthen... But I also think, in the aborigine tribes, someone who – I think – was to become a man, they inflicted some sort of... or tattoo, or branded him...*

As seen, Gianluca connects defensively utilised 'cultured' discourses with the experience of violent education as a rite of initiation, which toughens the subject and introduces him to the hardships of life (NC). It is significant that Cushion and Jones (2006) have discovered the same values in the soccer players admired by the hooligans. The complex defence mechanism used here is identification with the aggressor, whereby the maltreated infantile self is projected onto the new victim, and the former victim identifies with the former persecutor (Freud, 1936). Indeed, Gianluca goes on to connect the violence suffered when he was in a subordinate position with the violence perpetrated by himself on younger companions (PSC):

> G: *because maybe, when I did something wrong, I got a couple of slaps; they took me to one side and said 'look, you got that because it's right you should get your fingers burnt now, and if we hit you it was for this or that reason'; if you take it like the other 99%, in the end you say 'I could have avoided it'; you reason and you think 'I made a mistake; okay, it was my fault; next time...'. And then, later on, when a kid makes a mistake, you give him a crack and you explain why. And you'll see he won't make that mistake again.*

Thus, in the group of ultras, 'education' takes the form of authoritarian, institutional education, which is characterised by physical and verbal violence aimed at 'toughening' the 'novices'; this serves to prepare these youths to perpetrate violence outside, during clashes (NC):

> G: *But when you're out in the street on your own, and there's no mum or dad, it's all down to you. In the street, in a bar or anywhere else, you might have to take a couple of knocks. It makes you understand that you've got to make them respect you; that if you make a mistake... That's the law of the street. You can say what you like, but that's the way it is; ... the street's like that. If we want to bury our heads in the sand, let's do it; shit, let's say everything's okay. This*

world's full of bastards; the mother of the dick-heads is always pregnant. And when you find yourself face to face, if you believe in what, I mean, if he starts giving you shit, as soon as my freedom passes, my freedom ends, I mean, when you overstep that line, I use words to make you understand; but if you still don't understand, I mean, I'm not just going to let you do whatever you like. Wars happen however much you might be against war; some wars are inevitable. If someone invades your territory, takes your house, destroys what you've got, what are you going to do about it? And if you move away, go somewhere else, another one will turn up; you've got to learn to defend yourself.

Thus, when you are in the street and you come across rival ultras, the internalised good objects break down ('*no mum and dad...*'), and fighting breaks out; trust in others vanishes and the paranoid nucleus emerges, together with the unconscious reference to the peregrinations of the family (PSC). Gianluca takes pride in never backing off, because that would be like '*turning your back on the name of your group, on your symbols and on your friends, which are the same thing anyway, and so you go forward*'. While this type of argument may, on the one hand, make reference to the discourses of 'street culture' (Anderson, 1999), on the other, it also refers explicitly to the discourses of war; indeed, here, violence against enemy 'soldiers' is rationalised, while violence against 'civilians' (normal supporters) is not (NC). What we see is a sort of paramilitary organisation. Before or after the match, members of rival groups of ultras, the enemy, are sought out, as if there were a sort of 'pact to fight'. This recalls the reciprocal complicity of sadomasochistic rituals (Khan, 1979) (PSC) and the rules and rituals studied by scholars in the English context (Marsh et al., 1978):

> G: *The ultras don't go beating up ordinary fans; the ultras, true ultras, don't go wrecking cars or setting fire to trash cans; they take on the other ultras; it's just between us; we see things the same way; we take each other on... But there are rules: no knives; if someone's on the ground, you leave him alone; you don't want to kill anyone; it's a sort of challenge to see, like you were saying before, who's got the most courage to move forward. When you see the other group back off, you see them huddled together and moving back as you go forward, you get a burst of adrenaline and you keep going forward. Or if you see them break and run, it's like winning the league championship. Well, okay, not the league championship, but they're wankers (cowards).*

It is noteworthy that the sense of guilt is projected outward (PSC). Respectable members of society may well think that it is useless to get into fights '*over a match*', but Gianluca replies that '*there's much more violence outside the world of the ultras than there is inside*'. Moreover, he claims that, in addition to fighting, the group also carries out respectable, benevolent programs (NC), such as donating an ambulance to voluntary rescue workers, collecting money to aid the victims of natural disasters and helping an elderly person who has been robbed or someone who is sick; in short: '*a member of the ultras doesn't look the other way*'". He is the first to take the initiative – a hero, in Presser's terms (Presser, 2008). He exorcises shame and fear by stepping forward: '*maybe he's mad or something, but if he didn't make the first move he'd feel like a shit for not doing it; he'd feel in the wrong if he copped out. He's the one who'll take that first step*' (NC).

In saying all this, Gianluca strongly disagrees with the image painted by the media and is well aware of the social mechanisms whereby social panics are constructed. On the other hand, despite the neutralisation technique of condemnation of the condemners that Gianluca again puts forward, he does understand that the violence of the ultras '*is not justifiable from the point of view of a normal person*', although he again legitimises fighting as a '*consensual*' choice made by both parties (NC). Here, we can observe the copresence of different narrative explanations, which are apparently incongruous; however, some are directed towards insiders, while others are destined for outsiders, with the awareness that it is impossible to justify violence today (NC):

> G: *You know, some subjects are difficult, like violence. I mean, let's be honest... either you live it or you can't, you can't, like I said before, you can't even try to justify it... It's quite difficult to defend, seeing how they present it... when, even with the fact that we went on 'Porta a porta'* (a TV talk show), *or to Rome with the managers of the FIGC* (Italian Soccer Federation), *and on the way, you say 'Okay, guys, be careful'; if the question of violence comes up, we change the subject, because we're too vulnerable on that score, too vulnerable. I mean, you can't; it's too difficult; you can try, but you paint yourself into a corner; they'll put you with your back to the wall, and shit, 'yeah, we're violent as well', and then, if you say that, then public opinion... I mean, you get screwed. You've got to change the subject, like 'yeah, but you see fights in Parliament as well, or like the ones who have done it have owned up and have paid for it...' and you try to wriggle out of it. I mean, on 'Porta a Porta', with all those people watching... you say something... and that's it, you get screwed. And all the good stuff that you could talk about just falls to bits on the spot. In fact, the guy who went there did a great job; Trevor went on the program and he did a great job...*

Here the group of ultras is, again, compared to '*a group of brothers*', '*a family*', which, as we have seen, keeps tight hold of its secrets and solves its problems within its own ranks. Gianluca therefore seems to be aware of how much being a fan has made up for his childhood shortcomings, how much this affiliation has assuaged his feeling of loneliness and how it has provided him with support and intimacy, though also with secrecy and complicity (PSC).

Discussion

As seen in the case of Gianluca, the subject is born and grows in a 'pool' of relations and narrations, which simultaneously construct his familial, social and cultural environment, which in turn determines his position and in relation to which he positions himself. Such narrations can be 'retrieved' through the interview, which prioritises free associations. The approach of NC has therefore enabled us to study the plot and the particular characteristics of Gianluca's narration, as well as the characters, themes and discourses to which he refers. On the other hand, the PSC approach, through the analysis of the defensive use of such discourses, has highlighted the subject's peculiar anxieties and the ways of coping with them.

Thus, it is possible, fruitfully, to add to the various positionings of the subjects with respect to social, cultural and group discourses – the study of which is typical of the NC – the study of the construction of the subject's own peculiar discourse. On the one hand, the contribution of PSC to NC lies in the possibility of understanding self-narratives better, considering them as products of what Lacan defines as the imaginary structure of the Ego. In Lacanian terms, the subject is defined as 'barred' inasmuch is not simply equivalent to a conscious agent (a mere illusion): Lacan's 'subject' is the subject of the unconscious (cfr. Lacan, 1956), in the sense that it abruptly appears in the sudden blooming of an unexpected meaning that retrospectively gives a new sense to the narration (Freud's *Nachträglichkeit*, in English 'deferred action', 'afterwards-ness') (Lacan, 1961). In other words, and in Freudian terms, during self-narration, some unconscious trace appears, willingly or not, and a 'new' narrative possibility develops, which can also deny or contradict the 'official' one. Here, the presence of the other (the interviewer) is fundamental, even though both the narrator and the narratee are subject to higher norms (both are submitted to language and share cultural rules and values, which Lacan defines as belonging to the 'symbolic order') (Francia & Verde, 2015). The combination of the two traditions permits to discover that a sort of 'style', a 'unifying thread', runs through Gianluca's narratives, which better defines the motives of his positionings and the way in which he relates to his social environment. PSC also explains the contradictions and inconsistencies of what he tells about himself.

On the other hand, as seen, NC can help PSC by underlining the necessity for a precise and detailed analysis of authors' narratives, conceiving them as both inducing criminal and deviant actions and simultaneously explaining and justifying actions performed by subjects who are both narratively multidetermined and structurally and (sub)culturally positioned. In the present case, PSC alone would not have considered the details of Gianluca's interview transcripts so carefully. Hence, it would not have allowed us to detect the multiple narratives that define his complex East/West world and which led him to find a unifying plot in ultras' membership: a real master narrative, put forward in order to justify and harmonise normality and deviancy, peacefulness (and engagement in charity) and street violence.

Moreover, referring to NC also allowed PSC to consider the importance of the use of narratives as a way of constructing the Self at each stage of the story. Some of Gianluca's narrative passages are more defensive, while others are less so; above all, some are more imbued with emotivity than others and 'capture' the subject in a 'true' image. In this context, we define as 'true' the subject's feeling of being in the presence of a 'master plot' which weaves together experiences and emotions (Presser, 2013). This is clearly shown by the emphasis on Sampdoria as an idealised lover, whose achievements were followed from afar during childhood and who subsequently became the princess to be saved from the dragon. This truth is obviously subjective and binds the subject at both the social and individual levels. It is precisely where the emotions emerge most markedly (but also where they are totally absent) that it is possible to investigate what lies 'behind' the story that is constructed by the subject and to reconstruct the world of the less accessible affects by deciphering the defensive nature of certain emotional experiences (Mercan, 2018).

In sum, combining NC and PSC proved able to reveal the most significant aspects of Gianluca's history and his complex relationship with his parents (an inconsistent alcoholic father and a weak mother needing support) and to trace the drama back to its origins, i.e. the building blocks of his identity. These are very closely tied to the beloved soccer team and to its strong symbolic meaning. The continual separations and the moves from one country to another are exorcised through his identification with the soccer club – first as an ordinary fan and finally, in 'his' Camogli, as a member of the ultras – which constitutes a veritable transitional activity that has alleviated losses and separations. It may therefore even be hypothesised that, in this way, Gianluca succeeded in constructing a sort of prosthesis to replace his parents, who were unable to provide him with stability and a sense of identity, while at the same time healing and sustaining them.

In order to achieve this, Gianluca makes use of specific defence mechanisms, which are the expression of an adaptation and of a mode of functioning that have been achieved with great difficulty. Despite the difficulties revealed, however, Gianluca cannot be defined as irresponsible or impulsive; if anything, he is an adult with a difficult past, but he is also able to rationalise and to construct fairly satisfactory defensive narratives to assuage the anguish of being an affective 'stateless person', a foreigner to his own parents. These narratives allow him to deny the painful feelings connected with his solitude and abandonment, feelings that are exorcised through the group and through role reversal (the team to support, the parent to support). On examining the different adaptive levels of defence mechanisms used, in accordance with the criteria drawn up by the scholars (APA, 1994; Cramer, 2006, 2010; Perry & Hoglend, 1998), in Gianluca only altruism appears to be highly adaptive. We can also observe the presence of both mechanisms of mental inhibition (dissociation and intellectualisation) and minor image distortion (idealisation and omnipotence), and of more primitive functioning: mechanisms of disavowal (denial, projection, rationalisation) and major image distortion (projective identification and splitting). As we have seen, these last features are expressed through particular rhetorical artifices, such as iteration and psalmody (even the transcriptions convey the 'recited' nature of the subject's narrations). In this sense, like the Lacanian 'stolen letter' (Lacan, 1957), the unconscious is not what is 'deep', but often what is so evident that it escapes notice.

Frequently, Gianluca appears incoherent in his justifications: the contradictions and oxymora permeating his apparently inconsistent narrations (Verde, Angelini, Boverini, & Majorana, 2006) are, however, the effect of a successful management of their contents through the deliberate use of ambiguity (Sandberg, Tutenges, & Copes, 2015); this is achieved through the thoughtful use of defences and neutralisations. In this way, he succeeds in continuing his deviant activities, while integrating into society, like the offenders (carjackers) described by Jacobs and Copes (2015). This appears to be the most evolved aspect of his personality.

Conclusion

In order to develop this line of research further, NC and PSC could deepen the study of the defences and neutralisations that lead to the sometimes deliberate use of ambiguity. Adopting complex approaches, like the one advocated here, might be a fruitful strategy. From Gianluca, for example, we have learned that the use of ambiguity and the narrative complexity of his justifications could be ascribed to his relationship with his alcoholic and Muslim, reprehensible and perfect father. However, more cases are necessary in order to better articulate the possibility of being 'respectably deviant', or 'unrespectably normal', as Gianluca seems to suggest.

In conclusion, combining NC with PSC yielded a better understanding of the choice of deviancy, extending it to what (sometimes) can remain hidden to the consciousness of the subject. This connection, while requiring experience of the theoretical backgrounds of both NC and PSC, can be facilitated by the fact that both use very similar research tools: qualitative autobiographical interviews in which offenders freely narrate themselves. Moreover, from a theoretical standpoint, the differences between these traditions can stimulate discussion and promote a better understanding of what transgression 'means' to the offender and how it fits into his life.

Finally, by enabling us to frame subjects within collective discourses and the social context to which they belong, this strategy may prove very useful in the practical sphere to probation officers, social workers, psychologists and forensic psychotherapists.

References

American Psychiatric Association. (1994). *Diagnostic and statistical manual of mental disorders* (4th ed.). Washington, DC: American Psychiatric Association.

Anderson, E. (1999). *Code of the street: Decency, violence, and the moral life of the inner city*. New York, NY: W. W. Norton & Company.

Brookman, F. (2015). The shifting narratives of violent offenders. In L. Presser & S. Sandberg (Eds.), *Narrative criminology: Understanding stories of crime* (pp. 207–234). New York, NY: New York University Press.

Brookman, F., Copes, H., & Hochstetler, A. (2011). Street codes as formula stories: How inmates recount violence. *Journal of Contemporary Ethnography*, 40(4), 397–424.

Cramer, P. (2006). *Protecting the self: Defense mechanisms in action.* New York, NY: The Guilford Press.

Cramer, P. (2010). Defense mechanisms in psychology today: Further processes for adaptation. *American Psychologist*, 55(6), 637–646.

Cushion, C., & Jones, R. L. (2006). Power, discourse, and symbolic violence in professional youth soccer: The case of Albion soccer club. *Sociology of Sport Journal*, 23(2), 142–161.

DeWalt, K. M., & DeWalt, B. R. (2011). *Participant observation: A guide for fieldworkers.* Lanham, MD: AltaMira Press.

Doidge, M. (2015). *Soccer Italia: Italian soccer in an era of globalisation.* London: Bloomsbury Publishing.

Dunning, E., Murphy, P., & Williams, J. M. (1988). *The roots of football hooliganism: An historical and sociological study.* London: Routledge and Kegan Paul.

Fleetwood, J. (2016). Narrative habitus: Thinking though structure/agency in the narratives of offenders. *Crime, Media, Culture*, 12(2), 173–192.

Francia, A., & Verde, A. (2015). Il reo narra il suo delitto: Idee per una criminologia narrativa aperta alla complessità. *Rassegna Italiana di Criminologia*, 9(2), 116–126.

Freud, A. (1936). *The ego and the mechanisms of defense.* Abingdon and New York, NY: Routledge, 2018.

Freud, S. (1915). Instincts and their vicissitudes. In J. Strachey (Ed.), *The standard edition of the complete psychological works of Sigmund Freud, Volume XIV (1914–1916). On the history of the psycho-analytic movement. Papers on metapsychology and other works.* London: The Hogarth Press and the Institute of Psychoanalysis, 1957.

Freud S. (1921). Group psychology and the analysis of the ego. In J. Strachey (Ed.), *The standard edition of the complete psychological works of Sigmund Freud, Volume XVIII (1920–1922). Beyond the pleasure principle. Group psychology and other works.* London: The Hogarth Press and the Institute of Psychoanalysis, 1955.

Gadd, D. (2011). In-depth interviewing and psychosocial case-study analysis. In D. Gadd, S. Karstedt, & S. F. Messner (Eds.), *The Sage handbook of criminological research methods* (pp. 36–48). London: SAGE Publications.

Gadd, D., & Corr, M.-L. (2015). Psychosocial criminology: Making sense of senseless violence. In J. Miller & W. R. Palacios (Eds.), *Qualitative research in criminology* (pp. 69–84). Advances in Criminological Theory (Vol. 20). Piscataway, NJ: Transaction Publishers.

Gadd, D., & Jefferson, T. (2007). *Psychosocial criminology.* London: SAGE Publications.

Giulianotti, R. (2002). Supporters, followers, fans, and flaneurs: A taxonomy of spectator identities in soccer. *Journal of Sport & Social Issues*, 26(1), 25–46.

Harris, P. (2017). Inter-subjectivity and worker self-disclosure in professional relationships with young people: A psychosocial study of youth violence and desistence. *The Howard Journal of Crime and Justice*, 56(4), 516–531.

Harvey, A., & Piotrowska, A. (2013). Intolerance and joy, violence and love among male football fans: Towards a psychosocial explanation of 'excessive' behaviours. *Sport in Society: Cultures, Commerce, Media, Politics*, *16*(10), 1404–1413.

Hollway, W. (1984). Gender difference and the production of subjectivity. In J. Henriques, W. Hollway, C.Venn, & V. Walkerdine (Eds.), *Changing the subject*. London: Methuen Publishing.

Hollway, W., & Jefferson, T. (2013). *Doing qualitative research differently: A psychosocial approach* (2nd ed.). London: SAGE Publications.

Jacobs, B. A., & Copes, H. (2015). Neutralization without drift: Criminal commitment among persistent offenders. *British Journal of Criminology*, *55*(2), 286–302.

Jefferson, T. (2010). Psychosocial criminology. In E. McLaughlin & T. Newburn (Eds.), *The Sage handbook of criminological theory* (pp. 284–302). London: SAGE Publications.

Kerr, J. H. (1994). *Understanding soccer hooliganism*. Buckingham: Open University Press.

Khan, M. M. R. (1979). *Alienation in perversions*. New York, NY: Routledge, 2018.

Kohut, H. (1971). *The analysis of the self: A systematic approach to the psychoanalytic treatment of narcissistic personality disorders*. New York, NY: International Universities Press.

Lacan, J. (1956). The Freudian thing, or the meaning of the return to Freud in psychoanalysis. In B.Fink with R. Fink & R. Grigg (Trans.), *Écrits, the first complete edition in English*. New York, NY/London: W. W. Norton & Company, 2006.

Lacan, J. (1957). The stolen letter. In B.Fink with R. Fink & R. Grigg (Trans.), *Écrits, the first complete edition in English*. New York, NY/London: W. W. Norton & Company, 2006.

Lacan, J. (1961). The subversion of the subject and the dialectic of desire in the Freudian unconscious. In B.Fink with R. Fink & R. Grigg (Trans.), *Écrits, the first complete edition in English*. New York, NY/London: W. W. Norton & Company, 2006.

Maniglio, R. (2007). The hooligan's mind. *Journal of Forensic Sciences*, *52*(1), 204–208.

Marsh, P. (1978). *Aggro: The illusion of violence*. London: Dent, 1978.

Marsh, P., Rosser, E. Y. H., & Harré, R. (1978). *The rules of disorder*. London: Routledge and Kegan Paul.

Maruna, S., & Copes, H. (2005). What have we learned from five decades of neutralization research?. *Crime and Justice*, *32*, 221–320.

Maruna, S., & Matravers, A. (2007). N = 1: Criminology and the person. *Theoretical Criminology*, *11*(4), 427–442.

Mercan, B. A. (2018). Doing criminological research: Affective states versus emotional reactions. *Theoretical Criminology*, 1–18. 10.1177/2F1362480618779399, Online First.

Mitchell, S. A. (1988). *Relational concepts in psychoanalysis: An integration*. Cambridge, MA: Harvard University Press.

Perry, J. C., & Hoglend, P. (1998). Convergent and discriminant validity of overall defensive functioning. *The Journal of Nervous and Mental Disease*, *186*(9), 529–535.

Presser, L. (2008). *Been a heavy life: Stories of violent men*. Urbana, IL and Chicago, IL: University of Illinois Press.

Presser, L. (2009). The narratives of offenders. *Theoretical Criminology*, *13*(2), 177–200.
Presser, L. (2012). Getting on top through mass murder: Narrative, metaphor, and violence. *Crime, Media, Culture*, *8*(1), 3–21.
Presser, L. (2013). *Why we harm*. New Brunswick, NJ: Rutgers University Press.
Presser, L., & Sandberg, S. (2015). Introduction: What is the story? In L. Presser & S. Sandberg (Eds.), *Narrative criminology: Understanding stories of crime* (pp. 1–20). New York, NY: New York University Press.
Redl, F., & Wineman, D. (1951). *Children who hate*. New York, NY: Free Press.
Sandberg, S. (2009). A narrative search for respect. *Deviant Behavior*, *30*(6), 487–510.
Sandberg, S. (2010). What can "lies" tell us about life? Notes towards a framework of narrative criminology. *Journal of Criminal Justice Education*, *21*(4), 447–465.
Sandberg, S. (2013). Are self-narratives strategic or determined, unified or fragmented? Reading Breivik's Manifesto in light of narrative criminology. *Acta Sociologica*, *56*(1), 69–83.
Sandberg, S. (2016). The importance of stories untold: Life-story, event-story and trope. *Crime, Media, Culture*, *12*(2), 153–171.
Sandberg, S., & Fleetwood, J. (2016). Street talk and Bourdieusian criminology: Bringing narrative to field theory. *Criminology and Criminal Justice*, *17*(4), 365–381.
Sandberg, S., Tutenges, S., & Copes, H. (2015). Stories of violence: A narrative criminological study of ambiguity. *British Journal of Criminology*, *55*(6), 1168–1186.
Schafer, R. (1980). Narration in the psychoanalytical dialogue. *Critical Inquiry*, *7*(1), 29–53.
Segal, H. (1979). *Klein*. London: Fontana Modern Masters.
Spence, D. P. (1982). *Narrative truth and historical truth: Meaning and interpretation in psychoanalysis*. New York, NY: W. W. Norton & Company.
Stern, D. B. (2017). Interpersonal psychoanalysis: History and current status. *Contemporary Psychoanalysis*, *53*(1), 69–94.
Sykes, G., & Matza, D. (1957). Techniques of neutralization: A theory of delinquency. *American Sociological Review*, *22*(6), 664–670.
Taylor, I. (1971). Soccer consciousness and soccer hooliganism. In S. Cohen (Ed.), *Images of deviance* (pp. 134–163). Harmondsworth: Penguin Books.
Uriely, N., Ram, Y., & Malach-Pines, A. (2011). Psychoanalytic sociology of deviant tourist behavior. *Annals of Tourism Research*, *38*(3), 1051–1069.
Verde. A. (2018). Narrative criminology: Crime as produced by and re-lived through narratives. InN. Rafter & E. Carrabine (Eds.), *Oxford research encyclopaedia of crime, media, and popular culture* (Vol. 3). Oxford: Oxford University Press.
Verde, A., Angelini, F., Boverini, S., & Majorana, M. (2006). The narrative structure of psychiatric reports. *International Journal of Law and Psychiatry*, *29*(1), 1–12.
Winnicott, D. W. (1953). Transitional objects and transitional phenomena. In D. W. Winnicott (Ed.), *Collected papers: Through paediatrics to psycho-analysis*. London: Tavistock Publications, 1958.

Chapter 20

The Story of Antisociality: Determining What Goes Unsaid in Dominant Narratives

Lois Presser

Stories exclude far more than they include, and what is not said is as consequential as what is said. In fact, what is not said may be even more consequential because it affects us but is taken for granted, bypassing our critical faculties. I am interested in determining what storytellers leave out to significant effect. To discern what goes unsaid in stories, and to expound a method for doing so, I use the case of the story of antisociality related by American criminologists Michael Gottfredson and Travis Hirschi in their influential 1990 book *A General Theory of Crime*. That story identifies parental neglect as the preeminent cause of a person's lifelong propensity towards antisocial behaviour: the individual has not been adequately taught to restrain herself/himself early in life. This chapter both critiques the story/theory on the basis of its exclusions and presents a method for locating exclusions in stories generally.

My life experience led me to this critique. I am a single mother of two young children. Daily and nightly I meet the immense physical and mental demands of this role. The domestic labour that usually falls to women manifests as relational conflict in the case of two-parent heterosexual families with children (Hochschild, 2012) but remains invisible in the case of single-parent families. When the burdens of single mothers (the usual single parents[1]) are recognised, we are either characterised as having chosen those burdens (and maligned) or as extraordinary in our ability to manage them. Concealed either way are the socially planted and maintained hooks for hardship – the low visibility and devaluation of home and childcare, the off-duty requirements of paid labour and the paucity of resources other than one's own, especially in the US. I have a view, grounded in living, of how disregard sustains harm and hierarchies, and how gendered, raced and classed such disregard is, whether or not terms for gender, race and class are articulated.

---

[1]Single-parent families, around the world, are disproportionately single-mother families (OECD, 2018).

Likewise, Gottfredson and Hirschi's story of antisociality fails to articulate certain understandings of the world – it presupposes some and excludes others – in such a way that penal harm seems inevitable. In this way it does ideological work, 'legitimating the power of a dominant social group or class' (Eagleton, 1991, p. 5). Social theorist Terry Eagleton (1991) expounds the processes involved in such legitimation (pp. 5–6, emphases in original):

> A dominant power may legitimate itself by promoting beliefs and values congenial to it; *naturalizing* and *universalizing* such beliefs so as to render them self-evident and apparently inevitable; *denigrating* ideas which might challenge it; *excluding* rival forms of thought, perhaps by some unspoken but systematical logic; and *obscuring* social reality in ways convenient to itself.

In this chapter I sketch a method for determining textual exclusions that legitimise power positions. The method consists in (1) evaluating figurative language and other means of ambiguation; (2) assessing patterns of elaboration and explanation and (3) asking what and whose knowledge is missing.

It may seem implausible or nervy to assert that a particular thing has been left out of a text. First, that assertion seems to allege intent, which cannot be proven. Actually, powerful exclusions may not be intended by some communicator but are instead salient in the culture and supported unconsciously by the authors. In that regard I refer to Gee (1999) who, in presenting his view of discourse analysis, observes: 'It is sometimes helpful to think about social and political issues as if it is not just us humans who are talking and interacting with each other, but rather, the Discourses we represent and enact, and for which we are "carriers"' (p. 18, capitalisation in original). I submit that discourses contain omissions whether any human communicator intends them or is even mindful of them. Second, the project may seem foolhardy if only because *many* things, consciously or not, have in fact been left out of *any* text. And many exclusions are of little or no political consequence. Analysts make – *I* make – a judgement as to which unsaid things *matter*. We should be transparent vis-à-vis the positions (both roles and viewpoints) that guide such judgements, for these are inevitable and inevitably impactful. We should share what 'things left out' *we* deem vital and why.

Various social researchers have taken note of the not-said (e.g. Barak, 2007, pp. 198–199; Butler, 2004, p. 36; Gubrium & Holstein, 1997, p. 159; Hallsworth & Young, 2008; Loseke, 2003, pp. 56–57; Miles & Crush, 1993, p. 91; Polanyi, 1985, p. 49; Rosenberg, Rosenberg, & Farrell, 1992, p. 48). They commonly ascribe a constitutive role to not-saying. Historian Hayden White (1980, p. 14) considers narratives in particular as 'constructed on the basis of a set of events which *might have been included but were left out*' (emphasis in original). Marxist literary scholar Macherey (1978) points to the role of silence in meaning-making: 'the explicit requires the implicit' (p. 85). Philosopher Adam Knowles (2015) similarly observes that 'speech and silence cannot simply be read as standing in contrast with one another, but instead as at all times necessarily intertwined with one another' (p. 16). He notes: 'Philosophy has become philosophy by vesting itself with a silence, but equally so with the exclusions wrought by that silence' (p. 16). Psychoanalytic thinkers, beginning with Freud, are squarely attentive to absences, formulating them as that which is repressed because it provokes excessive anxiety; Lacan (1977) and others, including his feminist critics, have applied this idea to absences within language. A central problem of critical theories is silencing, represented in queer theory as the closet, for example. Ethnographies are well known for collecting the stories of research participants who have traditionally been silenced, their stories 'unlistened-to' (Colvin, 2017). The ethnographer effectively ends the silence. My exploration is more technical than any of these. My question is: How do we pin down with rigour what is not said?

The framework for my exploration is both critical theoretical, centring on hegemonic and subaltern knowing and speaking, and narrative criminology. Narrative criminology is based on the perspective that stories and features of stories influence harmful actions and patterns (Presser, 2009; Presser & Sandberg, 2015). To date narrative criminologists have explored the genres, plotlines and characters of stories that promote or prevent crime and other harm. We have been asking what influential stories *say*.[2] Determining what is *not said* is an important task for a critical narrative criminology (Presser & Sandberg, 2019). But first, what harm do criminology's prevailing stories cause?

Penal Harm and Criminology

Todd Clear (1994) coined the expression penal harm to describe the pains inflicted upon criminalised persons in the name of justice. The US is the definitive case of penal harm, with 2.2 million people behind bars (The Sentencing Project, 2018) and more than twice that number under community supervision (BJS, 2018). Specific strategies and effects of the harm project are well documented. They include imprisonment, solitary confinement, execution, substandard health care, rape and other physical victimisation, undercompensated and/or forced labour, blocked occupational and educational opportunities, political disenfranchisement, exclusion from public benefits, lifelong surveillance and risk of enhanced sanctions, and much more. Family members and whole communities of the criminalised targets are harmed as well (Chesney-Lind & Mauer, 2003; Clear, 2009). American history encompasses a series of politicised and especially racialized wars on crime and criminalised drugs. The US government launched an express penal harm project beginning in the 1970s, accelerating in the 1980s and 1990s, with policies such as harsh drug laws, determinate and mandatory minimum sentencing, increased use of life sentences and 'three strikes' laws (Gottschalk, 2015; The Sentencing Project, 2018; Travis, Western, & Redburn, 2014).

In the US context, deterrent and retributive rationales for punishment manifestly recommend that it be disagreeable. Yet, even when making targets suffer is

---

[2] I use story and narrative interchangeably, although valuable distinctions have been made, mainly along lines of story being more circumscribed, such as around particular episodes.

not the stated goal of punishment – as with incapacitation and rehabilitation rationales – it is criminal justice *policy* to treat the target's own interests as secondary or beside the point. The punishment harms because 'law violators are restricted, hampered, or prevented from acting in their own legitimate self-interest' (Clear, 1994, p. 17). As such, the settings for incapacitation or rehabilitation are generally hurtful and moreover individuals did not choose them. Penal harm is suffering and powerlessness.

Penal harm is clearly motivated by fiscal and political goals. Organisations, institutions and people amass money and power by imposing penal harm (Gottschalk, 2015; Henricks & Harvey, 2017; Shichor, 1995; Simon, 2007). At the same time, penal harm has discursive foundations. Before we can subject others to special treatment and get away with it, we must identify them as special. The special treatment in turn hones the identification. This is the insight of the labelling perspective and it is axiomatic for symbolic interactionism. The harm we do to 'criminals' (and others) requires that they be designated as different from the rest of us. Enter criminology, which expounds how criminals are different and does so with the imprimatur of science.[3] Historical and recent constructions of persons as born or hardened criminals and 'superpredators' have clearly shaped policy. Through their efforts to distinguish criminals 'criminologists have become the ancillary agents of power,' to quote Richard Quinney (1974, p. 27). Different theories of crime advance different notions of how mutable the condition of criminality is. Some mark out different circumstances or experiences, others different inheritances or traits. The more permanent the conditions marked out by a theory, the more sustained or irreversible the treatment that theory supports.

The General Theory of Crime as a Story

In their 1990 book *A General Theory of Crime*, Gottfredson and Hirschi advanced the perspective that individuals become criminals through inadequate self-control which stems from inadequate parenting. The 'major "cause" of low self-control (is) ineffective child-rearing' (p. 183). Parents must monitor the child's behaviour, recognise deviant behaviour in the moment and punish it (p. 97). After early childhood, the condition of low self-control is stable. Those 'who lack self-control will tend to be impulsive, insensitive, physical, risk-taking, short sighted, and nonverbal, and they will tend therefore to engage in criminal and analogous acts' (p. 179). Whether they engage depends on opportunity (p. 201). While all individuals seem to reduce their antisocial activity over time, a differential tendency to act badly remains constant. Thus, *A General Theory of Crime* supports penal harm and furthermore individualises the need for it. It is by no means the only work of criminology out of the US to do so, but its prominence in that realm (see Pratt & Cullen, 2000) makes it an important case.

---

[3]Criminology is like other social inquiry in this regard: consider theories of race that have primed policies of eugenics, slavery, segregation and so forth.

A General Theory of Crime begins with a discussion of what crimes are like. Crimes, for Gottfredson and Hirschi, are 'acts of force or fraud undertaken in pursuit of self-interest' (p. 15). The definition is explicitly rooted in criminology's classical theory. Crimes satisfy individual wants, or promise to.

In this (classical) view, all human conduct can be understood as the self-interested pursuit of pleasure or the avoidance of pain. By definition, therefore, crimes too are merely acts designed to satisfy some combination of these basic tendencies (p. 5).

Gottfredson and Hirschi furthermore stress that crimes are easy to commit and produce little gain. 'The skill required to complete the general run of crime is minimal' (p. 18); crime is 'usually of little lasting or substantial benefit to the offender' (p. 21). From the start of the book, Gottfredson and Hirschi make much of the fact that they derived their explanation of crime from their definition of crime. If crimes are acts promising immediate net benefit to the individual, then criminals are by nature people who pursue immediate net benefits. But, given presumed human nature, if not socialised the right way all people would commit crime and similarly reckless acts. Criminals have not been correctly socialised.

The book tells a story[4] of how antisocial people got to be that way. It is a *story of antisociality*, my expression for any account that describes the coming-into-existence of an antisocial person or people. Such stories support policies that isolate antisocial people for long or unending periods of time. Scholars are far more likely to call their accounts of a social phenomenon *theories* than stories. They might sense that in calling their theories stories, their objectivity is being called into question, and they would be correct. I mean to emphasise something more technical than that they are not objective, however. Theories are stories insofar as theories describe events happening over time and, on the basis of what transpires, make some point (Labov & Waletzky, 1967; see also; White, 1973). The general theory of crime is a story that makes the point that offenders are essentially different from the rest of us and must be controlled.

That the general theory of crime is a story has implications for social influence. Stories are authoritative guides to what people are like. They draw contrasts between individuals and between states of being for the same individual across time. Whereas language in general creates characterological distinctions (Lamont & Molnár, 2002), stories specialise in it. Frank (2010) observes: 'Stories have a singular capacity to delve the *character of the characters* who deal with trouble' (p. 29; emphasis in original). Relatedly, stories capture life as we live it. They are essentially about conflict and change, and they set out a common sense of action in the face of these. For these and other reasons, people get uniquely absorbed in stories. Hogan (2003) explains: 'our affective response to a situation, real or fictional, is not a response to an isolated moment, but to the entire sequence of events in which that moment is located' (p. 5). In short, stories are

---

[4]The authors also tell what I call a 'factional' story in the book, of their encounter with a discipline that fails to pin down the true nature of crime (see Presser, 2018, p. 113).

especially well suited for rationalising social arrangements and making emotional appeals.

Scholars call narratives that rule in a particular social milieu hegemonic, dominant, majoritarian or master narratives, and narratives that oppose these, subversive or counternarratives or counterstories (see e.g. Bamberg & Andrews, 2004; Ewick & Silbey, 1995; Halverson, Goodall, & Corman, 2011; Solórzano & Yosso, 2002). Discussions of hegemonic (and counter) narratives take obvious inspiration from the work of Antonio Gramsci, who identified hegemony, or control via ideas, as a principal instrument of state power under capitalism. Hegemonic ideas become common sense, and common sense requires little explication. As Steinberg (1998) puts it: 'an essential part of the power produced through discourse, and a cornerstone of hegemony, is the capacity to construct silences within common sense' (p. 855).

Absences in the Story of Antisociality

Gottfredson and Hirschi's story contains silences both on the real experiences and the social structuring of parenting, work, crime and acceptable conduct. The story upholds existing power relations and legitimises penal harm.

Gottfredson and Hirschi maintain that someone needs to monitor a child's behaviour, recognise bad behaviour and punish it, early in the child's life, or the child will develop a stable antisocial propensity, or criminality. According to Gottfredson and Hirschi, concern for children morphs naturally into the necessary manoeuvres. 'All that is required to activate the system is affection for or investment in the child. The person who cares for the child will watch his behaviour, see him doing things he should not do, and correct him' (Gottfredson & Hirschi, 1990, p. 97). Caring about the child (p. 98) and understanding the requirements of child development (p. 269) are the main drivers of successful socialisation. It follows that the ineffective parent is one who does not *feel* the right ways and does not *know* the right things. The labours of parenting – the material challenges of being present and attentive – are never discussed; the felt fallout of too much labour is referred to once: 'the parents, even if they care, may not have the time and energy to monitor the child's behaviour...finally, even if everything else is in place, the parents may not have the inclination or the means to punish the child' (p. 98). Yet, these practical deficits are not of particular interest to them, as seen by the fact that they are not mentioned at all in their practical recommendations.

Childcare is not work in Gottfredson and Hirschi's story, as in mainstream US culture. This misrecognition is significant in many ways, not least because it is the work that *women* do, disproportionately and historically, that is not presented as work. Thus Gottfredson and Hirschi (1990) can present a summary of research into the delinquency risk of 'children of women who work' (p. 104) and not remark on the codification of 'work' as paid work outside the home. Gottfredson and Hirschi acknowledge the fact that women are the main socialising agents of children, as when they concede that single parents are usually single mothers (p. 104), but take little from it. Feminists have long recognised this sleight of hand. Women who parent do not work unless they do the work associated, in the cultural imagination, with men. Mothers' efforts, and hence their hardships, are extraneous to social policy considerations.

Another of the book's ideological exclusions, related to the issue of women's (ir)responsibility, centres on social class. Gottfredson and Hirschi note the proximity of their conception of the properly socialised child to the bourgeois. They write: '[Albert] Cohen's description of middle-class values...is a detailed conceptualisation of what we mean by self-control' (Gottfredson & Hirschi, 1990, p. 143). In other words, the right way of behaving is that of the more affluent classes. This stray reference to social class does not come with any acknowledgement of the materiality of social class.

Generally speaking, Gottfredson and Hirschi's conceptualisation of crime as the province of poor people, particularly poor minorities, is more tacit than their remark concerning Cohen's theory suggests. They accomplish that conceptualisation, first, by excluding corporate crime, state crime and the legal harms perpetrated by both individuals and aggregates, from 'crime'. The crimes they take to be exemplary *as* crimes are conventional crimes: burglary, robbery, homicide, auto theft, rape, embezzlement and substance use. They call these ordinary, or common (p. 16). They *should* be common among crimes because the authors do not refer to any other harms and rely mostly on legal designations and police data. They hesitantly concede that corporations 'sometimes dispose of toxic chemicals in ways contrary to law' (p. 184). Their tepid claim about corporate crime receives none of the effort of cross-validating across data source that conventional crimes do. Second, Gottfredson and Hirschi treat hegemonic disappearances of domestic crime as factual. For example, their assertion that rape typically occurs 'between strangers' (p. 36) ignores the fact that both law and culture have traditionally constructed marital rape as an impossibility. They ignore the bank of knowledge of how criminal justice including data are structured by social hierarchies. Hence, 'research on racial differences' in crime 'should focus on differential child-rearing practices' (p. 153).

What do these exclusions achieve? As in all stories, characters and moral evaluations are in the making. Crimes (and other reckless acts) are the actions of lower-class individuals who have not been reigned in early in life. Parents, particularly mothers, construct their children's class position through their in/activity (see Smith, 1987). The parent is someone who could easily redirect her child from criminality *and* from the underclass, but does not. She is not someone for whom social support (e.g. paid afterschool care and sick leave) in raising her children could make a difference because her problem is her mindset. Among other things Gottfredson and Hirschi channel – though they do not explicate – storied ideologies, prevalent in the US, of women, poor and minority women in particular, with bad attitudes, unmotivated to do what maternal care requires – and furthermore unknowledgeable about good parenting. The deficits of individual mothers cause their children's deficits. What is not said is that caring takes time, that time is a material resource and that various social structures rob people of that resource. Important facts from people's lives are excluded. Both realms of the not-said – channelled ideologies and the facts of people's lives – construct harm-promoting myths concerning crime and persons associated with crime. How did I arrive at these absences methodologically?

A Method for Determining What Is Not Said

Some social researchers have deliberated, methodologically, on *silence* (Bengtsson & Fynbo, 2018; Mazzei, 2007), by which they mean people are not speaking for an atypically long period of time within a research setting. Other researchers have explored small stories (Bamberg & Georgakopoulou, 2008) and tropes (Sandberg, 2016) – texts that point to stories but recount them minimally if at all. What I am after are things that do not get said *when* other things *are* getting said – what is not said in a story that is otherwise told. How can one spot and isolate what has been expelled from the narrative? How did I do so in analysing the story of antisociality? In what follows I offer an approach to registering strategies for 'saying without saying' in storytelling. The approach moves from attention to stealthy integration of ideological understandings, to understatement, to silencing of other understandings and facts of people's lives.

Subtext: Evaluate Figuration and Multiple Meanings

Subtext is that which is implied but not overtly stated in discourse. Clues to subtext include the use of figurative language and polysemy, or multiple meanings.

Figurative language is various. So-called figurative devices include but are not limited to metonymy, simile, synecdoche, litote, personification, hyperbole and irony. The figurative device that has received the most scholarly attention by far is metaphor, which smuggles in the qualities of some 'source domain' (Lakoff & Johnson, 1980). ('Smuggles in' is a metaphor, its source domain theft, its target domain communication.) Metaphors are ubiquitous; communication without them is hard to imagine. The question is not whether, or how many, metaphors are in use but rather what work the metaphors-in-use do within the text.

The metaphor most fundamental to the story of antisociality is what Lakoff (2002) calls the 'metaphor of essence,' which constructs people as 'objects made of substances that determine how they will behave' (Lakoff, 2002, p. 87). The main substance in Gottfredsonn and Hirschi's version of the story is, of course, self-control. Metaphors of essence are so familiar, in both contemporary criminology and popular culture (think television shows like *Criminal Minds*), that they tend to escape notice. But Gottfredson and Hirschi also use a metaphor of socialisation as a machine and children as its products. 'Put in positive terms, several conditions appear necessary to produce a socialised child' (Gottfredson & Hirschi, 1990, p. 97). That metaphor is less familiar and therefore potentially more noticeable. This metaphoric structuring jettisons individual agency and changeability. Socialisation is 'successful' or it is not (p. 118). Some children are poorly produced, henceforth defective.

Another kind of vanishing act within texts – a means of achieving ambiguity – is polysemy, or multiple meanings. When a word has multiple meanings, communicators can smuggle in 'the other' meaning. An example appeared earlier, where I discussed Gottfredson and Hirschi's ideological deployment of *work* to mean paid labour outside the home. The authors also use the polysemous word *care*, which can mean either (emotional) concern or (mechanical) work when they write: 'All that is required to activate the system is affection for or investment in the child. The person who cares for the child will watch his behavior, see him doing things he should not do, and correct him' (Gottfredson & Hirschi, 1990, p. 97). Cares *for* signals work (as does 'takes care of') but the preceding sentence clearly signals an emphasis on care as concern. The story tacitly communicates that socialising children in the right way is effortless.

Abstracting from the various examples, my recommendation is that analysts document all figurative devices and all evident instances of double meaning and resulting equivocal expression. This is painstaking work. Figurative devices abound in communication. Ambiguity may be common as well. Furthermore, the clarity versus ambiguity of communication depends on what the recipient knows. Therefore, it is important that the analyst create an exhaustive inventory of figurative language and interrogate all text for straightforward exposition – not because these things are bad (figurative) or good (straightforward), but because they are potential signs of something important being erased (cf. Orwell, 1968).

Understatement: Assess Patterns of Elaboration and Explanation

Understatement is itself said to be a figurative device, but I mean it in the broad sense of relative muteness on some matter in the text, rather than as something artful. Varying patterns of elaboration and explanation give hints of what is of less or more interest to the narrator, and of what she/he deems true or factual. In particular, when narrators minimally elaborate or explain, they either convey that statements are common sense or that they are unimportant. Elaborating excessively, such as through a relative surplus of words, may indicate tension. The narrator 'doth protest too much,' working hard to make sure the audience knows something.

The analyst should ask: What claims is the narrator not elaborating – or supplying excessive detail, argumentation or evidence for? To address this question, one does well to look for *patterns*. One must ask what claims the narrator is failing to elaborate on when she/he elaborates on *other* claims. After all, some speakers say little, either in general or in the particular story being analysed. The key is nonuniform patterns of elaboration, such as Bengtsson and Fynbo (2018) found when 'after about 45 minutes into the interview, David stops using silence and begins elaborating his answers' (p. 25). He then tells a story of a crime that his social officer suspects he participated in. 'The interviewer attempts to learn more about the incident – for example, why was David blamed for burning the car – but David returns to short answers followed by silence' (Bengtsson & Fynbo, 2018). The pattern alerted these authors to resistance on David's part: 'he uses silence to resist talking in the way that the interviewer wants him to talk' (Bengtsson & Fynbo, 2018). But Riessman (2012) took her interviewee Gita to be simply uninterested in that which she said little about – her past inability to bear children: 'The lack of narrative detail in the plot up to this point suggests that the events are not particularly salient for her' (p. 375). Usually, when the speaker is reticent on some subject but verbose on a different subject, or outright 'changes the subject', analysts may infer that something provocative for the speaker or audience is being avoided or that something important is not being said. Often that 'something' has to do with issues of power, including deviance and stigma.

Gottfredson and Hirschi elaborate a great deal in their 275-page book, including on the history of various strands of criminology, the nature of crime, the typical features and 'logical structure' (p. 37) of particular crimes, various correlates of crime and how the general theory makes sense of them and how the theory should be tested. When Gottfredson and Hirschi do not elaborate on something, we should take notice. Gottfredson and Hirschi expound a large number of critiques. They critique positivistic theories, criminological arguments that white-collar crime differs from conventional crime, criminologists' failure to pin down the essential nature of crime and criminologists' concern with why offenders age out of crime. Given their critique of current understandings of crime, it is not surprising that Gottfredson and Hirschi are also critical of current strategies for reducing crime. They devote nearly seven pages of the book to a takedown of selective incapacitation, or targeting high-risk persons for social control. They also pan jail and other 'short-term institutional experiences' (p. 232). Meanwhile, they say nothing of general incapacitation or long-term institutionalisation – the policies that we have *actually* undertaken in the US. It is instructive to ask what they are not critical of. They are not critical of criminal justice.

Overlexicalization, or a surplus of words, is a special kind of elaboration the analyst may look for. In the preface of their book Gottfredson and Hirschi (1990) assert that they 'see little hope for important reductions in crime through modification of the criminal justice system' (p. xvi). The superfluous wording ('important' and 'modification of') is curious because the general theory unequivocally supports the futility of *any* intervention in adulthood – thus, whatever the system can mete out. The criminal justice system in general should be deemed unhelpful. In the abstract, 'modification of' (the criminal justice system) is ambiguous. It indicates change from what is, and therefore can mean more *or* less criminal justice. However, the context of the statement was the late 1980s (when the authors were in all likelihood writing) which saw historic climbs in the rate of imprisonment in the US. 'By 1990, the incarcerated population had increased to more than four times its 1972 level' (Travis, Western & Redburn, 2014, p. 39). Gottfredson and Hirschi are saying we ought not change this punitive course without saying it.

Like patterns of elaboration, patterns of *explanation* vary within a text. Communicators presuppose as self-evident what they do not bother to explain or support. Thus, Gottfredson and Hirschi's (1990) claim that: 'All that is required to activate the system is affection for or investment in the child' (p. 97) but do not explain why affection and investment are 'all that is required.' They are candid that their allegation that crime syndicates – organizations, the fact of which would counter their emphasis on individual conduct – tend to be short-lived is 'a good guess' (p. 213) but do not provide any research basis for their guess. More often they present truths about crime and its perpetrators as factual with neither qualification nor evidence (e.g. 'crimes are not a good source of stable income,' p. 164).

Silencing: Ask What and Whose Knowledge Is Missing

The story of antisociality omits some knowledge and elevates other knowledge. All theories and all stories do this. Theories, especially general theories, including my own (Presser, 2013), leave out much of the historical and contemporaneous context of a phenomenon in order to focus on just a few factors. The critical issue is being less than truthful about that exclusivity, framing some knowledge as the ultimate and entire truth of a matter.

Gottfredson and Hirschi reify their own perspective by failing to provide sources for some of their biggest claims – for example, the defining characteristics of criminal acts (pp. 89–90) – and by referring to 'concepts,' 'constructs,' 'images,' 'notions,' 'ideas' and 'scenarios' rather than phenomena that anyone experiences. Their concept of crime as self-gratifying, slapdash conduct is called 'the concept of crime' (p. 5). Here we see Gottfredson and Hirschi's tendency to objectify their perspective by using the definite article 'the' instead of the possessive determiner 'their.' 'The' concept of crime proceeds to operate as arbiter of what criminals are like. Gottfredson and Hirschi allege that little crime is organised because 'the idea of crime is incompatible with the pursuit of long-term cooperative relationships' (p. 213). Contesting strain theory, they argue that offenders are not 'concerned with equity' because: 'The notion of inequity at the point of crime is...incompatible with the image of the offender at the point of criminality' (p. 114). It is remarkable that a position on people's concerns is founded on the scholars' own conceptions – 'the image' – rather than even second-hand communication with those people. It is only via that methodological omission that 'large changes in circumstance' such as losing a job can, for the authors, come down (in the next sentence) to 'lack of perseverance' (p. 251). The blatant fiction of Gottfredson and Hirschi's story is that offenders are not (concerned with) any of a number of things that the authors' 'image' does not deem them to be.

Reification of one's own viewpoint appears to go hand in hand with the marginalisation of the viewpoint of others. To establish that knowledge is being excluded, the analyst must first establish some base of essential knowledge. One must obtain 'the big picture' of whatever is under discussion, however much we must acknowledge the constructed and delimited nature of any 'big picture.' A critical, reflexive awareness of the various politics of exclusion is generally necessary – for example, awareness of the rapes that do not get into the official counts. Also, I believe we can assume that people living in the situations under consideration have invaluable input. In the case of Gottfredson and Hirschi's story of antisociality, we need information on actual parenting from parents, children and other experts, especially those who actually engage with parents and children. Such information is entirely missing from their account (see Miller & Burack, 1993).

Working with other stories, analysts with various expertise and from various backgrounds will be able to identify other gaps in information that a story conveys or rests on. The basic task is to ask systematically if and how the perspectives of those dominated on the basis of such markers as gender, class, race, ethnicity, ability, sexuality, nationality, citizenship status, age, occupation and species are being considered in a text. Inviting subaltern expert informants to weigh in on findings and theories, and otherwise bridging the gap between analyst and data source, such as through autoethnography, can facilitate this effort as well.

Of the three methodological efforts I have described, this one – exposing the silencing of subaltern perspectives – is the one critical scholars have most commonly undertaken. They have demonstrated that whole groups are left out of the overarching narratives of academic disciplines and of academia at large (see Agozino, 2003; Beirne, 1999; Naffine, 1997; Nussbaum, 1997), and that social phenomena and individuals are selectively attended to. For example, critical criminologists have highlighted the omissions of a criminology that pays attention to violence by strangers over violence by familiars, intended over negligent violence, and street offences over offences perpetrated by social elites and the state (Box, 1983; Reiman, 2001). These scholars demonstrate that the hegemonic story of crime is based, among other things, on the exclusion of knowledge in such a way as to sustain hierarchical relations. I hope to contribute to a process for grasping particular strategies of exclusion.

Concluding Remarks

All communication leaves a myriad of things out as it assembles meaning. I am after exclusions that shape power positions. I developed a method for uncovering such exclusions in stories. The method moves from probing stealthy integration and understatement of ideological understandings to the silencing of other understandings along with facts of people's lives. The method has particular value for discerning the neoliberal logic of avowedly apolitical theories of crime. It is also well suited for the feminist project of revealing some of the 'conceptual strategies that obliterate women as active agents' (Smith, 1987, p. 164). But I envision more general use wherever hegemony is achieved narratively.

The method rests on subjective assessments. It cannot be neutral because no interpretation can be. My codification of what has been left out of dominant (and dominating) narratives is and must be selective. My selection bias is in the direction of subaltern understandings. Dominant narratives as a rule leave out the lived experiences and insights of subordinated others. They convey the perspectives and advance the projects of the powerful, yet they obscure their own role in power relations.

I used the story of antisociality formulated by criminologists Michael Gottfredson and Travis Hirschi to forge this new sort of inquiry. My treatment of theory as story in the first instance highlights a power move on the part of authors: outfitting their account as a theory is a means of denying the account's rootedness in a particular historical context. Approaching a theory as narrative, however, enables us to ask – *who and what is the story told for?* That question is a necessary step in discerning silences.

Gottfredson and Hirschi's general theory/story of antisociality is an important case because of its impact on criminology (Pratt & Cullen, 2000)[5] and, with other theories of offenders, American society. It has been criticised on grounds that are empirical (e.g. Benson & Moore, 1992; Geis, 2000; Goode, 2008), conceptual (e.g. Akers, 1991; Wikström & Treiber, 2007) and ideological (e.g. Miller & Burack, 1993). I join this last group. The authors' 'idea of crime' bolsters a program of harm. That idea guides highly selective consumption of research evidence – towards supposed individual lapses and flaws and away from public injustices.

The general theory/story of antisociality served my purpose of forging a method especially well because it 'stood still' for examination. My analysis presumes a story that is complete in itself rather than co-constructed, shifting and fragmented (see De Fina & Georgakopoulou, 2012): the written nature of the story facilitated that conceit. To analyse stories told during interviews and/or stories whose constitutional complexity the analyst would highlight will likely call for adjusting the method. Still, I believe that the basic strategies are viable generally – investigating: figuration and ambiguation generally, patterns of elaboration and explanation, and missing knowledge. I think that a very fruitful line of future research would explore the ways in which these moves are accomplished in actual social exchanges including research exchanges (see Presser, 2004).

The chapter's substantive critique concerns criminology and penal harm. The critique can and should be furthered by narrative criminologists. We should go bold with impactful stories and be candid about harms, by which I mean we should probe much more than the stories of apprehended offenders and their violations of law.

References

Agozino, B. (2003). *Counter-colonial criminology: A critique of imperialist reason*. London and Sterling, VA: Pluto Press.

Akers, R. L. (1991). Self-control as a general theory of crime. *Journal of Quantitative Criminology, 7*, 201–211.

Bamberg, M., & Andrews, M. (Eds.). (2004). *Considering counter-narratives: Narrating, resisting, making sense*. Amsterdam: John Benjamins Publishing Company.

Bamberg, M., & Georgakopoulou, A. (2008). Small stories as a new perspective in narrative and identity analysis. *Text & Talk, 28*, 377–396.

Barak, G. (2007). Doing newsmaking criminology from within the academy. *Theoretical Criminology, 11*, 191–207.

Beirne, P. (1999). For a non-speciesist criminology: Animal abuse as an object of study. *Criminology, 37*, 117–147.

---

[5]Evidence of its reach is the fact that *A General Theory of Crime* has been assessed with samples in Argentina, Canada, China, England, Hungary, India, Japan, Malaysia, The Netherlands, New Zealand, Nigeria, Russia, Spain, Switzerland, and Venezuela as well as the United States.

Bengtsson, T. T., & Fynbo, L. (2018). Analysing the significance of silence in qualitative interviewing: Questioning and shifting power relations. *Qualitative Research*, *18*, 19–35.
Benson, M. L., & Moore, E. (1992). Are white-collar and common offenders the same? An empirical and theoretical critique of a recently proposed general theory of crime. *Journal of Research in Crime and Delinquency*, *29*, 251–272.
Box, S. (1983). *Power, crime, and mystification*. New York, NY: Tavistock Publications.
Butler, J. (2004). *Precarious life: The powers of mourning and violence*. London: Verso.
Chesney-Lind, M., & Mauer, M. (2003). *Invisible punishment: The collateral consequences of mass imprisonment*. New York, NY: The New Press.
Clear, T. R. (1994). *Harm in American penology: Offenders, victims, and their communities*. Albany, NY: State University of New York Press.
Clear, T. R. (2009). *Imprisoning communities: How mass incarceration makes disadvantaged neighborhoods worse*. New York, NY: Oxford University Press.
Colvin, S. (2017). Unerhört? Prisoner narratives as unlistened-to stories (and some reflections on the picaresque). *The Modern Language Review*, *112*, 440–458.
De Fina, A., & Georgakopoulou, G. (2012). *Analyzing narrative discourse and sociolinguistic perspectives*. Cambridge: Cambridge University Press.
Eagleton, T. (1991). *Ideology: An introduction*. London: Verso.
Ewick, P., & Silbey, S. S. (1995). Subversive stories and hegemonic tales: Toward a sociology of narrative. *Law & Society Review*, *29*, 197–226.
Frank, A. W. (2010). *Letting stories breathe: A socio-narratology*. Chicago, IL and London: The University of Chicago Press.
Gee, J. P. (1999). *An introduction to discourse analysis: Theory and method*. London and New York, NY: Routledge.
Geis, G. (2000). On the absence of self-control as the basis for a general theory of crime: A critique. *Theoretical Criminology*, *4*, 35–53.
Goode, E. (Ed.). (2008). *Out of control: Assessing the general theory of crime*. Stanford, CA: Stanford University Press.
Gottfredson, M. R., & Hirschi, T. (1990). *A general theory of crime*. Stanford, CA: Stanford University Press.
Gottschalk, M. (2015). *Caught: The prison state and the lockdown of American politics*. Princeton, NJ and Oxford: Princeton University Press.
Gubrium, J. F., & Holstein, J. A. (1997). *The new language of qualitative method*. New York, NY: Oxford University Press.
Hallsworth, S., & Young, T. (2008). Crime and silence: 'Death and life are in the power of the tongue' (Proverbs 18:21). *Theoretical Criminology*, *12*, 131–152.
Halverson, J. R., Goodall, H. L., Jr., & Corman, S. R. (2011). *Master narratives of Islamist extremism*. New York, NY: Palgrave Macmillan.
Henricks, K., & Harvey, D. C. (2017). Not one but many: Monetary punishment and the Fergusons of America. *Sociological Forum*, *32*(S1), 930–951.
Hochschild, A. (2012). *The second shift: Working families and the revolution at home* (2nd ed.). New York, NY: Penguin Books.
Hogan, P. C. (2003). *The Mind and Its Stories: Narrative Universals and Human Emotions*. Cambridge: Cambridge University Press.
Knowles, A. (2015). A geneology of silence: Chōra and the placelessness of Greek women. *philoSOPHIA*, *5*(1), 1–24.

Labov, W., & Waletzky, J. (1967). Narrative analysis: Oral versions of personal experience. In J. Helms (Ed.), *Essays on the verbal and visual arts* (pp. 12–44). Seattle, WA: University of Washington Press.

Lacan, J. (1977). In A. Sheridan (Trans.), *Écrits: A selection*. London: Tavistock Publications.

Lakoff, G. (2002). *Moral politics: How liberals and conservatives think* (2nd ed.). Chicago, IL and London: The University of Chicago Press.

Lakoff, G., & Johnson, M. (1980). *Metaphors we live by*. Chicago, IL: The University of Chicago Press.

Lamont, M., & Molnár, V. (2002). The study of boundaries in the social sciences. *Annual Review of Sociology, 28*, 167–195.

Loseke, D. R. (2003). *Thinking about social problems: An introduction to constructionist perspectives* (2nd ed.). New York, NY: Aldine de Gruyter.

Macherey, P. (1978). *A theory of literary production*. London: Routledge & Kegan Paul.

Mazzei, L. A. (2007). *Inhabited silence in qualitative research: Putting poststructural theory to work*. Bern: Peter Lang.

Miles, M., & Crush, J. (1993). Personal narratives as interactive texts: Collecting and interpreting migrant life-histories. *The Professional Geographer, 45*, 84–94.

Miller, S. L., & Burack, C. (1993). A critique of Gottfredson and Hirschi's general theory of crime: Selective (in)attention to gender and power-positions. *Women & Criminal Justice, 4*, 115–134.

Naffine, N. (1997). *Feminism and criminology*. Cambridge: Polity Press.

Nussbaum, M. (1997). *Cultivating humanity: A classical defense of reform in liberal education*. Cambridge, MA: Harvard University Press.

Organisation for Economic Co-operation and Development (OECD). (2018). OECD family database. Retrieved from http://www.oecd.org/els/family/database.htm. Accessed on December 8, 2018.

Orwell, G. (1968). Politics and the English language. In S. Orwell & I. Angus (Eds.), *The collected essays, journalism and letters of George Orwell, Volume 4: In front of your nose, 1945–1950* (pp. 127–140). New York, NY: Harcourt Brace Jovanovich.

Polanyi, L. (1985). *Telling the American story: A structural and cultural analysis of conversational storytelling*. Norwood, NJ: Ablex Publishing Corporation.

Pratt, T. C., & Cullen, F. T. (2000). The empirical status of Gottfredson and Hirschi's general theory of crime: A meta-analysis. *Criminology, 38*, 931–964.

Presser, L. (2004). Violent offenders, moral selves: Constructing identities and accounts in the research interview. *Social Problems, 51*, 82–101.

Presser, L. (2009). The narratives of offenders. *Theoretical Criminology, 13*, 177–200.

Presser, L. (2013). *Why we harm*. New Brunswick, NJ and London: Rutgers University Press.

Presser, L. (2018). *Inside story: How narratives drive mass harm*. Berkeley and Los Angeles, CA: University of California Press.

Presser, L., & Sandberg, S. (Eds.). (2015). *Narrative criminology: Understanding stories of crime*. New York, NY and London: New York University Press.

Presser, L., & Sandberg, S. (2019). Narrative criminology as critical criminology. *Critical Criminology, 27*, 131–143.

Quinney, R. (1974). *Critique of legal order: Crime control in capitalist society*. Boston, MA: Little, Brown and Company.

Reiman, J. (2001). *The rich get richer and the poor get prison* (6th ed.). Boston, MA: Allyn & Bacon.

Riessman, C. K. (2012). Analysis of personal narratives. In J. F. Gubrium, J. A. Holstein, A. B. Marvasti, & K. D. McKinney (Eds.), *The Sage handbook of interview research: The complexity of the craft* (2nd ed., pp. 367–379). Los Angeles, CA: SAGE Publications.

Rosenberg, S. D., Rosenberg, H. J., & Farrell, M. P. (1992). In the name of the father. In G. C. Rosenwald & R. L. Ochberg (Eds.), *Storied lives: The cultural politics of self-understanding* (pp. 41–59). New Haven, CT: Yale University Press.

Sandberg, S. (2016). The importance of stories untold: Life-story, event-story, and trope. *Crime, Media, Culture, 12*, 153–171.

Shichor, D. (1995). *Punishment for profit: Private prisons/public concerns*. Thousand Oaks, CA: SAGE Publications.

Simon, J. (2007). *Governing through crime: How the War on Crime transformed American democracy and created a culture of fear*. New York, NY: Oxford University Press.

Smith, D. E. (1987). *The everyday world as problematic*. Boston, MA: Northeastern University Press.

Solórzano, D. G., & Yosso, T. J. (2002). Critical race methodology: Counter-storytelling as an analytical framework for education research. *Qualitative Inquiry, 8*, 23–44.

Steinberg, M. W. (1998). Tilting the frame: Considerations on collective action framing from a discursive turn. *Theory and Society, 27*, 845–872.

The Sentencing Project. (2018). Criminal justice facts. Retrieved from https://www.sentencingproject.org/criminal-justice-facts/. Accessed on January 28, 2019.

Travis, J., Western, B., & Redburn, S. (Eds.). (2014). *The growth of incarceration in the United States: Exploring causes and consequences*. Washington, DC: National Academies Press.

White, H. (1973). *Metahistory: The historical imagination in nineteenth-century Europe*. Baltimore, MD: The Johns Hopkins University Press.

White, H. (1980). The value of narrativity in the representation of reality. *Critical Inquiry, 7*(1), 5–27.

Wikström, P. H., & Treiber, K. (2007). The role of self-control in crime causation: Beyond Gottfredson and Hirschi's general theory of crime. *European Journal of Criminology, 4*, 237–264.

CONNECTING STORIES, POWER AND SOCIAL INEQUALITIES

Chapter 21

The Archived Criminal: Mandatory Prisoner Autobiography in China

Xiaoye Zhang and Xianliang Dong

Introduction

Since the early 1940s, Chinese penal institutions have required all prisoners to produce a written autobiographical essay as part of the prison admissions process. While this practice is not strictly defined in official regulations, it has been practiced locally under general guidance at the national level. The National Archive Administration, responsible for unified administration of archival work in China and development of archival laws and regulations, issued the *Archival Management of Criminals and Re-education-through-labour Personnel* (effective from 3 January 1994), in which Article 5 of Chapter 2 stated that 'Criminal's history, autobiographical material, and other important self-reflective materials written by the person himself/herself' should be included in each prisoner's file. The writing requirements can also be found in provincial prison bureaus' notices to the penal institutions within its jurisdiction. The title of the required writing may be 'My Autobiography' (*Wo de zizhuan*), 'Individual Autobiography' (*geren zizhuan*) or 'How I embarked on the road to crime' (*wo shi ruhe zoushang fanzuidaolu de*); Detailed writing instructions are often provided. This chapter discusses the written prisoner autobiography mandated by Chinese prison authority as a function of governmental power over subjectivities – in effect, a narrative correction (Fox, 1999).

Studies of prisoner autobiographies have categorised various subgenres of stories signalled by characterisations of 'unrepentant hardman,' 'cons' and 'straights' (Dearey et al., 2011; Morgan, 1999; Nellis, 2002; Weaver & Weaver, 2013). These are mostly commercially published autobiographies by ex-prisoners, and are commonly treated as descriptions and recounting of true experience (Morgan, 1999). The problems of utilising these published autobiographies have also been raised, such as the ambiguity of memory, alterations made by the professional editing process, as well as unclear methods of construction as compared to other social science narrative production (Nellis, 2002). These concerns have to do with the truth of what gets narrated, as does other critical work emphasising the subaltern story. Yet, in part under the umbrella of convict criminology, it has been argued that more attention should be paid to these narratives as an addition to or revision of criminology's claim of knowledge about the prison world, that these narratives contribute subjugated knowledge which challenges the dominance of mainstream criminology (Dearey et al., 2011; Weaver & Weaver, 2013). In general, offenders' autobiographical narratives are conceptualised as counternarratives, not only different but in opposition to official accounts. Little attention has been paid to the ways they interact with and influence each other. The mandatory autobiographies required by the Chinese prison admission education is an explicit example of institutional control and shaping of individual's narration of his/her own life story towards the broader aim of discipline and rehabilitation.

Brockmeier and Harré (2001) asked two essential questions for the analysis of narrative as discursive reality: 'What is the narrative process (and its situational context) through which (and in which) this reality is laid out?' and 'What are the narrative strategies and techniques that are used to evoke this idea of reality?' (p. 49). For our current study, we have investigated whether a metanarrative of criminal autobiography may be seen as underlying different prisoner's writings, and if so, what its mechanisms are. In their work on children's literature, Stephens and McCallum (2013) argued that metanarratives 'have the function of maintaining conformity to socially determined and approved patterns of behaviour which they do by offering positive role models, prescribing undesirable behaviour, and affirming the culture's ideologies, systems, and institutions' (pp. 3–4). Metanarratives structure and restructure individuals' social selves, functioning as 'a way of accessing cultural understandings as to what it is to be a human being – a self – in a particular context' (Juntunen & Westerlund, 2011). Autobiographical writing generates narratives of socially situated selfhood. We argue that our study of Chinese prison autobiographical writing not only can provide a narrative understanding of Chinese correctional ethos and practices but also of the engineering of 'offender selfhood' in the prison context (Brockmeier & Carbaugh, 2001; Sandberg, 2013).

Narrating the Self as Rehabilitation

Autobiographical narratives are an important aspect of offender rehabilitation in the modern Western penal institution, with cognitive and behavioural psychology as the main theoretical support (Andrews & Bonta, 2010; Bernfeld, Farrington, & Leschied, 2003; Cullen, 2012; McNeill, 2012; Ogloff & Davis, 2004). On this view, talking about past life experiences is essential for any psychological change to happen, therefore the narrative of one's experience, especially criminal offence in this context, becomes the key arena for intervention. Fox (1999) has drawn attention to the narrative struggle during mandatory Cognitive Self Change (CSC) treatment programme for violent offenders in Vermont, USA. Based on ethnographic enquiry into the treatment sessions, Fox exposed how the seemingly scientific and noncoercive discourse of psychology is supported by and supports governmental power, which manifested in offender's resistance to the treatment's attempt in correcting their telling about themselves. According to Fox's observation, resistance to narrative correction is not only futile but also further contributes to theories of criminality and neoliberal disciplinary ideology. Resistance validates and legitimises the judgement of 'faulty' cognition, and therefore the need for treatment. Also pertaining to cognitive psychology and consequently narrative intervention in the offender rehabilitation context, Waldram (2007) found that written and spoken autobiographical disclosures are an integral part of Cognitive Behavioural Therapy (CBT) in a Canadian therapeutic community prison, mandatory for sexual offenders. He argued that there is a 'judicial-correctional (…) official life story' on which the treatment process and goal are based, and the offender would be considered to have successfully rehabilitated 'in so far as he accepts the official truth, participates in the rewriting of his life story, and communicates a cognitive shift in its meaning' (p. 147). Therefore, the telling of individual offender's life story becomes a site of power struggle over the 'truth' of the offender's disclosure, in which the offender never wins.

The concern with subjugation of convicts' narratives is also echoed in research on desistance. Colvin (2015) argued in her paper for the importance of fiction in working with offenders and stated that 'exploring multiple, contradictory discourses might, then, be a more effective narrative path to change than a heavy focus on controlling or "making" sense' (p. 224). Narratives that contain and reconcile both the 'bad' and the 'good' may facilitate more long-lasting resilience, where simpler narratives suited to correctional purposes may cause confusion and frustration post release. This idea has been echoed in empirical studies where successful desisters' narratives – measured in terms of recidivism – are often multifaceted and complex, even with what can be called 'cognitive distortions' that exaggerate the positive aspects of selfhood. Such distortions may in fact contribute to resilience through the challenging process of desisting from reoffending (Gadd, 2003; Maruna, 2001). These studies provided evidence for the importance of narrative identity in rehabilitation and desistance, but the positive effects did not seem to be the result of official corrections nor did they fall neatly in line with its supporting theories.

While an interest in offender life stories and their relation to rehabilitation is found in both Western and Chinese practices, the mandatory use of narrative correction in interventions tends only to be used with offenders of specific offence or risk categories in the Western criminal justice systems. Sex offenders are the most common category of offenders who receive mandatory psychological interventions and treatment, as Waldram (2007, 2010, 2012) has written extensively. Our study of autobiographical writings by prisoners departs from those reviewed above as it is part of the prison's institutionalised official requirement without discrimination as to offence types, and at the same time outside the explicit framing of psychological discourse.

Studying Autobiographical Writing of Incarcerated Chinese

Narrative criminology as a distinctive field has been defined as the study of 'how narratives inspire and motivate harmful action, and how they are used to make sense of harm' (Presser & Sandberg, 2015a, p. 1). The importance of narrative has also been widely recognised in the broader field of crime and punishment (Dearey et al., 2011; DeValiant, McGrath, & Kougiali, 2018; Edney, 2005; Franzosi, 1998; Nellis, 2002). Offender narratives under study in both traditions have mostly been in oral form and generated during researcher-(ex)offender interviews or talking therapy sessions (Presser & Sandberg, 2015b; Sakacs, 2018; Sandberg, 2010; Waldram, 2007; Yardley, Wilson, Kemp, & Brookes, 2015). The subject of our study is unique not only because it is written autobiographies mandatorily required from all prisoners but also because these have been archived in individual files, and therefore we have integrated methods from historical and literary studies into the analytic process in order to thoroughly investigate different aspects of this type of narrative demand.

We collected and utilised four types of materials for this study: first-hand prisoner writings, fieldwork notes, historical archives such as government reports and policies. The focus of the study was not only narrative analysis of the current textual data but also of the formation and variations of this discursive reality in contemporary Chinese history, in order to understand its institutionalised production mechanisms.

Twenty-eight written prisoner autobiographies were collected during the author's fieldwork for a separate research project (Zhang, 2017). According to official publications and fieldwork, the written autobiographies were produced during the prisoner admission education period (the first 2–8 months), and consequently official regulations in regard to the requirement around autobiography writing, education and assessment were obtained from public records as well as during interviews with prison officers. Semi-structured interviews of ex-prisoners were also used to triangulate the textual data, which both validated the current state of the practice and also enriched our understanding.

In the process of historicising mandatory prisoner autobiography, documents such as self-critical writings by party cadres and writings in prisoner files in the form of booklets and files were obtained from Chinese second-hand book online shops.[1] These secondary archival materials were examined in relation to the prisoner autobiographies as they were under the broad genre of self-criticism. In particular, we focussed on self-criticism letters during the Yan'an rectification period, Party cadre and intellectual work unit files, and literature on *Laogai* management (Griffin, 1974; Hualing, 2005; Li, 1984; Shen, 1976; Wang, 1993; Xingrui Huang, 1991; Xue, 1986).

The research process started with thorough reading of the first-hand prisoner autobiographies and repentant letters obtained. After a few readings to gain a general impression of the collection of writings, we – the two authors – engaged in prolonged discussion around their perceptions in regard to the reading and research focus of these written narratives. As this is far from a well-researched topic, a period of exploration was made where extensive reading was undertaken between the two authors such as Chinese history, literature studies of narrative

---

[1] Mostly obtained from online second-hand material shopping platform Kong Fu Zi: http://www.kongfz.com/.

and autobiography in both the Western and Chinese traditions, accompanied by constant returning to the original texts (Bakken, 2000; Bodde, 1969; Chen, 1969; Prison Bureau of Chinese Criminal Justice Department, 2012; Dikötter, 2002; Hualing, 2005; Mühlhahn, 2009; Smith, 2013a, 2013b; Strauss, 2006; Williams & Wu, 2004; Xin, 2006; Xue, 1986). We then began to collect other related data regarding the justification for this reform method, including local and specific writing instructions, context of the writing production as well as written post-completion assessments.

A total of 14 interviews with 8 interviewees were conducted. Questions centred on autobiographical writing in prisons (such as if and how many time were they required to write them, under what circumstances and how the writing was evaluated, as well as its impact on their incarceration experience), the interviewees were also participants in regular theatre activities which Zhang has observed over the course of 2 years which significantly enhanced the credibility of the data. Four interviews of approximately 1 hour each were conducted with prisoners in the prison canteen or designated chat rooms and were recorded with prison-owned audio recorder; Zhang transcribed the interviews while inside the prison. The other 10 interviews were conducted with ex-prisoners and officers off of the prison premises for an estimated 2 hours each at cafés or interviewee's residences. With the exception of one interview with an officer as he did not give consent, these were all recorded. The interviews mostly helped to contextualise and verify changes and continuity in the demands of autobiography writing in practice, the focus of the research being on the written texts.

All names, personal and institutional details were crossed out in the original copies of autobiographies before the authors received the photocopied documents. The authors also confirmed that there are no high-profile offenders such as retired government officials or celebrities among the writers, as discussion of their stories might compromise anonymity. No details of the name nor location of the prison(s) was disclosed.

Unlike narrative data from interviews, the researcher's relationship with written narratives is distant and unobtrusive. The written narratives studied by criminologists, such as (ex)prisoner autobiographies, are typically developed with the general public as readers in mind, and therefore special attention would be paid to the relationship between the public and the (ex)prisoner-writer. Thus, the analyst might situate such publicly published written autobiographies among other public discourses on criminality, punishment, prison and deviance. When stories are told to the researcher in person, discussions of the interview situation and researcher–interviewee relationship are often discussed (Presser, 2004). In the case of our study, the autobiographies were written with the prison authority, including frontline officers and their leadership, in mind as readers, rather than the general public. This requires the researcher to read beyond the text itself and into the official requirements and production process, as they are essential to the narrative outcomes.

A writing structure and a narrative pattern became clear after the first stage of exploratory reading and analysis of the collection of autobiographical writings. We conceptualise mandatory prisoner autobiography as embedded in the self-criticism practice long ago adopted by the Chinese Communist Party's governance (Dittmer, 1973). Self-criticism is commonly understood as a rectification method used against party cadres or intellectuals during campaign-style rectifications, where they are required to criticise themselves on the particular struggle of the campaign (Dittmer, 1974; Eggli & Hasmath, 2016; MacFarquhar, 1966; Teiwes, 1976; Vogel, 1965; Wang, 2018). However, this is not to say that prison's required autobiographies amount only to self-criticism, as it has been adapted within a different institutional context. Little literature exists on why and how it has been utilised within the criminal justice system as a rehabilitative tool for convicts. The following section attempts to locate autobiography writing in the Chinese literary tradition, before moving on to examine its more contemporary forms.

Autobiographical Writing in the Chinese Literary Tradition

Autobiography, which aims at recounting one's own real-life events, marked a clear departure from fictional literary genres in the West (Kawai, 1998, p. 9), although later research pointed out the fictional aspect of autobiographical writings (Spengemann, 1980). In the Chinese tradition, autobiography's boundary with other literary genres is not as obvious: both autobiographical and fictional writings can be based on real-life stories and can also both take on fictional elements. The Chinese tradition of historiography has been considered to have higher value compared to other literary styles, and autobiographies are commonly considered as a subgenre of biographical writing, both of which are influenced by historiography (Kawai, 1998). The earliest widely recognised autobiographical writing was Sima Qian's self-statement of *The Grand Historian's Preface* in the *Record of the Grand Historian*. According to existing research, autobiography before the Song dynasty was a genre of writing where the author sets out to affirm his or her self-awareness by establishing distinction from other writers. Such writing normally demonstrates a more stylised tradition and allows the author to move closer to an ideal type of the genre in the writing process, which shows a tendency to de-emphasise the individuality in accordance with the orthodox aspects of Confucian ideology. This inclination of self-location's dependence on locating others can be argued to be a general method of self-identification in Chinese social psychology (Huang, 1995).

In the Chinese writing of autobiography, the writer tries to suppress the presentation of self-narration, to convey an impartial tone (Wu, 1990). The author of the autobiography, in spite of having experienced the narrative events first hand, would still utilise authoritative historical materials from official records to the point where the writer could become 'invisible': the writing of autobiography is thus situated between personal, historical and literary writing. Sometimes the author 'hides' himself or herself in the narrative until the end of the piece, and works on overcoming personal emotions, which produce highly regarded autobiographies (Wu, 1990). Other than autobiography, poetry is often used by an author to record the same events, and this is a genre where one's affections can be channelled and expressed more explicitly.

Chinese autobiography differs from its Western counterpart in both its literary tradition and its modern manifestation (Larson, 1991; Ng, 2003). Autobiography in the Western tradition did not appear in China until the 1920s and 1930s. With the introduction of Western literature and thought, reformers in Chinese literary circles began to engage in autobiographical writing. For them, autobiography was not about self-reflection or disclosure, nor about biographical documentation of extraordinary figures, but was a record of ordinary persons. Chinese autobiography in modern times does not seem to be centred on individualistic expressions, but rather 'a way of narrating the ordinary which is closely integrated with the social background of the era' (Kawai, 1998).

Chinese autobiographical writing is closely related to the field of literature which emphasises high achievement in narrative writing skills. From imperial China to modern times, only a very small percentage of the population has been literated, therefore, the ability to produce autobiographical writing as discussed above was only reserved for those who could master the complicated writing system until the beginning of the twentieth century. Indeed, the 28 prison autobiographies we collected from the 2000s included only two cases where the author demonstrated confident control over textual expression.

Chinese prisoner autobiography is situated strongly within the written language system, which differed significantly from spoken Chinese during the classical Chinese era across different Chinese-writing regions in East Asia. The shift in literacy and popularisation of the capable autobiographers originated in the earlier ideals of the Chinese Communist Party (CCP). The ideal of eliminating class divisions was related to the reduction of illiteracy, as the party believed that knowledge should not be restricted to a small elite group. Since the issuing of *Compulsory Education Law of the People's Republic of China* in 1986, even more children of school age were absorbed into the official educational system. The impact of this measure can be observed in the writing of prison autobiographies which demonstrated considerable compatibility with essay writing in Chinese school subject exams in their structure, style, figures of speech, etc. More than half of the other authors, similar to the majority of the prison population, had only received primary school level general education. Nevertheless, they have all produced their own autobiographical writings of varying complexity. Prisoner's archived autobiography should be considered as a contemporary form of Chinese autobiography which not only differs from its Western counterparts such as commercially published prisoner autobiographies but also departs significantly from what has been found in the Chinese literary tradition.

While the literary tradition of Chinese autobiography helped us to establish a distinction, a turn to contemporary Chinese politics is necessary in order to understand the prisoner autobiography as it is now, as autobiographical writing has been utilised explicitly at reforming individuals since the early years of the founding of CCP.

Autobiographical Writing as Ideological Reform

The autobiographical writing requirement in China was most prominently imposed during the Yan'an rectification period (1942–1945) as well as for the thought reform of intellectuals (mainly during 1940s–1950s), during which times

CCP would 'command that each Party member and cadre confess their personal history in detailed written form' (Gao, 2000, p. 419). Gao (2000) included a concise instruction of self-criticism writing for party cadres during the Yan'an rectification in his book (pp. 421–422):

Part 1: General personal information
Part 2: Educational background and other experiences before and after joining the revolution.
Part 3: Familial and social relations
Part 4: Changes in thoughts and understanding about the revolution
Part 5: Self-criticism on one's Party spirit

Apart from the Yan'an rectification campaign, during the 1950s and beyond, Chinese socialist reform was also extended to intellectuals beyond the bounds of the Party. The requirements for university students to write 'thought self-criticism' were, we discovered, very similar to those for Party cadres (Ding, 1949):

Part 1: Familial background: economic situation and political attitudes
Part 2: Personal history: educational background and other major life events
Part 3: Post college admission: motivations, performance appraisal, thought development and turning points
Part 4: Strength and weakness
Part 5: Future affirmations on thought reform of young intellectuals

The guidelines for both Party cadres and young intellectuals similarly include a small part in the beginning listing personal 'facts,' followed by the major narrative which combines life stories with self-examination and self-criticism. The autobiographies relate to a theme, which may vary with the institutional context and its demands – whether campaign or mobilisation needs such as intra Party rectification (Party spirit/loyalty as theme), thought reform of intellectuals (Party-related intellectual thinking as theme) or, in the penal context, offender reform (confession and repentance as theme).

Autobiographical Writing as Archived Criminality Reform

During Zhang's fieldwork, notes were taken regarding the writing requirements for newly admitted prisoners. A piece of paper with the title 'My Autobiography' (*wode zizhuan*) had the following instructions on the top of the page, followed by lined blank pages for prisoners to fill:

> *Write about personal history starting from childhood, focusing on people or events that have had a great impact;*
> *Focus especially on the process and activities of criminal offences;*
> *Present events and thoughts both good and bad during one's developmental process;*

> *Present how family, school, work organization, living environment, interpersonal relations and other social factors influenced one's development in positive and negative ways.*

These writing instructional guidelines clearly demonstrate the official requirement for the offender to reveal his life course development in his own words, but within a given narrative frame. While the instructions included 'positive and negative' influences, it emphasises that writing about the 'process and activities of criminal offences' would be the most important dimension of the writing. Instructions on how to write an autobiography for newly admitted prisoners are not limited to the written guidelines; according to interviews with prison officers, verbal instructions are also given in the writing sessions during the time-tabled admission education period. However, no public record has documented what is said and how it is said during face to face writing instructions.

By comparing the autobiographies produced by prisoners and examining their similarities against the above instructions, a common structure in their writings emerged as follows:

Part one: General information. Prison unit affiliation, name, conviction, sentence length, number of incarcerations, age, hometown, date of birth, ethnicity;
Part two: Personal history. Life events and relations, and narration of criminal offence;
Part three: Self-evaluation. Confession and repentance about convicted criminal offence (sometimes integrated into the narration of offence);
Part four: Future affirmation. During incarceration and beyond.

While part one and two could be found in every single one of the writings that we have obtained, part three was not always presented as a stand-alone section but sometimes fulfilled by narrating the offending experience in part two, which will be discussed further in this section. However, this does not mean that part three is of no importance, as there are separate writing requirements specifically on confession and repentance of their crime separate from this autobiography writing. The last part, which links what has been written about the prisoner's past to his future life in confinement after the writing of the autobiography, does not seem to be of great importance as it is often only one or a few sentences in length, and occasionally omitted.

Part one is statement of facts, which is chronicle but without moral message, and is highly uniform among all the writings, such as the following two examples suggest:

> *Respected Officer, I am offender DXX, sentenced to eight years for the conviction of burglary by court X of city X, with deprivation of political rights for one year. I arrived at X prison on 12 December to serve my sentence and be reformed.*

> Respected Officer, I am offender AXX, I am 40 years old this year. I was convicted of contract fraud and sentenced to fourteen years of imprisonment and three years of deprivation of political rights. I live in Z city of HL province. This is my first offence. I am currently receiving Admission Education at Unit 2 of prison V. The following is my autobiography.

The second part of the writing presents a wide variety of life story narratives, some detailed and consistently reflexive, some written at length about previous success or misfortunes, and some written poorly with little mastery of writing skills. For most of the autobiographies, the beginning of part two starts with the exact date, year and place of the author's birth, often followed by a description of family situation at that time, such as the following excerpt:

> On the 22rd of March 1980, I was born into a poor peasant family in F county of D province. I have a brother who is two years older than me, although our family was very poor, my mother still gave my brother and I plenty of love. In my memory, my earliest memory was when I was four. I was living at my grandma's home, she lives in a small village, my mother came and took me home to F county when I was five. In my memory as a child, I did not have my father's love, his shouting and yelling was all I remembered. He would go drinking and gambling every day, and he would get drunk and lose money every single time and come home and have fights with my mother (prisoner FX).

A few of the writings can be seen to consciously and actively adopt the narrative of 'criminal pathway' implied in the guidelines required by the authority, even before the telling of his life story:

> As the saying goes 'men at birth, are naturally good', and I have now deeply felt the meaning of this. Everyone's degradation and crime have their patterns and pathways, including greed and sins. No one became bad all at once, but it was little by little that one slips into the deep end until all is doomed (prisoner PXX).

The majority of the prisoner-authors, however, left the 'objective' narration related to their criminal identity to the later section, especially during and after the account of their offences. As noted previously, part three on self-evaluation is often achieved through the narration of the author's offending. One such example is the autobiography written by Nin who wrote at length about his father's sudden death, of unclear causes, at home, and how he subsequently began to hang out with a group of schoolmates to smoke, skip class and play computer games all day when he was about 11 years old. Nin quit school and began his life as a migrant worker when he was only 16 years old, and since then embarked on an unstable lifestyle until he committed several robberies with his friends back in his hometown and was apprehended soon after. During the narration of his offence, Nin used several legal terms (italics for emphasis by the authors):

> On the 5th of July 2001, ZQ[2] called me to go home and I did. I got to know my *accomplice* Ya, (...) They tried to persuade me to do something *against the law*, I strongly resisted. (...) they tried to persuade me to go with them to city O to *do some robbery* and I cave in. (...) on the way we saw two women (who are the victims of our case) ... the three of us robbed the *victim*'s money and mobile phones, (...) later we *committed crime again* in the same manner in a nearby town.

Most of the autobiographies incorporated some legal or criminological terms and discourse in their narrative of their offences, Part three self-evaluation is often only summarised with a couple of sentences, such as: 'I am currently receiving admission education, and through more than 1 month's study and education, I have deeply realised *the seriousness of my crime*. It has *caused great threat and harm to society, family and victim*' (prison H). Some provided a lengthy and explicit self-evaluation, which as mentioned before can be found in abundance in other writing the prison authority requires from the prisoners on the topic of confession and repentance. Prisoner R is one of the authors who wrote a separate paragraph on his regrets and self-criticism as well as his future affirmation to reform himself:

> I regret, I hate, I used to be my parent's utmost pride, bringing them fulfillment and joy, but today I brought them deep pain and endless worries (...) Now I *fight on the frontline of reformation, studying hard, obeying orders and becoming a changed man* so I can reunite with my family as soon as possible. I have paid a big price for my actions, painted an unharmonious stroke on the harmonious society, I have lost the right to be a good citizen. But I can feel the warmth of the Party and the country, sun still shines inside these walls. Coming to prison is the gift among the unfortunate events, I will cherish this opportunity to reform, to re-examine myself and totally wash away the dirt on my mind (prisoner R).

While the narrative of criminal offending experience utilised mostly legal terms, the above interwoven self-evaluation and promise evoked more tropes and expressions familiar in the context of Chinese official thought reform, such as 'fight,' 'sun shines' and 'wash away the dirt on my mind' (Smith, 2013a, 2013b). Familiarisation with multiple official discourses related to criminality facilitates the narrative fulfilment of the required criminal autobiography.

---

[2] Another accomplice in his case.

The discovery of the four parts among the writings pointed to the existence of a state-ordered writing structure which organised autobiographical narrative as presentation of an obedient criminal subject of the penal authority. In combination with the official writing requirements, mandatory prisoner autobiography demonstrated the autobiography-writing-as-reform's pedagogical ideal: self-reflection focussing on the criminal offence through the writing of life history.

Bruner's (1991) concept of 'narrative accrual' points out the centrality of cultural legitimacy to narratives. Bruner conceives of culture as a '"local" capacity for accruing stories of happenings of the past into some sort of diachronic structure that permits a continuity into the present' (p. 20). A very concise history of the present use of autobiographical self-criticism has shown that the method's use is interwoven with in-party rectification, thought reform of intellectuals as well as prisoner reform starting from 1940s until today. It is not clear to us when exactly this reform requirement was first imposed in the penal context, and how its requirements and assessments were adapted for the less educated offender population. However, the method of autobiography writing clearly stemmed from a bigger thought reform ideal of individuals and society under the CCP's ruling. This prior censorship of individual life story continued to dictate a meta-narrative structure for a confessional story of moral deterioration and (hope for) salvation through the reformation process.

The importance of the relationship between 'self' and 'other' in autobiographical writings cannot be overstated. One of the tasks of autobiographers, regardless of cultural variations, is to locate themselves within some social system, as noted by Kawai (1998) in his study on Chinese autobiography. However, as our analysis has shown, Chinese prison autobiography partly aims to eliminate such social situatedness as it structures personal life narratives via a controlled, uniform storyline and meaning. Therefore, writing ceased to be a creative process of self-expression, but rather a demonstration of compliance with the required rules and regulations.

Warr (2019) studied what he called the 'narrative labour' of prisoners with life and indeterminate sentences in the UK and found that the demonstration of being rehabilitated is based on very specific narrative tropes. For the prisoners in his study to be positively regarded by the prison officers and authority as well as to secure release, they needed to understand what is expected and to be able to convincingly perform a reformed self. Narrative labour is highly functional for the individual, and it pays off the most when it is performed during engagement in activities that are high in disciplinary capital, which are events that are most visible and can be recorded as proof, such as …. Warr coined the term 'disciplinary capital' to refer to 'information, data, and recommendations which communicate some symbolic connotation that achieves the disciplinary constraints the prison seeks to impose' (p. 6). The narrative expectations of autobiographical writing in the Chinese penal context not only restrict individual's narrative autonomy and produce similar copy, but the copy itself also reinforces such a mechanism. When the offender realises that certain gains, such as an improved relationship with officers could be achieved through contributing to fulfil the official requirements, they are very likely to comply with the narrative demand.

While almost all the autobiographies contain repentant self-criticism, such as: 'this was a big lesson in my life, I will start fresh here, reform myself, obey the regulations, reflect on myself and recognise the harm of crime' (prison T), we also found numerous instances within the prisoner-author's narration of the life course where attempts were made to contextualise the offence. One prisoner-author, for example, provided a kind of 'neutralization' (Sykes & Matza, 1957): '(To) think back on it now, what truly drove me to where I am now was the days after I arrived in city J. (..) I used to believe in legal and hard work, but since I came to Beijing, I realised how naive I was' (prisoner Y). Y expressed explicitly his perspective that his 'criminality' should be attributed to the problems associated with the social order of city J rather than his internal thoughts, even indicating that social reality in urban China has criminalised the law-abiding and honest person he used to be. Such denial of individual responsibility evidently does not belong to the 'repentant criminal' ideal, however, it had also passed the assessment as it was already archived. Warr (2019) argues that one person's narrative labour may result in profound cognitive dissonance where it becomes difficult for the prisoner to distinguish his or her original identity, and the above archived deviated narratives suggest there may be more space for the coexistence of both narrative identities, the private self and the self in corrections, in the Chinese penal context.

We argue that autobiographical writings in Chinese prisons serve multiple functions, as they can be used and understood as reformation method, tool of sustaining control and discipline as well as a mechanism for penal and governmental legitimacy. The dual presence of compliance with and resistance to the expected narrative in prisoner autobiographies demonstrate that the demand may be rather relaxed, and autobiography writing should be understood as co-constructed product between authority and its managed subjects. This is also echoed with the writing structure we discussed earlier where autobiography writing seems to be foremost a type of functional writing and perhaps a matter of bureaucratic paperwork than correctional intervention. We also argue that while Warr (2019) has noted that narrative demonstration of rehabilitated selfhood was most effective during highly visible and well-documented occasions, he did not raise the question of coperformance between officers and prisoners, as officers also have a role to play and a stake to lose or gain in the maintenance of the disciplinary image.

Conclusion

In their study of former senior CCP cadre Deng Kesheng's confessional writings across 3 years' time as a case study of thought reform, Eggli and Hasmath (2016) found that the writings were mostly aimed at achieving three goals: to express trust in the Party's leadership, to affirm Mao's absolute authority and to distinguish between Kesheng's political and intellectual selves, which justified his previous 'incorrect' expression. Ultimately, the writings would 'express conformity, and re-affirm prevailing power structures', and thus the language used 'functioned to communicate in a functionalist way, fulfilling (the narrator's) subordinated role in the process of thought reform' (pp. 13–14). In regard to our own research, we also found that the mandatory offender autobiographies are highly functional writings with clear requirements that embody the existing power structure, but with much less scrutiny over the narrative details than that of the thought reform period.

The writing guidelines and the finished autobiographies presented an ideal type metanarrative of criminality as well as repentant subjects of penal power. The metanarrative of repentant and corrected life stories are 'instruments assuring historical continuity if not legitimacy' (Bruner, 1991). As correctional institutions continue to require autobiographical reflections and insist on their correctional value, this narrative construction will continue to embody the self-legitimation effort of Chinese legal authority and Party leadership. The written autobiographies in this study suggest considerable commonality with findings in Western contexts of the importance of narrative compliance and rehabilitation, though they differ in extent, assessment and consequences of narrative labour. The prominence of the narrative imperative, including the requirement of conformity with moralistic and ideological discourse, which has continuity with CCP's earlier thought reform movements, also indicate that Chinese penal power has not yet moved to the 'actuarial consideration of aggregates' penological shift in the West famously heralded by Feeley and Simon (1992).

In the process of conducting this study, particularly conceptualising it and analysing data, it was important to synthesise Chinese literature, historical studies and criminology. A historical perspective was crucial to the understanding of narrative co-construction. In-depth analysis of offender narrative is embedded in local cultural memories and political heritage. However, it was challenging to navigate between the different disciplinary traditions, such as between Criminology and History, as the latter is less concerned with methodology and argument than the former. Analysts may still need to choose and conform to one of those traditions, especially in writing for a specific field.

Narrative criminology as a field of enquiry offers examples of literary, historical and criminological synthesis (see volume edited by Presser and Sandberg, 2015a, 2015b). The field has mostly looked at the narratives of offenders on the assumption that these are freely, if collaboratively, constructed, whereas our research focussed on narrative requirements with which subjects are governed by penal authority. We argue that the field needs to further its engagement with the practice and ethics of narrative censorship (both its destructivity and productivity) by criminal justice authority, as well as intervention programmes carried out inside the prison walls, as these take different forms in different historical–social contexts.

References

Andrews, D. A., & Bonta, J. (2010). *The psychology of criminal conduct*. Abingdon-on-Thames: Routledge.

Bakken, B. (2000). *The exemplary society: Human improvement, social control, and the dangers of modernity in China*. Wotton-under-Edge: Clarendon Press.

Bernfeld, G. A., Farrington, D. P., & Leschied, A. W. (2003). *Offender rehabilitation in practice: Implementing and evaluating effective programs*. Hoboken, NJ: John Wiley & Sons.

Bodde, D. (1969). Prison life in eighteenth century Peking. *Journal of the American Oriental Society*, *89*(2), 311–333.

Brockmeier, J., & Carbaugh, D. (2001). *Narrative and identity: Studies in autobiography, self and culture* (Vol. 1). Amsterdam: John Benjamins Publishing Company.

Brockmeier, J., & Harré, R. (2001). Narrative: Problems and promises of an alternative paradigm. In J. Brockmeier & D. Carbaugh (Eds.), *Narrative and identity: Studies in autobiography, self and culture* (pp. 39–58). Amsterdam/Philadelphia, PA: John Benjamins Publishing Company.

Bruner, J. (1991). The narrative construction of reality. *Critical Inquiry*, *18*(1), 1–21.

Chen, T. H.-e. (1969). The new socialist man. *Comparative Education Review*, *13*(1), 88–95.

Colvin, S. (2015). Why should criminology care about literary fiction? Literature, life narratives and telling untellable stories. *Punishment & Society*, *17*(2), 211–229.

Cullen, F. T. (2012). Taking rehabilitation seriously: Creativity, science, and the challenge of offender change. *Punishment & Society*, *14*(1), 94–114.

Dearey, M., Petty, B., Thompson, B., Lear, C. R., Gadsby, S., & Gibbs, D. (2011). Prison (er) auto/biography, 'true crime', and teaching, learning, and research in criminology. *Critical Survey*, *23*(3), 86–102.

DeValiant, G., McGrath, L., & Kougiali, Z. (2018). Through the prison walls: Using published poetry to explore current UK prisoners' narratives of past, present and future selves. *Qualitative Research in Psychology*, *0*(0), 1–18. doi: 10.1080/14780887.2018.1442701.

Dikötter, F. (2002). The promise of repentance. Prison reform in modern China. *British Journal of Criminology*, *42*(2), 240–249.

Ding, L. (1949). *Lun sixiang gaizao*. Tianjin, China: Duzhe shudian.

Dittmer, L. (1973). The structural evolution of 'criticism and self-criticism'. *The China Quarterly*, *53*, 708–729.

Dittmer, L. (1974). *Liu Shao-ch'i and the Chinese cultural revolution: The politics of mass criticism*. Oakland, CA: University of California Press.

Edney, R. (2005). Contested narratives of penal knowledge: H Division Pentridge Prison and the histories of imprisonment. *Current Issues in Criminal Justice*, *17*, 362.

Eggli, M., & Hasmath, R. (2016). Thought reform during the Chinese cultural revolution: The case of Deng Kesheng. Paper presented at the American Sociological Association Annual Meeting, Seattle, USA. Retrieved from https://ssrn.com/abstract=2712298; doi:10.2139/ssrn.2712298. Accessed on November 11, 2018.

Feeley, M. M., & Simon, J. (1992). The new penology: Notes on the emerging strategy of corrections and its implications. *Criminology*, *30*(4), 449–474.

Fox, K. J. (1999). Changing violent minds: Discursive correction and resistance in the cognitive treatment of violent offenders in prison. *Social Problems*, *46*(1), 88–103.

Franzosi, R. (1998). Narrative analysis—or why (and how) sociologists should be interested in narrative. *Annual Review of Sociology*, *24*(1), 517–554.

Gadd, D. (2003). Review essay: Making criminology good: A response to Shadd Maruna. *The Howard Journal of Criminal Justice, 42*(3), 316–322.
Gao, H. (2000). *How the red sun rose: The origin and development of the Yanan Rectification Movement, 1930–1945.* Hong Kong: The Chinese University Press.
Griffin, P. (1974). Prison management in the Kiangsi and Yenan periods. *The China Quarterly, 58,* 310–331.
Hualing, F. (2005). Re-education through labour in historical perspective. *The China Quarterly, 184,* 811–830.
Huang, M. (1995). *Literati and self-re/presentation: Autobiographical sensibility in the eighteenth-century Chinese novel.* Redwood City, CA: Stanford University Press.
Juntunen, M.-L., & Westerlund, H. (2011). The legacy of music education methods in teacher education: The metanarrative of Dalcroze Eurhythmics as a case. *Research Studies in Music Education, 33*(1), 47–58.
Kawai, K. (1998). In Y. Cai (Trans.), *Zhoongguo de zizhuan wenxue.* Beijing: Zhongyang Bianyi Chubanshe.
Larson, W. (1991). *Literary authority and the modern Chinese writer: Ambivalence and autobiography* (Vol. 2). Durham, NC: Duke University Press.
Li, J. (1984). *Chinese penal judicial history.* Taipei: Taiwan Shangwu Yinshuguan.
MacFarquhar, R. (1966). *The hundred flowers campaign and the Chinese intellectuals.* New York, NY: Praeger.
Maruna, S. (2001). *Making good.* Washington, DC: American Psychological Association.
McNeill, F. (2012). Four forms of 'offender' rehabilitation: Towards an interdisciplinary perspective. *Legal and Criminological Psychology, 17*(1), 18–36.
Morgan, S. (1999). Prison lives: Critical issues in reading prisoner autobiography. *The Howard Journal of Criminal Justice, 38*(3), 328–340.
Mühlhahn, K. (2009). *Criminal justice in China: A history.* Cambridge, MA: Harvard University Press.
Nellis, M. (2002). Prose and cons: Offender auto/biographies, penal reform and probation training. *The Howard Journal of Criminal Justice, 41*(5), 434–468.
Ng, J. (2003). *The experience of modernity: Chinese autobiography of the early twentieth century.* Ann Arbor, MI: University of Michigan Press.
Ogloff, J. R., & Davis, M. R. (2004). Advances in offender assessment and rehabilitation: Contributions of the risk–needs–responsivity approach. *Psychology, Crime and Law, 10*(3), 229–242.
Presser, L. (2004). Violent offenders, moral selves: Constructing identities and accounts in the research interview. *Social Problems, 51*(1), 82–101.
Presser, L., & Sandberg, S. (2015a). *Narrative criminology: Understanding stories of crime.* New York, NY: New York University Press.
Presser, L., & Sandberg, S. (2015b). Research strategies for narrative criminology. *Qualitative Research in Criminology, 1,* 85.
Prison Bureau of Chinese Criminal Justice Department (2012). *Renzui Huizui Jiaoyu.* Shenyang: Liaojing Renmin Chubanshe.
Sakacs, L. M. (2018). *Tell me who you are: Life histories of women beyond the prison walls.* Long Beach, CA: California State University.
Sandberg, S. (2010). What can "lies" tell us about life? Notes towards a framework of narrative criminology. *Journal of Criminal Justice Education, 21*(4), 447–465.

Sandberg, S. (2013). Are self-narratives strategic or determined, unified or fragmented? Reading Breivik's Manifesto in light of narrative criminology. *Acta Sociologica, 56*(1), 69–83.
Shen, J. (1976). *Lidai Yukao (on historical prisons)*. Tianjin, China: Taiwan Shangwu Yinshuguan.
Smith, A. M. (2013a). The dilemma of thought reform: Beijing reformatories and the origins of reeducation through labor, 1949–1957. *Modern China, 39*(2), 203–234.
Smith, A. M. (2013b). Thought reform and the unreformable: Reeducation centers and the rhetoric of opposition in the early People's Republic of China. *Journal of Asian Studies, 72*(4), 937–958.
Spengemann, W. C. (1980). *The forms of autobiography: Episodes in the history of a literary genre*. New Haven, CT: Yale University Press.
Stephens, J., & McCallum, R. (2013). *Retelling stories, framing culture: Traditional story and metanarratives in children's literature*. Abingdon-on-Thames: Routledge.
Strauss, J. (2006). Morality, coercion and state building by campaign in the early PRC: Regime consolidation and after, 1949–1956. *The China Quarterly, 188*, 891–912.
Sykes, G. M., & Matza, D. (1957). Techniques of neutralization: A theory of delinquency. *American sociological review, 22*(6), 664–670.
Teiwes, F. C. (1976). The origins of rectification: Inner–party purges and education before liberation. *The China Quarterly, 65*, 15–53.
Vogel, E. F. (1965). From friendship to comradeship: The change in personal relations in communist China. *China Quarterly, 21*, 46.
Waldram, J. B. (2007). Narrative and the construction of 'truth' in a prison-based treatment program for sexual offenders. *Ethnography, 8*(2), 145–169.
Waldram, J. B. (2010). Moral agency, cognitive distortion, and narrative strategy in the rehabilitation of sexual offenders. *Ethos, 38*(3), 251–274.
Waldram, J. B. (2012). *Hound pound narrative: Sexual offender habilitation and the anthropology of therapeutic intervention*. Oakland, CA: University of California Press.
Wang, F. (1993). *Zhongguo Laogai Gongzuo Jianshi (brief history of China reform though labor work)*. Beijing: Jingguan Jiaoyu Chubanshe.
Wang, J. (2018). What's wrong with corruption? Messages from confessions in China. *Crime, Law and Social Change, 69*(3), 447–463.
Warr, J. (2019). 'Always gotta be two mans': Lifers, risk, rehabilitation, and narrative labour. *Punishment & Society, 0*(0), 1–20.
Weaver, A., & Weaver, B. (2013). Autobiography, empirical research and critical theory in desistance: A view from the inside out. *Probation Journal, 60*(3), 259–277.
Williams, P. F., & Wu, Y. (2004). *The great wall of confinement: The Chinese prison camp through contemporary fiction and reportage*. Oakland, CA: University of California Press.
Wu, P.-y. (1990). *The Confucian's progress: Autobiographical writings in traditional China*. Princeton, NJ: Princeton University Press.
Xin, G. e. (2006). *Mao Zedong Gaizao Zuifan Lilun Yanjiu (study on Mao Zedong's theory of criminal reform)*. Tianjin, China: Renmin Chubanshe.

Xingrui Huang, M. G. (1991). *Dangdai Zhongguo Zuifan (contemporary Chinese criminal)*. Beijing: Zhongguo Zhengfa Daxue Chubanshe.

Xue, M. (1986). *Zhongguo Jianyu Shi (history of Chinese prison)*. Tianjin, China: Zhongguo Qunzhong Chubanshe.

Yardley, E., Wilson, D., Kemp, D., & Brookes, M. (2015). Narrative beyond prison gates: Contradiction, complexity, and reconciliation. *International Journal of Offender Therapy and Comparative Criminology, 59*(2), 159–179.

Zhang, X. (2017). Prison theatre as method: Focused ethnography and auto-ethnography in a Chinese prison. In S. Fletcher & H. White (Eds.), *Emerging voices: Critical social research by European group postgraduate and early career researchers*. Capel Dewi: EG Press.

Chapter 22

Opposing Violent Extremism through Counternarratives: Four Forms of Narrative Resistance

Sveinung Sandberg and Jan C. Andersen

Extremist jihadist groups have dominated the media since the terrorist attacks on the US on 11 September 2001. The rise of the Islamic State (IS)[1] in 2014 further increased the already extensive news coverage. For many outsiders, this presence has further bolstered a conflating of the religion of Islam with jihadist organisations, portraying the former as violent and totalitarian. Studying Western media, Ahmed and Matthes (2017, p. 219) show that Muslims 'tend to be negatively framed, while Islam is dominantly portrayed as a violent religion.' This portrayal in media can lead to Muslims feeling unjustly defined as a threat to national security (Mythen, Walklate, & Khan, 2012). Backing that sentiment, Kearns, Betus, and Lemeiux (2017) reveal that the word terrorism is more widely used in cases where the perpetrator is Muslim and that these cases receive media coverage that is four and a half times as great as that when the perpetrator is a non-Muslim.

The skewed media coverage creates and reinforces cultural notions of what and who should be feared. It alienates Muslims in general and may 'further enhance intergroup conflicts between Muslims and non-Muslims' (Von Sikorski, Schmuck, Matthes, & Binder, 2017). As part of a package that treats all Muslims as guilty, Muslims are being asked to account for acts of violence committed in the name of Islam (van Es, 2018). Many young Muslims consider doing so to be an unreasonable expectation and say that media coverage of Islam and social pressure ruins their quality of life and sense of belonging in Western societies. Western Muslims often refuse to denounce extremist groups. They believe it is not their responsibility, and argue that these groups have nothing to do with Islam (Sandberg et al., 2018). Their public silence has sometimes been interpreted as support, and Muslims have been criticised for not taking a clearer stance against terrorism and religious extremists (e.g. Maidment, 2017; Von Sikorski et al., 2017).

---

[1]Also known as ISIS, ISIL or Daesh.

This chapter explores how young Muslims reject jihadist organisations and points to the value of studying counternarratives in general populations instead of focussing on the dominant narratives that are reproduced in media and public representations. The Muslims we interviewed expressed their opposition to religious extremism not primarily through loud protests or large mobilisations aimed at creating media attention; rather, it emerged in everyday stories about religion and politics. There is an ongoing *narrative struggle* on how to understand Islam in Muslim communities. Combined with factors such as social and economic marginalisation, international and national politics, and social networks, the outcome of this narrative struggle explains the prevalence of religious extremism. Like all ideologies, jihadist ideology is primarily narrative in its structure (Halverson, Goodall, & Corman, 2011), which makes narrative analysis and narrative criminology central for terrorism studies. Narratives nurture the motivation to do harm and ignore harm by others (Presser, 2018), but telling stories can also be an important way to resist criminogenic and harmful ideologies.

Drawing on qualitative interviews with 90 young Muslims in Norway, we show the ways in which young Muslims reject violent extremist organisational actions and rhetoric. Their opposition to extremism varied from calmly and factually disproving such religious practice and theology, to using highly emotional language containing derogatory terms, humour and ridicule. Sometimes they attempted to ignore terrorist organisations and rhetoric altogether. We describe these counternarratives as narrative resistance, emphasising how the stories of 'ordinary' people can limit harm and challenge harm-doers. In terms of method, we touch upon how to research counternarratives and the advantages of qualitative team research in narrative studies.

Narrative Analysis, Power and Resistance

Narrative criminology has approached narratives in different facets (Sandberg, 2016) but has tended to emphasise narratives that may induce harm. In the initial conception of narrative criminology, however, the emphasis was on stories that perform the work of 'instigating, sustaining, or effecting desistance from, harmful action' (Presser & Sandberg, 2015, p. 1). That is, opposition to harm was on the agenda for research. The research preceding narrative criminology studied desistance (Maruna, 2001); however, one notable Canadian exception notwithstanding (Joosse, Bucerius, & Thompson, 2015), few works within narrative criminology have studied resistance to criminal and harmful action by non-offenders or the narrative struggles preceding engagement in harm.

Narratives are discourses that link one or more events temporally and causally (Polletta, Chen, Gardner, & Motes, 2011). We believe that narratives are extraordinary forms of discourse due to their potential for captivating narrators and arousing audiences (Presser, 2018). Characters are an essential part of narratives. Most stories include one or several easily recognisable characters, such as 'the villain' or 'the imposter' in folktales that are crucial for understanding the plot and morale of the story (Propp, 1968). Narratives sometimes appear as complete stories, which most people associate with narrative analysis, but in real life, narratives often appear as tropes, or 'single words or short phrases that only hint at familiar stories' (Sandberg, 2016, p. 155). In contemporary Western society tropes such as 'Islamic terrorism', can be used to identify stories that are so widespread that they need not be spelt out every time they are evoked. Another fundamental, but often-neglected, part of narrative analysis is narrative performances. Stories are not only transmitted through words but also gestures, body language, tone of speaking etc (Baumann, 1986). These displays of emotions are sometimes followed by the use of derogatory terms, as we will return to later.

The intense emotions that accompanied many of the stories in this dataset suggest that interviewees felt that they were up against powerful master narratives about Islam. A master narrative is one that is 'deeply embedded in a culture, provides a pattern for cultural life and social structure, and creates a framework for communication about what people are expected to do in certain situations' (Halverson et al., 2011, p. 7). What counts as a master narrative varies depending on context; different master narratives pertain in different situations, and they can sometimes conflict with each other. Sometimes it is relatively easy to identify a master narrative, as with stories of motherhood and pregnancy depicted in early work on narrative resistance (Talbot, Bibace, Bokhour, & Bamberg, 1996). At other times, it is more difficult: What counts as master narratives is to a large degree a question of interpretation and in many cases, it is better for researchers to argue it thoroughly or show it empirically instead of assuming their presence. In narrative analysis, the concepts of master narrative or even hegemony (Laclau & Mouffe, 1985) are important because they open up thinking about domination in a research field that is often accused of neglecting issues of power.

While conceptualising master narratives can be a way to identify powerful moments of consensus in society, researching counternarratives shows the many ways that this ideological domination can be challenged. Counternarratives exist in close relation to master narratives but these two types of narratives are not 'necessarily dichotomous entities' (Andrews, 2004). Instead, they are intertwined in complex ways; for example, a master narrative can be challenged through appeal to other master narratives or by working critically with components of them, providing new direction and meaning. Individuals and groups can mirror or challenge a master narrative, or develop it using their own personal stories (Andrews, 2002, see also; Bamberg, 2004). The association of Islam with war and terrorism for example, is thematised in a prominent master narrative, but is also continuously challenged by counternarratives in public discourse and opposed in narrative work on senses of self and social identities among Muslims.

Paradoxically, the idea of Islam as a religion of war and terrorism is shared by both jihadi extremist and anti-Islamic rhetoric (Ekman, 2015; Page, Challita, & Harris, 2011; Shaffer, 2016). The two master narratives that the young Western Muslims we interviewed countered were first, a jihadi master narrative that uses narratives of Muslim victimhood and religious apocalyptic utopianism to conclude that war and terror are justified, even inevitable, because Islam is at war with the West (Halverson et al., 2011; Karmon, 2015; McCants, 2015); and second, a Western master narrative based on the assumption that Islam is a singular world religion, and ideas of racial inferiority with a long history in

Western societies, concluding that 'Muslims are terrorists' (e.g. Ahmed & Matthes, 2017; Aydin, 2017; Kearns, Betus, & Lemieux, 2017). Islam is, for example, routinely associated with terrorism through the term 'Islamic terrorism', promoting 'the widely accepted "knowledge" that certain forms of Islam are by nature violent and terroristic' (Jackson, 2007, p. 405).

The frequency and urgency of the young Muslim interviewees' stories countering extremism indicate that these stories are of great importance to them. In this regard, we agree with Joosse et al. (2015, p. 815) that 'the most powerful counternarratives that work against radicalisation will already be in place within communities, reacting against the ideologies and radicalisation strategies of terrorist movements.' We describe the counternarratives to which we gained access in our interviews as narrative resistance to master narratives that describe Islam as a religion of war and terrorism. Our main aim in this chapter is to explore these forms of 'everyday' narrative resistance, to understand how narratives not only promote but also constrain harm. When extreme beliefs are challenged by friends, family or others who are socially, religiously or ideologically close to those holding them, it is more effective than when they are confronted by outsiders.

Study and Participants

The participants in this study were 90 young Muslims in Norway aged 18–32 years old; half of them were women and half men[2]. The main criteria for participation were age and that the subjects defined themselves as Muslims. Given the aim to research the everyday counternarratives of young Muslims, we tried to avoid activists, imams or other religious experts and leaders. The goal was to recruit and get access to the counternarratives of what we for want of a better word describe as 'ordinary' Muslims. This research focus also made it important to talk to young people instead of searching for coverage in newspapers or comments online. Open source data are often shaped by a public or (social) media context and usually comes with a heavy selection bias in favour of the more 'activist' and 'extreme' voices.

The interviews were conducted throughout Norway in 20 different municipalities. Most of the interviews took place in the capital, Oslo, or the surrounding areas, where most Norwegian Muslims live. It is estimated that approximately 200,000 people identify as Muslims in Norway, representing approximately 4 % of the population (Østeby & Dalgard, 2017). The participants in our study had backgrounds from 20 different countries, the most numerically prominent being Morocco, Somalia and Pakistan. Most of the young Muslims were Sunni (73), but we also interviewed Shiites (8) and those declaring some smaller Muslim affiliations. Some participants did not want to state their religious affiliation, for example because they refused to differentiate between what they described as 'sectarian' affiliations within Islam.

---

[2]This study was funded by the Norwegian Research Council, project number 259541.

A team of five researchers, three women and two men, from different cultural and academic backgrounds and with religious affiliations and beliefs, carried out the interviews, which were conducted over a 6-month period, from January to June 2017. Although it might be expected that the gender, religious and cultural backgrounds of the interviewer would impact the narrative, for example whether interviewers were Muslims, ethnic minority or ethnic majority, in fact respondents' narratives were more similar than different (see also Damsa & Ugelvik, 2017). The different ways in which Muslims rejected extremist narratives were often the same, and seemed to reflect a narrative habitus (Fleetwood, 2016) – their structured and embodied ways of experiencing and acting in the world – rather than specific responses in and to the interview situation.

The interviews lasted between 1 and 2 hours and were held in cafés or participants' homes. The interviewees were recruited using social networks, referral by university students, and social media such as Facebook, by contacting mosques and Muslim youth organisations and seeking out Muslim events. Interviewers followed a semi-structured interview guide on themes including positive Islamic narratives, marginalisation and discrimination, jihadi narratives, extremist organisations and deradicalisation. The interviews were designed to elicit storytelling: rather than having a checklist of questions, and the interviewers were encouraged to start a conversation about the aforementioned themes. Unlike many surveys of Muslims (e.g. Vestel & Bakken, 2016), where participants are encouraged to answer categorically yes or no if they support controversial themes such as sharia, and whether the West is at war with Islam, we attempted to elicit more nuanced answers to such controversial questions. Therefore, establishing trust was paramount. We did this by recruiting through interviewers' own social networks, establishing contact in advance of interviews and attempting to do interviews on premises where interviewees felt comfortable. Most importantly, we tried to create an atmosphere in interviews where participants felt free to state their opinions and explore controversial issues through storytelling.

The Pros and Cons of Team Research

Team research is especially useful in studies such as ours where the aim is to include many participants in a limited period of time and where participants are difficult to recruit or are spread out over a large geographical area. While qualitative researchers should not strive to make their samples representative, having a large sample makes it easier to obtain variety and to gain a sense of whether what is described is a widespread or a more individually or regionally specific phenomenon. In narrative studies where the primary interest is in the narrative repertoires of groups, societies and cultures, large qualitative samples can be useful to obtain a large variety of stories, and have the same story told in various ways to observe the different 'shapes' that it can take. It also makes it easier to gain a sense of which stories are the most important and to 'control' for interviewer effects. In our study, comparable stories coming forth in interviews with researchers of different age, gender, and cultural and religious background strengthens our view that they are not the result of any particular interview combination but rather pivotal narratives salient in Muslim communities.

Having a research team also means that there is a continuous discussion of how to interpret the research results after interviews, which is an advantage compared to research conducted by a single researcher. Our team included Muslims, others with great expertise in Islam and the associated language and culture – and researchers with other backgrounds and academic expertise. When doing qualitative research there are advantages of both being an insider and outsider (Bucerius, 2013), and team research can get the best of both. For example, when reading or listening to interview extracts we could sometimes discuss single words or expressions (e.g. in Arabic) for hours to agree upon an interpretation of how and why they were used. It was of great value to have a diverse team when interpreting complex narratives that often came in the form of tropes. Group research forces one to continuously challenge one's own presumptions and preliminary conclusions. These ongoing discussions and the experiences from the different interviewer–interviewee combinations strengthen the validity of the research conclusions. On a different note, qualitative research is also often a solitary and lonely project and team research can make research more social and fun.

While there are many advantages, there are naturally disadvantages to team research. It takes a considerable amount of logistics and organising, the interviewers need to be trained and followed up closely, and there is always the risk that individual researchers do things so differently that comparison across interviews is difficult. Having many researchers involved in studying sensitive and personal topics can also result in conflicts within the group. Coauthoring was in our experience more difficult than doing interviews as part of a team, and one should consider the advantages and disadvantages of having 'too many cooks' when writing and if choosing to do so, one should have a clear plan for how to go about it. However, based on this study and on our previous experience with team research projects studying different populations such as children in school, cannabis users, binge drinkers and large-scale imprisoned drug dealers, we strongly recommend team research for narrative studies.

Forms of Narrative Resistance

Through narrative team research (Sandberg et al., 2018), we discovered four ways that interviewees rejected religious extremism: disputing the jihadist rhetoric and interpretation of Islam on factual grounds, using derogatory, often highly expressive language to dismiss religious extremism, making fun of extremists, and trying to ignore their presence.[3] Taken together, our results show the variety of ways extremism is opposed and rejected narratively in Muslim communities. More generally, they reveal the various forms that counter-narratives can take.

---

[3] It was most often directed against the IS, the jihadist organisation that dominated the news at the time of the interviews.

Factual Counternarratives

The jihadi master narrative is based on the premise that Islam is under attack by the West and secular forces in Muslim countries, requiring Muslims to defend the religion by force. Jihadi organisations argue that terrorism and political violence are proportionally just and religiously sanctified countermeasures in an ongoing war against the *kuffar*, or disbeliever (Leuprecht, Hataley, Moskalenko, & McCauley, 2009). They also proclaim a strict interpretation of sharia as a repressive set of laws that should be deeply and comprehensively implemented in society, through the use of force if necessary (McCants, 2015). The majority of our participants opposed the general idea that the West was at war with Islam as well as violent and authoritarian interpretations of Islamic law. They disputed the jihadist account of Islam versus the West on factual grounds, by criticising the theological interpretations, the principles and the practices of Islamic teachings advocated by jihadi organisations. They adamantly insisted that jihadi organisations in no way or form represented Islam.

Yasmin,[4] a twenty-four-year-old Norwegian–Pakistani woman, argued that extremists 'abuse Islam in the worst kind of way.' Karim, a twenty-five-year-old Norwegian–Algerian man, made a similar point about the IS in particular:

> *It's really a war for their own interests, to get rich. Because when they took control of more land in Iraq or Syria, I think, the first thing they did was to secure the oil wells. So, this says it all. That is, they were not aiming to establish social justice or a fair society, no. They are simply there just to have their piece of the pie. That's it. It's just that they use religion or not that they use religion but, rather, their own ideology. Those kinds of people have nothing to do with Islam.*

By alleging that the IS has primarily acted only to secure its own economic interests, Karim dismissed it as being a truly Islamic organisation. It was important for our participants to explain that extremists do not represent Muslims and that they in fact act contrary to the teachings of Islam.

Jihadi organisations are known for their violence and brutality. The IS is especially notorious for its violent actions, displaying brutality not only as a by-product of war but also as a deliberate strategy (Byman, 2015). Terrorist organisations can use spectacles of violence to draw attention and supporters to their cause, but in doing so they risk losing mainstream support (Andersen & Sandberg, 2018). Indeed, the use of excessive violence displayed by the Somali group al-Shabaab has led the Somali diaspora in Canada to reject the organisation (Joosse et al., 2015). The excessive and violent behaviour perpetrated by

---

[4] All names are pseudonyms.

jihadi organisations was a major point of critique for the young Muslims whom we interviewed. Mina, a twenty-year-old Norwegian–Somali woman, stated:

I feel that the IS is using Islam. They don't follow Islam. They use the word 'Islam,' saying that they are Muslims, but they don't follow any of it. They kill lots of innocent Muslims every single day and torture and rape. It's like all that Islam says you should not do, they do.

For these young Muslims, violence was only legitimate in situations of self-defence, and they labelled jihadists as Muslim *imposters* because they failed to follow what they saw as the teaching of the Quran. Such characteristics are an efficient way to draw borders between 'good' and 'bad' people and sanction behaviour. Young Muslims frequently categorised jihadists as imposters who cynically misused the religion of Islam (see also Joosse et al., 2015). Sana, a nineteen-year-old Norwegian–Moroccan woman, highlighted the difference between 'a real Muslim' and the IS:

In the Quran, it says that one should not kill anyone or harm anyone. Not rape women, or force women, things like that. If you were one hundred percent Muslim, you would not do such things. But still they bomb people. Children who are innocent. Tell me where in the Quran it says that you must kill a baby and the world will be better? No, because a real Muslim wouldn't have done anything like that. He wouldn't hurt a little insect or spider.

Ayan, a twenty-two-year-old Norwegian–Somali woman, similarly rejected violent actions committed in the name of Islam, referring to verse 5:32 of the Quran: 'Killing a human being – it does not matter what religion he or she is – is like killing all humanity,' she said. Many of our participants referred to the same Quran verse and described Islam as a peaceful religion and 'real' Muslims as peaceful. To emphasise the importance of human dignity in Islam, the young Muslims referred to another phrase that also originated from verse 5:32 in the Quran: 'If you save a human being, it is like saving all mankind.' That extremist groups break with these principles was an important part of the argument for why they did not represent Islam.

Extremism is often linked to a conservative understanding of Islam. Nevertheless, there was a widespread scepticism about the IS even among the most conservative young Muslims whom we interviewed. Abdulllah, an eighteen-year-old Norwegian–Somali man, self-identified as Salafi, an ultraconservative interpretation of Islam. He expressed a more literate and sophisticated theological opposition to jihadi extremism, which differed from Muslims with less literate knowledge about Islam. Abdulllah explained, 'When talking about hadith and different types of classifications of authentic hadith, the IS has used a lot of hadith that is *daif*,' which means that the source material has little credibility (Barlas, 2002). Abdullah then argued against the IS' theological interpretation of judgement day:

> Among other things, that there will be black flags rising, that it will be an army, that they will be fighting in Afghanistan.[5] All this is daif. That is not something you can accept. So, hadith scholars have classified hadiths. Among the hadiths that are declared daif are the hadiths that the IS uses. So, people think that this is true, that the Prophet has said they should go there [to Syria].

Abdullah emphasised that supporters of the IS hide theological facts and use religious texts with little credibility. Like Abdullah, other young Muslims we interviewed referred to theological concepts using specific Arabic words or expressions to show their knowledge and expertise of Islam. This can be seen as highly effective symbolic boundary work to cultivate differences between Muslim in-groups and out-groups (Essers & Benschop, 2009). Many young Muslims denounced extremist jihadist group by questioning their use of sources and theological interpretations; their use of Arabic expressions demonstrated their own knowledge of Islam.

Amal, a twenty-four-year-old Norwegian–Moroccan woman, criticised jihadists for 'picking-and-choosing' when they advocated violent and authoritarian interpretations of Islamic law. In explaining the meaning of 'true' Islam as peaceful, many young Muslims also emphasised that Islam was consistent with international laws of war. Mustafa, a twenty-seven-year-old Norwegian–Moroccan man, pointed out that Islam contains 'rules when it comes to war and the treatment of other people who are not engaging in war against you.' He elaborated on how extremist groups violate these rules:

> If someone who is fighting against you loses his weapon or doesn't have any weapons and surrenders, then you have no right to do anything to him. You can capture him as a hostage and feed him as a guest. You have to feed him well, let him sleep well, and later release him so he can go back to his family. At the same time, if you fight someone and kill him, then you're not allowed to cut his body up in pieces. If he dies, then the body is supposed to be whole and delivered to his family, or you have to allow the others who are fighting against you to stop the war so they can take his body so they can bury him.

---

[5]The flags IS use refers to a story of how an army led by the Muslim Mahdi (Messiah) is prophesied to emerge under the black flag before the end of the world. In a decisive battle, Muslim forces will achieve victory against the enemies of Islam to restore the glory of Islam (Bahari & Hassan, 2014). The emergence and success of the IS is often attributed to the promotion of an apocalyptic worldview, describing how we are approaching the end of history (McCants, 2015).

This understanding of the humane and peaceful aspect of Islam even in the midst of combat constructed an immense divergence between his version of Islam and that of jihadist organisations.

In a Dutch analysis of newspaper articles concerning Muslims in media, van Es (2018) argues that they emphasised the humane dimension of Islam and framed Islam as a religion of peace as a direct response to the continuous call on Muslims to denounce terrorism. Stories depicting 'peaceful Islam' are important counternarratives disputing a master narrative promoted by jihadi and anti-Islamic rhetoric alike, stating that Islam promotes political violence and terrorism. With time and as they spread, these counternarratives can change the meaning of the phenomena itself. Muslims, for example, sometimes counter widespread 'negative' narratives of Islam by fundamentally redefining their own understanding of what the religion is (van Es, 2018). Stories emphasising that 'Islam is peace' can emerge as counternarratives but then gradually become master narratives in their own right.

This group of young Muslims in Norway argued calmly and factually against both the theology and the religious practice of jihadist organisations. In an ongoing narrative struggle with extremists and in an attempt to take control of their Muslim identity, they rejected violent extremism as being part of Islam. The most important way in which they did so was by stating that terrorism had nothing to do with Islam and by criticising the violence used by jihadist organisations. Counternarratives that factually reject or challenge master narratives appeal to what Aristotles (1991) described as logos or reasoning. In such means of persuasion, stories were often used to show that the narrator knows better than those being opposed. Importantly, narrative resistance is not only about language but also closely connected to body language and narrative performance. In discussions characterised by factual counternarratives, for example, it can be a pointed choice to stay calm and not be carried away by emotions to demonstrate a superior intellectual position. Such counternarratives can therefore sometimes be opposed to those we discuss below.

Emotional Counternarratives

Emotional outbursts, insults and derogatory terms are another important element of counternarratives. Stories with such elements expressed moral repugnance regarding the brutal violence perpetrated by extremists (Cragin, 2014). Derogatory terms and emotional involvement underlined the great importance of the issues at stake and proved the personal commitment of the narrator. The young Muslims whom we interviewed, for example, often described extremists as naïve and simple people who were 'brainwashed.' They characterised them as 'fake, ridiculous and stupid idiots' or as 'crazy psychopaths' who were 'completely extreme.' Such insults were common ways of rejecting extremist groups and an important part of the narrative resistance of young Muslims.

Maryam, a twenty-two-year-old Norwegian–Somali woman, stated with great passion that extremists are 'ruining the reputation of Islam,' and Melodi said that they are 'fucked up people who don't understand life.' In the young Muslims' narratives, jihadists were mainly characterised as what Propp (1968) describes as 'villains' or 'false heroes' (imposters). Magnus, a twenty-four-year-old Norwegian convert, criticised the IS because of its excessive use of violence, stating, 'They are just blood-thirsty. They are completely mad. They only punish because they are used to it, whether they are criminals or gangsters. There must be something wrong with their heads.' Others described them as 'living in their own little bubble.' Amir, a twenty-eight-year-old Norwegian–Pakistani man, described the IS as a group of 'provocateurs' without any clear form of vision. He stated that they lived in a fantasy world or, as he put it, 'They live in Disneyland.' Sometimes, the broad variety of insults and name-calling was so overwhelming that we had the impression that, as opposed to trying to present a consistent narrative, the young Muslims were searching for any available derogatory term to describe extremists. The urgent need for young Muslims to disassociate themselves from jihadists often led to such extreme othering.[6]

Young Muslims often claimed that those who sympathise with extremist groups are brainwashed or mentally ill. Jamal, a twenty-two-year-old Afghani man, explained that 'they have something in their minds' that makes it possible. Hassan, a twenty-four-year-old Palestinian man, explained that 'the leaders are extreme' and that the people in the IS are not necessarily evil but victims of brainwashing. He emphasised the difference between a general 'us' (including the interviewer) and 'them': 'We are not so kind that we let the others decide, control us and brainwash us.' In this way, the dichotomy between Muslim and non-Muslim was replaced with a dichotomy categorising people as either extremists or peaceful people. Hassan, a twenty-four-year-old Palestinian, compared the IS with other extremist religious groups, saying that they were 'just an extremist group, just like other extremist Christian groups in the West. Either way, the IS is just extreme people.' Some of the young Muslims we interviewed described extremists as losers or as victims needing help, and they portrayed them in the same way as previous research, as 'mindless instruments of someone else' (Joosse et al., 2015, p. 822). Esra, an eighteen-year-old Norwegian–Turkish woman, characterised extremists as being easily manipulable because they were 'those who are bullied, who don't have many friends, and who can't tell their friends about their problems, and those who are not included.' Such portrayals invalidated the narrative of 'jihadi cool' (Picart, 2015) and stripped extremists of agency, masculinity and anything remotely attractive or desirable, leaving them instead as victims in need of help.

When extremists portrayed themselves as true devout Muslims this evoked strong emotions. Sofia, a nineteen-year-old Norwegian–Somali woman, angrily expressed 'I hate, I hate that they use the name of Islam. And I hate that they try to represent Islam when that's not what it is... I hate them. I only say their punishment lies with God.' She pointed out how IS kills innocent people, but

---

[6]For an overview over symbolic boundary literature and othering, see e.g. Lamont and Molnar (2002) and Copes (2016).

highlighted that 'those they kill are mostly Muslims!' and was unable to understand how people could believe such frauds. Some interviewees described extremists as deceiving imposters that hurt innocent people, while calling attention to how 'actual' Muslims were the 'real victims' of the reign of terror by extremists. These young Muslims thus positioned themselves as the real victims of jihadi terrorism, and argued that mainstream society and the media overlooked this.

Sarah, a twenty-seven-year-old Norwegian–Pakistani woman, harshly defined extremists as savages and 'ignorant idiots running around with a shotgun.' She also described how 'Shaytan is over them. Shaytan is their god. They have gone off the rails.' Labelling jihadists as Satan's agents was a way to turn their own rhetoric against themselves. It is also another example of the extreme othering involved in the boundary work of young Muslims. By describing them as the ultimate evil, they drew the clearest and most powerful boundaries possible between themselves and the jihadists. Differentiating in-group from out-group is not just about the other, but also 'a way to reinforce and protect' the self (Dervin, 2012, p. 191). Whether described as genuinely evil or as struggling with mental issues, the main point was that jihadists were fundamentally *different* from 'normal' people and thus that their extremism had little to do with Islam, a major, mainstream religion.

Sometimes, the derogatory terms used in emotional counternarratives had very specific religious foundations. Combining factual rejection with specific religious insults, some characterised extremist groups as *khawarij*. This highly offensive term describes a group that appeared in the first century of Islam, creating the first *fitna* (schism) among Muslims. It is commonly used as a derogatory term to describe organisations with a fundamentalist interpretation of Islam that allows the killing of opponents and the holding of extreme religious literalism (Meijer, 2009). Abdullah explained how the Prophet had warned about such groups:

> *He said, when the day of judgement comes near, there will be a group that will enter the religion and exit it like an arrow goes through a prey. They read the Quran, they pray and all that. But what they read does not hit the heart. They are khawarij. The Prophet called them dogs of hell. The IS has a lot of signs of khawarij, and there are many scholars who call them that.*

The term was used to reject violent jihadists, often by participants with a great deal of knowledge about Islam. The use of such terms thus combined the two counternarrative strategies that we have discussed so far: using an offensive and emotionally laden term and deploying superior Islamic theological knowledge. Khawarij was therefore an effective trope to reject extremist among Muslim youths.

The emotional energy produced by all these condemnations can justify very harsh acts against groups or individuals perceived as being extremists. Aise, a nineteen-year-old Norwegian–Turkish woman, expressed her frustration over foreign fighters going to Syria, saying, 'One should really just shoot them. It's impossible to control them.' Describing foreign fighters as evil, mad or uncontrollable in other ways made it necessary to stop them through lethal force. Aisha, a nineteen-year-old Norwegian–Pakistani woman, similarly concluded, 'One should go to war with them to kill them. They are absolutely extreme. It's ridiculous.' Such recommendations may not have been meant literally and, instead, may have been a way to express frustration and strong emotional involvement in opposing jihadism. Nevertheless, these feelings can be a negative side effect of emotional counternarratives. The condemnation of extremist groups by our interviewees could sometimes go so far that it ended up defending the unlawful use of force to combat them, reflecting a strand of opinion within the majority population.

Jihadi narratives portray jihadists as heroes fighting for justice (Hegghammer, 2017; Sageman, 2008). Derogatory counternarratives challenge this portrayal and, in an intense othering, describe jihadists as either crazy and bloodthirsty or weak and vulnerable. Emotional counternarratives frame jihadists as the extremist 'other' in a way that more factual counternarratives do not. Symbolic boundaries are an integrated part of all narratives, but as Copes (2016, p. 194) argues, they are 'especially important for those who are members of stigmatised groups or who are socially close to them' (see also Ugelvik, 2014, 2015). Young Muslims might have felt stigmatised by being associated with jihadi organisations through religious affiliation, which may have made them more emphatic when denouncing them. By using derogatory terms and highly emotional language, young Norwegian Muslims drew important boundaries between themselves and stigmatised groups, underlining who they were by making clear who they were not (Copes, Hochstetler, & Williams, 2008).

Emotional counternarratives are good at mobilising audiences, and they highlight the significance of the issues at stake. Pathos refers to attempts at persuading by appealing to emotions. Such attempts can be made by telling stories that arouse strong emotions (Presser, 2018) – stories which, as we have emphasised here, reveal the emotional engagement of the narrator himself or herself. The frequent use of derogatory terms shows the intense emotions that were involved in the narrative resistance of young Muslims in Norway. Combined with extreme othering, it can be potentially problematic. As Presser (2013, p. 26) notes, collective stories fuelled by emotion licence harm-doing against an 'evil other', and the extreme othering we have described above can justify disproportionate counterterrorism policies and penal sanctions.

Humorous Counternarratives

Ridicule and humour are other important elements in narrative resistance against extremism. Humour is an ambiguous and multifaceted phenomenon, which can be effective as a form of critique targeting members of social out-groups. It also serves a social function, allowing individuals to release tension and to express emotions such as superiority, aggression and hostility (Gruner, 2000). Religious extremism was a sensitive subject, evoking complex feelings. Still the topic was sometimes discussed with laughter in an amused tone among the young Muslims whom we interviewed. Salam, a twenty-five-year-old Moroccan woman, was frustrated but laughingly answered our question of whether she felt that it was her responsibility to defend Islam:

> Yes, because every time anything appears on the news about how there has been a bomb or something, the first thing that's written in the newspaper is that the person said 'Allahu akbar!' Oh my God! Here we go again! 'General assembly! How are we going to solve this situation!?'

The young Muslims viewed excessive media coverage of jihadist terrorism as a problem for them personally. Nala, a twenty-year-old Norwegian–Somali woman, expressed her frustration over the media portrayal of Islam, but she was also able to joke sarcastically about the consequences for her:

> N: *No, it's, like, 'Nala, what are you?' So, I say I'm a Muslim, and then it's, like, 'Oh, you are Muslim, what do you think about the IS?' As if that's the first thing that they think about, right?*
>
> I: *A direct link between the two?*
>
> N: *Yes, it's direct. It's very stupid, really. But people ignore all the work Muslims generally do. All the ways they oppose the IS and terrorist groups, fighting against them. It is not taken into consideration at all. Like, if all Muslims were the IS, then we would not have had a stream of refugees, you know. Everyone would be 'chilling' in Syria, to put it bluntly. Everyone would have had a great time there because the IS is Islam, right?*

The association between Muslims and terrorism was sometimes countered with humour and sarcasm. Expressing out-group hostility by highlighting oppositional attitudes while enhancing in-group solidarity explains how Muslims themselves were victimised by extremists (Gruner, 2000). Houda, a twenty-seven-year-old Norwegian–Lebanese woman, criticised other Muslims for believing in jihadi propaganda or violent interpretations of Islam:

> *People, please! Hello, God has given us a brain, so read books, read the interpretations. And don't be the person who writes their own book and creates chaos in the world. God does not want chaos. God says the first words we should say to each other are 'As-salamu alaykum,' which means 'Peace be with you.' God does not say, 'Chaos be with you!' (laughs)*

Combining factual rejection with a joke, she made fun of people who believed in jihadi propaganda. By making a joke based on one of the basic phrases that all Muslims know, 'As-salamu alaykum,' she provided an effective humorous counternarrative to jihadi narratives. Humour that emphasises how those made fun of are comically stupid and irrational (Davies, 1988) can work to demonstrate superiority (Gruner, 2000).

The promise of 72 virgins in paradise for martyrs is an important jihadi narrative and frequently used in the rhetoric of extremist Islamic groups (Halverson et al., 2011). It is also a story frequently referred to in public debates about Islam. Among our participants, it was an important source for ridicule. The sexual undertones probably made it exciting, slightly taboo, and thus particularly fitting for jokes. Mitra, a twenty-five-year-old Norwegian–Iraqi woman, broke into laughter when we mentioned the story about the virgins and stated, 'Um, yes... yes, assume I see it... it's in a way a very childish approach to death, a little, like, "Oh, I know I'm gonna get this, so just let me kill a non-Muslim."' She paused for a while but then continued to elaborate on her thoughts of what it meant to be a 'real martyr.'

Humour and laughter can reduce the tension or stress associated with awkward situations and sensitive themes. Laughter and jokes can release negative energy and help make it possible to talk about difficult subjects (Lynch, 2002). This was evident, for example, when the participants explained the concept of jihad as being an inner struggle and then used laughter to transition to the concept of violent jihad. We asked Mustafa what jihad meant to him, and he explained how 'jihad is working on yourself, striving in everyday life. You strive when you study, you strive when you work, that is jihad.' He then laughed and asked, 'But it is probably the "holy war" you're looking for, al-Harb al-Muqaddasa?'[7] This comment is a reference to a controversial interpretation of the concept of 'holy war' in Islam (Kabbani, 2006). He thus implicitly criticised us by making a joke implying that we were mainly interested in the violent aspects of Islam. Humour works as a social corrective (Sandberg & Tutenges, 2018), in this case by posing a critique that is less direct and therefore easier to convey.

Anton, a twenty-five-year-old Norwegian–Moroccan man, was also familiar with the story about the virgins and laughingly stated, 'Rewarded with 72 virgins and so on... Yeah, I don't know. It would have been "nice" with 72 virgins. But I can't handle one, let alone if you are supposed to have 72.' In addition to releasing tension, jokes can express a sense of superiority (Gruner, 2000). In broad terms, humour is based on aggression and hostility (Martin, 2007), which was evident when young Muslims combined factual or emotional counternarratives to make fun of extremists by criticising their lack of theological knowledge, their intellectual capacity or their moral values. Doing so empowered young Muslims by constructing their status as 'the storyteller who knows better,' who can humorously see through jihadi propaganda (Joosse et al., 2015, p. 825).

Our distinction between different counternarratives, utilised by young Muslims, is analytical. In the 'real world,' these forms of narrative resistance are closely intertwined. For example, when Sana, in what we described as a factual counternarrative above, asked, 'Where in the Quran does it say that you must kill

---

[7] Referring to the Arabic term for jihad, which does not occur in the Quran (Kabbani, 2006).

a baby and the world will be better?,' she questioned the jihadists' knowledge of Islam by using a highly emotional trope. Mentioning killing a baby is also ambiguous and in this context open to different interpretations, expressing either humorous critique, tragic despair or both. Laughter and tears are closely connected, and humour often carries important messages and critiques (Sandberg & Tutenges, 2018). Many jokes about jihadists also played on the extremists' lack of knowledge about Islam, and derogatory terms and insults sometimes had a comic dimension. Because of the inherent ambiguity in much humour, the ways in which different forms of resistance are connected are therefore especially evident in humorous narratives.

Silencing as Resistance

Narrative resistance can also include silence. Many young Muslims did not 'want to know' or talk too much about the IS or other extremist groups. They felt that these groups did not deserve their attention, and they tried to ignore them to make a political statement. As Presser (2013, p. 119) emphasises, that which is not said speak volumes.[8] Many young Muslims also considered detailed knowledge of groups such as the IS, al-Qaeda, al-Shabaab or Taliban to be redundant and were frustrated over the expectation that Muslims should distance themselves from terrorism committed in the name of Islam. For example, Amina, an eighteen-year-old Norwegian–Somali woman, explained that the constant pressure to reject jihadism was exhausting, but she said that she had found a solution:

> *Now, I don't care anymore. I don't feel like explaining. It's one thing when a person asks you about something, but it annoyed me when it was always brought up during class. It was always the most, like, extreme stuff, like, 'What do you think, Amina?,' and I'm, like, 'Out of all thirty students, why do you ask me?,' get it? It was very frustrating. It was like you were supposed to have opinions about everything, and maybe, like, you didn't know. It was, like, 'No, a Muslim must have an already complete identity and know everything from A to Z.' So, it was sort of like, 'No!'*

Amina's story shows how the pressures to know a great deal about or to denounce jihadism sometimes resulted in Muslims attempting to disregard the subject entirely. Ahmed, a twenty-four-year-old Norwegian–Afghani man, expressed a similar point of view, saying, 'I don't think they represent Islam, and I'm not even interested in reading about them. So, why should I waste any energy on it?' Abdul, a twenty-one-year-old Norwegian–Kurdish man, also reflected this attitude when asked about the IS and radicalisation on the internet:

---

[8] See also her chapter in this volume.

> *I don't remember any websites because I want to block it. I keep away from it. I don't remember any websites. I don't remember, I'm so terrible with those names. Because they don't have any relevance in my life, get it? So, that's why I don't put any emphasis on it. I just put it in the trashcan in my memory.*

Abdul proceeded to discuss theological questions in Islam and elaborated between right and wrong. However, when asked in detail about jihadist organisations, he had problems recollecting details:

> A: *I've probably heard a lot, but I don't involve myself with it, but I'm just, like, 'Oh no, not this again.' So, it's like that. It's not like I involve myself with it and 'It's so interesting now, I'm going on jihad' [laughter]. I'm not exactly like that.*
>
> I: *No, you 'delete it from your memory' and don't bother with it?*
>
> A: *Yes, it's not so… It's not relevant. And it's not relevant in my everyday life. Why should I care about wrong knowledge? That's just stupid.*

Abdul's reply can be viewed as another example of how intertwined the different counternarratives in narrative resistance are. When he stated that he does not care about jihadist organisations, the reason he offered was that they have 'wrong knowledge,' thus emphasising their faulty theological command. He also makes a sarcastic joke in the middle of a narrative emphasising the importance of ignoring extremist organisations. Most importantly, however, jihadi rhetoric was viewed as either irrelevant or wrong, and many young Muslims therefore did not want to waste energy on remembering details or refuting the religious claims promoted by such organisations, even when the young people clearly disagreed. This refusal can be described as resistance by silencing. Along with humour and ridicule, it is an important – but hitherto undescribed – way of rejecting extremism.

As demonstrated above, in a narrative analysis, counternarrative forms are analytically separable categories that are nevertheless closely intertwined. The close relationship between these forms of narrative resistance can be observed in the way in which the young Muslims alternated between them in our interviews. This was even the case for silencing. Some participants who stated that they really did not want to talk about extremists could subsequently proceed to talk about them at length. Silencing as resistance can therefore be viewed as narrative resistance in two different ways. First, it is 'actual' silencing, where these organisations are ignored and not talked about. Second, it is a more explicit counternarrative verbally stating that these organisations are so obscure that they do not merit any attention. This kind of silencing was closely associated with other insults and othering more generally.

Conclusion

Interviews with young Norwegian Muslims reveal a broad narrative repertoire for rejecting religious extremism. The counternarratives they told reflect general forms of narrative resistance that carry out very different types of work for the narrator. Factual counternarratives calmly and factually explain that the other group is wrong. Such stories appeal to the mind and show that the narrators are intellectually 'above' their opponents. Emotional counternarratives, on the other hand, come with and appeal to the passions. They often include derogatory terms and familiar storied characters to construct an 'other' who is evil, mad or weak. Humorous counternarratives consist of all kinds of jokes and snubs intended to be funny. Using humour makes it easier to talk about difficult topics and removes some of the gravity in sensitive discussions; furthermore, it is a way of demonstrating superiority and entertaining audiences through both stories and humorous narrative performances. Finally, silencing as resistance or a more explicit narrative about not wanting to talk about particular people, organisations or topics is a way of denying them significance in society, attention and, not the least, meaning in the narrators' own lives.

The narrative resistance and counternarratives revealed in this chapter can be viewed as both 'narratives of gentle defiance and resistance' (Andrews, 2004, p. 5). For the young Muslims whom we interviewed, it was common to alternate between seriously and factually rejecting the claims of jihadists and insulting, making fun of, or even completely ignoring them; sometimes, these strategies changed within a short period of time. Some of these narrative responses lean more towards active resistance, while others may be better described as gentle defiance. However, we argue that their prominence across narratives and the spontaneity with which they were shared suggests that they were of great importance to the narrators. Even the attempts to ignore extremist organisations and rhetoric were clearly driven more by deep discontent than by ignorance, which is the main reason why we describe such attempts as important forms of resistance to extremism.

A possible critique of our argument is that we know little of what happens outside interviews, and that the stories we have identified are produced in the interview setting for the researcher. Although reasonable, such critique shows little sensitivity to the social character of narratives. People have a limited number of stories to their disposal, and the ones they have are co-constructed or sometimes even determined by the society and community they live in (Foucault, 1970). Although interviewees strategically amend stories within interviews, it is difficult, if not impossible, to 'invent' new narratives on the spot to please interviewers. We believe that the strong emotions displayed in our interviews revealed how much was at stake for the narrator. The overall strength and magnitude of the counternarratives we identified speak clearly to the depth and significance of opposition to extremism in Muslim communities. These qualities also suggest that the Muslim community has 'already developed narrative tools that render it largely resistant to the radicalisation process' (Joosse et al., 2015, p. 815). While this does not imply immunity against radicalisation, these counternarratives are powerful resources in an ongoing narrative struggle concerning the meaning of Islam in Muslim communities.

We believe that narrative criminological studies can benefit from delving more into counternarratives (Presser, 2018, p. 144). Large qualitative data sampling achieved through team research is one way to do this. It demands more resources than smaller interview-based studies, but if one has the time and money, having a large sample will make it possible to paint a broader picture of what is studied and to achieve more variation. It can also make it easier to decide which stories are important in a particular group, culture or society, and avoid speculations about stories being told because of specific interview constellations. Most importantly, a research team consisting of individuals with different expertise, background and knowledge is an invaluable resource and source of inspiration when doing interviews or ethnography and when discussing and interpreting preliminary results.

Studying counternarratives can be helpful for understanding why crime, and especially serious violence, is *not* the rule. It can also help make all kinds of stigmatised populations less marginal by showing the many ways in which crime and harm are 'fought from within' – and the potential dangers of such opposition. Extreme othering has the potential to licence disproportional harm in the name of good. Emphasising positive resistance and the people and processes that constrain harm can help in moving away from the overall negative focus of most criminology studies. In its search for the causes of crime, much research in criminology has been overlooking societal resistance and opposition to harmful action. The multitude of ways in which crime and harm is rejected should be at the core for anyone interested in understanding what instigates, sustains or impacts avoidance of harmful action.

References

Ahmed, S., & Matthes, J. (2017). Media representation of Muslims and Islam from 2000 to 2015: A meta-analysis. *International Communication Gazette, 79*(3), 219–244. doi:10.1177/1748048516656305

Andersen, J. C., & Sandberg, S. (2018). Islamic state propaganda: Between social movement framing and subcultural provocation. *Terrorism and Political Violence*, 1–21. doi:10.1080/09546553.2018.1484356

Andrews, M. (2002). Memories of mother: Counter-narratives of early maternal influence. *Narrative Inquiry, 12*(1), 7–21. doi:10.1075/ni.12.1.04and

Andrews, M. (2004). Counter-narratives and the power to oppose. In M. Bamberg & M. Andrews (Eds.), *Considering counter-narratives: Narrating, resisting, making sense* (pp. 1–7). Amsterdam: John Benjamins Publishing Company.

Aristotles. (1991). *On Rhetoric. A theory of civic discourse*. Oxford: Oxford University Press.

Aydin, C. (2017). *The idea of the Muslim world: A global intellectual history*. Cambridge, MA: Harvard University Press.

Bahari, M., & Hassan, M. H. (2014). The black flag myth: An analysis from Hadith studies. *Counter Terrorist Trends and Analysis, 6*(8), 15–20.

Bamberg, M. (2004). Considering counter narratives. In M. Bamberg & M. Andrews (Eds), *Considering counter-narratives: Narrating, resisting, making sense* (pp. 351–372). Amsterdam: John Benjamins Publishing Company.

Barlas, A. (2002). *"Believing in women" in Islam: Unreading patriarchal interpretations of the Qur'an*. Austin, TX: University of Texas Press.

Baumann, R. (1986). *Story, performance, and event. Contextual studies of oral narrative*. Cambridge: Cambridge University Press.

Bucerius, S. (2013). Becoming a "trusted outsider": Gender, ethnicity, and inequality in ethnographic research. *Journal of Contemporary Ethnography*, *42*(6), 690–721. doi:10.1177/0891241613497747

Byman, D. (2015). *Al Qaeda, the Islamic state, and the global jihadist movement: What everyone needs to know*. Oxford: Oxford University Press.

Copes, H. (2016). A narrative approach to studying symbolic boundaries among drug users: A qualitative meta-synthesis. *Crime, Media, Culture*, *12*(2), 193–213. doi:10.1177/1741659016641720

Copes, H., Hochstetler, A., & Williams, J. P. (2008). "We weren't like no regular dope fiends": Negotiating hustler and crackhead identities. *Social Problems*, *55*(1), 524–270. doi:10.1525/sp.2008.55.2.254

Cragin, R. K. (2014). Resisting violent extremism: A conceptual model for non-radicalization. *Terrorism and Political Violence*, *26*(2), 337–353. doi:10.1080/09546553.2012.714820

Damsa, D., & Ugelvik, T. (2017). A difference that makes a difference? Reflexivity and researcher effects in an all-foreign prison. *International Journal of Qualitative Methods*, *16*(1), 1–10. doi:10.1177/1609406917713132

Davies, C. (1988). Stupidity and rationality: Jokes from the iron cage. In C. Powell & G. E. C. Paton (Eds.), *Humor in society. Resistance and control*. London: Macmillan Press.

Dervin, F. (2012). Cultural identity, representation and othering. In J. Jackson (Ed.), *The Routledge handbook of language and intercultural communication*. Abingdon: Routledge.

Ekman, M. (2015). Online islamophobia and the politics of fear: Manufacturing the green scare. *Ethnic and Racial Studies*, *38*(11), 1986–2002. doi:10.1080/01419870.2015.1021264

van Es, M. A. (2018). Muslims denouncing violent extremism. *Journal of Muslims in Europe*, *7*(2), 142–166. doi:10.1163/22117954-12341374

Essers, C., & Benschop, Y. (2009). Muslim businesswomen doing boundary work: The negotiation of Islam, gender and ethnicity within entrepreneurial context. *Human Relations*, *62*(3), 403–423. doi:10.1177/0018726708101042

Fleetwood, J. (2016). Narrative habitus: Thinking through structure/agency in the narratives of offenders. *Crime, Media, Culture*, *12*(2), 173–192. doi:10.1177/1741659016653643

Foucault, M. (1970). *The order of things*. New York, NY: Pantheon Books.

Gruner, C. R. (2000). *The game of humor: A comprehensive theory of why we laugh*. New Brunswick, NJ: Transaction Publishers.

Halverson, J. R., Goodall, H. L., & Corman, S. R. (2011). *Master narratives of Islamist extremism*. New York, NY: Palgrave Macmillan.

Hegghammer, T. (2017). *Jihadi culture: The art of social practices of militant Islamists*. Cambridge: Cambridge University Press.

Jackson, R. (2007). Constructing enemies: 'Islamic terrorism' in political and academic discourse in political and academic discourse. *Government and Opposition, 42*(3), 394–426. doi:10.1111/j.1477-7053.2007.00229.x

Joosse, P., Bucerius, S. M., & Thompson, S. K. (2015). Narratives and counter-narratives: Somali-Canadians on recruitment as foreign fighters to Al-Shabaab. *British Journal of Criminology, 55*(4), 811–832.

Kabbani, S. M. H. (2006). Jihad in Islam. In V. Cornell (Ed.), *Voices of Islam* (pp. 205–256). Westport, CT: Greenwood Publishing.

Karmon, E. (2015). Islamic state and al-Qaeda competing for hearts & minds. *Perspectives on Terrorism, 9*(2), 71–79.

Kearns, E., Betus, A., & Lemieux, A. (2017). Why do some terrorist attacks receive more media attention than others? *Justice Quarterly.* doi.org/10.2139/ssrn.2928138

Laclau, E., & Mouffe, C. (1985). *Hegemony and socialist strategy.* London: Verso.

Lamont, M., & Molnar, V. (2002). The study of boundaries in the social sciences. *Annual Review of Sociology, 28*(1), 167–195. doi:10.1146/annurev.soc.28.110601.141107

Leuprecht, C., Hataley, T., Moskalenko, S., & McCauley, C. (2009). Winning the battle but losing the war? Narrative and counter-narratives strategy. *Perspectives on Terrorism, 3*(2), 25–35.

Lynch, O. H. (2002). Humorous communication: Finding a place for humor in communication research. *Communication Theory, 12*(4), 423–445. doi:10.1111/j.1468-2885.2002.tb00277.x

Maidment, J. (2017). Muslims must do more than just 'condemn' terror attacks, Sajid Javid says. *The Telegraph,* June 5. Retrieved from https://www.telegraph.co.uk/news/2017/06/05/muslims-must-do-just-condemn-terror-attacks-sajid-javid-says/. Accessed on November 10, 2018.

Martin, R. A. (2007). *The psychology of humor: An integrative approach.* Burlington, VT: Elsevier.

Maruna, S. (2001). *Making good. How ex-convicts reform and rebuild their lives.* Washington, DC: American Psychological Association Press.

McCants, W. (2015). *The ISIS apocalypse: The history, strategy, and doomsday vision of the Islamic state.* New York, NY: St. Martin's Press.

Meijer, R. (2009). *Global Salafism: Islam's new religious movement.* London: Hurst Publishers.

Mythen, G., Walklate, S., & Khan, F. (2012). 'Why should we have to prove we're alright?': Counter-terrorism, risk and partial securities. *Sociology, 47*(2), 383–398. doi:10.1177/0038038512444811

Østeby, L., & Dalgard, A. B. (2017, November 22). Det religiøse mangfoldet. 4 prosent Muslimer i Norge? SSB. Retrieved from https://www.ssb.no/befolkning/artikler-og-publikasjoner/4-prosent-muslimer-i-norge. Accessed on April 26, 2018.

Page, M., Challita, L., & Harris, A. (2011). Al Qaeda in the Arabian peninsula: Framing narratives and prescriptions. *Studies in Conflict & Terrorism, 23*(2), 150–172. doi:10.1080/09546553.2010.526039

Picart, C. J. S. (2015). "Jihad cool/jihad chic": The roles of the internet and imagined relations in the self-radicalization of colleen LaRose (jihad Jane). *Societies, 5*(2), 354–383. doi:10.3390/soc5020354

Polletta, F., Chen, P. C. B., Gardner, B. G., & Motes, A. (2011). The sociology of storytelling. *Annual Review of Sociology, 37,* 109–130.

Presser, L. (2013). *Why we harm*. New Brunswick, NJ and London: Rutgers University Press.
Presser, L. (2018). *Inside story. How narratives drive mass harm*. Oakland, CA: University of California Press.
Presser, L., & Sandberg, S. (2015). Introduction: What is the story? In L. Presser & S. Sandberg (Eds.), *Narrative criminology: Understanding stories of crime* (pp. 1–22). New York, NY: New York University Press.
Propp, V. (1968). *Morphology of the folk tale*. Austin, TX: University of Texas Press.
Sageman, M. (2008). *Leaderless jihad: Terror networks in the twenty-first century*. Philadelphia, PA: University of Pennsylvania Press.
Sandberg, S. (2016). The importance of stories untold: Life-story, event-story and trope. *Crime, Media, Culture*, *12*(2), 153–171. doi:10.1177/1741659016639355
Sandberg, S., Andersen, J. C., Gasser, T. L. U., Linge, M., Mohamed, I. A. A., Shokr, S., & Tutenges, S. (2018). *Unge Muslimske Stemmer: Om Tro og Ekstremisme*. [*Young muslim voices: On faith and extremism.*] Oslo: Oslo University Press.
Sandberg, S., & Tutenges, S. (2018). Laughter in stories of crime and tragedy: The importance of humor for marginalized populations. *Social Problems*, 1–16. doi:10.1093/socpro/spy019
Shaffer, R. (2016). Jihad and counter-jihad in Europe: Islamic radicals, right-wing extremists, and counter-terrorism responses. *Terrorism and Political Violence*, *28*(2), 383–394. doi:10.1080/09546553.2016.1140538
Talbot, J., Bibace, R., Bokhour, B., & Bamberg, M. (1996). Affirmation and resistance of dominant discourses: The rhetorical construction of pregnancy. *Journal of Narrative and Life History*, *6*(3), 225–251. doi:10.1075/jnlh.6.3.02aff
Ugelvik, T. (2014). 'Be a man. Not a bitch.' Snitching the inmate code and the narrative reconstruction of masculinity in a Norwegian prison. In I. Lander, S. Ravn, & N. Jon (Eds.), *Masculinities in the criminological field* (pp. 69–82). London & New York, NY: Routledge.
Ugelvik, T. (2015). The rapist and the proper criminal: The exclusion of immoral others as narrative work on the self. In L. Presser & S. Sandberg (Eds.), *Narrative criminology: Understanding stories of crime* (pp. 23–41). New York, NY & London: New York University Press.
Vestel, V., & Bakken, A. (2016). *Holdninger til ekstremisme. Resultater fra Ung i Oslo 2015*. NOVA/2016.
Von Sikorski, C., Schmuck, D., Matthes, J., & Binder, A. (2017). "Muslims are not terrorists": Islamic state coverage, journalistic differentiation between terrorism and Islam, fear reactions, and attitudes toward Muslims. *Mass Communication & Society*, *20*(6), 825–848. doi:10.1080/15205436.2017.1342131

Chapter 23

Researching Sex Work: Doing Decolonial, Intersectional Narrative Analysis

Floretta Boonzaier

Introduction

Contexts of deepening global and local inequalities require research approaches that not only humanise those who continue to exist and survive on the margins, but that explicitly advance social justice. This chapter takes a narrative criminological approach to the study of violence in the lives of sex workers in South Africa, arguing that it has much to offer for our understanding of how individual lives and experiences are shaped by broader categories of power and privilege. Specifically, decolonial, intersectional narrative analysis counteracts the marginalising tendencies of some approaches to research. The approach offered here also speaks back to the ways in which those on the margins (especially poor, black and marginalised women) continue to be (mis)represented in the knowledge-making machinery. The chapter begins by pointing to the ways in which research has been implicated in further marginalising oppressed groups and doing little to advance social justice. Next, I make a case for decolonial, intersectional, black and African feminist approaches to narrative criminological research. The third section of the chapter provides an analytic example of a decolonial, intersectional approach to narrative criminology using data from interviews with sex workers. The conclusion considers the contributions decolonial, intersectional feminist work can make to advancing narrative criminology, especially work with victims that might advance social justice.

Decolonising/Rehumanising Research

Contexts of increasing inequality, violence against and marginalisation of particular sectors of society call for research that can offer visibility to those marginalised and recognise the ways in which power intersects to shape the experiences of those who live precarious lives on the margins. Research that opens opportunities for shifting the status quo is more urgent than ever. Furthermore, we must recognise the ways in which the knowledge economy continues to exclude and disempower particular groups of people. Research, as a means of knowledge production that occurs mostly in academic institutions, has been recognised as being a dehumanising endeavour. As Walker (1981) states: 'Rarely do people emerge from our studies as people with their dignity intact. Worse still the report may read as though the evaluator was the most intelligent person present' (p. 148). Some social science research approaches have been implicated in perpetuating marginalisation, doing little more than collecting, repackaging and recirculating stories of pain, oppression and damage without explicitly addressing questions of social justice (Tuck & Wayne Yang, 2014). As well, the academy may be considered a colonising endeavour in the ways in which it utilises research participants in the service of the careers of individual academics (Paris & Winn, 2014; Tuck & Wayne Yang, 2014). A range of disciplines, including criminology, have been recognised as rooted in long colonial histories (Agozino, 2003). Recognising these histories and their continuing problematics is especially important when we are working with those whose lives have been shaped by colonial patriarchy and apartheid and its epistemic and material violence (Irwin & Umemoto, 2016).

In this chapter I argue for a decolonial, intersectional approach to research in narrative criminology and to the emerging field of narrative victimology (Walklate, Maher, McCulloch, Fitz-Gibbon, & Beavis, 2018) that goes beyond just the analysis of the data – although this aspect is foregrounded in the chapter. This approach builds on feminist research principles and practices that recognise the ways in which power and politics play out in knowledge production, and that centres the experiences of those who have been traditionally excluded, especially women (Boonzaier & Shefer, 2006). At the same time, the approach I articulate centres decolonial, black and African feminist theory and praxis. The term intersectionality emerged from Black US-based feminists (Collins, 1990; Crenshaw, 1991) to call attention to the ways in which social identities and experiences intersect to produce different outcomes for individuals and how these identities and experiences are shaped by power and sociostructural oppressions. African feminist approaches have also always been concerned with questions of intersectionality – even though not explicitly identified as such. African feminism has been described as involving ongoing debates about identity and culture (Msimang, 2002), has been 'mindful of the nexi of power relations at play in black women's lives whilst acknowledging the agency with which we engage with them' (Gqola, 2001, p. 12) and centred on the experiences of African women. The approach has additionally foregrounded an understanding of African women's experiences within African contexts of colonisation and imperialism that have so fundamentally shaped the history and politics on the continent. It considers the political, economic, historical and cultural contexts to be important for understanding gender and women's experiences (Kiguwa, 2004). Along the same lines, decolonial feminist approaches recognise the continuation of coloniality in contemporary times, as well as the important ways in which the process of colonisation involved racialisation and the simultaneous process of gendered subordination (Lugones, 2007, 2010).

Advancing a Decolonial, Intersectional Agenda for Narrative Criminology

At the same time that intersectional and African feminist approaches are important for challenging the ways in which oppressed groups are presented, the decolonising potential of narrative research has been acknowledged for its ability to highlight the multiplicity of contexts, the complexity of human existence and for disrupting power relationships (Sonn, Stevens, & Duncan, 2013). Historically marginalised groups, for example, often gain visibility and political traction through crafting public narratives about their oppression. It is often personal stories about everyday challenges or oppressions that capture the public imagination and that can advance social and policy change. This point was powerfully made in Walklate et al.'s (2018) analysis of how the narrative of Rosy Batty, whose son had been killed by his father, had significantly shaped Australian policy on family violence.

Narrative research, including narrative criminology, like feminist approaches has the potential to make visible previously silenced experiences and for these to be represented on narrators' own terms. As Banister et al. (2011) argue, 'The presentation of the self in narrative can be a source of enormous pride for narrators, particularly people whose stories have been ignored or stifled' (p. 138). Riessman (2008) further argues that narratives may be strategic, functional and purposeful, allowing narrators to rewrite past events that may have been painful, present a particular argument from their perspective, or advance an argument for political or social change. In these ways, narratives are understood to restore agency to the tellers (Parker, 2005; Sonn et al., 2013), while at the same time advancing feminist research and political agency.

Narratives have also been argued to be closely linked to the construction of identity, in narrative psychology, for example (Murray, 2003), as well as in narrative criminology (Fleetwood, 2015; McNay, 1999). The stories we tell about ourselves and our experiences in the world construct particular versions of ourselves, whether as coherent or consistent narratives, or as those deployed for strategic and functional purposes, for example to position ourselves as particular kinds of people in particular situations. The links between narratives and the construction of identity hold the potential for advancing an intersectional, decolonial, feminist research agenda. It is understood that the self is revealed and constructed through the narration of personal stories (Murray, 2003). These personal stories thus hold the potential to disrupt hegemonic scripts and discourses and so hold transformative power for the ways in which people come to see themselves and others (see Boonzaier, 2014b). These are especially important for black, poor women and other groups in society that continue to be oppressed, not only by the dire material circumstances that mark their lives but also by the circulating, stigmatising scripts about them and their lives. A feminist, decolonial, intersectional agenda for narrative criminology can thus be advanced through acknowledgement of the transformative power of narratives to challenge hegemony and, through so doing, to build community (Rappaport, 1995) – explicitly linking the personal and the political.

Narrative criminology has much to offer for our understanding of how individual lives and experiences are shaped by broader categories of power, privilege and subordination that may resonate with and emerge from histories of imperialism, colonialism and institutionalised racism. Narrative criminological approaches are important for showing not only how individual lives, behaviours and histories are recounted and accounted for, but also for illustrating how these link to subjective identities and possible action (Presser, 2009). The potential for articulating which particular narratives advance which actions and foreclose others offers productive ground for narrative criminologists and scholars concerned with theorising violence. On the one hand, taking an intersectional narrative criminological approach to understanding the experiences of women in sex work is important, given that sex work is considered 'criminal' behaviour. On the other hand, the research overwhelmingly shows that women involved in sex work are frequently poor women struggling to survive (Phoenix, 2000) and are often victims of multiple forms of oppression (Gould & Fick, 2008; Huysamen, 2011; Wojcicki & Malala, 2001), making it especially important to take an intersectional narrative approach to their experiences of victimisation. In addition, a decolonial approach is important because it allows us to see the historical roots of the contemporary oppressions faced by poor women sex workers that might otherwise be erased. What kinds of stories, for example, do women tell about why/how they came to be involved in sex work? How do they 'talk themselves into' (Presser, 2012, p. 9) and 'out of' engaging in sex work? And how are their identities, as women, mothers, partners and sex workers, implicated in and achieved via their narratives? The latter question brings to the fore the ways in which gender is implicated in narratives told. As Miller, Carbone-Lopez, and Gunderman (2015) illustrated in their work with women methamphetamine users in prison, narratives convey important messages around gender and gender is also 'accomplished' through narrative. Following from West and Zimmerman, Miller et al. see gender as a situated accomplishment, performed through narrative. Indeed, the performance of gender through narrative has been illustrated in work with offenders of serious crimes in prison (Presser, 2005), with perpetrators of intimate partner violence (Boonzaier, 2014a) and with men who buy sex (Huysamen, 2015).

Narrative criminology offers an understanding of the 'social nature' of stories, of 'when, why, and how stories come to be told, heard, and which resources speakers can draw upon' (Fleetwood, 2015, p. 372). In addition, it pays attention to structure and agency, illuminating how women subjectively make meaning of their experiences while showing how these are shaped and produced by social–structural systems and circumstances (Fleetwood, 2015). This issue of structure and agency has also been taken up in Phoenix's (2000) work on what she calls 'prostitute identities' (p. 37) – challenging the false dualism set up in sex work research (and criminological research more broadly) between agency (suggesting that sex work is women's choice) and structure (suggesting that women's choices are constrained by social–structural factors). As Fleetwood (2015) has argued: 'Narrative criminology offers tools for conceptualizing and researching the complex ways in which gender (as both a material and discursive structure) shapes women's lawbreaking' (p. 383). Phoenix (2000) similarly argues that it is through the creative exploration of discourses of meaning that we can work with the complex interplay between 'material and social conditions' and the 'symbolic landscape' (p. 53) to understand the ways in which women's sustained involvement in sex work are shaped by agency (and a lack thereof) and social–structural constraints (and facilitators). In this chapter a decolonial, intersectional narrative criminological approach is taken to understand the experiences of women who have chosen to break the law but also situating these choices within histories of oppression and growing contexts of inequality, shaped by gender, race, class and other intersecting factors – 'connecting (women's) personal agency and social structure through attention to personal narratives, and public discourses about gender and crime' (Fleetwood, 2015, p. 384).

Producing Knowledge in Decolonial, Intersectional Narrative Criminology

Feminist research approaches foreground the political nature of the research. They understand that research is embedded within multiple contexts and relations of power and that inquiry demands an ethically and politically reflexive stance from us as researchers (Boonzaier & Shefer, 2006). This stance is one that shapes how we ask the questions that guide our research. In the construction of the research questions, for example, researchers should be aware of the racist and sexist othering of marginalised groups (see Boonzaier, 2018). The implications of asking particular research questions that continue to frame oppressed groups as damaged and dysfunctional should thus be avoided. In addition, from a narrative theoretical perspective it is useful to think about the product of our research as a/the narrative/s we produce about the work we had undertaken. What kinds of stories do researchers seek to collect or tell in their work? What kinds of assumptions are embedded in the stories we tell? Thus, a decolonial, intersectional feminist narrative perspective requires one to think carefully about how the narratives we produce as researchers may be taken up to advance particular antitransformative agendas that may further marginalise and disadvantage oppressed groups.

This politically aware and ethically reflective stance should also be centred in the ways in which we choose to collect data from our research participants and the particular kinds of interventions we make in the encounters we have with people. Are we exploiting them, being invasive, mining for data without an awareness of their material and other needs and challenges? Are we centring our questions and concerns without being mindful of what kinds of stories participants are interested telling? What will our research encounters do for the participants we work with? Will it leave them feeling further disempowered? What promises have we made to participants? How will we honour these? These are some of the questions that must be addressed when attempting to produce knowledge from a perspective that centres feminist, decolonial and intersectional narrative approaches.

Doing Decolonial, Intersectional Narrative Analysis

The approach I am articulating in this chapter develops in different phases. These include: (Phase 1) An analysis of narrative content; (Phase 2) An analysis of decolonial, intersectional power; (Phase 3) Reading against the grain: Articulating resistance; and (Phase 4) Crafting a plurivocal narrative. These phases are guided by different approaches but centre a decolonial, intersectional lens. While the reader might like to follow these as 'phases' and employ them as a starting point for their analyses, it is important to acknowledge that a 'grounded', intuitive and credible analysis involves more than following a series of 'steps'. Our ways of knowing, our intuition and hunches about our research are important too for producing analyses that are situated in and would 'sit well' with our feminist politics and agendas and that would also be meaningful for the individuals and communities with whom we work.

I articulate the analytic approach I am expounding in this chapter through an analysis of interviews conducted with women engaged in sex work in Cape Town, South Africa. Specifically, the data drawn from two sets of interviews. The first (in 2011), were interviews with 11 women, recruited through a support group who considered themselves to be in the process of exiting from sex work. The support group, called Embrace Dignity, was established with the explicit purpose of facilitating women's exit from sex work and was founded with the understanding that sex work is a form of violence against women. The women ranged in age from 27 to 51 years old. These interviews were conducted by Monique Huysamen.[1] Women were asked, in unstructured interviews, about their experiences of violence in the sex industry, using the prompt: 'I would like to hear about your experiences of working in prostitution, perhaps you could begin by telling me how you started prostitution' (Huysamen, 2011, p. 12). In the second set of interviews from 2014, with 11 women (ages 31–51 years), they were asked specifically about their experiences of intimate partner violence and its intersections with their involvement in sex work, using the prompt: 'I would like you to tell me the story of your intimate relationship – how you met, how the relationship progressed, the challenges you experienced, that sort of thing' (Bartlett, 2014, p. 11). This question was followed up with: 'What connections can you draw between your experiences in the relationship and the work you do?' (Bartlett, 2014, p. 11). For the most part, these women were still involved in the sex industry and using the support of a sex worker rights organisation. These women were recruited via an agency called Sex Workers Education and Advocacy Taskforce (SWEAT), a group specifically established to lobby for the rights of sex workers and to provide them various forms of support during their engagement in sex work. These interviews were conducted by Elretha Bartlett.[2] Both sets of interviews progressed in relatively open-ended, unstructured formats, taking a

---

[1] Monique Husyamen was a postgraduate student in Psychology at the time the interviews were conducted.
[2] Elretha Bartlett was a postgraduate student in Psychology at the time the interviews were conducted.

conversational approach to allow for women to make meaning of their experiences and situations through the act of narration.

While both interviewers were young, middle-class, white women, all but one of the women interviewed were black.[3] Consistent with the sex workers generally, especially those who work on the street, the women interviewed were also all living in poverty. These race and class dynamics inevitability shaped the interviews and the kinds of stories that were told. A further contextual factor shaping the interviews would have been the agencies' divergent stances on sex work/prostitution. Both agencies take an explicitly political and firm stance on the nature of women's participation in sex work – each coming down strongly on a different side of the debate concerning sex work. In practical terms this means that they formulate their advocacy work around either women's agency and the idea that sex work is a choice (SWEAT) or the idea that women are compelled into 'prostitution' which is also a form of violence against women (Embrace Dignity).

I reanalyse these interviews here as someone who has had longstanding relationships with both agencies, and as a black feminist with a long history of feminist work on gender and sexual violence in South Africa. I had also, at the time, suggested the possibility of this work to both students and supervised the research projects they produced, with the agreement being made that the data would be available for reanalysis by any of the project participants. It is also important to note that the research questions in the original work undertaken (i.e. an exploration of the harms women encounter in prostitution (Huysamen, 2011) and an exploration of sex worker's experiences of intimate partner violence (Bartlett, 2014)) emerged at the request of the two organisations concerned (Embrace Dignity and SWEAT, respectively).

Phase One: An Analysis of Narrative Content

The thematic narrative analysis approach articulated by Riessman (2008) focuses on the content of particular narratives. As far as possible, attention is accorded to the holistic meaning of narratives and some attention is paid to time, place and historical context. The strength of thematic narrative analysis is that it foregrounds the content of participants' narratives and, in so doing, foregrounds the subjectivity and agency of participants (Riessman, 2008). A thematic narrative analysis is concerned with the meanings that stories have to narrators and the possibilities for creating social identity, group belonging and collective action. It also makes links between lifeworlds and power relations and inequalities – strengthening its synergies with feminist decolonial and intersectional approaches.

The first phase of this analysis takes Riessman's thematic narrative analysis as a starting point, exploring common narratives within and across the interview transcripts. This involves intimately familiarising oneself with the data to obtain a

---

[3]'Black' here is used to refer to all groups of people oppressed by and discriminated against through apartheid legislation in South Africa.

Table 23.1. Phase One: Useful Analytic Questions.

- What overall sense do I get from reading or listening to each transcript?
- What emotional reactions are evoked in reflecting on the interview interaction or afterwards?
- How does each interview start, unfold and end?
- What would I have liked to hear more about?
- What are the narratives being told? What are the themes in the transcript?
- What kind of narrative is it?
- What narratives appear common amongst participants? What are the differences?

Source: Adapted from Fraser (2004), Esterberg (2002) and Parker (2005).

sense of the different thematic areas that characterise each story. In relation to the project on sex work, the overarching questions addressed in this first phase ask: What stories do women tell about sex work and intimate relationships? (Table 23.1).

In the early stages of the first phase of this analysis the following thematic areas around women's experiences as sex work emerged. Women overwhelmingly told stories about multiple forms of violence in their lives. These included stories of physical violence; of economic abuse; of verbal violence; of psychological violence; and of sexual violence. As women narrated these experiences of violence they also showed how these multiple experiences overlapped. Women also articulated experiences of violence from the different men they encountered in their lives, namely clients, partners, the police and others.

Intersecting violence: partners and clients

This section briefly presents women's narratives about violence to give a flavour of their complexity; the following section discusses methodological issues. Women's narrations of their experiences as women who sell sex and as women in intimate relationships illuminate the overwhelming presence of violence in their lives. This violence was experienced from intimate partners, clients and sometimes from the police or others. Across the interviews, there were numerous stories told about being subjected to violence, in multiple forms. In addition to countless recollections of physical violence, participants also recounted many events that involved economic exploitation from clients, including refusing to pay at all or refusing to pay the agreed upon payment, and sometimes theft or robbery.

> *But in this business sometimes you (just) give up, especially when the men hurt you. I wasn't only hurt once. I was hurt a lot on the street. A lot! There in Rhodes they drop me there in the middle of the night. You know how dark it is? I had to find my way back to town again. Then the other one, he take your shoes and everything and leave you just there in the park. One day, I will never forget*

> that night, he was a coloured[4] guy, he took me to Malmesbury and dropped me there. He finished sexually, have sex with me and just said, 'Let me go take your money.' I thought, 'Why is he leaving me here and take the money? I must go with him.' When I go with him to the car, he was showing me the gun and just drive off. My shoes, my bag, everything... I had to walk from Malmesbury and Malmesbury is FAR! I got a lift (from) an OLD man. Even this old man is a Xhosa [...] So this Xhosa man still wants business. I didn't have (any) other option. I (had) to make business with him just to get out of that place. But at least he (gave) me money. (Jamiela).[5]

Jamiela begins her story by talking about the many instances of her being 'hurt' by men 'on the street', placing emphasis on the frequency of the harm ('A lot!'). She quickly moves to a description that complicates our understanding of harm to include harm beyond the physical; by choosing to talk about being robbed and left in deserted locations, compounding her risk of potentially experiencing further violence on the street. Many women narrated their experiences of being robbed by clients and/or being dropped off in isolated locations. Jamiela's story illustrates how multiple types of violence can intersect in one scenario. The economic violence that Jamiela experienced increased her vulnerability to sexual violence, as she felt she had 'no other option' but to 'do business' with a second man in order to obtain a lift back to Cape Town.

In women's descriptions of being subjected to violence and humiliation, they centre their identities as sex workers. The violence they experience, whether it is being subjected to psychological abuse or physical beatings by a partner, rape by a client or police officer, being robbed and dropped off in deserted places, being forced to perform degrading acts by a client, or being ostracised and humiliated by members of their communities, are constructed as misogynistic forms of punishment for their involvement in sex work, and simultaneously for their transgression of 'acceptable' notions of femininity, powerfully illustrated in Lindi's narrative below.

> Lindi: *And the guys like that they don't care, because what they do they first drug you. You must get drunk so that you mustn't know what is where, what is where, what is where. So I don't know. There are guys that are evil outside here. Other guys, they don't like this prostitution life. That is why they punish girls like that, they don't like it.*
>
> Interviewer: *So you think some guys pick up prostitutes because they against it?*

---

[4]The term 'coloured' is a racial term still commonly used to describe an apartheid-invented 'category' of oppressed people commonly understood to be of 'mixed ancestry'.
[5]Women who were interviewed are identified through the use of pseudonyms.

>Lindi: *They against that. In that very same time the other one experienced that from his wife.* [Interviewer: *Okay?*]
>
>Lindi: *The wife was a prostitute. The wife end up dead being a prostitute. Now he tell himself, 'you know, I hate somebody that is a prostitute. I hate a prostitute.'* [...]

Lindi's narrative above constructs an 'evil male predator', making little distinction between the man as a partner or the man as a client. She also powerfully conveys the misogyny in the violence perpetrated by 'the man' through repetition and emphasis on the word 'hate'. The significance of Lindi's narration of 'a life' in sex work is that she tells the listener that the extreme and frequent violence women are subjected to in sex work is not 'random' – it is intentional and explicitly gendered, directed at women, not only because they are women but because they are women who work on the streets.

Going against popular understandings of the safety and sanctuary that should be provided in intimate relationships, Faith below talks about the inability of women sex workers to negotiate condom use and sexual activity with intimate partners.

>Interviewer: *[after Faith talks about her lack of power in negotiation with her partner] So with clients you can negotiate condom use, but with your private relationship you can't?*
>
>Faith: *You can't negotiate much because he'd be like 'Who else are you sleeping with?' So the long-term relationships are more dangerous than sleeping with a client, because the client knows you're getting it for the money. But the long-term would not pay you as much and they'll wake up anytime and just open your legs. And you can't really stop them and say, 'Stop it.' Because I needed the shelter and I couldn't really fight or speak with him* [...]

In Faith's narration above there is an implicit message that one can expect to be subjected to violence from a client ('long-term relationships are more dangerous than sleeping with a client'). This construction was consistent with how other women in the research narrated their involvement in sex work – as dangerous and risky. It is also consistent with the 'men-as-expense symbolic landscape' (p. 48) crafted by the participants in Phoenix's research (2000), positioning any engagement with men as encompassing 'hidden costs' and risks.

Faith further amplifies several issues sex workers experience regarding health, safety and intimate relationships. Firstly, that insisting on condom use with an intimate partner can be complex if one's partner does not know about the sex work. Secondly, negotiating condom use and consent with a client is constructed as easier because there is a definitive limit on the interaction, whereas intimate partners, who spend time with the women on a daily basis, demand women's sexual availability. Making the same links between men and money that Phoenix (2000) found in her work, Faith constructs the intimate relationship as transactional too, like sex work but in the former she is unable to negotiate the timing of sexual activity as her partner likely views their relationship as him having 'ownership' of her body.

In their narrations women blur the boundaries between the violences 'at work' and 'at home'. This blurred boundary was evident in women's talk about being subjected to different kinds of violence. The example of verbal abuse is used below. The verbal abuse women pointed to in their narratives included being screamed, shouted, or sworn at, as well as being humiliated and degraded through the use of words.

> Interviewer: *[...] I'd like to know how your work influenced your relationship.*
>
> Camilla: *It actually made it a bit worse. Being a sex worker and being in a relationship, it doesn't ... it doesn't go hand-in-hand. It you have a partner and you stand on the road ... at the end of the day he doesn't have respect for you (because) he knows you're selling your body and because you have to sell your body. You sleep with different guys and when you come home your partner wants to sleep with you. And because your partner knows you're a prostitute, he treats you worse.*

Camilla's narrative above recalls the 'punishment' articulated by Lindi earlier, though she describes the violence as a result of the absence of 'respect'. Camilla, like other women in sex work (Phoenix, 2000), constructs her body as a commodity and as a result sex work is constructed as a job that lowers a woman's social value. The idea that women who sell sex have a 'lower' social value further perpetuates ideas that place sexuality at the centre of women's identities. When women's supposed and expected 'sexual purity' is 'violated' through her availability for sex work she is seen as having lost some of her worth as a woman, justifying violence against her.

Women's narrations about the links between their identities as sex workers and the violence they experience also suggests that, despite the multiple, intersecting and overlapping forms of violence they experience from a range of different men they encounter, an 'ideal victim' status may not be readily available to them. It has been established that ideas of victim worthiness are shaped by racialized, gendered and classed constructions, making the 'ideal' and 'innocent' victim someone identified as a white woman who is also heterosexual, middle-class, able-bodied and likely attractive (Jewkes, 2004). Women who more closely approximate the status of 'ideal victim' become more 'deserving' of public sympathy and also less likely to be blamed for their own victimisation. The status of an 'ideal victim' remains out of reach for the women interviewed, not only because of their involvement in sex work but also because, as poor black women, they wouldn't be deserving of sympathy anyway.

Thus far, paying close attention to the thematic content in women's narratives of violence allows for a reading of how (patriarchal and other forms of) power manifests in women's lives. Taking an inductive approach to the reading of women's narratives, simply answering the question – What is there? – allows us to see the overwhelming presence of violence in women's lives, as well as to see this as an aspect women themselves choose to foreground in their narrations.

Analysing intersecting 'violences'
Women's narrations of violence elucidate the entanglement between different types of violence. The women whose narratives we consider here, as in previous work, point to how violence of one 'type' cannot be considered in isolation of other 'types' (Boonzaier, 2014b), presenting a more complex understanding of what it means to be a victim of men's violence for the listener. Women's narratives also amplify how the larger issue of gendered oppression manifests in their lived experiences and their encounters with men.

In this first phase of the analysis we looked within and across the interview transcripts to assess the kinds of narratives told about violence. We read each woman's interview transcript multiple times to obtain a sense of what kinds of stories she told. These stories were coded and grouped to reflect different thematic areas that emerged from her interview. Once a strong sense of each individual transcript was obtained, we looked across interviews by paying attention to how these different stories about violence occurred in across women's transcripts.

These narratives of violence position women squarely in the role of gendered vulnerability to victimhood (like the participants in Phoenix's (2000) study), although women through their narrations had to work hard[6] to position themselves as 'victims', given that they were not automatically positioned as 'ideal' or 'worthy', by virtue of their sex worker identities, their race and their class. In addition, women's narrations about violence, in its different forms, construct themselves as being at 'risk' from men, whether they are clients, partners or the police. In this first phase of the analysis we stay close to the content of women's stories – attending to how they talk about the interconnectedness of violence. In their stories women blur the boundaries between the types of crime/violence, typically considered to be separate.

In narrative research, including narrative criminology, this lived reality, especially the realities of violence and oppression, is often bracketed off at the

---

[6] I suggest that women worked hard to position themselves as victims because of the countless stories of extreme and horrific violence they told about. I am certain that the interview extracts I have chosen to represent women's stories do not convey the extent of their suffering, nor do they convey how prevalent stories of violence and suffering were in the interviews. The days and weeks I spent working with the data were very difficult and amplified for me the personal costs of researching gendered violence – an issue not often dealt with in the literature but powerfully considered in the work of Rebecca Campbell (2002).

expense of a focus on the discursive. Although a focus on how realities (e.g. psychological and criminological) are constructed through language is important, this focus on the discursive is often privileged at the expense of other ways of theorising experience. In this choice to bracket off 'reality', the risk for obscuring women's material and embodied experiences, its intrapsychic dimensions and the ways in which social and political power shape their lives is real (Ussher, 2010). Taking an approach that attempts to bring in ways of seeing that might acknowledge dimensions of experience that have been negated or ignored allows us as decolonial, intersectional researchers to make the links between the larger oppressions faced by women and other marginalised groups and the lived, embodied experiences of victimisation revealed in their stories.

Phase Two: Analysing Decolonial, Intersectional Power

Whilst women's narratives reveal complex and intersecting forms of violence, we must also ask what these narratives obscure or exclude. At this point in the analysis the intersectional lens is more explicitly attentive to how participants' identities and experiences accord with power and social–structural oppressions. It engages questions of how the narratives of experiences are shaped by discourses on race, class, gender, sexuality, nationality, ability, religion, body size, occupation, marital status and age, amongst other identities and what this means in relation to the dynamics of power. At the same time, the analysis also centres questions of coloniality and an understanding of how these oppressive conditions, that may be considered 'contemporary', have long historical roots that demand analysis.

The aim thus, is not only to interpret findings 'within the sociohistorical context of structural inequality for groups positioned in social hierarchies of unequal power' (Bowleg, 2008, p. 320) but also to analyse how the enmeshed and co-constructed social divisions relate to 'political and subjective constructions of identities' (Yuval-Davis, 2006, p. 205). The guiding questions that are useful during this phase of analysis are included in Table 23.2 below.

In pointing to the overwhelming presence of violence in their lives, women also position themselves in the socially scripted role of 'victim', sometimes 'survivor'. To a large degree they position themselves as acted upon; as the subjects of men's violence. Narrative analysis leads us to question how women may take up the narrative category/identity of 'victim' and the purpose of such narrative positioning, but it should also bring in the tensions and struggle as women attempt to counteract this passive positioning of themselves. Asking analytic questions about what lived experiences are implicated in their narratives, about how the social contexts and structures and circulating public scripts are implicated in the stories, reveals two further narratives in the research on sex work and violence. These are: Stigmatised/Shameful Identities and Narratives of Struggle, discussed below.

Stigmatised/Shameful identities

A close reading of women's interviews illuminates the ways in which their lives are shaped by mainstream moral discourses about sex work. The ways in which their

480 Floretta Boonzaier

Table 23.2. Phase Two: Useful Analytic Questions.

- What meanings do the narratives hold for the tellers?
- What kinds of identities are being constructed?
- Beyond the manifest meanings in the narratives, what else might participants be calling attention to in their narratives? What are its meanings?
- How do the stories implicate the lived, intersectional experiences of race, class, gender, sexuality, age, disability, location, religion, occupation, nationality, etc.
- Whose perspectives are privileged in the story? Whose are left out?
- What is the social context in which the story is being told? What kinds of social and cultural resources might the storyteller have access to? How does this frame the telling?
- Are there aspects of the narratives that highlight intrapersonal, interpersonal experiences? Are there aspects of the stories that highlight cultural conventions and social structures?

Source: Adapted from Fraser (2004), Esterberg (2002) and Parker (2005).

experiences of violence from clients, partners and others are shaped, facilitated and enabled by the stigma attached to sex work and the stigmatized identities imposed on them. Women narrate about how sex work is constructed as a degrading kind of work and the implications of the 'spoiled identity' (Goffman, 1963) this manufactures for them. The stigma attached to sex work is entangled, not only with the physical and other types of violence women experienced from their partners, but also with humiliation and shame.

Interviewer: *Can you tell me a bit more about the relationship?*

Daphne: *Every day, I was being beaten up every day, because he was using drugs and if he get too high, I'm always the problem. Every night. I was abused every night. I couldn't go to my family, because I got bruises, blue eyes. And then he locked me up. I had to stay a few days inside, because, if I go to my family maybe for one day then he come and pick me up again.*

Interviewer: *He cut you off from all other relationships by locking you up in the house.*

Daphne: *Yes. So that I could be his punching bag. Every time. Every day.*

Interviewer: *Was he emotionally abusive towards you, by putting you down?*

Daphne: *Yes he was.*

Interviewer: *What did he say to you?*

Daphne: *I'm a bitch. I'm a whore. Why couldn't he just treat me as the whore he met, though I was his wife that time too. I told him, 'Why didn't you just pass this whore or this prostitute or this hotnot[7] as you say?' Because he was a white man, a German. So his family didn't want him, because he was with me. The culture mustn't be mixed. So he became, treated me also as they treated him. 'Why do you want this (black) woman? ... tell us you picked her up on the street, this prostitute who put her family in shame.' So he became aggressive.*

Above, Daphne articulates an interconnectedness between her experiences of physical abuse, control and isolation and verbal abuse. Daphne works hard to amplify the frequency of the violence she was subjected to 'every day' and 'every night'. Daphne also constructs the physical evidence her partner's abuse leaves on her body as shameful – resulting in her avoidance of contact with her family. Like other abused women, Daphne carries the burden of shame for the violence, the physical evidence thereof (bruises and blue eyes) marking her as a woman who is 'unloved' (Boonzaier, 2014b). The narration from Daphne above also powerfully intersects with the gendered shame she carries (as a woman sex worker) with a history of racialised shame (cf. Wicomb, 1998). For her, the abuse from her partner manifests as a result of his own internalisation of his family's racism and sexism – resulting in the packaging together of the shameful identities of being a black woman and a sex worker.

From women's narrations of their experiences it is clear that sex work is discursively constructed as something that is dirty and shameful. The degradation, humiliation and stigma of sex work emerged in many of the stories women told about how they were humiliated by their partners, by their clients (through language, violence and degrading sexual acts), by the police, as well as by family or the general public. In their narratives women clearly show that the stigma of sex work shapes their experiences as women, as partners, family and community members. They also show how the stigma of sex work intersects with misogyny and manifests as deep contempt for them as women. This, women illustrate through reference to the language of contempt used against them by men, especially repetitive uses of the words 'bitch', 'prostitute' and 'whore'. These words recurred in women's talk about their lives as women sex workers.

It is clear that women's experiences are shaped by stigmatising discourses about sex work – that powerfully intersect with their identities as women who are also black and poor. The prevailing ways in which women are 'marked' by the stigma on sex work provide few opportunities for resistance, although women, through their narrations in this research, point to the ways in which this stigma (that might be invisible to those of us who are not involved in sex work) is damaging to them and their ability to engage in dignified ways of 'making a living'. The ways in which women's narrations about sex work and stigma reveal

---

[7] A racially denigrating term.

small acts of resistance are also illustrated below through their stories on what it means to 'survive'.

Narratives of struggle: 'Life Is Hard'
This analysis reveals that women articulate the difficulties of what it means to be a poor black woman trying to make their way in the world – in a racist, sexist, neoliberal, capitalist environment that provides few forms of protection and dignity for them and their families. Like other poor women on the margins who experience intimate partner violence, they speak against dominance to counter the individualising, pathologizing narratives of them as somehow being responsible for their continuing victimisations (Boonzaier, 2014b) by pointing to systemic issues that shape their lives. Across almost all of the interviews, women described their entry into sex work as a result of an unfortunate life event (such as the death of a partner or breadwinner) that propelled them into poverty or else was a result of poverty and the need for survival.

> *It's hard, but I want to change. I want to change. And then what I'm struggling too it's like, now this year I pray to God that I must get a job, because I want any job. Any! I don't mind.* (Busisiwe)

Pointing to the ways in which neoliberal economies and other forces push those already on the margins further away, women narrate the difficulties of their existences in how they shift between different kinds of precarious work such as sex work, domestic work or employment as cleaners. In their narratives of struggle women articulate the difficulties of survival by pointing to the need for formal employment, for social support from family and the state. They counter notions of individual failure or success by showing how their current conditions are a manifestation of their positioning on the social hierarchy and as a result of oppressive structural forces shaping their lives. Women's narratives provide evidence of structural forms of violence.

Beyond being propelled into poverty and sex work as a means of survival, structural violence also took other forms. Given the ways in which women constructed themselves as at risk of constant violence from men, safety and security were key features of their narratives of life on the streets. Women pointed to the failures of the police in helping to keep them safe from harm, sometimes naming the police as the perpetrators of violence against them.

> *And the police also, they they are supposed to be our protectors; but some of the police when they they pretend that they are arresting us they also rape us and we don't lay the charges because we are afraid to be locked up, and they told us that if you go you won't have evidence because they throw the condoms when they finished what they doing.* (Gina)

Some women also point to how they were not protected from further abuse from partners, being failed by the criminal justice system, despite their efforts to assert their legal rights through obtaining protection or restraining orders for example.

This second phase of the analysis was concerned with attending to the complexity of women's narrations of their experience – asking how the lived intersectional experiences of race, class and gender emerged in their narratives. It also asked about the social and cultural resources they drew upon in the telling and the implications for the subjective construction of their identities.

In this phase of the analysis we see how the violence women are subjected to intersects with the stigmatisation of sex work. Women's narrative choices to attend to the ways in which the stigma of sex work intersects with misogyny and violence provide powerful evidence of how the 'symbolic landscape' (Phoenix, 2000) or the realm of representation has 'real' effects in their lives. They clearly show these effects by narrating about what it means to live and survive as a 'stigmatised woman'.

We also see that women call attention to the ways in which they are positioned on the structural hierarchy as poor, black women engaged in sex work. Through 'narratives of struggle' they call attention to the ways in which they are oppressed by social structures that provide little to no support to enable them to live dignified lives. Women's narratives of struggle may be interpreted as one way in which they counteract the stigma associated with being poor and being involved in sex work. Calling attention to systemic issues that make their lives hard as women means that they are asking their audiences to look beyond individualised notions of success and failure – rather to read their stories as evidence of systemic failures and as a challenge to the normalisation of neoliberal ways of being.

Phase Three: Reading Against the Grain: Articulating Resistance

In the context of this overwhelming violence, stigmatisation and degradation a feminist decolonial, intersectional narrative reading also needs to listen carefully to the ways in which women talk against dominance (Boonzaier, 2014b) in order to recognise how they counteract their imposed positionalities and the ways in which they are represented as poor black women on the periphery. It involves attention to how women navigate the tightrope, what McKenzie-Mohr and Lafrance (2011) call 'tightrope talk' to refer to the ways in which they negotiate dominant discourses on femininity while at the same time giving voice to their own resistance.

Collins (2000) argues that intersectional work must involve changing consciousness and producing social change. She argues that foregrounding new ways of knowing, new knowledges that centre the realities of marginalised groups, will advance these aims. This latter point is also applicable to decolonial work. At the same time, Lugones (2010) argues that feminist decolonial work involves an attempt to not only study the coloniality of gender, which includes an analysis of racialisation, colonisation, capitalist exploitation and gendered oppression, but also involves attempts to overcome it. In this regard, phase three of the analysis asks the analyst to look to the ways in which women's narratives articulate resistance (Table 23.3).

484   Floretta Boonzaier

Table 23.3. Phase Three: Useful Analytic Questions.

- What possibilities do the narratives create for social identity, group belonging and collective action (Riessman, 2008)
- In which ways do the narratives 'speak back' to hegemonic, 'othering' discourses about the particular group of participants being researched?
- Where are the possibilities for collective identification and resistance? What feminist narratives can be identified?

Talking against dominance
Although the women interviewed take up the discursive position of 'victim' in their narratives about violence, they also counteract this positioning in a number of ways. A feminist decolonial, intersectional narrative analysis is decidedly political and allows us to point to the ways in which consciousness about oppression might be shifted to produce social change. Along these lines it is important to consider how women's narratives 'produce' resistance. Firstly, they point to gendered inequalities and oppression as the root of men's violence against them. In some women's narratives this manifests as a deep scepticism, hatred or distrust of men more generally. The various violent partners, clients, or police are described fundamentally as men, who benefit from the control and violence against them, as women. Secondly, women in this research also make links with other women, especially poor, black women engaged in sex work. They recognise their collective struggles as women in sex work, poor black women on the margins attempting to survive in increasingly constraining contexts that make it difficult to do so. Thirdly, the women counteract the 'spoiled identity' constructed for sex workers by positioning themselves as fully responsible citizens who take active ownership of their health. The concern with health appears most visibly in women's narrations about condom use to prevent contracting HIV.

> *In this sex business you must go for your tests regularly, 'cause if the condom breaks, I run immediately ... I run to the first hospital that I can get hold of. I (just) run into the emergency room and I tell the doctor, 'Doctor the condom (broke). Maybe I'm gonna get AIDS. Please, just do something please.' Yeah I go straight. I don't go and sit and keep myself shy like a virgin.* (Elmarie)

Above Elmarie draws on the same discourse of femininity (the Madonna/Whore dichotomoy, Macdonald, 1995) that positions sex workers as shameful to situate herself as fully responsible and active by seeking medical assistance when a condom breaks during sexual intercourse. By not being 'shy like a virgin', and incidentally not taking up the gendered role that society and others construct for her, she is able to play this active role.

Other ways in which women similarly construct health and well-being within the context of sex work is through talk about working at their own pace, reducing the number of clients they have – a discourse that simultaneously works to counteract the idea of sex work as a 'dirty job'.

> ... But I don't overwork myself. I maybe go out three times a week and I'll maybe do two clients a night. So I will make sure that it's not like a constant uhm... not that it's always busy either. But if it's a busy night, I'll do two clients and I'll finish and I'll go home. It's more than enough for me, 'cause I do take care of myself, my body, my emotions, my physical and mental state. (Gail)

The narratives of self-care and 'being healthy' are constructed in opposition to mainstream discourses of ill health and lack of care. The ability to 'take care' of the self, particularly through the reduction of the number of clients one accommodates is of course dependent on one's socioeconomic circumstances and the obvious issue of financial need.

Finally, women speak against dominance by narrating about survival against all odds and telling stories about motherhood, another readily available discourse for women (Phoenix, 2000). Sex work is work in a context of deepening gender inequities, of the feminisation of poverty and the normalisation of the neoliberal economy. Without exception, women constructed narratives of entry into sex work as a consequence of socioeconomic struggles or dire financial need – often in response to crisis situations. Sex work is described as a choice within constraining contexts in which the choices available to some women are limited. Through their stories of sex work therefore, women take up a form of active socioeconomic citizenship in the face of a broader context in which their choices for survival are limited. This active citizenship is most pertinently foregrounded when women discuss their responsibilities as mothers.

> So just focused on my kids. So I get the second pregnancy of him. The last pregnancy I thought no, I don't care what my family is going to think or say about me. I'm just going to focus on being a healthy mother, being a stable mother, just trying to get my kids out of this life, being abused, so I split my kids. (Daphne)

Daphne's construction of herself as a 'healthy mother' involves making difficult decisions to protect her children from her partner's abuse. She sent her children to live with different family members but she continues to support them through her earnings from sex work.

> How am I supposed to get an income? My children need to go to school. I have four mouths to feed. And I can't go begging and asking every day. How many meals can you give me when I need three meals a day? So I'm not asking like, 'Oh, give me stuff'. I can work it myself. And if I can sell sex and make money, I think you should respect my choices and a human being because at least I'm trying to make a better life for my children. (Faith)

Within hegemonic notions of femininity, the identity of sex worker is constructed as shameful for women; however, many participants counter this by positioning themselves within a discourse of good motherhood, one that positions them as proud and restores a 'respectable' version of femininity, as illustrated by both Daphne and Faith above. Positioning themselves as active socioeconomic citizens within the context of responsible mothering works to counteract the widespread stigma surrounding sex work and presents a source of pride for women, some who revealed that they had been able to afford to sustain their children through their school careers and some into university. Because the notion of being a 'good woman', like an 'ideal victim', is coloured by race and class, it is not readily available to all women. These women on the margins therefore (re)construct ideas about what it means to be a good woman, drawing upon their identities as mothers and as breadwinners, taking care of their families. Aulette-Root-Toyer, Boonzaier, and Aulette (2014) found a similar discourse on 'good womanhood' in the narratives of HIV-positive women in South Africa. These women drew on notions of conventional femininity to foreground the care work they do for men, children and others in their lives to counteract the stigma associated with living with HIV. These women, like other socially marginalised women (Fleetwood, 2014), draw on a 'safe' discourse of respectable personhood, womanhood in particular that involves notions of care for others, being good mothers and homemakers.

In this penultimate 'phase' of the analysis we attempted to look closely at the broader significance of women's narratives on their lives as sex workers. Given women's marginalised positions on the social hierarchy and the associated stigmas imposed on them, we asked specifically how women's narratives reflected and resisted these. In recognition that resistance may not always be easily articulated in language, especially for the oppressed, we attended very closely to women's narrations and attempted an understanding of the significance thereof given their various social identities, contexts and locations – both discursive and material. This process involved further reading and listening to women's narrations beyond an attempt to find themes. It also involved 'staying close' to women's narrations and deep reflection on the significance thereof.

Phase Four: Crafting a Plurivocal Narrative

For now, the story I want to craft about the experiences of the women involved in this research ends here. I have not yet written the larger story I would like to tell about the lives and experiences of the women, although this work has appeared in different formats elsewhere (see Bartlett, 2014; Huysamen, 2011; Kessi, Kaminer, Boonzaier, & Learmonth, 2018). In writing up my feminist decolonial, intersectional narrative analysis based on the research with women sex workers I, like you, will have to ask myself the following questions:

- What are your research questions? How will your analysis address these?
- What narrative will you craft about the lives and realities of those you engaged with? Why are you electing to tell this particular story? Are there any other stories to tell?

- Who are you writing this narrative for?
- Where are you in this narrative? How has your own identity, history, politics and context been implicated, not only in the interviews but throughout the research and especially in the crafting of the narrative?
- What commitments have you made to your participants and your politics? How will you keep these? Who will benefit from this research?

In our crafting of the narrative, we must attempt to honestly address these questions and hold in the balance our commitment telling the story demanded of us (through our respective disciplinary, work and other demands) and using the research to advance social justice for those with whom we work. The writing will attempt to weave together multiple, situated stories bringing together our reading of participants' worlds, our analyses of existing scholarship in the field as well as bringing in our awareness and attention to the sociopolitical and historical contexts in which we work.

Conclusion

In this chapter I articulated a decolonial, intersectional narrative analysis, working with the data generated in interviews with women sex workers on their experiences of violence from men, sometimes clients, sometimes intimate partners. The chapter outlines how a decolonial, intersectional narrative analysis may be accomplished, taking Riessman's articulation of a thematic narrative analysis as the starting point and building thereon to analyse the intersections of power at material, representational and structural levels. The chapter illustrates the importance of a decolonial, intersectional feminist lens for clarifying the complexity of women sex workers' experiences of gendered violence and for understanding the multiple forms of material, symbolic and institutionalised subordination they experience in increasingly unequal and oppressive contexts.

Sex work has long been an arena that is highly stigmatised, suffering from moral scrutiny and conservative attitudes around sex, although this paradoxically occurs as public and other contexts have become increasingly sexualised. For a large proportion of women who make up the sex work industry, this stigma is intersected with their identities as women who are also poor and black. Women who work on the streets selling sex may arguably be of the most marginalised in South Africa (with South Africa being just one geographical example but by far not the only one). In this regard it is important that we understand these women's encounters with 'crime' and deviance from a decolonial, intersectional perspective – ensuring that our methodologies, approaches to asking questions and ways of working with them don't further contribute to their stigmatisation and marginalisation. In this regard the decolonial, intersectional narrative approach offered in this chapter is important.

In the research, women revealed the powerful ways in which their lives were shaped by the stigma attached to sex work and how this shaped their experiences of violence with partners, family and others they encountered. Their narratives also revealed how the stigma of sex work intersected with misogyny and manifested as contempt for them as women, women who were also poor and black. Women's narrative choices to foreground the intersectional ways in which their lives are shaped by the symbolic landscape (Phoenix, 2000) shaped by stigma offers a powerful example of the effects of harmful discourse on embodied material realities – illustrating for listeners and readers what it means to live and survive as 'stigmatised women'. In addition, women's personal stories called attention to the ways in which gendered (and other forms of) structural oppressions manifested in their everyday experiences, especially experiences of violence. In so doing, the approach allowed for the linking of women's personal lives and experiences to symbolic, structural, historical and political systems that fundamentally impact them.

A decolonial, intersectional narrative perspective to criminology is important for offering space for women themselves to challenge the ways in which they are positioned as poor black women on the margins of society. This 'space' may include physical and discursive space offered in the context of the interview (Hydén, 2008), but importantly as illustrated in this chapter, it also refers to 'analytical space' and the ways in which we read and make meaning of women's narratives told to us in the context of our research. This chapter shows that this approach to narrative criminology offers a space for women to speak back to and to disrupt harmful circulating scripts about them and their lives – through countering victim-blaming discourses; through graphic illustration of the harms of stigma; through providing a challenge to the normalisation of neoliberal, individualised discourses about success and failure; and through speaking themselves into discourses of respectable personhood.

The analytical space offered through the method, however, cannot be taken for granted. It involves thinking through and listening beyond the words to the ways in which it might be possible for oppressed people to engage in what Wade (1997) has called, small acts of living and resistance, what McKenzie-Mohr and Lafrance (2011) have called tightrope talk and what I have referred to as 'talking against dominance' (Boonzaier, 2014b). It involves listening for the ways in which the subaltern does indeed speak (Spivak, 1988). Listening beyond the words offers the opportunity for dignity in the stories we tell about our participants and guards against the recolonising potential still prevalent in much academic research endeavours.

Overall, this chapter fundamentally illuminates the potential of narrative criminological research to advance a decolonial, intersectional feminist agenda that might repoliticise research in the interests of social justice and contribute to broader aims of rehumanising those who are dehumanised and decolonising criminological research.

References

Agozino, B. (2003). *Counter-colonial criminology. A critique of imperialist reason.* London: Pluto Press.

Aulette-Root-Toyer, A., Boonzaier, F., & Aulette, J. (2014). *South African women living with HIV: Global lessons from local voices.* Bloomington, IN: Indiana University Press.

Banister, P., Bunn, G., Burman, E., Daniels, J., Duckett, P., Goodley., ... Whelan, P. (Eds.). (2011). *Qualitative methods in psychology. A research guide* (2nd ed.). Berkshire: Open University Press.

Bartlett, E. (2014). *The subjective experiences of intimate partner violence among female sex workers.* Unpublished honours research report. University of Cape Town, South Africa.

Boonzaier, F. (2014a). Methodological disruptions: Interviewing domestically violent men across a 'gender divide'. *NORMA: International Journal for Masculinity Studies, 4,* 232–248.

Boonzaier, F. (2014b). Talking against dominance. South African women resisting dominant discourse in narratives of violence. In M. N. Lafrance & S. McKenzie-Mohr (Eds.), *Creating counter-stories. Women voicing resistance* (pp. 102–120). London: Routledge.

Boonzaier, F. (2018). Challenging risk: The production of knowledge on gendered violence in South Africa. In K. Fitz-Gibbon, S. Walklate, J. McCulloch, & J. Maree Maher (Eds.), *Intimate partner violence, risk and security: Securing women's lives in a global world.* London: Routledge.

Boonzaier, F., & Shefer, T. (2006). Gendered research. In T. Shefer, F. Boonzaier, & P. Kiguwa (Eds.), *The gender of psychology* (pp. 3–11). Cape Town: UCT Press.

Bowleg, L. (2008). When black + lesbian + woman ≠ black lesbian woman: The methodological challenges of qualitative and quantitative intersectionality research. *Sex Roles, 59,* 312–325. doi:10.1007/s11199-008-9400-z

Campbell, R. (2002). *Emotionally involved: The impact of researching rape.* New York, NY: Routledge.

Collins, P. H. (1990). *Black feminist thought: Knowledge, consciousness, and the politics of empowerment* (1st ed.). Boston, MA: Unwyn Hyman.

Collins, P. H. (2000). *Black feminist thought: Knowledge, consciousness, and the politics of empowerment* (2nd ed.). New York, NY: Routledge.

Crenshaw, K. W. (1991). Mapping the margins: Intersectionality, identity politics, and violence against women of color. *Stanford Law Review, 43,* 1241–1299.

Esterberg, K. G. (2002). *Qualitative methods in social research.* Boston, MA: McGraw-Hill.

Fleetwood, J. (2014). Keeping out of trouble: Female crack cocaine dealers in England. *European Journal of Criminology, 11*(1), 91–109. doi:10.1177/1477370813491177

Fleetwood, J. (2015). A narrative approach to women's lawbreaking. *Feminist Criminology, 10*(4), 368–388.

Fraser, N. (2004). Doing narrative research. Analysing personal stories line by line. *Qualitative Social Work, 3*(2), 179–201.

Goffman, E. (1963). *Stigma: Notes on the management of spoiled identity.* New York, NY: Simon & Schuster.

Gould, C., & Fick, N. (2008). *Selling sex in Cape Town: Sex work and human trafficking in a South African city.* Cape Town: Institute for Security Studies.

Gqola, P. D. (2001). Ufanele uqavile: Blackwomen, feminisms and postcoloniality in Africa. *Agenda: Empowering Women for Gender Equity, 16*(50), 11–22.

Huysamen, M. (2011). *Women's experiences of harm in prostitution: A feminist inquiry.* Unpublished honours research report. University of Cape Town, South Africa.

Huysamen, M. (2015). Constructing the 'respectable' client and the 'good' researcher: The complex dynamics of cross-gender interviews with men who pay for sex. *NORMA: International Journal for Masculinity Studies, 11*, 1–15.

Hydén, M. (2008). Narrating sensitive topics. In M. Andrews, C. Squire, & M. Tamboukou (Eds.), *Doing narrative research* (pp. 121–136). Los Angeles, CA: SAGE Publications.

Irwin, K., & Umemoto, K. (2016). *Jacked up and unjust: Pacific Islander teens confront violent legacies.* Berkeley, CA: University of California Press.

Jewkes, Y. (2004). *Media and crime.* London: SAGE Publications.

Kessi, S., Kaminer, D., Boonzaier, F., & Learmonth, D. (2018). Photovoice methodologies for social justice. In A. Fynn, S. Kramer, & S. Laher (Eds.), *Transforming research methods in the social sciences.* Johannesburg: Wits University Press.

Kiguwa, P. (2004). Feminist critical psychology in South Africa. In D. Hook, N. Mkhize, P. Kiguwa, A. Collins, E. Burman, & I. Parker (Eds.), *Critical psychology* (pp. 187–209). Lansdowne: UCT Press.

Lugones, M. (2007). Heterosexualism and the colonial/modern gender system. *Hypatia, 22*(1), 186–209.

Lugones, M. (2010). Toward a decolonial feminism. *Hypatia, 25*(4), 742–759.

Macdonald, M. (1995). *Representing women: Myths of femininity in the popular media.* London: Edward Arnold.

McKenzie-Mohr, S., & Lafrance, M. (2011). Telling stories without the words: 'Tightrope talk' in women's accounts of coming to live well after rape or depression. *Feminism & Psychology, 21*(1), 49–73.

McNay, L. (1999). Gender and narrative identity. *Journal of Political Ideologies, 4*(3), 315–336.

Miller, J., Carbone-Lopez, K., & Gunderman, L. V. (2015). Gendered narratives of self, addiction and recovery among women methamphetamine users. In L. Presser & S. Sandberg (Eds.), *Narrative criminology: Understanding stories of crime* (pp. 69–95). New York, NY: New York University Press.

Msimang, S. (2002). Introduction African Feminisms II: Reflections on politics made personal. *Agenda: Empowering Women for Gender Equity, 54*, 3–15.

Murray, M. (2003). Narrative psychology. In J. A. Smith (Ed.), *Qualitative psychology: A practical guide to research methods* (pp. 111–131). London: SAGE Publications.

Paris, D., & Winn, M. T. (2014). To humanize research. Preface. In D. Paris & M. T. Winn (Eds.), *Humanizing research. Decolonizing qualitative inquiry with youth and communities* (pp. xiii–xxii). Los Angeles, CA: SAGE Publications.

Parker, I. (2005). *Qualitative psychology: Introducing radical research.* New York, NY: Open University Press.

Phoenix, J. (2000). Prostitute identities. Men, money and violence. *British Journal of Criminology, 40*, 37–55.

Presser, L. (2005). Negotiating power and narrative in research: Implications for feminist methodology. *Signs: Journal of Women in Culture and Society, 30*, 2067–2090. doi:10.1086/428424

Presser, L. (2009). The narratives of offenders. *Theoretical Criminology, 13*(2), 177–200. doi:10.1177/1362480609102878

Presser, L. (2012). Getting on top through mass murder: Narrative, metaphor, and violence. *Crime, Media, Culture, 8*(1), 3–21.

Rappaport, J. (1995). Empowerment meets narrative: Listening to stories and creating settings. *American Journal of Community Psychology, 23*(5), 795–807.

Riessman, C. K. (2008). *Narrative methods for the human sciences*. Thousand Oaks, CA: SAGE Publications.

Sonn, C. C., Stevens, G., & Duncan, N. (2013). Decolonisation, critical methodologies and why stories matter. In G. Stevens, N. Duncan, & D. Hook (Eds.), *Race, memory and the apartheid archives: Towards a psychsocial praxis* (pp. 295–314). Johannesburg: Wits University Press.

Spivak, G. C. (1988). Can the subaltern speak? In N. Cary & L. Grossberg (Eds.), *Marxism and the interpretation of culture* (pp. 271–313). Urbana, IL: University of Illinois Press.

Tuck, E., & Wayne Yang, K. (2014). R-Words: Refusing research. In D. Paris & M. T. Winn (Eds.), *Humanizing research. Decolonizing qualitative inquiry with youth and communities* (pp. 223–247). London: SAGE Publications.

Ussher, J. M. (2010). Are we medicalizing women's misery? A critical review of women's higher rates of reported depression. *Feminism & Psychology, 20*, 9–35.

Wade, A. (1997). Small acts of living: Everyday resistance to violence and other forms of oppression. *Contemporary Family Therapy, 19*(1), 23–39.

Walker, R. (1981). On the uses of fiction in educational research. In D. Smetherham (Ed.), *Practising evalution*. Driffield: Nafferton.

Walklate, S., Maher, J., McCulloch, J., Fitz-Gibbon, K., & Beavis, K. (2018). Victim stories and victim policy: Is there a case for a narrative victimology. *Crime, Media, Culture*, 1–17. doi.org/10.1177/1741659018760105

Wicomb, Z. (1998). Shame and identity: The case of the coloured in South Africa. In D. Attridge & R. Jolly (Eds.), *Writing South Africa: Literature, apartheid, and democracy, 1970–1995* (pp. 91–107). Cambridge: Cambridge University Press.

Wojcicki, J. M., & Malala, J. (2001). Condom use, power and HIV/AIDS risk: Sex-workers bargain for survival in Hillbrow/Joubert Park/Berea, Johannesburg. *Social Science & Medicine, 53*(1), 99–121.

Yuval-Davis, N. (2006). Intersectionality and feminist politics. *European Journal of Women's Studies, 13*(3), 193–209. doi:10.1177/1350506806065752

Index

Absences, 10, 11–12, 17, 411, 414–416
Active interviewing, 93–96
Actor-network theory, 228
Agency, 239–257
   organic agency, 14
   personal agency, 70, 345, 361
   human agency, 167, 343
   political agency, 469
Agonistic interviews, 93
Allegories of environmental harm, 155, 165–167
Allegory, 165–166
Al-Shabaab, 27, 133, 143, 460
Analytical dialogue, 381–384
Andrews, M., 65
Animating interest, 371
Anti-jihadism, 39
Armed conflict and war, 4
Art, 9, 36, 66–68, 121, 180, 197–200, 203, 207, 217
Articulating resistance, 472, 483–486
As-salamu alaykum, 458
As-told-to autobiography, 135
Attentiveness, 96, 102–103
Attorney stories, 156–160
Australia, 250
Autobiographical resources, 67
Autobiographical writing, 13, 64, 429
   archived criminality reform, 434–439
   Chinese Literary Tradition, 432–433
   ideological reform, 433–434
   incarcerated Chinese, 429–432
Autobiography
   analysis in practice, 140–145
   defining, 134–136

   paratexts, 136–140
   terrorism, 133–134
Autoethnography, 7, 63, 68–71, 79, 420

Bad apple hypothesis, 323
Bakhtin, M., 78, 136, 368, 370, 383
Becker, H., 2
Belgium, 8, 90, 101
Belgian bureaucratic system, 101
Biography, 9, 73, 135
The Birth of Purgatory, 218
Bourdieu, Pierre, 3, 369

Canadian treatment programme for men, 280
Capriccio, 212–214
Carceral, 5, 7, 109, 113, 122, 161, 197–216
Character, 29, 36, 52, 54, 79, 100, 178, 181, 184, 283, 296, 329, 371, 419, 462
Chico's visual narratives
   Chico the friend, 189–190
   economic and social marginalisation, 181
   friend, 189–190
   menacing rebel, 184–188
   methamphetamine, 180
Children's stories, 162–164
China, 13, 117, 202, 427–440
Chinese Communist Party (CCP), 431, 433
Class
   class status, 114, 143, 265
   middle-class values, 4, 49, 79, 413, 415

494 Index

social class, 410, 415
working-class, 75
Coding, 12, 48, 134, 378
Collective representations, 7, 63, 142, 163, 397, 484
Co-conspirators, 55
Collecting stories, 6
Colonialism. *See also* 'Race', 16, 198, 225, 470
Compulsory Education Law of the People's Republic of China, 1986, 433
Confucian ideology, 432
Constitutive perspective, 2, 46–48, 67, 92, 104, 134, 219, 283, 410
Conversation, 34, 35, 37, 51, 93, 95, 102, 114, 193, 282, 317, 391, 449
Convict criminology, 63–80
Corporate offenders, 156–160
Counterinsurgency, 335
Counternarratives, 7, 13, 65, 66, 103
   narrative analysis, 446–448
   narrative resistance, 450–461
   power, 446–448
   resistance, 446–448
   study and participants, 448–449
   team research, 449–450
Court case files, 87, 89, 90
Co-victim narratives, 265, 269, 270
Crime
   crime narratives, 389
   crime-involved populations, 110
   criminality, 131
   criminological facts, 72
   drug crime, 4
   environmental crime, 153–172
   general theory, 412–414
   narrative scripts, 2
   personality disorders, 5
   proximal antecedents to, 345
   serious crimes, 180
   types, 13
   victims' narratives, 265–272

Crime Victims' Rights Week programs, 270
Criminal justice
   crafting language, 50
   ethnography, 45–47
   honesty, 52–54
   impartiality, 57–59
   making evidence intelligible, 50–52
   performance, 54–57
   prosecutorial narratives, 47–50
   real-time narrative creation, 45–47
   The Trial, 217
Criminal Justice Institutions
   courts, 16, 90, 92, 99, 243, 294, 314
   police, 5, 11, 31, 35, 39, 90, 92, 191, 131, 184, 189, 296, 321–341
   prisons, 9, 16, 65, 72, 76, 115, 197, 204, 211, 212, 297, 431
   youth justice, 5, 8, 87–108
Criminal justice professionals, attorney stories, 156–160
Criminal law, 309–314
Critical criminology, 4, 66
Culture, 3, 5, 9, 15, 28, 37, 89, 119, 136, 155, 176, 197, 217–233, 226, 271, 321–341, 346, 414, 416, 438, 463, 468
Cultural criminology, 4, 153–172

Daya's story, 113–115, 119, 120, 125
Decolonial analysis, 467–491
Deconstruction, 200, 202, 214
Decontextualized images, 179
Defence mechanism, 12, 390, 395, 400, 404
Derogatory counternarratives, 457
Dialogical narrative analysis (DNA), 367–385
   analytical dialogue, 381–384
   animating interest, 371
   apocalyptic stories, 377–381
   definition, 370
   forms of, 372–374
   implications, 384–385

Dictated autobiography, 135
Discipline and Punish, 70
Discourse, 2, 8, 87, 111, 156, 253, 335, 416, 428, 447, 485, 486
Discourse analysis, 8, 156, 199, 253, 410
Documentary analysis, 179, 330
Documents
  case file documents, 101
  forged signature, 57
  forgery of bank documents, 53
  legal, 296
  official documents, 8, 27
  photocopied documents, 431
  textual analysis, 8
Dominance, 484–486
Double consciousness, 68
Doxastic interviews, 94
Drugs policy war, 383–384

Elastic narratives, 391
Elites, 59, 198, 420
Elite and expert interviews, 47, 59, 93, 96
Emotions, 32, 432, 447, 454, 455, 457
Empathy, 28, 100–102, 178, 267, 272, 285, 288, 297
England, 38, 203, 285, 394
Environmental crime, 153–172
Environmental harm, 8, 154, 155
  fictionalised depictions and representations, 160–162
Epiphany, 33, 248, 251
Episodic narratives
  offence narrative roles, 346–357
Epistemic and doxastic modes, 97–99
Epistemic interviews, 93, 94, 103
Establishing trust, 36, 449
Ethnicity. See also 'Race', 72, 87, 420, 435
Ethnocentrism. See also 'Race', 329
Ethnography, 6–7, 27–43, 46, 56, 60, 68, 178, 392, 463

Existential narratives, 35
Extremism, 14, 133, 445–446, 461

Factual counternarratives, 451–454, 457, 462
Faith, 75, 79, 240, 245, 248, 250, 252, 304, 476
Feminism, 198, 282, 468
  black and African feminist theory, 474
  eco-feminist, 208
  intersectional feminism, 473
Feminist research, 88
  interviewing, 95–96
  practice, 93–96
Ferguson
  community, 332
  effect, 333
  Ferguson Police Department (FPD), 332
Fiction, 8, 59, 109, 111, 142, 155, 160, 161, 162, 166, 327, 419, 429
Figurative devices, 12, 416, 417
First-time offender, 124, 312, 313, 314
Formula stories, 104, 177, 391
Football Hooliganism, 12, 350
Frank, A. W., 220, 229, 367–374, 382, 384, 413
Free Association Narrative Interview (FANI), 390, 392
Frye, N. 343, 344, 353, 354, 355, 357

Galli de Bibiena, Ferdinando, 206
A General Theory of Crime, 409, 412–414
Gender
  cultural norms, 225, 329
  race. See Race
  regimes imposed on women, 65
  transgender, 109, 113, 114
  women's prison, 46
Genre, 8, 102, 112, 123, 142–143, 146, 201, 204, 359, 376, 381, 383, 432

Germany, 3, 11, 305, 310, 312, 314
German Youth Courts Act, 314
Globalisation, 14, 16, 153, 334, 467
Goffman, E., 2, 229
Godka, 27, 31–36
Green criminology, 8, 153
Green cultural criminology, 4, 153–168
Gubrium, J., 28, 46
Gulliver's Travels, 111, 125

Habitus, 3, 104, 369, 370, 449
Hall, S., 303, 305
Haunting, 205, 206, 214, 282, 298
Harm, 1, 2, 8, 240
  power and inequality, 15–16
  self-harm, 77
  penal harm, 87, 91–104, 153–172, 411–412
  environmental harm, 156–162
  disaster, 157
  environmental harm, 160–167
Heart of Darkness, 70
Hegemonic narratives, 17, 104, 411, 414, 415, 420, 469, 486
Heteroglossia, 368, 381
Homonarrativus, 92
Honesty, 52–54
"How-to" bias,' 47
Holstein, J., 28, 46
Humility topos, 138
Humour, 29, 37, 185, 190, 193, 457–460, 462
Hegemony, 66, 414
Human Rights, 374, 382

'Ideal' victimhood, 267
Ideologies, 322, 446, 448
Ideology, 189, 396, 397, 429, 466
Images, 9, 70, 175–193, 197–214, 398
Imaginative small talk, 34, 35, 46
Impartiality, 57–59
Implicit authority, 267
Implicit psychological content, 360

Imposter syndrome, 75
Individual offenders, 29, 78, 87, 111, 131–132, 281, 156, 283, 286, 343, 345, 347, 390, 405, 428–429
Inference rich, 308
Institutional narratives, 91–104
  empathy, 100–102
  engagement, 100–102
  infusing insights, 95–96
  interview, 103–104
  judicial-correctional 'truth discourse', 280
  judicial truth, 4
  penal harm, 91–104
  police, 92
  research context and interaction, 102–103
  researching up, 93–95
  respect, 100–102
  self-narratives, 92, 97
  shifts and porous, 97–99
  Socratic interviews, 96–97, 99–100
Institutions, 5, 11, 16, 95, 158, 161, 298, 305, 373, 385, 427, 440, 468
Insurgency, 335
Intersectionality, 17, 468
Intersectional narrative criminology, 471
Interviews/interviewing, 7–8, 181
  contextualising photographs, 178–180
  convict criminology, 72
  Dave, 11
  document studies, 29
  epistemic interviews, 94
  ethnographies, 9
  individuals accused, 4
  narrative inquiry, 40
  semi-structured dialogue, 72, 430
  Socrates Light, 87–105
  texts, 8

ISIS, 27, 37
Italy, 207, 395

Jihadism, 27, 32, 39, 41
Jihadist organisations, 445, 454, 461
Justice
　criminal justice, 5, 70, 75, 192, 240–241, 259, 283, 289, 298, 321, 327, 385, 418, 432
　Immanent Justice, 213
　social justice, 13, 104, 467–491
　storied Justice, 45–62
　youth justice, 5, 8, 87–108
June's story, 244–251
　practising faith, 245–247
　redemptive suffering, 249–251
Jurors' interpretations, 49, 50

Katz, J., 2, 177, 229, 373

Labelling perspectives, 347
Labelling theories, 2
Labov, W., 371
Landscape art, 203, 204
Law enforcement
　community members, 324
　culture and officer behaviour, 322, 323, 326
　narrative methods, 321
　visual pictures, 328
　witnesses in contact, 57
Law, legal narratives, 5, 47, 45, 46, 59, 65, 68, 73, 78, 79, 80, 92, 110, 122, 156, 159, 198, 213, 271, 309–313, 321, 323, 325, 328, 330, 332, 378, 382, 412, 439
Lawyers, 45, 47–49, 56, 58, 158
Lay decision-makers, 50–52
Lies, 8, 109–113, 125, 200, 252, 403, 455
Life as book, 358

Life As A Film (LAAF) approach, 11
　criminal narratives, 358–359
　elicitation interview, 359–360
　explicit processes, 360
　implicit psychological content, 360
Life event calendars (LECs), 113
'Light' Socratic dialogues, 96–103
Loseke, D. R., 176

Maruna, S., 2, 242, 249, 279, 345, 347, 359, 390
Marxism, 198, 214
Masculinity, 123, 139, 227, 228, 231, 336, 379
Master plot, 404
Material culture, 9, 217–218
Material objects, 223–224
Matza, D., 2, 390
Mauser 98K, 220–222
McAdams, D., 134, 343, 344, 358–360
Melancholy dilapidation, 197
Membership Categorisation Analysis (MCA), 304, 306–309
　categories, 303–304, 306–308
　categorisation, 317–318
　category-bound construction, 309–316
　Dave's story, 309–316
Memoir. *See also* Autobiography, 134, 135
Metaphors, 8, 11, 39, 213, 334, 416
Migration/migrants, 87, 92, 100, 123, 155, 166
Mills, C. W., 2, 63, 64, 76, 77, 79
Motherwood, Absent Mother Syndrome, 120, 248
Mothers Against Violence, 242, 243, 248
Murder/homicide, 10, 115, 250, 263, 361
Muslims, 13, 39, 119, 144, 445–467

498   Index

Narrative analysis
  material culture studies, 217–218
  Mauser 98K, 220–222
  narratives, 218–220
  objects, 218–220
Narrative convictions, 63–83
Narrative dialogue, 11–12
Narrative ethnography, 7, 47, 60, 264
  criminology, 28–31
  Godka, 31–36
  trust, 36–39
Narrative habitus, 104, 369, 370, 449
Narrative identity, 180
Narrative labour, 5, 71, 438, 439
Narrative resistance, 446–447, 450–461
Narrative Role Questionnaire (NRQ), 11, 348, 358, 362
Narrative strategies, 45–62
Narrative victimology. *See also* June's story, 244–246
  audience, 271–275
  challenges, 256–258
  features, 269–276
  researching, 267–268
  situating, 264–267
  speaker, 269–271
  storytelling, 263
  timing, 275–276
Nations/nationality, 164, 224, 420, 479, 480
Neutralisations. *See also* Techniques of Neutralisation, 389, 390, 405
News media, 14, 154, 379
Norway, 35, 217, 220, 222, 225, 446, 448, 454, 457

Objective reality, 111
Objects, 6, 9, 175–195, 218–220, 222–231, 304, 416
  intended purpose, 224–225
  owner/user, 226–228
  own story, 228–231
  past, 223–224

  sociocultural context, 225–226
  storytelling prop, 222–223
Observations, 6–7, 46, 93, 95, 157, 178, 192, 263–264, 267–268
Offender Assessment System (OASys) report, 289
Offender's narratives
  cognitive distortions, 279
  'innocent,' 282
  judicial-correctional 'truth discourse,' 280
  missing victim, 290–293
  offender and victim, 293–297
  offenders and victims narratives, 286–297
  penitent offender, 286–290
  punished offender, 290–293
  real victim, 286–290
  slipperiness, 279
  stories and justice, 297–298
  victims in the prison, 283–286
Online research
  Google, 282, 375
  YouTube.com, 375
Organisations, antisociality, 412
Overlexicalization, 418

Paintings, 199, 201, 202, 208
Panini, Giovanni Paolo, 208, 209
Paratexts, 132
  covers, 138–140
  written introductions, 137–138
Participant observation. *See also* Ethnography, 30, 45, 46, 48, 49, 60, 262, 274, 281, 295, 374
Penal harm, 12, 91–104, 411–412
Penology, 5
Personal narratives, 5, 7, 79, 156, 343, 345, 471
Phatic talk, 34
Phenomenal testimony, 67
Philippines, 12, 367, 374, 376, 377, 384, 385

Photo-elicitation, 179, 190–192
Photo-elicitation interviews, 190
Photographs, 178–180
Phronetic approach, 97
Pictures
  dark visions, 203–207
  fascinating ruins, 207–210
  image and narrative, 198–200
  landscapes, 200–203
  sublime effects, 211–213
  visual criminology, 194, 198
Piranesi, Giovanni Battista, 9, 197, 205, 210, 212
Plot, 35, 115, 166, 189, 229, 230, 293, 359, 403, 404, 446
Plurivocal narrative, 472, 486–487
Police
  police culture, 5, 321–341
Police narratives
  culture, 321–323
  development, 323–327
  growth areas, 333–336
  methodological challenges, 333–336
  popular culture, 327–329
  storytelling, 323–327
  thin blue line, 329–331
  'truth,' 331–333
Polkinghorne, D., 134
Polletta, F., 135, 253, 369, 373
Polyphony, 318, 368, 381
Positivism, 35, 52, 74, 109, 138, 180, 244, 251, 260, 264, 273, 313, 327, 335, 361, 416, 418, 429
Postcolonialism. *See also* 'Race', 198
Poststructuralism, 198
Power
  harm, 15–16
  inequality, 15–16
  narrative analysis, 446–448
  resistance, 446–448
  social inequalities, 12–13
Prisoner autobiography. *See also* Autobiographical writing, 64–66
  individual autobiography, 427
  rehabilitation, 428–429
Prisons/prisoners, 3, 5, 9, 16, 64–66, 72, 76, 115, 197, 204, 211, 212, 281, 297, 431
Prisoners' narratives, 298
Professional role, 355, 358
Prosecutorial narratives, 47–49
Prostitution. *See also* Sex work, 291, 472, 473
Psychiatry, 11, 309–312
Psychoanalysis, 198
Psychological approach
  Agency and Communion, 343
  Leary's personality dimensions, 344
  moral justification, 345–346
Psychological complexity, 360–361
Psycho-social criminology
  free association narrative interview, 390
  Gianluca's life story, 394–402
  methods, 393
Punishment, 15, 67, 72, 155, 159, 162, 197, 217, 285, 292, 312, 314, 316, 361, 412, 431, 477

Quantitative analysis, 5, 68

Rapport, 36, 37, 55, 94, 95, 103, 264, 266, 272, 282
'Race'. *See also* Ethnicity
  black and African feminist theory, 474
  black perspectives, 80
  black prisoners, 65
  Caucasian youth, 90
  colonialism, 16, 198, 225, 470
  ethnocentrism, 329
  intersectional feminism, 473
  marginalized black women, 473, 475, 483, 487, 488, 489, 490
  Northern Caucasian migrants, 89

postcolonialism, 198
white narratives, 80
"white pride", 191, 195
white prisoners, 65
Racism, 14, 470
Redemption, 239–257
Reflexivity, 63, 88, 96, 103, 270
Religion, 13, 32, 35, 38, 248, 253, 266, 334, 446, 448, 452, 456, 479
Religious narratives. *See also* Redemption; Epiphanies; Faith, 10, 14, 32, 33, 34, 35, 38, 154, 207, 240, 253, 266, 445, 446, 448, 449, 451
finding a 'calling,' 247–249
redemptive suffering, 249–251
Researching up. *See* Active interviewing
Reissman, C. K., 321
Resistance, 446–448
Respectable femininity, 114
Revengeful mission, 349, 351, 352, 357
Ricoeur, P., 80, 369, 373
Roles, categorisations, 10–11

Self-categorisation, 313, 314, 316
Self-help groups, 262, 266, 267, 269, 270
Sex Offender Treatment Programme facilitators (SOTP), 287
Sexualities, 122, 420, 477, 479, 480
Sex Workers Education and Advocacy Taskforce (SWEAT), 472, 473
Sex work, 115, 123, 467–491
  decolonising/rehumanising research, 467–468
  intersectional agenda, 469–471
Shameful identities, 479–482
Side grip, 230
Silences, 11, 16, 35, 414
Silencing, 419–420
Social harm, 105

Socio-narratology, 12, 368–374, 385
Socrates light, 87–105
Socratic dialogues, 88, 96–97
Socratic interviews, 99–100
South Africa, 13, 15, 467, 472, 473, 486, 487
Sri Lanka, 109, 113–115, 117, 119, 121–123
Stigmatised identities, 479–482
The State, 10, 16, 78, 94, 159, 164, 213, 295, 352, 482
Street culture, 32, 35, 36, 37, 40, 401
Storytelling, 15, 28, 36–39, 177, 222–223, 232, 243
Structures of feeling, 71
Subculture, 11, 32, 119, 334
Sublime effects, 211–213
Subtext, 416–417
Superpredators, 412
Symbolic boundaries, 177
Symbolic interactionism, 2, 261, 347, 412
Symbolic interactionist, 92, 261, 346

Team research, 449–450
Techniques of neutralisation, 2, 390
Television, 283, 328, 329, 416
Terrorism, 133–134
Terrorist autobiographies, 134
Testimony, 49, 54, 57, 60, 67, 253, 295
Thin blue line, 329–331
The Three Little Pigs, 155, 166, 167
Toch, H., 344, 359
Tragic hero role, 353, 354, 357
Translation, 122, 201, 252
Trauma narratives, 241
Travelling stories, 14–15
Trial narratives, 47, 48, 213
Trust, 36, 41, 52, 100, 266, 333, 439
Truth, 4, 8, 35, 57, 63–64, 109–113, 115–120, 223, 248, 397, 331–333

Truth/lies, 35, 109–113
  factural truths, 35
  slants on truth, 63–64

Ugelvik family Mauser, 221, 222
UK, 10, 15, 64, 66, 67, 74, 250, 271, 273, 438
Understatement, 58, 417–418
Unsaid, 12, 409–424
USA, 428
US federal prosecutors, 45–61

Validity, 110, 125
Verisimilitude, 112, 120–122
Victim impact statements, 243, 262, 263
Victimhood, 9, 240, 251, 254, 261, 267, 447, 478
Victimology. *See* Narrative victimology
Victims, 4, 10, 58, 124, 158, 239–257, 259, 261, 263, 264, 265–272, 279–300, 382, 402, 455
Victim stories
  June's story, 240, 244–251
  lethal violence, 240, 241, 242–244

Violence, 3, 4, 39, 79, 121, 139, 161, 180, 240, 241, 242–244, 270, 308, 392, 393, 400
  atrocity, 4
  conceptual violence, 202
  finding a 'Calling' in the aftermath, 247–249
  gun violence, 265
  Jihadi organisations, 451
  mass violence, 4
  mothers against violence, 244
  political violence, 142
  redemptive suffering, 240, 249–251
  visual symbols, 139
Visual criminology, 3, 198, 214
Visual narratives, 9, 180–190
Vocabularies of motive, 2

War/armed conflict, 4, 12, 13, 115, 139, 184, 220, 447–448, 451, 453
War stories, 325, 334, 335, 376
Whimsical fantasises, 208

Youth justice, 89–108
YouTube.com, 375